Europe For Dummies, 3rd Edition

Cheat Sheet

A List of Handy Foreign-Language Words and Phrases

English	French	Italian	German	Spanish
My name is...	**Je m'appelle...** (zhuh mah-*pell*)	**Mi chiamo...** (me key-*ah*-mo)	**Ich heisse...** (eek *high*-suh)	**Me llamo...** (male) **Me llama...** (female) (may yah-moe/*yah*-mah)
Thank you	**Merci** (mair-*see*)	**Grazie** (*grat*-tzee- yay)	**Danke** (*dahn*-kah)	**Gracias** (*grah*-thee-yahs)
Please	**S'il vous plaît** (seel-vou-*play*)	**Per favore** (pair fa-*vohr*-ray)	**Bitte**	**Por favor** (por fah-*bohr*)
Yes/No	**Oui/Non** (wee/no)	**Sì/No** (see/no)		**Sí/No** (see/no)
Do you speak English?	**Parlez-vous anglais?** (par-lay-*vou* on-glay)	**Parla Inglese?** (par-la een-glay-zay)		een-glish)	**Habla usted inglés?** (ah-blah oo-sted een-glais)
Good day	**Bonjour** (bohn-*szourh*)	**Buon giorno** (bwohn *jour*-noh)		**Buenos días** (*bway*-nohs *dee*-hs)
Goodbye	**Au revoir** (oh-ruh-*vwah*)	**Arrivederci** (ah-ree-vah-*dair*-chee)	n)	**Adiós** (ah-dee-yohs)
Excuse me	**Pardon** (pah-*rdohn*)	**Scusi** (*skoo*-zee)	*h*-tuh)	**Perdóneme** (pair-*dohn*-eh-meh)
I'm sorry	**Je suis desolée** (zhuh swee day-zoh-*lay*)	**Mi dispiace** (mee dees-pee-*yat*-chay)	E..., ... (ef...	**Lo siento** (lo see-*yen*-toh)
How much is it?	**Combien coûte?** (coam-bee-*yehn* koot)	**Quanto costa?** (*kwan*-toh coast-ah)	**Wieviel kostet es?** (*vee*-feel *koh*-steht es)	**Cuánto cuesta?** (*kwan*-toh *kway*-stah)
1/2/3	**un** (uhn)/ **deux** (douh)/ **trois** (twah)	**uno** (*oo*-no)/ **due** (*doo*-way)/ **tre** (tray)	**eins** (eye'nz)/ **zwei** (zv'eye)/ **drei** (dr'eye)	**uno** (*oo*-noh)/ **dos** (dohs)/ **tres** (trays)

A List of Handy Foreign-Language Words and Phrases

English	French	Italian	German	Spanish
Where is the bathroom?	**Où est la toilette?** (ou *eh* lah twah-*let*)	**Dov'é il bagno?** (doh-*vay* eel *bahn*-yoh)	**Wo ist die toilette?** (voh eest dee toy-*leht*-tah)	**Dónde está el servicio/ el baño?** (*dohn*-day eh-*stah* el sair-*bee*-thee-yo/el *bahn*-yoh)
I would like this/that	**Je voudrais ce/ça** (zhuh vou-*dray* suh/sah)	**Vorrei questo/quello** (voar-*ray* *kway*-sto/ *kwel*-loh)	**Ich möchte dieses/das** (eek mowk-tah dee-zes/dahs)	**Quisiera éste/ése** (kee-see-*yair*-ah *eh*-stay/ *eh*-seh)
...a double room for X nights	**une chambre pour dux pour X soirs** (oou-n *shaum*-bra pour douh pour X swa)	**una doppia per X notte** (ooh-nah *dope*-pee-ya pair X *noh*-tay)	**ein Doppelzimmer für X nachts** (eye'n *doh*-pel- tzim-merr fear X nahkts)	**una habitacióndoble por X noches** (*oo*-nah ah-bee-ta-thee-*yon* doh-blay poar X *noh*-chays)
with/without bath	**avec** (ah-*vek*)/ **sans** (sahn) **bain** (baahn)	**con/**(coan)/ **senza** (*sen*-zah) **bagno** (*bahn*-yoh)	**mit** (miht)/ **ohne** (oh-nuh) **bad** (baad)	**con** (cohn)/ **sin** (seen) **baño** (*bah*-nyoh)
Check, please	**La conte, s'il vous plaît** (lah kohnt-ah seel-vou-play)	**Il conto, per favore** (eel *coan*-toh, pair fah-voar-ay)	**Die Rechnung, bitte** (dee rek-noong bit-tuh)	**La cuenta, por favor** (lah kwain-tah por fah-bohr)
Is service included?	**Le service est-il compris?** (luh sair-*vees* eh-teal coam-pree)	**É incluso il servizio?** (ey een-clou-so eel sair-veet-zee-yo)	**Ist die Bedienung inbegriffen?** (ihst dee beh-dee-nung in-beh-grih-fen)	**Está el servicio incluido?** (eh-stah el sair-bee-thee-yo een-clu-*wee*-doh)

FOR DUMMIES®

The fun and easy way™ to travel!

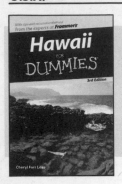
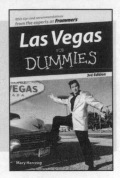

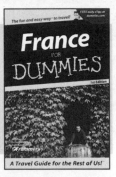
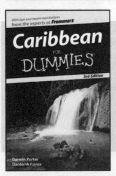

Europe FOR DUMMIES®

3RD EDITION

by Reid Bramblett

WILEY

Wiley Publishing, Inc.

Europe For Dummies, 3rd Edition

Published by
Wiley Publishing, Inc.
111 River St.
Hoboken, NJ 07030-5774
www.wiley.com

Copyright © 2005 by Wiley Publishing, Inc., Indianapolis, Indiana

Published simultaneously in Canada

For general information on our other products and services or to obtain technical support, please contact our Customer Care Department within the U.S. at 800-762-2974, outside the U.S. at 317-572-3993, or fax 317-572-4002.

Wiley also publishes its books in a variety of electronic formats. Some content that appears in print may not be available in electronic books.

Library of Congress Control Number: 2004117339

ISBN: 0-7645-7529-5

Manufactured in the United States of America

10 9 8 7 6 5 4 3 2 1

3B/QV/QR/QV/IN

WILEY

About the Author

Reid Bramblett has lived in Europe on and off since the age of 11, and is the author of ten travel guides, including *Frommer's Tuscany & Umbria* and *Frommer's Northern Italy*. He is Associate Editor of *Budget Travel* magazine, the creator of the award-winning TravelTools.net, and a contributor of travel articles to such publications as *Newsweek, The Miami Herald,* and the *Dallas Morning News*. When not on the road, he splits his time between New York and his native Philadelphia.

Dedication

This book is dedicated to Frances C. Sayers, who is largely responsible for it being (a) finished, and (b) accurate.

Author's Acknowledgments

My editor, Christine Ryan, did an excellent job of pointing out all the many, many places where what I originally wrote was confusing, out of place, or simply defied all laws of physics. Readers have her to thank for any coherence they might find within these pages. My parents first brought me to Europe (kicking and screaming) at the age of 11 to live in Rome, and proceeded to teach me all about vagabonding around the Continent over the next two years. These pages are, in large part, just me cribbing from those two masters at the art of travel. James Sayers and Matt Finley have both contributed greatly to this book over its various editions — I made them do all the difficult bits — and are both living proof that no one really lasts more than one season as a travel writer's assistant. And finally, my gratitude to Boy Scout Troop 116, which — over the course of three weeks in the summer of 2000 — reminded me (a) of all those minor aspects of life on the road we travel writers take for granted yet would save first-timers hours of agony and confusion if only someone would have warned them first, and (b) that the promise to lead a group of teenage boys across Europe is a serious thing and should probably never be agreed upon after one's sixth pint of Guinness.

Publisher's Acknowledgments

We're proud of this book; please send us your comments through our Dummies online registration form located at www.dummies.com/register/.

Some of the people who helped bring this book to market include the following:

Editorial

Editors: Elizabeth Kuball and Christine Ryan

Copy Editor: Elizabeth Kuball

Cartographer: Elizabeth Puhl

Editorial Manager: Carmen Krikorian

Editorial Assistant: Nadine Bell

Senior Photo Editor: Richard Fox

Cover Photos: Front, Bob Krist/ eStock Photo; back, Larry Fisher/ Masterfile

Cartoons: Rich Tennant, www.the5thwave.com

Composition

Project Coordinator: Kristie Rees

Layout and Graphics:
Lauren Goddard, Joyce Haughey, Shelley Norris, Barry Offringa, Lynsey Osborn, Heather Ryan, Julie Trippetti

Proofreaders: David Faust, Leeann Harney, Jessica Kramer, Carl William Pierce, TECHBOOKS Production Services, Inc.

Indexer: TECHBOOKS Production Services, Inc.

Publishing and Editorial for Consumer Dummies

Diane Graves Steele, Vice President and Publisher, Consumer Dummies

Joyce Pepple, Acquisitions Director, Consumer Dummies

Kristin A. Cocks, Product Development Director, Consumer Dummies

Michael Spring, Vice President and Publisher, Travel

Brice Gosnell, Associate Publisher, Travel

Kelly Regan, Editorial Director, Travel

Publishing for Technology Dummies

Andy Cummings, Vice President and Publisher, Dummies Technology/General User

Composition Services

Gerry Fahey, Vice President of Production Services

Debbie Stailey, Director of Composition Services

Contents at a Glance

Maps at a Glance

Table of Contents

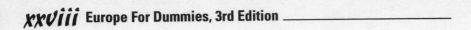

Introduction

● ●

*F*inally, you're taking that long-awaited trip to Europe. Congratulations! You're about to embark on a great adventure, and part of you may feel a bit overwhelmed. You have lots of plans to make: where to stay, where to dine, how long to remain in each country, and which attractions to see — but I can help you every step of the way. You already took the first step in the right direction by buying *Europe For Dummies,* 3rd Edition!

About This Book

You have in your possession a reference tool, not a guidebook that you have to read from cover to cover. Open up this book to any chapter to find the answers on how to make your European travel dreams come true. You *can* read *Europe For Dummies* from start to finish if you want, but if you're already familiar with some aspects of international travel, for instance, skip over the first two parts and jump right into the destination descriptions.

This is a selective guidebook to Europe. My goal throughout is to give you a really good selection of each country's highlights. That means I exclude places that other, more exhaustive guidebooks routinely include. Brussels, Copenhagen, and Lisbon are important cities, but from the perspective of the first-time visitor to Europe, they can't compete with London, Paris, and Madrid. In addition, so much is really worth seeing in Europe that you don't need to waste your time with the second-rate, the overrated, or the boring.

Please be advised that travel information is subject to change at any time — and this is especially true of prices. I, therefore, suggest that you write or call ahead for confirmation when making your travel plans. The authors, editors, and publisher cannot be held responsible for the experiences of readers while traveling. Your safety is important to us, however, so we encourage you to stay alert and be aware of your surroundings. Keep a close eye on cameras, purses, and wallets, all favorite targets of thieves and pickpockets.

Dummies Post-it® Flags

As you're reading this book, you'll find information that you'll want to reference as you plan or enjoy your trip — whether it be a new hotel, a must-see attraction, or a must-try walking tour. Mark these pages with the handy Post-it® Flags included in this book to help make your trip planning easier!

Conventions Used in This Book

If you've tried to extract some information from a guidebook and felt that you needed training in hieroglyphics to interpret all the different symbols, I'm happy to report you won't have that problem with user-friendly *Europe For Dummies*. The use of symbols and abbreviations is kept to a minimum.

The few conventions that I do use include the following:

- ✔ **Abbreviations for credit cards:** AE (American Express), DC (Diner's Club), MC (MasterCard), and V (Visa).

- ✔ **Two prices for everything:** First in the local currency (often the euro, €) and second in the U.S. dollar equivalent. These dollar conversions were calculated using the exchange rate listed in each destination chapter and were accurate at the time I was writing that chapter.

  Exchange rates can and will fluctuate, and the rate probably will not be the same when you visit. However, because the fluctuations tend to stay within around 10 to 20 percent, my conversions give you a fair idea about how much you'll pay (assuming the price itself doesn't go up, of course).

- ✔ **Dollar-sign ratings for all hotels and restaurants:** The number of signs indicates the range of costs for one night in a double-occupancy hotel room or a meal at a restaurant (excluding alcohol), from $ (budget) to $$$$$ (splurge). Because of the number of countries covered in this book, these ratings are relative, applied on a city-by-city basis. So a $ hotel in pricey London may be a quirky bed-and-breakfast in a residential neighborhood with mismatched furniture and shared baths; but a $ hotel in far-cheaper Athens may well be a centrally located but plain mid-scale hotel. The same goes for restaurants: At a rustic $$$$ joint in Madrid you may get a delicious, stick-to-your-ribs stew for about $22; but a $$$$ restaurant in Paris dishes up fancy, haute-cuisine dishes that can cost as much as $85 per course.

✔ **Two categories for hotels and restaurants:** My personal favorites (the "tops") and those that don't quite make my preferred list but still get my hearty seal of approval (the "runners-up"). Don't be shy about considering those in the second category if you're unable to get a room or a table at one of my favorites or if your preferences differ from mine. The amenities that the runner-up hotels offer and the services that each provides make all of them good choices to consider as you determine where to rest your head at night. The runner-up restaurants are all enjoyable standbys that are sure to serve up a tasty meal.

✔ **Cross-references to maps:** For those hotels, restaurants, and attractions that are plotted on a map, a page reference is provided in the listing information. If a hotel, restaurant, or attraction is outside the city limits or in an out-of-the-way area, it may not be mapped.

Foolish Assumptions

As I wrote this book, I made some assumptions about you and what your needs may be as a traveler. Here's what I assumed about you:

✔ You may be an inexperienced traveler looking for guidance when determining whether to take a trip to Europe and how to plan for it.

✔ You may be an experienced traveler, but you don't have a lot of time to devote to trip planning or you don't have a lot of time to spend in Europe once you get there. You want expert advice on how to maximize your time and enjoy a hassle-free trip.

✔ You're not looking for a book that provides all the information available about Europe or that lists every hotel, restaurant, or attraction available to you. Instead, you're looking for a book that focuses on the places that will give you the best or most memorable experience in Europe.

If you fit any of these criteria, then *Europe For Dummies* gives you the information you're looking for.

How This Book Is Organized

I divide *Europe For Dummies* into six parts. The first two parts cover planning and travel skills. The next three parts divide Europe into three regions; you get the lowdown on 15 of Europe's most popular destinations, and all destinations read as mini-guidebooks. You find all you need to conquer each city: historical background, local customs, the best hotels and restaurants for every budget, out-of-the-way gems, and more. I even recommend how much time to spend at each major attraction. The last part includes some fun top-ten lists as well as an appendix packed with helpful travel info you can use on the go.

Part 1: Introducing Europe

This part covers where to go, how to link it all together, and how to budget for your dream trip. I give you my picks of the best destinations and sights and my recommendations for the most fun-packed itineraries to fit your interests and vacation schedule.

Part 11: Planning Your Trip to Europe

If you're looking for a deal (and isn't everybody?), read on. This part reveals the tricks of the trade for finding the best prices on plane tickets, rail passes, and car rentals. I help you find the best hotel in any price range and share budgeting tricks so you can travel Europe without breaking the bank. I discuss tips for students, seniors, families, the physically challenged, and gay and lesbian travelers. Then I guide you through applying for passports; making reservations; dealing with trip insurance, health issues, and Customs; and figuring out how to keep in touch while traveling. I do everything but pack your bag!

Part 111: The British Isles

First, I help you tackle London and side trips in England to Bath; Salisbury and Stonehenge; and Oxford. Then I bring you north to Edinburgh and other Scottish highlights such as Loch Ness, Inverness, and Glasgow. Finally, I take you across the waters to Dublin and the best of Ireland's countryside, from the Wicklow Mountains to the Ring of Kerry.

Part 1V: Central Europe

Many adventures await you in Central Europe. From the much-loved and often-visited city of Paris, I take you to the palaces at Versailles and the Gothic cathedral at Chartres. After cruising Amsterdam's canals and red-light district, I help you explore the Dutch tulip fields in Haarlem and the Hoge Veluwe Park with its Kröller-Müller Museum. In Germany, I bring you to Munich and Bavaria, where you can drink beer with oompah bands and explore Neuschwanstein, the ultimate Romantic castle.

You raise a glass (of coffee) to the Hapsburgs in genteel Vienna before heading to Innsbruck in the Austrian Alps. Finally, you head to the magical baroque cityscape of Prague, which rarely disappoints (nor do the Czech Republic's cheap prices).

Part V: Mediterranean Europe

The bright Mediterranean basin has been home to Europe's great Empires. From the multilayered city of Rome, I show you the ancient Roman town of Ostia Antica, just a daytrip away. Then you journey to Florence, the city of the Renaissance, and the nearby Tuscan towns of Pisa, Siena, and San Gimignano, which help bring the Middle Ages back to life. I round up my Italian tour with the canal city of Venice, one of the most beautiful and unusual cities on Earth.

Next I take you to Spain. You start in Madrid, which houses great museums and tapas bars, and the nearby towns of Toledo and Segovia, which provide medieval respites from city sightseeing. Then you visit the great city of Barcelona, with its modernismo architecture and Gothic quarter.

Part VI: The Part of Tens

I fill this part with ten of Europe's must-see sights (and ten overrated ones) as well as ten affordable European souvenirs for $20 or less and advice on ten ways to break out of the tourist mold.

In back of this book I've included an *appendix* — your Quick Concierge — containing lots of handy information you may need when traveling in Europe, like average rail times between different European cities, clothing size conversions, and contact information for various tourism agencies. You can find the Quick Concierge easily because it's printed on yellow paper.

Icons Used in This Book

Throughout this book, helpful little icons highlight particularly useful information. Here's what each icon means.

This icon highlights money-saving tips and/or great deals.

This icon highlights the best the destination has to offer in all categories — hotels, restaurants, attractions, activities, shopping, and nightlife.

This icon gives you a heads-up on annoying or potentially dangerous situations such as tourist traps, unsafe neighborhoods, rip-offs, and other things to beware of.

This icon, in addition to flagging tips and resources of special interest to families, points out the most child-friendly hotels, restaurants, and attractions.

This icon is a catchall for any special hint, tip, or bit of insider's advice that helps make your trip run more smoothly.

Sometimes a great hotel, restaurant, or sight may require a bit of effort to get to. I let you in on these secret little finds with this icon. I also use this to peg any resource that's particularly useful and worth the time to seek out.

Where to Go from Here

Think of me as your advance scout. These pages are chock-full of insider tips, hints, advice, secrets, and strategies that I collected while criss-crossing the British Isles and the Continent. I explored. I took notes. And I made mistakes — and learned from them — so that you don't have to make the same errors, even if you're a first-time traveler.

From here, you depart on your big European adventure. Keep in mind that Europe is not a giant museum from the past, but a living and vital culture. If you open yourself to all its possibilities — new friends, experiences, sights, and sounds — you're bound to have a vacation that will stay with you long after you return.

Bon voyage!

Part I
Introducing Europe

The 5th Wave   By Rich Tennant

"Let me ask you a question. Are you planning to kiss the Blarney Stone, or ask for its hand in marriage?"

In this part . . .

What comes to mind when looking at a map of Europe? So many beautiful countries, so many glamorous cities, and so many possible itineraries. Before you jump on that plane, you need a travel plan that will allow you to visit all the places on your wish list without having to get a second mortgage on your home. This part guides you through all the necessary steps that you need to take in order to build your ideal travel plan. These chapters introduce you to Europe, help you decide when and where to go, and give you five great itineraries.

Chapter 1

Discovering the Best of Europe

In This Chapter
▶ Finding the best museums, historic sights, food, and architecture
▶ Discarding misconceptions before you go
▶ Traveling to the most intriguing cities and sights

*Y*ou need to get started on plenty of details a few months before you leave — things such as passports (see Chapter 9), rail passes (see Chapter 6), plane tickets (see Chapter 5), and traveler's checks (see Chapter 4). But for now, just sit back and dream of the possibilities.

In Europe, you find some of the world's most outstanding museums, historic sights, culinary creations, and architectural wonders. In this book, I guide you to the best of the best.

You can sail past decaying palaces and sinking churches on Venice's Grand Canal for the price of a bus ticket. You can drain creamy mugs of Guinness while clapping along to traditional Celtic music on a pub-crawl through Dublin. You can splurge on a 5-star meal in Paris, the mecca of haute cuisine.

You may want to stare for hours at the famed finger-almost-touching scene of *God Creating Adam* on Michelangelo's Sistine Chapel ceiling in Rome. Or sit atop Switzerland's Schilthorn Mountain, surrounded by peaks covered with snow and glacier-filled valleys, while eating breakfast in a revolving restaurant at 10,000 feet. Or enjoy a picnic lunch on the Greek island of Santoríni hundreds of feet above the Mediterranean amidst the ruins of a Mycenaean city.

Europe is yours to discover and experience. This book opens the doors.

Europe

The Top Museums

I give away no secrets by admitting that Europe is home to some of the world's greatest museums, displaying a cultural kaleidoscope of Western culture from classical busts and Renaissance frescoes to Impressionist landscapes and postmodern sculptures.

✔ **The Louvre (Paris):** The short list has to start with the **Louvre** (see Chapter 13), one of those great catchall museums that opens with ancient sculptures (including that armless beauty *Venus de Milo*), runs through Egyptian mummies and medieval artifacts, and then showcases some true icons of Renaissance art, including Da Vinci's *Mona Lisa* and Delacroix's ultra-French *Liberty Leading the People*.

✔ **Musée d'Orsay (Paris):** After exhausting yourself at the Louvre, you can cross the Seine River to visit an old train station that's been transformed into the **Musée d'Orsay** (see Chapter 13). The Orsay picks up the thread of French art where the Louvre leaves off, highlighting the best from the Romantic period onward, including the world's greatest collection of crowd-pleasing Impressionists like Manet, Monet, Degas, Cézanne, Renoir, Gaughin, van Gogh, Seurat, and more.

✔ **The Vatican Museums (Rome):** Arguably, Europe's greatest collection of museums all in one place belongs to the **Vatican Museums** (see Chapter 19). The Vatican's Painting Gallery houses Raphael's *Transfiguration* and Caravaggio's *Deposition*. A slew of antiquities collections together preserve some of the best bits of ancient Greek, Egyptian, Etruscan, and (naturally) Roman sculpture on the continent. Then you find the former private papal apartments frescoed by the likes of Pinturicchio and Raphael, and, of course, the Sistine Chapel with its ceiling frescoed by Michelangelo.

✔ **The British Museum (London):** You can get up close and personal with artifacts from the dawn of human history at London's renowned (and admission-free) **British Museum** (see Chapter 10). No nook or cranny of the ancient European, Mediterranean, or Middle Eastern worlds is overlooked, from Celtic treasure hordes to the Elgin Marbles of Greece's Parthenon, from the remains of Assyrian palaces to the Rosetta Stone that helped archaeologists crack the language of hieroglyphics, and from intricately decorated Greek vases to room after room stacked with Egyptian mummies and their fabulous treasures.

✔ **Museo del Prado (Madrid):** The **Museo del Prado** (see Chapter 22) stands on equal footing with the Louvre and Vatican Museums but is (quite unfairly) not nearly as well known. So much the better, really, because that means you get to enjoy its paintings by the greats of Spanish art — the courtly and insightful Velazquez, the creepy and dark Goya, the weirdly lit and uniquely colorful El Greco, and the truly warped and surreal Hieronymus Bosch — without the huge crowds and long lines.

✔ **The Uffizi Galleries (Florence):** Take a spin through the **Uffizi Galleries** (see Chapter 20), a veritable textbook on the development of painting during the Renaissance. Compared to the great museums of other cities, the Uffizi is small, but it houses an embarrassment of riches, from earlier works by Giotto, Fra' Angelico, and Botticelli (the goddess-on-a-half-shell *Birth of Venus* and flower-filled *Primavera* both hang here) through the height of the Renaissance represented by Leonardo da Vinci, Raphael, and Michelangelo.

✔ **The Deutsches Museum (Munich):** Overloaded on art and ancient relics? Head to the **Deutsches Museum** (see Chapter 15), one of the greatest science and technology museums on Earth. Whether you're turned green with envy at the fleets of early Mercedes, wowed by eye-popping electrical demonstrations, impressed by a hangar full of historic aircraft, intrigued by the lab benches where some of the earliest experiments in nuclear physics took place, or entertained by the giant machines they use to dig tunnels under the Alps, this informative and often hands-on museum is a delight for all ages.

The Top Historic Sights

Europe is the wellspring of Western culture, a living textbook of human history. People think in terms of centuries and millennia here, not decades. Americans may speak of fond memories of the '60s; Italians just as breezily refer to fond collective memories of *il seicento* (the 1600s). Europe allows you to dip into history at just about any point.

✔ **Best Greek and Roman Ruins:** You can see remnants of the ancient Greek and Roman empires, some 1,500 to 3,000 years old, with half-ruined temples at the **Acropolis** or **Ancient Agora** in Athens or at **Delphi** in inland Greece (see Chapter 24). Or how about the **Roman Forum,** the ghost town of **Ostia Antica,** or the ultimate sports arena, the **Colosseum** — all in or near Rome (see Chapter 19)?

✔ **Best Prehistoric Sites:** Prehistoric standouts include sites such as **Stonehenge** (see Chapter 10) in England, **Akrotiri** (see Chapter 24) on the Greek island of Santoríni, the passage tomb of **Newgrange** (see Chapter 12) in Ireland, and the remnants of the earliest settlements of what is now Paris excavated under the square in front of **Notre-Dame Cathedral** (see Chapter 13).

✔ **Best Castles:** You'll find castles from the Dark Ages and Middle Ages (from A.D. 500 to 1500) strewn across Europe, such as the **Tower of London** (see Chapter 10), with its bloody legends and famed crown jewels; **Edinburgh Castle** (see Chapter 11), glowering atop a volcanic hill in the center of the city; and **Prague Castle** (see Chapter 18), with its soaring cathedral and half-timbered lane of old alchemists' shops.

✔ **Best Medieval Neighborhoods:** This era also saw the development of major cities, leaving the world with cobblestone medieval quarters such as the **Altstadt** of Bern (see Chapter 17), the **Staré Mesto** in Prague (see Chapter 18), **Trastevere** in Rome (see Chapter 19), and the **Barri Gòtic** in Barcelona (see Chapter 23).

✔ **Best Hill Towns:** Tiny hill towns and hamlets sprang up between A.D. 500 and 1500, too, and this book describes the best of them, including **Chartres** in France (see Chapter 13), **Innsbruck** in Austria (see Chapter 16), the Tuscan hill towns of **Siena** and **San Gimignano** (see both in Chapter 20), and Spain's time capsules of **Toledo** and **Segovia** (see both in Chapter 22).

The Top Culinary Delights

European cuisine runs the gamut from the rib-sticking *röschti* (deluxe hash browns spiked with ham and eggs) of the Swiss Alps to France's traditional *coq au vin* (chicken braised in red wine with onions and mushrooms); from 101 types of **sausage** in Prague to the incredible yet unknown **cheeses** of Ireland nibbled after dinner in a countryside B&B.

✔ **Best Mediterranean Meals:** The cooking of Italy (see Chapters 19 through 21) goes far beyond **pasta** — though it's so good here you may not care. You can sample Adriatic **fish** in a Venetian trattoria patronized by local gondoliers, a mighty *bistecca fiorentina* (an oversized T-bone brushed with olive oil and cracked pepper then grilled) in Florence, or *gnocchi al pomodoro* (potato dumplings in tomato sauce) followed by a *saltimbocca* (wine-cooked veal layered with sage and prosciutto) in a Roman restaurant installed in the ruins of an ancient theater.

A night out in Madrid (see Chapter 22) — where dinner starts at 10 p.m. — may mean a traditional **roast suckling pig** in a restaurant unchanged since the days when Hemingway was a regular, or a giant Valencian *paella* (rice tossed with a seafood medley) to share with everyone at the table under the wood beams of a country-style inn.

✔ **Best British Meals:** England (see Chapter 10) once had a reputation for serving what was considered the worst cooking in Europe, featuring *shepherd's pie* (beef stew capped by whipped potatoes) and *bangers and mash* (sausages and mashed potatoes). But, oh, how times have changed. Much to Paris's chagrin, London now enjoys the **hottest restaurant scene** in Europe, and its celebrity chefs and designer dining spots surf the crest of modern cooking trends and serve the hippest fusion cuisines.

✔ **Best Bets for a Sweet Tooth:** Sure, French and Italian pastries are divine, but you can also sate your sweet tooth in Vienna (see Chapter 16), home of the **Sachertorte,** the original Death by Chocolate.

And what better way to cap off a night of clubbing in Madrid than to join the locals for *churros y chocolada* (fried dough strips you dip in thick hot chocolate) as the sun rises? Don't worry: You'll do so much walking on your trip that you probably won't gain too much weight . . . assuming of course you don't discover the *gelato* (super-rich ice cream) of Florence (see Chapter 20) or **toffee trifle cakes** in England (see Chapter 10).

✔ **Best Beer and Wine:** Most travelers know that, to wash it all down, you can tipple some of the finest wines in the world in France and Italy or take a swig from a liter-sized mug of beer in Germany. But did you know that **Eastern European beers** are finally getting the recognition they deserve in Prague (see Chapter 18)? And rightly so, because all Pilsners, and what became Budweiser, originally hail from the Czech Republic. And how about the *heuriger* in Vienna (see Chapter 16)? These small family-run wine estates serve up samples of their white wines accompanied by simple, hearty Austrian dishes.

The Architectural Highlights

Europe is home to some of the world's greatest cathedrals, palaces, and castles. You can marvel at the diversity of gargoyles and sparkling rose windows on Paris's **Notre-Dame Cathedral** (see Chapter 13), gape at Michelangelo's *Pietà* sculpture and Bernini's towering altar canopy in Rome's **St. Peter's** (Chapter 19), and admire many creations of medieval masonry or Renaissance engineering in between.

✔ **Chartres Cathedral (Beyond Paris): Chartres Cathedral** (see Chapter 13) is a study in formal Gothic, from its 27,000 square feet of stained glass to its soaring spires and flying buttresses.

✔ **Salisbury Cathedral (Beyond London):** Britain's answer to Chartres is **Salisbury Cathedral** (see Chapter 10), spiking the English countryside with one of the medieval world's tallest spires.

✔ **St. Mark's Basilica (Venice):** The multiple domes, swooping pointed archways, and glittering mosaics swathing **St. Mark's Basilica** (see Chapter 21) hint at how this great trading power of the Middle Ages sat at the crossroads of Eastern and Western cultures; it's as much Byzantine as it is European.

✔ **The Duomo (Florence):** When the Renaissance genius Brunelleschi invented a noble dome to cap **Florence's Duomo** (see Chapter 20), Europe's architectural landscape changed forever. Domes started sprouting up all over the place. Visit Florence's original, and you can clamber up narrow staircases between the dome's onion layers to see just how Brunelleschi performed his engineering feat — and get a sweeping panorama of the city from the top.

✓ **Residenz Palace and Schloss Nymphenburg (Munich):** In the 17th and 18th centuries, powerful kings governing much of Europe felt they ruled by divine right — and built palaces to prove it. The Bavarian Wittelsbach dynasty ruled for 738 years from Munich's **Residenz Palace** and the pleasure palace outside town, **Schloss Nymphenburg** (see Chapter 15).

✓ **Hofburg Palace (Vienna):** The Hapsburg emperors set up housekeeping in the sprawling **Hofburg Palace** (see Chapter 16), where the chapel is now home to a little singing group known as the Vienna Boy's Choir, and where museums showcase everything from classical statuary and musical instruments to medieval weaponry and the imperial treasury.

✓ **Buckingham Palace (London):** You can line up to watch the changing of the guard at **Buckingham Palace** (see Chapter 10), and even tour the royal pad, assuming Her Majesty Elizabeth II isn't at home.

✓ **Versailles (Beyond Paris):** You can ride the RER train from downtown Paris to the palace to end all palaces, **Versailles** (see Chapter 13), where Louis XIV held court, Marie Antoinette kept dangerously out of touch with her subjects (who were brewing revolution back in Paris), and the Treaty of Versailles was signed, ending World War I.

✓ **Neuschwanstein (Beyond Munich):** Tourists aren't the only ones looking to recapture a romantic, idealized past. Mad King Ludwig II of Bavaria was so enamored by his country's fairy-tale image that he decided to build **Neuschwanstein** (see Chapter 15) in the foothills of the Alps south of Munich. This fanciful 19th-century version of what Ludwig thought a medieval castle *should* look like is a festival of turrets and snapping banners that later inspired Uncle Walt's Cinderella castle in Disney World.

✓ **Sagrada Famiglia (Barcelona):** Lest you think the architectural innovations are all relics of the past, head to Barcelona, where one of the early 20th centuries' greatest architects, Antoni Gaudí, used his own unique riff on Art Nouveau to design everything from apartment blocks to a cathedral-size church, **Sagrada Famiglia** (see Chapter 23), still under construction.

Chapter 2

Deciding Where and When to Go

●　●

In This Chapter

▶ Deciding on the best season to travel
▶ Participating in Europe's many festivals and feasts
▶ Sightseeing survival tips

●　●

T his chapter takes you through the pros and cons of traveling to
Europe at different times of the year. You also find a rundown of the
most popular festivals, as well as some strategies for staving off sightseeing sensory overload.

Going Everywhere You Want to Be

Europe is huge, and rich with possible destinations. Narrowing my coverage was tough, but a guidebook only contains so much room and you
only have so much time in your vacation schedule. Keeping that in mind,
I present the 15 must-see cities and the best of all possible side trips to
give you a true, wide-ranging flavor of all that Europe has to offer.

The splendors of the British Isles

The best place to start is **London** (see Chapter 10), capital of the old
British Empire. From the medieval Tower of London, where Henry VIII's
wives lost their heads, to the neo-Gothic halls of Westminster, where you
can watch Parliament in heated debate, London offers a wealth of sightseeing possibilities.

It vies with New York as the hotbed of English-language theater, and its
museums cover everything from Old Masters (National Gallery) and decorative arts (the Victoria & Albert Museum) to naval history (Greenwich's
Maritime Museum) and World War II (the War Cabinet Rooms). The city
contains the pomp and circumstance of the royal family and the bump
and grind of the trendiest nightclubs. You can dine on everything from
pub grub to Indian fare to modern British fusion cuisine.

Easy daytrips from London include the Georgian splendors and Roman ruins of **Bath,** the mysterious prehistoric stone circles of **Stonehenge** and **Avebury,** the Gothic cathedral of **Salisbury,** and the sine qua non of world academia, the hallowed halls of **Oxford** University.

Edinburgh (see Chapter 11), the capital of Scotland, is a vibrant university town whose old city is presided over by one of the best glowering castles in Europe, and whose Georgian new city is a genteel grid of streets for shopping and finding cheap town-house accommodations. You can haunt the pubs once frequented by local son Robert Louis Stevenson, find out about Scottish Impressionism at the National Gallery, and stroll the Royal Mile in search of tartan scarves and memorable sights (from the hokey whisky tour to the royal Holyrood Palace).

You can also day-trip to **Inverness** and search for the Loch Ness Monster from the ruins of Urquart Castle, or head down to happening **Glasgow,** an industrial city revitalizing itself as a cultural center.

Although a visit to the Irish capital of **Dublin** (see Chapter 12) has its charms, such as admiring the Book of Kells at Trinity College, exploring Celtic history at the Archaeological Museum, following in the footsteps of James Joyce and other Irish scribes, and pub crawling through Temple Bar, the best way to enjoy Ireland is to rent a car and drive through the Irish countryside.

To that end, I offer plenty of coverage of the passage tombs at **Newgrange,** the Celtic crosses and windswept heaths of the **Wicklow Mountains** and **Glandalough,** and the fishing villages and ancient sites of the **Ring of Kerry** and **Dingle Peninsula.**

The heart of the Continent

Many people consider **Paris** (see Chapter 13) the capital of European sightseeing. From the masterpieces in the Louvre and the Impressionists collection of the Musée d'Orsay to climbing the Eiffel Tower, cruising the Seine, or simply whiling the day away at a cafe in the St-Germain-de-Pres or Marais neighborhoods, Paris has enough to keep you busy for a lifetime. And I haven't even mentioned the bistros and brasseries, where you can sample everything from the finest 5-star cuisine in town to cheap fixed-price menus.

But do take the time to day-trip from Paris to over-the-top **Versailles,** one of the greatest royal residences in Europe, or to **Chartres,** one of the world's great Gothic cathedrals and a holy spot since ancient Druid days.

Amsterdam (see Chapter 14) is as famed for its examples of Dutch tolerance (from the libidinous — the red-light district and "smoking" cafes — to the serious — the Dutch house that hid Anne Frank and her family during the Nazi occupation) as it is for its canals lined by genteel 17th-century town houses and artistic giants such as Rembrandt and van Gogh. And don't forget the Indonesian feasts in the Leidesplein district, rib-sticking dinner pancakes, and local brews Heineken, Amstel, and gin.

Nearby, you can sample a less hectic Dutch way of life in the smaller city of **Haarlem** or tour tulip gardens, windmills, and re-created villages in the countryside. You can also ride bikes for free in **Hoge Veluwe National Park** with its Kroller-Müller Museum dedicated to van Gogh and other modern-era artists.

The pulsing heart of life-loving, beer-happy Bavaria is **Munich** (see Chapter 15), an industrial powerhouse packed with a bevy of fine museums and two outstanding baroque palaces — and host to the biggest fraternity party in the world, the annual September Oktoberfest. You can munch on bratwurst and pretzels in beer halls and stroll the old center and expansive Englisher Garten city park.

Half the fun of Munich is traveling out of town to visit **Neuschwanstein,** the ornate fairy-tale castle of Mad King Ludwig. The darker side of history is here, too, of course. Just outside Munich, the town where the Nazi Party got its start, you can tour the sobering concentration camp of **Dachau.**

Over the Alps in **Austria** (see Chapter 16), you can sip from the cup that was the Austro-Hungarian Empire in Vienna, a city that retains its refined 19th-century air such as no other in Europe. Steep yourself in this heritage by climbing the cathedral towers, sipping coffee at a famous cafe, taking in the masterpieces of the Kunsthistoriches Museum, or waiting in line for standing-room tickets ($3) at the renowned State Opera house. Another popular Austrian destination is **Innsbruck,** a great little town tucked away in the heart of the Austrian Alps.

After a quick visit to the Swiss capital of **Bern** (see Chapter 17) to admire hometown boy Paul Klee's masterpieces, see where Einstein came up with $E=mc^2$, feed the town mascots at the Bear Pits, and float down the river with the locals, you can delve into the heart of the **Swiss Alps,** the Bernese Oberland region around the towering Jungfrau peak. Here, small resort towns and Alpine villages cling to the lips of the mighty Lauterbrunnen and Grindlewald Valleys, surrounded by glaciers and ribbon-thin waterfalls accessible by miles of hiking and skiing trails, scenic cog railway runs, and gravity-defying cable cars.

Finally, take a foray into Eastern Europe to see how the medieval and baroque masterpiece city of **Prague** (see Chapter 18) has come roaring out from behind the defunct Iron Curtain to become one of Europe's greatest destinations. This dreamy city of fairy-tale spires, castles, and churches is one of the world's top centers for sampling beer and classical music. You find a plethora of cheap concerts every night and in every venue imaginable — from symphonies playing in grand halls to street trios improvising under an acoustically sound medieval bridge abutment.

The charms of the Mediterranean

Rome (see Chapter 19) has both ancient sites and over 900 churches, from massive St. Peter's Cathedral to tiny medieval chapels. The city's dozens of museums house everything from ancient Roman statues, frescoes, and mosaics to Renaissance masterpieces. You can also see Michelangelo's Sistine Chapel ceiling. The cityscape itself is a joy to wander, a tangle of medieval streets and Renaissance-era boulevards punctuated by public squares (like Piazza Navona and Piazza del Popolo) sporting baroque fountains (such as famed Trevi Fountain) and Egyptian obelisks.

You can also day-trip to **Tivoli** (home to the ruins of Hadrian's villa and some palatial gardens) or **Ostia Antica,** the ancient port of Rome.

Florence (see Chapter 20) is the birthplace of the Renaissance, with more world-class museums and frescoed churches than you can shake a Michelangelo at. Here you find his *David,* Botticelli's *Birth of Venus,* Leonardo's *Annunciation,* and other artistic icons. Florence is also a great place to chow down on succulent steaks, sample fine Italian wines, and wander Dante's old neighborhood.

Florence is the capital of **Tuscany,** one of Europe's most (deservedly) popular regions. Here the tower of **Pisa** leans, wineries squash grapes into Brunellos or Chiantis, and hill towns such as **Siena** and **San Gimignano** still bring the Middle Ages to life with their tall stone towers, friendly atmospheres, and beautifully decorated churches.

Venice (see Chapter 21) floats like a dream city on its lagoon, with ornate palaces and tiny footbridges springing over a network of canals. The only modes of transportation here are boats and your own two legs. The interior of St. Mark's Cathedral glitters with more mosaics than you would think possible, and the works of great Venetian artists, such as Titian, Tintoretto, and Veronese, cover the walls of both the Accademia Gallery and Doge's Palace.

After feasting on Venice's seafood delicacies, take the public ferry to explore the outlying islands of **Murano** (where Venetian glassblowing was invented), **Burano** (a colorful fishing village), and **Torcello** (a desolate, undeveloped island hiding another gorgeously mosaicked church). And don't forget to set aside a day on the Veneto mainland to see the Giotto frescoes in **Padova (Padua).**

The Spanish capital of **Madrid** (see Chapter 22) also grabs you with its museums, from the masterworks in the Museo del Prado to Picasso's Guernica in the Reina Sofia. Tour the Royal Palace, take in a professional bullfight, or move from bar to bar sampling appetizer-size tapas before indulging in a hearty 10 p.m. dinner and resting up to party in the clubs until dawn.

If you still have the energy, take a few days to explore the medieval capital of **Toledo,** the kingly monastery at El Escorial (both boasting many El Greco paintings), and the impressive Roman aqueduct and Gothic cathedral of **Segovia.**

Barcelona (see Chapter 23), the capital of Spain's Catalonia region, boasts a great Gothic quarter to explore (Barri Gòtic), Las Ramblas (one of Europe's most fun pedestrian promenades), and the work of local early 20th-century greats. You find the work of Picasso, Joan Miró, and especially Antoni Gaudí, whose modernismo take on Art Nouveau architecture pops up in everything from town houses to a city park to the only great European cathedral still (slowly) being built, his Sagrada Famiglia.

Last, but certainly not least, head off to the heart of the Mediterranean, the ancient Greek capital of **Athens** (see Chapter 24), a sprawling modern city with the ruins of the 2,500-year-old Parthenon looming over it from atop the Acropolis Hill. Packed around the inexpensive *tavernas* and bargain-friendly shops lie more crumbling reminders of the Greek Golden Age such as Temple of the Olympian Zeus and Temple of the Winds. The city's archaeological museums highlight not only Classical Age remains but also statues from the Cycladic era and earlier ages, when ancient Egypt was the arbiter of artistic taste.

The side trips from Athens are phenomenal. Visit the romantic ruins of **Delphi,** where the ancient world's premier oracles advised kings and commoners alike. Or take off for the island of **Santoríni,** a haven for sun-worshippers, with its beaches, white wine, summer nightlife, and Minoan and Mycenaean ruins.

The Secret of the Seasons

Europe brings few seasonal surprises, for the most part, with the weather being similar to that of the Northeastern United States — although you may run into a warm, breezy day in December in Sicily, or a cold snap in summer in Scotland.

Europe tends to be slightly wetter than the United States (not including the Pacific Northwest) in autumn, winter, and spring; and drier (not including Arizona and New Mexico) in summer. Rain seems to fall an awful lot in England, and the peaks of the Alps never entirely lose their snow.

Be prepared for all varieties of weather by packing clothes that you can layer, long underwear, a folding pocket umbrella, and lightweight clothes for warmer days.

Spring is great because . . .

- ✔ During this *shoulder season* (in between low and high seasons), the weather tends to be pleasantly mild, but unpredictable. Temperatures may still be cool enough for skiing in the Alps but already warm enough for a dip in the Mediterranean. As at home, spring can be notoriously fickle, though; be prepared for rain, cold spells, sudden heat waves . . . and/or perfect weather.

✔ Airlines usually offer more-reasonable rates than in summer.

✔ Europe is neither too crowded nor too solitary.

✔ Tulips bloom in Holland and elsewhere.

But keep in mind . . .

✔ Shoulder season is becoming ever more popular (read: crowded) as frequent travelers tire of the summer hordes and take advantage of airlines' reduced rates.

✔ The off-season often runs October to Easter, so in early spring, many things may still be closed — from hotels to some sights to rural tourism destinations such as vineyards or farms.

Summer is great because . . .

✔ All the services that cater to tourists open their welcoming arms — this is the height of the tourist season, with the exception of ski resorts. Early summer is the most popular time to visit Europe, especially June and July.

✔ Colorful folk festivals, open-air music, and theatrical performances abound in early summer.

But keep in mind . . .

✔ In summertime, Europe can feel like one giant bus tour. In fact, the crowds are the season's biggest drawback.

✔ The prices are the highest of the year — especially for airfares and hotels, which book quickly.

✔ Popular museums have long lines. You may have to wait for hours to get inside at peak times.

✔ The temperatures really heat up across Europe in August, especially during the second half of the month. Europeans go to the beaches, leaving the sweaty cities to the tourists.

✔ In the southern climates, the heat can be unbearable all summer long.

Fall is great because . . .

✔ The bulk of the tourists have left.

✔ Crops ripen, and wine and harvest festivals celebrate the season.

✔ As in spring, the fall shoulder season brings reasonable rates on airlines and some hotel bargains.

✔ The opera and concert seasons for Europe's best companies and grand performance halls tend to begin in mid- to late fall.

But keep in mind . . .

✔ The weather can turn on you suddenly, with lots of drizzle, and the occasional downright wintery cold snap.

✔ Some tourist facilities — hotels, restaurants, and some sights — close for the season in October and November.

✔ Crowds are beginning to increase at this time of year as visitors try to escape the masses of summer.

Winter is great because . . .

✔ During low season (from mid- or late November through Easter, excluding Christmas week), hotel and travel expenses drop and you often have entire churches, museums, or even small towns to yourself.

✔ Christmas in Paris — or Rome, or Madrid, or Venice — can be beautiful and an experience to remember.

✔ You haven't really skied until you've been to the Swiss Alps and gone downhill for more than an hour without ever having to catch a lift.

But keep in mind . . .

✔ You may not want to spend your vacation bundled up, shielding yourself from the cold.

✔ Tourism destinations tend to freshen up during this period of calm. Museums review and reorganize their exhibits. Churches and monuments undergo restorations or cleanings. And local transportation, tourist offices, and shops shorten their hours, while some restaurants and hotels close for a week or even a month.

✔ Some of the most popular destinations, such as islands, smaller tourism-based cities, and spas, close up almost entirely.

Europe's Calendar of Events

A great way to tour is to plan an entire vacation around a single large festival. Even though the traditional sights of a particular location may be closed, especially in smaller towns, just attending a festival can be a great vacation. You can witness a slice of European life most tourists never get to see. Celebrate the festival with the locals, take tons of pictures, and make some unforgettable memories.

Book your accommodations as soon as possible if your plans include traveling to a location where a major festival or other cultural event is taking place. Attendees snatch up accommodations quickly at festival time, sometimes months in advance. For big festivals in smaller places, such as the Palio in Siena, Italy, all the hotels within the town walls may be sold out over a year beforehand. If necessary, book a room in a neighboring town.

What follows is a subjective list of the top ten festivals in Europe. Country guidebooks, such as *Frommer's* (Wiley), list many, many more festivals. For specific dates or more information, contact the local tourist offices (see the "Fast Facts" sections of Chapters 10 through 24 for listings) or visit the event Web site (if one is listed).

✔ **Carnevale,** Venice, Italy (and just about everywhere else): Carnevale is a feast of food and wine and a raucous celebration of spring — a true pagan holdover grafted onto the week preceding Christian Lent. Carnevale turns the world upside down: The lowly hobnob with the elite, and everyone has a roaring good time. The whole Christian world celebrates Carnevale (called "Carnival" in Rio and "Mardi Gras" in New Orleans). The most famous celebration in Europe, however, is Venice's Carnevale (www.venice-carnival. com), a series of elegant-yet-drunken masked balls reminiscent of Casanova's 18th century. But you find eventful celebrations throughout Europe. You can see chariot parades and a wild bacchanal in the Greek city of Pátras; the solemn burial of a sardine in Madrid, Spain; satiric political floats in the port of Livorno, Italy; and flower battles and bonfires in Nice, France. Carnevale starts a week or two before Ash Wednesday (usually in late February) and culminates on the final Tuesday, called "Fat Tuesday" (*Mardi Gras* in French). Fat Tuesday immediately precedes the sober period of Lent.

✔ **Shakespeare season,** Stratford-upon-Avon, England: Fans of great theater relish this experience. The Royal Shakespeare Company (www.rsc.org.uk) performs its season here, where Shakespeare was born and where he also retired. You can purchase tickets in advance on its Web site. The season runs from February through October.

✔ **Easter,** throughout Europe: In London, you can see multicolored floats parade around Battersea Park. You can hear hooded processioners sing love songs to the Virgin Mary in Seville, Spain. In Florence, you can watch an ox-drawn cart stuffed with fireworks explode in front of the cathedral. Celebrations vary widely between Good Friday and Easter Monday; Easter falls approximately in late March or early April.

✔ **Palio,** Siena, Italy: One of the highlights of the Italian summer is this breakneck, bareback, anything-goes horse race around the sloping, dirt-covered main piazza of medieval Siena. Even a horse that's thrown its rider (not uncommon) can take the prize, and whips are used as much on the other riders as on the horses. The parties held before and after the horse race are street feasts to behold, no matter who wins. The horse race occurs twice each summer, July 2 and August 16.

✔ **Running of the Bulls** (www.sanfermin.com), Pamplona, Spain: One of the more dangerous festivals you can see is this one, where couragous fools dress in white with red kerchiefs and run while enraged bulls chase them through the narrow streets of Pamplona. The wild chase ends when the bulls chase the last runners into the harbor, after forcing most of them to jump the fences for safety. After that, all involved drink much wine, set off fireworks, and, of course, attend the many bullfights. You can experience the event vicariously by reading Hemingway's *The Sun Also Rises,* or see it yourself from July 6 to 14.

✔ **Bastille Day,** Paris, France: France celebrates its nation's birthday with street fairs, parades, feasts, and pageants, starting with a procession along the Champs-Elysées and ending with fireworks over Montmartre. Bastille Day is July 14.

✔ **Edinburgh International Festival and Fringe Festival,** Edinburgh, Scotland: One of Europe's premier cultural extravaganzas, the festival features the art, dance, film, plays, and music of some of the world's top creative talents and performers. The traditional bagpipes-and-kilt Military Tattoo at the castle is the festival's highlight. The Edinburgh International Festival (www.eif.co.uk) takes place over three weeks in August and early September. The August **Fringe Festival** (www.edfringe.com) started off as a small, experimental offshoot to the main festival, but over the past decade it has exploded in popularity (and ticket sales, topping 1 million in 2003) and now boasts more than 1,500 shows and events — compare that to the 111 offered as part of the official Edinburgh Festival in 2004. Either way, August is a fantastic time to be in Edinburgh.

✔ **Bloemencorso,** Amsterdam, the Netherlands: This major flower festival takes place in a country obsessed with blooms. The event begins with a colorful parade of floral floats in the nearby flower market town of Aalmeer and ends in Amsterdam on the Dam Square. And get this — tulips are not included. The festival (☎ 029-793-9393) takes place on the first Saturday in September.

✔ **Oktoberfest,** Munich, Germany: Welcome to the world's biggest keg party! This festival attracts tens of thousands of people who listen to brass bands oompah, watch as a whole ox roasts on a spit, and sit under giant tents drinking liter-size mugs of beer. (I'm told that 5 million liters of beer are consumed here nearly every year.) Oktoberfest (www.oktoberfest.de) actually begins in mid-September. The first weekend in October is the final flourish.

✔ **Christmas,** throughout Europe: You can enjoy the Christmas fun and festivities anywhere in Europe from a few weeks before the holiday until January 6 (the Epiphany). Christmas is not completely commercialized in Europe, luckily. Look carefully and you can see *crèches* (Nativity scenes) in public squares and church chapels across the Continent. Some of these crèches are live, some ultratraditional, and others postmodern. I love the ones in Naples, where the holy manger seems an insignificant detail in a very Italian Bethlehem, complete with pizza parlors. On Christmas Eve, you can go to Oberndorf, north of Salzburg, Austria, to sing *Silent Night* in the town where the song was written. Or you can receive a blessing from the Pope on Christmas Day when he leans out his window in Rome at noon to give a mass blessing broadcast around the world.

Tips for Successful Trip Planning

 When planning your trip — both the whole trip and the daily schedule — make sure to leave room for downtime, changing plans, and spontaneity:

- ✔ **Make time for relaxation.** For every 10 to 15 days of rigorous sightseeing, plan at least 2 days for doing little or nothing.

- ✔ **Mentally prepare yourself for those inevitable changes in your plans.** You never know when circumstances will cause you to miss a train, for example. Try to rethink your unlucky situation in order to make the most of your new circumstances.

- ✔ **Be spontaneous.** Take advantage of unexpected opportunities, such as daytrips or festivals, and don't be scared to spend more or less time in a place after you get to know it.

Often, travelers who return to Europe for the second or third visit discover that they can see many sights outside of the major cities by renting cars and staying in villas. They can go hill-town-hopping and explore one tiny corner of Europe at a time, enabling them to travel at a leisurely pace away from the crowds and pressures of the big cities. But on your first visit, you may want to visit as many major cities and sights as possible, and nothing is wrong with that.

The whirlwind tour is still the best way to sample all of Europe's offerings during your first trip. You can get the "required" sights out of the way, so when you come back (and you *will* return), you can concentrate on lesser-known attractions or explore an area in depth.

Seeing it all without going nuts

 The idea of planning a large-scale trip can seem overwhelming — so much history and culture, so little time! Here are six ways to maximize your time and still see as much as possible:

- ✔ **Don't duplicate types of sights.** You know that many sights in Europe are unique and worth seeing in their own right. But let's face it: Visit some royal palaces or famous Gothic cathedrals, and they all start to look the same. Pick one or two examples of each and move on.

✔ **Stay centrally located.** Use your limited time to see as much of Europe as you can, rather than taking days to travel to a peripheral corner, especially on your first trip. Think about skipping some of the more geographically remote countries, such as Scandinavia, Portugal, Spain, and especially Greece, because — unless you take advantage of no-frills airlines — traveling to them takes forever. See Parts III through V to help you choose destinations that keep this idea in mind.

✔ **Select side trips prudently.** I highly recommend daytrips because they ordinarily add variety. But pick your excursions wisely, and make sure these trips don't take time away from the major city you're visiting. If you're in Florence for just one day, don't plan to see Pisa, because you'll end up seeing neither. Reserve a full day to see any destination that's more than a city-bus ride away.

✔ **Go your separate ways.** If you plan six days in London to accommodate the sightseeing wishes of each member of the family, you're wasting time unnecessarily. You don't have to tour Europe as Siamese triplets. Your partner can spend a few more hours in the British Museum and your kids can take a tour out to Windsor Castle while you check out Shakespeare's Globe Theatre. That way you all spend a single afternoon doing what otherwise would have taken one and a half days.

✔ **Practice extreme time-saving techniques.** No matter how pretty the countryside en route is, you can save a lot of precious vacation time by taking night trains between major cities so as not to use a whole day just getting from Point A to Point B, even though this may not be the most comfortable way to spend the night. Because you arrive at your destination so early, this strategy also allows you to visit a museum before the crowds arrive; you can always take a siesta later.

✔ **Know that you'll probably come back.** Assume it. Europe still has a lot left to see, no matter how much you pack in. Europe will wait for you.

Staying sane on the museum trail

Europe has generated quite an output of history and art over the past millennium, and you may feel like you've seen it all by the time your vacation is over. These hints can help you get the most out of your visits to the great museums without overloading your brain:

✔ **Plan to go to big museums twice.** Spread the visit over several days, if you have the time and inclination, because some museums are just too big to get through in one day. Consider this strategy for the Louvre, Museo del Prado, Vatican Museums, British Museum, Uffizi, and the National Gallery (London).

✔ **Split up.** Nothing is as subjective as taste in art. You and your companions don't have to stick together in museums and spend all your time looking at the same paintings. You can each go through at your own pace and peruse your own pleasures if you part ways at the front door and set a time to meet. This strategy also gives you and your companions some time apart. (Even the closest of friends and family can get on each other's nerves.)

✔ **Try out the audio tour.** Audio tours in museums have become quite sophisticated. You no longer have to deal with those barely understandable cassette audio guides that make everyone go in a big group from one masterpiece to the next. Now, most audio tours are digital, and you go at your own pace. The exhibited works have numbers next to them, which you just punch into the wand's keypad. It then gives you the facts and background of the work, artist, era, and so on. You can just press Stop when you want to and continue on to the next painting. That way, you get the lowdown on just the works that intrigue you.

✔ **Do the guided-tour thing.** Most museum tours are led by certified experts who explain the background and significance of the most important works and can answer all your questions.

✔ **Do your homework.** When you've informed yourself as to what you're looking at, the art can be much more engaging and interesting. Whether you skim your guidebook for the information or take a class in art history before your trip, a little brushing up on European artists and movements can enrich any museum-going experience.

✔ **Create your own story.** Look for humorous details the artist included, and try imagining dialogue next to the figures on the canvas. Any large canvas of a courtly scene or a banquet usually features details like two servants getting frisky with each other in the background, or a monkey and dog eyeing each other warily under the table. Most people get a little punchy after too many hours spent soberly contemplating creative genius. Feel free to make up stories to go with the scenes.

✔ **Keep the museum hours in mind.** In the later hours, museums empty out, especially the big museums that may stay open until 7 or 8 p.m. In summer, some museums may stay open as late as 10 p.m. or even midnight. If you're a fan of museum books and postcards and plan to stay until closing, check to see when the gift shop closes. Gift shops often close 30 minutes before the museum itself closes.

✔ **Spend your time on the masterpieces.** Even a moderate-size museum can overwhelm you if you don't pace yourself. Don't feel obligated to see it all. Many museums include a list of the masterpieces on their floor plans, and you can skip whole wings that you don't feel like going through.

Dealing with cultural overload

The French writer Stendhal, while visiting Florence, was so overwhelmed by the aesthetic beauty of the Renaissance — and so exhausted by trying to see absolutely everything — that he collapsed. Stendhal's case is an extreme one, perhaps, but he's not the last one to break down from too much Europe.

Even if you don't faint in the piazza, after a few days or weeks of full-steam-ahead sightseeing, you may become irritable and tired, catch a cold, or just stop caring whether you see another Giotto fresco in that church. When the idea of visiting the Louvre makes you merely groan and want to take a nap, it's time to recharge your mental batteries.

Check out these hints for remedying traveler's burnout:

- ✓ **Just because something is famous, don't feel obligated to do or see it.** If you're going to wear yourself out, do it on the stuff you like. Feel free to skip what doesn't interest you and go see what really floats your boat.

- ✓ **Pace yourself.** Go a little bit at a time in soaking up the variety of Europe's cultural offerings. Schedule rest periods. I say again what is worth repeating: Leave room to picnic, to breathe, and to stop and smell the cappuccino. Do not pack too much into either your trip itinerary or your daily sightseeing agenda.

- ✓ **Put variety into your sightseeing.** Visit a church, ruin, or park, or relax in a cafe in between sights. Don't hit one big museum after another. Give other areas of your brain a workout for a while. Your whole trip doesn't then blur into one large, colorful mirage of Gothic cathedrals and old masters from which your memory can't distinguish where Prague left off and Paris began.

- ✓ **Do the siesta thing.** In Mediterranean countries, almost all businesses are closed in the early afternoon anyway, so why not do as the Europeans do: Take a nap! A nap in the middle of the day can do you a world of good, both physically and mentally. You can take a *riposo* along with the Italians, and you'll not only appreciate the culture more, but also be able to finish the sightseeing in Florence that Stendhal started.

- ✓ **Take a break when the sightseeing starts getting to you.** Whatever it takes to bring your cultural appreciation back from the brink, do it. Take a day to get off the beaten path. Go shopping. Go to a soccer match. But stop trying to rack up sightseeing points. Sit down and write postcards. Chances are you'll get psyched to get back on the sightseeing wagon after describing to your friends back home the once-in-a-lifetime experiences you've had.

How to Schedule Your Time

Table 2-1 gives you an idea of the minimum amount of time that's needed to "see" Europe's major cities. This schedule allows time to settle in, visit the major sights, get a taste for the place, and maybe go on one daytrip.

Table 2-1	How Much Time to Spend in Each City
City	*Amount of Time*
Amsterdam	2 to 3 days
Athens	1 to 2 days
Barcelona	2 to 3 days
Bern/Alps	1 to 3 days
Dublin	1 to 2 days
Edinburgh	1 to 2 days
Florence	2 to 3 days
London	3 to 4 days
Madrid	2 to 3 days
Munich	1 to 2 days
Paris	3 to 4 days
Prague	2 to 3 days
Rome	3 to 4 days
Venice	2 to 3 days
Vienna	1 to 3 days

Remember to add on at least one extra day for each overnight side trip you want to take. Also, try to stay longer in some of the major cities, such as London, Paris, or Rome — you won't run out of things to do.

Chapter 3

Presenting Five Great Itineraries

*B*efore you start gathering information on specific destinations or looking for airfares, you need to hammer out the skeleton of your trip: your very own European itinerary. Choosing all the places you want to visit is the easy part. Figuring out which of them you have time to see takes some work. To ease the burden, I present five possible itineraries in this chapter.

Most of these tours fit into a one- or two-week timeframe, because most Americans get just one or two precious weeks of vacation. I also include a three-week whirlwind extravaganza in case you can carve out that extra bit of time.

 These itineraries include two extra "freebie" days that the weekends snag for you when planning a vacation. Most flights from the United States to Europe leave in the evening, so if you can get off work a little early on Friday to get to your closest gateway city, you get all day Saturday in Europe as well. And forget about taking a day to rest when you get home before going back to the office — life's too short; don't bother coming home until the last Sunday. All of a sudden, your "week" is nine days long! Sure, you'll be exhausted at work on Monday, but will you have stories!

Keep in mind that open hours vary from season to season. Because summer is the most popular travel time, I arrange these itineraries assuming summer schedules. You may have to tweak them if you're visiting in the off-season or if one of the days you happen to be in town falls on a Monday, a Sunday, or another day when some sights may be closed.

Occasionally, I include specific train times and schedules, but remember that this is just to get you thinking about how early to catch a train. Rail timetables can and will change regularly, so always check the train times listed here against more-current schedules (Chapter 6 shows you how to do just that).

The Everything-but-the-Kitchen-Sink-in-Two-Weeks Tour

If you're determined to see as much as you can on your trip, here's the way to do it. But rest up first — you'll be on the go nonstop.

Take an overnight plane that lands early in **London** (see Chapter 10). Spend **Days 1 through 4** as outlined in Chapter 10 — taking the extra, fourth day to side-trip out to whichever most intrigues you: **Oxford, Bath,** or **Stonehenge.** This itinerary gets in all the greatest sights and experiences of London, from the National Gallery and British Museum to the Tower of London and Westminster Abbey; from shopping at Harrods and peeking at a session of Parliament to joining a London Walks tour and taking in a Shakespearean play at the Globe.

On **Day 5,** take the earliest Eurostar train through the Channel Tunnel to **Paris** (see Chapter 13). Get settled in your hotel, have lunch, and head to the Rodin Museum. Then, leave the sightseeing until tomorrow and instead spend the late afternoon in a classic French cafe followed by a sunset cruise on the Seine.

Spend **Days 6 through 8** as outlined in Chapter 13 (the "If you have three days" suggested itinerary), marveling at Notre-Dame and Sainte-Chapelle, indulging yourself with the art treasures of the Louvre and Musée d'Orsay, and climbing the Eiffel Tower.

Leave plenty of strolling time: through the genteel Marais, along the banks of the Seine River, and around the bohemian-turned-touristy (but still fun) Montmartre. Day-trip to the extravagant Versailles, the palace to end all palaces. Treat yourself to at least one first-class dinner to celebrate your arrival in one of the world capitals of cuisine.

On the morning of **Day 8,** be sure to get up early and head to the Gare de Lyon train station to leave your bags and reserve a couchette for that night's train to Venice, leaving around 7 or 8 p.m.

When you arrive in **Venice** (see Chapter 21) on **Day 9,** check out the next morning's schedule for trains on to Florence and leave your bag in the lockers; you can live out of your daypack for one day by stuffing in it a fresh set of underclothes and your toothbrush.

Then dive (well, not literally) into the city of canals. Cruise the Grand Canal on the *vaporetto* (public ferry) to one of Europe's prettiest squares, Piazza San Marco. Tour the glittering mosaic-filled St. Mark's cathedral and ride the elevator to the bell tower for sweeping views across the city and its canals.

Take the Secret Itineraries tour of the Doge's Palace (described in Chapter 21) at 10:30 a.m. for a behind-the-scenes look at Venetian history and intrigue. Have a snack on your way to check into your hotel in the early afternoon, and then see the masterpieces of the Accademia in the mid-afternoon. Take a gondola ride before dinner and wander the quiet, romantic streets after your meal. Try to get to bed at a reasonable hour because you'll have to get up early.

On the morning of **Day 10,** head to the train station at least 90 minutes before your train (this gives the slow public ferry time to get there). Retrieve your bag, and take the first morning train you can to **Florence** (see Chapter 20), and drop your bags at your hotel.

Have a lunch on the go so you don't waste time that's better spent seeing the Duomo (cathedral), climbing its ingenious and noble dome to get a city panorama, and marveling at the mosaics inside the adjacent baptistery. By 3 p.m., start heading a few blocks down to the world's premier museum of the Renaissance, the Uffizi Galleries. Have a Tuscan feast at Il Latini before bed.

Be in line at the Accademia on **Day 11** when it opens so you can see Michelangelo's *David* before the crowds arrive. If you don't linger too long, you'll have time to swing by Santa Maria Novella church before lunch for a look at its Renaissance frescoes (a young apprentice named Michelangelo helped out on the Ghirlandaio fresco cycle).

After lunch, while the city is shut down for the midday *riposo* (nap), make your way over to the Giotto frescoes in Santa Croce church, Florence's version of Westminster Abbey and the final resting place of Michelangelo, Galileo, and Machiavelli. On your way back to the heart of town, stop by Vivoli for their excellent *gelato* (ice cream).

Cross the jewelry shop–lined medieval bridge called Ponte Vecchio to get to Oltrarno, the artisan's quarter, and the Medicis' grand Pitti Palace, whose painting galleries will keep you occupied until closing time at 7 p.m. Oltrarno is full of good, homey restaurants where you can kick back, toast your 36 hours in Florence, and vow a return.

Get up extra early on **Day 12** to catch the 7:30 a.m. train to **Rome** (see Chapter 19), which pulls in around 9:15 a.m. Spend **Days 12 through 14** as outlined in Chapter 20 in the "If you have three days" section. See the glories of ancient Rome at the Forum, Colosseum, and Pantheon, and the riches of the capital of Christendom at St. Peter's and the Vatican Museums.

Rome's world-class museums include both the well known — Capitoline Museums, Galleria Borghese (which you should book before you leave home), Galleria Doria Pamphilij — and the relatively new, such as Palazzo Altemps and Palazzo Massimo alle Terme.

Spend **Day 15,** your last full day in Europe, outside the big city at **Tivoli,** a nearby hill town full of palaces, gardens, and the ruins of Emperor Hadrian's eclectic villa. Return to Rome in time for dinner and then make your way to the famous Trevi Fountain. It's tradition to toss a few coins in the water to ensure that one day you'll return to the Eternal City.

Most flights from Rome back to the United States leave either in the morning or early afternoon. Either way, **Day 16**'s a wash; spend the morning getting to the airport and the day in the air.

The Three-Week Grand Tour of Europe

Slightly less intense than the two-week tour outlined in the previous section, this itinerary allows a little leisure time to get out and enjoy the countryside, with a few scenic drives and mountain hikes thrown in for good measure.

Days 1 through 4 are the same as those in the Everything-but-the-Kitchen-Sink-in-Two-Weeks trip described in the previous section — you start in **London** (Chapter 10).

On the morning of Day 5, take an early no-frills flight to **Amsterdam** (see Chapter 14). EasyJet (www.easyjet.com) usually offers cheap fares. After you settle in, spend **Days 5 and 6** as described in Chapter 14 in the "If you have two days" section — relaxing with a canal cruise, ogling all those skinny, gabled 17th-century town houses.

Continue with that two-day itinerary, enjoying the masterpieces in the Rijksmuseum and van Gogh Museum, a Dutch-style tool around town on two wheels, titillation in the red-light district, an Indonesian feast in the hopping Leidseplein neighborhood, and a sobering tour of the Anne Frank House. Dine early on the evening of Day 6, because you need to grab the overnight train to Munich, which leaves around 7:30 p.m.

First thing to do when you arrive in **Munich** (see Chapter 15) is pause at the train station to book an overnight couchette to Venice for the next evening. Spend **Days 7 and 8** in Munich as recommended in Chapter 16. For the evening of Day 8, know that the overnight train to Venice leaves very late (around 11:30 p.m.), so after a rib-sticking dinner, bide your remaining time in Munich in true Bavarian style at the Augustinerkeller beer hall, five long blocks past the train station.

When you get to **Venice** (see Chapter 21), check into your hotel, and then head to the center of town. Spend **Day 9** as described as Day 1 under "If you have two days" in Chapter 21, drinking in the three big sights: St. Mark's Cathedral, the Doge's Palace, and the Accademia Gallery.

Spend **Day 10** visiting the outlying islands of the Venetian lagoon with their glass- and lace-making traditions, fishing villages, and glittering church mosaics.

Then, for **Day 11,** flip-flop the second day described in Chapter 21's "If you have two days" itinerary — spend the morning in the museums such as the Peggy Guggenheim and Ca' Rezzonico, and then the early afternoon simply lost in Venice's enchanting back alleys. Be sure to find yourself in plenty of time to hop on a late-afternoon train to **Florence** (see Chapter 20), arriving in time to check into your hotel and grab a late (10 p.m.) dinner.

For **Days 12 through 14** follow my two-day Florentine itinerary in Chapter 20. You get Michelangelo's *David,* the Uffizi Galleries, the Pitti Palace museums, Fra' Angelico's frescoes in San Marco monastery, the Medici Tombs, the cathedral and its dome, Bargello sculpture gallery, and the shop-lined Ponte Vecchio spanning the Arno River.

Starting with an early-morning train to **Rome** (Chapter 19), spend **Days 15 through 18** exactly as Days 12 through 15 in the preceding section, with one addition: on the morning of Day 18, take your bags to the train station to check them at the left-luggage office and to book a couchette for the overnight train to Paris before heading out to Tivoli for the day. Leave Tivoli by 4 p.m. at the latest so that you will be back in Rome by 5 p.m. — enough time to pick up some picnic supplies for dinner on the train. The Paris train leaves around 7:30 p.m.

Spend **Days 19 through 22** in **Paris** (see Chapter 13), following the schedule for Days 5 through 8 under the two-week itinerary in the preceding section.

Most flights from Paris back to the United States leave in the morning or early afternoon, so spend the morning of **Day 23** getting to the airport and the day flying home.

Two Weeks in Europe for Lovers of Art

For this trip, you can work out the daily sightseeing schedules on your own, depending on what best floats your artistic boat. Most cities have two-and-a-half days of sightseeing time budgeted, which should be enough to give the major museums a good once-over.

Head to **London** (see Chapter 10) for **Days 1 through 3.** Your first order of business should definitely be the medieval, Renaissance, and baroque masterpieces of the National Gallery. The other great art collection is the Tate Gallery, now divided between two buildings, one on each side of the Thames; the original neoclassical gallery covers the British greats and the vast new space in Southwark, the Tate Modern, concentrates on international art in the 19th and 20th centuries (from Impressionism to contemporary works), with stellar temporary exhibits.

While at the National Gallery, you may also want to nip around the corner to stop in by the National Portrait Gallery (same building, different entrance). Although the collection exists more for the historical interest of its subjects, some artistically fine portraits reside here as well (especially by Holbein, Reynolds, and Warhol).

No museum buff should miss the Victoria & Albert Museum, which has London's best sculpture collection (Donatello, Giambologna, and Bernini) and a fascinating exhibit on artistic fakes and forgeries, in addition to miles of decorative arts.

If you're into Christopher Wren's brand of Renaissance architecture, you're in luck — the city's full of it — but his greatest hit is St. Paul's Cathedral. And I can't imagine a trip to London without calling on the British Museum, at least briefly, where you can get the best overview of the ancient world's art forms (Greek, Roman, Egyptian, Assyrian, Asian, Indian, and Islamic).

On the morning of Day 4, catch a Eurostar train to **Paris** (see Chapter 13). Spend **Days 4 through 6** in the City of Light, exploring the treasures of the Louvre over a full day at least. Fans of Impressionism and French art in general should devote at least two-thirds of a day to the Musée d'Orsay.

Paris has so many smaller art museums that choosing from among them can be difficult and squeezing them all in can be nearly impossible. Whole museums are devoted to single artists (Rodin, Picasso, Delacroix, Le Corbusier, and Dalí), and others are devoted to eras — such as the medieval at underrated Thermes de Cluny, or the modern at the incomparable Georges Pompidou.

 Two of my favorite, slightly lesser-known art treasures are the Delacroix murals in the church of St-Suplice and Monet's 360-degree *Waterlilies* in specially built basement rooms of the Orangerie, off Place de la Concorde. At the end of Day 6, hop on the overnight train to Florence.

Days 7 through 9 are for **Florence** (see Chapter 20). Reserve one entire day for the Uffizi galleries, a living textbook of Renaissance development. The Pitti Palace's Galleria Palantina covers the High Renaissance and baroque eras thoroughly. Michelangelo's *David* and his unfinished *Slaves* in the Accademia are a must, and Donatello reigns supreme at the Bargello sculpture museum.

Fra' Angelico frescoed his brothers' cells at his monastery of San Marco, and they're now open as a fine museum of his works. Florence's churches are so richly decorated I scarcely know where to begin: Giotto in Santa Croce; Ghirlandaio in Santa Maria Novella and Stana Trìnita; Donatello and Michelangelo at San Lorenzo and again in the Museo dell'Opera dell' Duomo; Masaccio in Santa Maria della Carmine (the restored St. Peter's frescoes by him and teacher Masolino) and in Santa Maria Novella (his *Trinità* fresco is the first work in history using true linear perspective).

Then you can see Brunelleschi's architecture, from the Duomo's dome to Santo Spirito to the Pazzi chapel at Santa Croce. Florence is one place where you'll definitely run out of time long before you run out of art.

Days 10 through 12 find you in **Rome** (see Chapter 19). Take the morning train here from Florence on Day 10 and start exploring the baroque period with Bernini's sculptures on Piazza Navona, Piazza Barberini, and in the Galleria Borghese.

The Vatican Museums (home to the Raphael Rooms, the Pinacoteca painting gallery, and Michelangelo's Sistine Chapel) take at least two-thirds of a day. The Capitoline Museums split their collections between ancient sculpture and mosaics and Renaissance and baroque painting. Some smaller museums include the Doria Pamphilij collections and the Galleria Nazionale d'Arte Antica, split between the Palazzo Barberini (near Via Veneto) and Palazzo Corsini (in Trastevere).

Rome's churches are blanketed with art, from Filippino Lippi's frescoes in Santa Maria Sopra Minerva (where you also find Michelangelo's *Risen Christ*) to the Caravaggios in Santa Maria del Popolo and Michelangelo's *Moses* in San Pietro in Vincoli. Again, you're unlikely to run out of art to ogle in just three days here.

On the evening of Day 12, get on the overnight train for the long haul to Barcelona. If you don't like those overnight trains, wait until morning and hop the 8:55 a.m. train. Volareweb.com (http://buy.volareweb.com) sells no-frills flights to Barcelona for around $65.

Spend **Day 13** in the Catalonian capital of **Barcelona** (see Chapter 23). You should definitely take in the intriguing early Picasso works at the museum dedicated to this hometown hero and make a survey of Antoni Gaudí's whimsical architecture. At the end of the day, hop the overnight train to Madrid.

Plunge into the myriad museums of **Madrid** (see Chapter 22) on **Days 14 and 15.** Spain is the land of Picasso, Velázquez, Goya, El Greco (by adoption), Murillo, and Ribera. You have a day to devote to the Museo del Prado and another day to split between the Reina Sofía museum (home of Picasso's Guernica), the Thyssen-Bornemisza Museum, and — if you can stand any more art at this point — the Museo Làzaro Galdiano.

Day 16 is your travel-home day.

A Week of Romance, European Style

I leave much of the daily scheduling up to you in this tour — nothing kills a romantic mood more than shuttling hurriedly from place to place.

The mere mention of **Paris** (see Chapter 13) conjures up romantic images, so it's a great place to spend **Days 1 through 3.** See your fair share of Paris's famed museums — the Musée d'Orsay has both French Romantic-era painters and scads of those lovable Impressionists, but take time to enjoy the finer points of Parisian life.

Linger at cafe tables for hours, spend an evening strolling Montemartre, have long meals at fine restaurants and cozy bistros, explore Paris's gorgeous parks, take a dinner cruise along the Seine river, and ascend the Eiffel Tower one evening for a panorama of Paris that lives up to its nickname, City of Light.

To indulge in the romance of yesteryear, make a palatial daytrip to Versailles, the palace to end all palaces. On the evening of Day 3, board the overnight train or a late-evening flight on no-frills SmartWings (http://smartwings.net; about $102) to Prague.

Prague (see Chapter 18), your focus for **Days 4 and 5,** is a city of baroque palaces and mighty fortresses, church concerts and powerful beers, hidden gardens and classical street musicians who play a mean Dvořák. Pass an afternoon delving into Prague's rich Jewish heritage at its synagogues and museums; take a sunset stroll across the statue-lined Charles Bridge.

Spend a day (or at least a morning) exploring Prague Castle, both for its soaring Gothic cathedral and to see how a fortress-city of the Middle Ages looked and worked. Whatever else you do, try to fit in as many of Prague's delightful evening concerts as you can.

At the end of Day 5, hop an overnight train — or a Volareweb.com flight (http://buy.volareweb.com; about $45) — to **Venice** (see Chapter 21) for **Days 6 through 8.** Venice — La Serenissima, "The Most Serene" city of canals, palaces, Byzantine mosaics, and delicate blown glass — has made a romantic out of everyone, from Shakespeare and Thomas Mann to Casanova and Woody Allen. Venice has always been a haven of secrets, so I leave you to your own devices in exploring.

Don't pass up a spin in a traditional gondola (despite the outrageous prices). Make sure you have a couple of long, drawn-out Italian feasts by candlelight, a cruise down the majestic sweep of the Grand Canal, and some moonlit strolls through the narrow, winding alleys and over countless tiny canals.

 I suggest one personal favorite among romantic Venetian experiences: Set aside one full day to explore the smaller fishing, glassblowing, and lace-making islands in the Venetian lagoon.

You'll most likely have to fly home from (or at least connect through) Milan, so leave all of **Day 9** free for the return trip. Remember in Venice, with its languid pace, to allow at least an hour from the time you leave the hotel until you get to the train station (either to take the train to Milan in 2½ to 3½ hours, or to catch the shuttle to the Venice airport in 20 minutes).

A Week in Europe the Kids Will Love

 For this trip, fly open-jaws into London and out of Rome. Leave plenty of time for the kids to rest, and remember that kids' constitutions and ability to appreciate even the finest art and coolest palace wears out quickly. You may want to spend five hours in the Louvre, but the tykes'll be lucky to last two. Take Europe at their pace so you can all get something out of it and have a fantastic, rewarding, and (*shh!* don't tell) educational time.

Your overnight plane lands early on **Day 1** in **London** (see Chapter 10). Check into your hotel, and then head for the Tower of London, London's bastion of the Middle Ages, where knights were knighted, heroes and villains alike were beheaded, and even the famous could be held prisoner. The Crown Jewels glitter as brightly as the armor and battleaxe blades on display in the armory-and-torture-device museum.

The Yeoman Warders (or Beefeater Guards) give some of the most entertaining tours in all of Europe, turning a millennium of dry history into the most fantastic tales of intrigue and swordplay, heroic kings and tragic princelings, foul murders and fair damsels in distress.

After lunch, head to Westminster Abbey to see the tombs of great poets, explorers, and kings and queens. In the cloisters, the kids can grab giant sheets of black paper and fat gold and silver crayons, then engage in brass rubbing, a fun pastime (from the 19th century) of making imprints from floor tomb slabs featuring knights lying in repose and coats of arms.

From Westminster, you can walk past the houses of Parliament, lorded over by the Clock Tower, in which tolls a bell named Big Ben. You may have time to pop into the War Cabinet Rooms where Churchill's best and brightest kept track of troop movement and planned daring World War II offensives. You can also cross St. James's Park to peer through the gates at the queen's home, Buckingham Palace (although the changing of the guard is, in all honesty, rather overrated; I didn't particularly enjoy it at age 11, and I still find it a big yawn).

Start off **Day 2** with a cruise down the Thames to **Greenwich,** which still retains a bit of its village ambience and is home to a bevy of exciting sights. Start off at the Maritime Museum, finding out about the famed Royal British Navy in the days when the sun never set on the British Empire. Moored nearby is the most famous of the multi-sailed Clipper Ships — and liquor icon — the *Cutty Sark.*

Greenwich is a town of world standards. You can tight-rope-walk down the Prime Meridian (the line that separates the Earth's two hemispheres; have fun jumping from one to the other), and set your watch at the source from which all the world's clocks get their reading: Greenwich mean time.

Take the late afternoon to relax back in London proper, and in the evening, get cultural. See a big production musical such as *Phantom of the Opera*, a cutting-edge play in the West End, or Shakespeare performed in the

Globe Theatre or under the stars in Regent's Park. Take in whatever you're in the mood for and think the kiddies will enjoy (or at least tolerate). Get to bed early to finish off that jet lag and be ready for a daytrip the next day.

Take **Day 3** to side-trip out to **Salisbury,** with its towering Gothic cathedral, and evocative **Stonehenge** where your imagination can run wild over ancient tales of Druids and star-worshipers.

Take the earliest Eurostar train through the Channel Tunnel to Paris (see Chapter 13) on **Day 4.** Get settled in your hotel, have lunch, and head to Notre-Dame Cathedral, which you can make even more interesting if you take the time to clamber up the North Tower so the kids can examine those famed gargoyles up close (though Quasimodo — animated or otherwise — is a no-show). On a sunny day, even the most jaded of teenagers can't fail to be impressed by the delicate spectacle of light and color courtesy of Saint-Chapelle's stained-glass windows.

After a quick lunch, spend the obligatory two hours in the Louvre to see the *Mona Lisa* and other artistic treasures. Try to get to quai d'Orsay by 4 p.m. (3 p.m. in winter) so you can tour one of the oddest sights in Paris, Les Egouts, the sewers — as much to see a marvel of 19th-century metropolitan engineering as to conjure up images of *Les Misérables* and partisans hiding from the Nazis during World War II.

From here, it's just a short stroll to the ultimate Parisian sight, the Eiffel Tower. If your kids are anything like I was at age 12, you won't get away without climbing to, and pausing at, every level up to the top. Here's something fun: Have them call relatives from the pay phones halfway up ("Hey, Grandma, guess where I am?").

In the morning of **Day 5,** take your bags to Gare de Lyon train station and leave them in lockers so you can catch the overnight train to Rome that night (it leaves around 7:30 p.m.).

Then take the RER out to **Versailles,** the biggest, most impressive palace in all of Europe. Even all this lavishness gets pretty boring pretty quickly, so just take a quick tour of the highlights (a guided tour that reveals the daily life of Louis XIV or something of that nature may hold the children's attention a little longer), and then head out to enjoy the vast gardens. Visit Marie Antoinette's Hameau, a fake thatched village she had built so she could sort of slum it as a peasant girl, shepherding perfumed lambs and feeding ducks on the pond.

Be back in Paris in plenty of time to grab supplies for a picnic dinner on the train and be back at the station by 7 p.m.

Your train pulls into **Rome** (see Chapter 19) on **Day 6** around 10 a.m. Check into your hotel, splash some water on your faces, and head off to the Markets of Trajan, where the kids can wander down a block of an ancient Roman street and explore the empty shops pigeonholing the remarkably intact ruins of the world's first multilevel shopping mall.

Truth be told, this section of the Imperial Fori is a bit more impressively intact than the far more famous Roman Forum across the street, but you may still want to wander through that seat of Roman Imperial power — if only to pose as Vestal Virgins on the few empty pedestals in between the remaining statues in the Vestal's ancient home.

In the middle of touring the Forum — which is now free, so you can come and go as you like — detour out the back door to pop into the portico of Santa Maria in Cosmedin church and test your children's veracity with the help of the Mouth of Truth (you also find two midget temples to admire, and just around the corner, the Circus Maximus, where chariot races were once held).

Return to the Roman Forum to finish seeing its sights, and then show the kids the original model for sports stadiums the world over. The massive Colosseum has recently reopened much more of its interior to visitors so the kids can clamber around and imagine tournaments of wild beasts and gladiator fights with Russell Crowe (though *you* may picture Charlton Heston in the role instead).

If you finish with the Forum and Colosseum by 2 p.m. — and I suggest you try to — you have enough time to get in a visit to one or two catacombs along the Appian Way. The littlest kids may be afraid, but most will get a thrill out of wandering miles of spooky underground tunnels lined with the niched tombs of ancient Christians. The best catacomb to visit is the Catacombe di San Domitilla.

On **Day 7** head across the Tiber to the holiest side of Rome, St. Peter's Basilica and the Vatican Museums. St. Peter's may yet be another church to drag the kids into, but its sheer size is impressive to anyone — especially if you make sure to tour the subcrypt of papal tombs and climb the dome. Inspire the kids by pointing out that Michelangelo carved his *Pietà* sculpture when he was just 19 years old.

Then walk around the wall to plunge into the Vatican Museums, home to loads of ancient sculpture, the Raphael Rooms, and of course, the Sistine Chapel frescoed by Michelangelo.

Just a few blocks away on the riverbanks squats the massive Castel Sant'Angelo, the papal stronghold for centuries and a great medieval fortress to explore.

If you can manage to make it to Piazza Barberini before 5:30 p.m., pop into the Capuchin crypt where generations of silent monks — after whose dun-colored robes cappuccino was named — used their dead brothers' bones to craft mosaics, make chandeliers, or simply stack skulls in a series of cryptlike chapels under the church. Mosey from here to the Spanish Steps in time for the *passeggiata,* a see-and-be-seen stroll in the surrounding streets. Be sure before you head to bed for the night that you all stop by the Trevi Fountain (best after dark) to toss in a few coins and ensure your return to the Eternal City.

Day 8 is daytrip time again, this time out to **Ostia Antica,** ancient Rome's port. It's an Imperial-era ghost town of crumbling temples, weed-filled shops, mosaic-floored houses, dusty squares, cavernous baths, and paved streets deeply rutted by cart wheels — on a par with Pompeii, but without the hordes of tourists and just a Metro ride away from downtown Rome.

Most flights from Rome leave in the early afternoon, so plan on spending **Day 9** just getting packed and to the airport two hours before your flight.

Part II
Planning Your Trip to Europe

The 5th Wave   By Rich Tennant

"It says, children are forbidden from running, touching objects or appearing bored during the tour."

In this part . . .

Now I get down to the nitty-gritty of trip planning, from managing your money to shopping for plane tickets to choosing a tour operator to reserving a room at a hotel. You find the resources that cater to every sort of traveler — from students to seniors and everyone in between — and get the bottom line on how to pack, get your passport, and get the most miles out of your rental cars and rail passes. In short, I help you dispense with the details so you can wing your way across the Atlantic with all the information you need to fulfill your European vacation dreams.

Chapter 4

Managing Your Money

- -

In This Chapter

▶ Getting a general idea of your trip's total cost
▶ Working out a budget
▶ Deciding which is best for you: ATMs, credit cards, or traveler's checks
▶ Beating the exchange-rate game
▶ Understanding the VAT tax and getting it back
▶ Avoiding theft

- -

*E*ven though other guides may gloss over the money issue, this chapter addresses such questions as, "Can I afford this?" and "What are the real expenses involved?" Let's face it: Overcoming the expense of a trip to Europe usually makes for the biggest hurdle.

This chapter tells you straight-out how much you should budget for every major aspect of your trip and how to keep the total to a reasonable amount. But that's not all! I also give you hints, tips, and secrets on how you can trim your budget down to a price that you can actually afford.

Vacationing frugally does *not* mean you must cut out the fun. One of my rules of travel states that the less money you spend while traveling, the closer you get to experiencing the real people and culture, whether by sleeping in budget pensions and hotels with European families or eating heartily at local bistros. Although you can't realistically manage a trip to Europe on just $5 a day anymore, you can still squeak by on $90 a day — plus transportation costs — which is still a great value in this era of a strong Europe, a weak dollar, and "euroflation" (prices on everything in Europe went up with introduction of the euro single currency).

After you have your budget planned out, you need to know how to handle your money when you get to Europe. As you travel, you have many payment options, including ATM cards, credit cards, traveler's checks, and local currency. This chapter weighs the benefits and annoyances of each method and shows you how to get the most out of your dough. I also discuss the once-confusing realm of exchange rates, which has been simplified a bit with the advent of the euro, and talk a bit about taxes. Finally, I provide safety tips for securing your money and yourself.

Planning Your Budget

You can make two different trips to the same city for the same amount of time and see all the same sights, but come out with a total bill that differs by thousands of dollars. This book shows you how to maintain the quality of your trip while stretching every dollar along the way.

Traveling frugally means looking for clean, comfortable, central, and safe hotels rather than those with minibars and massage services; knowing when to splurge, when to skimp, and how to spot rip-offs; buying rail passes and museum cards instead of individual tickets; and chowing down on authentic meals in local *trattorie* (family-run restaurants) rather than on Continental slop at overpriced tourist-oriented restaurants.

Before you delve into the specific tips on saving money, plan out a rough trip budget. Your total cost depends greatly on your means and taste. If you look through the listings in the destination chapters of this book, you can easily figure out what price level of hotel and restaurant appeals to you. Just plug the average cost for these accommodations into your expected daily expenses. As long as you round all dollar amounts up to allow for some padding, you should get a good idea of your costs. As always, overestimating is wise. End your trip with some surprise leftover cash, rather than a disastrous shortfall.

In addition to the prices listed later in this book, here are some general guidelines:

- ✔ **Transportation:** One of your biggest expenses will be transportation. Airfares vary dramatically, depending on the season. See Chapter 5 for ways to get the best deal. Around Europe, use a rail pass to travel between regions or countries. Make long trips at night, upgrading to a couchette. See Chapter 6 for options and prices. You can pay individually for short rail trips, such as those within Italy and the uncovered train ride from the Netherlands/Germany border to Amsterdam.

- ✔ **Lodging:** Hotels range in price from around $70 to $100 per double for a budget hotel — from around $30 or $50 if you're willing to stay in hostels, B&Bs, or other extremely cheap options — to $250 and up (into the thousands!) for a luxury room.

- ✔ **Dining:** To me, sampling an area's local cuisine plays as large a role in my vacation as sightseeing does. So I allow a generous budget for my meals. I plan to spend $15 on an average lunch — I may spend more on one day for a restaurant meal, and considerably less the next day for a picnic. For dinner, I assume I'll indulge in a big meal every night (appetizer, two courses, table wine or beer, dessert, and coffee) and budget around $35 per person at dinner.

I don't allow myself any money for breakfast because most hotels offer a roll and coffee along with a room. If not, buying a small breakfast at a cafe costs $2 to $4, which can come out of the lunch allowance.

✔ **Attractions/shopping:** Museum hounds and sightseeing fanatics should figure enough cash into their budgets to cover the rising costs of admission. Don't be chintzy here. I usually estimate an average of $8 per sight ($10–$15 for biggies and $3–$6 for smaller sights). Therefore, stopping at three major sights per day adds up to roughly $24. Budget at least $10 a day for postcards and other minor souvenirs, more if you're a chronic shopper.

Using the three-week grand tour from Chapter 3 as a sample (making one change: instead of flying home from Paris, on the last day you take a no-frills flight back to London and fly home from there), I worked out a cost-per-person budget for two adults traveling together (see Table 4-1). I used only the information and suggested hotels contained in this book (plus ten minutes online: a quick stop at www.easyjet.com to search for transatlantic airfares).

Table 4-1 Expenses for a Three-Week Trip to Europe during High Season (Per Person)

Expense	*Cost*
Airfares, including taxes (roundtrip NYC–London $486; London–Amsterdam $22; Paris–London $39)	$547
Eurail Selectpass Saver (four countries/five days; per-person price for two people)	$340
Three nights in train couchettes ($38 each, because you can reserve a second-class couchette even on a first-class pass)	$114
18 days of city transportation ($4 a day)	$72
19 nights in hotels ($52 per person per night, averaged from hotel prices in this book)	$988
44 meals (22 lunches at $15, plus 22 dinners at $35; breakfast usually comes with hotel room, but if not, grab a quick cafe breakfast and picnic for lunch to offset the cost)	$1,100
Sightseeing admissions ($24 a day for 18 days, leaving out Paris; for Paris, $58 covers the museums pass and Eiffel tower admission)	$490
Souvenirs, postcards, gelato, and miscellaneous stuff ($10 a day)	$220
TOTAL	**$3,871**

(Not) Worrying About the Cost

You *can* afford a trip to Europe. No one should deny themselves the gift of such an experience. As you can see in Table 4-1, you can finance a thrilling three-week trip, which hits most of Europe's must-see sights, for around $3,873 per person. If that amount is still too rich for your blood, don't give up hope — the budget has some leeway.

To trim more money from your budget, for example, you can cut out $114 by sleeping in unreserved compartments on overnight trains (the pull-out seat kind) instead of couchettes. Pack picnic lunches (around $7 a person) and keep your dinner costs down to $20 apiece — plenty for a full, hearty meal — and your dining total magically shrinks from $1,100 to $594. Reduce your miscellaneous expenses to $5 a day by making your photos your postcards and skipping the souvenirs.

Factoring in these adjustments, the new grand total comes to around $3,143 — certainly not peanuts, but still a great value for everything that you're getting. You can even manage a two-week trip to Europe for as little as $2,000, if you travel smart, go during the off-season, and keep your budget in mind. The next section presents some tips to help you do just that.

Keeping a Lid on Hidden Expenses

No matter how carefully you plan a budget, it seems like you always end up shelling out for expenses that you didn't expect. The following is a list of common (yet completely avoidable) travel expenses, and ways to keep them from putting a dent in your vacation fund:

- ✔ **Find out what your rental covers.** When shopping for car rentals, always make sure you know what the quoted rate includes — and excludes. Some charges the rental agent may or may not mention to you are: airport pickup/drop-off surcharge, drop-off fee for renting in one city and dropping off in another, *CDW* (collision damage waiver), local taxes, mileage (limited or unlimited?), and a tank of gas. See Chapter 7 for more information.

- ✔ **Ask whether taxes are included.** In most of Europe, taxes are automatically included in the hotel rates. In some countries, however, hotels may quote you the prices before tax — usually the case in Spain (7 percent), sometimes in England (17.5 percent), and occasionally at expensive hotels in the Czech Republic (22 percent). Always ask to be sure.

- ✔ **Never place a phone call from a hotel.** On long-distance calls, the markup is often 200 percent. They even charge for what should be free calls to the local AT&T, MCI, or Sprint calling card number. Always use a pay phone (see Chapter 9).

✔ **Look before you tip.** Many restaurants include a service charge in your bill, so tipping another 15 percent is tossing your money out the window. Always ask if service is included. If not, tip about 15 percent, just like at home. If service is included, and you felt that your server did a good job, leave a bit extra on the table anyway (one euro, for example, or in England, a pound coin).

✔ **Watch out for high commission on exchange rates.** Find out the bank's commission fee or percentage before exchanging traveler's checks, or you could end up leaking a little extra cash each time you change money.

Cutting Costs — but Not the Fun

The following list just gives you a taste of all the budget strategies that exist. No doubt you'll encounter more ways to stretch your travel dollar.

Planning

Airfare to Europe can make you blow your budget before you even leave home, but fear not — there are plenty of ways to save.

✔ **Go off-season.** If you can travel at non-peak times (October through May for most major cities and tourist centers), you'll find hotel rates up to 30 percent below the prices of peak months.

✔ **Travel midweek.** If you can travel on a Tuesday, Wednesday, or Thursday, you may find cheaper flights to your destination. When you ask about airfares, see if you can get a cheaper rate by flying on a different day. For more tips on getting a good fare, see Chapter 5.

✔ **Try a package tour.** For many destinations, you can book airfare, hotel, ground transportation, and even some sightseeing just by making one call to a travel agent or packager, for a price much less than if you put the trip together yourself. (See Chapter 5 for more on package tours.)

✔ **Always ask for discount rates.** You may be pleasantly surprised to discover that you're eligible for discounts on sights, transportation, hotels, you name it. Members of AAA, trade unions, or AARP; frequent fliers; teachers; students; families; and members of other groups sometimes get discounted rates on car rentals, plane tickets, and some chain-hotel rooms. Ask your company if employees can use the corporate travel agent and corporate rates even for private vacations. You never know until you ask.

If your family emmigrated from Europe, you may get another discount. Many ethnic travel agencies (usually found in major cities) specialize in getting forgotten sons and daughters rock-bottom rates when returning to the Old Country. It's worth looking into if you can find one near you.

Transportation

Getting to Europe uses up most of your transportation budget, but just getting from place to place can add up too. Here are a few ways to make the most of your remaining transportation dollars:

- ✔ **Reserve your rental car before you leave.** If you know you want to have a car for some or all of your trip, rent it before you leave through a major U.S. company to save big bucks over the cost of renting on the spot in Europe (see Chapter 6 for details).

- ✔ **Don't rent a gas guzzler.** Renting a smaller car is cheaper, and you save on gas to boot. Unless you're traveling with kids and need lots of space, don't go beyond the economy size. For more on car rentals, see Chapter 6.

- ✔ **Invest in a rail pass.** Europe's extensive train system constitutes its greatest transportation asset. The train system's best value is its family of Eurorail passes (see Chapter 6).

- ✔ **Walk a lot.** A good pair of walking shoes can save lots of money in taxis and other local transportation. As a bonus, you'll get to know your destination more intimately because you explore at a slower pace.

Lodging

Hotel costs in Europe can be sky-high — especially in big cities. If you don't relish the thought of shelling out big buck for a swank room you won't be spending much time in anyway, try some of the following tips:

- ✔ **Catch 20 winks on an overnight train for $0 to $38.** Armed with your trusty rail pass, you can jump on an overnight train and fork out just $38 for a reserved bunk in a sleeping couchette. Or if you're feeling lucky, take your chances on finding an empty sitting couchette, slide down the seat back, and — voilà! — you have a bed for free! In the morning, you'll have reached your destination plus saved yourself a night's hotel charge.

- ✔ **Leave the private plumbing at home; take a room without a bathroom.** You can get a hotel room that shares a bathroom down the hall for about two-thirds as much as you pay for a virtually identical room with its own plumbing.

- ✔ **Get a triple or cots, not two rooms, if you have kids.** At most European hotels, kids stay for free in a parent's room. At the worst, a hotel may charge a small fee ($10–$20) for the extra bed.

- ✔ **Rent a room instead of staying at a hotel.** At $20 to $50 a night, private rooms for rent beat out even the cheapest B&Bs or pensions. You may also get the experience of staying in a real European home, which no 5-star hotel can give you for any price (see Chapter 7).

✔ **Give the ultra-cheap accommodations a try.** If sleeping near 150 roommates (mostly students) on a wooden floor under a big tent sounds appealing, you can spend a night in Munich for $11, breakfast included. Budget options abound in Europe, from hostels (dorm bunks cost $20) to convents ($20–$50) to extreme options like Munich's aforementioned mega tent. Check out www.beyond hotels.net, and see see Chapter 7 for more details.

✔ **Opt for a double bed instead of two singles.** Fewer sheets for the hotel to wash equals savings for you. Though this "twin versus double" option is disappearing in many places, it still holds true in some countries. Even noncouple buddies can travel this way — although if your traveling partner is of the opposite sex, pretend you're married just to put traditionalist Europeans more at ease.

✔ **Get out of town.** In many places, big savings are just a short drive or taxi ride away. Hotels outside the historic center, in the next town over, or otherwise less-conveniently located are great bargains.

✔ **Never allow the hotel to handle your laundry** — unless you enjoy being taken to the cleaners, so to speak. You can wash a few pieces of clothes in the sink each night, roll them in towels to sop up the dampness, and hang them on the radiator to dry — or even better, on the heated towel racks (a silly amenity even cheap places are installing). Or look for a laundry shop that washes and dries clothes based on weight (an average load costs $10). Most European cities have them; start looking near the local university.

✔ **Rent a room that doesn't include breakfast.** Often hotels charge an extra $10 to $15 a night when breakfast is "included." You can get the same food for about $3 at a nearby cafe.

Dining

Don't worry — you won't have to starve or even eat bad food to keep dining costs to a minimum. There are plenty of ways to eat well in Europe without breaking the bank:

✔ **Stuff yourself if your hotel room rate includes breakfast.** Don't be shy about loading up on the food that comes with your room. Have three rolls and a big bowl of cereal or as much meat and cheese as you can eat. Trust me; you're paying for the food. To avoid an expensive lunch, stick an orange and an extra roll in your pocket for later.

✔ **Reserve a hotel room with a kitchenette.** Doing your own cooking and dishes may not be your idea of a vacation, but you can save a lot of money by not eating in restaurants three times a day. Even if you only make breakfast or cook the occasional dinner, you'll save in the long run.

✔ **Try expensive restaurants at lunch instead of dinner.** Lunch menus often boast many of the same specialties, but at a fraction of the dinnertime cost.

✔ **Lunch on pub grub in Britain and Ireland.** An authentic, yet cheap, meal in a British pub includes a sandwich and a sturdy pint of ale. You can find options for sandwiches and snacking in every country.

✔ **Order from fixed-price and tourist menus.** Fixed-price meals can be up to 30 percent cheaper than ordering the same dishes à la carte. Although the options on a fixed-price menu are limited, you can't beat the price.

✔ **Picnic often.** For well under $10, you can dine like a king wherever you want — on a grassy patch in the city park, in your hotel room, or on the train.

Attractions/shopping

Some of the best sights in Europe are absolutely free, and you can often find ways to get a discounted rate on the rest:

✔ **Purchase a Paris Museum Pass.** The Paris Museum Pass gives you unlimited entry for three full days to virtually all Parisian museums and sights (the Eiffel Tower is the only major one not on the list) for only $45. It also saves you the hassle of waiting in ticket lines. You can find similar passes in other cities (Austrian and Scandinavian ones are particularly great on this) that also grant you free travel on city buses and subways and other benefits.

✔ **Visit the free or near-free sights.** You can, for example, witness first-hand Paris cafe culture for the price of a cup of coffee ($2) or cruise the Grand Canal in Venice for under $8 on the public *vaporetto* (water ferry). Other free sights and experiences include London's British Museum, Tate, and National Gallery; Rome's Pantheon and lively piazzas; and throughout Europe, most churches and cathedrals, church services where choirs sing, medieval quarters, sidewalk performers, baroque fountains, city parks, and street markets. Check out www.europeforfree.com for city-by-city lists.

✔ **Take advantage of free or reduced-price museum days.** See the Vatican for free on the last Sunday of every month. You can uncover such policies at many other museums as well. The Louvre, for example, waives admission on the first Sunday of the month and is also almost half price after 3 p.m. Read your guidebooks carefully, check the status of freebie days at www.europeforfree.com, and take advantage of the free days and hours of reduced admission, but remember that other people have the same idea — the museums will be most crowded during these free times.

✔ **Skip the souvenirs.** Your photographs and memories serve as the best mementos of your trip. Ten years down the road, you won't care about the T-shirts, key chains, Biersteins, and the like.

✔ **Use traveler's checks wisely.** Trade traveler's checks at the bank for local currency or you'll get a bad exchange rate. Also, exchange booths at major tourist attractions give the most miserable rates.

Handling Money

A traveler's check and the local American Express or Thomas Cook office used to be your only means of obtaining local currency abroad. Nowadays, however, traveler's checks are the dinosaurs of European travel. ATM cards and credit-card cash advances are much cheaper and easier. The inconvenience of waiting in line at banks or exchange booths, digging your passport out of your money belt, and getting charged sometimes high commissions has led most frequent travelers to abandon traveler's checks in favor of a trip to a street-corner ATM.

Using your ATM card

In Europe, your bank card was useless plastic about a decade ago. These days, however, you can saunter up to an ATM in virtually any city or small town and retrieve local cash, just as you would in the United States. Using the ATM is the fastest, easiest, and least expensive way to exchange money. When you use an ATM, you take advantage of the bank's bulk exchange rate (better than any rate you would get changing, say, traveler's checks at a bank), and the fees your home bank may charge you for using a nonproprietary ATM are usually less than a commission charge would be.

Both the **Cirrus/Maestro** (☎ 800-424-7787; www.mastercard.com) and **PLUS** (☎ 800-843-7587; www.visa.com) networks offer automated ATM locators that list the banks in each country that will accept your card. Look at the back of your bank card to see which network you're on, and then call or check online for ATM locations at your destination. Or, as an alternative, you can search for any machine that carries your network's symbol. In Europe, as in America, nearly every bank ATM is on both systems.

Be sure you know your personal identification number (PIN) before you leave home, and find out your daily withdrawal limit before you depart (usually around $200). Also, keep in mind that many home banks impose a fee every time your card is used at a different bank's ATM, and that fee can be higher for international transactions (up to $5 or more) than for domestic ones (where they're rarely more than $1.50). To compare banks' ATM fees within the U.S., use www.bankrate.com. For international withdrawal fees, ask your bank.

Increased internationalism has essentially eliminated the worry that your card's PIN needs special treatment to work abroad, but you should still check with the issuing bank before you leave. Most European systems use four-digit PINs; six-digit ones sometimes won't work.

If you get a strange message at the ATM that says your card isn't valid for international transactions, most likely the bank simply isn't able to make the phone connection to check your PIN (occasionally this epidemic occurs citywide). Don't panic. Try another ATM, cash a traveler's check, or try again the next day or in the next town that you visit.

Pulling out the plastic

Visa and **MasterCard** are now almost universally accepted — and in many places preferred — at most European hotels, restaurants, and shops. The majority of these places also take **American Express,** although its high commissions and unhurried reimbursement process is leading more and more small businesses to deny acceptance. The **Diners Club** card has always been more widely accepted in the cities and at more expensive establishments than in smaller towns and budget joints, but its partnership with MasterCard, announced in 2004, means that the card may soon be welcomed at establishments that take MasterCard.

 Except in the most exclusive restaurants and hotels, most Europeans have never heard of **Carte Blanche.** You rarely find a place that accepts **Discover,** and gas station and department-store credit cards are worthless overseas. Leave all those at home. Likewise, when visiting smaller, cheaper, family-run businesses, such as some inexpensive hotels and cheap restaurants, most rental rooms, and some neighborhood shops, you may find that *all* your plastic is useless, even Visa. Therefore, never rely solely on credit cards.

You can also use your credit card to get a **cash advance** through Visa or MasterCard, as long as you know your PIN. If you've forgotten yours, or didn't even know you had one, call the number on the back of your credit card and ask the bank to send it to you. It usually takes five to seven business days. But these days, cash advances can prove to be an expensive option. Keep in mind that when you use your credit card abroad, most banks assess a 2 to 3 percent fee on top of the 1 percent fee charged by Visa, MasterCard, or American Express for currency conversion on credit charges. But credit cards still may be the smart way to go when you factor in things like ATM fees and higher traveler's check exchange rates (and service fees).

 Adding insult to injury, when you use your credit cards overseas, you pay the premium interest rate (usually around 19 percent) on cash advances, not the low introductory rate that many credit cards offer. Likewise, with most cards, you start to accrue interest *immediately* when you make a cash advance (rather than at the end of the month and only if you don't pay up, as with purchases). If you use American Express, you can usually only obtain a cash advance from an American Express office.

 Some credit-card companies recommend that you notify them of any impending trip abroad so that they don't become suspicious when the card is used numerous times in a foreign destination and block your charges. Even if you don't call your credit-card company in advance, you can always call the card's toll-free emergency number if a charge is refused — a good reason to carry the phone number with you. But perhaps the most important lesson here is to carry more than one card with you on your trip; a card may not work for any number of reasons, so having a backup is the smart way to go.

Cashing traveler's checks

Take your traveler's checks (along with your passport for i.d.) to any bank, American Express office, or exchange booth in Europe, and they'll change the checks for the equivalent amount of local currency, minus exchange-rate fees (more on shopping for exchange rates later in the chapter). You sign traveler's checks once at the bank or issuing office when you buy them and again in the presence of the person who accepts or cashes the check.

These days, traveler's checks are less necessary because most cities have 24-hour ATMs that allow you to withdraw small amounts of cash as needed. However, unlike an ATM card, when you cash in your traveler's checks, you only get the street exchange rate (about 4 percent below prime), and you have to wait in long bank lines, then wait again while the teller checks and photocopies your passport. If you're comfortable doing so, using the ATM is the better, all-around choice.

So why do so many people still use traveler's checks? Insurance. Unlike regular currency, if you lose your traveler's checks, you haven't lost your money.

 If you choose to carry traveler's checks, keep a record of their serial numbers *separate from your checks* in case they're stolen or lost. (You can't get reimbursed if you can't cite the numbers of the checks that you haven't yet cashed.)You can get traveler's checks at almost any bank. **American Express** offers denominations of $20, $50, $100, $500, and (for cardholders only) $1,000. You'll pay a service charge ranging from 1 to 4 percent. You can also get American Express traveler's checks over the phone by calling ☎ **800-221-7282;** American Express gold and platinum cardholders who use this number are exempt from the 1 percent fee.

Visa offers traveler's checks at Citibank locations nationwide, as well as at several other banks. The service charge ranges between 1.5 and 2 percent; checks come in denominations of $20, $50, $100, $500, and $1,000. Call ☎ **800-732-1322** for information. AAA members can obtain Visa checks without a fee at most AAA offices or by calling ☎ **866-339-3378.** **MasterCard** also offers traveler's checks. Call ☎ **800-223-9920** for a location near you.

 Buy your traveler's checks in U.S. dollar amounts (as opposed to, say, euros) because they're more widely accepted abroad. You should also buy your traveler's checks in different denominations. For example, you can cash $100 checks when you're visiting a town for a while and $50 checks closer to the end of your visit to ensure that you don't end up with currency that you'll never use. Likewise, if you're just passing through a country, $20 checks are good to use.

Most places in Europe (excluding the town barber or the elderly couple with the five-table bistro perhaps) accept traveler's checks, especially American Express traveler's checks. However, paying for a hotel room, purchase, or meal directly with a traveler's check virtually ensures that you get the worst possible exchange rate. Exchange your traveler's checks for local cash at a bank or the American Express office.

Exchanging Money at the Best Rate

Make sure that you do some research before you change your money, or you risk getting ripped off. Exchange rates are the best and easiest way small-time financiers can take advantage of inattentive tourists. Avoid exchanging your money in the branch offices of banks you see in airports (and, to a lesser extent, train stations). Bank branches located in airports and train stations often offer a rate inferior to that of the same bank's downtown office.

Shop around for the best exchange rate. If you do, you often notice that exchange rates at banks right next door to each other can differ by 40 percent. The business section of major newspapers (and Europe's main English-language paper, the *International Herald Tribune*) lists the current rates for European currencies. The figures published are prime rates, so although you won't find a street price that's as attractive, they're a good guide to follow when shopping for rates.

In each destination chapter in this book, I give you the exchange rate for that country in the "Fast Facts" section. Although currency conversions in this guide are accurate as of this writing, European exchange rates fluctuate constantly. For up-to-date rates, look in the business pages or travel section of any major U.S. newspaper, and check online at the **Oanda Classic Currency Converter** (www.oanda.com).

Most banks display a chart of the current exchange rates that they offer, often in an outside window or inside at the international teller's window. Make sure that you look at the rate the bank buys, not sells, U.S. dollars. When you compare the rates at different banks, look for the chart with the highest number in the buying dollars column to find the best rate.

Remember to factor in the commission, if any, when comparing rates. The commission can be a flat fee that equals a few dollars or a percentage (usually 2 to 10 percent) of the amount you exchange. (Banks display commission costs in the fine print at the bottom of the daily rate chart.) Occasionally, a slightly less attractive exchange rate coupled with a low or flat-fee commission can cost you less in the long run (depending on how much you exchange) than a great-looking rate with a whopping commission.

Before you shop for an exchange rate, decide the amount that you're going to exchange. Doing so helps you figure out which rate-and-commission combo best suits your needs. I usually exchange enough money to last a few days, because I save myself the hassle of visiting the bank every day and I can save money using a flat-fee commission. However, remember to stow most of this cash in your money belt — carry in your wallet only enough for the day. (For more safety tips, see "Avoiding Theft," later in this chapter.)

You can also exchange money at commercial exchange booths (multilingually labeled as *change/cambio/wechsel*). The rates here are generally lousy and the commissions high, but they do keep longer hours than banks. Only use commercial exchange booths as a last resort if all the banks are closed and you can't access an ATM. Hotels and shops also offer terrible rates. However, multinational travel agencies such as American Express and Thomas Cook usually offer good rates and will exchange their own traveler's checks for no commission.

Buying Currency before You Leave

Though the age of ATMs makes this less necessary, some people still purchase about $50 worth of local currency for each country that they'll visit even before they leave home. Doing so gets you from the airport or train station to the better exchange rates of a downtown bank. Likewise, this money can tide you over until you get your hands on some more, if you arrive in town late at night or on a bank holiday.

AAA offices in the United States sell ready-to-go packs of several currencies at relatively reasonable rates, although you can get better ones at any bank (call ahead — usually only banks' main downtown branches carry foreign cash). Shop around for the best rate, and ask the teller to give you small bills (close to $10 denominations) because you need the cash primarily to buy inexpensive items like maps, bus tickets, and maybe food.

One big merger: The euro

In 2002, most Western European nations finally did away with their francs, marks, pesetas, and lire and finalized the adoption of a single European currency called the *euro* (€). As of this writing, one euro equals about $1.15, and conversions in this guide were calculated at this exchange rate.

Countries in this guide that use the euro include Austria, France, Germany, Greece, Ireland, Italy, the Netherlands, and Spain. The United Kingdom (which includes Scotland) and Switzerland have not adopted the euro, and the Czech Republic, which joined the European Union (EU) in May 2004, has yet to jump the appropriate economic hurdles to be able to join the more exclusive club of the single currency zone (though of the ten new EU nations, it will likely be first in line to trade in its korun for euros sometime in the next few years).

Paying and Redeeming the VAT

Most purchases that you make in Europe have a built-in **value-added tax (VAT)** of approximately 17 to 33 percent, depending on the country. Theoretically, most European Union (EU) countries are supposed to adopt the same VAT tax across the board (especially the euro countries because, technically, they share a single economic system), but that's a convention still being worked out.

The VAT tax is the European version of a state sales tax, only it's already embedded in the price instead of tacked on at the register. The price tag on merchandise is the price you pay.

If non–European Union citizens spend more than a certain amount at any one store (always before tax), they're entitled to some or all the VAT via refund. This amount ranges from as low as $80 in England (although some stores, like Harrods, require as much as $150) to $200 in France or Italy. You can also avoid the VAT if you have your purchases shipped directly from the store, but this can get expensive quickly.

To receive a VAT refund, request a VAT-refund invoice from the cashier when you make your purchases and take this invoice to the Customs office at the airport of the last EU country that you visit. Have all your VAT-refund invoices stamped before you leave Europe. After you've returned to the United States, and within 90 days of your purchase, mail all your stamped invoices back to the stores, and they'll send you a refund check. This process usually takes from few weeks to a few months, but I've waited as long as 18 months.

Many shops now participate in the Tax Free for Tourists network (look for a sticker in the store window). Shops in this network issue a check along with your invoice. After Customs stamps the invoice, you can redeem it for cash directly at the Tax Free booth in the airport (usually near Customs or the duty-free shop), or you can mail it back to the store in the envelope provided within 60 days for your refund.

Avoiding Theft

Random, violent crime rates, although increasing, are still much lower in Europe than in the United States. Murder is rare. On the whole, Europe's big cities are safer than U.S. cities. Therefore, the two biggest things you need to worry about are pickpockets and the crazy traffic.

Stay safe by sticking to populated streets after dark, and know the locations of bad neighborhoods. Each destination chapter in this book includes discussions of neighborhoods, as well as sections on safety (under "Fast Facts"), which list the less savory parts of town.

Beware of thieves young and old

As you make your way around Europe, be aware that you may encounter masterful thieves and pickpockets (although you won't realize it until you reach for your wallet and find it missing). Often, these thieves are gypsies — easy to spot, in their colorful but dirty, ragged clothes. Although you may find them anywhere — especially around major tourist attractions — they're most prevalent in southern Europe.

The adults mainly beg for money and can be very pushy doing so. The ones you really need to watch out for, however, are the children. They'll swarm you while babbling and sometimes holding up bits of cardboard with messages scrawled on them to distract you, during which time they rifle your pockets faster than you can say "Stop...." If you're standing near a wall or in a metro tunnel, they'll even be so bold as to pin you against the wall with the cardboard message so as to fleece you more easily.

Although not physically dangerous, they're very adept at taking your stuff, and they're hard to catch. Keeping on the lookout is your best defense. If a group of scruffy-looking children approaches, yell "No!" forcefully, glare, and keep walking; if they persist, yell "Politz!" (which sounds close enough to "police" in any language). If they get near enough to touch you, push them away — don't hold back just because they're children.

Usually, if your wallet is missing and you didn't leave it in a restaurant or hotel, it's gone for good. If you heed my advice in Chapter 9 and keep all your important stuff in your money belt, all you've lost is a day's spending money (and a wallet).

 Make two copies each of your itinerary, your plane tickets, and your vital information, including the information page of your passport, your driver's license, and your student or teacher's identity card. Also, include your traveler's check numbers, your credit-card numbers (write the numbers backward to "code" them), and the phone numbers that I list later in this chapter for the issuers of your bank cards, credit cards, and traveler's checks. (If you lose any of these items on the road, call those numbers collect to report your loss immediately.) Leave one copy of each of these items with a friend at home and carry the second copy with you in a safe place (separate from the originals) while you travel.

Hazard #1: The pickpocket

 Pickpockets target tourists, especially Americans. Pickpockets know that the United States is a wealthy country and that American tourists often carry lots of money and decent cameras. Make sure you're especially careful in crowded areas (buses, subways, train stations, and street markets) as well as most touristy areas (the Eiffel Tower, the Colosseum, and so on).

Don't tempt thieves. Leave your jewelry at home and don't flaunt your wallet or valuables. Follow these tips to theft-proof yourself:

✔ **Keep all valuables (plane tickets, rail passes, traveler's checks, passport, credit cards, driver's license, and so on) in your money belt and wear it at all times (see Chapter 9 for more on this).** Keep only a day's spending money in your wallet.

✔ **Carry your wallet in a secure place, such as a back pocket that buttons or in the front pocket of your jeans.** When riding buses, casually keep one hand in your front pocket with your wallet.

✔ **Don't hang your purse strap off one shoulder where a thief can easily grab it.** Instead, hang your purse across your chest. If your purse has a flap, keep the flap and latch side against your body, not facing out where nimble fingers have easy access. When on the sidewalk, walk against the wall instead of close to the curb, and keep your purse toward the wall. Also, beware of thieves who zip up on their scooters and snatch away purses.

✔ **Don't leave your camera bouncing around on your belly when you aren't using it.** Instead, stow your camera in a plain bag (a camera bag announces "steal my camera" to thieves).

✔ **Travel in a trench coat (good for warmth, rain, a makeshift blanket, and fitting into European crowds).** You can fit all your valuables inside your coat or pants pockets, and with the trench coat wrapped around you, you can feel pickpocket-proof. *Remember:* Always button up your coat before stepping on a bus, metro, or train.

Hazard #2: The scam artist

Each con artist uses his own specific tactics to rip you off. What follows are some of the most common swindles:

✔ **In countries that count pocket change in increments of hundreds (not so much of a concern since the introduction of the euro), watch out for dishonest types who confuse new arrivals with all those zeros.** For example, some people will give you change for 1,000,000 Turkish lire when you paid with a 10,000,000 bill, unless you catch them. Until you're used to the money system, examine each bill carefully before you hand it over and make sure you show the receiver that you know what you're doing.

✔ **Waiters sometimes add unordered items to your tab, "double" the tax (allocating 15 percent for the state and 15 percent for the waiter), or simply shortchange you.**

✔ **A stranger may offer to help you exchange money, befriend you, and walk off with your wallet after hugging you good-bye.** Decline any stranger's offer for assistance and continue on your way.

✔ **Hotels may sneak in minibar, phone, or other charges.** So, if your bill is any higher than the rate (plus tax) you agreed upon times the nights that you stayed, ask a manager to explain your bill.

✔ **Hotels charge obscenely high telephone rates, with markups anywhere from 150 to 400 percent — especially on long-distance calls, and their scam is perfectly legal.** In fact, hotels often charge you for the free local call to your calling-card company! Do your wallet a favor and pretend that the hotel phone doesn't exist. Use pay phones or the post office instead.

✔ **If your escort on a guided bus tour recommends a shop for buying local crafts or souvenirs, she may be getting a kickback from that store.** In return, the store charges heavily inflated prices for items. (In defense of tour guides, however, this kickback system is one of the only ways they can make a living, because they're notoriously underpaid — in part because companies unofficially expect them to take advantage of this option as an unlisted perk.)

Keeping Valuables Safe on Trains

Here are some tips for keeping your stuff safe and secure on an overnight train:

✔ **Don't flaunt your valuables.**

✔ **Lock your door and make sure that everyone in the couchette understands the importance of keeping your door locked.** Conductors usually emphasize this point, but doing it yourself doesn't hurt either.

✔ **Reserve the top bunk.** Although the top bunk is hotter, it puts your goods above the easy reach of most thieves, and you can sleep with your head next to your bags.

✔ **Stow your bags in the luggage niche above the door.** If you strap or lock your bags to this railing, a thief can't easily tug them down and run off with them.

✔ **Wear your money belt while you sleep.** After you take care of your tickets and passports with the conductor (you may have to give your passport to the conductor if your train crosses a border overnight), excuse yourself to the bathroom and strap your waistbelt around your upper thigh. This will sound creepy, but thieves with light touches sometimes unzip your pants and deftly empty your money belt while you sleep. If you strap your money belt around your thigh, they can't get away with your goods without you noticing.

✔ **Turn your valuables into a pillow.** You may not experience the most comfortable sleep, but if you wrap your valuables in your clothes and put it in a sack, the discomfort is worth the reward.

✔ **Take special precautions when sleeping in unreserved sitting couchettes.**

Coping with a Stolen Wallet

If you lose your wallet, don't panic. If you follow my tips in the "Avoiding Theft" section, earlier in this chapter, you won't have more than a day's spending money in your wallet.

If you lose your **traveler's checks** and you remembered the all-important rule of writing down the check numbers and keeping them in a separate and safe place, you can easily replace them in any big European city. Just call the issuer of your checks for details (see "Cashing traveler's checks," earlier in this chapter, for telephone numbers).

 If you lose **credit** or **ATM cards,** you'll need to cancel them immediately. Before you leave on your trip, create a list of the international customer-service numbers given on the back of each card. Keep the list in a safe spot — but not with your cards! Note that these are special U.S. numbers set up explicitly for emergencies abroad. Go to any pay phone in Europe and dial an international operator to connect your collect call.

Your credit-card company or insurer may require a police-report number or record of the loss. The collect-call numbers for the most common credit cards include:

> ✔ **American Express** (credit cards or traveler's checks):
>   ☎ 801-945-9450
>
> ✔ **Visa** (checks): ☎ +44-171-937-8091 or 813-623-1709
>
> ✔ **Thomas Cook** (checks): ☎ +44-1733-318-950

Your credit-card or ATM-card issuer may be able to wire you a cash advance or issue an emergency replacement card in a day or two. In situations such as these, carrying traveler's checks, which are easily replaced, can save your entire vacation, as American Express commercials waste no time trumpeting.

 Some major credit cards offer a service (usually for a small fee) in which you can register the numbers of all your major cards (credit, bank, and calling card), and they'll cancel them for you with one phone call, as well as provide you with emergency cash or traveler's checks. (You can pick up the traveler's checks at a local American Express, Thomas Cook, or Western Union office.)

An alternative to gaining quick cash is to have a friend wire you money. Reliable, international services include **Western Union** (☎ **800-CALL-CASH;** www.westernunion.com) and American Express's **MoneyGram** (☎ **800-666-3947;** www.moneygram.com), which allows someone back home to wire you money in an emergency in less than ten minutes.

When traveling abroad, you're a nonentity without your **passport**. If you lose your passport, go immediately to the nearest U.S. consulate. Make sure that you bring a photocopy of your passport's information pages (the two pages facing each other with your picture and vital information), passport-sized photos (bring some with you), and any other form of identification that wasn't lost.

Identity theft and fraud are potential complications of losing your wallet, especially if you've lost your driver's license along with your cash and credit cards. Notify the major credit-reporting bureaus immediately; placing a fraud alert on your records may protect you against liability for criminal activity. The three major U.S. credit-reporting agencies are **Equifax** (☎ 800-766-0008; www.equifax.com), **Experian** (☎ 888-397-3742; www.experian.com), and **TransUnion** (☎ 800-680-7289; www.transunion.com).

Chapter 5

Getting to Europe

• •

In This Chapter

▶ Consulting a travel agent
▶ Considering package tours
▶ Choosing an escorted tour
▶ Arranging your own flights

• •

*Y*our destination rolls through your thoughts like a richly colored banner. You know where you're headed, and your mind is reeling with all the sights, scenes, and excitement you expect to experience. You have just one more fine point to figure out before you connect with those places you're imagining: how to get there.

Airline options are far from limited. To check out the offerings, you can tap a travel agent for assistance, call flight reservation desks on your own, or cruise the Internet for the best deals. Also, you can choose to set out on your European explorations with or without a professional guide.

Before you get down to the business of booking a flight, take time to wing your way through this chapter.

Seeking a Travel Agent's Advice

Word of mouth goes a long way toward finding a qualified, reliable travel agent. If the brother of the friend of your Aunt Tillie's dog groomer speaks highly of his travel expert's treatment, stay tuned to clues about level of service. Finding a cheap deal on airfare, accommodations, and a rental car is the least an agent can do. A more helpful agent goes the extra mile to give you vacation value by weighing comfort with expense.

Great agents can give advice on several travel issues, including how much time to spend in a particular destination and how to choose an economical and practical flight plan. They can also make reservations for competitively priced rental cars and find deals at better hotels.

To help your travel agent help you, do a little research before you sit down to talk; picking up this book is a great start. Have a general idea of where you want to stay and what you want to do by reading up on locations. If you have access to the Internet, check prices on the Web to get a ballpark feel for prices (see "Booking your flight online" later in this chapter for shopping ideas).

When you have enough information in hand, pack up your notes and trot off to the travel agency. Agents rely on a variety of resources, so your arrangements are likely to cost less than if you seal the deal by yourself. Plus, your agent can suggest alternatives if your first choice of hotels is unavailable, and issue airline tickets and hotel vouchers.

 The travel industry is built on commissions. When you book a vacation, your agent earns a paycheck from the airline, hotel, or tour company with which you're doing business. Be on the lookout for unscrupulous travel agents who are bent on coaxing you to go for the plan that brings them the most bucks in commissions.

Some airlines and resorts started waving good-bye to agents' commissions several years ago. Customers now have to make specific mention of certain hotels or airlines if they're interested in booking; otherwise, the agent may not bring them up as options.

Exploring Package-Tour Possibilities

For lots of destinations, package tours can be a smart way to go. In many cases, a package tour that includes airfare, hotel, and transportation to and from the airport costs less than the hotel alone on a tour you book yourself. That's because packages are sold in bulk to tour operators, who resell them to the public. It's kind of like buying your vacation at a buy-in-bulk store — except the tour operator is the one who buys the 1,000-count box of garbage bags and resells them ten at a time at a cost that undercuts the local supermarket.

Comparing packages

When dealing with packagers, keep in mind that differences exist among the available options — differences that may significantly affect your travel experience. Set side by side, one combo may top another in any of the following ways:

- ✔ Better class of hotels.
- ✔ Same hotels for lower prices.
- ✔ Accommodations and travel days (days of departure and return) may be limited or flexible.
- ✔ Escorted and independent packages available — not one or the other only.
- ✔ Option to add on just a few excursions or escorted daytrips (also at discounted prices) without booking an entirely escorted tour.

Some packagers specialize in overpriced, international chain hotels. Spending time shopping around can yield rewards; don't hesitate to compare deals and details before you fork over your funds.

Hunting down the deals

You can find a tour package on your own. In fact, the information is right under your nose: Start by looking for packagers' advertisements in the travel section of your local Sunday paper. Also check national travel magazines such as *Arthur Frommer's Budget Travel, Travel + Leisure, National Geographic Traveler,* and *Condé Nast Traveler.*

Reputable packagers include these standouts:

- ✔ **Go-Today.com** (☎ 425-487-9632; www.go-today.com)

- ✔ **OffPeakTraveler.com** (www.offpeaktraveler.com)

- ✔ **Euro Vacations** (☎ 877-471-3876; www.eurovacations.com)

- ✔ **American Express Vacations** (☎ 800-346-3607; www.american express.com/travel)

- ✔ **Liberty Travel** (☎ 888-271-1584; www.libertytravel.com)

Airlines themselves often package their flights together with accommodations. When you check out the airline choices, look for one that offers both frequent service to your airport and frequent-flier miles.

The following airlines offer tour packages:

- ✔ **American Airlines Vacations** (☎ 800-321-2121; http://aav6.aavacations.com)

- ✔ **Continental Airlines Vacations** (☎ 888-898-9255; www.cool vacations.com)

- ✔ **Delta Vacations** (☎ 800-872-7786; www.deltavacations.com)

- ✔ **Northwest Airlines World Vacations** (☎ 800-800-1504; www.nwaworldvacations.com)

- ✔ **United Vacations** (☎ 888-854-3899; www.unitedvacations.com)

- ✔ **US Airways Vacations** (☎ 800-455-0123; www.usairways vacations.com)

Most European airlines offer competitive packages as well (see the appendix for their Web sites and toll-free numbers).

Several big **online travel agencies** — Expedia, Travelocity, Orbitz, Site59, and Lastminute.com — also do a brisk business in packages. If you're unsure about the pedigree of a smaller packager, check with the Better Business Bureau in the city where the company is based, or go online to www.bbb.org. If a packager won't tell you where it's based, don't book with them.

The biggest hotel chains and resorts also offer packages. If you already know where you want to stay, call the hotel or resort and ask about land/air packages.

Joining an Escorted Tour

Many people love escorted tours. The tour company takes care of all the details and tells you what to expect at each leg of your journey. You know your costs up front, and you don't get many surprises. Escorted tours can take you to see the maximum number of sights in the minimum amount of time with the least amount of hassle.

If you decide to go with an escorted tour, I strongly recommend purchasing travel insurance, especially if the tour operator asks to you pay up front. But don't buy insurance from the tour operator! If the tour operator doesn't fulfill its obligation to provide you with the vacation you paid for, there's no reason to think that it will fulfill its insurance obligations, either. Get travel insurance through an independent agency. (I tell you more about the ins and outs of travel insurance in Chapter 9.)

When choosing an escorted tour, along with finding out whether you have to put down a deposit and when final payment is due, ask a few simple questions before you buy:

- ✔ **What is the cancellation policy?** Can the tour operator cancel the trip if it doesn't get enough people? How late can you cancel if you're unable to go? Do you get a refund if you cancel? What if the tour operator cancels?

- ✔ **How jam-packed is the schedule?** Does the tour schedule try to fit 25 hours into a 24-hour day, or does it give you ample time to relax by the pool or shop? If getting up at 7 a.m. every day and not returning to your hotel until 6 or 7 p.m. sounds like a grind, certain escorted tours may not be for you.

- ✔ **Can you opt out of certain activities?** Does the tour allow picking and choosing activities; or does the bus leave once a day, and you're out of luck if you're not onboard?

- ✔ **How large is the group?** The smaller the group, the less time you spend waiting for people to get on and off the bus. Tour operators may be evasive about this, because they may not know the exact size of the group until everybody has made reservations, but they should be able to give you a rough estimate.

- ✔ **Is there a minimum group size?** Some tours have a minimum group size, and may cancel the tour if they don't book enough people. If a quota exists, find out what it is and how close they are to reaching it. Again, tour operators may be evasive in their answers, but the information may help you select a tour that's sure to happen.

✓ **What exactly is included?** Don't assume anything. You may have to pay to get yourself to and from the airport. A box lunch may be included in an excursion but drinks may be extra. Beer may be included but not wine. Are all your meals planned in advance? Can you choose your entree at dinner, or does everybody get the same chicken cutlet?

Making Your Own Arrangements

So you want to plan the trip on your own? This section tells you all you need to know to research and book the perfect flight.

Booking your flight

With the introduction of *codesharing* — one carrier selling flights as its own on another carrier — customers now enjoy more travel options and an easier time making flight arrangements. Chances are, you can call your favorite airline and come up with a plan that flies you from just about anywhere in the United States to just about anywhere in Europe.

Listed in the Appendix are the phone numbers and Web sites for all the major U.S. and European airlines that offer direct flights from North America to Europe. In these days of airline alliances, widespread code-sharing, and carrier consolidation, it barely seems to matter which airline you call to make your booking. Chances are, their interlocking partnerships will ensure you can flit from your hometown to your European destination on any combination of carriers, foreign or domestic, and any one of them can arrange this for you.

You may have to travel first to a U.S. hub, such as New York, in order to pick up a direct flight to your destination, and to reach smaller European cities you'll probably be routed through a major European hub such as Paris or Frankfurt.

Shopping for the best airfare

Competition among the major U.S. airlines is unlike that of any other industry. Every airline offers virtually the same product (basically, a coach seat is a coach seat is a . . .), yet prices can vary by hundreds of dollars.

Business travelers who need the flexibility to buy their tickets at the last minute and change their itineraries at a moment's notice — and who want to get home before the weekend — pay (or at least their companies pay) the premium rate, known as the *full fare*. But if you can book your ticket far in advance, stay over Saturday night, and are willing to travel midweek (Tuesday, Wednesday, or Thursday), you can qualify for the least expensive price — usually a fraction of the full fare. On most flights, even the shortest hops within the United States, the full fare is close to $1,000 or more, but a 7- or 14-day advance-purchase ticket may cost less than half of that amount. Obviously, planning ahead pays.

The airlines also periodically hold sales in which they lower the prices on their most popular routes. These fares have advance-purchase requirements and date-of-travel restrictions, but you can't beat the prices. As you plan your vacation, keep your eyes open for these sales, which tend to take place in seasons of low travel volume — for Europe that's generally September 15 through June 14. You almost never see a sale around the peak summer-vacation months of July and August, or around Thanksgiving or Christmas, when many people fly regardless of the fare they have to pay — though this is obviously less true if you can get a direct flight to Europe from your home airport (most folks travel domestically for the holidays). Often, flying into Europe's major cities (usually London and Paris) brings the price of a ticket down. Also, look into purchasing an *open-jaw* plane ticket, one that allows you to fly into one European city and depart from another — say, flying into London but out of Madrid on your way home. Open-jaw tickets can sometimes be a more expensive option — although usually no more than half the price of a round-trip ticket to London plus half the round-trip Madrid fare — but it's a wonderful way to keep your itinerary flexible, and you don't have to backtrack to the first city on your trip.

Consolidators, also known as bucket shops, are great sources for international tickets. Start by looking in Sunday newspaper travel sections; U.S. travelers should focus on the *New York Times, Los Angeles Times,* and *Miami Herald.* For less-developed destinations, small travel agents who cater to immigrant communities in large cities often have the best deals.

 Bucket-shop tickets are usually nonrefundable or rigged with stiff cancellation penalties, often as high as 50 to 75 percent of the ticket price, and some put you on charter airlines with questionable safety records.

Some reliable consolidators include the following:

- ✔ **AutoEurope** (☎ 888-223-5555; www.autoeurope.com)
- ✔ **Cheap Tickets** (☎ 800-377-1000; www.cheaptickets.com)
- ✔ **STA Travel** (☎ 800-781-4040; www.statravel.com)
- ✔ **Lowestfare.com** (☎ 866-210-3289; www.lowestfare.com)
- ✔ **ELTExpress** (☎ 800-TRAV-800; www.flights.com)
- ✔ **Air Tickets Direct** (☎ 800-778-3447; www.airtickets direct.com)

Booking your flight online

The "big three" online travel agencies, **Expedia** (www.expedia.com), **Travelocity** (www.travelocity.com), and **Orbitz** (www.orbitz.com) sell most of the air tickets bought on the Internet. (Canadian travelers should try www.expedia.ca and www.travelocity.ca; U.K. residents can go for expedia.co.uk and opodo.co.uk.). Each has different business deals with the airlines and may offer different fares on the same flights, so shopping around is wise. Expedia and Travelocity will also send you an **e-mail notification** when a cheap fare becomes available to your favorite destination.

Of the smaller travel agency Web sites, **SideStep** (www.sidestep.com) receives good reviews from users. It's a browser add-on (PCs only) that purports to "search 140 sites at once," but in reality only beats competitors' fares as often as other sites do. Also check out **Cheapflights.com** — a fantastic meta-search engine that will give you the going rate for any destination from the airlines sites, the booking engines like Expedia, and the major consolidators.

 Great **last-minute deals** are available through free weekly e-mail services provided directly by the airlines. Most of these deals are announced on Tuesday or Wednesday and must be purchased online. Most are only valid for travel that weekend, but some can be booked weeks or months in advance. Sign up for weekly e-mail alerts at airline Web sites or check mega-sites, such as **Smarter Living** (www.smarterliving.com), that compile comprehensive lists of last-minute specials. For last-minute trips, www.site59.com in the U.S. and www.lastminute.com in Europe often have better deals than the major-label sites.

If you're willing to give up some control over your flight details, use an *opaque fare service* like **Priceline** (www.priceline.com) or **Hotwire** (www.hotwire.com). Both offer rock-bottom prices in exchange for travel on a "mystery airline" at a mysterious time of day, often with a mysterious change of planes en route. The mystery airlines are all major, well-known carriers — and the possibility of being sent from Philadelphia to Chicago via Tampa is remote. But your chances of getting a 6 a.m. or 11 p.m. flight are pretty high. Hotwire tells you flight prices before you buy; Priceline usually has better deals than Hotwire, but you have to play their "name our price" game. *Note:* In 2004, Priceline added non-opaque service to its roster. You can still bid on opaque fares, but you now also have the option to pick exact flights, times, and airlines from a list of offers — most of which are comparable to the prices you'll find on sites like Expedia and Travelocity. For more information on the ins and outs of Priceline, look for a copy of *Priceline.com For Dummies,* by Sascha Segan (published by Wiley).

Chapter 6

Getting Around Europe

● ●

In This Chapter

▶ Discovering low-cost, European air travel
▶ Riding the rails of Europe
▶ Taking buses and ferries
▶ Renting a car

● ●

*E*urope is a very interconnected place. Between planes, buses, rental cars, and especially trains, moving from country to country is easier than getting from state to state in the United States.

Choosing the right rail pass, knowing the ground rules for figuring out schedules, and remembering some helpful hints on getting the best deal out of no-frills airlines, train stations, and rental-car agencies can slash your travel time and budget in half.

Flying Around Europe

Air travel within Europe makes sense only if you need to cover very large distances in a limited amount of time, possibly traveling to/from Scandinavia, Spain, Portugal, Greece, or Sicily. The good news is that, with the advent of **no-frills airlines,** air travel in Europe is now open even to those on the strictest of budgets.

When is flying more worthwhile than taking the train? Compare the extra money you spend on a plane ticket with the time that you waste traveling by train. If you find that you have to spend close to a full day on the train — or if a plane ride is actually cheaper — fly.

You have three main choices for air travel within Europe:

> ✔ **Regular flights on major European carriers:** Although this is your best bet, it also tends to be the most expensive option. You can call the airlines' toll-free numbers before you leave for Europe to arrange these flights (see the appendix), or you can contact a travel agent or the airline's office in any European city.

✔ **Consolidator tickets:** Budget travel agencies across Europe, especially in London and Athens, often sell cheap tickets from consolidators (also known as *bucket shops*). Although these tickets aren't totally unreliable, they constitute the least-safe way to fly. Shady consolidators can go out of business overnight (make sure you pay by credit card for insurance), they have a higher rate of cancellation, and many of the airlines (often Middle Eastern and Asian carriers) follow lower safety standards than major U.S. and European carriers.

✔ **Small, no-frills airlines:** Over the past few years, Europe has developed a fabulous system of **no-frills airlines,** dozens of small outfits — modeled on American upstarts like Southwest and JetBlue — selling one-way tickets crisscrossing Europe for well under $100. By keeping their overhead down — electronic ticketing (often via Web sites exclusively, no phone calls allowed), no meal service, and using either major cities' secondary airports or flying from smaller cities — these airlines are able to offer amazingly low fares. In fact, one of the biggest, Ryanair (www.ryanair.com), frequently runs promotions during which it gives away tickets *for free* (though taxes bring the total to around $25). Seriously, this happens all the time. The system is still evolving, with new players appearing every year and a few failing or, more commonly, being gobbled up by the growing competition. The phenomenon started in London, and many are still based there (although they now also have smaller hubs across Europe).

The two big boys in the business are **easyJet** (www.easyjet.com), which has hubs in London, Liverpool, Bristol, Barcelona, Amsterdam, and Paris; and **Ryanair** (www.ryanair.com), which flies out of London, Glasgow, Dublin, Shannon, Frankfurt, Stockholm, Brussels, and Milan. The current short-list of the most dependable among the other choices includes: **Virgin Express** in Brussels (www.virgin-express.com); **Germanwings** (www.germanwings.com) and **Hapag-Lloyd Express** (www.hlx.com) in Germany; **Volare** (www.volareweb.com) and **Air One** (www.air-one.it) in Italy; **Sterling** (www.sterlingticket.com) and SAS's offshoot **Snowflake** (www.flysnowflake) in Scandinavia; and **Air Europa** (www.air-europa.com) and **Spanair** (www.spanair.es) in Spain.

There are many more. Independent Web sites such as www.low costairlines.org and www.nofrillsair.com keep track of the industry. Another site, applefares.com, will do a pricing metasearch of some two dozen low-cost European airlines, including some — but not all — of those listed above, plus some other, smaller ones. That way, you can see the going rate for, say, a London to Rome ticket — though it's not a booking engine, just a search engine. You'll have to go to the individual airline's Web site to buy a ticket.

Taking the Train

Fast, efficient, relatively cheap, and incredibly well-interconnected, trains rule European travel. As a rule, European trains run on time, are clean and comfortable, and have a vast network that covers almost every major and minor city.

For average travel times by rail between the destinations in this book, see the appendix.

Figuring out the basics of train travel

In the United States, most folks hop in the car or book a plane ticket for long-distance travel, but in Europe, everyone and his grandmother take the train to get where they're going — and you'll probably get into a interesting conversation with that grandmother along the way (bring a picnic and offer to share it with your neighbors to jump-start conversations). Though no-frills airlines (discussed earlier) are now the best way to cover great distances between far-flung countries, the train is still king when it comes to exploring a single nation or smaller region of Europe. But before you ride the rails, you should know a few things.

Understanding train classifications

Europe offers several train classifications that range from local runs that stop at every tiny station to high-speed bullet trains (France's TGV, Italy's ETR/Pendolino, Spain's AVE), new international high-speed runs (Thalys from Paris to Brussels; Artesia from Paris to Turin and Milan in Italy), and the **Eurostar** Channel Tunnel train. Beyond these, the fastest trains you'll probably take are the popular **EC** (Eurocity), **IC** (Intercity — same as Eurocity, but doesn't cross an international border), or **EN** (Euronight).

The **Eurostar** train (☎ **08705-186-186** in London; **0892-35-35-39** in France; **02-528-2828** in Belgium; **800-EUROSTAR** in the U.S.; www.eurostar.com) runs through the Channel Tunnel and connects London's Waterloo Station both with the Gare du Nord in Paris and Central Station in Brussels. Both trips take about three hours (plus or minus the one-hour time-zone difference). Because the old train-ferry-train route (through Dover and Calais) takes all day and costs almost the same, the Eurostar option is a great deal.

Many high-speed trains throughout Europe require that you pay a supplement of around $10 to $20 in addition to your regular ticket price. If you buy point-to-point tickets, this supplement is included in the full price, but sometimes it's printed on a separate ticket. If so, validate both tickets (usually you do this by stamping the tickets in a little box at the beginning of each track). With a pass such as Eurail, you may have to purchase a supplement separately (only with some specialty trains). You can buy a supplement from the train conductor, but he'll also charge you a small penalty fee. To avoid the penalty, check at the ticket office and pay for the supplement in advance.

Europe's Primary Train Routes

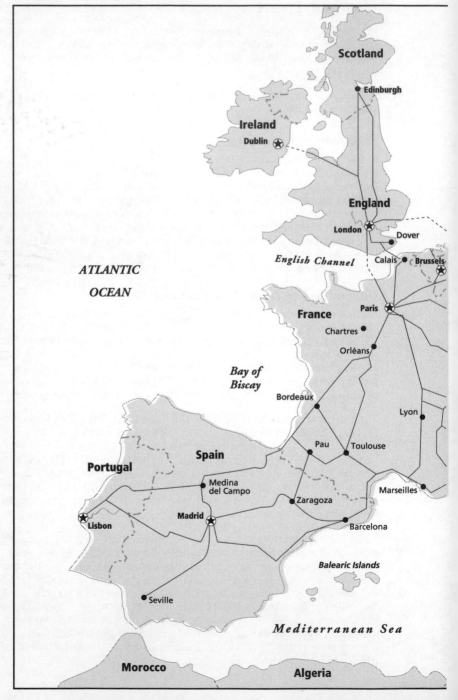

Finding schedule and fare information

Contact **Rail Europe** (☎ 800-4-EURAIL; www.raileurope.com) to receive more information about train travel in Europe, as well as automated schedule information online or by fax.

I've never really needed to buy the rail schedule bible, the **Thomas Cook European Timetable** (available at travel specialty stores or by calling ☎ 800-FORSYTH), through some people would never travel without this 500-page tome. Updated monthly (but rumored to go quarterly soon), the timetable contains the daily schedules of all major European train and ferry routes. I find looking at Rail Europe's Web site to get an idea of schedules much easier — or, even better, go directly to the sources and visit the Web sites of the individual national rail systems in Europe, which always have the latest schedules and prices (occasionally even in English). You can find lots more advice on riding the rails at www.europetrains.org.

 Most train schedules and signs use native names for cities, not the English equivalent. For example, Athens is Athinai, Cologne is Köln, Copenhagen is København, Florence is Firenze, Lisbon is Lisboa, Munich is München, Naples is Napoli, Pamplona is often Iruñea, Prague is Praha, Venice is Venezia, Vienna is Wien, and so on.

Making reservations

Some of the speediest high-speed trains require reservations, including Eurostar (the Channel Tunnel train), TGV in France, Pendolino in Italy, and long-distance trains in Spain.

You must reserve ahead of time, for a fee, any train marked with an *R* on the schedule — usually around $15, but the price can reach beyond $75 if you include a meal. You can almost always reserve a seat within a few hours of the train's departure, but booking a few days in advance at the station assures that you have a seat. You must also reserve any **sleeping couchettes** or **sleeping berths** (see the next section, "Taking overnight trains" for more information).

 Aside from those, there's no need to buy or reserve individual train tickets through your travel agent before leaving the United States. Doing so only locks you into a schedule that you may want to change after you've hit the road, and the travel agent will charge you a few extra dollars for his assistance. (Remember, though, you do need to buy your rail pass before leaving the United States; see "Saving time and money with rail passes," later in this chapter.)

I make only two exceptions to this rule:

> ✔ The high-speed Artesia train (connecting Paris with major Italian cities) requires a supplement. If you have a rail pass, you can receive a substantial discount, but only if you buy the supplement in the United States at the same time that you purchase your rail pass.

✔ Reserving a seat on the Eurostar (between London and Paris) is always a good idea. Tour groups and England's frequent bank holidays (three- or four-day weekends) book the train solid, because many Londoners take short vacations to Paris.

Traveling without a reserved seat on a regular train is rarely a problem (unless you happen to catch a train toward the beach on a holiday weekend) — though many overnight trains now require you to make at least a seat reservations for around 5€ ($5.75), if not a couchette or sleeper (see earlier in this section).

Outside each couchette, you find a little plastic window where bits of cardboard are inserted if someone at this stop or at a stop down the line has reserved a seat. To save yourself the trouble of getting booted out later in your trip, check to make sure that you're occupying an unreserved seat before you claim the couchette.

Taking overnight trains

Go to bed in Paris; wake up in Rome. Convenience doesn't get any easier. Why waste an entire day watching the countryside pass you by (no matter how pretty it is) when you traveled to see the cities? On an overnight train, not only do you get a cheap (if uncomfortable) bed for the night, but you also eliminate wasted travel time. To maximize your time and money in Europe, make any trip over six hours an overnight ride.

Don't drink the water on the trains, not even to rinse your mouth. Use this water for hand washing only. Trains, especially overnight trains, dehydrate you quickly, so make sure that you bring bottled water to sip throughout the night as well as to rinse your mouth and toothbrush the next morning.

On an overnight train, you have four sleeping choices:

✔ **Regular seats:** Use this as a last resort, because you won't get much sleep sitting up.

✔ **Fold-out seats:** In regular couchettes, you can often pull facing seat bottoms out toward each other, collapsing the seat backs. If you collapse all the seat backs on the couchette, you have a little padded romper room in which to nap, but usually no doors lock. Your privacy isn't guaranteed, so as soon as you find an unoccupied couchette, pull out all the seats, close all the curtains, turn out the lights, and lie down as though you're asleep — even if it's only 5 p.m. Hopefully, potential roomies will pass by your couchette in search of a more inviting one.

✔ **Flip-down bunks:** These are always my first choice. Sleeping couchettes can sleep six in minor discomfort on narrow, flip-down, shelflike bunks. Doors lock (make sure they're locked before you go to bed) and the conductor watches over your car (and your passport; he holds it overnight for border crossings). For 30€ ($35) a reservation, this option is one of the cheapest sleeping deals that you can find in Europe. Unless you reserve an entire couchette, prepare to share your room with strangers. (Don't flash anything valuable, and sleep with your moneybelt on.)

✔ **A sleeping-car berth:** Usually, sleeping-car berths are only a first-class option. For 40€ to 95€ ($46–$109), depending on distance traveled and how many bunks there are, you get a tiny room with two to four bunks and a private sink. Berths are a smidgen comfier than a couchette, but strangers may populate the other bunk if you're traveling alone.

Saving time and money with rail passes

The *rail pass* — a single ticket that allows you unlimited travel or a certain number of days of travel within a set period of time — was always the greatest value in European travel (until no-frills airlines came along). If your trip covers countless kilometers on the rails, a pass ends up costing you considerably less than buying individual train tickets. A rail pass also gives you the freedom to hop on a train whenever you feel like it, making a daytrip out of town cheap and easy. An extra bonus of the rail pass is that you don't have to wait in ticket lines.

The granddaddy of passes is the **Eurail** pass, which covers 17 countries (most of Western Europe except the U.K.). If you're taking a whirlwind, pan-European tour, this is your single best investment. The more modest but flexible **Selectpass** covers three to five contiguous countries for more focused trips.

These rail passes also often make you eligible for discounts on private rail lines (such as those in the Alps) and the Eurostar between London and Paris or Brussels, as well as give you discounts or free travel for ferry crossings (Italy to Greece) and some boat rides on rivers (Rhine, Mosel) and lakes (especially Swiss lakes). These bonuses can change from year to year, so check with the agency that issues your pass and read the literature that it sends with your pass to find out about any extra goodies you may receive.

Layout of the train

Some European trains still have the old-fashioned couchette configuration. Each car has a corridor along one side, off of which ten small couchettes, or compartments, reside. Each couchette seats six to eight people each, or, in first-class compartments, four to six people in slightly plushier chairs. (First class isn't worth the added expense.)

However, most trains are switching to modern, straight-through cars with seats running down both sides of an open aisle.

Rail passes are valid all the way to the borders of the countries they cover. For example, if you're traveling from a Eurail country to a non-Eurail country — say Vienna, Austria, to Prague, Czech Republic — you can visit the ticket window in Vienna and purchase a ticket for the stretch of your trip from the Austrian/Czech border to Prague. Your pass covers the Vienna-to-the-border segment.

Using a rail pass

From the date that you buy your rail pass, you have six months to begin using it. You have to validate your pass at a European train station the day you want to start using the pass. Aside from reserving couchettes or buying supplements, validating your rail pass is the only time that you have to wait in a ticket line. With consecutive-day, unlimited-use Eurail passes, you can just hop on trains at whim.

Rail passes are available in either **consecutive-day** or **flexipass** versions (in which you have two months to use, say, 10 or 15 days of train travel). Consecutive-day passes are best for those taking the train very frequently (every few days), covering a lot of ground, and making many short train hops. Flexipasses are for folks who want to range far and wide but plan on taking their time over a long trip and intend to stay in each city for a while.

The flexipass gives you a certain number of days (5 to 15) to travel within a two-month window. Printed on your flexipass are a number of little boxes that correspond with the number of travel days you bought. Write the date in the next free box (in ink) every time you board a train. The conductor comes around, checking your ticket to make sure that you've put down the right date.

 What date do I write down for overnight trains, you say? A Eurail day begins at 7 p.m. and runs 29 hours until the following midnight. In other words, when you board an overnight train after 7 p.m., write the next day's date in the box. Doing so clears you for that night and any traveling that you do the next day.

Eurail covers Austria, Belgium, Denmark, Finland, France, Germany, Greece, Hungary, Ireland, Italy, Luxembourg, the Netherlands, Norway, Portugal, Spain, Sweden, and Switzerland. *Note:* The United Kingdom (England, Scotland, Wales, and Northern Ireland) isn't included.

Knowing your options

 There are also **saverpasses** for families and small groups, and **rail/drive** passes that mix train days with car-rental days. If you're under age 26, you can opt to buy a regular first-class pass or a second-class youth pass; if you're 26 or over, you're stuck with the first-class pass. Passes for kids 4 to 11 are half price, and kids under 4 travel free.

The following prices that I list for the various rail passes are for 2004, but keep in mind that they rise each year:

✔ **Eurailpass:** Consecutive-day Eurailpass $588 for 15 days, $762 for 21 days, $946 for 1 month, $1,338 for 2 months, or $1,654 for 3 months.

✔ **Eurailpass Flexi:** Good for 2 months of travel, within which you can travel by train for 10 days (consecutive or not) for $694 or 15 days for $914.

✔ **Eurailpass Saver:** Good for 2 to 5 people traveling together, costing $498 per person for 15 days, $648 for 21 days, $804 for 1 month, $1138 for 2 months, or $1408 for 3 months.

✔ **Eurailpass Saver Flexi:** Good for 2 to 5 people traveling together, costing $592 per person for 10 days within 2 months or $778 per person for 15 days within 2 months.

✔ **Eurailpass Youth:** The second-class rail pass for travelers under age 26, costing $414 for 15 days, $534 for 21 days, $664 for 1 month, $938 for 2 months, or $1,160 for 3 months.

✔ **Eurailpass Youth Flexi:** Only for travelers under age 26, allowing for 10 days of travel within 2 months for $488 or 15 days within 2 months for $642.

✔ **Eurail Selectpass:** For the most tightly focused of trips, covering 3 to 5 contiguous Eurail countries connected by rail or ship. It's valid for 2 months, and cost varies according to the number of countries you plan to visit. A pass for 3 countries is $356 for 5 days, $394 for 6 days, $470 for 8 days, and $542 for 10 days. A 4-country pass costs $398 for 5 days, $436 for 6 days, $512 for 8 days, and $584 for 10 days. A pass for 5 countries costs $438 for 5 days, $476 for 6 days, $552 for 8 days, $624 for 10 days, and $794 for 15 days.

✔ **Eurail Selectpass Saver:** Same as the Eurail Selectpass, (and slightly less expensive), but for two to five people traveling together. Per person, the three-country pass is $304 for five days, $336 for six days, $400 for eight days, and $460 for ten days. A pass for four countries is $340 for five days. $372 for six days, $436 for eight days, and $496 for ten days. A 5-country pass is $374 for 5 days, $406 for 6 days, $470 for 8 days, $530 for 10 days, and $674 for 15 days.

✔ **Eurail Selectpass Youth:** Good in second class only for travelers under age 26. Cost varies according to the number of countries you plan to visit, but all passes are valid for 2 months. For 3 countries, it's $249 for 5 days, $276 for 6 days, $329 for 8 days, $379 for 10 days. A 4-country pass costs $279 for 5 days, $306 for 6 days, $359 for 8 days, and $409 for 10 days. A 5-country pass is $307 for 5 days, $334 for 6 days, $387 for 8 days, $437 for 10 days, and $556 for 15 days.

✔ **EurailDrive Pass:** This pass offers the best of both worlds, mixing train travel and rental cars (through Hertz or Avis) for less money than it would cost to do them separately (and it's one of the only ways to get around the high daily car-rental rates in Europe when you rent for less than a week). You get four first-class rail days and two car days within a two-month period. Prices (per person for one adult/two adults) vary with the class of the car: $452/$409 economy, $481/$423 compact, $496/$431 midsize, $531/$447 small automatic (Hertz only). You can add up to six extra car days ($49 each economy, $64 compact, $75 midsize, $95 small automatic [Hertz only]). You have to reserve the first "car day" a week before leaving the United States but can make the other reservations as you go (subject to availability). If you have more than two adults in your group, the extra passengers get the car portion free but must buy the four-day railpass for about $365 (about $183 for children 4–11).

✔ **Eurail SelectPass Drive:** This pass, like the EurailDrive Pass, offers combined train and rental car travel, but only for very focused trips: within any three to five adjoining Eurail countries. A flexipass, it includes three days of unlimited, first-class rail travel and two days of unlimited mileage car rental (through Avis or Hertz) within a two-month period. Prices (per person for one adult/two adults) are $335/$291 economy, $365/$305 compact, $392/$315 midsize, $429/$331 small automatic. You can add up to seven additional rail days for $39 each and unlimited extra car days for $49 to $95 each, depending on the class of car.

There are also **national rail passes** of various kinds (flexi, consecutive, rail/drive, and so on) for each country, **dual country passes** ("France 'n' Italy," or "Switzerland 'n' Austria"), and **regional passes** like ScanRail (Scandinavia), BritRail (covering Great Britain — which Eurail and Europass don't), and the European East Pass (good in Austria, the Czech Republic, Slovakia, Hungary, and Poland).

Purchasing your rail pass

To get the rates I quote in the preceding section, you must buy passes for Eurail and its offshoots in the United States before you leave. (You can purchase passes in some major European train stations, but you pay up to 50 percent more.) You can buy rail passes from most travel agents, but the largest supplier is **Rail Europe** (☎ **877-257-2887;** www.raileurope.com), which also sells most national passes, except German passes.

You must buy some types of national passes in the United States, whereas others you can get on either side of the Atlantic, and still others you can only purchase in Europe. In some countries, seniors, students, and youths can usually get discounts on European trains by simply asking for a discount, while in others, they can buy a discount card good for a fixed period. Rail Europe can give you all the details.

Passing on passes

Nifty as they are, rail passes aren't the wisest investment for every trip. If you're on an extended tour of Europe, Eurail is for you. However, if you're taking shorter, more focused trips, Europass is handier, but even it may be overkill if you plan to take only a few train rides over the course of your visit.

Is any pass right for you? The answer is different for every trip, so prepare to do some math. After you create an itinerary, you can estimate how much you think you'll spend on individual tickets by contacting **Rail Europe** (☎ 800-438-7245; www.raileurope.com) for prices. Choosing which pass is right for you can be tricky as well. For example, you have to travel at least 22 days (24 days with the youth pass) to make a 2-month consecutive-day pass a better deal per trip than the 15-days-within-2-months flexipass. You have to decide if the extra days are worth it, depending on your travel plans and how much freedom you want to jump trains on a whim.

Navigating the train station

Like the trains themselves, European train stations are generally clean and user-friendly. They also offer good snack bars (in case you forget to pick up train picnic supplies in town). Spending 20 minutes there when you first arrive in a city can help orient you and prepare you for your visit.

Here are my suggestions for taking advantage of the train station's resources:

- ✔ **Hit the ATM.** Most stations have a bank or ATM where you can pick up some of the local currency. Don't get more than you need — a downtown branch may offer better rates.

- ✔ **Find the tourist board kiosk.** Pick up all the free info, maps, and brochures you can get.

- ✔ **Visit a newsstand.** Unless the free map that you picked up from the tourist office is better (a rare thing), buy a map. While you're there, pick up a phone card (if you'll be in the country long enough to use it), grab a few city bus or metro tickets to get you on your way, and buy the local English-language information/events magazine.

- ✔ **Find the lockers.** Now that you have some pocket change and a map that you can use to discover your destination, you may want to dump your main bag in a locker or left-luggage office for $2 to $10 a day, keeping only your daypack. You'll definitely want to do this if you're only in town for a half-day visit, but even if you're spending the night, I suggest you go hotel hunting *without* your luggage. You'll have more stamina and bargaining leverage to find the best deal.

- ✔ **Make some calls.** Find a phone and call around for a hotel, or use the station's hotel booking service. See Chapter 7 for more hotel advice.

In smaller towns, the tiny station bar may double as the ticket office. Most stations, however, have banks of ticket windows. Try to figure out which window you need before getting in the invariably long lines. The bulk of windows are for purchasing regular tickets, and a few windows are for people who need reservations only (if, for example, you have a Eurail pass but plan to take a reservations-required train or want to reserve a sleeping couchette). You may find a few windows for international or special high-speed trains only.

 Before you exit the train station, check your options for when you leave town, as well as for any daytrips that you plan to make. You can then swing by the train station a day or two before you leave to buy your tickets and reserve seats or couchettes rather than wait until the last minute, when the lengthy ticket lines may thwart your plans.

The rail information desk — not to be confused with the city tourist board's desk (the two won't answer each other's questions) — usually has a long line and a harried staff. Use the do-it-yourself information sources as much as possible. Modern stations in big cities often have computerized rail information kiosks/automatic ticketing machines.

When the lines at the information desk are long, you can still access the information you need the old-fashioned way. Almost all stations (except some in Paris) have schedule posters that list the full timetables and regular track numbers for all trains that pass through the station. Usually, but not always, arrivals are on a white poster and departures are on a yellow one. These posters show you the number of trains per day that go where you want to go, their departure times, whether you need a reservation (usually marked by a prominent *R*), and the ultimate destination for that train. For example, you may want to travel from Paris to Pisa, but the train's final destination is marked Rome.

Keep in mind that track assignments may change on a daily basis. In larger stations, check the big, electronically updated departure boards. You can then seek out a conductor on the indicated platform and say your destination in a questioning voice while pointing at the train-in-waiting for reconfirmation before boarding. After you're onboard, you may also want to triple-check with one of the other passengers.

 Make sure that you get on the right car, and not just the right train. Individual train cars may split from the rest of the train down the line and join a different train headed to a different destination. Making sure that you're on the right car is especially important when taking a night train (if you have a reserved spot, you needn't worry). Each car has its own destination placard, which may also list major stops en route.

 Most train stations are fairly safe, but because they're central clearinghouses for tourists, pickpockets flourish. Never abandon your bags, always take caution, and don't become distracted by the many hotel touts who will swarm you offering rooms.

Ticketing tips for public transport

Although most metros (subways) have turnstiles, most public transportation (buses, trams, cable cars) in European cities operate on the honor system. As soon as you board, you're expected to punch your ticket in a little box on the bus. Make sure that you hold on to all tickets (metro, bus, or otherwise) for the duration of your ride, because spot inspectors board regularly or stop you in the metro tunnels. If they discover that you don't have a valid ticket, they fine you on the spot; fines range from $20 to $300. On the London subway, you need your ticket to get back out at the end of your journey.

In many countries now, you *must* stamp your ticket in a little box — usually attached to a column at the beginning of each track — in order to validate it before boarding the train. Conductors are increasingly issuing fines for not validating the ticket, even to unknowing tourists who plead ignorance.

Floating to Your Destination by Ferry

Throughout the length of your stay, you may occasionally cross the waters in Europe, whether you do so over the traditional English Channel crossing from Dover, England, to Calais, France; en route to Greece from Italy; or just off to an island somewhere. Ferry travel is often scenic and can be cheap, but it's also invariably slow. Don't think of it as a cut-rate cruise or you'll be disappointed. Ferry rides are strictly a mode of public transportation.

For approximately double the money of a ferry, you can often take a *hydrofoil* (a sort of a ferry on steroids). A hydrofoil travels about twice as fast as the ferry, but you're stuck below deck for the entire trip.

I recommend taking the Eurostar train through the Channel Tunnel to get from England to France or Belgium rather than taking a hydrofoil across the waters. The time you save, and the aggravation and seasickness you avoid, more than offset the difference in fare.

Getting Around by Bus

Regional and long-haul bus service in Europe mirrors the trains in its efficiency and remarkable network density. If a train in Europe can't take you where you want to go, a bus can almost certainly get you there.

Although prices are comparable to train prices, buses take two to four times as long, and they're five to ten times more uncomfortable. Avoid uncomfortable overnight bus trips.

I only take buses when a train isn't running to my destination point (as is often the case in rural areas), or if the bus makes a better connection (Florence to Siena, for example). In some countries — especially Ireland, Greece, Turkey, Portugal, and parts of Spain and Scandinavia — the bus network is more vast and better connected than the train service.

Driving in Europe

Although trains are great, a car is sometimes the best way to see Europe — with the wind in your hair and the freedom to turn down any road and visit vineyards, medieval hamlets, and crumbling castles. With a car, you can make your own schedule and get away from the set time structures of trains. Using a car is the only way to explore any small region in depth.

Of course, driving a car also has its downfalls. For example, you have to deal with aggressive drivers, navigate nerve-racking and confusing city traffic on occasion, and find and pay for parking whenever you stop. Likewise, you can't relax and do research on the trip between towns when you're behind the wheel, and the gasoline prices in Europe are shocking. Regardless, unless you walk or bike through Europe, you can't get any closer to the land and have the true freedom to go where you want than you can renting a car.

Obtaining an International Driver's Permit

If you plan to drive in Europe, you may want to bring along and carry, in addition to your regular driver's license, an *International Driver's Permit* (this permit isn't required; it merely translates your data into several languages). The permit costs $10 from AAA (call ☎ 407-444-7000 to find the office nearest you). You don't have to be a AAA member to get the pass, but if you are, ask for any free info and maps that they can send you to cover the countries in which you'll drive.

Knowing when to rent a car

 If you want to cover lots of ground, concentrate on the cities, or go solo, taking the train is better than renting a car. However, if you're exploring a single country or region, planning to visit many small towns, and you're traveling in a party of three or more, rent a car. Splitting the cost of one car rental is cheaper than train tickets when you're traveling with a group, and renting a car allows you more flexibility if you're traveling with kids. Tuscany, Provence, southern Spain, and Ireland are among the most scenic and rewarding areas in Europe to explore by car.

Avoid renting and having a car in cities. I can think of no aspect of European travel less exciting or more stressful. Plus, parking fees gobble at your travel budget. Between hotel charges and garage and lot fees, you can expect to pay anywhere from $15 to $70 a day just to park your rental. Save renting the car for exploring the countryside. Arrange to pick up your rental car the morning you leave the first city on your driving itinerary and to drop it off as soon as you pull into your final destination.

The best trips mix and match modes of transportation. For example, you can take the train to Florence, and then spend two or three days driving through the vineyards and hill towns of Tuscany to Rome. Rail-and-drive passes (see "Figuring out the basics of train travel," earlier in this chapter) can sometimes offer you bargain rates. I recommend breaking up your metropolis itinerary with some jaunts through the countryside to smaller towns to ensure that you don't miss out on a big part of the continent in your travels.

Saving time and money on rental cars

Car-rental rates vary even more than airline fares. The price depends on the size of the car, the length of time you keep it, where and when you pick it up and drop it off, where you take it, and a host of other factors. Asking a few key questions may save you hundreds of dollars.

Follow these tips to get the best deal on a rental car:

✔ **Rent in the United States.** You can get the best rates on car rental if you rent ahead of time directly through a U.S. company. If you're on the road and decide that you want a car, contact a friend or relative back home and ask him to cut the deal and fax the confirmation directly to your hotel — the money you save is worth the hassle. I list the numbers for the major rental companies, plus those that specialize in European travel, in the appendix.

✔ **Shop around.** You may think that the rental-car companies offer similar rates, but nothing is further from the truth. For the same four-day weekend, you may hear $50 from one company and $130 from another. I find that Europe specialists Auto Europe (☎ 800-223-5555; www.autoeurope.com) and Europe By Car (☎ 800-223-1516; www.europebycar.com) invariably offer the best rates. Make sure to find out what your rental rate includes — or *excludes* — such as a collision-damage waiver (CDW), taxes, mileage (you definitely want unlimited), and any other restrictions that may apply.

✔ **Shop online.** As with other aspects of planning your trip, using the Internet can make comparison shopping for a car rental much easier. You can check rates at most of the major agencies' Web sites. Plus, all the major travel sites — **Travelocity** (www.travelocity.com), **Expedia** (www.expedia.com), **Orbitz** (www.orbitz.com), and **Smarter Living** (www.smarterliving.com), for example — have search engines that can dig up discounted car-rental rates. Just enter the car size you want, the pickup and return dates, and the location, and the server returns a price. You can even make the reservation through any of these sites.

✔ **Be flexible.** When giving the rental company your dates for pickup and delivery, inform them that you're also open to other dates as well, if changing your dates means saving money — sometimes picking up the car Thursday instead of Friday, or keeping it over the weekend, saves you big bucks. You may also save money if you rent for a full week rather than two days. Finally, check whether the rate is cheaper if you pick up the car at a location in town rather than at the airport.

✔ **Know your restrictions.** Most rental companies restrict where you can drive. With some companies, you must stay in the country of rental (usually only smaller, national outfits mandate this rule). Likewise, most don't allow you to take a car that you rented in England to Ireland or the continent. Few let you drive from any Western European country into Eastern Europe, so if you're planning to drive to Prague, make sure that you make arrangements with the rental agency before you leave.

✔ **Check any age restrictions.** Many car-rental companies add on a fee for drivers under 25, while some don't rent to them at all. If you're under 25, research which companies will rent to you without a penalty.

✔ **Lease for longer periods of time.** Companies don't always remind you of the leasing option, but if you want a car for more than 17 days (up to 6 months), tell them that you want to short-term-lease the car (Auto-Europe and Europe By Car both offer this option). Leasing a car gives you a brand-new car and *full* insurance coverage with no deductible. You can also get around a technical loophole for those too young to rent under official company policy if you lease. The minimum age for renting a car ranges from 18 to 27, but it's usually 21 to 25. Anyone over 18, however, can usually lease a car.

✔ **Mention the ad.** If you see an advertised price in your local newspaper, be sure to ask for that specific rate; otherwise you may be charged the standard (higher) rate. Don't forget to mention membership in AAA, AARP, and trade unions. These memberships usually entitle you to discounts ranging from 5 to 30 percent.

✔ **Check your frequent-flier accounts.** Not only are your favorite airlines likely to have sent you discount coupons, but most car rentals add at least 500 miles to your account.

✔ **Consider a stick shift instead of an automatic.** You can save up to 40 percent on the price of car rental if you rent a stick-shift car instead of an automatic. As an added bonus, stick shifts often give you better control on Europe's many narrow, windy, hilly roads and tight streets in ancient cities.

✔ **Look into coverage you may already have.** The *collision damage waiver* (CDW), basically allows you to total the car and not be held liable. Your credit card may cover the CDW if you use it to pay for the rental, so make sure that you check the terms of your credit card before purchasing CDW. However, keep in mind that some rental agencies in Italy won't accept credit-card CDW for rentals. You must purchase it separately instead. Travel Guard (☎ 800-826-4919; www.travelguard.com) sells independent CDW coverage for a mere $7 a day — a sight better than the $10 to $20 a day rental agencies tend to charge.

✔ **Carefully consider the other insurance options.** The car-rental companies also offer additional *liability insurance* (if you harm others in an accident), *personal accident insurance* (if you harm yourself or your passengers), and *personal effects insurance* (if your luggage is stolen from your car). Your insurance policy on your car at home probably covers most of these unlikely occurrences. However, if your own insurance doesn't cover you for rentals or if you don't have auto insurance, definitely consider the additional coverage (ask your car-rental agent for more information). Unless you're toting around the Hope diamond, and you don't want to leave that in your car trunk anyway, you can probably skip the personal effects insurance, but driving around without liability or personal accident coverage is never a good idea. Even if you're a good driver, other people may not be, and liability claims can be complicated.

✔ **Remind the company that you've already paid.** Make sure that you know exactly what you paid for when you arranged your car rental. Many times, the car pickup offices in Europe overlook the fact that your credit card was already charged for the rental cost, and they try to double-charge you. Usually, you end up with one charge on your card from the European office for the first full tank of gas that it provides (which is almost never included in the original rental price).

✔ **Inspect the car before driving away.** If the rental agency doesn't know that something is wrong with the car you rented when you drive it off, it'll assume that you broke the car and charge you accordingly. If the car's condition doesn't match the inspection form that they want you to sign, point out the discrepancy. Otherwise, you're legally liable for the condition after you drive away. Make sure that all locks and doors work, check the various lights, and quickly scan the entire car for dents, scratches, and fabric rips.

✔ **Check for repair and safety equipment.** Check the trunk to make sure that your rental car is equipped with a jack, inflated spare, snow chains (for winter driving), and a hazard triangle (most countries require that you hang this on your trunk if you're broken down on the side of the road). Likewise, check the glove compartment for a parking disc. (Ask the rental agency about the parking disc; they'll explain the country's honor-system parking lots, if the system applies.)

✔ **Gas up before you return the car.** When leaving the rental company, make sure the car has a full tank of gas so you don't have to worry about dealing with local gas stations immediately. Also make sure that you return the car with a full tank of gas. Similar to rental-company practices in the United States, if you forget to fill up the car before you return it, the company will kindly fill it for you at obscenely jacked-up prices. Before you return the car, find a gas station and top off the tank.

Understanding European road rules

Except for driving on the left in Great Britain and Ireland, European road rules are similar enough to American ones that you can drive without further instruction. However, the following important differences do exist:

✔ **Watch out for aggressive drivers.** Most European drivers are much more aggressive than American drivers.

✔ **Don't cruise in the left lane.** You *do not* ride in the left lane on a four-lane highway; it's truly for passing only. Or for Mercedes with the pedal down and their hazards blinking to let you know they don't intend to use the brake pedal.

✔ **Help other drivers pass you.** If a vehicle comes up from behind and flashes its lights at you, it's signaling for you to slow down and drive more on the shoulder of the road, so it can pass you more easily. Two-lane roads in Europe routinely become three cars wide.

✔ **Be aware of speed limits.** Except for parts of the German Autobahn, most highways list speed limits of approximately 60 to 80 mph (100–135 km/h).

✔ **Remember to convert from kilometers.** European measurements relating to vehicles are in kilometers (mileage and speed limits). For a rough conversion, remember that 1 kilometer equals about 0.6 miles.

✔ **Watch out for gas prices.** Gas may look reasonably priced, but remember that the price is per liter. Remember that 3.8 liters equals 1 gallon, so multiply by 4 to guestimate the equivalent per-gallon price.

✔ **Buy a toll sticker.** Some countries, such as Austria and Switzerland, require highway stickers in lieu of paying tolls (or as a supplement to cheap tolls). If you rent a car within such a country, your car already has a sticker. But, if you're crossing a border, check at the crossing station to see whether you need to purchase a sticker on the spot for a nominal fee.

✔ **Drive defensively.** Assume that other drivers have a better idea of what they're doing than you do, and take your hints from them.

Chapter 7

Booking Your Accommodations

● ●

In This Chapter

▶ Preparing for a stay in a European hotel
▶ Finding the best hotels at the best rates
▶ Considering alternatives to traditional hotels

● ●

*I*n an era when round-trip plane tickets cost as little as $300, including taxes, but you're lucky to find a hotel room for under $100 per night (what with the weak dollar/strong Euro phenomenon), accommodations will probably eat up the biggest slice in your travel budget. But because you usually have so many options of where to stay, lodging is also an area in which you can save a lot of money. In Paris, for example, you can spend several hundred dollars on a lavish palace, stay in a clean but simple 2-star hotel down the street for around $60, or check into a hostel for just $26 per person per night.

Understanding European Hotels

Hotels in Europe tend to have fewer frills and features than hotels in the United States. For example, free cable television is standard at even the cheapest U.S. motel chains. In Europe, however, few moderately priced and inexpensive hotel rooms even have televisions.

Europe's more traditional hotels and *pensions* (smaller, family-run places) typically differ from American hotels in the following ways:

✔ **The appearance of the lobby rarely reflects the appearance of the rooms.** Never judge a European hotel by the front entry; expensive hotels sometimes invest heavily in the lobby but cut corners on the rooms, and cheaper hotels often have just a dingy desk in a hallway, but spotless, fine accommodations upstairs.

✔ **"Double" beds are often two side-by-side twin beds made with a single sheet and blanket (or overlapping twin sheets).** If you're worried about that crack between the two widening over the course of the night and your slipping through (it happens), turn the mattresses perpendicular to the springs. Also, watch out for ancient mattresses that sag in the middle.

✔ **Hotels in old European buildings often don't have elevators.** If they do, the few elevators that are available are likely to be so rickety and slow that they belong in a museum.

✔ **Floors are often covered with tile or linoleum instead of carpet.**

✔ **Bathrooms are vastly and surprisingly different from the American norm** (see the next section, "The bathroom: The big culture shock").

✔ **You can trust hotel staff to provide you with general information and pamphlets about sightseeing and attractions, but be wary of anything beyond that.** A restaurant recommended by an employee may be one owned by a relative or someone who has agreed to give the hotel a kickback. Usually the place is fine, but never count on a hotel to direct you to the best food in town. Hotel staff members may also offer to get you tickets for the theater or cultural shows, but tickets are usually cheaper from the box office or local tourism office.

In short, think of the hotel simply as a safe, clean place that's reasonably close to the sights, with a room where you can rest between long days of sightseeing. Oh, and unless you're in a 3- to 5-star property, don't expect to see chocolates on your pillow or little bottles of shampoo and conditioner in the bathroom, either.

The bathroom: The big culture shock

People who haven't traveled in Europe think that language, architecture, and food best illustrate the cultural differences between the United States and the Continent. Sorry, guess again. Americans traveling in Europe experience the greatest culture shock in the bathroom. It all starts in your first cheap pension, when you find out that the only bathroom is down the hall and shared by everyone on the floor — of *both* sexes.

European hoteliers have trouble understanding why so many American travelers don't want to share a bathroom. Although more and more European hotels are installing bathrooms in every room, this is far from the norm. If you simply can't bear the thought of sharing a bathroom, you'll have to pay extra for a private bathroom in your room.

Europeans usually refer to the bathroom itself simply as the *toilet.* You may also hear the term *W.C.* (short for the British euphemism "water closet").

See the section on electricity in Chapter 9 for information on what is not safe to plug into European bathroom outlets. (Here's a hint: everything.)

The shower: Another new adventure

In many European hotels, the concept of a shower is something like this: a nozzle stuck in the bathroom wall and a drain in the floor; curtains optional. In some cramped private baths, you have to remove the toilet paper from the bathroom to keep it dry while you drench the whole room with your shower.

Bath-takers are not home-free, either. Some European hotels still have half-tubs, in which you can only sit, not stretch out. The half-tub usually sports a shower nozzle that has nowhere to hang — your knees get very clean, but the floor gets very wet.

 Although this has been changing in recent years, in smaller, cheaper hotels it's still sometimes true that hot water may be available only once a day — and not when you want it. This is especially true in hotels with shared baths. Because heating water is costly, many smaller hotels only do it once a day, in the morning; after the hot water is used up, you won't be able to get any more until the next day. So when you check in, ask, "When is the water hot?" Try to be the first in line, shower quickly, and soap up with the water off. In some countries, especially Britain, you may have to turn on the hot water yourself at a small water heater either inside or just outside the stall.

 Before you take your shower or bath, remember that traditional European towels are annoyingly nonabsorbent. Carry your own towel for just such an emergency (a terry-cloth hand towel is less bulky than a full-size one; camping towels work great).

That extra thing: Not a toilet

The extra porcelain fixture that looks like another toilet is called a *bidet* (bi-*day*). *Do not use the bidet as a toilet.* The water that jets up and out is supposed to clean your private parts more thoroughly than toilet paper. Some non-European travelers wash clothes or store fruit or beverages in the bidet, but if you think about what the bidet is supposed to be used for, you'll see the sink is a much better place to do your laundry.

Finding the Best Room at the Best Rate

One of the biggest disappointments of any trip is getting to your hotel room and realizing that it's too small, too dirty, or too expensive. This section offers information and advice that helps you find the accommodations that meet your needs — and your budget.

Comparing room rates and ratings

The hotels listed in this book are rated from $ to $$$$$. These ratings are not an official ranking system, nor do they reflect the overall quality of a hotel. Rather, these categories reflect the approximate price range of the hotels that I recommend, related to their overall value. A ranking of $ indicates a budget gem, $$ means a pretty cheap hotel, $$$ is applied to moderate joints, $$$$ means more upscale accommodations, and $$$$$ is for a recommended splurge. These ratings are comparable only within the same city, meaning that a $ joint in an expensive place like London may cost nearly the same as a $$$$ hotel in a far cheaper area like Athens.

For the top hotels, in addition to these categories I include the hotel's actual rates, which should make finding something in your price range much easier. Of course, rates can and will go up regularly, but barring massive renovations, a budget gem or moderate choice this year will fall in the same category next year, even if the price tags are $10 higher.

The *rack rate* (referred to in this book's hotel listings simply as *rates*) is the maximum rate a hotel charges for a room — they usually fix it pretty high because, legally, that's the most they can ever charge and they want a nosebleed-high number in case some event or holiday comes along and demand outstrips supply, allowing them to charge a premium. It's the rate you get if you walk in off the street and ask for a room for the night. You sometimes see these rates printed on the fire/emergency-exit diagrams posted on the back of your door — and at least posted, in most countries by law, on the wall near the reception desk.

 Hotels are, of course, more than happy to charge you the rack rate, but you can almost always do better. Perhaps the best way to avoid paying the rack rate is surprisingly simple: Just ask for a cheaper or discounted rate. You may be pleasantly surprised. You'll stand a better chance of receiving a lower rate if you're traveling in the off-season or if you're staying several days at that one hotel. If you're booking ahead, many hotel's Web site often run specials that clock in well below the official rack rates.

Room rates (even rack rates) change with the season as occupancy rates rise and fall. But even within a given season, room prices are subject to change without notice, so the rates quoted in this book may be different from the rate you receive when you make your reservation. If you're booking at a major international chain, be sure to mention membership in AAA, AARP, frequent-flier programs, or any other corporate rewards programs. You never know when the affiliation may be worth a few dollars off your room rate. (Mom-and-pop hotels or European chains, of course, couldn't care less that you have a membership in some American automobile club or senior citizens' network, so don't bother asking them.)

 Something else that applies only to major international chains: Reserving a room through the hotel's toll-free number may also result in a lower rate than calling the hotel directly. On the other hand, the central reservations number may not know about discount rates at specific locations. For example, local franchises may offer a special group rate for a wedding or family reunion, but they may neglect to tell the central booking line. Your best bet is to call both the local number and the toll-free number and see which one gives you a better deal.

Settle all hotel charges when you check in. You don't need to pay in advance (though occasionally, a budget hotel may require it), but make sure that you and the hotel clerk agree on the rate. Does it include breakfast, taxes, and showers? What are the phone rates (although you should never make long-distance calls from the hotel)? Do they charge even for you to dial your calling card's toll-free number? Also, be sure that the quoted rate is per room, *not per person,* as may be the case in resort-type coastal towns and islands.

In most European destinations, taxes are automatically included in the quoted rates. However, in some countries (often in Spain, where it's 7 percent; in England, where it's 19 percent; and in France, where it varies depending on the classification of the hotel), these local taxes are not included in the price quoted over the phone. Always ask, "Does that price include all taxes?"

When you check in, always take one of the hotel's business cards. You'd be surprised by how many people forget their hotel's name or location after a long day of sightseeing. Many cards have a little map on the back. If you're clueless about where your hotel is, hop in a cab and show the driver the card with the hotel's address. He can get you home.

Making reservations

I always reserve at least the first night's stay before leaving home, especially if I'll be arriving on a weekend. Having somewhere to base yourself right away minimizes the stress and uncertainty when you arrive tired and in a strange place. But don't book the room for more than a few days; having the option of changing your travel plans at the last minute or looking for other accommodations if your choice isn't what you expected is nice. I often book my first night's stay in a new city simply by phoning from the train station when I arrive.

You should be aware that making last-minute arrangements can cause headaches. If you're traveling with young children, you don't want to be fumbling for coins in the train station as you simultaneously try to reserve a room and keep the kids from running off for parts unknown.

You should also find out whether you'll be arriving in town during a festival or trade fair. If you are, the gala may be the highlight of your trip, but you could end up sleeping under the stars if you haven't booked a room well in advance (before you leave home).

If you reserve a room before leaving home for your vacation, *always confirm the reservation with a follow-up fax.* Most hotels prefer this, and it gives you printed proof that you've booked a room. Faxes to hotels should use simple language and include the following:

  ✔ Your name

  ✔ The number of people in your party

✔ What kind of room you want (Make sure you say "double with one bed with private bathroom" or "double with two beds and a shared bathroom," and specify "two adults, one child, in the same room.")

✔ The number of nights you want to stay

✔ The date of the first night

To avoid confusion, always spell out the full name of the month — Europeans numerically abbreviate dates day/month/year, not month/day/year as Americans do (so "5/6/2004" would be read May 6 in the United States, but June 5 in Europe).

Smaller, less expensive hotels often won't take reservations for short stays (fewer than three nights). This policy protects them from cancellations, which can be particularly damaging to smaller hotels' bottom lines, and no assurance you offer will convince the hotelier that you'll show up. Even when you have a reservation, these hotels will hold your room only if you call from the station to say you're on the way.

Using a hotel booking service

Either the train station or the local tourism office in most European towns has a desk that serves as a central reservation service for the city. To use the service, tell the people working there your price range, the part of the city you'd like to stay in, and sometimes even the type of hotel, and they can use a computer to find you a room. In each city chapter in this book, I list booking services at the beginning of the hotel section.

Here are the advantages of booking services:

✔ **They do all the legwork for you.** Staff members speak English, and many individual hoteliers may not, so they can act as interpreters while calling around for you.

✔ **They're helpful when rooms are scarce.** If everything's booked — during a convention or festival, or maybe just in high season — they can often find rooms in hotels that aren't listed in the guidebooks or other popular resources.

✔ **They know the hotels.** The best ones can find accommodations that perfectly match your needs and price range.

But booking services do have their drawbacks:

✔ **Contacting hotels directly is generally cheaper.** Booking services usually charge a fee — a nominal one (say, $3–$10), but a fee nonetheless. And in many countries, hotels often charge higher rates for bookings they receive through services.

✔ **A tourism office booking-desk clerk offers no opinion about the hotels.** Agents just provide you a list to choose from that may include amenities and prices, but little else.

✔ **They may be biased.** A booking agency, especially a private one (which is probably run by a group of local hotels), may try to steer you to places on its "push list." Rather than an honest evaluation, its "advice" is frequently a biased sales pitch dictated by the hotel itself.

You get mixed results from the information that booking services provide. I've found wonderful little bed-and-breakfasts in Ireland through the glossy promotional catalog the tourist office sent me. I've also had a Prague hotel agency stick me in what appeared to be an old high school almost an hour from the city center; the room made me long for my college dorm. The only way to protect yourself is to read promotional fluff with a skeptical eye and ask tough questions when you call around.

In most cities — Prague and Rome come to mind — and on popular islands, hotel reps will swarm you as you step off the train or boat. Some are honestly drumming up business, but others are out to fleece you. If an offer interests you, make sure the rep pinpoints the exact location of the hotel on a map and get the price in writing before you go off with him. Pay close attention to any photos he shows you — a little photo retouching and some strategic furniture rearrangement can make a dismal cell look more like a palatial suite.

Surfing the Web for hotel deals

Shopping online for hotels is generally done one of two ways: by booking through the hotel's own Web site or through an independent booking agency (or a fare-service agency like Priceline.com). These Internet hotel agencies have multiplied in mind-boggling numbers of late, competing for the business of millions of consumers surfing for accommodations around the world. This competitiveness can be a boon to consumers who have the patience and time to shop and compare the online sites for good deals — but shop they must, because prices can vary considerably from site to site. And keep in mind that hotels at the top of a site's listing may be there for no other reason than that it paid money to get the placement.

Of the "big three" sites, **Expedia** offers a long list of special deals and "virtual tours" or photos of available rooms so you can see what you're paying for (a feature that helps counter the claims that the best rooms are often held back from bargain-booking Web sites). **Travelocity** posts unvarnished customer reviews and ranks its properties according to the AAA rating system. Also reliable are **Hotels.com** and **Quikbook.com.** An excellent free program, **TravelAxe** (www.travelaxe.net), can help you search multiple hotel sites at once — even ones you may never have heard of — and conveniently lists the total price of the room, including the taxes and service charges. Another booking site, **Travelweb** (www.travelweb.com), is partly owned by the hotels it represents (including the Hilton, Hyatt, and Starwood chains) and is, therefore, plugged directly into the hotels' reservations systems — unlike independent online agencies, which have to fax or e-mail to the hotel all reservation requests, a good portion of which get misplaced in the shuffle. More than once, travelers have arrived at their hotel, only to be told that they have no reservation. To be fair, many of the major sites are undergoing improvements in service and ease of use, and Expedia will soon be able to plug directly into the reservations systems of many hotel chains — none of which can be bad news for consumers. In the meantime, it's a good idea to get a confirmation number and make a printout of any online booking transaction.

In the opaque Web site category, **Priceline.com** and **Hotwire.com** are even better for hotels than for airfares; with both, you're allowed to pick the neighborhood and quality level of your hotel before offering up your money. Priceline's hotel product even covers Europe and Asia, though it's much better at getting 5-star lodging for 3-star prices than at finding anything at the bottom of the scale. On the downside, many hotels stick Priceline guests in their least desirable rooms. Be sure to go to the **BiddingForTravel** Web site (`www.biddingfortravel.com`) before bidding on a hotel room on Priceline; it features a fairly up-to-date list of hotels that Priceline uses in major cities. For both Priceline and Hotwire, you pay up front, and the fee is nonrefundable. *Note:* Some hotels do not provide loyalty-program credits or points or other frequent-guest amenities when you book a room through opaque online services.

One of the pluses of Web sites is that they often include virtual brochures, so you can see pictures of the rooms ahead of time. You can also usually get the latest hotel rates, plus any discounts the booking service may be able to secure (especially at pricier inns).

But these sites also have some big minuses. Because most of them charge a fee to the hotels they list and the hotels themselves provide the write-ups and other info, you must take any descriptions or recommendations with a grain of salt. Travel guidebooks like this one provide unbiased recommendations, but most hotel booking Web sites are just a new form of promotional material. Also, the bulk of the hotels that choose to be listed on these sites are high-end, business-oriented, owned by chains, or all the above. The best small hotels in the historic city centers, mom-and-pop pensions, and outright cheap places are usually absent.

Some lodging sites specialize in a particular type of accommodation, such as *bed-and-breakfasts* (B&Bs), which you don't find on mainstream booking sites. Others offer weekend deals at chain properties, which cater to business travelers and have more empty rooms on weekends.

Finding deals at the last minute

If you arrive at your destination with no hotel reservation, a guidebook like this can come in very handy. Before you get to town (perhaps on the train ride in), study the hotel reviews and figure out which ones best fit your taste and budget. Then rank your top choices by writing 1, 2, 3, and so on in the guide's margin. Prioritizing the hotels prepares you to move quickly to the next-best option if your first choice is full.

Checking in at the chains

International chain hotels, which you can usually reserve from the United States, are often located on the edge of town in the business or industrial district. They're huge, impersonal, and expensive, but you can count on a certain level of amenities and services.

There is one chain that does it a bit differently in Europe. By partnering with existing downtown hotels, **Best Western International** (☎ 800-528-1234; www.best western.com) usually offers personality *and* location. Often a European Best Western is a local bastion of a hotel that's been a solid low-end-of-luxury choice in that city for decades, if not a century or more.

 After your train pulls into the station, get some change or buy a phone card at a newsstand and immediately start calling hotels to check for vacancies. This strategy gives you a head start on the many people who look for a room by marching out of the station with their bags and walking to the nearest hotel. If you're uncomfortable making the calls yourself, the train station or tourism office may have a reservation service that can do this for you (see "Using a hotel booking service," earlier in this chapter).

If you can't find a room this way, you can try wandering the streets checking each hotel you pass. But the areas around city train stations usually are full of cheap hotels, but they're also often bland — sometimes seedy — neighborhoods and not centrally located.

 Try expanding the scope of your search, but only as a last resort. Hotels outside the center of town often have more rooms available and are cheaper than centrally located ones. You may be able to get an even better deal in the next town over, but it won't be worth the trouble if it's more than a 30-minute train ride away.

To get the best price on the best room, follow these tips:

✔ **Compare different hotels.** Many people don't want to run from place to place, but if you have some time and are counting your pennies, it's probably worth a try. Don't assume that the first hotel you visit is the best. If you've called around and lodging seems in short supply around town, take a room where you can get it. But if rooms seem plentiful, tell the first hotel you stop in that you'll think about it and head to another one nearby.

 ✔ **Ask to see different rooms.** When you get to the hotel, don't take the first room you're shown. Ask to see some other ones. Open and close windows to see how well they block out noise. Check the rates posted on the room door (usually there by law) to make sure they match the rate you were quoted and the rate that's posted in the lobby. Ask whether some rooms are less expensive than others. After you make your reservation, asking one or two more pointed questions can go a long way toward making sure you get the best room in the house. Always ask for a corner room. They're usually larger, quieter, and have more windows and light than standard rooms, and they don't always cost more. Also ask if the hotel is renovating; if it is, request a room away from the renovation work. Inquire, too, about the location of the restaurants, bars, and discos in the hotel — all sources of annoying noise. And if you aren't happy with your room when you arrive, talk to the front desk. If they have another room, they should be happy to accommodate you, within reason.

✔ **Bargain.** Room prices are rarely set in stone, especially in pensions and mom-and-pop joints. The more empty rooms a hotel has to fill for the night, the lower you can get the price. If you're staying a single night during high season, you'll have to pay the going rate. But for off-season stays and for longer than three nights, ask for a discount. Many places have weekend discounts, too.

For more tips on saving money on hotel costs, see Chapter 4.

Discovering Other Options

The reviews in this book include standard hotels (along with a few traditional and charming family-run pensions), which are generally large and likely to have rooms available. But hotels aren't your only lodging option. In fact, compared to the other options available, they're usually among the most expensive and are rarely the most fun or memorable. Even if your room truly is just a place to rest your weary body, if you can get a bed that's both cheaper and in unique surroundings, why not do it?

The most popular alternatives

Each country seems to have its own hotel alternatives, from Alpine hikers' shacks to rental villas in Tuscany. Far too many different options exist — some 36 in Europe by my last count — to do justice to each of them here. However, here's a quick rundown on the most popular substitutes for the traditional hotel (for more information on each of these, check with the local tourism office):

✔ **B&Bs or pensions:** When Europeans go on vacation, these small, family-run versions of hotels are where they stay. If the hotels in town charge $130 for a double, a pension usually costs only $60 to $90. Upscale B&Bs — often offering what amounts to a chic apartment — can be found in such cities as London and Paris.

Some B&Bs require you to pay for breakfast or *half* or *full board* (all meals included); private baths are still rare (although this is changing); and the service is almost always genial and personable. Don't accept the meal options unless you have no other choice, as is often the case in resort locations like spas and beaches. You usually get better food and more variety in a local restaurant.

✔ **Private room rentals:** Even the cheapest B&B can't beat the price of renting a room in a private home, which can run as low as $20 to $50 for a double. This is a great option for single travelers because you don't pay the single-occupancy rate that most hotels charge.

The quality of the accommodations in rental rooms is less consistent than at standard hotels, but at worst you're stuck in a tiny, plain room. At best, you get comfortable furniture, a homey atmosphere, a home-cooked breakfast, and a feel for what it's like to be part of a European family.

✔ **Motels:** Europe has adopted this American form of modular innkeeping, but most travelers don't know this because — as in the United States — motels cluster around city outskirts at highway access points. If you're doing your travel by car and are arriving late, these places are a great, cheap lodging option. They're completely devoid of character, but they're often real bargains. Some are even fully automated so you check yourself in and out.

✔ **Converted castles and other historic buildings:** These usually high-quality lodgings can be outrageously expensive, or they can be surprisingly cheap state-run operations. (Spain's *paradores* are the best example of the latter.)

✔ **Rental apartments or villas:** If you're planning a long stay in one location and want to feel like a temporary European, or if you have a large traveling party (a big family or two families traveling together), these options are the best.

Rental apartments or villas are easiest to book through a travel agent or rental consortium, such as **Barclay International Group** (www.barclayweb.com), but you can sometimes get better rates by contacting the owners directly (with addresses or phone numbers from newspaper travel sections, magazines, English-language magazines, and tourism boards).

Before you reserve an apartment or villa, shop around, ask many questions, and look at pictures — both of the rooms and of the views in every direction. For particularly long stays, it may pay for one member of the party to make a quick trip to the country in question to tour the top options before you settle on one.

Hostels and other bargain options

If you're on a severely limited budget, or if you like hanging out with primarily youthful backpackers, you may want to stay in a hostel. They used to be called *youth hostels,* but the only ones that still follow the under-26-only rule are in southern Germany. Most hostels are now open as cheap digs for travelers of all ages, with nightly rates ranging from $15 to $40 per person.

Some are affiliated with the official hostel organization, Hostelling International (or IYH, as it's known abroad), which means they have to live up to a certain set of standards. Increasingly, private, unaffiliated hostels are opening up (often closer to the center of town than the official hostel), and although they may not have the IYH stamp of approval, in some cases they're actually nicer joints (by the same token, they may also be squalid dumps).

In a hostel, you stay in bunks in shared, dormlike rooms — though increasingly hostels are offering private rooms sleeping two to four people as well. You find anywhere from 4 to 8 beds per room (the current trend) to as many as 100 beds in one big gymnasium-like space (this sort of arrangement is slowly disappearing); most hostels have a mix of different-sized rooms at varying prices. Families can often find hostels with four-bunk rooms. Many hostels separate the sexes into different rooms or floors and supply lockers for safe bag storage. Bathrooms are usually shared (but this, too, is changing as more private rooms are made available), breakfast is often included, and other cheap but school cafeteria–like meals may be available.

Hostels (especially the official IYH ones) are often far from the city center, occasionally on the outskirts of town, and they fill up with high-school students in the summer. Year-round, many seem to be little more than giant backpacker singles' bars — great for meeting your fellow travelers, but terrible for getting to know the local city and culture.

Almost all hostels impose evening curfews (usually between 10 p.m. and midnight), midday lockout periods, and length-of-stay limits (often a maximum of three days). You may only be able to make reservations one day ahead of time, or not at all, so be sure to show up early.

To stay in many "official" IYH hostels — or at least to get a discount — you must be a card-carrying member of **Hostelling International,** 8401 Colesville Rd., Suite 600, Silver Springs, MD 20910 (☎ **301-495-1240;** www.hiusa.org for the U.S. site and joining; www.hihostels.com for the international site). Membership is free for people under 18, $28 per year for people ages 18 to 54, and $18 for those 55 and older. You can also buy the card at many hostels abroad. You can find hostel listings on Hostelling International's Web site (www.hihostels.com) and at the private sites www.hostels.com, www.hostels.net, and www.europe hostels.org.

Most hostels furnish a blanket but require you to have your own sleep-sack, which is basically a sleeping bag made out of a sheet. If you plan to stay in hostels on your trip, before you leave buy one (from Hostelling International) or make one (fold a sheet in half and sew it closed across the bottom and halfway up the side). Some hostels sell sleep-sacks, and a few insist that you rent one of theirs.

In addition to hostels, several other options exist for low-budget lodging (ask for details at the tourism office):

✔ **Convents:** Especially in predominantly Catholic countries such as Italy, Spain, and France, staying in convents and other religious buildings enables you to save a lot of money and get an immaculate and safe room, no matter what your religious affiliation. Rooms in convents, available in many major cities and pilgrimage sites, cost as little as $5 to as much as $250 per night — though the latter is a bit of an exception; they're usually pretty cheap, and well under $100 in most cases. Your room probably won't be any fancier than the cells that the nuns or monks occupy, but a few are quite posh. Many convents do give preference to visitors of their own denomination or from that religious order's country of origin.

✔ **University housing:** During the summer when school is not in session, checking with local universities to see whether any unused dorm rooms are for rent (at rates comparable to hostels) can be worthwhile.

✔ **Tent cities:** Some cities (including Munich, London, Paris, Venice, and Copenhagen) have hangarlike rooms or large tents open at the height of the summer season for travelers on an extremely tight budget. For anywhere from $7 to $20, you get a floor mat and a blanket, more than 100 roommates, and a cup of tea in the morning. Most of the people at these giant slumber parties are students, but the tent cities are open to everyone. Essentially, this is one step above sleeping on a park bench (which, by the way, is dangerous, not recommended, and usually illegal).

If you use any type of shared-space lodging, such as hostels or tent cities, be very careful with your belongings. Always play it safe; leave your pack in the lockers (if you're staying in a hostel) or at the train station (if you're staying in another type of communal lodging). For safety tips on overnight trains, see Chapter 9.

Chapter 8

Catering to Special Travel Needs or Interests

*I*f you're headed to Europe with a particular interest or concern in mind, here is the place to look for information. This chapter has resource information and travel tips for families, senior citizens, gays and lesbians, and travelers with disabilities.

Traveling with the Brood: Advice for Families

If you have enough trouble getting your kids out of the house in the morning, dragging them thousands of miles away may seem like an insurmountable challenge. But family travel can be immensely rewarding, giving you new ways of seeing the world through younger pairs of eyes. Europeans expect to encounter traveling families, because that's how they travel. You're likely to run into caravanning European clans, including grandparents and babes in arms. Locals tend to love kids, especially in Mediterranean countries. You often find that hotels and restaurants give you an even warmer reception if you have a child in tow.

 In addition to cooing over infants and toddlers, most Europeans offer loads of encouragement and attention to a teenager struggling to order a meal in the local lingo. Ask for a half portion to fit Junior's appetite. Your best bet for help with small children may be 3- and 4-star hotels. The babysitters on call and a better infrastructure for helping visitors access the city and its services more than offset the higher cost of the hotel. Still, even cheaper hotels can usually find you a sitter.

When you travel with children, you can usually expect lower rates for them. Most museums and sights offer reduced prices or free admission for children under a certain age (which can range from 6 to 18), and getting a cot in your hotel room won't cost you more than 30 percent extra, if that. Always ask about discounts on plane and train tickets for kids, too.

A number of books that offer hints and tips on traveling with kids are available. *Take Your Kids to Europe: How to Travel Safely (and Sanely) in Europe with Your Children* by Cynthia Harriman (Globe Pequot Press) offers practical advice based on the author's four-month trip with her hubby and two kids, along with tips from other familial travelers. Two other books, *Family Travel & Resorts* by Pamela Lanier (Lanier Publishing International) and *How to Take Great Trips with Your Kids* by Sanford and Joan Portnoy (The Harvard Common Press; now out-of-print, but worth searching for), give some good general advice that you can apply to travel in the United States, Europe, and elsewhere. You also may want to check out the reliable *Adventuring with Children: An Inspirational Guide to World Travel and the Outdoors* by Nan Jeffrey (Avalon House), which includes specific advice on dealing with everyday family situations, especially those involving infants, which become Herculean labors when you encounter them on the road.

Familyhostel (☎ 800-733-9753; www.learn.unh.edu/familyhostel) takes the whole family, including kids ages 8 to 15, on moderately priced domestic and international learning vacations. Lectures, field trips, and sightseeing are guided by a team of academics. You can find good family-oriented vacation advice on the Internet from sites like the **Family Travel Forum** (www.familytravelforum.com), a comprehensive site that offers customized trip planning; **Family Travel Network** (www.familytravel network.com), an award-winning site that offers travel features, deals, and tips; **Traveling Internationally with Your Kids** (www.travelwith yourkids.com), a comprehensive site that offers customized trip planning; and **Family Travel Files** (www.thefamilytravelfiles.com), which offers an online magazine and a directory of off-the-beaten-path tours and tour operators for families. The highly regarded (albeit expensive) **Smithsonian Study Tours** has inaugurated a Family Adventures division (☎ 877-338-8687; www.si.edu/tsa/sst) that runs escorted educational and adventure trips specifically designed for the whole clan.

Making Age Work for You: Advice for Seniors

If you're a senior citizen, you can discover some terrific travel bargains. Members of **AARP** (formerly known as the American Association of Retired Persons), 601 E St. NW, Washington, DC 20049 (☎ 888-687-2277; www.aarp.org), get discounts on hotels, USAirways airfares (though not its U.S.-Europe flights), and car rentals. AARP offers members a wide range of benefits, including *AARP: The Magazine* and a monthly newsletter. AARP deals in Europe aren't as easily found, however, because generally they're offered only by American chains operating in Europe. Anyone over 50 can join.

Don't look for discounts from the big car-rental agencies while in Europe. Only Avis, Hertz, and National give an AARP discount (5 to 30 percent). On the other hand, the many rental dealers that specialize in Europe — Auto Europe, Kemwell, Europe by Car, and so forth — offer rates 5 percent lower to seniors. Take a look in the appendix for contact information.

Make sure to ask about senior discounts when you book your flight. People over 60 or 65 also get reduced admission at theaters, museums, and other attractions in most European cities. Additionally, they can often get discount fares or cards on public transportation and national rail systems. Make sure to carry identification that proves your age.

Besides publishing the free booklet *101 Tips for the Mature Traveler,* **Grand Circle Travel,** 347 Congress St., Boston, MA 02210 (☎ **800-959-0405;** www.gct.com), specializes in vacations for seniors (as do hundreds of travel agencies). Beware of the tour-bus style of most of these packages, however. If you're a senior who wants a more independent trip, you should probably consult a regular travel agent.

 Many reliable agencies and organizations target the 50-plus market. Give **Interhostel** (☎ **800-733-9753;** www.learn.unh.edu) or **Elderhostel** (☎ **877-426-8056** or 617-426-8056; www.elderhostel.org) a ring if you want to try something more than the average guided tour or vacation. Foreign universities host these trips, which cost around $2,700 to $3,700 (European cruises cost significantly more). Interhostel and Elderhostel fill your days with seminars, lectures, field trips, and sightseeing tours, all led by academic experts. You must be over 55 to participate in Elderhostel (a spouse or companion of any age can accompany you), and the programs range from one to four weeks. Interhostel requires its participants to be over 50 (any companion must be over 40) and offers two- and three-week programs.

In Spring 2004, Elderhostel launched **Road Scholar** tours (☎ **800-466-7762;** www.roadscholar.org), aimed at giving adults (not just seniors) a tour that combines learning with travel. Resident experts — local professors and professionals — join the group for on-site talks, culture and language lessons, and field trips. There's freedom in the schedule, though, allowing you to do a fair amount of exploring on your own.

ElderTreks (☎ **800-741-7956;** www.eldertreks.com) offers small-group tours to off-the-beaten-path or adventure-travel locations, restricted to travelers 50 and older. **INTRAV** (☎ **800-456-8100** or 314-655-6700; www.intrav.com) is a high-end tour operator that caters to the mature, discerning traveler, not specifically seniors, with trips around the world that include guided safaris, polar expeditions, private-jet adventures, and small-boat cruises down jungle rivers.

Unfortunately, all specialty books on senior travel focus on the United States. Nevertheless, some do provide good general advice and contacts. Try *The 50+ Traveler's Guidebook* by Anita Williams (St. Martin's

Press), *Travel Tips & Trips for Seniors* by James Toland (Bridgeway), and *Unbelievably Good Deals and Great Adventures That You Absolutely Can't Get Unless You're Over 50* by Joan Rattner Heilman (Contemporary Books). *Travel 50 & Beyond* (☎ 713-974-6903; www.travel50andbeyond.com), a quarterly magazine, also offers sound advice.

Accessing Europe: Advice for Travelers with Disabilities

A disability shouldn't stop anybody from traveling to Europe, even though the Continent has never won any medals for handicapped accessibility. After all, the big cities have made an effort to accommodate people with disabilities in the past few years, and more options and resources are out there than ever before. You'll find plenty of organizations to help you plan your trip and provide specific advice before you go.

Organizations that offer assistance to disabled travelers include the **MossRehab** (☎ 215-456-9603; www.mossresourcenet.org), which provides a library of accessible-travel resources online; **SATH (Society for Accessible Travel and Hospitality)** (☎ 212-447-7284; www.sath.org; annual membership fees: $45 adults, $30 seniors and students), which offers a wealth of travel resources for all types of disabilities and informed recommendations on destinations, access guides, travel agents, tour operators, vehicle rentals, and companion services; and the **American Foundation for the Blind (AFB)** (☎ 800-232-5463; www.afb.org), a referral resource for the blind or visually impaired that includes information on traveling with Seeing Eye dogs.

The worldwide organization known as **Mobility International,** P.O. Box 10767, Eugene, OR 97440 (☎ 541-343-1284 V/TDD; Fax: 541-343-6812; www.miusa.org), promotes international disability rights, provides reference sheets on travel destinations, and hosts international exchanges for people with disabilities. Its *A World of Options* book lists information on everything from biking trips to scuba outfitters.

Many travel agencies offer customized tours and itineraries for travelers with disabilities. **Flying Wheels Travel** (☎ 507-451-5005; www.flyingwheelstravel.com) offers escorted tours and cruises that emphasize sports and private tours in minivans with lifts. **Access-Able Travel Source** (☎ 303-232-2979; www.access-able.com) offers extensive access information and advice for traveling around the world with disabilities. **Accessible Journeys** (☎ 800-846-4537 or 610-521-0339; www.accessiblejourneys.com) offers wheelchair travelers and their families and friends resources for travel.

Avis Rent a Car has an Avis Access program that offers such services as a dedicated 24-hour toll-free number (☎ 888-879-4273) for customers with special travel needs; special car features such as swivel seats, spinner knobs, and hand controls; and accessible bus service.

For more information specifically targeted to travelers with disabilities, the community Web site **iCan** (www.icanonline.net/channels/ travel/index.cfm) has destination guides and several regular columns on accessible travel. Also check out the quarterly magazine *Emerging Horizons* ($14.95 per year, $19.95 outside the U.S.; www.emerging horizons.com); **Twin Peaks Press** (☎ 360-694-2462; http://home. pacifier.com/~twinpeak), offering travel-related books for travelers with special needs; and *Open World Magazine,* published by SATH ($13 per year, $21 outside the U.S.).

Following the Rainbow: Advice for Gay and Lesbian Travelers

Much of Europe now accepts same-sex couples, and homosexual sex acts are legal in most countries. Do some research on the city or area you're planning to visit, however, to ensure your safety. Many European cities have blossomed into centers for gay lifestyles, including parts of London, Paris, Berlin, Milan, and Greece. As is usually the case, smaller, more traditional towns are often not as accepting.

Your best all-around resource is the **International Gay and Lesbian Travel Association (IGLTA)** (☎ 800-448-8550 or 954-776-2626; www. iglta.org), the trade association for the gay and lesbian travel industry. IGLTA offers an online directory of gay- and lesbian-friendly travel businesses; go to its Web site and click on Members.

Many agencies offer tours and travel itineraries specifically for gay and lesbian travelers. **Above and Beyond Tours** (☎ 800-397-2681; www. abovebeyondtours.com) is the exclusive gay and lesbian tour operator for United Air Lines. **Now, Voyager** (☎ 800-255-6951; www.nowvoyager. com) is a well-known San Francisco–based gay-owned and -operated travel service. **Olivia Cruises & Resorts** (☎ 800-631-6277 or 510-655-0364; www.olivia.com) charters entire resorts and ships for exclusive lesbian vacations and offers smaller group experiences for both gay and lesbian travelers.

 An excellent resource is *Frommer's Gay & Lesbian Europe* (Wiley; www.frommers.com), one of the first guidebooks focusing on gay-friendly hotels, restaurants, and nightlife. The following travel guides are available at most travel bookstores and gay and lesbian bookstores, or you can order them from **Giovanni's Room** bookstore, 1145 Pine St., Philadelphia, PA 19107 (☎ 215-923-2960; www.giovannisroom.com) or **A Different Light Bookstore** (☎ 800-343-4002 or 212-989-4850; www.adl books.com): *Out and About* (☎ 800-929-2268 or 415-644-8044; www. outandabout.com), which offers guidebooks and a newsletter ($35/year; 10 issues) packed with solid information on the global gay and lesbian scene; *Spartacus International Gay Guide* (Bruno Gmünder Verlag; www.spartacusworld.com/gayguide/) and *Odysseus,* both good, annual English-language guidebooks focused on gay men; the *Damron guides* (www.damron.com), with separate, annual books for gay men and lesbians; and *Gay Travel A to Z: The World of Gay & Lesbian Travel Options at Your Fingertips* by Marianne Ferrari (Ferrari International; Box 35575, Phoenix, AZ 85069), a very good gay and lesbian guidebook series.

The Out Traveler (www.outtraveler.com) gives a gay perspective to the travel experience, covering not only destinations but also gay-specific travel issues. It is distributed to subscribers of *The Advocate* (24 issues/year, $39.97 in the U.S., $69.97 in Canada) and *Out* magazine ($14.95 in the U.S., $39.95 in Canada). *Our World,* 1104 North Nova Rd., Suite 251, Daytona Beach, FL 32117 (☎ 386-441-5367; www.ourworld publishing.com), a slick monthly magazine, highlights and promotes travel bargains and opportunities. The annual subscription rate for this magazine is $25 in the United States, $35 in Canada, and $50 outside North America. A one-year online subscription is available for $12.

Chapter 9

Taking Care of the Remaining Details

- -

In This Chapter

▶ Obtaining passports and travel insurance

▶ Keeping illness from ruining your trip

▶ Booking plays, restaurants, and sights before you leave

▶ Packing light and loving it

▶ Staying in touch by phone or e-mail

▶ Keeping up with airport security

▶ Going through Customs

- -

*B*esides choosing your itinerary and making your plans, what else do you have to do? This chapter helps you answer that question — from getting a passport (or renewing the one you have) to deciding whether to purchase additional insurance, to offering tips on packing and staying in touch while you're away from home.

Getting a Passport

A valid passport is the only legal form of identification accepted around the world; you can't cross an international border without it. Wherever you enter Europe, an official stamps your passport with a visa that is valid for 90 days within the same country. (If you plan to visit longer in any one country, you can get a specific visa by contacting any of the country's consulates in the United States before you leave, or any U.S. consulate when you're abroad.)

 Getting a passport is easy, but the process takes some time. For an up-to-date country-by-country listing of passport requirements around the world, go to the Foreign Entry Requirement Web page of the U.S. State Department at http://travel.state.gov/foreignentryreqs.html.

Applying for a U.S. passport

If you're applying for a passport for the first time, follow these steps:

1. Complete a **passport application** in person at a U.S. passport office; a federal, state, or probate court; or a major post office. To find your regional passport office, check the **U.S. State Department** Web site, http://travel.state.gov/passport_services.html, or call the **National Passport Information Center** (☎ 877-487-2778) for automated information.

2. Present a **certified birth certificate** as proof of citizenship. (Bringing along your driver's license, state or military ID, or Social Security card is also a good idea.)

3. Submit **two identical passport-size photos,** measuring 2 x 2 inches. You often find businesses that take these photos near a passport office. *Note:* You can't use a strip from a photo-vending machine because the pictures aren't identical.

4. Pay a **fee.** For people 16 and over, a passport is valid for ten years and costs $85. For those 15 and under, a passport is valid for five years and costs $70.

If you have a passport in your current name that was issued within the past 15 years (and you were over age 16 when it was issued), you can renew the passport by mail for $55. Whether you're applying in person or by mail, you can download passport applications from the U.S. State Department Web site at http://travel.state.gov/passport_services.html. For general information, call the **National Passport Agency** (☎ 202-647-0518). To find your regional passport office, either check the U.S. State Department Web site or call the **National Passport Information Center** toll-free number (☎ 877-487-2778) for automated information.

 Allow plenty of time before your trip to apply for a passport; processing usually takes three weeks, but can take longer during busy periods (especially spring). Expedited service will cost you an additional $60, whether you're applying for your first passport or are simply renewing it.

Applying for other passports

The following list offers more information for citizens of Australia, Canada, New Zealand, and the United Kingdom:

   ✔ **Australians** can visit a local post office or passport office; call the **Australia Passport Information Service** (☎ 131-232 toll-free from Australia), or log on to www.passports.gov.au for details on how and where to apply.

   ✔ **Canadians** can pick up applications at passport offices throughout Canada, at post offices, or from the central **Passport Office,**

Department of Foreign Affairs and International Trade, Ottawa, ON K1A 0G3 (☎ 800-567-6868; www.ppt.gc.ca). Applications must be accompanied by two identical passport-size photographs and proof of Canadian citizenship. Processing takes five to ten days if you apply in person, or about three weeks by mail.

✔ **New Zealanders** can pick up a passport application at any New Zealand Passports Office or download it from their Web site. For information, contact the **Passports Office** at ☎ 0800-225-050 in New Zealand or 04-474-8100, or log on to www.passports.govt.nz.

✔ **United Kingdom** residents can pick up applications for a standard ten-year passport (five-year passport for children under 16) at passport offices, major post offices, or travel agencies. For information, contact the **United Kingdom Passport Service** (☎ 0870-521-0410; www.ukpa.gov.uk).

Request four to six extra copies of your passport photo. Tote the extras with you; they'll come in handy if — heaven forbid! — you need to replace a lost passport.

If you lose your passport while traveling, *immediately* find the nearest U.S. embassy or consulate. Bring any forms of identification (hopefully you haven't lost these, too), so they can process a new passport for you.

Always carry your passport with you — safely tucked away in your money belt. Take it out only on necessary occasions: at the bank while changing traveler's checks (they will need to make a photocopy); for the guards to verify when crossing borders or for the train conductor on overnight rides; if any police or military personnel request it; and *briefly* to show to the concierge while checking into your hotel.

European hotels customarily register all guests with the local police. When you check in to your hotel (particularly in southern Europe), the concierge may ask to keep your passport overnight (to fill out the paperwork when business is slow), in which case it is dumped into a drawer with everyone else's. To avoid having your passport lost in the shuffle, ask the concierge to fill out your paperwork while you wait, or arrange to pick it up in a few hours.

Playing It Safe with Travel and Medical Insurance

Three kinds of travel insurance are available: trip-cancellation insurance, medical insurance, and lost luggage insurance. The cost of travel insurance varies widely, depending on the cost and length of your trip, your age and health, and the type of trip you're taking, but expect to pay between 5 and 8 percent of the vacation itself. Here is my advice on all three:

✔ **Trip-cancellation insurance** helps you get your money back if you have to back out of a trip, if you must go home early, or if your travel supplier goes bankrupt. Allowed reasons for cancellation can range from sickness to natural disasters to the State Department declaring your destination unsafe for travel. (Insurers usually won't cover vague fears, though, as many travelers, wary of flying after September 11, 2001, discovered when they tried to cancel their trips that fall.)

A good resource is **"Travel Guard Alerts,"** a list of companies considered high-risk by Travel Guard International (www.travelguard.com). Protect yourself further by paying for the insurance with a credit card — by law, you can get your money back on goods and services not received if you report the loss within 60 days after the charge is listed on your credit-card statement.

Note: Many tour operators, particularly those offering trips to remote or high-risk areas, include insurance in the cost of the trip or can arrange insurance policies through a partnering provider, a convenient and often cost-effective way for the traveler to obtain insurance. Make sure the tour company is a reputable one, however. Some experts suggest you avoid buying insurance from the tour or cruise company you're traveling with, saying you're better off buying from a third-party insurer than you are putting all your money in one place.

✔ Buying **medical insurance** for your trip doesn't make sense for most travelers. For travel overseas, most health plans (including Medicare and Medicaid) do not provide coverage, and the ones that do often require you to pay for services up front and reimburse you only after you return home. Even if your plan does cover overseas treatment, most out-of-country hospitals make you pay your bills up front, and send you a refund only after you've returned home and filed the necessary paperwork with your insurance company. As a safety net, you may want to buy travel medical insurance, particularly if you're traveling to a remote or high-risk area where emergency evacuation is a possible scenario. If you require additional medical insurance, try **MEDEX Assistance** (☎ 410-453-6300; www.medexassist.com) or **Travel Assistance International** (☎ 800-821-2828; www.travelassistance.com; for general information on services, call the company's Worldwide Assistance Services, Inc., at ☎ 800-777-8710).

✔ **Lost luggage insurance** is not necessary for most travelers. On domestic flights, checked baggage is covered up to $2,500 per ticketed passenger. On international flights (including U.S. portions of international trips), baggage coverage is limited to approximately $9.07 per pound, up to approximately $635 per checked bag. If you plan to check items more valuable than the standard liability, see if your valuables are covered by your homeowner's policy, get baggage insurance as part of your comprehensive travel-insurance package, or buy Travel Guard's BagTrak product. Don't buy insurance at the airport — it's usually overpriced. Be sure to take any valuables or irreplaceable items with you in your carry-on luggage; many valuables (including books, money, and electronics) aren't covered by airline policies.

If your luggage is lost, immediately file a lost-luggage claim at the airport, detailing the luggage contents. For most airlines, you must report delayed, damaged, or lost baggage within four hours of arrival. The airlines are required to deliver luggage, once found, directly to your house or destination free of charge.

For more information, contact one of the following recommended insurers: **Access America** (☎ 866-807-3982; www.accessamerica. com); **Travel Guard International** (☎ 800-826-4919; www.travel guard.com); **Travel Insured International** (☎ 800-243-3174; www.travelinsured.com); and **Travelex Insurance Services** (☎ 888-457-4602; www.travelex-insurance.com).

Don't pay for more insurance than you need. For example, if you need only trip-cancellation insurance, don't buy coverage for lost or stolen property. Trip-cancellation insurance costs about 6 to 8 percent of the total value of your vacation.

Staying Healthy When You Travel

Getting sick on vacation is bad enough, but trying to find a trustworthy doctor can make you feel even worse. Bring all your medications with you, as well as an extra prescription in case you run out. (Ask your doctor to write out the generic, chemical form rather than a brand name to avoid any confusion at foreign pharmacies.) Pack an extra pair of contact lenses in case you lose one. And don't forget the medicine for common travelers' ailments like upset stomach or diarrhea.

Check with your health-insurance provider to find out the extent of your coverage outside your home area. For travel abroad, you may have to pay all medical costs up front and be reimbursed later. For information on purchasing additional medical insurance for your trip, see the previous section. Be sure to carry your identification card in your money belt.

Talk to your doctor before leaving on a trip if you have a serious and/or chronic illness. For conditions such as epilepsy, diabetes, or heart problems, wear a **MedicAlert identification tag** (☎ 888-633-4298; www.medicalert.org), which immediately alerts doctors to your condition and gives them access to your records through Medic Alert's 24-hour hotline. Contact the **International Association for Medical Assistance to Travelers (IAMAT)** (☎ 716-754-4883 or, in Canada, 416-652-0137;

Avoiding "economy class syndrome"

Deep vein thrombosis, or as it's know in the world of flying, "economy-class syndrome," is a blood clot that develops in a deep vein. It's a potentially deadly condition that can be caused by sitting in cramped conditions — such as an airplane cabin — for too long. During a flight (especially a long-haul flight), get up, walk around, and stretch your legs every 60 to 90 minutes to keep your blood flowing. Other preventative measures include frequent flexing of the legs while sitting, drinking lots of water, and avoiding alcohol and sleeping pills. If you have a history of deep vein thrombosis, heart disease, or other condition that puts you at high risk, some experts recommend wearing compression stockings or taking anticoagulants when you fly; always ask your physician about the best course for you. Symptoms of deep vein thrombosis include leg pain or swelling, or even shortness of breath.

---

www.iamat.org) for tips on travel and health concerns in the countries you're visiting, and lists of local, English-speaking doctors. The United States **Centers for Disease Control and Prevention** (☎ 800-311-3435; www.cdc.gov) provides up-to-date information on health hazards by region or country and offers tips on food safety. If you do get sick, ask the concierge at your hotel to recommend a local doctor — even his own doctor, if necessary — or contact the local U.S. embassy for a list of English-speaking doctors.

Dealing with European Health Care

You seldom have to wait at the doctor's office in Europe. Europeans often rely on their local pharmacist to treat their ailments. So even if you don't speak the language, just walk (or crawl, depending on how bad you feel) up to the counter, groan, and point to whatever hurts.

If your condition requires further medical attention, you can visit any European hospital. (Don't worry: Most hospitals have English-speaking doctors.) Many European countries practice semi- or fully socialized medicine, so they may send you on your way with a generous prescription and a small medical bill (sometimes the visit is free or costs no more than $35 to $40).

If you must pay for health care, especially overnight care or other costly procedures, most health-insurance plans and HMOs foot some of the bill. Many plans require you to pay the expenses up front but reimburse you when you get back. (Save your hospital receipt; you need it to fill out claim forms.) Members of **Blue Cross/Blue Shield** can use their cards at certain hospitals in most major cities worldwide, which means lower out-of-pocket costs. For more information, call ☎ 800-810-BLUE or visit the Web site at www.bluecares.com/blue/bluecard/wwn for a list of participating hospitals.

Making Reservations for Popular Restaurants, Events, and Sights

Planning ahead not only takes the fun out of spur-of-the-moment activities but can shackle your trip to a schedule that may not work out after you get there. But to avoid missing out on the opera, dinner, or museum of your dreams, you may want to book these activities before you leave (or at least a few days ahead while on the road).

Top restaurants in Paris and London (and, to a much lesser extent, other major cities) can have waiting lists up to two or three weeks long. More than likely, you can call the day before (or the day of) your planned dinner and get a spot with no problem, but you may want to call further ahead to ensure a table at Gordon Ramsey, Alain Ducasse, or any other restaurant of stratospheric reputation (and price!).

Increase your chances of landing a coveted eatery by reserving for lunch rather than the more popular dinner hour. Also, while traveling, you may want to reserve dinners a day or so ahead of time even at undistinguished restaurants if missing a meal there would be a big disappointment.

If you want to avoid missing a performance — a musical or play in the West End, the Vienna Boys Choir, an opera at the ancient Roman amphitheater in Verona, or standing-room-only Shakespeare at the Globe — reserve your tickets several weeks before you leave. Call the box office direct, book at the theater's Web site (which allows you to peruse the schedule and pick your performance), or contact the local tourist office.

You can also contact a ticketing agency like **Keith Prowse** (the U.K., France, Italy, Czech Republic, Austria, and Ireland; ☎ **800-669-8687;** www.keithprowse.com), **Edwards & Edwards/Global Tickets** (all of Europe; ☎ **800-223-6108;**), or **Tickets.com** (the U.K., Netherlands, Germany, Ireland, and Belgium).

If you don't have time before you leave, try to reserve tickets when you first arrive in town. To find out what's playing, pick up the local events magazine — like *Time Out* in London or *Pariscope* in Paris — at a newsstand.

At several museums and sights across Europe (especially in Italy), you can call ahead and reserve an entry time. This feature can save you hours of standing in line at popular places like Florence's Uffizi and Rome's Galleria Borghese (where reservations are mandatory and sell out weeks ahead of time).

Of course, you don't need to book in advance at all museums or sights that allow you to do so. The sights worth reserving are the Lippizaner Horse Show in Vienna, the Galleria Borghese and Papal Audiences in Rome, the Uffizi Galleries and the Accademia (Michelangelo's *David*) in Florence, and the Secret Itineraries tour of the Doge's Palace in Venice.

Cities whose museums don't offer advance reservations may still offer a way for you to skip to the head of the line: Paris's Carte Musées et Monuments, for example, allows you immediate entry at dozens of museums — no waiting.

Packing It Up

My packing suggestion: Take everything you think you need and lay it out on the bed. Now get rid of half. Why get a hernia from lugging around half your house? Believe me — you'll have a better trip, and be more mobile, if you carry less.

So what are the bare essentials? Comfortable walking shoes, a camera, a versatile sweater and/or jacket, a belt, toiletries, medications (pack these in your carry-on bag in case the airline loses your luggage), and something to sleep in. Unless you attend a board meeting, a funeral, or one of the city's finest restaurants, you don't need a suit or a fancy dress. You can rely on a pair of jeans or khakis and a comfortable sweater.

Put things that may leak, like shampoo and suntan lotion, in zippered plastic bags. Finally, put a distinctive identification tag on the outside so your bag is easy to spot on the carousel.

Sensible carry-on items include a book, any breakable items you don't want to put in your suitcase, a personal headphone stereo, a snack in case you don't like the airline food, any vital documents you don't want to lose in your luggage (like your return tickets, passport, and wallet), and some empty space to stuff a sweater or jacket while waiting for your luggage in an overheated terminal.

Dressing like the locals

Clothed in bargains or brand names, most urban Europeans are known for their savvy fashion sense. But what most Americans wear for an expensive meal out or a night on the town, many Europeans throw on for an evening walk before dinner.

Of course, comfort is essential, but you may feel more at ease looking less like a tourist. Leave the silly garments at home (you know what they are); pack a sensible, sporty outfit; and mingle with the locals on the town's main drag.

If your travel plans include visiting churches and cathedrals, keep in mind that some adhere to strict dress codes. St. Peter's Basilica in Rome turns people away who show too much skin. Plan ahead: Wear shorts or skirts that fall past the knee and shirts that cover your shoulders. During warmer seasons, layer a shirt under a sleeveless jumper, and in cooler temperatures, an oversized scarf (check out nearby souvenir stands for a good bargain) can substitute for a wrap — a very chic look! Men may not want the same fashion statements as women, but if necessary, they can drape one of these handy scarves over the bare parts as well.

Sporting money belts

Tote your most important documents, such as your plane tickets, rail passes, traveler's checks, credit cards, driver's license, and passport, in a money belt.

Money belts are flat pouches worn under clothing. You can choose from three kinds: one that dangles from your neck; one that fastens around your waist, over your shirt tails but under your pants (larger and more safely concealed, but less comfortable); and one that sways by your pants leg, attached to your belt by a loop.

Don't take any keys except your house key and leave behind any unnecessary wallet items (department store and gas-station credit cards, library cards, and so on).

Traveling without electronics

Electronics take up valuable luggage space, waste too much time, and blow hotel fuses. In other words, leave them at home. Take a small battery-operated alarm clock and one of those tiny flashlights for poking around ancient ruins and finding stuff in the dark.

Still determined to lug around half of an electronics store? Then you need to know the following: American current runs on 110V and 60 cycles, and European current runs on 210V to 220V and 50 cycles. Don't expect to plug an American appliance into a European outlet without harming your appliance or blowing a fuse. You need a converter or transformer to decrease the voltage and increase the cycles.

You can find plug adapters and converters at most travel, luggage, electronics, and hardware stores.

Travel-sized versions of popular items such as irons, hair dryers, shavers, and so on come with dual-voltage, which means they have built-in converters (usually you must turn a switch to go back and forth). Most contemporary camcorders and laptop computers automatically sense the current and adapt accordingly (first check either the manuals on the bottom of the machine or with the manufacturer to make sure you don't fry your appliance).

Mastering Communication

This section helps you figure out how to call another country — if you need to make advance reservations or book a hotel before you leave — as well as how to stay in touch while you're away from home.

Calling Europe from the United States

When calling Europe from the United States, you must first dial the **international access code, 011,** then the **country code,** and then (sometimes) the **city code** (usually dropping the initial zero, or in Spain's case, a nine). Country and city codes are listed in the "Fast Facts" section of each destination chapter.

Only when you're calling a city from another area within the same country do you dial the initial zero (or nine).

 However, as in some areas of the United States, many countries (France, Italy, and Spain, among others) are now incorporating the separate city codes into the numbers themselves. In some cases you still drop the initial zero; in others you do not. If all this seems confusing, don't worry: The rules for dialing each city are included in the chapters themselves.

Calling home from Europe

 No matter which calling method you choose, overseas phone rates are costly. But some money pits are avoidable. For example, *never* make a transatlantic call from your hotel room, unless you can spare lots of cash.

Phone charges are one of hotels' greatest legal scams. Surcharges tacked on to your hotel bill can amount to a whopping 400 percent over what you pay if you make the call from a public pay phone. They even overcharge for local calls. Just ignore your hotel-room phone; look for one in a nearby bar or cafe instead.

 Using a calling card is the simplest and most inexpensive way to call home from overseas. (Some credit cards even double as calling cards.) You just dial a local number — which is usually free — and then punch in the number you're calling plus the calling-card number (often your home phone number plus a four-digit PIN). The card comes with a wallet-sized list of local access numbers in each country (I list these numbers in the "Fast Facts" section of each destination chapter). Before leaving home, set up a calling card account with MCI, AT&T, or Sprint.

If you're calling from a non-touch-tone country like Italy, just wait for an American operator, who will put your call through, or for the automated system in which you speak your card's numbers out loud.

To make a collect call, dial a phone company's number and wait for the operator.

 Phone companies offer a range of calling card programs. When you set up an account, tell the representative that you want the program and card most appropriate for making multiple calls from Europe to the United States.

When dialing directly, calling from the United States to Europe is much cheaper than the other way around, so whenever possible, ask friends and family to call you at your hotel rather than you calling them. If you must dial direct from Europe to the United States, first dial the international access code (often, but not always, 00), then the country code for the United States (which is 1). After that 001, just punch in the area code and number as usual.

Using European pay phones

European and American pay phones operate similarly, but the major difference is that European ones accept phone cards. You'll find three types of phones in Europe: coin-operated (a rapidly disappearing species), phone-card only (most common), and a hybrid of the two. Phone-card units are quickly replacing coin-operated phones all over the continent (the old special phone tokens are a relic of the past).

Slide the phone card into the phone like an ATM card at a cash machine. You can buy prepaid cards in increments equivalent to as little as $2 or as much as $30, depending on the country. Phone cards come in handy only if you plan on staying for a while or if you want to make direct long-distance calls. If you're visiting for only a few days and expect to make mainly local calls, just use pocket change.

Calling cards (described in the preceding section) have made phoning the United States from Europe cheap and easy from any pay phone, but some traditionalists still prefer heading to the post office or international phone office, where you make your call on a phone with a meter and then pay when you're done. This method is no cheaper than direct dialing from a pay phone, but at least you don't need a bag full of change (when phone cards caught on at public pay phones, phone offices lost business).

Staying connected by cellphone

The three letters that define much of the world's **wireless capabilities** are GSM (Global System for Mobiles), a big, seamless network that makes for easy cross-border cellphone use throughout Europe and dozens of other countries worldwide. In the U.S., T-Mobile, AT&T Wireless, and Cingular use this quasi-universal system; in Canada, Microcell and some Rogers customers are GSM; and all Europeans and most Australians use GSM.

If your cellphone is on a GSM system, and you have a world-capable multiband phone such as many Sony Ericsson, Motorola, or Samsung models, you can make and receive calls across civilized areas on much of the globe, from Andorra to Uganda. Just call your wireless operator and ask for international roaming to be activated on your account. Unfortunately, per-minute charges can be high — usually $1 to $1.50 in Western Europe and up to $5 in places like Russia and Indonesia.

That's why buying an "unlocked" world phone is important. Many cell-phone operators sell "locked" phones that restrict you from using any removable computer memory phone chip (called a **SIM card**) other than the ones they supply. Having an unlocked phone allows you to install a cheap, prepaid SIM card (found at a local retailer) in your destination country. (Show your phone to the salesperson; not all phones work on all networks.) You'll get a local phone number — and much, much lower calling rates. Getting an already locked phone unlocked can be a complicated process, but it can be done; just call your cellular operator and say you'll be going abroad for several months and want to use the phone with a local provider.

For many, **renting** a phone is a good idea. (Even world phone owners will have to rent new phones if they're traveling to non-GSM regions, such as Japan or Korea.) Although you can rent a phone from any number of overseas sites — including kiosks at airports — we suggest renting the phone before you leave home. That way you can give loved ones and business associates your new number, make sure the phone works, and take the phone wherever you go — especially helpful for overseas trips through several countries, where local phone-rental agencies often bill in local currency and may not let you take the phone to another country.

Phone rental isn't cheap. You'll usually pay $40 to $50 per week, plus airtime fees of at least a dollar a minute. If you're traveling to Europe, though, local rental companies often offer free incoming calls within their home country, which can save you big bucks. The bottom line: Shop around.

Two good wireless rental companies are **InTouch USA** (☎ **800-872-7626**; www.intouchglobal.com) and **RoadPost** (☎ **888-290-1606** or 905-272-5665; www.roadpost.com) — though you may find cheaper rates by simply renting through one of the big car-rental agencies, such as AutoEurope (www.autoeurope.com) or Avis (www.avis.com). Give them your itinerary, and they'll tell you what wireless products you need. InTouch will also, for free, advise you on whether your existing phone will work overseas; simply call ☎ 703-222-7161 between 9 a.m. and 4 p.m. EST, or go to http://intouchglobal.com/travel.htm.

Accessing the Internet in Europe

Travelers have any number of ways to check their e-mail and access the Internet on the road. Of course, using your own laptop — or even a personal digital assistant (PDA) or electronic organizer with a modem — gives you the most flexibility. But even if you don't have a computer, you can still access your e-mail and even your office computer from cybercafes.

Nowadays, finding a city that *doesn't* have a few cybercafes is difficult. Although no definitive directory for cybercafes exists — these are independent businesses, after all — two places to start looking are www. cybercaptive.com and www.cybercafe.com.

Aside from formal cybercafes, most **youth hostels** nowadays have at least one computer you can use to access the Internet, and most **public libraries** across the world offer Internet access free or for a small charge. Inexpensive hotels often have an Internet terminal in the lobby you can use for free or pretty cheaply, but avoid **business centers** in the pricier hotels or in international chain properties, unless you're willing to pay exorbitant rates.

Most major airports now have **Internet kiosks** scattered throughout their gates. These kiosks, which you'll also see in shopping malls, hotel lobbies, and tourist-information offices, give you basic Web access for a per-minute fee that's usually higher than cybercafe prices. The kiosks' clunkiness and high price mean they should be avoided whenever possible.

To retrieve your e-mail, ask your **Internet Service Provider (ISP)** if it has a Web-based interface tied to your existing e-mail account. If your ISP doesn't have such an interface, you can use the free **mail2web** service (www.mail2web.com) to view and reply to your home e-mail. For more flexibility, you may want to open a free, Web-based e-mail account with **Yahoo! Mail** (http://mail.yahoo.com) or Microsoft's **Hotmail** (www. hotmail.com). Your home ISP may be able to forward your e-mail to the Web-based account automatically.

If you need to access files on your office computer, look into a service called **GoToMyPC** (www.gotomypc.com). The service provides a Web-based interface for you to access and manipulate a distant PC from anywhere — even a cybercafe — provided your "target" PC is on and has an always-on connection to the Internet (such as with a cable modem or DSL). The service offers top-quality security, but if you're worried about hackers, use your own laptop rather than a cybercafe computer to access the GoToMyPC system.

If you're bringing your own computer, the buzzword in computer access to familiarize yourself with is **wi-fi** (wireless fidelity), and more and more hotels, cafes, and retailers are signing on as wireless hot spots from which you can get high-speed connection without cable wires, networking hardware, or a phone line. You can get wi-fi connection one of several ways. Many laptops sold within the last year have built-in wi-fi capability (an 802.11b wireless Ethernet connection). Mac owners have their own networking technology, Apple AirPort. For those with older computers, an 802.11b/**wi-fi card** (around $50) can be plugged into your laptop.

You sign up for wireless access service much as you do cellphone service, through a plan offered by one of several commercial companies that have made wireless service available in airports, hotel lobbies, and coffee shops, primarily in the U.S. (followed by the U.K. and Japan). **Boingo** (www.boingo.com) and **Wayport** (www.wayport.com) have set up networks in airports and high-class hotel lobbies. IPass providers also give you access to a few hundred wireless hotel-lobby setups. Best of all, you don't need to be staying at the Four Seasons to use the hotel's network; just set yourself up on a nice couch in the lobby. The companies' pricing policies can be byzantine, with a variety of monthly, per-connection, and per-minute plans, but in general you pay around $30 a month for limited access — and as more and more companies jump on the wireless bandwagon, prices are likely to get even more competitive.

There are also places that provide **free wireless networks** in cities around the world. To locate these free hotspots, go to www.personal telco.net/index.cgi/WirelessCommunities.

If wi-fi is not available in your destination, most business-class hotels throughout the world offer dataports for laptop modems, and a few thousand hotels in the U.S. and Europe now offer free high-speed Internet access using an Ethernet network cable. You can bring your own cables, but most hotels rent them for around $10. Call your hotel in advance to see what your options are.

In addition, major Internet service providers (ISP) have **local access numbers** around the world, allowing you to go online by simply placing a local call. Check your ISP's Web site or call its toll-free number and ask how you can use your current account away from home, and how much it will cost. If you're traveling outside the reach of your ISP, the **iPass** network has dial-up numbers in most of the world's countries. You'll have to sign up with an iPass provider, who will then tell you how to set up your computer for each of your destinations. For a list of iPass providers, go to www.ipass.com and click on Individual Purchase. One solid provider is **i2roam** (www.i2roam.com; ☎ 866-811-6209 or 920-235-0475).

Wherever you go, bring a **connection kit** of the right power and phone adapters, a spare phone cord, and a spare Ethernet network cable — or find out if your hotel supplies them to guests. European phone-jack converters and line testers are available from some travel and electronics stores and from catalogues such as Magellan's (www.magellans.com) or Travel Smith (www.travelsmith.com). Many European phone lines use the pulse system rather than touch-tone, so you may need to configure your dial-up software settings to cope.

Keeping Up with Airline Security Measures

With the federalization of airport security, security procedures at U.S. airports are more stable and consistent than ever before. Generally, you'll be fine if you arrive at the airport at least **two hours** before an international flight; if you show up late, tell an airline employee and she'll probably whisk you to the front of the line.

Obviously, bring your **passport.** Be prepared to show it several times — to airline employees asking security questions, to the clerks checking you in, to the TSA officials at the security checkpoint, and sometimes even to the gate attendants.

In 2003, the TSA phased out **gate check-in** at all U.S. airports. And **e-tickets** have made paper tickets nearly obsolete. With an e-ticket, you may often be required to have with you **printed confirmation** of purchase, and perhaps even the credit card with which you bought your ticket. This varies from airline to airline, so call ahead to make sure you have the proper documentation.

Many travelers have grown accustomed to curbside check-in, time-saving kiosks, and even checking in for flights online, but when you're flying internationally, you're still often required to wait in line for check-in, answer those inane security questions, and then proceed to the security checkpoint with your boarding pass and photo ID.

Security checkpoint lines are getting shorter than they were in 2001 and 2002, but some doozies remain. If you have trouble standing for long periods of time, tell an airline employee; the airline will provide a wheelchair. Speed up security by **not wearing metal objects** such as big belt buckles and by sending your shoes through the X-ray. If you have metallic body parts, a note from your doctor can prevent a long chat with the security screeners. Keep in mind that only **ticketed passengers** are allowed past security, except for folks escorting disabled passengers or children.

Federalization has standardized **what you can carry on** the plane and **what you can't.** The general rule is that sharp things, including nail clippers, are out. (I've noticed some inconsistencies, however; in Atlanta, a friend's nail clippers were confiscated at security, but he was able to buy a new pair at the newsstand near our gate.) Food and beverages must be passed through the X-ray machine — but security screeners can't make you drink from your coffee cup. Bring food in your carry-on rather than checking it, because explosive-detection machines used on checked luggage have been known to mistake food (especially chocolate, for some reason) for bombs. Travelers are generally allowed one carry-on bag, plus a personal item such as a purse, briefcase, or laptop bag. Carry-on hoarders can stuff all sorts of things into a laptop bag; as long as it has a laptop in it, it's still considered a personal item. The TSA has issued a list of restricted items; check its Web site (www.tsa.gov/public/index.jsp) for details.

Airport screeners may decide that your checked luggage needs to be searched by hand. Although the TSA recommends that you not lock your checked luggage (because, should they search it, they have to break the locks), you can now purchase **TSA-approved locks** (also called Travel Sentry–certified and marked with a red diamond logo), which agents are able to unlock with a special key and secret combination (although, as I write this six months after those locks were introduced, not all TSA agents yet know what the things are — internal memos in the TSA are infamously slow to disperse and often disregarded — and there are still reports of ignorant agents destroying the locks to remove them). Check www.tsa.gov for a list of approved locks and the retailers who sell them. For more information on the locks, visit www.travelsentry.org.

Bringing Your Goodies Back Home

You *can* take your goodies with you — to a point. Restrictions exist for how much you can bring back into the United States for free. If you go over a certain amount, the Customs officials impose taxes.

In 2003, the personal exemption rule — how much you can bring back into the States without paying a duty on it — was doubled to $800 worth of goods per person. On the first $1,000 worth of goods over $800, you pay a flat 3 percent duty. Beyond that, it works on an item-by-item basis. There are a few restrictions on amount: 1 liter of alcohol (you must be over 21), 200 cigarettes, and 100 cigars. Antiques more than 100 years old and works of fine art are exempt from the $800 limit, as is anything you mail home.

 You can mail yourself $200 worth of goods duty-free once a day; mark the package "For Personal Use." You can also mail gifts to other people without paying duty as long as the recipient doesn't receive more than $100 worth of gifts in a single day. Label each gift package "Unsolicited Gift." Any package must state on the exterior a description of the contents and their values. You can't mail alcohol, perfume (it contains alcohol), or tobacco products worth more than $5.

 Items bought at a duty-free shop before returning to the United States still count toward your U.S. Customs limit. The "duty" that you're avoiding in these shops is the local tax on the item (like state sales tax in the United States), not any import duty that may be levied by the U.S. Customs office.

If you need more information or would like to see a list of specific items you can't bring into the United States, check out the **U.S. Customs and Border Protection** Web site (www.cbp.gov) or write to them at 1300 Pennsylvania Ave. NW, Washington, DC 20229, to request the free *Know Before You Go* pamphlet.

Part III
The British Isles

The 5th Wave   By Rich Tennant

"It's the room next door. They suggest you deflate your souvenir bagpipes before trying to pack them in your luggage."

In this part . . .

Britain can be a good place to start your journey because everyone speaks English, so the culture shock isn't as great. A visit to the British Isles makes for a memorable, adventurous stop on any European vacation. You can choose from such activities as hiking the highlands of Scotland, going on a pub-crawl in Ireland, or visiting world-class museums in London.

Chapter 10

London and the Best of England

. . . .

In This Chapter

▶ Getting to London
▶ Checking out the neighborhoods
▶ Discovering the best places to sleep and eat
▶ Exploring the city's highlights
▶ Side-tripping to Bath, Salisbury, Stonehenge, or Oxford

. . . .

*T*he wondrous city of London — home to Buckingham Palace and Big Ben, Sherlock Holmes and Scotland Yard, Prince William and a stiff upper lip, pubs and pints, tea time and scones, Harrods and the British Museum. You can spend the evening at the latest West End production, dance until dawn at the hippest clubs, and have a pint in the same pubs where Shakespeare hung out. And if that's not enough, you have the Tower of London, the River Thames, the Tate Modern, and the Crown Jewels. London also has some of the world's foremost museums, including exhaustive collections of historical artifacts, paintings, antiquities, wax figures, and film memorabilia.

Anything less than less than three days in London is simply not enough time to appreciate more than a smidgen of what the city has to offer; four or five days is more reasonable.

Getting There

Air travel is the most convenient option for getting to London, although if you're coming from the Continent you can always hop a ferry or take the train from Paris or Brussels through the Channel Tunnel (*Chunnel* for short).

Arriving by air

Transatlantic flights usually land west of the city at **Heathrow Airport** (☎ 0870-000-0123; www.baa.co.uk), from where you can take either a 15-minute ride on the Heathrow Express bullet train (☎ 0845-600-1515; www.heathrowexpress.com), with departures every 15 minutes to London's Paddington Station, or a leisurely 50-minute Underground ride on the Piccadilly Line, which runs through the center of town and may more conveniently drop you off right at your hotel.

Some flights (especially from the Continent) and charter planes land at **Gatwick Airport** (☎ 0870-000-2468; www.baa.co.uk), 30 miles south of London and a 30-minute ride on the Gatwick Express to London's Victoria Station (☎ 0845-850-1530; www.gatwickexpress.com); or at **London Stansted Airport** (☎ 0870-000-0303; www.baa.co.uk), 35 miles northeast of town and a 45-minute ride to London's Liverpool Street Station on the Stansted Express (☎ 0845-850-0150; www.stanstedexpress.com).

Some flights from Britain and northern Europe land at **London City Airport** (☎ 020-7646-0000), 9 miles east of the center, where a shuttle bus whisks you to the nearby Liverpool Street Station in 25 minutes. EasyJet and other no-frills/low-cost European airlines are making little **London Luton Airport** (☎ 01582-405-100), 30 miles northwest of the city, into a busy hub for their budget flights from other parts of Britain and the Continent. From Luton Airport, the hourly Greenline Coach 757 (☎ 0870-608-7261) departs to a bus shelter on Buckingham Palace Road (a 70-minute trip) near the corner with Eccleston Bridge (a block from Victoria Rail and Victoria Coach stations); or you can take a bus (eight minutes) to Luton's rail station and connect to a train (30 minutes) to London's King's Cross Station or next-door neighbor St. Pancras Station.

Arriving by rail

Trains coming from Dover (where ferries from the Continent land) arrive at either **Victoria Station** or **Charing Cross Station,** both in the center of town (10½ hours total travel time from Paris via the ferry route).

The direct Eurostar trains (www.eurostar.com) that arrive from Paris and Brussels via the Channel Tunnel (a trip of three hours — two after you factor in the time change) pull into **Waterloo Station** in Southbank. If you're coming from Edinburgh, you arrive at **King's Cross Station** in the northern part of London.

Orienting Yourself in London

London is a large and sprawling city. Urban expansion has been going on around London for centuries, and the 618 square miles of London consist of many small towns and villages that slowly have been incorporated over time. Officially, 33 boroughs divide London, but most of its 7.2 million residents still use traditional neighborhood names, which I do as well in this guide.

England

Most of central London lies north of the Thames River (west of it when the river turns southward) and is more or less bounded by the two loops of the District and Circle Tube lines. Central London can be divided into **The City** and the **West End.**

Introducing the neighborhoods

Located on what now is the eastern edge of London's center, **The City** is the ancient square mile where the Romans founded the original *Londinium.*

This area is now home to St. Paul's Cathedral, the Tower of London, world financial institutions, and the one-time center of newspaper publishing, Fleet Street.

The **West End** is much larger and harder to classify. This lively center of London's shopping, restaurant, nightlife, and museum scene includes many neighborhoods.

One old district West End neighborhood, **Holborn,** lies alongside The City and today is filled with the offices of lawyers and other professionals. North of this district, the British Museum and the University of London lend a literary, academic feel to **Bloomsbury.** West of Bloomsbury, **Fitzrovia** is an old writer's hangout with shops and pubs that fade into Soho to the south. Farther to the west, the bland residential grid of **Marylebone's** streets attracts visitors to Madame Tussaud's Wax Museum and the stomping grounds of the fictional Sherlock Holmes.

The area below Bloomsbury gets livelier. **Covent Garden** and **the Strand** comprise an upscale restaurant, entertainment, and funky shopping quarter. To the west, **Soho,** once a seedy red-light district, is cleaned up and contains numerous budget eateries and London's Chinatown. To the south is **Piccadilly Circus/Leicester Square** — party central, with the bulk of London's theaters; lots of crowded pubs, bars, and commercial clubs; the biggest movie houses; and Piccadilly Circus, which is a bustling square of traffic and tacky neon.

Southwest of Piccadilly Circus are the exclusive, old residential streets of **St. James** (imagine an old gentlemen's club and expand it several blocks in each direction). Northwest of St. James (and west of Soho) is fashionable **Mayfair,** which is full of pricey hotels. **Westminster,** running along the western bank of the Thames's north-south stretch, is the heart and soul of political Britain, home to Parliament and the royal family's Buckingham Palace. Westminster flows into **Victoria** to the south. Centered on Victoria train station, this neighborhood remains genteel and residential. Northwest of Victoria and west of Westminster is **Belgravia,** an old aristocratic zone full of stylish town houses that's just beyond the West End.

West of the West End, the neighborhoods are divided north-south by enormous **Hyde Park.** South of Hyde Park stretch the uniformly fashionable residential zones of **Knightsbridge, Kensington,** and **South Kensington,** which are also home to London's grandest shopping streets. (Harrods department store is in Knightsbridge.) South of Belgravia and South Kensington is the artists' and writers' quarter of **Chelsea,** which manages to keep hip with the changing times — Chelsea debuted miniskirts in the 1960s and punk in the 1970s.

North of Hyde Park are the more middle-income residential neighborhoods of **Paddington, Bayswater,** and **Notting Hill,** popular among budget travelers for their abundance of bed-and-breakfasts (B&Bs) and inexpensive hotels. Nearby **Notting Hill Gate** is similar and is becoming a hip fashion and dining center in its own right.

On the other side of the Thames is **Southwark** — where tourism has recently exploded, thanks to the opening of Shakespeare's Globe Theatre, the Tate Modern (now connected to St. Paul's Cathedral and The City by the funky pedestrian Millennium Bridge), and a motley assortment of lesser sights. It's also an arts and cultural center, home to some of London's premiere performance halls as well as the National Theatre.

On a first-time or quick visit, you probably won't venture too far beyond this huge area of central London. If you do, the most likely candidates are the revitalized **Docklands,** home to many businesses and grand, upscale housing developments of the 1980s, or the **East End,** ever an economically depressed area — part of the real, working class of London and home to many recent immigrants.

 If you're exploring London to any extent, one of your most useful purchases will be **London A to Z,** one of the world's greatest street-by-street maps. This publication is the only one that lists every tiny alley and dead-end lane of the maze that is London's infrastructure. You can buy one at any bookstore and most newsstands.

Finding information after you arrive

London's tourist office (see the "Fast Facts" section at the end of this chapter) will provide useful information, as will a copy of *Time Out: London,* sold at any newsstand.

The **London Information Centre** (☎ 20-7292-2333), smack-dab in the middle of Leicester Square right next to the TKTS booth, offers information to visitors and provides a free hotel booking service. Like the square, the info center is open late — from 8 a.m. to 11 p.m. seven days a week.

Getting Around London

The city of London is too spread out for you to rely on your feet to get from here to there, and driving in the city is a nightmare. Fortunately, London has an extensive public transportation system. At any Tube stop or tourist center, pick up a copy of the map/pamphlet "Tube & Bus," which outlines the major bus routes and includes a copy of the widespread Tube map. For information on all London public-transport options (Tube, buses, light rail) call ☎ 020-7222-1234 or visit www. tfl.gov.uk.

You can hop aboard London's buses, Tube, and light rail systems with the **Travelcard** (in this section I just discuss "off-peak" prices, which are valid after 9:30 a.m. Monday through Friday and anytime weekends and public holidays). You buy tickets according to how many zones you'll need to ride through. Zone 1 covers all of central London — plenty for the average visit; Zone 2 is the next concentric ring out, getting in most of the outlying attractions. Charts posted in Tube stations help you figure out in which zones you'll be traveling.

By Tube (subway)

The quickest and most popular way to get around town is London's subway system, although in British the word *subway* means "pedestrian underpass." Known locally as the Tube, the Underground is a complex network of lines and interchanges that make getting anywhere in London easy. For travel time, count on an average of three minutes between Tube stops. For a map of the system, pick up a free pamphlet in one of the stations, or see the inside back cover of this book.

You can buy tickets from machines (they take coins only) or manned booths in Tube stations. A single ticket in Zone 1 costs £2 ($3.60) adults or 60p ($1.10) children (ages 5 to 15), or you can buy a "carnet" package of ten tickets for £15 ($27) adults or £5 ($9) children.

Because single tickets are so pricey, unlimited-ride tickets called Travelcards make much more sense. Kids ages 5 to 15 usually get discounts of up to 40 or 50 percent on most cards, and 16- to 17-year-olds can get discounted student versions. One-day Travelcards are valid in zones 1 and 2 and cost £4.30 ($8) adults and £2.60 ($5) children. Weekly Travelcards covering Zone 1 cost £17 ($31) adults and £7 ($13) children, or £20.20 ($36) and £8.20 ($15), respectively, if you want to cover zones 1 and 2. **Weekend** and **Family Travelcards** are also available. Old hands at London travel will be happy to hear that you no longer need a photograph to buy weekly passes.

By bus

Although you can use the Tube and its many transfer stations to tunnel your way just about anywhere in London, I suggest you ride the bus a few times — but not during rush hour — because you can see where you're going. Riding the bus gives you a much better feel for the city layout than when you travel underground. Bus-stop signs with a red slashed circle on white are compulsory stops, so you just wait and the bus will stop for you; if the slashed circle is white on red, you're at a request stop, and you have to wave down the bus.

The bus system in London is slowly changing — and, sadly, that includes replacing the famous double-decker buses with ones that are twice as long and bend in the middle. It's also changing the way you pay, and during this long (multiyear) transition, things will be a bit complicated. Normally, you just board the bus and — if you don't have a Travelcard — pay the conductor cash. However, on newer, Pay Before You Board (PBYB) lines — distinguishable by the fact that the route numbers have a yellow background on bus-stop signs — you must either have a Travelcard or other pass, or buy a ticket from a machine before you board (all bus lines that have become PBYB have machines at each stop).

Either way, a regular ride costs £1 ($1.80) adults or 40p (72¢) children. Carnets of six tickets cost £4.20 ($8) adults, £2.10 ($3.80) children. **One-day bus passes** are available for £2.50 ($4.50) adults or £1 ($1.80) children; **weekly passes** are £9.50 ($17) adults or £4 ($7) children for zones 1, 2, 3, and 4.

By taxi

London's Tube and buses can get you around town nicely, but for longer distances, more-convenient travel, travel at night, or just the novelty of riding in one of those fabled, incredibly spacious, London black cabs, opt for a taxi instead. The drivers are highly trained and experienced, and also incredibly knowledgeable about London information. In fact, many people use these drivers as auxiliary city guides, asking them for information as they ride. Prices, however, are far from a bargain.

Hail a taxi on the street or find one at a taxi rank (stand) outside major rail stations, hotels, department stores, and museums. Keep in mind that you pay for your fun; London's taxi fares are steep. As of April 2004, the initial charge just for starting the meter is £2 ($3.60). The minimum for any trip 1 mile or less is £3.60 ($6), 2 miles is £5.40 ($10), 4 miles is £9 ($16), and 8 miles is £18 ($32). Expect to pay surcharges for travel between 8 p.m. and 6 a.m., on the weekends, and on holidays. To call for a taxi (an extra £2/$3.60 charge), dial ☎ **020-7272-0272, 020-7253-5000,** or **020-7432-1432.** Take note, though: The meter begins running as soon as the driver picks up the call. For more info, visit www.pco. org.uk.

Minicabs are meterless taxis that operate out of offices rather than drive the streets for fares. Minicabs are more useful at night when the Tube stops running and few regular taxis are available. Make sure you get one that is licensed by the Public Carriage Office (by 2005, all will have stickers in the windows with the diamond-shaped "Licensed Private Hire Vehicle" hologram) Negotiate the fare before you get into the minicab. You can find minicab stands in popular spots such as Leicester Square; or call the numbers in the preceding paragraph. Women may prefer Lady Cabs, with only women drivers (☎ **020-7254-3501**).

By foot

London sprawls, and what appears to be a short jaunt may actually be an epic trek. There are, however, pleasant walks throughout the city. Try out the new Millennium Bridge between St. Paul's and the Tate Modern in Southwark or the colorful back streets of Soho.

Staying in London

Hotel rates in London come at premium prices, especially when compared to other large European cities, such as Paris. To avoid exorbitant room rates, your best bet is to find a B&B, pension, or small hotel offering low rates. You may not sleep in luxury, but you'll be able to afford the rest of your trip. Many hotels — especially those owned by chains, such as Forte, which runs the Regent Palace (see review later in this section) — offer **Weekend Breaks** that can get you 20 to 50 percent off a room rented for two or three weekend nights.

The two best **hotel booking services** are run by the Visit London tourist board (☎ **08456-443-010** or 020-7932-2020; www.visitlondonoffers. com) and the private LondonTown (www.londontown.com).

Britain sports two types of **bed-and-breakfasts** these days: the old pension-type inn — cheap, worn about the edges, and pretty hit or miss, but costing from only £35 ($63) — and the upscale private-home type of B&Bs that burgeoned in the 1990s (at rates from £65/$117 on up). The place to find the cream of the crop among the latter type is **The Bulldog Club** (☎ **877-727-3004** in the United States, 020-7371-3202 in the U.K.; Fax: 020-7371-2015; www.bulldogclub.com), a reservation service that charges a £25 ($45) three-year membership fee. Not quite as exclusive, but still representing upscale B&Bs and apartments, is **Uptown Reservations** (☎ **020-7351-3445**; Fax: 020-7351-9383; www.uptownres.co.uk). Solid midrange agencies include **London Homestead Services** (☎ or fax **020-7286-5155**; www.lhslondon.co.uk), **London Bed & Breakfast Agency** (☎ **020-7586-2768**; Fax: 020-7586-6567; www.londonbb.com), **London B and B** (☎ **800-872-2632** in the United States; www.londonbandb.com), **At Home in London** (☎ **020-8748-1943**; Fax: 020-8748-2701; www.athome inlondon.co.uk), and the **Independent Traveller** (☎ **01392-860-807**; www.gowithit.co.uk).

For general tips on booking and what to expect from European accommodations, see Chapter 7.

London's top hotels and B&Bs

The Cadogan
$$$$$ Chelsea

This inn on chic, boutique-lined Sloane Street still gives you the feeling of living in one of the posh 19th-century homes that were linked together over a century ago to make a hotel. The antiques-stuffed rooms unfold above a series of genteel lounges and bars. Suites have much larger sitting rooms than do junior suites — plus marble-finished baths and nonworking fireplaces — but all the rooms are huge, quiet, and absolutely lovely. No. 118 is a smallish corner suite furnished with fin-de-siècle décor, just as it was in 1895 when guest Oscar Wilde was arrested here for "offenses against young men" and carried off for two years of hard labor.

See map p. 136. 75 Sloane St. (at Pont Street). ☎ 888-452-8380 in the United States, 020-7235-7141 in the U.K. Fax: 020-7245-0994. www.cadogan.com. Tube: Knightsbridge or Sloane Square. Rates: £288–£352 ($518–$634) double; £411–£646 ($740–$1,163) suites. Continental breakfast £12 ($22); English breakfast £16.50 ($30). AE, DC, MC, V.

11 Cadogan Gardens
$$$$ Chelsea

Of all London's boutique inns, this one succeeds the best at creating a cozy private-home feel — with discreet hotel comforts — in a building from the 1800s. Victorian antiques and artwork abound, and the choicest room overlooks a private garden. The inn has a restaurant, a small gym, and a sauna, and you can treat yourself to in-room massages.

See map p. 136. 11 Cadogan Gardens (just off Sloane Square). ☎ *020-7730-7000. Fax: 020-7730-5217.* www.number-eleven.co.uk. *Tube: Sloane Square; from the Tube stop, walk the long way across the square, and turn right (north) out the far corner onto Pavilion Road; take an immediate left onto Cadogan Gardens, and then your first right onto another Cadogan Gardens (you find four "Cadogan Gardens" streets that all intersect). The hotel is on the right. Rates: £235–£355 ($423–$639) double; £355–£525 ($639–$945) suite. Low-calorie breakfast £8.50 ($15), continental breakfast £10.50 ($19), English breakfast £13.50 ($24). AE, DC, MC, V.*

The Leonard
$$$ Marylebone

The Leonard links four 18th-century town houses for a British atmosphere with an Imperial touch — the furnishings in public areas are often of Indian origin or inspiration and the air is lightly scented with exotic spices. The enormous Grand Suites have high stuccoed ceilings and tall windows opening onto balconies. Two-bedroom suites feature marble fireplaces, oil paintings, and old-fashioned settees — it's like renting your own posh little London pad. Even the simple doubles are elegant (although some can verge on cramped), and all come with a CD stereo. A tiny exercise room is available.

See map p. 136. 15 Seymour St. (between Old Quebec Street and Park Street). ☎ *020-7935-2010. Fax: 020-7935-6700.* www.theleonard.com. *Tube: Marble Arch. Rates: £212–£258 ($382–$464) double; £329–£588 ($592–$1,058) suite; £540–£646 ($972–$1,163) two-bedroom suite. Continental breakfast £14 ($25), English breakfast £18.50 ($33). AE, DC, MC, V.*

Norfolk Court & St. David's Hotel
$ Paddington

Accomodations aren't fancy at this comfortable old B&B (only six rooms have showers), but the clients who sing this hotel's praises stretch all the way back to the 19th century. The furniture is mismatched, which is the decorative flair of late, the atmosphere is welcoming, and the price for a B&B in this neighborhood can't be beat. Rates include a full English breakfast, and they offer lower rates for longer stays. The price and casual atmosphere make this a good place for families.

See map p. 136. 16–20 Norfolk Square. ☎ *020-7723-4963 or 020-7723-3856. Fax: 020-7402-9061. Tube: Paddington, and then exit onto Praed Street; catty-corner to Paddington Station is Norfolk Square. Rates: £59 ($106) double without private bathroom; £69 ($124) double with private bathroom. English breakfast included. MC, V.*

The Pelham
$$$$ South Kensington

The Pelham is an oasis of tranquility in a busy road hub, mere steps from a Tube stop and blocks from the shopping of Brompton Road. Tom and Kit Kemp, the owners, love antiques. She is an interior decorator and has given

Accommodations, Dining, and Attractions in Central London

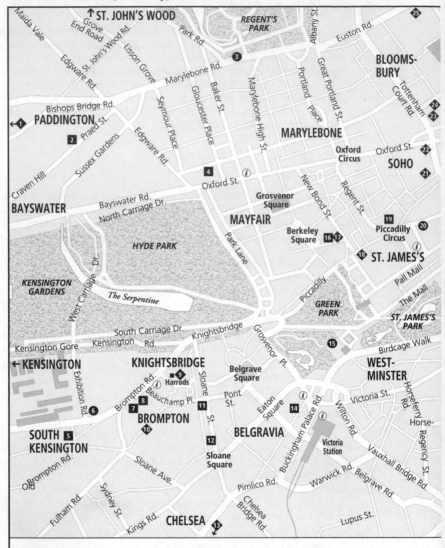

HOTELS ■
Brown's Hotel **16**
The Cadogan **11**
Egerton House **7**
11 Cadogan Gardens **12**
Fielding Hotel **31**
The Franklin **8**
The Leonard **4**
Norfolk Court &
   St. David's Hotel **2**

The Pelham **5**
Regent Palace Hotel **19**
The Savoy **34**
St. Margaret's Hotel **26**
Topham's Belgravia **14**

RESTAURANTS ◆
Belgo Centraal **29**
Cafe Spice Namaste **43**
Chor Bizarre **17**

The Cow **1**
The Eagle **42**
The Enterprise **10**
Gay Hussar **22**
Georgian Restaurant
   (Harrods) **9**
Gordon Ramsay at
   Claridge's **13**
The Ivy **28**
Malabar Junction **24**

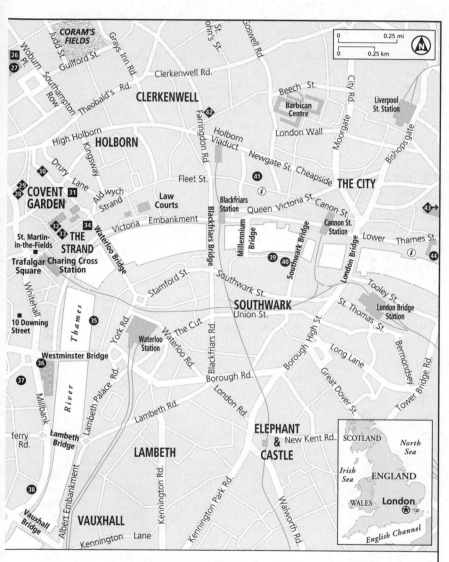

North Sea Fish Bar **25**
Pollo **21**
Porters English Restaurant **32**
The Rock and Sole Plaice **30**
Rules **33**
St. James's Restaurant
  (Fortnum and Mason's) **18**
Wagamama **23**

ATTRACTIONS ●
British Museum **27**
Buckingham Palace **15**
Globe Theater **40**
London Eye **35**
Madame Tussaud's **3**
National Gallery **20**
Parliament and Big Ben **36**
St. Paul's Cathedral **41**
Tate Britain **38**

Tate Modern **39**
Tower of London **44**
Victoria & Albert Museum **6**
Westminster Abbey **37**

Information ⓘ

each room its individual style, with beds piled high with pillows and walls sheathed in carefully chosen rich fabrics. Rooms also include TVs and VCRs. The suites feel nothing like a hotel and feel very much as if you're in your own London flat. The Pelham has an Olde English front lounge for afternoon tea and modern British cuisine in the downstairs restaurant.

See map p. 136. 15 Cromwell Place (between South Kensington Tube station and Cromwell Road). ☎ *020-7589-8288. Fax: 020-7584-8444.* www.firmdale.com. *Tube: South Kensington. Rates: £212–£294 ($382–$529) double or mews studio; £529–£811 ($952–$1,460) suite. Continental breakfast £14.50 ($26), full English breakfast £17.50 ($32). AE, MC, V.*

Regent Palace Hotel
$ Piccadilly Circus

This huge (908-room), institutional hotel operates much like a small city, with restaurants, bars, boutiques, and an after-hours pub. Rooms are rather nondescript, but the location is wonderful. Your first impression may be that it looks like a dorm or hostel, but the clientele is a mix of students, businesspeople, families looking for value, and seniors in town for two weeks of theater. Longer stays come with lower rates.

See map p. 136. Piccadilly Circus (between Glasshouse and Sherwood streets. ☎ *0870-400-8703. Fax: 020-7734-6435.* www.regentpalacehotel.co.uk. *Tube: Piccadilly Circus; take exit 1 from the Tube station, and the hotel is opposite where you emerge. Rates: £39–£89 ($70–$160) double without private bathroom; £69–£139 ($124–$250) double with private bathroom. Continental breakfast £5 ($9), full English breakfast £6.50 ($12). AE, DC, MC, V.*

The Savoy
$$$$ The Strand

This is one of London's grandest hotels, a monument to Art Deco from the chrome-plated entrance to the mirrored desks and curved dressers in half of the huge bedrooms. The other half of the accommodations are Victorian, harking back to the hotel's 1889 origins. Those on the front are all doubles, while suites overlook the Thames with Parliament and Big Ben beyond. This place is posh. A call box by your bed allows you to summon a maid, valet, or waiter 24 hours a day. There are several bars and lounges — including the Thames Foyer, where Elizabeth II was crowned, and the American Bar, where the martini was invented — and a trio of elegant restaurants. The Savoy's best-kept secret: You can get the envied Thames view without breaking the bank by renting out just the bedroom half of a suite and paying for it as a double.

See map p. 136. The Strand (near Waterloo Bridge). ☎ *800-63-SAVOY in the U.S.; 020-7836-4343 in the U.K. Fax: 020-7240-6040.* www.the-savoy.com. *Tube: Embankment or Charing Cross. Rates: £262–£336 ($472–$605) double; from £606 ($1,091) suite. Continental breakfast £18.50 ($33), full English breakfast £24.50 ($44). AE, DC, MC, V.*

St. Margaret's Hotel
$ Bloomsbury

This clean and comfortable old hotel is the best of a cluster of inexpensive accommodations that line a quiet street. The Marazzi family has offered kind, homey service for over 50 years. Rooms are carpeted and the furniture is worn but cared-for. Ask for a room in the rear of the hotel — those are the nicest. Though not all rooms have private bathroom, they do boast sinks, TVs, and telephones. The breakfast is large and is included in the low rates. The British Museum is just around the corner — a huge plus. Stay more than one day, and the Marazzis will knock a couple of pounds off the nightly rate.

See map p. 136. 26 Bedford Place (near the Russell Square end of the street, 2 blocks west of the British Museum). ☎ *020-7636-4277. Fax: 020-7323-3066.* www.st margaretshotel.co.uk. *Tube: Russell Square; turn left out of the Tube station for the half-block to the square; turn left down the square, and then right across the south end of it to Bedford Place, where you turn left; the hotel is on the right. Rates: £65 ($117) double without private bathroom, £80 ($144) doubles with shower but no toilet, £95–£99.50 ($171–$179) double with private bathroom. Rates include breakfast. MC, V.*

Topham's Belgravia (Ebury Court Hotel)
$$ Belgravia

This excellent choice is in a fine residential area near the station (Margaret Thatcher is a neighbor). The smaller rooms are quite cozy. The owner — part of a second generation of family management — is an interior decorator and has decorated the rooms in an English country-house style. The rooms are Laura Ashley–like without being too floral and feminine. Guests over 60 get a 10 percent discount.

See map p. 136. 28 Ebury St. (1 block east of, and parallel to, Buckingham Palace Road). ☎ *020-7730-8147. Fax: 020-7823-5966.* www.tophams.co.uk. *Tube: Victoria; from Victoria Station walk 1 block west on Eccleston Street (which dead-ends at the station) and turn right on Ebury Street. Rates: £140 ($252) double. Rates include breakfast. AE, DC, MC, V.*

London's runner-up accommodations

Brown's Hotel

$$$$$ Mayfair Brown's Hotel has, since 1837, hosted the likes of Agatha Christie (*At Bertram's Hotel* is set here), Rudyard Kipling (he finished *The Jungle Book* while a guest here), Napoleon III, and Teddy Roosevelt. The hotel still serves one of London's best afternoon teas in the genteel Drawing Room. It was closed from Apr 2004 to Mar 2005 for a complete overhaul and refurbishing under the new management of Sir Rocco Forte. *See map p. 136. Albemarle Street, 2 blocks off Picadilly.* ☎ *020-7493-6020. Fax: 020-7493-9381.* www.brownshotel.com.

Egerton House

$$$ **Knightsbridge**   Egerton House offers Victorian comfort (if smallish rooms) with a modern touch overlooking grassy Egerton Gardens. The location puts you near the chicest boutiques, Harrods, and the Victoria & Albert Museum. Go for the "deluxe" rooms. *See map p. 136. 17 Egerton Terrace, off Brompton Road.* ☎ *800-473-9492 in the U.S., 020-7589-2412 in the U.K. Fax: 020-7584-6540.* www.egertonhousehotel.co.uk.

Fielding Hotel

$$ **Covent Garden**   This old-fashioned hotel has small, worn, but comfortable rooms and traditional charms. The hotel is located in one of the best parts of town, on a gas lamp–lit pedestrian street across from the Royal Opera House and near the busy Covent Garden. *See map p. 136. 4 Broad Court, Bow Street.* ☎ *020-7836-8305. Fax: 020-7497-0064.* www.the-fielding-hotel.co.uk.

The Franklin

$$$$$ **Knightsbridge**   The Franklin is the slightly more expensive sister hotel to Egerton House, with elegantly posh suites, high ceilings, and garden-view rooms. *See map p. 136. 28 Egerton Gardens.* ☎ *020-7584-5533. Fax: 020-7584-5449.* www.franklinhotel.co.uk.

Dining in London

Granted, the British have long been mocked for the drab quality of their national cuisine (mushy peas, anyone?). And certainly you can still go to a corner pub in London and get food lousy enough to curl your toenails. But over the past decade, London's top chefs have started paying attention to the quality of old-fashioned dishes, while adopting new culinary techniques and using more international ingredients. This fusion of old-world tradition with new-world foodstuffs has led to the rise of Modern British cuisine. Add to this London's variety of ethnic restaurants — locals go out for Indian the way Americans go out for Chinese — and you won't ever have to touch steak and kidney pie unless you want to.

When you're not dining high on modern innovations, Britain still has a formidable array of time-tested dishes for you to try. The *ploughman's lunch* is a hunk of bread, a chunk of cheese, butter, pickle (relish), and chutney. The two most familiar of the many meat pies you find are *Cornish pasty* (beef, potatoes, onions, and carrots baked in a pastry shell) and *shepherd's pie* (lamb and onions under mashed potatoes — if they use beef, it's called *cottage pie*). The English are masters of roast beef, which is often served with *Yorkshire pudding* (a popover-like concoction cooked under the meat joint so the juices drip into it).

You can also partake of oddly named British dishes such as *bangers and mash* (sausages, of which the best are Cumberland, and mashed potatoes), *bubble-and-squeak* (fried cabbage and potatoes), or *toad in the hole* (what Americans call pigs-in-a-blanket). *Fish 'n' chips* (fried fish with french fries) is a greasy delight, and oysters from Colchester can also be fabulous.

Traditional English breakfasts — scarce in these days of the continental croissant-and-coffee breakfast — are tasty, but really high in cholesterol: ham and/or sausage, fried eggs, fried tomatoes, and toast or scones with butter and jam. Even better is the tea ritual, detailed in the "More cool things to see and do" section, later in the chapter.

If the British are masters of anything culinary, it's their cheeses and puddings (British for "desserts"). Of the former, blue-veined Stilton is the king and is best enjoyed with a glass of port wine. Regional delicacies pop up on the cheese board as well, one of the most famous being cheddar. If you prefer your meal to end with something sweet, try an English pudding. *Trifle* is sponge cake soaked with brandy, smothered in fruit or jam, and topped with custard. Light cream whipped with fresh fruit is called a *fool*, and a *treacle pudding* is a steamed trifle without the sherry and with syrup instead of fruit.

Wash down your meal with a pint of bitter — but make sure it's a proper English ale and not a wimpy import or lager. A few of the most widely available bitters are listed under the pub section of "More cool things to see and do."

London's top restaurants

Belgo Centraal

$ Covent Garden   BELGIAN

This bastion of Belgian beer and *bangers* (sausages) is one of the best dining deals in London. You take a freight elevator down to the basement eatery, where rows of communal bench-lined tables fill room after room, the waiters dress as monks, the Belgian grub (pots of mussels, wild boar sausages, and roast chickens) is excellently prepared, and the beer flows freely. The restaurant offers several bargain meals, including a lunch menu — from noon to 5 p.m., £5.95 ($11) buys you a basic dish plus beer (from 5:30 to 7 p.m., you pay whatever the clock shows at the time you order). Plus, two kids eat free with each paying adult.

See map p. 136. 50 Earlham St. (3 blocks north of the Covent Garden Piazza, off Shaftesbury Avenue). ☎ **020-7813-2233.** www.belgo-restaurants.com. *Tube: Covent Garden. Main courses: £5.95–£13 ($11–$22); fixed-price menus from £5.95 ($11). AE, DC, MC, V. Open: Lunch and dinner daily.*

Cafe Spice Namaste

$$$$ The City   INDIAN/EASTERN

Don't let the atmosphere fool you. The restaurant is a large, Victorian Hall without any style or character, but the Indian cuisine is some of the best in London. The owner, who hails from the Indian island of Goa, has added specialties from his own land (try the three-alarm sorpotel pork), but you also taste Thai, Malay, Sri Lankan, and Singaporian influences. The daily specials are usually a sure thing, or try the complex chicken curry dish of galinha xacutti.

See map p. #136. 16 Prescott St. (between Mansell and Leman streets). ☎ *020-7488-9242. Reservations recommended. Tube: Tower Hill or Aldgate. Main courses: £9.95–£16 ($18–$29). AE, DC, MC, V. Open: Lunch Mon–Fri, dinner Mon–Sat.*

Gay Hussar
$$$$ Soho HUNGARIAN

This Soho standby is a perennial favorite of left-wing politicians and paprika lovers. The Hungarian grub is outstanding, and the wood-paneled interior with deep red velvet-cushioned benches and bow-tied service is a comfortable throwback to an earlier era. Try the veal goulash with thimble egg dumplings after a bowl of the soup of the day, perhaps cold wild cherry or a light lemon and chicken.

See map p. 136. 2 Greek St. (1 block off Soho Square, 1 block west of Charing Cross Road). ☎ *020-7437-0973.* www.simplyrestaurants.com/thegayhussar. *Reservations recommended. Tube: Tottenham Court Road. Main courses: £9.50–£17 ($17–$30); fixed-price lunch menus: £16–£19 ($28–$33). AE, MC, V. Open: Lunch and dinner Mon–Sat.*

Gordon Ramsay at Claridge's
$$$$$ Mayfair MODERN BRITISH

Gordon Ramsay is the hottest chef in London today and his flavorful yet light, inventive cooking needs to answer to no one, save the palates of an appreciative and fashionable clientele. The menu changes frequently, but try the filets of baby red mullet on a juniper-flavored sauerkraut or the breast and confit leg of guinea fowl with vegetables and foie gras. The three-course lunch and early supper menu (until 6:45 p.m. Monday to Satruday) are steals at £30 ($54) for either.

See map p. ###. Brook Street, W1. ☎ *020-7499-0099.* www.gordonramsay.com. *Reservations required as far in advance as possible. Tube: Bond Street. Fixed-price meals £30–£65 ($54–$117). AE, DC, MC, V. Open: Lunch and dinner daily.*

Malabar Junction
$$ Bloomsbury INDIAN

The owner comes from the southern Indian province of Kerala, spice capital of the subcontinent and a region renowned for its cuisine. The subdued décor may not be as funky as Chor Bizarre (see the following section), but the cooking is perhaps a notch or two better and is surprisingly well-priced.

See map p. 136. 107 Great Russell St. (1 block off New Oxford Street, near the British Museum). ☎ *020-7580-5230. Reservations recommended. Tube: Tottenham Court Road. Main courses: £3.50–£11 ($6–$20). AE, MC, V. Open: Lunch and dinner daily.*

Porters English Restaurant

$$$ Covent Garden   BRITISH

With so many pricey traditional restaurants in London, the Earl of Bradford took a gamble that the city had room for reasonably priced, well-prepared British cuisine. His instinct was correct and Porters has become popular with people looking for the tastes they remember from old-fashioned family dinners. The meat pies and puddings are particularly good; try the unusually flavored lamb and apricot pie with mint and Lady Bradford's famous banana and ginger steamed pudding.

See map p. 136. 17 Henrietta St. (½ block off the Covent Garden square). ☎ *020-7836-6466.* www.porters.uk.com. *Reservations highly recommended. Tube: Covent Garden. Main courses: £8.95–£13 ($16–$23); fixed-price menu (not available before 9:30 p.m.): £10 ($18). AE, DC, MC, V. Open: Lunch and dinner daily.*

Rules

$$$$$ Covent Garden   BRITISH

In a clubby, 19th-century setting, Rules is the oldest restaurant in London, established in 1798. The restaurant serves up game from its own preserve and some of the most staunchly British food in town, beloved of everyone from Charles Dickens to Graham Greene. You can't go wrong with the venison or wild fowl. Try the sea trout, mussels, or a delicious pie — just make sure you cap the meal off with one of Rules's famous puddings. This truly is a special place, well worth a splurge.

See map p. 136. 35 Maiden Lane (1 block off the Strand). ☎ *020-7836-5314.* www.rules.co.uk. *Reservations recommended. Tube: Charing Cross or Covent Garden. Main courses: £16–£20 ($11–$36). AE, DC, MC, V. Open: Lunch and dinner daily.*

London's runner-up restaurants

London is chock-a-block with restaurants, but perhaps the neighborhood with the densest concentration of inexpensive eateries (Indian, Italian, Asian, and more) is in no-longer-so-seedy **Soho. Leicester Square/ Piccadilly** is the easiest place to grab a *Döner kebab* (a pita wrap with spiced lamb and a picante sauce) or other vaguely Middle Eastern street food from a hole-in-the-wall joint. Some of the cheapest (but still excellent) Indian and Asian restaurants now cluster just south of the British Museum in the south end of **Bloomsbury** (around, although usually not on, New Oxford Street).

Several of London's museums and sights have extremely good cafeterias or restaurants on the premises, so that you don't have to leave the museums at lunchtime. You may want to plan on a meal in the **Tate, National Gallery,** or **St. Martin-in-the-Fields** church (where you get to eat in the crypt atop tomb slabs).

The most discriminating diners shop for their picnic delicacies in the gourmet food departments of **Harrods** at 87–135 Brompton Rd. or **Fortnum and Mason** at 181 Piccadilly. **Marks and Spencer,** at 458 Oxford St., has a cheaper grocery department for less fancy staples.

Chor Bizarre

$$$ **St. James**   Come here to see the unusual, fun décor — an assortment of items picked up at Indian bazaars — and the maharaja thali, a sampler feast of specialties from across the subcontinent. Seeing a show? Their four-course, pre-theater dinner at £11 ($20) for two courses, £18 ($32) for four, includes a car ride to the theater. *See map p. 136. 16 Albemarle St. (between Piccadilly and Grafton Street).* ☎ *020-7629-9802.* www.chorbizarre restaurant.com.

The Cow

$$$ **Notting Hill**   The Cow is the spot for high-quality pub grub from the new school of British cooking. *See map p. 136. 89 Westbourne Park Rd.* ☎ *020-7221-0021.*

The Eagle

$$$ **The City**   The Eagle, specializing in Mediterranean-style dishes, pioneered the concept of a pub actually serving edible food, though it can be snooty about it. *See map p. 136. 159 Farringdon Rd.* ☎ *020-7837-1353.*

The Enterprise

$$ **Brompton**   Try this place for tasty pub grub. *See map p. 136. 35 Walton St.* ☎ *020-7584-3148.*

The Ivy

$$$ **Covent Garden**   Dine on well-prepared international and French dishes while hob-nobbing with the stars of the London theater scene after (or before) the show, as well as business moguls, London movers and shakers, and any mere mortal lucky enough to get a reservation. *See map p. 136. 1 West St. (just off Cambridge Circus).* ☎ *020-7836-4751.*

North Sea Fish Bar

$$ **Bloomsbury**   This beloved London institution serves some of the best chips in town. *See map p. 136. 7–8 Leigh St.* ☎ *020-7387-5892.*

Pollo

$ **Soho**   A Soho legend for laughably cheap, enormous portions of Italian home-cooking in a convivial, crowded, no-frills atmosphere. *See map p. 136. 20 Old Compton St. (2 blocks north of Shaftesbury Avenue).* ☎ *020-7734-5917.*

The Rock and Sole Plaice

$ **Covent Garden** Founded in 1871, this is London's oldest fish 'n' chips joint. *See map p. 136. 47 Endell St.* ☎ *020-7836-3785.*

Wagamama

$ **Bloomsbury** This popular, and hectic, basement Japanese noodle house provides a perfect break from the British Museum. *See map p. 136. 4 Streatham St. (off Coptic Street, around the corner from the British Museum).* ☎ *020-7436-7830.* www.wagamama.com.

Exploring London

Not only is London home to some of the world's greatest museums — the antiquities of the British Museum, the Old Masters of the National Gallery, the contemporary greats in the Tate Modern, the globe-spanning decorative arts in the V&A — but all the biggies are absolutely free of charge! On the other hand, London's major churches *do* charge admission. Go figure.

London's top sights

British Museum
Bloomsbury

The Brits have quite possibly the world's greatest archaeological collection. You can spend several days exploring this intriguing museum, or do the highlights in two to three hours. My advice: Spend a couple of half-days here. After all, it's free.

The British Museum has treasures that span history as well as the globe, from the Rosetta Stone — the key that cracked the code of Egyptian hieroglyphics — to the towering winged bull/men that guarded the gates to Assyrian palaces in 880 B.C. You can also see the 2,000-year-old Lindow Man, who was ritually strangled and drowned in a peat bog that preserved his shriveled body, and the famous Elgin Marbles, the grandest of the carved reliefs that once decorated Athens's Parthenon. Kids seem fascinated by room after room of Royal Egyptian mummies.

Recent highlights include the recently opened central courtyard and high-tech visitor's center. Guided tours of the museum's highlights cost £6 ($11) per person, but specialized Eye Openers tours of themed parts of the collections are free.

See map p. 136. Great Russell Street (a block off of Oxford Street). ☎ *020-7323-8299.* www.thebritishmuseum.ac.uk. *Tube: Holborn, Tottenham Court Road, or Russell Square; from Tottenham Court Road, take Exit 3 out of the station, and then take the first right outside of the station. Admission: Free, but donations are greatly appreciated. Open: Sat–Wed 10 a.m.–5:30 p.m., Thurs–Fri 10 a.m.–8:30 p.m.*

London Eye
South Bank

London's latest major attraction towers 450 feet above the River Thames, adding a dramatic modern element to the London skyline. The British Airways–funded London Eye is the largest observation wheel in the world — technically, because of the way it's constructed, it's not a Ferris wheel. Bascially, it's a giant bicycle wheel — only 200 times as big as the one on your Schwinn, with 80 spokes held together by more than 3.6 miles of cables. You're in "the tire," one of 32 capsules that hold 25 people each. The wheel whips around at the glacial speed of 0.6 miles per hour, and you board every half-hour. On a clear day, from the dizzying top of the circle, you can see 25 miles in every direction — though most people are looking down at St. Paul's Cathedral, Westminster, and other icons of London spread below. A Champagne Flight costs £35 ($63); bubbly plus a Thames cruise afterward runs £45 ($81) total.

See map p. 136. Jubilee Gardens (on the banks of the Thames, right across the river from Big Ben, between Hungerford Bridge and Westminster Bridge). ☎ *0870-500-0600.* www.londoneye.com. *Tube: Waterloo. Admission: £12 ($21) adults, £5.75 ($10) kids aged 5–15. Open: Daily 9:30 a.m.–8 p.m. (until 9 p.m. Fri–Sun); open until 10 p.m. in July–Aug (and weekends in June).*

National Gallery
Trafalgar Square, St. James's

A huge, neoclassical edifice houses some of the finest works the 13th to 20th centuries have to offer (start with the oldest paintings, in the modern Sainsbury wing way off to the left of the main entrance). Give your tour about two to three hours. The works include da Vinci's *Virgin of the Rocks,* one-third of Uccello's *Battle of San Romano,* Botticelli's erotic *Venus and Mars,* and Michelangelo's unfinished *Entombment.* El Greco's *Agony in the Garden* hangs alongside works by other Spanish greats, Goya and Velázquez. Rubens, Vermeer, and a pair of Rembrandt self-portraits represents the northern European Renaissance.

The 19th-century British artists are well-represented with Gainsborough, Constable, and Turner, but are outshined by Impressionist masters Monet, Degas, Renoir, Seurat, and Cézanne. My favorite hidden treasures are da Vinci's huge drawing of the *Virgin and Child,* in an antechamber off the first room, and Hoogstraten's masterful optical illusion *Peepshow.* Free guided tours are available, but to set your own pace, donate £3 ($5) and carry along the informative digital audio tour. The onsite Brasserie restaurant is surprisingly excellent for museum chow.

See map p. 136. Trafalgar Square (at the top of the square; you can't miss it). ☎ *020-7747-2885.* www.nationalgallery.org.uk. *Tube: Charing Cross. Admission: Free (admission for special exhibitions varies). Open: Thurs–Tues 10 a.m.–6 p.m., Wed 10 a.m.–9 p.m.*

Parliament and Big Ben
Westminster

The many debates of British Parliament ensue inside this series of neo-Gothic 1840 buildings — a complex most famous for its 336-foot Victoria Tower, which is home to the world's most famous timepiece (still wound by hand) and is often referred to by the name of its chime's biggest bell, the 13.5-ton Big Ben. You're welcome to watch debates from the Strangers' Gallery in either the House of Lords, which is more formal, or the House of Commons, which is much more lively and controversial — you're likely to eavesdrop on shouting matches of often witty personal attacks and learned obscenities. Sessions can last until 11 p.m., although you'll probably just want to stick around for an hour or so. The houses go into recess for two weeks around Easter, and from mid-July to early October (save one week in early September).

See map p. 136. Bridge Street and Parliament Square (the line to get inside forms at the St. Stephen's entrance). ☎ *020-7219-4272.* www.parliament.uk. *Tube: Westminster; Parliament is right across the street. Admission: Free. Open: House of Commons, public admitted Mon 2:30–10:30 p.m., Tues–Wed 11:30 a.m.–7:30 p.m., Thurs 11:30 a.m.–6:30 p.m., and Fri (only when they're sitting) 9:30 a.m.–3 p.m.; House of Lords, public admission Mon–Wed 2:30 p.m.–10 p.m. (approximately), Thurs 11 a.m.–1:30 p.m. and 3–7:30 p.m. (approximately).*

St. Paul's Cathedral
The City

Christopher Wren's architectural Renaissance masterpiece, St. Paul's Cathedral, was one of the few structures to withstand the Nazi air raids of World War II. Captured on newsreel footage, the image of the church's survival became a rallying point for Britain's pride and indomitable spirit during the darkest days of the war. This embodiment of the British stiff upper lip continues into the crypt, where national heroes such as the Duke of Wellington (who defeated Napoleon at Waterloo) and Lord Nelson are buried, alongside architect Wren, painters Constable and Turner, and adventurer/hero T. E. Lawrence (also known as Lawrence of Arabia).

Visitors can climb the 365-foot-high dome that glitters with mosaics, enjoy the acoustic effects of the whispering gallery halfway up (murmur against the wall and someone 158 feet away on the opposite side can hear you), and see the 360° panorama of London from the top (after climbing 426 steps). Half-hour guided tours of the church depart at 11 a.m., 11:30 a.m., 1:30 p.m., and 2 p.m., and cost an additional £2.50 ($4.50) adults, £2 ($3.60) seniors and students, and £1 ($1.80) children under 16. Tours include church admission and get you into bits normally closed to the public. Merely eyeballing the church is a 20-minute deal; give yourself at least 45 more minutes to climb the dome.

See map p. 136. St. Paul's Churchyard. ☎ *020-7246-8348.* www.stpauls.co.uk. *Tube: St. Paul's, then walk down New Change Street toward the large golden dome. Admission: Cathedral and crypt, £5 ($9) adults, £4 ($7) seniors/students, £2.50 ($4.50) ages 16 and under. Open: Mon–Sat 8:30 a.m.–4 p.m.*

Tate Britain
Millbank

The Tate Britain houses the national collections of British art (15th century to today), which means room after room filled by Gainsborough, Reynolds, Stubbs, Blake, Constable, and especially Hogarth and J. M. W. Turner. Since the gallery's modern art collection decamped to Bankside (see "Tate Modern," following), the British collection has expanded to fill the entirety of the museum's traditional seat in a neoclassical building on Millbank. Unless you're really into British art, or decide to have lunch at the Tate's excellent cafe, only expect to spend about 30 minutes here.

See map p. 136. Millbank. ☎ *020-7887-8000.* www.tate.org.uk. *Tube: Pimlico, and then walk to Vauxhall Bridge Road and turn right (walking toward the river); make a left onto John Islip Street; the Tate Gallery is on your right. Admission: Free (fees for special exhibitions vary). Open: Daily 10 a.m.–5:50 p.m.*

Tate Modern
Bankside

The Tate's famed international modern art collection has moved to a huge renovated former power station on Bankside, just across the pedestrian Millennium Bridge from The City and St. Paul's. The collection includes art from the Impressionists to today — from Rodin's *The Kiss* and dozens of pieces by Picasso, Matisse, and van Gogh to Dalí, Giacometti, and Modigliani, and later works by Mark Rothko, Jasper Johns, Henry Moore, Julian Schnabel, Frank Stella, Anselm Keifer, and a host of other contemporary-era artists. Count on spending at least an hour here, longer if there's an interesting temporary show on.

See map p. 136. Bankside. ☎ *020-7887-8000. Tube: London Bridge or Southwark. Admission: Free (fees for special exhibitions vary). Open: Sun–Thurs 10 a.m.–6 p.m., Fri–Sat 10 a.m.–10 p.m.*

Tower of London
The City of London

Come early to beat the long lines at London's best medieval attraction, a site of intrigue, murder, and executions galore. The hour-long tours guided by Beefeater guards are highly entertaining and informative. Count on at least another full hour to explore on your own, and to investigate the Crown Jewels, the Armory, and such. The Beefeaters take you past the Bloody Tower where Sir Walter Raleigh awaited execution for 13 years and where King Edward IV's two young sons were murdered. You walk through the 900-year-old White Tower, still housing an armory of swords and plate mail, as well as a gruesome collection of torture instruments, and into Tower Green, where Thomas Moore, Lady Jane Grey, and two of Henry VIII's wives (Anne Boleyn and Catherine Howard) were beheaded.

All the gore should be enough trade-off for the kids when you have to wait in line to be whisked past the Crown Jewels on a moving sidewalk. Be sure to drool over the world's largest cut diamond, the 530-carat Star of Africa (set in the Sovereign's Sceptre), and to gape at Queen Victoria's Imperial State Crown (still worn on occasion), studded with over 3,000 jewels. Say hello to the resident ravens, who are rather pampered because legend holds that the Tower will stand as long as they remain.

See map p. 136. Tower Hill. ☎ *0870-756-6060.* www.hrp.org.uk. *Tube: Tower Hill; head across Tower Hill Road to the Tower of London. Admission: £14 ($24) adults, £9.50 ($17) seniors/students, £8 ($14) ages 5–15. Tickets cost £1 ($1.80) less if bought in advance online or by phone. Open: Mar–Oct, Tues–Sat 9 a.m.–6 p.m., Sun–Mon 10 a.m.–6 p.m.; Nov–Feb, Tues–Sat 9 a.m.–5 p.m., Sun–Mon 10 a.m.–5 p.m. Last admission 1 hour before closing. Beefeater Tours: Mon–Sat every half hour starting at 9:30 a.m. and continuing until 2:30 p.m. (3:30 p.m. in summer), Sun tours begin at 10 a.m.*

Victoria & Albert Museum
South Kensington

While reading my lists of London's offerings, you must wonder if the only descriptive adjectives in my vocabulary are "greatest," "wonderful," and "fascinating." But the Victoria & Albert Museum truly is the greatest museum of decorative arts in the world. If your interest is mild, 90 minutes will suffice; plan on 2½ hours or more if you're into it. While interior decorating aficionados are perusing a quite amazing collection of 14th-century embroidery, Chinese vases, Indian furnishings, and historic British candlesticks, less enthusiastic companions can amuse themselves with the largest collection of Renaissance sculpture outside Italy (featuring Donatello, Rossellino, and Bernini) and the "Fakes and Forgeries" gallery, cataloging some of the best knockoffs of Old Masters.

See map p. 136. Cromwell Road. ☎ *020-7942-2000.* www.vam.ac.uk. *Tube: South Kensington; the museum is directly across Cromwell Road from the station. Admission: free. Open: Thurs–Tues 10 a.m.–5:45 p.m., Wed and the last Fri of the month 10 a.m.–10 p.m.*

Westminster Abbey
Westminster

This grandiose early English Gothic abbey is one of Europe's major churches and the burial ground of many famous Brits — one of the country's greatest honors is to be buried in this hallowed hall. A tour only takes about 30 to 45 minutes, although history buffs may want to linger longer over their heroes. Every English monarch from William the Conqueror in 1066 to Elizabeth II in 1953 was crowned here (save Edwards V and VIII), and most of them (up to 1760) are buried here as well, some in fantastic tombs. Many of the early 16th-century royal tombs were carved by Pietro Torrigiani, a Florentine who studied sculpture with — and bullied — the young Michelangelo.

The right transept is known as Poet's Corner, with memorials to Britain's greatest writers and creative types, plus the graves of Chaucer, Robert Browning, Rudyard Kipling, D. H. Lawrence, Dylan Thomas, Noel Coward, and Sir Laurence Olivier. Other notables who rest in peace inside the abbey include Sir Isaac Newton, Charles Darwin, and composers Benjamin Britten and Handel. You can take an audio tour for an additional £3 ($5) or sign up for a £4 ($7) guided tour. Although the Royal Chapels are closed on Sundays, you can explore the rest of the abbey unless a service is in progress.

See map p. 136. Broad Sanctuary. ☎ 020-7654-4900. www.westminster-abbey. org. *Tube: Westminster or St. James Park; enter through the north transept. Admission: £7.50 ($14) adults, £5 ($9) seniors/students/children 11–17; free for children under 11. Open: Mon–Tues and Thurs–Sat 9:30 a.m.–4:45 p.m., Wed 9:30 a.m.–8 p.m. Last admission 1 hour before closing.*

More cool things to see and do

✔ **Strolling Portobello Road Market:** Antique collectors, bargain hunters, tourists, and deals on everything from kumquats to Wedgewood are what you find at London's most popular market street. Vendors set up by 5:30 a.m.; the outdoor fruit and veggie market runs all week (except Sunday), but on Saturday the market balloons into an enormous flea and antiques mart. About 90 antique shops line the roads around this section of London, so even during the week you can browse their dusty treasures (serious shoppers pick up the Saturday Antique Market guide). To get to the market, take the Tube to Notting Hill Gate.

✔ **Embarking on a London pub crawl:** Theater aside, the real traditional London evening out starts around 5:30 p.m. at your favorite pub. Among the most historic and atmospheric ale houses are the sawdust-floored and rambling **Ye Olde Cheshire Cheese** at Wine Office Court, off 145 Fleet St. (☎ 020-7353-6170); Dryden's old haunt the **Lamb and Flag,** 33 Rose St. (☎ 020-7497-9504), known as "Bucket of Blood" from its rowdier days; the Art Nouveau **Black Friar,** 174 Queen Victoria St. (☎ 020-7236-5474); and **Anchor Inn,** 34 Park St. (☎ 0870-990-6402), where the present pub dates from 1757 — but a pub has been at this location for 800 years, with Dickens and Shakespeare as past patrons. Make sure you order some true English bitters, hand-pumped and served at room temperature. Try Wadworth, Tetley's, Flowers, and the London-brewed Young's and Fuller's. Most pubs are open Monday through Saturday from 11 a.m. to 11 p.m. and on Sunday from noon to 10:30 p.m.

✔ **Making a shopping pilgrimage to Harrods:** Posh and a bit snobbish (they may turn you away if you look too scruffy), **Harrods,** 87–135 Brompton Rd. (☎ 020-7730-1234; www.harrods.com), is the only store in the world that offers you any item you can possibly want and backs up its word. Legend has it that a customer jokingly asked if the Harrods staff could procure him an elephant — then he got the bill. With 1,200,000 square feet and 300 departments, the store carries just about everything. Its fabulous food halls are still the highlight of a visit — 500 varieties of cheese, anyone?

✔ **Raising your pinkies at a proper afternoon tea:** Possibly the best British culinary invention was deciding to slip a refined, refreshing extra meal into the day, between 3:00 and 5:30 p.m. — a steaming pot of tea accompanied by a tiered platter of delicious finger sandwiches, slices of cake, and scones with jam and clotted cream. A full tea serving can run anywhere from £10 ($18) to £25 ($45). One of London's classiest (and most expensive) afternoon teas is at the ultratraditional **Brown's Hotel,** 29–34 Albemarle St. (☎ 020-7493-6020; www.brownshotel.com; Tube: Green Park). Less pricey — but just as good — are the teas at two of London's legendary department stores: the inimitable **Harrods Georgian Restaurant,** on the fourth floor at 87–135 Brompton Rd. (☎ 020-7730-1234; www.harrods.com; Tube: Knightsbridge), and **Fortnum and Mason's** St. James's Restaurant, 181 Piccadilly (☎ 020-7734-8040; www.fortnumandmason.co.uk; Tube: Piccadilly Circus or Green Park).

✔ **Taking in the changing of the guard at Buckingham Palace:** The Queen's London home on Buckingham Palace Road, St. James Park (☎ 09068-663-344 in the U.K. only at a premium charge; www.army.mod.uk), is one of Europe's most overrated attractions, but I include the spectacle here for its fame alone. Watching the guard change is like sitting through a bad halftime show by an overdrilled marching band. Come to the palace to make faces at the stoically unresponsive (and long-suffering) Beefeater guards if you must, but I advise you to skip the changing of the guard. If you decide to go anyway, it's at 11:30 a.m. daily from mid-April to July; every second day the rest of the year. In August and September, you can take a spin through the palace if the Queen's not in — if the flag's a-waving, she's home.

✔ **Reciting Romeo, oh Romeo — Shakespeare at the Globe Theatre:** If you saw *Shakespeare in Love,* you know what the rebuilt Globe Theatre looks like. Shakespeare was once part owner of, as well as performer in and main playwright for, a theater called The Globe at the Thames Bankside. Shakespeare's Globe Theatre is a recently built replica of the O-shaped building, with an open center and projecting stage — the sort of space for which Shakespeare's plays were written. Performances are May to October; tickets for seats run £13 to £29 ($23–$52). For only £5 ($9), you can stand in the open space right in front of the stage (tiring, and not so fun if it rains). Call ☎ 020-7401-9919 for the box office. Even if you don't stop for a show, make some time during the day to come for a tour (☎ 020-7902-1400; www.shakespeares-globe.org).

✔ **Club hopping:** The city that gave the world punk, new wave, techno, and electronica still has one of the world's most trend-setting clublands. The nature of the art means that any place I pen in this book will be considered out before the guide is, so do yourself a favor and pick up the *Time Out London* magazine to find out what's hottest each week. A few perennial favorites (sure to be full of tourists) include the once-fab-now-touristy-but-still-gloriously-tacky-in-neon **Hippodrome** (☎ 020-7437-4311) at Charing Cross Road and Cranbourne Street; the formerly massively hip, and still massively loud, garage and house beats of the **Ministry of Sound,** 103 Gaunt St. (☎ **020-7378-6528;** www.ministryofsound.com); the '70s retro, er, charm of **Carwash** (☎ **020-7434-3820**); and the joyful sacrilege of dancing to house tunes in a converted church at **Walkabout Shaftesbury Avenue** (formerly Limelight), 136 Shaftesbury Ave. (☎ **020-7255-8620;** www.walkabout.eu.com).

✔ **Joining the thespians — an evening at the theater:** London rivals New York for the biggest, most diverse theater scene. The West End has dozens of playhouses, but you find many other venues as well. The *Time Out London* and *What's On* magazines list (and often review) the week's offerings, as does the online Official London Theatre Guide (www.officiallondontheatre.co.uk). Plus, you can pick up plenty of pamphlets at the tourist office. You're best off going directly to the individual theatre's box offices to get your tickets, which can cost anywhere from £10 to £50 ($18–$90), although you can also buy them from **Keith Prowse** (☎ **800-223-6108** in the U.S., 0870-842-2248 in the U.K.; www.keithprowse.com), which has a desk in the main tourist office on Regent Street. If you want to try to get last-minute tickets at a discount, the *only* official spot is Leicester Square's half-price TKTS ticket booth (www.official londontheatre.co.uk/tkts), open Monday to Saturday 10 a.m. to 7 p.m., Sunday noon to 3 p.m. The tickets there are half-price (plus a £2.50/$4.50 fee) and are sold on the day of the performance only. The seats are usually up in the rafters, and don't count on getting into the biggest, hottest productions.

✔ **Waxing historic at Madame Tussaud's:** Famous **Madame Tussaud's,** Marylebone Road (☎ **0870-400-3000;** www.madame-tussauds.co.uk), is something between a still-life amusement ride and a serious gallery of historical likenesses. Madame herself took death masks from the likes of Marie Antoinette (which was easy, what with her head already detached and all); Ben Franklin (while very much alive) personally sat for her to mold a portrait. Some of the historical dioramas are interesting — although whether they're £19.99 ($36) worth of interesting (£17.99/$32 if you skip the Chamber Live house of horrors in the basement) I leave up to you to decide. They knock £2 ($3.60) off if you enter after 5 p.m. weekdays, £3 ($5) after 3 p.m. weekends (between 5 and 6 p.m., it falls to the "bargain" rate of £12/$22). The museum is open Monday to Friday from 10:00 a.m. to 5:30 p.m. and Saturday and Sunday from 9:30 a.m. to 5:30 p.m.

✔ **Setting your watch — a day in Greenwich:** London may set its watches by Big Ben, but Ben looks to the **Old Royal Observatory** at Greenwich for the time of day. This Thames port and shipping village keeps Greenwich mean time, by which the world winds its clock. Come to the observatory to straddle the prime meridian (0° longitude mark) and have one foot in each hemisphere, and, at the **National Maritime Museum** immerse yourself in the history of the proud Navy that maintained the British Empire for centuries. Both are admisison-free and open daily from 10 a.m. to 5 p.m. (☎ **0870-780-4552** or 020-8312-6565; www.nmm.ac.uk). During the same hours, you can board that most famous of clipper ships, the *Cutty Sark,* down near the ferry docks (☎ 020-8858-3445; www.cuttysark.org.uk); admission is £4.25 ($8). **The Greenwich Tourist Centre,** 46 Greenwich Church St. (☎ 0870-608-2000; www.greenwich.gov.uk), can give you more information. To get here, take the Jubilee Tube line to North Greenwich, the train from Charing Cross Station, the Docklands Light Railway from the Tower Hill Tube stop, the 188 bus from Russell Square, or my favorite option: an hour's float down the Thames in a ferry from Westminster or Charing Cross Piers.

Guided tours

You can get an excellent overview of the city's layout, and see many of the architectural sights at a snappy pace, from the top of a double-decker bus on **The Original London Sightseeing Tour** (☎ 020-7877-1722; www.theoriginaltour.com). You'll find flyers all over the city outlining the different tours offered by this hop-on/hop-off bus with running live commentary. At £15 ($27), the Original Tour is the best overall, spinning a two-hour loop of the top sights with 5 minutes (15 in winter) between buses. Tickets are good all day — if you buy tickets after 2 p.m., they're good the next day as well.

Of the many walking tour outfits in this city, by far the biggest and best is **London Walks** (☎ 020-7624-3978; www.walks.com). I can think of no better London investment for fun, education, and entertainment. Just £5.50 ($10) ($4.50/$8 for adults over 65 or students under 26, free for children under 15 with a parent) buys you two hours with an expert guide on a variety of thematic walks: neighborhood jaunts, museums, pub crawls, or walks in the footsteps of Shakespeare, Churchill, Christopher Wren, or Jack the Ripper. They also run Explorer Days jaunts out into the rest of England.

Suggested itineraries

In case you're the type who'd rather organize your own tours, this section offers some tips for building your own London itineraries.

If you have one day

To see London in a day takes full-throttle sightseeing. Reserve ahead for the 9:30 a.m. Beefeater tour at the **Tower of London.** After perusing the Crown Jewels there, take off for the **British Museum** (grab lunch along the way) to ogle the Rosetta Stone, Egyptian mummies, and Elgin Marbles. Be at **Westminster Abbey** by 3 p.m. to pay homage to the British monarchs, English poets, and other notables entombed therein. Have an early pre-theatre dinner at **Rules** or **The Ivy,** and then spend the evening doing whatever floats your boat: attending a play or a show, indulging in a pub crawl (an early play may leave you time to pub-crawl a bit afterward), or just drinking in the street acts and nighttime crowds milling around Leicester Square.

If you have two days

Begin Day 1 marveling at the spoils of the old empire in the **British Museum.** Move along to the stellar collection of Renaissance paintings in the **National Gallery,** stopping early on for a sandwich in the excellent cafeteria. Lunch tides you over until you get to fabled **Harrods** department store, where you can take a break from the window-shopping to indulge in an afternoon tea in the **Georgian Restaurant.** Spend the late afternoon however you like, but make sure you get tickets ahead of time for a play or show (whether it's Shakespeare at the Globe or a West End musical), and book ahead at **Rules** or **The Ivy** for a late, post-theatre dinner (in fact, try to reserve a week or so beforehand).

Start off Day 2 at the **Tower of London** on one of the excellent Beefeater tours. Spend the late morning climbing the dome of Christopher Wren's masterpiece, **St. Paul's Cathedral.** After a late lunch, be at the meeting place for the **London Walks** tour that intrigues you most (several leave from near St. Paul's itself). Try to get to **Westminster Abbey** early enough to pop into the Royal Chapels before they close at 4 p.m.; the rest of the church stays open until 7 p.m. Duck out and head to the neighboring **Parliament House** to get inside and witness British Government in session. If it's a Friday or Saturday, you still have time afterward to hit the **Tate Modern,** which doesn't close until 10 p.m.

If you have three days

Spend the morning of Day 1 in the **British Museum,** which catalogues human achievement across the world and throughout the ages. During lunch, call the **Globe Theatre** to see whether a play is on for tomorrow at 2 p.m. (if so, book tickets). Try to finish lunch by 2 p.m. and then head to the nearest stop on the map for the **Original London Sightseeing Tours** and take the 90-minute bus loop past the major sights of London. After you're good and oriented, plunge right into the Old Masters of the **National Gallery.** Have a traditional British dinner at **Rules** or **Porters** and try to get to bed early; you need to wake up early the next morning.

Day 2 is the day for the London of the Middle Ages and Renaissance. Be at the **Tower of London** by 9:30 a.m. to get in on the first guided tour of this medieval bastion and its Crown Jewels. Afterward, visit **St. Paul's Cathedral** and grab some lunch. Then head across the Thames River to visit the **Tate Modern,** then stroll Bankside walkway along the Thames to tour Shakespeare's **Globe Theatre** and — if possible — experience one of the Bard's plays in the open-air setting the way he intended (plays start at 2 p.m.). The tour itself only takes an hour; a play takes two to four hours.

If you see a play, grab a quick dinner; if you just do the tour, you have the late afternoon to spend as you like — perhaps squeeze in a visit to **Tate Britain** to indulge in the best of British art, or take a ride on the **London Eye.** Either way, finish dinner by 6:30 or 7:00 p.m. so that you can join whichever historic pub walk **London Walks** is running that evening (they start at either 7 or 7:30 p.m.; the brochure tells you where to meet). After your introduction to British ales and pub life, call it a night.

Yesterday was medieval, but for Day 3 you're going to stiffen your upper lip with some Victorian-era British traditions. Start out at 9 a.m. by paying your respects to centuries of British heroes, poets, and kings buried at **Westminster Abbey.** Drop by the **Victoria & Albert Museum** for miles of the best in decorative arts and sculpture. Have a snack (not lunch) on your way to the world's grandest and most venerable department store, **Harrods.** After a bit of high-class browsing inside, stop by the fourth floor's **Georgian Restaurant** at 3 p.m. sharp for a proper British after-noon tea. Linger and enjoy your teatime.

Head over to **Big Ben** and the buildings of **Parliament** around 5:30 p.m. and, if government is in session (October through July), get in line to go inside and watch Parliament at work, vilifying one another in a colorfully entertaining way that makes the U.S. Congress seem like a morgue. Or, if you go ga-ga over musicals (or are itching to see a cutting-edge London play), go see a show. Either way, because you'll eat late, make sure you've reserved a restaurant that specializes in late, after-theatre meals (**Chor Bizarre** is a good choice).

Traveling Beyond London

Although you can find enough to do in London to keep you busy for weeks, a daytrip into the English countryside is a magnificent way to escape the bustle of the city. My top choices are Bath, with its ruins and stately 18th-century mansions; Salisbury, with its imposing Gothic cathedral and Stonehenge nearby; and Oxford, one of the world's great-est college towns.

 If planning your own daytrips is too much trouble, check out **Green Line** (☎ 0870-608-7261; www.greenline.co.uk) in London, which offers guided bus trips. Bath, Stonehenge, and the Cotswolds are grouped into a very full day; the cost is £20 ($36) for adults and £25 ($45) for those under age 15 or over 60.

Bath: Ancient Rome in Georgian clothing

When Queen Anne relaxed at the natural hot springs here in 1702, she made the village of Bath fashionable again, but she wasn't exactly blaz-ing new territory. The Romans built the first town here in A.D. 75, a small spa village centered around a temple to Sulis Minerva — mixing the Latin goddess of knowledge, Minerva, with Sulis, the local Celtic water goddess. When the Georgians were laying out Britain's most unified cityscape in the 18th century with the help of architects John Wood, Sr., and John Wood, Jr., they also unearthed Britain's best-preserved Roman ruins.

Bath, today, is a genteel foray into the Georgian world. The highlights include having high tea in the 18th-century Pump Room, perusing Roman remains, and admiring the honey-colored stone architecture that drew, in its heyday, the likes of Dickens, Thackeray, Nelson, Pitt, and Jane Austen. These luminaries enjoyed the fashionable pleasures of a city whose real leader was not a politician, but rather the dandy impresario and socialite Beau Nash. Although doable as a daytrip from London, Bath's charms really come out after the day-trippers leave, and savvy travelers plan to stay the night and next morning.

Getting there

Trains to Bath leave from London's Paddington Station at least every hour; the trip takes about one and a half hours. The **Tourist Information Centre** (☎ 01225-477-101; www.visitbath.co.uk) is in the center of town in the Abbey Chambers, on a square off the lower flank of Bath Abbey.

 Free, two-hour Mayor's Guides walks leave from outside the Pump Room Monday through Sunday at 10:30 a.m. and Sunday to Friday at 2 p.m. From May through September, there are also walks at 7 p.m. on Tuesday, Friday, and Saturday.

Seeing the sights

Bath's top attractions are clustered together on the main square. A spin through the **Roman Baths Museum** (☎ 01225-477-785; www.romanbaths. co.uk) with your digital audio guide in hand gives you an overview of the hot springs from their Celto-Roman inception (the head of Minerva is a highlight) to the 17th/18th-century spa built over the hot springs. Starting in Autumn 2004, the spa itself will reopen at a nearby site for soaks and beauty treatments; precise details were not yet released when we went to press, except a number for info and reservations: ☎ 01225-331-234 (www.thermaebathspa.com). Until then, you can always drink a cup of its waters (taste: *blech!*) upstairs in the elegant **Pump Room** (☎ 01225-477-785). This cafe/restaurant offers one of England's classic afternoon tea services, but you can also get a good lunch here, all to the musical accompaniment of a live trio or solo pianist. Lunch and tea are served daily. The museum is open daily March to October from 9:30 a.m. to 6:00 p.m.; July to August from 9 a.m. to 10 p.m.; and November to February from 9:00 a.m. to 5:30 p.m. Admission is £9 ($16).

While you're waiting for your seating in the Pump Room, head out to the square to examine **Bath Abbey** (☎ 01225-422-462), the focal point of Bath's medieval incarnation as a religious center. The 16th-century church is renowned both for the fantastic, scalloped fan vaulting of its ceilings and the odd, carved Jacob's ladders flanking the facade, which were inspired by a dream of the bishop who rebuilt this church on the site of an earlier one. April to October the Abbey is open Monday to Saturday from 9 a.m. to 6 p.m.; November to March, hours are Monday to Saturday from 9:00 a.m. to 4:30 p.m. Around to the right you can enter the **Heritage Vaults,** whose meager displays trace the history both of the abbey, which in some form dates back to the sixth century, and of the city itself (☎ 01225-303-314); admission is £2 ($3.60).

Bath's newest attraction, **The Jane Austen Centre,** 40 Gay St. (☎ **01225-443-000;** www.janeausten.co.uk), is located in a Georgian town house on an elegant street where Austen once lived. Exhibits and a video convey a sense of what life was like in Bath during the Regency period, and how the city influenced Austen's writing. The center is open Monday to Saturday from 10:00 a.m. to 5:30 p.m. and Sunday from 10:30 a.m. to 5:30 p.m. Admission is £4.45 ($8).

Aside from its major attractions, Bath in and of itself is a sight. Visit especially the architectural triumphs of **The Circus** and the **Royal Crescent,** both up on the north end of town. The latter has a highly recommended **Museum of Georgian Life** at No. 1 (☎ **01225-428-126**), where the guides can answer all your questions on life during Bath's glory days. It's open Tuesdays to Sundays, February 10 to October 23 from 10:30 a.m. to 5:00 p.m., and October 24 to November 28 from 10:30 a.m. to 4:00 p.m.; admission is £4 ($7).

Where to stay

If you can swing the £240-and-up ($432) per-double price tag, *the* place to stay in Bath is bang in the middle of one of the city's architectural triumphs at the **Royal Crescent Hotel,** 16 Royal Crescent (☎ **888-295-4710** in the U.S., 0800-980-0987 or 01225-823-333 in the U.K.; Fax: 01225-339-401; www.royalcrescent.co.uk). If you stay here, you get to live in that restrained Georgian splendor for a few days with a private boat and hot air balloon at your disposal. Otherwise, the elegant Victorian **Leighton House,** 139 Wells Rd. (☎ **01225-314-769;** Fax: 01225-443-079; www.leighton-house.co.uk), is a small, traditional British B&B that's much more affordable. Rates are £55 to £105 ($99–$189) double (no credit cards).

Where to dine

One of Bath's leading restaurants and wine bars, the **Moon and Sixpence,** 6A Broad St. (☎ **01225-460-962**), is an unbeatable value. The bar is open for lunch and dinner daily. Quaint **Sally Lunn's,** 4 North Parade Passage (☎ **01225-461-634;** www.sallylunns.co.uk), is where the monstrous brioche-like Bath bun was invented in the 17th century. The location is reputedly the oldest house in Bath.

Salisbury and Stonehenge: A mix of the Gothic and prehistoric

Many visitors hurrying out to see the famous Stonehenge are surprised to find that they stumble across one of Europe's greatest Gothic cathedrals along the way. Salisbury, gateway to South Wiltshire and its prehistoric remains, is a medieval market town that's a deserved attraction in its own right. Although you can see the cathedral and Stonehenge as a daytrip from London, you have to rush to do it.

Getting there

About 18 trains make the 90-minute trip from London's Waterloo Station to Salisbury daily. From here, you can grab a Wilts and Dorset bus for the half-hour leg out to Stonehenge, 12 miles north of the city at the junction of the A303 and A344/A360.

Salisbury's **Tourist Information Centre** (☎ **01722-334-956;** www.visit salisburyuk.com) is on Fish Row.

Seeing the sights

 The overpowering sight in town is the **Cathedral** (☎ **01722-555-120** or 01722-555-113; www.salisburycathedral.org.uk), the spire of which dominates the landscape and the construction of which started in 1220 and took a remarkably short 38 years. You can go halfway up the spire for a view of both the church architecture and the surrounding city and then visit the octagonal chapter house for a peek at some medieval manuscripts and one of the four surviving copies of the Magna Carta. Don't miss the peaceful cloisters or the brass-rubbing center. The cathedral is open daily from 7:15 a.m. to 6:15 p.m. (to 7:15 p.m. June 9 through August 30); "voluntary donations" are £3.80 ($7) adults, £3.30 ($6) students and seniors, £2 ($3.60) children 5 to 17.

History buffs can stop by the **Salisbury and South Wiltshire Museum**, 65 The Close (☎ **01722-332-151;** www.salisburymuseum.org.uk), to get information about early humans and the remains of nearby prehistoric sites such as Stonehenge and Old Sarum. The museum is open Monday to Saturday from 10 a.m. to 5 p.m. (July and August also Sundays from 2 p.m. to 5 p.m.). Admission is £4 ($7) adults, £1.50 ($2.70) children.

The tourist office can fill you in on the other Salisbury sights, mostly 17th- and 18th-century homes, such as the **Mompesson House** on The Close (☎ **01722-335-659;** www.nationaltrust.org.uk), which is open April 9 to October 31, Saturday to Wednesday from 11:00 a.m. to 5:30 p.m.; admission to the house and garden is £4 ($7) adults, £2 ($3.60) children (gardens only, 80p/$1.45).

 Stonehenge (☎ **01980-624-715;** www.english-heritage.org.uk/ stonehenge) itself is, in some ways, a bit of a letdown. Don't get me wrong — Stonehenge is still one of the most incredible sights in Europe, highly conducive to contemplating the earliest dawn of human endeavor and terribly romantic when the sun sets behind the ancient ruins. But keep in mind that a rope barrier keeps you 50 feet away from the concentric circles of enormous standing stones; unfortunately, past visitors were fond of scratching their names into the venerable rocks, which gave rise to the barriers. A new walkway allows you to circle the stones but seriously mars the beauty of the site.

Stonehenge was begun by an unknown people before 3,000 B.C. and added to up until 1,500 B.C. (many people associate Stonehenge with the Druids, but they didn't appear on the scene until around the first century B.C.).

All we really know about Stonehenge is that it represents a remarkable feat of engineering — some of the stones came from dozens of miles away. Also, the stones act like a huge astronomical calendar; they align with the summer equinox and still keep track of the seasons after more than 5,000 years.

The site is open daily, June to August from 9 a.m. to 7 p.m., March 16 to May 31 and September 1 to October 15 from 9:30 a.m. to 6:00 p.m., and October 16 to March 15 from 9:30 a.m. to 4:00 p.m. Admission is £5.20 ($9) adults, £3.90 ($7) students, and £2.60 ($4.70) children.

Where to stay

Try a £120 ($216) double at **White Hart** (☎ 0870-400-8125; Fax: 01722-412-761; www.whitehart-salisbury.co.uk), opposite Salisbury Cathedral, with a Georgian old wing and a motel-like new one. You can get a less pricey room at **The Kings Arms**, 7A–11 St. Johns St. (☎ 01722-327-629; Fax: 01722-414-246; E-mail: thekingsarmshotelsalisbury@fsmail.com), a Tudor coaching inn where the doubles cost £99 ($178) and an open fire warms the pub.

Where to dine

Salisbury's finest dining is on the outskirts of town, but the city center does have **Salisbury Haunch of Venison**, 1 Minster St. (☎ 01722-322-024), a 1320 chophouse with tasty roasts and grilled meats. **Harper's Restaurant**, 6–9 Ox Row, Market Square (☎ 01722-333-118; www.harpersrestaurant.co.uk), does a good three-course lunch menu of British/International cooking.

Oxford: The original college town

The City of Dreaming Spires, robed dons, budding intellectuals, and punting on the Cherwell is today surrounded by sprawling suburbs and clogged with the bustle of both a university town and a small industrial city. But don't let that keep you from making a pilgrimage to the school that has matriculated the likes of John Donne, Samuel Johnson, Christopher Wren, William Penn, Charles Dodgson (otherwise known as Lewis Carroll), Graham Greene, and Percy Bysshe Shelley. Actually, Shelley never graduated; he was kicked out for helping write a pamphlet on atheism. (Now he has a memorial on Magpie Lane — go figure.)

Getting there

Oxford is a comfortable daytrip from London, but to really get to know the place takes a few days' stay (or enrollment at the university). Regular trains from London's Paddington Station take just over an hour. **Oxford Express** provides coach service from London's Victoria Station (☎ 01865-785-400; www.oxfordbus.co.uk) to the Oxford bus station. Coaches usually depart about every 20 minutes during the day from Gate 10 (trip time: about 90 minutes). One-way is £9 ($16); a same-day round-trip ticket costs £11 ($20).

The **Tourist Information Centre** (☎ 01865-726-871; www.visitoxford. org) is opposite the bus station on Gloucester Green at 15–16 Broad St. The private Web site www.oxfordcity.co.uk is also packed with good Oxfordian resources.

Seeing the sights

The city itself is the "campus" of Oxford University (☎ 01865-270-000; www.ox.ac.uk); it spreads over the town in a series of 36 colleges, each with its own long history and arcane traditions — such as Christ Church College, whose Great Tom bell rings every evening at 9:05 p.m. to signal the closing of the school gates, pealing 101 times in honor of the college's original 101 students. Many of the colleges incorporate architectural tidbits from their foundings in the 13th to 16th centuries. Because the primary business here is education, not tourism, fairly strict rules keep visits limited to certain areas at certain times and in small groups (six people maximum). Most colleges, when they're open, allow visitors to poke around discreetly (check the notice boards outside each college for specifics).

I don't have room to detail all of Oxford's colleges here, but the top ones include **Christ Church** (☎ 01865-276-492; www.visitchristchurch. net), dating from 1525 with the largest quadrangle in town and that big ol' bell (the top half of the bell tower was designed by Christopher Wren). The college chapel also happens to be the local cathedral, one of the tiniest in England. *Alice in Wonderland's* Lewis Carroll once studied here, but perhaps its most famous "students" are fictional — many scenes in the Harry Potter movies were set here. The college is open to visitors Monday to Saturday from 9:00 a.m. to 5:30 p.m., Sunday from noon to 5:30 p.m.; admission is £4 ($7).

Try also to fit in **Merton College** (☎ 01865-276-310; www.merton.ox. ac.uk), the oldest (1264), with a library the odd collections of which include Chaucer's astrolabe. Merton is open weekdays 2 to 4 p.m., weekends 10 a.m. to 4 p.m.; admission is free, but tours of the Old Library run £1 ($1.80).

Perhaps the prettiest overall, **Magdalen College** (☎ 01865-276-000; www. magd.ox.ac.uk) is a 15th-century gem surrounded by a park and overlooking the Cherwell River. It's open from 1 p.m. (from noon July through Sept) to 6 p.m. or dusk, whichever comes first; admission is £3 ($5).

You can also finally pay a visit to the famed **Bodleian Library** (☎ 01865-277-224; www.bodley.ox.ac.uk), long closed to visitors. It's one of the oldest libraries in Europe — operating continuously since 1602, but begun long before that — and the second largest in England (after the British Library), containing copies of every book copyrighted in the U.K. It also has some terribly scenic rooms and architectures — it stood in for Hogwart's Library in the *Harry Potter* films. It's open for hour-long guided tours Monday to Friday at 10:30 a.m., 11:30 a.m., 2:00 p.m., and 3:00 p.m. (no morning tours Nov to Feb), and year-round Saturdays at 10:30 a.m. and 11:30 a.m. Admission is £3.50 ($6).

Of course, the campus isn't all that Oxford has to offer. Perhaps your first order of business in town should be to climb **Carfax Tower** (☎ 01865-792-653) in the center of town. Aerial maps are handed out at the bottom to help you get a bird's-eye handle on the city layout. The tower is open daily from 10 a.m. to 5 p.m.; admission is £1.40 ($2.50) adults, 60p ($1.10) children ages 5 to 15.

If you only visit one museum in town, make it the **Ashmolean Museum** (☎ 01865-278-000; www.ashmol.ox.ac.uk), founded in 1683 and one of Britain's best. The impressive painting collection features works by Bellini, Raphael, Michelangelo, Rembrandt, and Picasso. The museum is open Tuesday to Saturday from 10 a.m. to 5 p.m. and Sunday from 2 to 5 p.m.; admission is free.

Where to stay

You can hole up for the night at the **Eastgate Hotel,** 23 Merton St., The High (☎ 0870-400-8201; Fax: 01865-791-681; www.eastgate-hotel.com). The hotel is near the river, with modern £96 ($173) doubles in a country-inn setting.

Where to dine

Oxford's classic eatery is the **Cherwell Boathouse Restaurant,** Bardwell Road (☎ 01865-552-746; www.cherwellboathouse.co.uk), right on the river. The French cuisine features fresh ingredients and half-priced kids' meals. For pub grub, follow in the footsteps of Thomas Hardy, Elizabeth Taylor, and Bill Clinton (who studied at Oxford), all former regulars of **The Turf Tavern,** 4 Bath Place (☎ 01865-243-235; www.o-h-m.co.uk/turf), a venerable 13th-century watering hole.

Fast Facts: London

Area Code

The country code for the United Kingdom is **44.** The city code for most of Greater London is **020.** Many businesses instead use the new, non-geographical code of **0870.** When dialing either from abroad, drop the initial zero. To call London from the United States, dial **011-44-20,** and then the local number. See also "Telephones," later in this section.

American Express

London has several offices, including 30–31 Haymarket, SW1 (☎ 020-7484-9600; Tube: Charing Cross), near Trafalgar Square.

Hours are Monday through Saturday 9 a.m. to 6 p.m., Sunday 10 a.m. to 5 p.m.

Currency

Britain has so far opted out of adopting the euro. The basic unit of currency is the pound sterling (£), divided into 100 pence (p). There are 1p, 2p, 10p, 20p, 50p, £1, and £2 coins; banknotes are issued in £5, £10, £20, and £50.

The rate of exchange used to calculate the dollar values given in this chapter is $1 = 56p (or £1 = $1.80). Amounts over $5 have been rounded to the nearest dollar.

Doctors and Dentists

Ask the concierge if your hotel keeps a doctor or dentist on call. Otherwise, for 24-hour emergency care, go to the Royal Free Hospital, 11 Pond St., NW3 (☎ 020-7352-8121) or the University College Hospital, 25 Grafton Way, WC1 (☎ 020-7380-9964).

Embassy

The U.S. Embassy and Consulate is at 24 Grosvenor Square, W1A 1AE (☎ 020-7499-9000; www.usembassy.org.uk). For passport and visa information, visit the Special Consular Services Monday to Friday from 8:30 to 11:30 a.m. and 2 to 5 p.m.

Emergency

Dial ☎ **999** or **112** to call the police, report a fire, or call for an ambulance.

Hospitals

See "Doctors and Dentists," earlier in this section.

Information

The Tourist Information Centre in Victoria Station is always busy, but the folks who work there are amazingly helpful. Much better is the British Visitor's Centre, at 1 Lower Regent St., 3 blocks down from Piccadilly Circus (☎ 020-7808-3838). It has plenty of information on all of Britain, plus a convenient travel bookshop, BritRail ticket window, and both travel and theatre ticket agencies. It is open Monday from 9:30 a.m. to 6:30 p.m.; Tuesday through Friday from 9:00 a.m. to 6:30 p.m.; and Saturday and Sunday from 10 a.m. to 4 p.m. (late June to late Sept, Saturday hours are from 9 a.m. to 5 p.m.).

Heathrow Airport and Liverpool Street station also have information desks, but unfortunately no office answers phone inquiries.

The London Information Centre in Leicester Square is open late seven days a week. See "Finding information after you arrive," earlier in this chapter.

Online you can get information at the national Visit Britain site (www.visitbritain.org), London's www.visitlondon.com, and the private but officially sanctioned www.londontown.com.

Internet Access and Cybercafes

The best cybercafes in London are the easyInternetCafe shops (www.easyinternetcafe.com), open daily from 8 or 9 a.m. to 11 p.m. or midnight. They offer hundreds of terminals and charge the lowest rates in town — £1 ($1.80) per hour. Branches include 456–459 The Strand, just off Trafalgar Square across from Charing Cross Station (Tube: Charing Cross); 9–13 Wilton Rd., opposite Victoria Station (Tube: Victoria); 9–16 Tottenham Court Rd. (Tube: Tottenham Court Road or Goodge); and 43 Regent St., in the Burger King on Picadilly Circus (Tube: Picadilly Circus).

Maps

The *London A to Z* (pronounced ay-to-zed) is a widely available booklet that maps every teensy alleyway, mews, close, and street in all of London. Makes a great souvenir, too.

Newspapers/Magazines

The best way to find out what's going on around town, from shows to restaurants to events, is to buy a copy of the *Time Out London* magazine, published every Tuesday and available at newsstands. You can also get listings from *Time Out London* magazine's competitor, *What's On*, as well as from the *Evening Standard*.

Pharmacies

Boots (www.boots.com) is the largest chain of London chemists (drugstores). You find them located all over London — with some 156 branches in London alone, there are far too many to list. They are generally open Monday through Saturday from 9 a.m. to 10 p.m. and Sunday from noon to 5 p.m.

Police

In an emergency, dial ☎ 999 from any phone; no money is needed. At other times, dial the operator at ☎ 100 and ask to be connected with the police.

Post Office

The most central post office is the Trafalgar Square branch at 24–28 William IV St. (☎ 020-7930-9580), open Monday through Saturday from 8 a.m. to 8 p.m.

Safety

London is a friendly city to its visitors; areas where you may be a bit uneasy — Tottenham, South London, and Hackney — lie far beyond central London. Even so, London is a very large city, so you're wise to take general precautions to prevent being targeted by thieves or pickpockets. Another borough to be wary of is Soho; it has a few borderline areas.

Taxes

In England, a 17.5 percent value-added tax (VAT) is figured into the price of most items. Foreign visitors can reclaim a percentage of the VAT on major purchases of consumer goods (see Chapter 9 for more on this).

Taxis

See the "Getting Around" section, earlier in this chapter.

Telephone

London has three kinds of pay phones — one that accepts only coins; the Cardphone, which takes only phone cards; and one that accepts both phonecards and credit cards. The minimum charge for a local call is 10p (18¢) for 55 seconds. Stick to small coins at coin-operated phones because they don't make change. Phone cards are sold at newsstands and post offices for £1 ($1.80), £2 ($3.60), £4 ($7), £10 ($18), or £20 ($36). Credit-card pay phones accept the usual credit cards — Visa, MasterCard, American Express — but the minimum charge is 50p (90¢); insert the card and dial 144. For directory assistance, dial 192 for the United Kingdom or 153 for international; for operator-assisted calls, dial 100 for the United Kingdom or 155 for international.

To call the United States direct from London, dial 001 followed by the area code and phone number. To charge a call to your calling card or make a collect call home, dial AT&T (☎ 0800-890-011 or 0500-890-011), MCI (☎ 0800-279-5088), or Sprint (☎ 0800-890-877 or 0500-890-877). See also "Area Code," earlier in this section.

Transit Info

See "Getting Around London," earlier in this chapter.

Chapter 11

Edinburgh and the Best of Scotland

- -

In This Chapter

▶ Getting to Edinburgh
▶ Checking out the neighborhoods
▶ Discovering the best places to sleep and eat
▶ Exploring the city's highlights
▶ Heading into the Highlands or wandering west to Glasgow

- -

*I*f you believe every Hollywood movie about Scotland, you would think that Highlanders only wear tartan kilts, are all named Heather or Angus, and wear blue face paint while fighting for liberty from the British. Oh, and don't forget the bagpipes that play in the background while woolly sheep graze in the glen.

Hollywood aside, the people of Scotland are proud of their heritage, and local political parties are constantly striving for further autonomy from the English.

But then again, while visiting Balmoral, Prince Charles is more likely to wear a kilt than the average Scotsman. And whether anyone actually enjoys eating *haggis* — Scotland's answer to "mystery meat" — is unclear. Incidentally, use the word *Scotch* only to describe the whisky, broth, or prevailing northern mist. Calling a person by that word is considered an insult. Refer to the locals here as *Scots* or *Scottish*.

A clearer picture of modern Scotland emerges in the industrial and agricultural center of Glasgow and in Edinburgh, the gateway to the Highlands. Edinburgh is called the "Athens of the North," partly for its renowned university and intellectual life (Sir Walter Scott and Robert Burns lived here, and Robert Louis Stevenson is a native son) and partly because some neoclassical ruins top one of its hills.

Edinburgh is a town of fine arts and shopping, plus some of the most happening nightlife in Britain. The city is a cultural capital of Europe and hosts a performing arts blowout every August called the Edinburgh

International Festival (see "More cool things to see and do," later in this chapter). I've toured Edinburgh in a day before, but the town deserves two or three days — more if you can spare it.

Getting There

Scotland borders England to the north, so if you're coming to Edinburgh from London, the best choices are a quick one-hour flight or a scenic five-hour train ride that lets you off right in the middle of town.

Arriving by air

Edinburgh Airport (☎ **0870-040-0007;** www.baa.com/main/airports/edinburgh) is just 8 miles west of town and handles flights from all over Great Britain and major cities on the continent (Amsterdam, Brussels, Frankfurt, Paris, and Zurich). The airport is small and quite manageable. The information desk is located in the arrivals hall. You can grab **Airlink 100** bus (☎ **0131-555-6363;** www.flybybus.com) every 10 minutes or so (30 minutes at night — and the bus follows a slightly different route) for the 25-minute trip to downtown's Waverly Station. One-way is £3.30 ($6); round-trip is £5 ($9). You can buy tickets at the airport information desk or onboard the bus. A 20-minute taxi ride from the airport to Edinburgh runs about £16 ($29). The taxi *rank* (stand) is to the left outside the arrivals hall.

Arriving by train or bus

Nearly every hour, trains from London (www.scotrail.co.uk or www.gner.co.uk) pull into **Waverley Station,** at the east end of Princes Street. The trip takes five to seven and a half hours. *Coaches* (the term for buses here) from London cost less, but take eight miserable hours (sleep is impossible) and arrive at a bus depot on St. Andrew Square.

Orienting Yourself in Edinburgh

Edinburgh is a port town of sorts; its outskirts rest on the **Firth of Forth,** an inlet of the North Sea. The center of town is an ancient volcanic outcrop atop which glowers **Edinburgh Castle.** Due east of the castle is Waverley train station. Between the two run **Princes Street Gardens** and the sunken train tracks. These gardens effectively divide the city between the Old Town to the south and the grid-like New Town to the north.

Introducing the neighborhoods

Hotels and shops fill **New Town,** developed in the 18th century. The major east-west streets of New Town are **Princes Street,** bordering the gardens named after it, and **George Street,** which runs parallel to Princes Street 2 blocks north.

Scotland

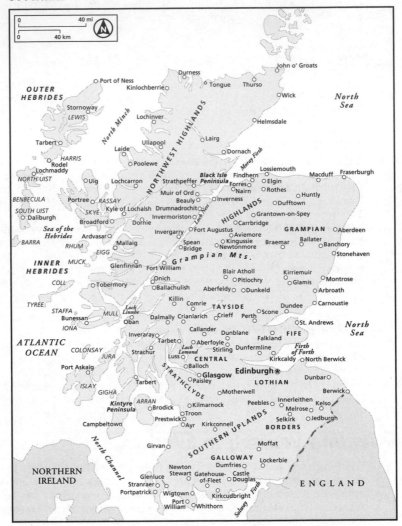

The **Royal Mile,** the main thoroughfare of the **Old Town,** spills off the castle's mount and runs downhill to the east. It's a single road, but the Royal Mile carries several names: Lawnmarket, High Street, and Canongate. Farther to the south is the **University District,** one of the hot spots for Edinburgh's famed nightlife.

Finding information after you arrive

Edinburgh's tourist office (see the "Fast Facts" section at the end of this chapter) is an excellent resource.

Getting Around Edinburgh

Because historic Edinburgh is not a big area, you can walk most of it easily. But if you plan to travel across town to catch a show or see a sight, consider hopping a bus or hailing a cab.

By bus

City buses (☎ 0131-555-6363; www.lothianbuses.co.uk) are cheap and offer quick access to the residential districts that surround the city center — where you find the more inexpensive hotels and B&Bs. On Edinburgh buses, you pay by the mile, so you tell the driver where you're getting off and drop *exact change* in the slot. Single rides cost 60p, 80p, or £1 ($1.10, $1.45, or $1.80).

The **Daysaver Ticket** costs £2.50 ($4.50) for a full weekday of unlimited rides; weekends, the Daysaver costs just £1.80 ($3.25). If you plan to be around for a week, you can get a **City GoSmart Ridacard** good for unlimited travel for £12 ($22) adults and £8 ($14) children. Purchase tickets and passes at the **Edinburgh and Scotland Information Centre** at 3 Princes Street, right above the train station.

By taxi

You can reach Edinburgh's tourist sites easily on foot, but a taxi may be useful if you're traveling longer distances or carrying luggage. Hail a cab or find one at a taxi rank at Hanover Street, Waverley Station, or Haymarket Station. To call a taxi, dial ☎ 0131-229-2468 or 0131-228-1211. The initial charge is £1.80 ($3.25), plus £1.98 ($3.55) for each mile.

By foot

Edinburgh is an easily walked city, and most of the sights listed in this chapter won't take you too far from the city's center. An especially pleasant walk is down the Royal Mile (see "Exploring Edinburgh," later in this chapter).

Staying in Edinburgh

Edinburgh hotels are not cheap. Plus, all the hotels charge three different rates: off-season, high season, and Festival season. If you don't book well in advance for Festival time (the annual Edinburgh International Festival, see "More cool things to see and do," later in this chapter), you probably won't find a room — at least not anywhere near the city center. Even if you do book in advance, staying near the city center costs more than double the off-season price.

 Luckily, Edinburgh has many pleasant suburbs no more than 20 minutes by bus from the center of town — neighborhoods where the rooms cost less year-round and where you can find some of the only free space during the Festival. Inexpensive guesthouses fill one such area, around Dalkeith Road between Holyrood Park and The Meadows, just a ten-minute bus ride south of the Old Town.

 The tourist office has a booklet listing local B&Bs and guesthouses, and the staff can help you find room in one or space in a regular hotel for a small fee.

For general tips on booking and what to expect from European accommodations, see Chapter 7.

Edinburgh's top hotels and B&Bs

Balmoral Hotel
$$$$$ **New Town**

Edinburgh's premier luxury hotel perches atop Waverley Station, a 1902 city landmark with a clock tower, where kilted doormen welcome you to a slightly contrived Scottish experience. The RF chain redecorated the hotel in 1998 and 1999, and the large rooms are now outfitted in a Victorian-meets-contemporary-comfort style, discreetly cushy and with full amenities. The refined Number One restaurant, which earned Michelin stars in both 2003 and 2004, is highly recommended for international cuisine, as is the modern brasserie-style Hadrian's. The popular NB's pub has live music on weekends, while the more sedate Bar at Palm Court specializes in single-malt whiskies. You can take afternoon tea in the Palm Court after a workout in the gym, a trip to the spa or sauna, or a dip in the indoor pool.

See map p. 170. 1 Princes Street (at the east end of the street, practically on top of the train station). ☎ *800-225-5843 in the U.S. or 0131-556-2414. Fax: 0131-557-3747.* www.roccofortehotels.com. *Bus: 3, 3A, 4, 8, 15, 26, 30, 31, 33, or 44 (but if you're arriving by train, you're already there). Rates: £225–£340 ($405–$612) double. Full Scottish breakfast £17 ($31), continental breakfast £14 ($25). AE, DC, MC, V.*

Dalhousie Castle
 $$$$ **Bonnyrigg**

Staying right in charming Edinburgh is convenient, but you can travel just outside the town to find a 15th-century castle that offers all the medieval romance that you expect to find in Scotland. Henry IV, Sir Walter Scott, and Queen Victoria all resided at Dalhousie Castle, before it was renovated to provide luxurious, modern comforts. The castle's sylvan setting beside a flowing stream appeals both to romantic and outdoorsy types. The hotel organizes salmon and trout fishing, shooting, and horseback riding expeditions. Try the Dungeon Restaurant for a unique dining experience. The novelty of staying in a castle is usually a big hit with kids. Children under 12 stay for free with their parents.

See map p. 170. Bonnyrigg (8 miles southeast of Edinburgh). ☎ *01875-820-153. Fax: 01875-821-936.* www.dalhousiecastle.co.uk. *By car: Take the A7 8 miles southeast of Edinburgh toward Carlisle and turn right onto B704; the castle is just outside the village of Bonnyrigg. Rates: £165–£195 ($297–$351) double. Rates include full Scottish breakfast. AE, DC, MC, V.*

George Inter-Continental
$$$ New Town

The core of this hotel on tony George Street is a 1755 Georgian house. The refurbished hotel rooms feature all the amenities that modern standards prefer. You can enjoy the atmosphere of the original town house in the Scottish restaurant, but the new wing has the best rooms (fourth floor and above), which overlook the street.

See map p. 170. 19–21 George St. (steps away from St. Andrews Square). ☎ *800-327-0200 in the U.S. or 01312-251-251. Fax: 0131-226-5644.* www.edinburgh.inter continental.com. *Bus: 24, 28, or 45. Rates: £99–£114 ($178–$205) double. Rates include breakfast. AE, DC, MC, V.*

Greenside Hotel
$$ New Town

The recently remodeled Greenside Hotel is a four-floor Georgian house that dates back to 1786. Antiques blend perfectly with the hotel's decor. All rooms come with private bath and open onto views of a private garden or the Firth of Forth. Drinks are served in the bar.

See map p. 170. 9 Royal Terrace. ☎ *0131-557-0121. Fax: 0131-557-0022.* www. townhousehotels.co.uk/green.html. *Bus: 1, 4, 5, 15, 15A, 19, 34, 44, or 45. Rates: £45–£100 ($81–$180) double. Rates inlcude breakfast. AE, DC, MC, V.*

Hotel Ibis
$ Old Town

Hotel Ibis is a rare commodity in Edinburgh — an inexpensive hotel with plenty of rooms in a good location. All this after inflation has affected so much of the rest of Europe! After you see the décor, you may understand why: You wake up thinking you're in Miami (you wouldn't think turquoise and pink could be used together anywhere else). But the rooms are clean and spacious, as are the bathrooms, and some of the rooms look out onto the Royal Mile.

See map p. 170. 6 Hunter Square (just west of South Bridge on the Royal Mile). ☎ *0131-240-7000. Fax: 0131-240-7007.* www.accor-hotels.com. *Bus: 3, 3A, 5, 7, 14, 29, 30, 31, 33, 35, or 41. Rates: £50–£60 ($90–$108) single or double. Breakfast £4.95 ($9). AE, DC, MC, V.*

Accommodations, Dining, and Attractions in Edinburgh

HOTELS ■
Balmoral Hotel **20**
Dalhousie Castle **36**
George Inter-Continental **16**
Grassmarket Hotel **8**
Greenside Hotel **29**
Hotel Ibis **18**
Jury's Inn Edinburgh **22**
Radisson SAS Hotel
   Edinburgh **21**
Terrace Hotel **30**
Travel Inn **5**

RESTAURANTS ◆
The Atrium **3**
Baked Potato Shop **19**
Cafe Byzantium **9**
Deacon Brodie's Tavern **12**
Indian Cavalry Club **2**
Kebab Mahal **33**
La Cuisine d'Odile **1**
Nicholson's **34**
Witchery by the Castle **14**

ATTRACTIONS ●
Arthur's Seat **35**
Calton Hill **28**
Canongate Tollbooth/
   People's Story Museum **26**
Edinburgh Castle **6**
Edinburgh Zoo **4**
Gladstone's Land **11**
High Kirk of St. Giles **17**
John Knox House **23**
Museum of Childhood **24**
Museum of Edinburgh **27**
National Gallery
   of Scotland **15**
Our Dynamic Earth **32**
Outlook Tower
   and Camera Obscura **13**
Palace of Holyroodhouse **31**
The Royal Mile **25**
Scottish Whisky
   Heritage Centre **7**
Writer's Museum **10**

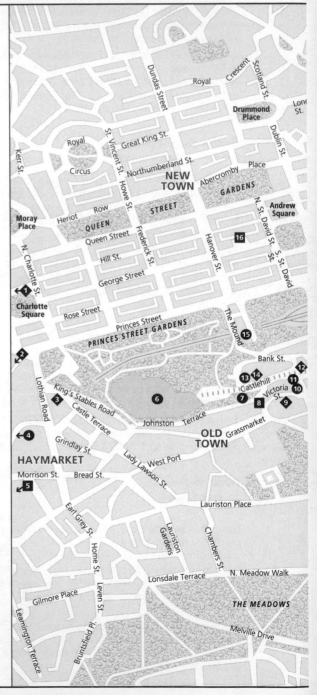

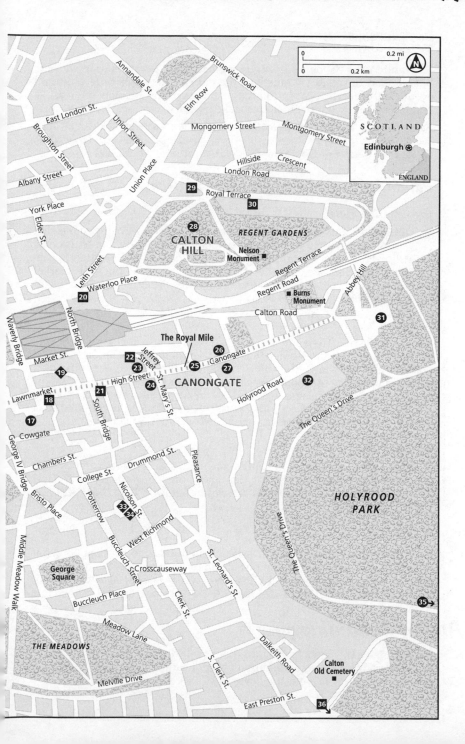

Jury's Inn Edinburgh
$$ Old Town

The modern Jury's, on a side street connecting the train station with the bottom end of the Royal Mile, is aimed at business folk here to attend events in the nearby convention center, but its prime location, often excellent prices, and modern amenities make it perfect for vacationers as well. *See map p. 170. 43 Jeffrey St. (just off East Market Street at North Bridge).* ☎ *0131-200 3300. Fax: 0131-200-0400.* www.jurysdoyle.com. *Bus: 3, 3A, 5, 7, 14, 29, 30, 31, 33, 35, or 41. Rates: £49–£98 ($88–$176). Breakfast £9 ($16). AE, DC, MC, V.*

Edinburgh's runner-up accommodations

Grassmarket Hotel

$ Old Town This lodge has an ultramodern interior with tidy rooms that range from adequate to extra large; reasonably sized beds; and bathrooms with showers that are spotless. Of course, it's the central location (a cannonball's shot from the castle) that most recommends it, but Grassmarket can be busy and noisy on weekend nights. *See map p. 170. 94 Grassmarket.* ☎ *0131-220-2299. Fax: 0870-990-6401.*

Radisson SAS Hotel Edinburgh

$$$ Old Town The almost castle-like Radisson — formerly a Crowne Plaza — looks centuries older than its 11 years due to Edinburgh's strict zoning rules for the Royal Mile. The hotel has smallish, amenity-filled rooms and a stellar location, plus a health club, pool, and restaurant (appetizing international cuisine in a dull subterranean environment). *See map p. 170. 80 High St. (on the Royal Mile just east of South Bridge).* ☎ *800-333-3333 in the U.S., 0131-557-9797 in Scotland. Fax: 0131-557-9789. www.radisson.com.*

Terrace Hotel

$ New Town Terrace Hotel offers elegance — and 14-foot ceilings — at a reasonable price in an historic Georgian home. *See map p. 170. 37 Royal Terrace (on the north side of Calton Hill near Regent Gardens).* ☎ *0131-556-3423. Fax: 0131-556-2520.* www.terracehotel.co.uk.

Travel Inn

$ Old Town Travel Inn is a massive chain hotel: zippo atmosphere, but some 278 institutional rooms at dirt-cheap rates (plus a full Scottish breakfast for under $10). *See map p. 170. 1 Morrison Link (a ten-minute walk west of Edinburgh Castle).* ☎ *0131-228-3319. Fax: 0131-228-9836.* www.travelinn.co.uk.

Dining in Edinburgh

Traditionally, the Scots have started out their days with a bowl of delicious porridge. Canned soup doesn't hold a candle to genuine Scotch *broth soup* (barley in a mutton-flavored stock). Angus beef makes great steaks and roast beef; Scottish lamb is excellent, as are the many game dishes (rabbit, woodcock, red deer, and grouse).

When it comes to fish, this country excels at preparing haddock, whitefish, herring (usually kippered and eaten for breakfast), and the mighty river salmon. At a Scottish high tea, you can sample freshly baked scones alongside some of the best fresh jams (especially raspberry), heather honeys, and marmalades in Europe. Also excellent are Scottish cheeses — look for cheddars; the creamy, oatmeal-coated Caboc; and cottage cheeses in particular.

 Scotland's national "dish" is the infamous *haggis,* a fat, cantaloupe-size sausage made from sheep lungs, liver, and hearts mixed with spices, suet, oatmeal, and onions. Haggis smells horrible, and you have to wonder whether the Scots themselves ever touch the stuff. Whether haggis is actually a national practical joke played on unsuspecting visitors or an earnest patriotic meal, I still think you should try it — if only once. **Charles MacSween and Son,** Dryden Road (☎ **0131-440-2555**), will be happy to inflict one upon you.

Edinburgh's Top Restaurants

The Atrium
$$$$ New Town   CONTEMPORARY MEDITERRANEAN

The stylish and upscale Atrium opened to acclaim in 1993. Although located in the atrium of an office building, the restaurant atmosphere consists of oil lamps and rusted metal. The menu changes with the trends and the chef's inspiration, but the dishes are always tasty and primarily of Mediterranean ingredients, such as sun-dried tomatoes, couscous, and arugula. The well-presented dinners may center on anything from seared scallops to roast duck. Upstairs is the Atrium's sister restaurant, **Blue Bar Cafe** (☎ **131-221-1222;** www.bluebarcafe.com), which offers lighter fare at lesser prices.

See map p. 170. 10 Cambridge St. (off Lothian Road, beneath Saltire Court). ☎ 0131-228-8882. www.atriumrestaurant.co.uk. *Reservations highly recommended. Bus: 2, 10, 11, 15, 15A, 16, 17, or 24. Main courses: £10–£21 ($18–$38) lunch, £17–£22 ($31–$39) dinner. Fixed-price dinner menu: £25 ($45) without wine, £40 ($72) with wine. AE, DC, MC, V. Open: Lunch Mon–Sat, dinner Mon–Fri. Closed Christmas week.*

 ### Deacon Brodie's Tavern
$$ Old Town   SCOTTISH/PUB GRUB

This tavern, established in 1806, is a favorite among the locals and tourists who are drawn to the old pub atmosphere, the good food, and the unusual story of its namesake: the real-life model for one of Edinburgh's most famous fictions. A responsible, respectable city councilor and inventor by day, Brodie was by night a thief and murderer. In 1788, his dark side caught up with him, and after a trial, he was hanged on a gibbet he himself helped perfect. The story inspired R. L. Stevenson to write *The Strange Case of Dr. Jekyll and Mr. Hyde*. Morbid history aside, the tavern serves decent pub food on the ground floor, but head upstairs to the wood-lined restaurant, where you may want a second helping of the beef steak pie (a variant on shepherd's pie).

See map p. 170. 435 Lawnmarket (the western spur of the Royal Mile, near St. Giles's Church). ☎ *0131-225-6531. Reservations recommended. Bus: 23, 27, 28, or 41. Main courses: £7.95–£15 ($14–$27). Open: Lunch and dinner daily.*

Indian Cavalry Club
$$$ New Town   INDIAN

This restaurant serves the best of Edinburgh's Indian fare. Nepalese and Burmese dishes join the tandoori and other classic Indian cuisine found in Britain. The decor, with a different theme for each room, is reminiscent of the days when Britain's imperial flag flew over India. No one in town does curry better, and you can't go wrong with the fixed-price, five-course dinner that gives you a taste of the kitchen's best.

See map p. 170. 3 Atholl Place (between Shandwick Place and Haymarket train station). ☎ *0131-228-3282. Reservations required. Bus: 2, 3, 3A, 21, 26, 31, or 33. Main courses: £8.75–£15 ($16–$26); five-course dinner for minimum of two people £20 ($35) per person; lunch buffet £7.50 ($14). AE, DC, MC, V. Open: Lunch and dinner daily.*

La Cuisine d'Odile
$ New Town   FRENCH

Here you'll find hearty French home cooking with no pretensions and loads of flavor, set in the basement of the French Institute (but of course!) — though in fine weather, there are tables outside as well. The cooking is fresh and the menu ever-changing; Odile whips up lunches based on whatever was freshest at the market that morning. Shame it's not open for dinner, too — and that it's BYO if you want a bottle of French wine to go with your grub.

See map p. 170. 13 Randolph Crescent (off Queensferry Street, 3 blocks west of Charlotte Square). ☎ *0131-225-5685.* www.ifecosse.org.uk. *Reservations highly recommended. Bus: 13, 19, 36, 37, 37A, 41. Set-price menus: £6.65 ($12) for two courses; £7.35 ($13) for three courses. No credit cards. Open: Lunch Tues–Sat.*

Witchery by the Castle
$$$$$ Old Town   SCOTTISH

Witchery by the Castle is a bit of a tourist magnet — and heinously expensive (though the light lunch and pre-theater menus are an option for penny-pinchers) — but still a lot of fun. The restaurant serves dyed-in-the-wool Scottish classics and advertises itself as being the oldest in town. In fact, this building is where the Hellfire Club met in the Middle Ages and where witches were once burned; one witch still reportedly haunts the place. Witchery boasts an impressive wine list (1,000 in the cellar, 16 of which are available by the glass), plus 40 malt whiskies.

See map p. 170. Castlehill (at the west end of the Mile, very near the Castle). ☎ *0131-225-5613;* www.thewitchery.com. *Reservations recommended. Bus: 23, 27, 28, 41, or 42. Main courses: £14–£50 ($25–$90); two-course light lunches and pre-theater dinners £9.95 ($18). AE, DC, MC, V. Open: Lunch and dinner daily.*

Edinburgh's runner-up restaurants

Baked Potato Shop

$ **Old Town** Baked Potato Shop is a health-conscious and environmentally aware purveyor of scrumptious stuffed potatoes, Indian bhajias (curried dumplings), and (of all things) vegetarian haggis. The single table seats only six. *See map p. 170. 56 Cockburn St.* ☎ *0131-225-7572.*

Cafe Byzantium

$ **Old Town** Located above an antiques market, Cafe Byzantium is an Indian buffet with beefy portions of everything from sandwiches and crisps (potato chips) to curries and other Indian delicacies. *See map p. 170. 9 Victoria St.* ☎ *0131-220-2241.*

Kebab Mahal

$ **Old Town** Kebab Mahal is the perfect spot to partake in a tasty donner kebab (spicy lamb sandwich) and other Middle-Eastern takeout. *See map p. 170. 7 Nicholson Square.* ☎ *0131-667-5214.*

Nicholson's

$$ **Old Town** This is the now-hallowed spot where one struggling writer sat in a booth, sipped coffee, and wrote out the manuscript for a quirky book about a magical lad named Harry Potter. Don't come expecting the dining room at Hogwart's, though (or in hopes of a J.K. Rowling sighting); this place is Art Deco, and the food modern Scottish. *See map p. 170. 6a Nicholson Square.* ☎ *0131-557-4567.*

Exploring Edinburgh

With the exception of the National Gallery, you find most of Edinburgh's most popular sights concentrated in Old Town, the rocky outcropping that overlooks the rest of the city.

Edinburgh's top sights

Calton Hill
Old Town

Off Regent Road in eastern Edinburgh rises this odd Romantic paean to classical architecture. Besides a great view of the city and Edinburgh Castle (and behind you, the Firth of Forth), the hill is scattered with a collection of 19th-century "instant ruins." A half-finished Parthenon, started in 1822 to honor Scottish soldiers killed in the Napoleonic wars, is probably the most famous. The Parthenon ended up being no more than a colonnade after funding ran out by 1829 (the unfinished temple was eventually dubbed "Scotland's Shame"). At the summit stands the 100-foot Nelson Monument. *See map p. 170. Entrance to Regent Gardens off of Regent Road.* ☎ *0131-556-2716.* www.cac.org.uk. *Bus: 5, 7, 14, 22, 25, 29, 37, or 37A. Admission: £2.50 ($4.50). Open: Nelson Monument, Apr–Sept, Mon 1–6 p.m., Tues–Sat 10 a.m.–6 p.m.; Oct–Mar, Mon–Sat 10 a.m.–3 p.m.*

Edinburgh Castle
Old Town

The castle, a huge part of this city's history, ascends over Edinburgh. The center of the castle protects the 12th-century, Norman-style St. Margaret's Chapel. In the Royal Apartments, you can see the bedroom of Mary, Queen of Scots — the very place she gave birth to James VI (later James I of England).

The best feature is the Crown Chamber, where you learn all about the Scottish Honours (the crown jewels) and more than you ever wanted to know about the inauguration of the Scottish king. But my favorite part of the tour is being in the prison cells to see the drawings etched into the walls by early 19th-century prisoners of the Napoleonic wars. You can whip through in 45 minutes or spend 2 hours taking all the tours and exploring the nooks and crannies.

See map p. 170. Castlehill. ☎ *0131-225-9846.* www.historic-scotland.gov.uk. *Bus: 23, 27, 28, 41, or 42. Admission: £9.50 ($17) adults, £7 ($13) seniors, £2 ($3.60) children. Open: Apr–Oct daily 9:30 a.m.–6 p.m.; Nov–Mar daily 9:30 a.m.–5 p.m. Last admission 45 minutes before close.*

National Gallery of Scotland
Princes Street Gardens

This honey-colored neoclassical temple houses one of the best midsized art museums in Europe, hung with a well-chosen selection of Old Masters and Impressionist masterpieces. Spend a morning (or at least half of one) here in the company of Rembrandt, Rubens, Andrea del Sarto, Raphael, Titian, Velázquez, El Greco, Monet, Degas, Gainsborough, and van Gogh. You may find yourself pleasantly surprised by the many works of largely unknown Scottish artists.

See map p. 170. 2 The Mound (in the center of Princes Street Gardens, behind the train station). ☎ *0131-624-6200 or 0131-332-2266.* www.nationalgalleries.org. *Bus: 23, 27, 28, 41, 42, or 45. Admission: Free. Open: Daily 10 a.m.–5 p.m.; Thurs until 7 p.m.*

Our Dynamic Earth
Old Town

This high-tech multimedia museum purports to take you on a journey through time, to witness the creation of Earth and everything the planet has done since. Occasional special exhibitions have featured topics as diverse as re-creations of natural disasters and environmental photography.

See map p. 170. On Holyrood Road, in between South Bridge and Holyrood Park. ☎ *0131-550-7800.* www.dynamicearth.co.uk. *Bus: 35 or 64. Admission: £8.95 ($16) adults, £5.45 ($10) children ages 5–15 and seniors, free children under 5. MC, V. Open: Apr–June and Sept–Oct daily 10 a.m.–6 p.m.; July–Aug daily 10 a.m.–6 p.m.; Nov–Mar Wed–Sat 10 a.m.–5 p.m. Last admission 70 minutes before close.*

Palace of Holyroodhouse
Old Town

The royal palace of Scotland was originally the guesthouse of a 20th-century abbey (now in ruins). Of James V's 16th-century palace, only the north tower — rich with memories of his daughter, the political pawn Mary, Queen of Scots — remains. You can see a plaque where Mary's court secretary Riccio was murdered by her dissolute husband and his cronies, and some of the queen's needlework is on display. Most of the palace was built in the late 17th century. Although Prince Charles held his roving court here at one time, the palace was only recently restored after years of neglect; it opened in November 2002. A quick visit takes about 45 minutes. Admission is by timed entry and includes an audio guide. You must book ahead of your visit.

See map p. 170. Canongate (east end of the Royal Mile). ☎ *0131-556-5100 for required reservations.* www.royal.gov.uk. *Bus: 35 or 64. Admission: £8 ($14) adults, £6.50 ($12) seniors, £4 ($7) children under 17. Open: Daily 9:30 a.m.–6 p.m. Last admission 45 minutes before close. Closed two weeks in May, two weeks in November, and Dec 25–26.*

The Royal Mile
Old Town

Walking down the Royal Mile — the main drag of the Old Town that changes names from Lawnmarket to High Street to Canongate — takes you from Edinburgh Castle on the west end downhill to the Palace of Holyroodhouse on the east. The various small museums of the Royal Mile tend to be open Monday through Saturday from 10 a.m. to 6 p.m. (a few stay open until 7:30 p.m. in summer and are open on Sunday afternoons during the Festival).

Most museums along the Royal Mile are free, but some (Whisky Centre, Camera Obscura, John Knox House, Gladstone's Land) charge admission ranging from £1 to £7.95 ($1.80–$14). Simply strolling the Mile from one end to the other takes 20 to 30 minutes. Add in another 20 to 30 minutes for each stop you want to make along the way.

Begin your mile tour at the **Scottish Whisky Heritage Centre,** 354 Castlehill (☎ **0131-220-0441;** www.whisky-heritage.co.uk) where you find out all that you could possibly want to know about the making of single malts; the tour is somewhat cheesy, but you get to swig a few free samples at the end.

Across the street is the **Outlook Tower and Camera Obscura** (☎ **0131-226-3709;** www.camera-obscura.co.uk), the top of which has retained the live image of Edinburgh-out-the-peephole, projected onto a white tabletop, that made it famous 150 years ago. The exhibits are updated to include modern advances in optics, such as laser holography.

At 477B Lawnmarket, **Gladstone's Land** (☎ **0131-226-5856;** www.nts.org. uk) is a restored 17th-century home inside and out (open Apr–Oct only). A nearby alley leads to Lady Stair's House, home to the **Writer's Museum** (☎ **0131-529-4901;** www.cac.org.uk), which celebrates the lives and works of Scotland's three great scribes: Burns, Scott, and Stevenson.

Briefly a cathedral in the past, the **High Kirk of St. Giles** (☎ **0131-225-9442;** www.stgiles.net) has changed so much over the ages that today the main draw is the Thistle Chapel, built onto the church's corner in 1911. The fiery John Knox, leader of the Scottish Reformation and perpetual antagonist to Mary, Queen of Scots, served as the church's minister from 1559 to 1572.

Supposedly Knox lived a few doors down at 43–45 High St., although no actual historical evidence supports this theory. The **John Knox House** (☎ **0131-556-9579**) is the only 16th-century building still existing on the Royal Mile with projecting upper floors.

Across the street at No. 42 is the **Museum of Childhood** (☎ **0131-529-4142;** www.cac.org.uk), a museum full of toys from Victorian to recent times. Patrick Murray founded the museum even though he was a confirmed bachelor who insisted he was opening a museum of social science, not a romper room for kids — whom he reportedly detested.

As the Royal Mile becomes Canongate, you pass at No. 142 the **Museum of Edinburgh,** formerly called **Huntly House** (☎ **0131-529-4143**). It resides in a restored 16th-century house filled with period rooms and collections detailing Edinburgh's past. Across the street is the clock-faced 1591 **Canongate Tollbooth,** a one-time council room, law court, and prison, now housing the **People's Story Museum** (☎ **0131-529-4057;** www.cac.org.uk), an exhibit on working life in Edinburgh from the 18th century to today.

More cool things to see and do

✔ **Scaling Arthur's Seat:** At 820 feet, Arthur's Seat is a hill in Holyrood Park created by volcanic action. The hill feels more like a mountain after you make the 30-minute climb. After reaching the summit, your efforts are rewarded with a grand view that sweeps across the city below to the Firth of Forth in the distance.

✔ **Donning a kilt:** Thinking of sizing yourself for a kilt? The Highlander's dress used to be a 16-foot-long plaid scarf wrapped around and around to make a skirt, with the excess thrown across the chest and up over the shoulder. After an 18th-century ban on the wearing of such traditional clan tartans, kilts became a fierce symbol of Scottish pride, and an industry was born. Today, a handmade kilt with all its accessories can run you upward of £500 ($900), but even if a tartan scarf or tie is more your stripe, the **Tartan Gift Shop,** 54 High St. (☎ **0131-558-3187**), can help you identify your clan (or one close enough) and match you to one of its traditional tartans.

✔ **Visiting a few old Edinburgh haunts:** The most entertaining walks around the city are led after dark by the "dead" guides working for **Witchery Tours** (☎ **0131-225-6745;** www.witcherytours.com). Each guide wears a costume representing an officially deceased Edinburgher whose ghost haunts this city. Your spirit guide leads you on a sometimes spooky, often goofy, and occasionally educational 90-minute tiptoe around the city's key historical and legendary spots in Ghosts and Gore and Murder and Mayhem. Reserve a spot in advance for this tour.

✔ **Witnessing the penguin parade at the zoo:** From April to September, at 2 p.m. daily, the **Edinburgh Zoo,** 134 Corstorphine Rd. (☎ **0131-334-9171;** www.edinburghzoo.org.uk; take bus 12, 26, or 31), herds the largest penguin colony in Europe out of its enclosure to run a few laps around a grassy park. Don't miss the gorillas, either (or the great view that stretches to the Firth of Forth).

✔ **Sampling the city's pubs and nightlife:** Edinburgh is an unsung nightlife capital, with a lively performing arts and theater scene year-round. More nighttime fun can be had at discos, such as the always-trendy **Buster Browns,** 25 Market St., and the enormous **Century 2000,** 31 Lothian Rd. The city is saturated with pubs and bars, especially in the Old Town around Grassmarket (**Black Bull,** No. 12), Candlemaker Row (**Greyfriars Bobby's Bar,** No. 34), Cowgate (**The Green Tree,** No. 182), and other university-area streets. In New Town, the slightly rundown Rose Street has a good row of pubs (try **Kenilworth,** No. 152). Toss back a pint of bitter or set up your own tasting marathon of wee drams of single-malt Scotch whisky — the night is yours.

For a more archetypal Scottish evening, you can either go with the hokey or the traditional. A bagpipe-playing, kilt-swirling Scottish Folk Evening is staged at big hotels such as the Carlton Highland or King James. A less forced *ceilidh* (pronounced *kay-*lee, a folk-music jam session) happens nightly at the Tron Tavern on South Bridge or at any of the musical pubs listed in *The Gig* (available at newsstands and in pubs).

✔ **Attending the big festival:** Since 1947, in August, Scotland's capital celebrates two to three weeks of theater, opera, arts, dance, music, poetry, prose, and even traditional culture (the bagpiping Military Tattoo parade uses the floodlit castle as a backdrop) during the **Edinburgh International Festival,** headquarters at The Hub on the Royal Mile on Castlehill (☎ **0131-473-2000** or 0131-473-2001; www.eif.co.uk).

The festival has also spawned multiple minifestivals, including celebrations that center around jazz, film, television, and books, and the famous **Fringe Festival,** headquarters at 180 High St. (☎ 0131-226-0026; www.edfringe.com), also held in August and offering many more acts.

Guided tours

Lothian Buses (☎ 0131-555-6363; www.lothianbuses.co.uk) runs circles around the major Edinburgh sights, and a full-day ticket lets you hop on and off at any of its two dozen stops. You can get tickets (valid for 24 hours) for the tour bus — £8.50 ($15) adults, £7.50 ($14) seniors/ students, and £2.50 ($4.50) children — at the starting point, Waverley Station. The **Edinburgh Tour: Guide Friday** (☎ 0131-220-0770) offers a similar tour at the same prices. You can hop on the tour at Waverley Bridge, Lothian Road, Royal Mile, Grassmarket, or Princes Street.

But perhaps the best way to see Edinburgh with a guide is to join one of the walking tours described in the "More cool things to see and do" section, earlier in this chapter.

Suggested itineraries

If you're the type who'd rather organize your own tours, this section offers some tips for building your own Edinburgh itineraries.

If you have one day

Start your early morning admiring Old Masters and Scottish Impressionists in the **National Gallery of Scotland.** Cross The Mound and climb Lawnmarket/Castlehill to glowering **Edinburgh Castle.** Tour the bits you like, and then start making your way down the **Royal Mile,** popping into the sights and shops that catch your fancy and stopping for a late Scottish lunch at Witchery by the Castle or, if your purse strings are tighter, Deacon Brodie's Tavern. Finish up with the Royal Mile in time to meet the **Witchery Tours** guide for 90 minutes of Ghosts & Gore. Spend the evening hopping from pub to pub, with a pause to dine at Pierre Victoire or the Indian Calvary Club.

If you have two days

Begin Day 1 exploring Edinburgh's single greatest sight: **Edinburgh Castle.** After you have your fill of medieval battlements and royal history, head to the **National Gallery of Scotland** for a spell of art appreciation. Window-shop your way through New Town en route to **Calton Hill** in the late afternoon for a panorama over the city.

Take Day 2 to take in the bustle, shopping, atmosphere, and some dozen modest attractions that line the **Royal Mile.** Start from the top end at Edinburgh Castle and work your way down to the 16th-century royal palace of **Holyroodhouse** anchoring the other end. Pop into **Our Dynamic**

Earth on your way to **Holyrood Park,** where you can clamber up Arthur's Seat for the sunset. Finish the day off with a pub-crawl through the Old City and the University district.

If you have three days

Spend the first two days as I discuss previously and take Day 3 to get out of town, either to track down the Loch Ness Monster or get funky in Glasgow. (Both excursions are described in the next section.)

Traveling Beyond Edinburgh

If you have a day or so to spare, consider heading out of town. I recommend either traveling north to the Highlands, where you witness spectacular scenery (and perhaps catch a glimpse of that fabled sea monster), or going west to Glasgow, recently reinvented as a splendid museum and shopping town.

On Nessie's trail: Inverness and Loch Ness

Many first-time visitors to the Highlands on a tight schedule view Inverness — ancient seat of the Pictish kings who once ruled northern Scotland — merely as a stepping stone. Their quest is for that elusive glimpse of the monster said to inhabit the deep waters of Loch Ness, which stretches its long finger of water along a fault line southwest from Inverness. The largest volume of water in Scotland, the loch is bigger than it looks — only 1 mile wide and 24 miles long, but at its murkiest depths, it plunges 700 to 800 feet to the bottom.

In truth, the Highlands hold more beautiful and rewarding spots, but no one can deny the draw of Loch Ness and its creature. Visiting the loch in a single day from Edinburgh is tough, but it can be done. Take the early train to Inverness, take in the loch in the late morning and early afternoon, and then bus back to Inverness to spend an afternoon seeing a few sights and grabbing an early dinner before jumping a late train back to Edinburgh or the overnight train to London.

Getting there

Seven trains daily connect Edinburgh and Inverness, and the trip is three and a half hours long. From Inverness, buses run hourly down the loch to Drumnadrochit (a 30-minute trip; exiting the Inverness train station, turn right and then right again on Strothers Lane to find the bus station).

Inverness's tourist office (☎ **01463-234-353;** Fax: 01463-710-609; www. visithighlands.com), at Castle Wynd off Bridge Street, is more than used to teaching visitors the basics of Nessie-stalking and other loch activities, from lake cruises to monster-seeking trips in a sonar-equipped boat for around £7.50 to £25 ($14–$45).

Nessie, the monster of the loch

The legend started in the sixth century after St. Colomba sent a monk swimming across the loch and a giant creature attacked. After a harsh scolding from the saint, the monster withdrew. The legend, however, lives on.

Is Nessie the Loch Ness Monster that surfaced from the dark waters in the 16th century coming to shore while knocking down trees and crushing three men with her tail? Or is she *Nessitera rhombopteryx,* a vestigial survivor from the age of the dinosaurs (her basic description sounds somewhat like that of a plesiosaur — then again, it also kind of matches some species of sea snake).

No one knows for sure, but one definite fact is that the monster sightings increased in number after 1933, when the A82 road was built by blasting lakeshore rock. Shortly thereafter, innkeeps Mr. and Mrs. Spicer thought they saw something break the surface of the waters one night. The incident was reported on a slow news day in the local paper, and the rumor spread like wildfire.

In the end, the monster may be no more than the collective effect of faked photographs, water-surface mirages brought on by too much whiskey, a few unexplained lake phenomena, and a string of lochside villages whose economies are based on spinning tall tales to visitors. Sonar soundings and a host of keen-eyed watchers have not yet managed to prove, or disprove, Nessie's existence, and that is more than enough reason for 200,000 visitors annually to come, cameras and binoculars in hand, to search for the monster of Loch Ness.

If you just want a quick spin to Nessie's lair, **Highland Experience,** 2 Stoneycroft Rd., South Queensferry in Edinburgh (☎ **0131-331-1889;** www.highlandexperience.com), offers a full-day bus tour of Loch Ness — including an hour-long lake cruise, a stop at Glen Coe, and a drive through the scenic countryside where Rob Roy, William "Braveheart" Wallace, and other cinematic icons of Scottish history made their names — that leaves from Waterloo Place in Edinburgh at 8 a.m. on Wednesdays, Thursdays, Saturdays, and Sundays. It costs £32 ($58) adults and £29 ($52) for under 16s or over 60s. (You have to provide your own suspension of disbelief.)

In Inverness, **Jacobite Coaches and Cruises,** Tomnahurich Bridge on Glenurquhart Road (take a taxi or bus 3, 3A, 4, or 4A from Church Road, 1 block straight ahead from the train station; ☎ **01463-233-999;** www.jacobitecruises.co.uk), runs half- and full-day tours of the loch. You can tour by boat (£12.50/$23 adults, £10.50/$19 children round-trip, which means you don't get to get off, but must admire the castle from the boat), or coach-and-cruise (£19.50/$35 adults, £14.50/$26 children; bus to Drumnadrochit, cruise the loch a bit, and bus back). The £6 ($11) admission to **Urquhart Castle** (described under "Seeing the sights"), part of the coach-and-cruise itinerary, is in addition to the cost of the cruise. Jacobite runs tours year-round, though fewer cruises run October to March.

In Drumnadrochit, **Loch Ness Cruises,** behind The Original Loch Ness Visitor Centre (☎ **01456-450-395;** www.lochness-centre.com), runs hourly Nessie-hunting cruises on the loch for ₤8 ($14) adults, ₤5 ($9) children, Easter to October, weather permitting.

Seeing the sights

Despite being one of the older towns in Scotland, **Inverness** looks rather modern. After burnings and other usual destructions over time, Inverness was rebuilt over the last 150 years or so. So although the Castle is impressive enough, it dates only from 1834 to 1847.

A short distance to the east of Inverness, on Auld Castlehill of the Craig Phadrig, is the most ancient area in town. This rise was the original site of the city castle, one of several Scottish contenders for the title of the infamous spot where Macbeth murdered King Duncan in 1040.

Next to the modern castle sits the free **Inverness Museum and Art Gallery** (☎ 01463-237-114; www.invernessmuseum.com), which gives you the lowdown on the life, history, and culture of the Highlands. You can reach the museum by walking up Castle Wynd from Bridge Street. You can also learn about Gaelic language and culture from the **Highlands Association,** headquartered in the 16th-century Abertaff House on Church Street.

 Across the river are the Victorian **St. Andrew's Cathedral** (☎ **01463-225-553;** www.invernesscathedral.co.uk) on Ardoss Street (check out the Russian icons inside) and the excellent **Balnain House,** 40 Huntly St. (☎ **0463-715-757),** whose exhibition of Highland music displays include instruments you can play and a great CD and gift shop. They also sponsor fantastic jam sessions Thursday nights year-round (plus Tuesdays in summer). Farther west lies **Tomnahurich,** or the "hill of the fairies," with a cemetery and panoramic views.

 For tooling around the lake, you have to make a choice: the main A82 along the north shore, passing such monster haunts as Drumnadrochit and Urquhart castle, or the more scenic southern shore route of natural attractions — pretty woodlands and the Foyers waterfalls. On a quick trip, the A82 gives you more to remember.

 About halfway (14 miles) down the A82 from Inverness is the hamlet of **Dumnadrochit,** unofficial headquarters of Nessie lore. You find two museums here devoted to Nessie. The **Official Loch Ness 2000 Exhibition Centre,** in a massive stone building (☎ **01456-450-573;** www.loch-ness-scotland.com), is a surprisingly sophisticated look at the history of the loch (geological as well as mythological) and its famously elusive resident. The show takes a strict scientific view of the whole business of Nessie-hunting, really doing more to dispel and discredit the legends and sightings than to fan the flames of speculation.

The older, considerably more homespun **Original Loch Ness Monster Exhibition** (☎ 01456-450-342; www.lochness-centre.com), is more of a believers' haunt, running down the legend of the monster with a hackneyed old film, a lot of photographs, accounts of Nessie sightings (along with other mythological creatures throughout the world, such as unicorns and Bigfoot), and a big ol' gift shop.

Almost 2 miles farther down the road (a half-hour walk), **Urquhart Castle** (☎ 01456-450-551; www.historic-scotland.gov.uk) sits near ruins on a piece of land jutting into the lake. This castle holds the record for the most Nessie sightings. For the history buffs: The 1509 ramparts encompass what was once one of the largest fortresses in Scotland, blown up in 1692 to prevent it from falling into Jacobite hands. When not packed with summer tourists, the grassy ruins can be quite romantic, and the tower keep offers fine loch views.

Where to stay and dine

One of the nicest, yet more inexpensive, places to stay in Inverness is the **Glen Mhor Hotel** (☎ 01463-234-308; Fax: 01463-713-170; www.glen-mhor.com), on the River Ness with great views for £59 to £120 ($106–$216) per small double and excellent Scottish cuisine in its restaurants. Cheaper fare (steaks, seafood, or pizza) can be had at the modern, laid-back Irish music pub **Johnny Foxes** (☎ 01463-236-577; www.johnnyfoxes.co.uk), on Bank Street at Bridge Street. If you want to stay immersed in monster tales, shack up in Drumnadrochit at the **Polmaily House Hotel** (☎ 01456-450-343; Fax: 01456-450-813; www.polmaily.co.uk) for £55 to £72 ($99–$130); prices are per person, depending on the season, and include breakfast.

Glasgow: A Victorian industrial city discovers culture

Glasgow was an Industrial Revolution powerhouse, the "second city of the British Empire" from the 19th to the early 20th century. With its wealth came a Victorian building boom, the architecture of which is only beginning to be appreciated as the city comes off a decade-long publicity blitz.

This civic and mental makeover of the 1980s has turned Glasgow from the depressed slum the city had been for much of this century into a real contender for Edinburgh's title of cultural and tourist center of Scotland. With friendlier people, more exclusive shopping than the capital, and a remarkable array of art museums, Glasgow has made a name for itself. Spend at least one night, two if you can, to drink in its renewed splendors.

Getting there and around

Half-hourly trains arrive in 50 minutes from Edinburgh, and the 8 daily trains (4 on Sunday) from London take almost 6 hours to arrive in Glasgow. **CityLink** (www.citylink.co.uk) runs about three buses an hour from Edinburgh to Glasgow. The helpful tourist board's office (☎ 0141-204-4480; www.seeglasgow.com) is at 11 George Square.

The old section of Glasgow centers around the cathedral and train station. The shopping zone of **Merchant's City** is west of High Street. Glasgow grew westward, so the finest Victorian area of the city is the grid of streets known as the **West End.** All these areas are north of the River Clyde. The city has a good bus system and an underground (subway) that swoops from the southwest in an arc back to the northwest. Rides on either cost anywhere from 50p to £1.50 (90¢ to $2.70), depending on how long the ride is; you just board the bus and tell the driver where you're going, he tells you how much. The £1.70 ($3) Discovery Ticket allows you unlimited travel on Glasgow's subway after 9:30 a.m. Monday to Saturday (Sat tickets include Sun for free).

Seeing the sights

As far as sightseeing goes, Glasgow offers art, art, and yet more art. Luckily, admission to almost all of Glasgow's attractions is, ahem, scot-free. You'll find additional information about many of the museums listed in this section at www.glasgowmuseums.com. Make sure you fit in at least the **Kelvingrove Art Gallery and Museum** (☎ 0141-287-2699), which is strong on Italian and Dutch Old Masters, such as Botticelli, Bellini, and Rembrandt, as well as the moderns — Monet, Picasso, van Gogh, Degas, Matisse, Whistler, and Ben Johnson. A whole horde of Scottish artists is represented, too, with works dating from the 17th century to the present. Take your time perusing the collections of sculpture, ethnological artifacts, arms and armor, natural history, decorative arts, and relics of Scotland's Bronze Age. The museum is closed for refurbishment until 2006, but in the meantime, some of the prize pieces are on display at the **McLellan Galleries,** 270 Sauchiehall St. (☎ 0141-565-4137).

The other great gallery of Glasgow is the **Burrell Collection,** (☎ 0141-287-2550), about 4 miles southwest of the city center in Pollok Country Park. The huge assortment of art and artifacts was once a private collection. The collection is global and spans from the Neolithic era to the modern day, with special attention to ancient Rome and Greece as well as paintings by Cézanne, Delacroix, and Cranach the Elder. Also in the park is the 18th-century mansion **Pollok House** (☎ 0141-616-6410), with a fine series of Spanish paintings by El Greco, Goya, Velázquez, and others. From April to October admission is £6 ($11) adults, £4 ($7) children and seniors.

The **Hunterian Art Gallery,** University Avenue (☎ 0141-330-5431; www.hunterian.gla.ac.uk), controls the estate of the great artist James McNeill Whistler (born American, but proud to be of Scottish blood). The gallery is housed in a painstaking reconstruction of Charles Rennie Mackintosh's home, an architectural treasure designed and built by the Art Nouveau innovator, which was demolished in the 1960s.

Across the street from the Hunterian Art Gallery is the **Hunterian Museum** (☎ 0141-330-4221; www.hunterian.gla.ac.uk), which has a unique archaeological collection, ranging from Roman and Viking artifacts to paleontology, geology, and dinosaur fossils — in short, enough relics to give naturalists and the kids a welcome break from all those paintings. You can also see an exhibit on the exploits of Captain Cook.

 The kids — and certainly history buffs — may also get a kick out of the **People's Palace and Winter Gardens** (☎ **0141-554-0223**) on Glasgow Green (Britain's first public park). Beyond a lush greenhouse filled with palms and a tea room, the museum contains a few drips and drabs of artifacts from the Middle Ages and Mary, Queen of Scots, but the main collections bring to light the life of an average Victorian Glasgowian.

Where to stay

The huge **Quality Hotel Central,** 99 Gordon St. (☎ **0141-221-9680;** Fax: 0141-226-3948; www.quality-hotels-glasgow.com), near the central station, has tatty turn-of-the-last-century charm for £44 to £125 ($79–$225) per double; the tourist office can help you book a room.

Where to dine

Revitalized Glasgow has plenty of refined international eateries these days, and the best of the lot has to be oddball **Rogano,** 11 Exchange Place, Buchanan Street (☎ **0141-248-4055;** www.rogano.co.uk) serving slightly pricey traditional seafood in an atmosphere intended to re-create the Deco styling of the *Queen Mary.*

Fast Facts: Edinburgh

Area Code

The country code for the United Kingdom is **44.** Edinburgh's city code is **0131.** If you're calling Edinburgh from outside the United Kingdom, drop the zero. In other words, to call Edinburgh from the United States, dial 011-44-131 and the number. To call the United States direct from Edinburgh, dial 001 followed by the area code and phone number.

American Express

Edinburgh's branch at 69 George St. (☎ 0131-718-2501), is open Monday through Friday from 9 a.m. to 5:30 p.m. and Saturday from 9 a.m. to 4 p.m.

Currency

As a member of the United Kingdom, Scotland is one of several European countries that has chosen not to adopt the euro.

The basic unit of currency is the pound sterling (£), divided into 100 pence (p). There are 1p, 2p, 10p, 20p, 50p, £1, and £2 coins; banknotes are issued in £5, £10, £20, and £50. Scottish banks can print their own money, so you may find three completely different designs for each note, in addition to regular British pounds. All different currency designs are valid.

The rate of exchange used to calculate the dollar values given in this chapter is $1 = 55p (or £1 = $1.80). Amounts over $5 have been rounded to the nearest dollar.

Doctors and Dentists

Your best bet is to ask your hotel concierge to recommend a doctor or dentist.

Embassies and Consulates

The U.S. Consulate, 3 Regent Terrace
(☎ 0131-556-8315; www.usembassy.
org.uk/scotland), is open Tuesday
from 1 to 4 p.m. by appointment only. The
after-hours emergency number for U.S.
citizens is ☎ 0122-485-7097.

Emergency

For police assistance, fire, or ambulance,
dial ☎ 999 or 112.

Hospitals

Try the Royal Infirmary, 1 Lauriston Place
(☎ 0131-536-1000; www.show.scot.
nhs.uk/rie/; Bus: 23, 27, 28, 37, 45).

Information

The main Edinburgh and Scotland Tourist
Information Centre, 3 Princes St. (☎ 0131-
473-3800; www.edinburgh.org; Bus:
all city-center buses), is at the corner of
Princes Street and Waverley Bridge,
above the underground Waverley Market
shopping center. During May, June, and
September, hours are Monday through
Saturday from 9 a.m. to 7 p.m. and Sunday
from 10 a.m. to 7 p.m. During July and
August, hours are Monday though Saturday
from 9 a.m. to 8 p.m and Sunday from
10 a.m. to 8 p.m. In April and October,
hours are Monday through Saturday from
9 a.m. to 6 p.m. and Sunday from 10 a.m.
to 6 p.m. From November through March,
hours are Monday through Saturday from
9 a.m. to 6 p.m. and Sunday from 11 a.m.
to 6 p.m. You also find an info desk at the
airport. Scotland's tourism board runs
www.visitscotland.com, another
useful resource.

For transit info, call the Lothian Region
Transport Office (☎ 0131-554-4494). For
train info, contact ScotRail (☎ 0191-
269-0203; www.scotrail.co.uk).

Internet Access and Cybercafes

You can check your e-mail or send messages at easyEverything, 58 Rose St., just
behind Princes Street (www.easyevery
thing.com; Bus: all Princes Street
buses), open seven days a week from
7:30 a.m. to 10:30 p.m. Rates are around
£1 ($1.80) for an hour, but if you don't use
your full-time allocation, your ticket (issued
before you log on) is valid for 28 days and
can be used repeatedly until your hour
allocation has expired. You can also get
access at the International Telecom Centre,
52–54 High St., on the Royal Mile (☎ 0131-
558-7114; Bus: 3, 3A, 5, 7, 8, 29, 35, 37),
where the rates are £4 ($7.20) per hour. The
center is open daily from 9 a.m. to 10 p.m.

Maps

The tourist office sells maps of Edinburgh
for a small fee, or you can visit any
bookstore.

Newspapers/Magazines

Both *The Scotsman* and the *Daily Record
& Sunday Mail* list goings on about town.

Pharmacies

Edinburgh has no 24-hour pharmacies,
but a branch of the drugstore Boots the
Chemist, 48 Shandwick Place (☎ 0131-
225-6757), is open Monday through
Saturday from 9 a.m. to 9 p.m. and Sunday
from 10 a.m. to 5 p.m

Police

For police assistance, dial ☎ 999.

Post Office

You find Edinburgh's main post offices at
7 Hope St., off Princes Street (☎ 0131-226
6823), and 40 Frederick St. (☎ 0131-226-
6937). Hours are Monday through Friday
from 9 a.m. to 5:30 p.m. and Saturday from
9 a.m. to 12:30 p.m.

Safety

Violent crime is rare in Edinburgh, so you should feel safe walking around the city day or night. But keep in mind that the city's drug problem has produced a few muggings.

Taxes

In Scotland a 17.5 percent value-added tax (VAT) is figured into the price of most items. Foreign visitors can reclaim a percentage of the VAT on major purchases of consumer goods. See Chapter 4 for more on this, or visit www.hmce.gov.uk/public/vatrefunds/vatrefunds.htm.

Taxis

See "Getting Around Edinburgh," earlier in this chapter.

Telephone

A local call in Edinburgh costs 20p (30¢) for the first three minutes. Pay phones accept either coins or phone cards, which are sold at post offices or the tourist board. A three-minute phone call to the United States costs about £4.50 ($7).

To charge a call to your calling card or make a collect call home, dial AT&T (☎ 0800-890-011 or 0500-890-011), MCI (☎ 0800-279-5088), or Sprint (☎ 0800-890-877 or 0500-890-877).

Transit Info

See "Getting Around Edinburgh," earlier in this chapter.

Chapter 12

Dublin and the Best of Ireland

C alled the Emerald Isle with good reason, Ireland is a lush, green land with a deep history and unique inhabitants. Ancient ruins and medieval monasteries, structures once inhabited by Celts, Vikings, Normans, and the English, dot the countryside. Ireland is the renowned home to literary giants, Irish whiskey, and astounding music.

Although part of the British Isles, Ireland is *not* part of the United Kingdom. The Irish fiercely fought for their independence from the British crown (some 750 years) and have been an independent republic since 1921. However, a few counties in the northern region of Ireland did not agree to become independent and are still part of the United Kingdom.

Unfortunately, Northern Ireland has been faced with "The Troubles" ever since the decision to stay with the United Kingdom. The Troubles consist of a long-standing political and paramilitary conflict between the Protestant minority, which supports British rule, and the Catholic majority, which favors independence from Britain. Terrorist attacks plagued Belfast and London in the 1980s and 1990s as each side sought to subvert the other's legitimacy. Although both sides continue to work toward a peaceful resolution, for now Ireland remains a land divided.

The city of Dublin has exquisite museums and a thriving nightlife. But even more appealing is the beautiful, rural landscape and friendly townspeople who await you. I say give Dublin a day or two at most and then take off to the Irish countryside. Renting a car in Ireland to explore the landscape is a great idea.

Getting There

You can fly to Dublin from London in just one hour, making that by far the most convenient way to get to town — especially in light of the plodding train-to-overnight-ferry-to-commuter-rail alternative. But I cover all your options in the following sections.

Arriving by air

Dublin International Airport (☎ 01-814-1111; www.dublin-airport. com) lies about 8 miles (30 minutes) north of the city. Inside the arrivals hall are multiple ATMs and a cellphone rental shop. The **Tourist Information** desk (☎ 1-800-668-668 within Ireland or 00-800-6686-6866) can help with hotel reservations. It's open daily 8 a.m. to 10 p.m.

AirCoach (☎ 01-844-7118; www.aircoach.ie) makes 60 runs a day to Dublin's City Centre at 15-minute intervals between 4:30 a.m. and midnight. The one-way fare is 7€ ($8.05); round-trip is 12€ ($14). You can buy a ticket onboard. The 747 and 748 Dublin Bus **Air Link** (☎ 01-873-4222; www.dublinbus.ie) also run between the airport and City Centre. The 747 will drop you off at O'Connell Street or the Busaras Central Bus Station; the 748 stops at the same bus station and the Tara Street DART station. A one-way trip is 5€ ($5.75) for adults, 2€ ($2.30) for children.

Taxis line up outside the terminal for a quick, easy trip into town; fares average 15€ to 25€ ($17–$29).

Arriving by land

Most trains (from the west, south, and southwest) arrive at **Heuston Station** (☎ 01-836-6222), on the west end of town. Those from the north pull in to the more central **Connolly Station** (☎ 01-703-2358). **Buses** arrive at the **Busaras Central Bus Station** (☎ 01-836-6111) on Store Street near Connolly Station. For information on train schedules, call **Irish Rail** (☎ 1-850-366-222).

Orienting Yourself in Dublin

The city of Dublin is sprawling, but most of its sights are concentrated along the **River Liffey** — a nice area for a walk. A lot of the sights that may interest you lie south of the Liffey, except some literary sights to the north around **Parnell Square**.

Introducing the neighborhoods

North of the Liffey, the main thoroughfare is called **O'Connell Street**. O'Connell Street crosses a bridge of the same name to the south side, where it becomes a large traffic circle in front of **Trinity College**. The street then narrows again into the pedestrian **Grafton Street**. Grafton

Ireland

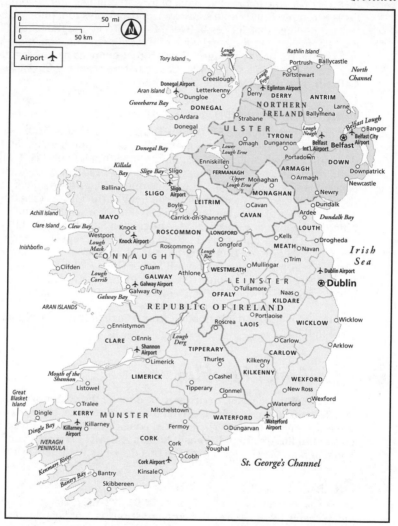

Street continues south to spill into **St. Stephen's Green,** which is something between a square and a gorgeous city park. Off the northeast corner of this square is a complex of huge buildings that house the government and various national museums and libraries. To the east of the square lie several more luxuriant city spaces, such as **Merrion Square** and **Fitzwilliam Square.** Farther to the southeast is the fashionable embassy and hotel-filled neighborhood of **Ballsbridge.**

Back at that traffic circle in front of Trinity College, College Green leads due west past the impressive Bank of Ireland building and becomes **Dame Street. Temple Bar,** Dublin's always trendy, always fun, pub-, club-, and restaurant-filled district lies between Dame Street and the Liffey. (Temple Bar is connected to the north side of the Liffey by the slim, picturesque span of the **Ha'penny Bridge.**) Dame Street changes names regularly as it moves west, passing Dublin Castle before reaching **Christ Church Cathedral** on the edge of the city center.

Finding information after you arrive

The main phone number for **Dublin Tourism** (☎ 01-605-7700; www.visit dublin.com) merely gets you a recording of the numbers to call for info depending on whether you're calling from within Ireland (☎ 1-850-230-330), from the United Kingdom (☎ 080-0039-7000), or from anywhere else (☎ +353-66-979-2083). The office operates six tourism centers throughout the city. In addition to the desk at the airport (see "Getting There," earlier in this chapter), you can find information at the main office in the former **Church of St. Andrew** on Suffolk Street (July–Aug Mon–Sat 9 a.m.–7 p.m. and Sun 10:30 a.m.–3 p.m., Sept–June Mon–Sat 9 a.m.–5:30 p.m.); the **Dun Laoghaire Harbour** (Mon–Sat 10 a.m.–1 p.m. and 2–6 p.m.); **14 Upper O'Connell Street** (Mon–Sat 8 a.m.–5 p.m.); **Baggot Street Bridge** (Mon–Fri 9:30 a.m. to noon and 12:30–5 p.m.); and the Square Towncentre at **Tallaght** (same hours as Baggot Street).

You can also get good information from **Tourism Ireland** (☎ 800-223-6470 in the U.S.).

Getting Around Dublin

If you prefer to ride a lot, or are staying outside the center of town, the 5€ ($5.75) one-day bus pass (also available for three, five, or seven days, see the following section) or 7.70€ ($8.85) one-day bus-and-rail pass (good on the Dublin Area Rapid Transit, known as DART) is worth your while. You can purchase either one at the bus depot at 59 Upper O'Connell St.

By bus

Dublin's green double-decker buses (☎ 01-873-4222; www.dublinbus.ie) can transport you all over the city and suburbs, but keep in mind that Dublin's core is very easily walked. To take a bus, hop on, say where you want to get off, and pay the driver (nothing bigger than a 5€ note). Your fare is calculated by the distance traveled and runs from .85€ to 1.75€ ($1–$2) — except at night when the rate is a flat 4€ ($4.60) fare. A **Rambler Ticket** is valid for one, three, or five days of travel on the bus system, and costs 5€ ($5.75), 10€ ($12), and 15€ ($17), respectively. For a ticket that combines travel on the bus and DART systems, see the following section.

By DART (light rail)

The speedy Dublin Area Rapid Transit (**DART**) electric train (☎ 01-703-3504; www.dart.ie) is really for commuters, with only five stops you may need to know: three in the city center (Connolly, Tara Street, and Pearse), the Lansdowne Road station in Ballsbridge, and the Dun Laoghaire station at the ferry docks. DART tickets cost 1.25€ to 3.35€ ($1.45–$3.85). A **one-day pass** is 6.50€ ($7.50) for DART only and 7.70€ ($8.85) if you want to ride the buses as well. A **three-day pass** is 13.40€ ($15), or 15€ ($17) including bus travel. If you arrive in Ireland by ferry, you can take DART into town (trains run from 6:30 a.m. to midnight). If your ferry arrives at dawn, take bus 46A; it runs from the ferry docks to Parnell Square West from 6:25 a.m. to 10:30 p.m.

As of this writing, Dublin is lengthening the DART trains and upgrading the stations to make them fully accessible. As a result, weekend DART travel — especially that north of Pearse Station in City Centre — will be disrupted until 2005; buses will provide transportation between stations. Be prepared, but be flexible: Carry bus and DART maps, allow extra time, and know that bus routes referred to in this chapter may have changed by the time you visit.

By taxi

Do not try to hail a taxi as it whizzes by you on the street. Instead, line up at one of the city's many *ranks* (stands), where taxis wait for their fares. You find ranks outside all the major hotels and transportation centers as well as on the busier streets, such as Upper O'Connell Street, College Green, and the north side of St. Stephen's Green.

You can also call a taxi. Try **ABC** (☎ 01-285-5444), **Blue Cabs** (☎ 01-802-2222), **Co-op Taxis** (☎ 01-676-6666), or **National Radio Cabs** (☎ 01-677-02222). The minimum charge for one passenger is 3.25€ ($3.75), plus 0.15€ (20¢) for each ⅛ mile (0.18km) — which is 1.35€ ($1.55) per mile. Each additional passenger or suitcase costs 0.50€ (60¢) — though they only charge for the first two suitcases. Between 10 p.m. and 8 a.m. and all day Sunday, taxis charge "Tariff 2" rates: 3.50€ ($4) minimum, and 1.80€ ($2.05) per mile. If you take a taxi to or from the airport, or if you call ahead for one at the numbers earlier in this paragraph (rather than lining up at a rank), there's a 1.50€ ($1.70) surcharge.

By foot

The heart of Dublin is small and, with so many garden squares to stroll, eminently walkable — and you can't cross Ha'penny Bridge any other way.

Staying in Dublin

You can find a lot of nice, if expensive, hotels in central Dublin, but you can also find some great values if you look hard enough. Most of the larger hotels in Dublin are the huge, uniform chains that are fine for a good night's sleep, but lack much in the way of charm. My advice is to seek out one of the number of hotels converted from historic Victorian and Georgian buildings, or something funky — like the Temple Bar neighborhood's **Oliver St. John Gogarty** (☎ 01-671-1822; www.gogartys.ie), listed as a pub under "More Cool Things to See and Do," which has converted its upper floors into a hostel (60€–90€/$69–$104 — or 18€–24€/ $21–$28 per person in the dorms) and, at the top, a chichi penthouse (105€–190€/$121–$219). Heading outside the city center a bit, one of the nicest (and safest) neighborhoods is in the eastern, embassy-filled residential zone of **Ballsbridge,** a short DART ride from downtown.

In addition to the hotels listed in this chapter, Dublin has a surplus of B&Bs, which generally offer inexpensive lodging in a friendly, small inn atmosphere. **Dublin Tourism** (☎ 01-605-7777; Fax: 01-605-7787; www. visitdublin.com) can help you find a B&B room for a 4€ ($4.60) fee; the agency books rooms in traditional hotels as well (see "Finding information after you arrive," earlier in this chapter).

Note that Dublin hotels often quote their prices *per person,* not per room. The prices listed in this chapter are per room, but wherever you stay, double-check the hotel's pricing policy so that you won't be in for any surprises when you check out.

For general tips on booking and what to expect from European accommodations, see Chapter 7.

Dublin's top hotels

Jurys Inn Christchurch
$$ Old City

One of Dublin's great central bargains, Jurys has rooms large enough to hold a family of four for just 96€ ($110). The rates are great and the location superior (near Dublin's top sights), but Jurys isn't dripping with charm. Still, the hotel is very clean and furnished with contemporary good taste and all your basic amenities.

See map p. 196. Christ Church Place (across from Christ Church, where Werburgh Street, Lord Edward Street, and High Street meet). ☎ *800-448-8355 in the United States, or 01-454-0000 in Ireland. Fax: 01-454-0012.* www.jurys.com. *Bus: 49X, 50, 50X, 51B, 54A, 77X, 78A, 123, or 206. Rates: 108€ ($124) double; full Irish breakfast 8€ ($9.20). AE, DC, MC, V.*

The Morgan
$$$ Temple Bar

In just a few short years, this stylized boutique hotel has developed a cult following among fashion- and music-industry types. Rooms, designed by John Rocha, are airy and minimalist, featuring light beechwood furnishings and crisp, white bedspreads against creamy neutral tones, with a smattering of modern artworks adding visual punch. Downstairs, the Morgan Bar offers similarly sophisticated taste — and drinks. Although this may sound like a contradiction in terms, the place manages to be both trendy and a classic at the same time.

See map p. 196. 10 Fleet St. ☎ 01-679-3939. Fax: 01-679-3946. www.themorgan.com. *DART: Tara Street. Bus: 14, 14A, 46, 63, 83, 117, 118, or 150. Rates: 99€–240€ ($114–$276) double, 151€–253€ ($174–$291) deluxe double; continental breakfast 9.50€ ($11), full Irish breakfast 17.70€ ($20). DC, MC, V.*

Shelbourne
$$$$$ St. Stephen's Green

An imposing red-and-white facade on Dublin's most stately square of greenery announces this historic hotel. Built in 1824, the Shelbourne has been host to actors, writers, and the signing of Ireland's constitution. Crackling fires and Waterford chandeliers greet you in the clubby entrance lounges; the comfortable, varied-size guest rooms mix modern conveniences with antique furnishings. Take afternoon tea in the Lord Mayor's Lounge.

See map p. 196. 27 St. Stephen's Green (right in the center of town, on the north side of the Green). ☎ 01-663-4500. Fax: 01-661-6006. www.shelbourne.ie. *DART: Pearse Station. Bus : 10, 11, 13B, 15A, 15B, 25X, 32X, 39X, 46N, 58X, 67X, 70X, or 84X. Rates: 185€–234€ ($213–$269) double; buffet breakfast 7€–18€ ($8.05–$21). AE, DC, MC, V.*

Stauntons on the Green
$$$ St. Stephen's Green

Although only just over a decade old, this hotel on Dublin's central square has a historic feel — thanks in large part to the fact that it occupies a series of three eighteenth-century Georgian town houses. The windows are tall, ceilings high, and furnishings traditional, with fireplaces blazing in the public rooms. You see green every way you look; the back rooms open onto Iveagh Gardens.

See map p. 196. 83 St. Stephen's Green (on the south side of the Green). ☎ 01-478-2300. Fax: 01-478-2263. www.stauntonsonthegreen.ie. *DART: Pearse Station. Bus: 10, 11, 13B, 15A, 15B, 25X, 32X, 39X, 46N, 58X, 67X, 70X, or 84X. Rates: 126€–152€ ($145–$175) double. Rates include full Irish breakfast. AE, DC, MC, V.*

Accommodations, Dining, and Attractions in Dublin

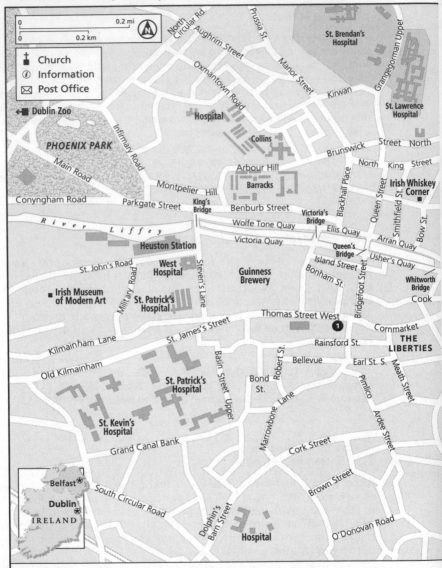

HOTELS ■
Blooms **17**
Harding Hotel **10**
Jurys Inn Christchurch **11**
Lansdowne Hotel **33**
The Morgan **18**
The Morrison **5**

Shelbourne **27**
Stauntons on the Green **29**
Temple Bar Hotel **16**

RESTAURANTS ◆
Bewley's Cafe **22**
Davy Byrnes **23**

Dobbins Wine Bistro **34**
Gallagher's Boxty House **15**
L'Ecrivain **31**
Leo Burdock's **12**
Mao **21**
Mermaid Cafe **14**
Pier 32 **30**

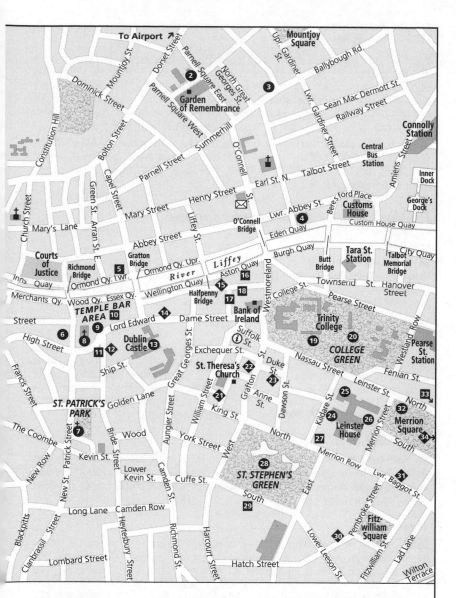

ATTRACTIONS ●

Abbey Theatre **4**
Christ Church Cathedral **8**
Dublin Castle **13**
Dublin Experience **19**
Dublinia **6**
Dublin Writers Museum **2**

Guinness Storehouse **1**
James Joyce Cultural Centre **3**
Merrion Square **32**
National Gallery of Ireland **26**
National Library of Ireland **25**
National Museum **24**
St. Patrick's Cathedral **7**

St. Stephen's Green **28**
Temple Bar **9**
Trinity College and the
  Book of Kells **20**

Temple Bar Hotel
$$$$ **Temple Bar**

You find yourself in the midst of all the action at the Temple Bar Hotel. Built in 1993, this trendy hotel with a Victorian facade has more than 100 rooms decorated in a traditional style with modern facilities. Bonuses include a good pub, acceptable restaurant, and Dublin's liveliest neighborhood right out the front door. The hotel occasionally runs specials, so check its Web site; you may be able to get a room for less than the prices listed here.

See map p. 196. Fleet Street (off Westmoreland Street, a block from the Liffey). ☎ *01-677-3333. Fax: 01-677-3088.* www.templebarhotel.com. *DART: Tara Street. Bus: 14, 14A, 46, 63, 83, 117, 118, or 150. Rates: 145€–195€ ($167–$224) double. Rates include full Irish breakfast. AE, MC, V.*

Dublin's runner-up accommodations

Blooms
$$ **Temple Bar** A large, modern hotel wedged strategically between Trinity College and Temple Bar. Guests receive complimentary passes to Club M (www.clubm.ie), the hotel's sister nightclub. *See map p. 196. Anglesea Street, off Dame Street.* ☎ *01-671-5622 in Ireland. Fax: 01-671-5997.* www.blooms.ie.

Harding Hotel
$$ **Temple Bar** Harding Hotel was built in 1996 for traveling students and other budgeteers (although all types patronize this hotel — this is not a hostel). The hotel offers comfortable, if uninspiring, rooms complete with coffeemaker on the edge of trendy Temple Bar at the cheapest rates in central Dublin. *See map p. 196. Copper Alley, Fishamble Street, Christchurch off High Street.* ☎ *01-679-6500. Fax: 01-679-6504.* www.hardinghotel.ie.

Lansdowne Hotel
$ **Ballsbridge** You find large rooms in this inn, located near the Rugby Grounds. The neighborhood is packed with Georgian architecture and shopping. *See map p. 196. 27 Pembroke Rd.* ☎ **01-668-2522.** *Fax: 01-668-5585.* www.lansdownehotel.ie.

The Morrison
$$$$ **North of the Liffey** This stunning, contemporary hotel is a five-minute walk from O'Connell Street and across the river from Temple Bar. Irish designer John Rocha used minimalist clean lines, warm neutral colors, and natural elements to evoke a sensuous, luxurious feeling of space and relaxation. *See map p. 196. Lower Ormond Quay.* ☎ *01-887-2400. Fax: 01-878-3185.* www.morrisonhotel.ie.

Dining in Dublin

Ireland has surpassed even Britain in the reinventing-your-national-cuisine department. Irish grub is no longer limited to blackened meats and overcooked veggies. The chefs of Ireland have studied both California cooking and French nouvelle to put a new spin on traditional dishes. Plus, in cosmopolitan Dublin, you can find plenty of Continental, French, Italian, and other ethnic restaurants to satisfy any hunger craving.

The Irish have a reputation of being a meat-and-potatoes — and nothing else — sort of people. This reputation isn't entirely true, but even if it were, Irish lamb and mutton are quite excellent (you're in sheep country now). So is the steak, especially the beef from central Ireland around Mullingar. As for those potatoes, the Irish have managed to cultivate them from a poor man's food almost into an art form; some varieties of potatoes are so buttery and soft that they need no condiments or accompaniment.

People tend to forget that Ireland is an island, and as such has excellent seafood, too. The wild salmon caught in the Shannon River is a tasty treat, as are the Dublin Bay prawns.

Other Irish foods that may grace your table are roast chicken, *boxty* (potato pancakes wrapped around meaty fillings), *coddle* (boiled bacon, sausages, onions, and potatoes), and lamb stew. Alongside almost every meal, you find slabs of incredible, dense Irish breads, the best being brown bread and the dry soda bread. The most common pub snack is a simple toasted ham and cheese sandwich.

You should partake of a traditional, hearty Irish breakfast, if only once. This feast can include a bowl of deliciously lumpy porridge, eggs, country bacon, scones with marvelous jams and marmalades, black and white puddings (scrumptious, especially if you don't think about the innards and other unknown bits that are in them), and a slice of tomato, all of it fried — well, except for the scones and porridge.

You can't discuss Irish cuisine without mentioning beer, the mainstay of any meal. The Irish say that drinking Guinness from a can or bottle rather than enjoying a fresh pint drawn straight from the tap is like eating canned peaches rather than a ripened peach fresh off the tree. Some beer purists adamantly patronize only the pub at the brewery itself (see "Dublin's top restaurants" for more brewery information) in order to guzzle the rich, black, creamy, yeasty elixir straight from the proverbial vat. Guinness's lager is called *Harp,* and don't miss out on the Guinness rival from Cork, the dark *Murphy's.* Kilkenny's *Smithwicks* is the best when it comes to ales. For a break from the brew, quality hard cider is also on tap.

The Irish invented whiskey — the legend pins it on a sixth-century monk. Old Bushmills (established in 1608) is the oldest distillery in the world. The "e" isn't the only difference between Irish whiskey and Scotch or English *whisky;* the unique Irish distillation process gives the stuff a cleaner, less smoky flavor. Other brands to sample include John Jameson, Powers, Paddy's, Tullamore Dew, Murphy, and Dunphy. The Irish drink their whiskey *neat* — straight out of the bottle at room temperature. A few decades ago, they started dumping Irish whiskey into coffee, mixing in sugar, topping it off with whipped cream, and serving it to arrivals at the Shannon airport, hence Irish Coffee. This concoction may be touristy, but it's very, very tasty.

Dublin's restaurants often add a service charge of 10 to 17 percent to your bill, so when you're calculating a tip, double-check the bill to see if it's already been done.

Dublin's top restaurants

Bewley's Cafe
$ Near St. Stephen's Green IRISH

This huge, old-fashioned, high-ceilinged tearoom on Dublin's main shopping walkway has been a preferred tearoom of Dubliners since 1840. You can get well-prepared light foods, cafeteria-style, but Bewley's is most famous for its teas with scones and jams. You can find other branches at 11–12 Westmoreland St. and 13 S. Great George St.

See map p. 196. 78 Grafton St. (on the main strolling path in town). ☎ *01-677-6761. www.bewleys.com. Reservations not required. DART: Pearse Street. Bus: 10, 11, 13B, 15A, 15B, 25X, 32X, 39X, 46N, 58X, 67X, 70X, or 84X. All foods: 4€–9.30€ ($4.60–$11). AE, DC, MC, V. Open: Breakfast, lunch, and dinner daily (Sun–Thurs until 11 p.m., Fri–Sat until 1 a.m.).*

Dobbins Wine Bistro
$$$$ Near Merrion Square IRISH-CONTINENTAL

Dobbins's cozy, country interior and tropical patio are perfect spots for intimate dining. The chef uses many traditional Irish ingredients in his inventive dishes. The menu changes often but may include roast herbed lamb; black sole stuffed with salmon, crab, and prawn; or duckling with orange and port sauce.

See map p. 196. 15 Stephen's Lane (between Upper and Lower Mount streets, a block east of Merrion Square). ☎ *01-676-4679. Reservations required. DART: Pearse Street. Bus: 7, 7A, 10, 11, 13, 13A, 25, 25A, 66, 67, or 90. Main courses: 14€ ($16) lunch, 23€ ($26) dinner. AE, DC, MC, V. Open: Lunch Mon–Fri, dinner Tues–Sat.*

Gallagher's Boxty House
$$$ Temple Bar TRADITIONAL IRISH

Welcoming, homey Gallagher's is a Temple Bar fixture. Gallagher's specialties are the grilled potato pancakes called *boxty,* rolled around fillings of beef, lamb, chicken, or fish. The open-faced lunchtime sandwiches and salmon are excellent here. The clientele is a mix of tourists seeking real Irish cooking and locals doing the same, trying to recapture that old "dinner at Grandma's" feeling.

See map p. 196. 20–21 Temple Bar (between Essex and Fleet streets). ☎ *01-677-2762.* www.boxtyhouse.ie. *Reservations recommended but not always accepted. DART: Tara Street. Bus: 14, 14A, 46, 63, 83, 117, 118, or 150. Main courses: 12€–21€ ($14–$24). AE, MC, V. Open: Lunch and dinner daily.*

Mao
$$$ Near St. Stephen's Green   ASIAN FUSHION

Amazingly popular ever since it opened in 1997, Mao is where to go when you feel like Asian cooking laced with a fun and exhilarating attitude. An exposed kitchen lines an entire wall, and the rest of the space is wide open — fantastic for peoplewatching on weekends. Everything is well prepared and delicious, so you can't go wrong.

See map p. 196. 2 Chatham Row (between William Street and Clarendon Street). ☎ *01-670-4899.* www.cafemao.com. *Reservations not accepted. Bus: 10, 11, 13B, 15A, 15B, 25X, 32X, 39X, 46N, 58X, 67X, 70X, or 84X. Main courses: 9.95€–18€ ($11–$21). MC, V. Open: Lunch and dinner daily.*

Mermaid Cafe
$$$$ Temple Bar   INVENTIVE INTERNATIONAL

Since 1996, this uprepossesing cafe has been wowing Dublin's cheapskate gourmands with its innovative take on international cuisine. Owner Ben Gorman and his co-chef Temple Garner may pair seared salmon with an orange, fennel, and mint yogurt dressing, or plop a pile of sage-and-mustard–flavored mashed potatoes next to a juicy chargrilled Angus ribeye. It'll be hard, but by all means save some room for the divine desserts, such as pecan pie with maple ice cream, or rhubarb and ginger crème brûlée — after all, it's all included in Mermaid's set-price lunch menus, which rank among the best dining deals in town.

See map p. 196. 69–70 Dame St. (at Sycamore Street, near Dublin Castle). ☎ *01-670-8236.* www.mermaid.ie. *Reservations highly recommended. Bus: 49X, 50, 50X, 51B, 54A, 77X, 78A, 123, or 206. Lunch set-price menus: 20€–24€ ($23–$28); dinner main courses: 7.30€–30€ ($8.40–$35). MC, V. Open: Lunch and dinner daily.*

Dublin's runner-up restaurants

Davy Byrnes
$$ Near St. Stephen's Green   Dublin's most famous literary and Joycean pub — it pops up both in Dubliners and as one of Leopold Bloom's hangouts in Ulysses — was established in 1889 and still does a brisk business in exquisite traditional pub grub, heavy on the seafood variety (don't miss salmon in any variety). *See map p. 196. 21 Duke St.* ☎ *01-677-5217.* www.davy byrnespub.com.

L'Ecrivain

$$$$$ **Near Fitzwilliam Square** A traditional Irish restaurant that puts on a bit of French flair (in the kitchen and in the refined dining rooms) to add to the class. Book a table on the garden terrace in warm weather. *See map p. 196. 109 Lower Baggot St.* ☎ *01-661-1919.* www.lecrivain.com.

Leo Burdock's

$ **Old City** An absolute shrine of the fish-and-chip crowd, where you get some of the British Isles' greatest chips (french fries) along with your light and flaky fried cod or whiting fish. *See map p. 196. 2 Werbaugh St. (just around the corner from Christ Church Cathedral).* ☎ *01-454-0306.*

Pier 32

$$$$ **Near St. Stephen's Green** Pier 32 serves seafood (great cups of seafood chowder) and traditional Irish fare (angus steaks are excellent) amid bare bricks, beams, and fireplaces. The homemade soda bread is beyond compare. *See map p. 196. 22–23 Upper Pembroke St.* ☎ *01-676-1494.*

Exploring Dublin

With the exception of the Dublin Writers Museum, the top sights in town are concentrated south of the River Liffey.

In May 2004, the city launched the new **Dublin Pass** (www.visitdublin. com/dublinpass), a card that allows you free transportation (including a ride from the airport on AirCoach) and expedited and "free" entry to more than 30 of Dublin's sights (the pass, of course, is not free). All the major attractions listed in the "Dublin's top sights" section are covered by the pass except the Book of Kells; it also covers a few of the minor attractions in town, such as the James Joyce Cultural Centre and the Dublin Literary Walking Tour. The pass, which you can buy at any of Dublin's tourism centers, is available for one, two, three, or six days. The **one day pass** is 29€ ($33) for adults, 19€ ($22) for children; the **two-day pass** is 49€ ($56) adults, 34€ ($39) children; the **three-day pass** costs 59€ ($68) for adults and 39€ ($45) for children; and the **six-day pass** is 89€ ($102) for adults and 49€ ($56) for children.

Dublin's top sights

Christ Church Cathedral
Old City

The remaining bits of the 12th-century Norman-style church erected here by a Welsh Norman, Richard de Clare (better known as Strongbow), and his followers represent the oldest stone building in Dublin.

Strongbow himself, who helped conquer Ireland for the Normans, supposedly rests in peace inside. Purists insist the sarcophagus was made about 170 years after Strongbow's death, and that the grave effigy is modeled after the Earl of Drogheda. Others argue that no matter who built the tomb, Strongbow's entrails at least are interred within, and a few people think that the curious, small half-figure tomb right *next* to the main tomb is Strongbow's. (Myth followers believe that this smaller tomb is that of Strongbow's son, who was sliced in half by his father when Strongbow suspected that junior lacked in the bravery department.)

Because the church was rebuilt in the 1870s, the design is mostly Gothic. The church was once used as an indoor market and you can check out the huge crypt underneath, which was once full of taverns. Allow 30 minutes for a look around.

See map p. 196. Christ Church Place (off Lord Ebury Street). ☎ *01-677-8099.* www. cccdub.ie. *DART: Pearse Station. Bus: 49, 50, 50X, 51B, 54A, 56A, 65, 77, 77A, 78A, or 123. Suggested donation: 5€ ($5.75) adults, 2.50€ ($2.90) students and children under 15. Open: Mon–Fri 9:45 a.m.–5 p.m., Sat–Sun 10 a.m.–5 p.m.*

Dublin Castle
Old City

Dublin Castle sounds nice and medievally Irish, and, indeed, this was the site of the first earthen fort established by the Vikings. But the castle today, which you can easily tour in 30 to 45 minutes, is mainly 17th- and 18th-century state apartments and assembly rooms that served the ruling British government for 700 years. Of more ancient lineage, you do get to see the 13th-century Record Tower (Norman era) and, in the undercroft, the foundations of that Viking bunker and bits of medieval city wall.

See map p. 196. Palace Street (off Dame Street). ☎ *01-677-7129.* www.dublin castle.ie. *Bus: 49X, 50, 50X, 51B, 54A, 77X, 78A, 123, or 206. Admission: 4.50€ ($5) adults, 3.50€ ($4) seniors and students, 2€ ($2.30) children under 12. Open: Mon–Fri 10 a.m.–5 p.m., Sat–Sun and holidays 2–5 p.m. 45-minute guided tours every 20 to 25 minutes.*

Dublin Writers Museum
North of the River Liffey

Ireland has produced a multitude of great writers — the short list includes Jonathan Swift, Oscar Wilde, James Joyce, Thomas Mann, Roddy Doyle, and Nobel Prize winners George Bernard Shaw, W.B. Yeats, and Samuel Beckett. This 18th-century house commemorates Ireland's famed scribes with first editions, letters, busts, and photos. The museum could definitely be more entertaining, but the audio tour enhances the tour a bit (and stretches a visit to about 30 minutes). Only true literary types need apply.

See map p. 196. 18 Parnell Square N. ☎ 01-872-2077. www.writersmuseum.com. *DART: Connolly Station. Bus: 10, 11, 11A, 11B, 13, 13A, 16, 16A, 19, 19A, or 123. Admission: 6.25€ ($7.20) adults, 5.25€ ($6) seniors/students, 3.75€ ($4.30) ages 3–11, 17.50€ ($20) family. Open: Mon–Sat 10 a.m.–5 p.m. (until 6 p.m. June–Aug); Sun and holidays 11 a.m.–5 p.m.*

Guinness Storehouse
Near The Liberties

Alec Guinness refined his rich, black variant on stout in 1759, and by the mid-18th century his brewery was the biggest in the world. You can't get into the plant itself anymore, but an entertaining audiovisual display in the little Hop Store museum offers features on Guinness's long and clever advertising history and the lost art of the *cooper* (barrel maker). The highlight, of course, is the pub, where you get a free half-pint of the famed brew. A purely academic visit only takes about half an hour; a more in-depth survey of Guinness's velvety pleasures at the pub can go on until last call.

Guinness — like any other beer — is best pulled from a tapped keg. If you see the bartender fluidly cranking down the tap arm over and over, he's pulling a proper pint. After ordering Guinness, don't grab the glass after the barkeep first puts it down, because he's letting the foam settle and will top it off after a minute or two. The famously thick head on a Guinness should stay intact until you get to the bottom of the glass. The old trick is to carve your initials into the froth with a knife blade and watch as it remains undisturbed and intact all the way to the bottom.

See map p. 196. Crane Street (off Thomas Street). ☎ 01-453-8364 for recorded information, or 01-408-4800. www.guinnessstorehouse.com. *Bus: 51B, 78A, 90, or 123. Admission: 14€ ($16) adults, 9€ ($10) seniors over 18 and students, 7€ ($8.05) students under 18, 5€ ($5.75) children under 12, 30€ ($35) family. Open: Daily 9:30 a.m.–5 p.m. (until 9 p.m. July and Aug).*

National Gallery of Ireland
Merrion Square

In the realm of Europe's art galleries, the National Gallery in Dublin is not superior, yet you do find a few major works that make a 30-minute tour a requisite for appreciators of art. The highlights are Caravaggio's tumultuous 1602 *Arrest of Christ,* Paolo Uccello's oddball 1440 *Virgin and Child,* and Vermeer's richly lit 1665 *Woman Writing a Letter.* The collections are fleshed out with works by Titian, van Dyck, Goya, Velazquez, Gainsborough, El Greco, and Degas. Free tours are offered Saturdays at 3 p.m. and Sundays at 2, 3, and 4 p.m.

See map p. 196. Merrion Square W. ☎ 01-661-5133. www.nationalgallery.ie. *DART: Pearse Station. Bus: 5, 7, 7A, 10, 13A, 44C, or 48A. Admission: Free (there may be a charge for special exhibitions in the Millennium Wing). Open: Mon–Sat 9:30 a.m.– 5:30 p.m., Thurs 9:30 a.m.–8:30 p.m., Sun noon to 5:30 p.m. (last admission 15 minutes before close).*

National Museum
Merrion Square

Celtic-civilization or antiquities buffs should head straight to Ireland's foremost archaeological collection, which spans prehistory to the Middle Ages. Among the National Museum's treasures are the eighth-century Tara Brooch, an intricately designed jewel of white bronze, and the famed Ardagh Chalice (also eighth century), a cup of beaten silver embellished with engravings, embossing, enamels, and gold filigree.

You can also see row after row of golden *torcs,* those thick yoke-shaped necklaces that were a symbol of royalty among Celtic peoples (and the only article of clothing Celtic warriors wore into battle according to Roman historians). Antiquities aficionados may want to spend 90 minutes or more; the mildly curious can be out in half an hour.

See map p. 196. Kildare Street and Merrion Row. ☎ *01-677-7444. DART: Pearse Station. Bus: 7, 7A, 10, 11, 13, 25, 25A, 66, 67, or 90. Admission: Free. Open: Tues–Sat 10 a.m.–5 p.m., Sun 2–5 p.m.*

St. Patrick's Cathedral
City Centre

Why does the city have two cathedrals? Primarily because a falling out with Christ Church's clergyman led Dublin's archbishop to name St. Patrick's a cathedral. This Gothic cathedral is believed to be founded on the same site where St. Patrick baptized converts in A.D. 450. The cathedral was raised in 1190 and then rebuilt in the 14th century. You can easily tour the cathedral in ten minutes; the main attraction is the floor tomb of Jonathan Swift, of *Gulliver's Travels* fame.

See map p. 196. Patrick's Close (off Patrick Street). ☎ *01-453-9472.* www.stpatricks cathedral.ie. *Bus: 65, 65B, 50, 50A, 54, 54A, 56A, or 77. Admission: 4.20€ ($4.85) adults, 3.20€ ($3.70) students and seniors, 9.50€ ($11) family. Open: Year-round Mon–Fri 9 a.m.–6 p.m.; Nov–Feb Sat 9 a.m.–5 p.m., Sun 10–11 a.m. and 12:45–3 p.m.; Mar–Oct Sat 9 a.m.–6 p.m., Sun 9–11 a.m., 12:45–3 p.m., and 4:15–6 p.m. Closed except for services Dec 24–26 and Jan 1.*

Trinity College and the Book of Kells
College Green

Most visitors to the 18th- and 19th-century buildings of Trinity College — whose illustrious graduates include Jonathan Swift, Thomas Moore, Oscar Wilde, Bram Stoker, and Samuel Beckett — go directly to the library. Here, in about an hour, you can examine a fine display on the medieval art of manuscript illumination — a craft at which Irish monks excelled.

The library is home to a precious trinity of illuminated manuscripts, including one of Ireland's most richly decorated, the eighth-century *Book of Kells.* Stolen from its monastery in 1007, the book was miraculously recovered from a bog three months later. The book's gold-rich cover was

missing, but the near disastrous experience did little harm to the vibrant colors and remarkable detail in what is perhaps the most beautiful, important, and cherished illuminated manuscript in the world.
See map p. 196. College Green (enter where Dame Street runs into Grafton Street). ☎ *01-608-2320 or 01-677-2941.* www.tcd.ie/Library. *DART: Pearse or Tara Street Stations. Bus: All City Centre buses. Admission: 7.50€ ($8.60) adults, 6.50€ ($7.50) seniors/students, 15€ ($17) families, free for children under 12. Open: Year-round Mon–Sat 9:30 a.m.–5 p.m.; June–Sept Sun 9:30 a.m.–4:30 p.m., Oct–May Sun 12:30–4:30 p.m.*

More cool things to see and do

✔ **Spending an evening in the pubs and clubs of Temple Bar:** The eclectic, hopping **Temple Bar** area is most people's favorite district of Dublin. This area, a few streets along the Liffey, is packed with pubs, shops, bars, cafes, galleries, entertainment venues, and fun. The neighborhood even has its own tourist office at 12 East Essex St. (www.temple-bar.ie). In summer, ask at the tourist office about "Diversions Temple Bar," an arts and culture program that includes movie screenings, dance performances, and Irish music and storytelling sessions. Events are free of charge, but tickets (available at the Temple Bar tourist office) are required.

Strolling about is the best way to visit Temple Bar, but proper pub-hopping here includes **Flannery's** (48 Temple Bar), **The Norseman** (Essex Street East), **Oliver St. John Gogarty** (58–59 Fleet St.), and its catty-corner neighbor **Auld Dubliner** (Temple Bar and Anglesea streets). Clubbers can dress up to wait in line for **Club M** (in Blooms Hotel at Anglesea Street) or **The Kitchen** (6–8 Wellington Quay, in the basement of the Clarence Hotel), a hip joint partly owned by the Irish band U2. (In recent years, Dublin's hottest disco, though, has been **POD**, far from Temple Bar on Harcourt Street. As this is written, POD is under renovation, but expect it to reemerge on top.) No need to pub-hop just to Temple Bar, though. Make sure you also hit Dublin's oldest and greatest pub, the **Brazen Head** (west of Temple Bar at 20 Lower Bridge St.), as well as the Victorian **Doheny and Nesbitt** (5 Lower Baggot St.), the literary **Davy Byrnes** (21 Duke St.), and two musical bars, **Kitty O'Shea's** (23 Upper Grand Canal St.) and **O'Donoghues** (15 Merrion Row). Officially, Dublin's pubs are open Sunday to Thursday from 10:30 a.m. to 11:30 p.m. and until 12:30 a.m. Friday and Saturday nights. Some pubs are licensed to stay open even later on weekends.

✔ **Tapping your feet on a musical pub-crawl:** An interesting tour for anyone who enjoys traditional Irish music or even the New Age music of Enya or Clannad, the **Musical Pub Crawl** (☎ 01-478-0193) is an entertaining two-and-a-half-hour guided walk of four Dublin pubs with musicians as tour guides. They introduce you to several traditional instruments and styles, teach you a couple of songs, and give you plenty of time to introduce yourself to Ireland's beer as you go. The nightly tour begins in the upstairs room at **Oliver St. John Gogarty's pub** at the corner of Fleet and Anglesea streets in Temple Bar. Show up at 7:30 p.m. (from May through October).

✔ **Succumbing to a hokey audiovisual "History o' Dublin" experience:** For a Disneylike tour of Dublin, check out the audiovisual tours that attempt to bring different past eras of Dublin back to life. Trinity College has a 45-minute **Dublin Experience** video (☎ 01-608-1177 or 01-608-2320) that looks more like a tourist promo than a historical chronicle; you find it in the Davis Theater on Nassau Street. The most corny version is **Dublinia** (☎ 01-679-4611), at Christ Church Place off High Street, which tries to evoke medieval Dublin from the Norman era through the 1530s.

✔ **Researching your Irish roots:** If you're like me — and approximately 40 million other Americans out there — you've got some Irish in ya. Hundreds of Americans come to Ireland every year to seek out their ancestors here, and the Irish are much obliged to help (sometimes for a modest fee). First, the freebie services. The **National Library** (☎ 01-603-0200; www.nli.ie) and the **National Archives** (☎ 01-407-2300; www.nationalarchives.ie — for Northern Ireland, use ☎ +44-(0)20-8876-3444; www.nationalarchives.gov.uk) are great places to start your search. The **Office of the Registrar General** (☎ 01-635-4000; www.groireland.ie) retains all the records on births, deaths, and marriages in the Republic of Ireland (if your ancestors hailed form Northern Ireland, contact the U.K. Public Record Office at ☎ +44-(0)20-8876-3444; www.pro.gov.uk). The Web sites of commercial (for-a-fee) ancestor-research firms **Irish Geneaology** (www.irishgenealogy.ie) and **Irish Roots** (www.irishroots.net) both have a good links lists to lots of local resources.

✔ **Discovering literary Dublin:** If the Dublin Writers Museum (see "Dublin's top sights" earlier in this chapter) isn't enough, immerse yourself in literary Dublin by checking out the definitive **James Joyce Cultural Centre,** 35 North Great George's St. (☎ 01-878-8547; www.jamesjoyce.ie), and the **Abbey Theatre** (☎ 01-878-7222; www.abbeytheatre.ie), founded at Lower Abbey Street by W.B. Yeats and Lady Gregory in 1904 (plays are performed Mon–Sat at 8 p.m.).

One of the most fun ways to visit the Dublin of books is to take the **Literary Pub Crawl** (☎ 01-670-5602; www.dublinpubcrawl.com), a popular guided walking tour that meets at the Duke Pub at 9 Duke St. nightly at 7:30 p.m.; on Sundays, a tour is also offered at noon. December through March, tours are offered only Thursday through Sunday. Or try the **James Joyce Dublin Walking Tour** (☎ 01-878-8547), led by Ken Monaghan, the curator of the James Joyce Cultural Centre and Joyce's nephew.

✔ **Shopping (finally!):** This is the country that invented duty-free, so you'd be remiss not to purchase a few items of local craft and tradition, from tweeds and tin whistles to Waterford crystal, woolen sweaters, and whiskey. Dublin has several "anything and everything Irish" stores, which are like department store–sized gift shops that cater exclusively to tourists. A few, though, have high quality control and are great if you're on a tight time schedule (all but one of the following are on Nassau Street, across from the south flank of Trinity College). Head for **House of Ireland,** 37–38 Nassau St. (☎ 01-671-4543; www.houseofireland.com), or the nearby **The Kilkenny Shop,** 5–6 Nassau St. (☎ 01-677-7066). You don't have to go all the way to the Aran Islands to pick up thick Irish woolen sweaters. Try the **Blarney Woollen Mills,** 21–23 Nassau Street (☎ 01-671-0068; www.blarney.com), or, even better, **Monaghan's,** 15–17 Grafton Arcade on Grafton Street (☎ 01-677-0823).

Guided tours

For a general feel of the city, **Dublin Bus** (☎ 01-873-4222; www.dublinbus.ie) operates a very good, 75-minute hop-on, hop-off **Dublin City Tour** that connects 19 major points of interest, including museums, art galleries, churches and cathedrals, libraries, and historic sites. The tour departs from the Dublin Bus office at 59 Upper O'Connell St. Fares are 12.50€ ($14) adults, 6€ ($6.90) children under 14, and 11€ ($13) students and senior citizens; the ticket is valid for 24 hours. Tours are offered daily from 9:30 a.m. to 6:30 p.m.

City Sightseeing (☎ 01-605-7705; www.guidefriday.com) covers all the same major sights as the Dublin Bus's Dublin City Tour but is slightly more expensive at 14€ ($16) adults, 12€ ($14) seniors and students, 5€ ($5.75) children, and 32€ ($37) family. The first tours leave at 9:30 a.m. from 14 Upper O'Connell St., and they run every 10 to 15 minutes thereafter. Tours last about 90 minutes.

Suggested itineraries

If you're the type who'd rather organize your own tours, this section offers some tips for building your own Dublin itineraries.

If you have one day

Begin with **Trinity College** and its library, which preserves perhaps the world's greatest illuminated manuscript, the *Book of Kells*. Stay in a historical mood with a visit to the treasures of the **National Museum** before heading over to Grafton Street to grab lunch at **Bewley's Cafe.**

After lunch, you're off to **Christ Church Cathedral** (the moody medieval church) and its rival **St. Patrick's Cathedral** (Jonathan Swift's old haunt). After a good dose of religion, tour the **Guinness Brewery** — for many, the highlight of any trip to Dublin. Continue the beery fun with a **pub-crawl through Temple Bar,** stopping for dinner at **Gallagher's Boxty House.**

If you have two days

Start **Day 1** back in school at **Trinity College** to marvel at the *Book of Kells*. Head south to indulge in Dublin's two top museums, the **National Museum** of history, archaeology, and Celtic and Viking culture, and the **National Gallery of Ireland**. After lunch and a stroll down the banks of the Liffey and across **Ha'penny Bridge,** pop into some stores for some Irish souvenirs (those bulky wool sweaters are truly a worthwhile splurge). Stop by your hotel to drop off your shopping bags so that you can be ready to embark on whichever guided walk tickles your Irish fancy: a musical or a literary pub-crawl. Round out the night amid the pubs and bustle of trendy **Temple Bar.**

After the pub-crawling excesses of yesterday, begin **Day 2** at church, visiting Dublin's competing cathedrals, **Christ Church** and **St. Patrick's.** Tour **Dublin Castle** before heading off to the true cathedral of Ireland: the **Guinness Brewery.** Take the evening to sample some of Dublin's historic pubs outside the Temple Bar district.

If you have three days

Spend **Day 1** and **Day 2** as described in the preceding section, and take **Day 3** to tour either the prehistoric **mound tombs north of Dublin** or the **Wicklow Mountains** and **Glendalough** to the south (both covered in the following section).

Traveling the Irish Countryside

Lovely as Dublin is, you should really see a bit of Ireland's famed countryside. Scenic drives abound, and the excursions in this section take you past ruined churches and impressive mansions, along rocky shorelines and stunning, verdant landscapes.

North of Dublin to passage tombs and ruined medieval abbeys

Several sights just north of Dublin around the Boyne River Valley characterize two of the greatest attractions of Ireland — prehistoric sites and ruined abbeys. You can easily visit both on a daytrip.

Getting there

The most convenient base for the region is the town of Drogheda, which has regular rail and bus links with Dublin. The **tourist office** here has an unusual arrangement: Spring through fall, it's located in Drogheda's Bus Eireann Depot (☎ 041-983-7070; Fax: 041-984-5340; www.eastcoast midlandsireland.com), but in winter it's run by Drogheda on the Boyne Tourism at 1 Millmount (☎ 041-984-5684). For additional information, you may have to visit the regional office (☎ 042-933-5485) on Jocelyn Street in the city of Dundalk, farther up the road.

Seeing the sights

Top honors for sightseeing go to **Newgrange,** Ireland's most famous and most accessible passage tomb. This 36-foot-high mound of stones — some weighing up to 16 tons — was fitted together into a watertight engineering triumph well over 5,000 years ago, before Stonehenge or the Pyramids were even contemplated. You can take part in a guided visit down the 60-foot passage to the center of the tomb — a fun exploration for kids. Tours begin not at Newgrange, but at the **Brú Na Bóinne Visitor Centre,** south of the river Boyne on the L21, 2 miles west of Donore (☎ 041-988-0300; www.heritageireland.ie) and some distance from Newgrange itself.

The center is open daily year-round, but hours vary: October through April it's open 9:30 a.m. to 5:30 p.m.; May and the last two weeks of September it's open 9:00 a.m. to 6:30 p.m.; and June through the first two weeks of September it's open 9 a.m. to 7 p.m. The last tour is offered 90 minutes before close; the last admission to the visitor center is 45 minutes before close. The center restricts the number of people visiting the site so, as a result, you'll likely have a wait before your tour. Expect to spend about an hour viewing the center before your 45-minute tour of Newgrange.

The center also handles tours of **Knowth,** a nearby series of Neolithic grassy mound tombs — amazing, but not as popular as Newgrange.

Located 6 miles northwest of Drogheda are the remains of the monastery **Monasterboice,** now represented mainly by its quiet, monumental cemetery. Here you can see plenty of Celtic high crosses, including the best preserved in Ireland, **Muiredeach's High Cross,** a 17-foot-tall example from A.D. 922 (look at the beautifully preserved "Taking of Christ" panel just above the base). Nearby are the ruins of **Mellifont Abbey,** a 12th-century religious community of which little remains.

Where to stay and dine

You can stay in Drogheda at the modern **Westcourt Hotel** (☎ 041-983-0965; Fax: 041-983-0970; www.westcourt.ie) on West Street for 150€ ($173) per double. For food, check out the pub down the street at **Weavers** (☎ 041-983-2816); for a more complete meal, try the pricey French cuisine at the **Buttergate Restaurant** (☎ 041-983-4759) on Millmount Square.

South of Dublin: Mansions and monasteries in County Wicklow

Just an easy 15-minute drive south of downtown Dublin gets you to the gardens of County Wicklow. The sights south of Dublin can easily be visited on a daytrip, and then you can be back in town for dinner.

Getting there

Dublin's tourist office has information on County Wicklow; otherwise, you'd have to drive all the way through the region to Wicklow Town and the area **tourism office** (☎ 0404-69-117; www.wicklow.ie) on Fitzwilliam Square. You can see the best of this area by car, but if you're not renting a car, you can catch a ride with **Bus Eireann** (☎ 01-836-6111; www.bus eirann.ie), which takes busloads of tourists from Dublin to the major sights year-round.

Seeing the sights

A few miles south of Dublin on the N11, just past the town of Enniskerry, lies **Powerscourt Gardens** (☎ 01-204-6000), a thousand acres of late 18th-century gardens, grottoes, and fountains that make up one of the prime examples of "civilized naturalism" in Europe. The gardens are supposed to appear wild and natural . . . but with a civilized hand (holding pruning shears) guiding it, it became the epitome of nature—better than nature, even. The way nature would have done things, if only she had consulted some Brits beforehand. (They were pretty full of themselves, those 18th-century folks.) In 1974, the massive manor house was nearly destroyed by fire, but renovations have been taking place. About 4 miles on is the 400-foot **Powerscourt Waterfall,** the tallest in Ireland, but I don't recommend walking the narrow road unless you're very surefooted.

The old Military Road (R115) slices through the wildest heights of the **Wicklow Mountains.** This eerie peatscape covered with heather and reddish scrub looks as if it belongs somewhere on Mars, with only the Sally Gap pass and Glenmacnass waterfalls breaking up the moody boglands.

At Laragh, detour west to visit one of the most magical of Ireland's ruined monastic sites, **Glendalough** (☎ 0404-45-325, 0404-45-352, or 0404-45-688), filled with high crosses, round towers, pretty lakes, and medieval stone buildings. During the summer, the tour buses can be frequent. All the sights listed here are open daily from about 9:30 a.m. to dusk.

To partake in Celtic culture at its best, check out County Kerry. Ancient Irish traditions flourish here, from music and storytelling to good pub *craic,* or conversation, and some of the country's few remaining Gaelic-speaking pockets. The 110-mile **Ring of Kerry,** a scenic route circling the Inveragh Peninsula, is Ireland's most famous — and most tour bus–engulfed — drive.

Because this area is heavy with tour buses, most visitors take the Ring counterclockwise from Killarney, to make the heavy traffic easier to manage. The only thing less fun than driving on the left side of a twisty, narrow, two-lane road along a cliff and sharing it with a constant stream of giant buses much too wide for their lane is doing the same thing with all those buses *coming directly at you.*

County Kerry

You can easily visit the Ring in a day, but I'd give the area two or three days if you can in order to spend time in **Killarney,** tour the less-visited **Dingle Peninsula,** and see some of the other less-frequented sights off the Ring.

Getting there

Frequent daily train service arrives from Ireland's big cities into Killarney, the region's main town and tourist center. Killarney also houses the region's main **tourist office** (☎ 064-31-633; www.corkkerry.ie/killarneytio) in the Town Hall off Main Street.

Seeing the sights

Driving the Ring in County Kerry, a stretch of route N70 with plenty of sign designations, is a must-do. While driving the Ring, you can visit coastal villages, take pictures of inland lakes, and stare in wonder at the mountainous heights of the Inveragh Peninsula along the way. Highlights include the **Kerry Bog Village Museum** at Glenbeigh (thatched cottages re-created for tourists), **Cahirciveen** (the main town), **Staigue Fort** (a well-preserved, Iron Age, drystone fortress), and the towns of **Sneem** (cottages in festive colors) and **Kenmare** (known for its handmade lace).

About halfway around the Ring, you can detour onto **Valentia Island,** connected to the mainland by a bridge and home to the **Skellig Island Experience.** This video and display center introduces you to the endangered natural habitats and medieval monastery of the dramatic Skellig Islands off the coast. The islands' interiors are off-limits to visitors in order to preserve the ecosystem.

You can avoid the crowds by driving a similar, much less visited, and (in my opinion) even more scenic circle around the **Dingle Peninsula,** one inlet to the north of the Inveragh. Dingle's **tourist office** (☎ 066-915-1188; www.corkkerry.ie/dingletio) is on the Quay in Dingle Town. Dingle is the main town; at the pier there you can hire a boat to take you out to meet Fungi, the resident dolphin of Dingle Bay, if he's in a playful mood.

Relax from all the nerve-racking driving on the Ring in the touristy city of **Killarney,** gateway to a beautiful National Park full of lakes, waterfalls, castles, woodlands, bogs, and the manor house, gardens, and romantically ruined abbey of **Muckross.**

Where to stay and dine

Three miles west of Killarney, near Fossa and right on the Lower Lake, sits the picturesque Victorian-era **Hotel Europe** (☎ 064-71-350; Fax: 064-32-118; www.killarneyhotels.ie), with doubles running 194€ to 256€ ($223–$294). **Foley's** (☎ 064-31-217), in Killarney at 23 High St., serves excellent Irish food and seafood from Dingle Bay in a Georgian atmosphere.

Fast Facts: Dublin

Area Code

Ireland's country code is **353.** Dublin's city code is **01.** If you're calling from outside Ireland, drop the initial zero. To call Dublin from the United States, dial 011-353-1 followed by the number.

American Express

American Express no longer has any offices in Ireland.

Currency

In January 2002, Ireland's national currency changed from the Irish punt to the euro (€). The euro is divided into 100 cents, and there are coins of .01, .02, .05, .10, .20, .50, 1, and 2. Paper-note denominations are 5, 10, 20, 50, 100, 200, and 500. Rates of exchange used to calculate the dollar value given in this chapter are 1€ = $1.15. Amounts over $10 have been rounded to the nearest dollar.

Doctors and Dentists

In an emergency, ask your hotel to call a doctor for you, or go to the hospital (see "Hospitals," later in this section). Otherwise, call the Eastern Health Shared Services, Dr. Steevens' Hospital (☎ 01-679-0700; www.ehss.ie) or the Irish Medical Organisation, 10 Fitzwilliam Place (☎ 01-676-7273; www.imo.ie). Temple Bar Medical Center, 26 Wellington Quay, near the Millennium Bridge (☎ 01-670-7255; www.templebardoc.com), is another option if you're seeking a general practice.

Embassies and Consulates

The U.S. Embassy (☎ 01-668-8777; Fax: 01-668-9946) is at 42 Elgin Rd.

Emergency

Dial ☎ 999 or 122 in any emergency.

Hospitals

For an emergency room, go to Mater Misericordiae Hospital, Eccles Street (☎ 01-830-1122) or St. James's Hospital, St. James's Street (☎ 2774; www.stjames.ie).

Information

The main Dublin Tourism office is in St. Andrew's Church (☎ 01-605- 7700; www.visitdublin.com), at Suffolk Street, a block west of Grafton Street. For specifics on it, and on other offices, see "Finding information after you arrive," near the beginning of this chapter.

The Temple Bar District has its own tourist office at 12 East Essex St. (www.temple-bar.ie).

Visit the Irish Tourist Board (Fáilte Ireland) at Baggot Street Bridge (☎ 1-602-4000; www.ireland.travel.ie), if you're planning to venture outside Dublin. They'll provide you with information about the entire country.

The Dublin Bus number is ☎ 01-873-4222. The number for Dublin Area Rapid Transit (DART) is ☎ 01-703-3504; its Web site is www.dart.ie. For Bus Eireann (coaches throughout Ireland), call ☎ 01-836-6111 or visit www.buseirann.ie.

Internet Access and Cybercafes

Central Cyber Cafe, 6 Grafton St. (☎ 01-677-8298; www.centralcafe.ie), is open in the heart of town Monday through Friday from 9 a.m. to 10 p.m., Saturday and Sunday from 10 a.m. to 9 p.m. Its sister, Global Internet Cafe at 8 Lower O'Connell St. (☎ 01-878-0295;www.centralcafe.ie), is open Monday through Friday from 8 a.m. to 11 p.m., Saturday from 9 a.m. to 11 p.m., and Sunday from 10 a.m. to 11 p.m. Both charge from 0.75€ (85¢) for 15 minutes, with discounts for students and seniors.

Maps

You can pick up a map of Dublin at any tourist center or bookstore.

Newspapers/Magazines

The *Irish Times* (www.ireland.com) publishes a daily arts and entertainment guide. The *Dublin Events Guide* (www.dublinevents.com) and *The Event Guide* (www.eventguide.ie) are similar weekly publications. All can be bought at newsstands throughout Dublin.

Pharmacies

Leonard's Corner Pharmacy, 106 S. Circular Rd. (☎ 01-453-4282) is open daily from 9 a.m. to 10 p.m. Crowley's Pharmacy, at 53 Kilbarrack Rd., is open late at night. Call ☎ 01-832-5332 for hours.

Police

Dial ☎ **999** or **112** in an emergency to get the Garda (police). Dublin's Tourist Victim Support Service (☎ 1850-661-771 for the national hotline, or ☎ 1478-5295; www. touristvictimsupport.ie) is in the Garda headquarters on Harcourt Square.

Post Office

Dublin's main post office is on O'Connell Street (☎ 01-705-7000), open Monday through Saturday from 8 a.m. to 8 p.m., and Sunday from 10:00 a.m. to 6:30 p.m.

Safety

Violent crime is not the norm in Dublin, but with increased drug traffic, crime has risen. As with anyplace else, don't let yourself become careless.

Taxes

In Ireland, a value-added tax (VAT) of 17.36 percent is figured into the price of most items. Foreign visitors can reclaim this VAT on major purchases of consumer goods (see Chapter 4 for more on this).

Taxis

See "Getting Around Dublin," earlier in this chapter.

Telephone

Pay phones accept both euro coins (in denominations of 0.10€, 0.20€, 0.50€, 1€, and 2€) and phone cards, which you can buy at post offices. The minimum charge is 0.50€ (60¢).

To call the United States from Ireland directly, dial 001 followed by the area code and phone number. To charge a call to your calling card, or to make a collect call home, dial AT&T (☎ 1-800-550-000), MCI (☎ 1-800-551-001), or Sprint (☎ 1-800-552-001).

Transit Info

See "Getting Around Dublin," earlier in this chapter.

Part IV
Central Europe

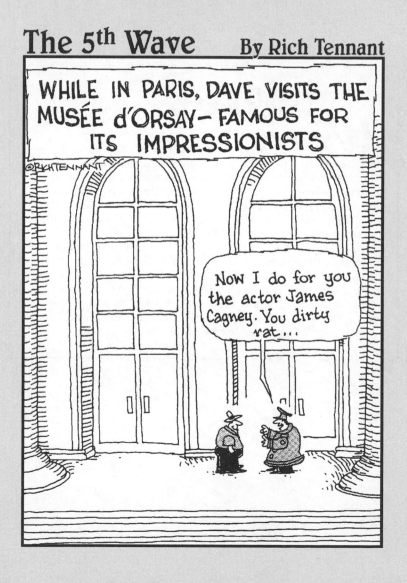

In this part . . .

*W*elcome to Central Europe, the home of dreamy Prague, the showcase city of Eastern Europe, and sophisticated Paris — fine food, high fashion, and great art. In Amsterdam, you can cruise the 17th-century canals to discover the Rembrandts and van Goghs, the red-light district, and Anne Frank's hiding place from the Nazis. In Munich, you can hoist a beer stein and discover a city that boasts the oompah-band cheeriness of Bavaria and the refinement of a cultural center financed by a progressive industrial sector. In genteel Vienna of the Hapsburgs, you can explore the city that taught Paris a thing or two about cafes and the world a lesson in how to build an opera house. In the Berner Oberland of Switzerland, you can scale the Alps on thrilling gondola rides, visit ice palaces carved into glaciers, and witness sky-scraping vistas from Europe's snowy summit.

Chapter 13

Paris and Environs

● ●

In This Chapter

▶ Getting to Paris

▶ Checking out the neighborhoods

▶ Discovering the best places to sleep and eat

▶ Exploring the highlights of the City of Light

▶ Side-tripping to Versailles and Chartres

● ●

*P*aris is the City of Light — the world capital of romance, birthplace of bohemians and Impressionists, muse to Hemingway and the Lost Generation, and the high temple of haute cuisine. You can overdose on art at the Louvre, cruise past 18th-century palaces on the Seine, write poetry at a sidewalk-cafe table, dance in the colored glow of Notre-Dame's stained glass, dine stupendously in a tiny bistro, or steal long kisses atop the Eiffel Tower.

Romanticizing this city is easy — and it's just as easy to belittle it. No doubt you've heard that the people are rude, the museums are crowded, the traffic is horrendous, the Champs-Elysées has become a commercialized strip mall, and everything is far, far too expensive.

You shouldn't let these obstacles keep you from having a good time. Don't expect everyone to be as warm and welcoming as folks in the Sicilian countryside, and you won't be disappointed. Go early to beat the museum crowds. To avoid traffic, take the Métro (subway) — the Métro is very convenient, and you have no reason to drive here.

Sure, McDonald's and movie multiplexes now dominate the Champs-Elysées, but you can find elegant, authentic Paris elsewhere. And although you can spend all your dough in Paris, I also know of no city more chockablock with great values on everything from meals and hotels to shopping and museums. You have to be willing to search those bargains out, and I'm here to help you do just that.

Finally, although those positives and negatives exist, they are by no means the sum of the city. Paris strikes a lively balance between the vibrant, modern metropolis of the 21st century and the majestic, historic city of Napoleon and Hemingway. Paris is a city of hip nightclubs, cutting-edge cuisine, and the highest fashion, as well as one of venerable museums, cafe legends, and sweeping 18th- and 19th-century grandeur. This balance keeps Paris intriguing, keeps it attractive, and keeps visitors and faithful admirers coming back year after year.

Getting There

Getting to the center of Paris is easy whether you're arriving by plane or train. Getting around the city is a breeze, too, thanks to the efficient Métro subway system.

Arriving by air

Most international flights land at **Charles de Gaulle Airport** (☎ 01-48-62-22-80; www.adp.fr), also known as Roissy, 14 miles northeast of the city. Transatlantic flights on carriers other than Air France arrive at Terminal 1; Air France arrives at Terminal 2. The May 2004 collapse of a section of Terminal 2E, which hosts some Air France and other European carriers, has thrown services at the airport into confusion. As of this writing, officials are debating whether to raze or rebuild the structure, and it's not clear what effect this or any other effort will have on travelers, although some officials were speculating that the terminal could be closed for about a year.

In the arrivals halls of both terminals are several ATMs. Information desks are located between doors 34 and 36 in Terminal 1 and in the center of each of the halls of Terminal 2.

An RER (commuter train) line runs into the center for 7.75€ ($8.90), or you can take a taxi for around 38€ ($44) from 7 a.m. to 8 p.m. and about 40 percent more at other times.

Some charter flights, as well as many national flights, land 5.3km (8½ miles) south of town at **Orly Airport** (☎ 01-49-75-15-15; www.adp.fr). The Orly Sud terminal handles international flights, and Orly Ouest terminal hosts domestic flights. ATMs and information desks are located in the arrivals hall of both terminals. RER trains to the Gare d'Austerlitz in the city center cost 5.25€ ($6); a taxi costs around 35€ ($40).

Arriving by rail

Paris has many rail stations, but most international trains arrive at one of three places. The **Gare du Nord** serves the Netherlands, Belgium, Denmark, northern Germany, and trains from London. Gare du Nord is the destination for both the **Eurostar** direct train that comes through the **Channel Tunnel** — a dozen trains daily for a three-hour trip, four hours with the time change — as well as trains arriving on the last leg of the old-fashioned and highly *not* recommended route: London to Dover by train; Dover to Calais by ferry; and Calais to Paris by train (four trains daily; 10½ long hours for the trip). **Gare de Lyon** serves the south (Italy and parts of Switzerland), and **Gare de l'Est** handles trains from Switzerland, southern Germany, and Austria.

France

Orienting Yourself in Paris

The Seine River divides Paris between the Right Bank *(Rive Droite)* to the north and the Left Bank *(Rive Gauche)* to the south. Paris began on the **Ile de la Cité,** an island in the Seine that is still the center of the city and home to **Cathédrale de Notre-Dame.**

Twenty districts called *arrondissements* divide Paris. These districts start with the first arrondissement and then spiral out from there. At the end of each address in this chapter, you see a number followed by an *e* (or in the case of 1, an *er*), such as *8e* or *5e*. That number refers to the arrondissement. A Parisian address, spoken or written, isn't complete unless the neighborhood name or arrondissement is included. The last two digits of a zip code are the arrondissement, so an address listed as

Paris Neighborhoods

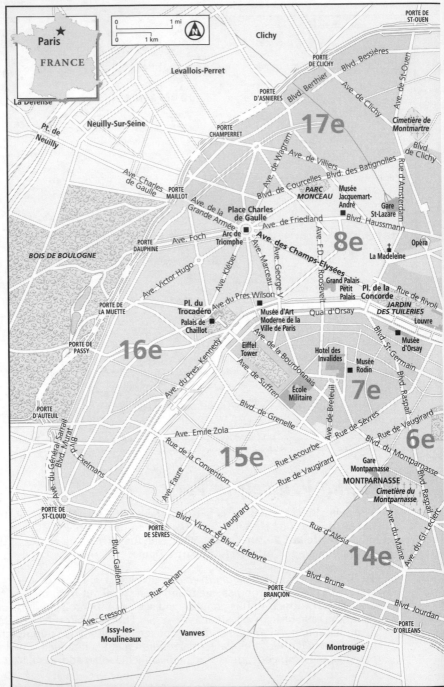

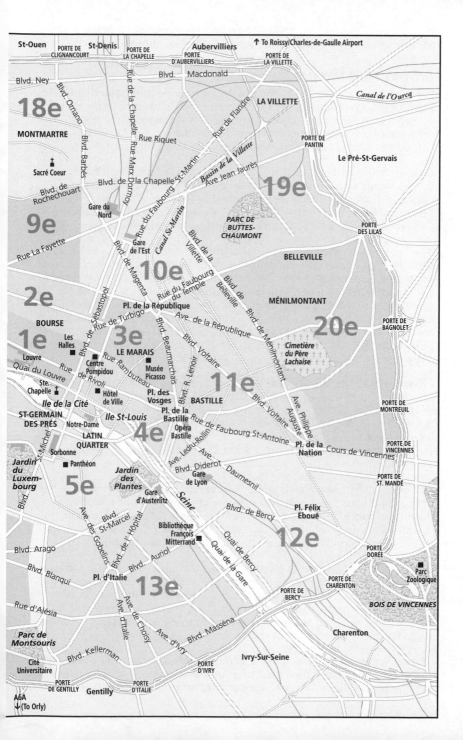

"Paris 75003" would be in the third arrondissement. (Most of these districts also correspond with traditional, named neighborhoods.)

Introducing the neighborhoods

Ile de la Cité is connected to the nearby posh residential island of **Ile de Saint-Louis**. Traditionally, people consider the Right Bank to be more upscale, with Paris's main boulevards such as **Champs-Elysées** and museums such as the **Louvre**. The old bohemian half of Paris is on the Left Bank with the **Latin Quarter** around the university.

Among the major arrondissements (for visitors) on the Right Bank is the 3e. Called **Le Marais,** this up-and-coming neighborhood manages to remain genuinely Parisian amid the swirl of tourism in the city center. The 4e includes most of the **Ile de la Cité**, **Ile St-Louis**, the **Beaubourg pedestrian zone,** and the **Centre Pompidou** modern-art complex.

The 1er includes the **Louvre** neighborhood and the tip of the **Ile de la Cité**. The 8e — a natural extension westward of the 1er — is Paris's most posh area, consisting of ritzy hotels, fashion boutiques, fine restaurants, and upscale town houses. The 8e arrondissement centers around the grandest boulevard in a city famous for them: the **Champs-Elysées.** The sidewalks of this historic shopping promenade were recently cleaned up and widened. Now no more than a string of international chain stores and movie theaters, the Champs-Elysées has become merely a shadow of its former elegant self.

From the **Place de la Concorde** — an oval plaza at the western end of the **Louvre** complex where French royalty met the business end of a guillotine during the Revolution — the Champs-Elysées beelines east-west to the **Arc de Triomphe.** The Arc is one of the world's greatest triumphal arches, a monument to France's unknown soldier and to the gods of car-insurance premiums (surrounding the Arc is a five-lane traffic circle where, it seems, anything goes).

Still echoing with the ghosts of Bohemian Paris, in the northerly reaches of the Right Bank lies **Montmartre,** topped by the fairy-tale gleaming white basilica of **Sacré-Coeur,** and tramped by tourists. The neighborhood is so distinct and (despite the tour buses) charming, it gets its own write-up under "More cool things to see and do," later in this chapter.

Left Bank arrondissements include the 5e, the famous old **Latin Quarter,** named for the language spoken by the university students who gave it its once colorful, bohemian atmosphere. These days, the quarter is another sad Parisian shadow of former glory, its bohemia replaced by gyro stands, souvenir shops, and hordes of tourists wondering why the Latin Quarter was ever famous.

The adjacent 6e retains some of its counterculture charm. The students of **Paris's Fine Arts School** help liven up things here, especially in the now highly fashionable but still somewhat artsy **St-Germain-des-Prés** neighborhood of cafes, brasseries, and restaurants. Tucked into a wide arc of the Seine, the 7e intrudes a bit on the **St-Germain** neighborhood, but its major features are the **Musée d'Orsay**, the **Tour Eiffel** (Eiffel Tower), and the **Musée Rodin.**

Finding information after you arrive

The city's **tourist information office,** Office de Tourisme de Paris, maintains two full-service welcome centers. Both offer basic information about attractions in the city, help with last-minute hotel reservations, make booking for daytrips, and sell transportation and museum passes — but for a small fee. The first, in Gare du Nord (Métro: Gare du Nord) beneath the glass roof, is open daily from 8 a.m. to 6 p.m. The second, at 11 rue Scribe (Métro: Opéra or Chaussée d'Antin) is open Monday to Saturday from 9:00 a.m. to 6:30 p.m.

Several auxiliary offices are scattered throughout the city. The Eiffel Tower office (Métro: Bir Hakeim or Trocadéro) is open daily from 11 a.m. to 6 p.m., May through September. The office in Gare de Lyon (Métro: Gare de Lyon) is open Monday through Saturday from 8 a.m. to 6 p.m. Both the office in Montmartre, 21 place du Tertre (Métro: Abbesses), and the office in the Louvre (Métro: Palais Royal or Musée du Louvre) are open daily from 10 a.m. to 7 p.m.

Getting Around Paris

Paris has an extensive public-transportation system that makes it easy for you to get around without having to rent a car. Transport tickets are good on the Métro, bus, and RER lines. Individual tickets cost 1.30€ ($1.50), but a *carnet* (pack of ten) costs only 10€ ($12).

Two types of cards offer unlimited travel on all forms of public transportation: the tourists' Paris Visite and the Parisian's Carte Orange Hebdomadaire. I say "tourists'" and "Parisians," because you won't find mention of the less-expensive Carte Orange on the English-language version of www.ratp.fr. But that doesn't mean you can't get the same savings a Parisian can; you just have to ask for it.

The **Carte Orange** costs 14.50€ ($17) for zones 1 and 2 and 19.40€ ($22) for zones 1 to 3. You'll need to provide a passport-size photo (or snap one at photo booths in major train and Métro stations). Make sure you get the *hebdomadaire* ("weekly") one.

Buy the **Paris Visite** (the regular pass covers zones 1 through 3, which include all of central Paris and many of its suburbs) if you're in Paris for only a day or two. At 8.35€ ($10) for one day or 13.70€ ($16) for two days (kids 4 to 11 pay half price; kids under four ride free), you'll still beat the price of the Carte Orange. However, the three-day 18.25€ ($21) and the five-day 26.65€ ($31) Visites are a waste of money.

More comprehensive Visite passes covering zones 1 through 5 (all the 'burbs, including Disneyland Paris) cost twice as much, and passes for zones 1 through 8 (the entire Ile-de-France region) cost three times as much.

Don't pay for passes that carry you beyond Zone 3; most of the interesting monuments lie within zones 1 and 2.

By Métro (subway) and RER

The Paris Métro (☎ 08-36-68-41-14 for information in English at .34€/39¢ per minute; www.ratp.fr) is one of the best subways in Europe, a clean, efficient, and well-interconnected system. Using a Métro map, find which numbered line you want to take and the name of the last station in the direction you want to go. In the Métro tunnels, follow signs for that line and that last station to get on the train going the right way.

You may have to transfer to another line to get to your destination (although usually not more than once per trip). When transferring, follow the signs labeled *correspondance* to the next line. Don't follow a *sortie* sign, unless you want to exit. You can make unlimited transfers on one ticket as long as you don't exit the system — although you may often find yourself walking long distances in the tunnels that connect some transfer stations.

Most of the lines are numbered, but some are assigned letters. The lettered lines (A, B, C, and D) are technically not the Métro but are part of the overlapping RER network. This high-speed commuter light-rail system services only major stops within the city and extends much farther out into the suburbs. The RER uses the same tickets as the Métro (except when you're traveling way out into the 'burbs, for which you have to buy a separate ticket), and you can transfer freely between the two systems.

Some RER lines are particularly useful; the C line, for instance, follows the left bank of the Seine closely (no Métro line does this) and also heads out to Versailles. Both ends of all RER lines split off like the frayed ends of a rope as they leave the city, so make sure the train you board is heading out to the numbered fork you want (for example, the C line has eight different end destinations, C1 through C8). Maps on the platforms show you the routes of each fork, and TV displays tell you when the next half-dozen trains will be arriving and which number each one is.

By bus

In all my trips to the City of Light, I've never needed to use the bus system, because I find that the Métro works well and is faster than plodding through aboveground traffic. Although buses use the same tickets as the Métro, a single ticket is only good for two *sections* to reach your destination, which can make bus trips expensive. If you're traveling through three or more sections, you need to punch two tickets.

You can find separate maps for each bus route posted at bus stops, and each map has a blue-and-red bar running along the bottom. You can also find maps and information online at www.ratp.fr. The stops that appear directly above the blue section of this bar are within that stop's two-section limit. For stops appearing above the red section(s) of the bar, you need to use two tickets. When the number of a bus route is written in black on a white circle, it means that the bus stops there daily; when it's written in white on a black circle, it means the bus doesn't stop there on Sundays or holidays.

By taxi

Because cabs in Paris are scarce, hiring one at a stand may be easier than hailing one in the street. Be careful to check the meter when you board to be sure you're not also paying the previous passenger's fare, and if your taxi lacks a meter, make sure to settle the cost of the trip before setting out. Calling a cab to pick you up is more expensive because the meter starts running when the cab receives the call, but if you need to do it, call ☎ **01-45-85-85-85**, 01-45-85-45-45, or 01-47-39-47-39.

The initial fare for up to three passengers is 2€ ($2.30) and rises .62€ (70¢) every kilometer between 7 a.m. and 7 p.m. Between 7 p.m. and 7 a.m., the standing charge remains the same, but the per-kilometer charge rises to 1.06€ ($1.20). An additional fee of .90€ ($1.05) is imposed for luggage weighing more than 5kg (11 lbs.), plus you pay .70€ (80¢) if you catch your taxi at a major train station. A fourth passenger incurs a 2.60€ ($3) charge.

By foot

Paris sprawls, yet it's a wonderful city for walking. Tourist attractions are spread throughout the city, but many areas — along the Seine, in the cemeteries, across the Pont Neuf — make for lovely strolls. Don't expect to take the Métro to the Eiffel Tower and then duck back underground quickly; you'll want to savor the scene.

On Sundays and public holidays between March and November, many Paris streets are closed to traffic and open to pedestrians. The "Paris Respire" initiative includes the Seine expressway on the Left Bank between the Eiffel Tower and the Musée d'Orsay, the expressway on the Right Bank between Place de la Concorde and Pont Charles de Gaulle, and the streets just south of Jardin de Luxembourg. Also included are two areas beyond Paris's ring road: the Boie de Boulogne and Boie de Vincennes.

Staying in Paris

Paris has some 73,000 hotel rooms, so you're sure to find a bed. The tricky part is finding a quality room in a desirable location and in your price bracket. This city is full of overblown, overpriced hotels and fleabag dives even the scruffiest backpackers would turn up a nose at. Stick with me, though, and I can help you find something that meets your needs, including some budget hideaways. I've had some of my best stays in Paris in small, fourth-floor walk-ups with unforgettable views across the rooftops.

The general assumption, still holding true (but tenuously) these days, is that the Right Bank has more upscale hotels, while the bohemian Left Bank boasts more inexpensive options. On your first visit, you may want to stay pretty close to the center of town, but don't fret if the only room you can find is out in *les boondocks*. Getting to the **Louvre** by Métro from the 16e only takes a few minutes longer than it does from the **Latin Quarter**. Besides, most repeat visitors find themselves drawn away from the tourist center in favor of a more authentic Parisian neighborhood. For a price, you can find that authenticity as close by as the **Marais** or **St-Germain-des-Prés**.

In addition to the November-to-February low season, July and August are also slow in Paris. You can bargain for good rates at hotels because many of them shut down. Multiple trade fairs during May, June, September, and October tend to book up the city's 4-star and luxury hotels.

The tourist office (see "Fast Facts: Paris" at the end of this chapter) will book a room for you, and they also broker last-minute rooms that upper-class hotels are having a hard time moving, so you may luck into a deep discount on a posh pad.

Although Paris bed-and-breakfasts (B&Bs) vary greatly in style and room décor, they're usually cheaper than hotels (prices typically range anywhere from $50 to $130), and you can guarantee a certain level of quality by booking a government-approved B&B through a private reservation agency: **Bed & Breakfast France** (☎ 01-42-01-34-34 in France; www.bed break.com), **Paris Bed & Breakfast** (☎ 800-872-2632 in the United States; www.parisbandb.com), or, for stays of a week or longer, **My Apartment in Paris** (☎ 01-45-44-54-97; www.my-apartment-in-paris.com).

Paris's top hotels

Grande Hôtel Jeanne d'Arc
$ The Marais (4e)

This place sort of reminds me of Grandma's comfortable guest room, with Sears & Roebuck furnishings, fresh carpeting, and fabric on the walls. Its rooms are larger — and certainly cleaner — than your standard French budget pension, and there are amenities galore, such as satellite TV. The location is right in the heart of the charming Marais district and often booked up to two months ahead of time by regulars, so be sure to make reservations.

See map p. 230. 3 rue de Jarente (between rue de Sévigné and rue de Turenne, off rue St-Antoine). ☎ 01-48-87-62-11. Fax: 01-48-87-37-31. www.hoteljeannedarc.com. Métro: St-Paul. Rates: 80€–95€ ($92–$109) double. Breakfast 6€ ($8). MC, V.

Hôtel d'Angleterre
$$$ Saint-Germain-des-Prés (6e)

The high-beamed ceilings of this 18th-century Breton-style inn offer a slice of U.S. history — when this was the British Embassy in 1783, the English finally signed the papers here recognizing American independence. Some rooms have exposed stone walls and four-poster canopy beds, and all boast period furnishings, carved-wood closet doors, and silk wall hangings. The "apartments," with two bedrooms, are ideal for families. The homey common lounge has a piano, and there's a small lush courtyard where you can breakfast in summer.

See map p. 230. 44 rue Jacob (off rue Bonaparte). ☎ *01-42-60-34-72. Fax: 01-42-60-16-93.* www.hotel-dangleterre.com. *Métro: St-Germain-des-Prés. Rates: 140€–230€ ($161–$265) double. Rates includes breakfast. AE, DC, MC, V.*

Hôtel de la Bretonnerie
$$ The Marais (4e)

The Sagots keep a cozy, friendly hotel where each room is done in a classic French style but with a unique décor, from Empire divans or Louis XIII chairs to Napoleon III tables. The nicest are the so-called *chambres de caractère,* some with canopy beds, some country-style with heavy beams and floral-print walls. All rooms were renovated in 2003. *Classique* rooms are smaller but still have nice touches, such as the occasional four-poster bed. The cozy duplexes are defined by beamed ceilings and huge curtained windows.

See map p. 230. 22 rue Saint-Croix-de-la-Bretonnerie (between rue des Archives and rue Vieille-du-Temple). ☎ *01-48-87-77-63. Fax: 01-42-77-26-78.* www.hoteldela bretonnerie.com. *Métro: Hôtel de Ville. Rates: 110€–145€ ($127–$167) double. Breakfast 9.50€ ($11). MC, V.*

Hôtel de L'Elysee
$$$ Champs-Elysées (8e)

This small, exceedingly friendly inn has been overhauled in Restoration style, with wallpaper of stamped 18th-century etchings, built-in closets, half-testers over many beds, and stuccoed ceilings in a few suites. Smallish mansard suite no. 60 features wood beams crisscrossing the space and skylights set into the low, sloping ceilings that provide peek-a-boo vistas of Parisian rooftops, including a perfectly framed view of the Eiffel Tower. All fifth- and sixth-floor rooms enjoy at least rooftop views, the former from small balconies (nos. 50–53 even glimpse the Eiffel Tower).

See map p. 230. 12 rue des Saussaies (off rue Faubourg St-Honoré at place Beauvau, 2 blocks north of Champs-Elysées). ☎ *01-42-65-29-25. Fax: 01-42-65-64-28.* www. france-hotel-guide.com/h75008efsh.htm. *Métro: Champs-Elysées-Clemenceau or Miromesnil. Rates: 135€–225€ ($155–$259) double. Breakfast 11€ ($13). AE, DC, MC, V.*

Accommodations, Dining, and Attractions in Paris

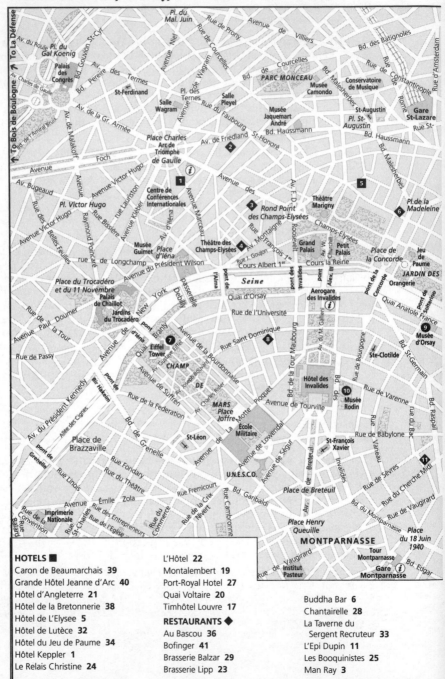

HOTELS ■
Caron de Beaumarchais **39**
Grande Hôtel Jeanne d'Arc **40**
Hôtel d'Angleterre **21**
Hôtel de la Bretonnerie **38**
Hôtel de L'Elysee **5**
Hôtel de Lutèce **32**
Hôtel du Jeu de Paume **34**
Hôtel Keppler **1**
Le Relais Christine **24**

L'Hôtel **22**
Montalembert **19**
Port-Royal Hotel **27**
Quai Voltaire **20**
Timhôtel Louvre **17**

RESTAURANTS ◆
Au Bascou **36**
Bofinger **41**
Brasserie Balzar **29**
Brasserie Lipp **23**

Buddha Bar **6**
Chantairelle **28**
La Taverne du
    Sergent Recruteur **33**
L'Epi Dupin **11**
Les Booquinistes **25**
Man Ray **3**

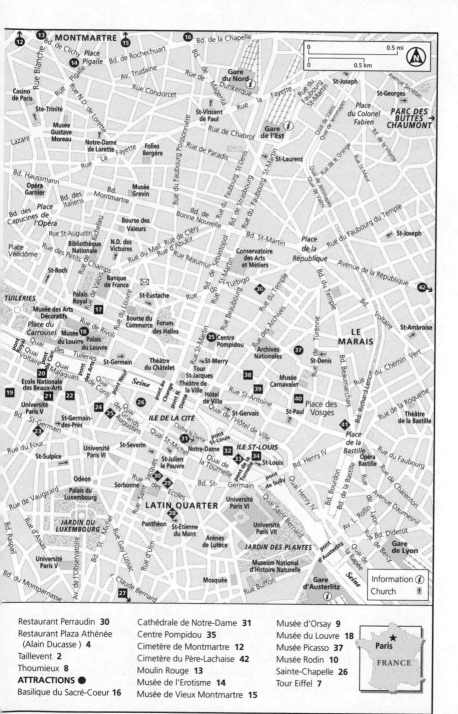

Restaurant Perraudin **30**
Restaurant Plaza Athénée
  (Alain Ducasse) **4**
Taillevent **2**
Thoumieux **8**
ATTRACTIONS ●
Basilique du Sacré-Coeur **16**

Cathédrale de Notre-Dame **31**
Centre Pompidou **35**
Cimetière de Montmartre **12**
Cimetière du Père-Lachaise **42**
Moulin Rouge **13**
Musée de l'Erotisme **14**
Musée de Vieux Montmartre **15**

Musée d'Orsay **9**
Musée du Louvre **18**
Musée Picasso **37**
Musée Rodin **10**
Sainte-Chapelle **26**
Tour Eiffel **7**

Hôtel de Lutèce
$$$ Ile Saint-Louis (4e)

The Lutèce occupies a converted 17th-century house accented with rustic details, such as wood-beam ceilings and terra-cotta floors. This refined hotel in a chic neighborhood has comfy rooms that are large for such a central location, even if a few bathtubs could use curtains; the last renovation was in 1998. The location, on a street lined with restaurants and shops, is just a five-minute stroll from Notre-Dame. **Des Deux-Iles** (☎ **01-43-26-13-35**), a sibling hotel, is a few doors down; between the two of them, there's a pretty good chance you can get a room.

See map p. 230. 59 rue Saint-Louis-en-l'Ile (on the main drag of the island). ☎ *01-43-26-23-52. Fax: 01-43-29-60-25.* www.hotel-ile-saintlouis.com. *Métro: Pont-Marie. Rates: 158€ ($182) double. Breakfast 10€ ($12). AE, MC, V.*

Hôtel du Jeu de Paume
$$$$ Ile Saint-Louis (4e)

Built in 1634 as a *Jeu de Paume* court (a precursor of tennis), this hotel is a successful marriage of 17th-century wood beams and plaster with 20th-century burnished steel and glass. The impressive, airy, three-story, ancient wood skeleton inside incorporates public lounges, an indoor breakfast terrace, a hanging corridor, and a glass elevator. Most accommodations are on the cozy side of medium, but the simplicity of the stylishly modern décor under hewn beams keeps them from feeling cramped. The three standard duplexes with spiral stairs are roomier (and don't cost any more than a double), but for true bliss check into the 750€ ($863) suite, a duplex with a lounge below and bedroom above, two baths, and a private terrace overlooking the small stone garden rimmed with flowers where guests — the suite can accommodate five people — can breakfast in nice weather.

See map p. 230. 54 rue Saint-Louis-en-L'Ile. ☎ *01-43-26-14-18. Fax: 01-40-46-02-76.* www.jeudepaumehotel.com. *Métro: Pont-Marie. Rates: 215€–285€ ($247–$328) double. Breakfast 15€ ($17). AE, DC, MC, V.*

Le Relais Christine
$$$$$ Saint-Germain-des-Pres (6e)

Passing through the cobbled courtyard to enter this early-17th-century building, you feel less like you're checking into a hotel and more like the baron and baroness arriving at your own country manor house. Most of the largish rooms are done in a contemporary relaxed style, but a few make a splash with grand, repro–Louis XIII décor. Most suites are duplexes, with sitting areas downstairs, marble bathrooms sporting double sinks, and a lofted bedchamber. The basement breakfast/dining room is installed under the low rough vaulting of a 13th-century abbey founded by Saint Louis himself.

See map p. 230. 3 rue Christine (off rue Dauphine, between bd. Saint-Germain and the Pont Neuf). ☎ *800-447-7462 in the U.S., 01-40-51-60-80 in Paris. Fax: 01-40-51-60-81.* www.relais-christine.com. *Métro: Odéon or St-Michel. Rates: 335€–430€ ($385–$495) double. Breakfast 20€–25€ ($23–$29). AE, DC, MC, V.*

Port-Royal Hotel

$ **Latin Quarter (5e)**

Although this hotel is on the far edge of the Latin Quarter, the Métro stop down the block keeps you only minutes from the city's center. These incredible rates come with surprisingly nice, if often smallish, rooms. The breakfast room has a TV. You have to pay a nominal fee for showers (unless you have a bathroom en suite), but they're modern and don't run out of hot water. In short, it's a decent hotel at hostel prices.

See map p. 230. 8 bd. Port-Royal (near av. des Gobelins). ☎ *01-43-31-70-06. Fax: 01-43-31-33-67.* www.portroyalhotel.fr.st. *Métro: Gobelins. Rates: 82€–87€ ($94–$100) double with bathroom; 48€–73€ ($55–$84) double without bathroom. Breakfast 5€ ($5.75). No credit cards.*

Paris's runner-up accommodations

 Caron de Beaumarchais

$$ **The Marais (4e)** Caron de Beaumarchais is a boutique hotel at budget rates, with a small antique-style salon in place of a reception area and rooms outfitted as befits an 18th-century Marais town house — wood ceilings and a touch of gold about the carved filigree on curving chair backs and mirror frames. Rooms in the front are largest. *See map p. 230. 12 rue Vieille-du-Temple (off rue de Rivoli).* ☎ *01-42-72-34-12. Fax: 01-42-72-34-63.* www.carondebeaumarchais.com.

Hôtel Keppler

$$ **Trocadéro (16e)** This older hotel could stand to replace the aging carpets and knockabout pine veneer modular furnishings, but the property is clean, resides in a quiet, bourgeois neighborhood just a few blocks away from the Champs-Elysées, and offers killer rates. *See map p. 230. 12 rue Keppler (between av. Marceau and av. d'Iéna, south of the Arc de Triomphe).* ☎ *01-47-20-65-05. Fax: 01-47-23-02-29.* www.hotelkeppler.com.

L'Hôtel

$$$$ **Germain-des-Prés (6e)** This hotel is no longer the flophouse where Oscar Wilde died in 1900. Today it's a funky velvet-and-pink-marble monument to curves, with smallish rooms and furnishings ranging from Louis XV and Empire styles to Art Nouveau. *See map p. 230. 13 rue des Beaux-Arts (between rue Bonaparte and rue de Seine, 1 block from the Quai Malaquais).* ☎ *01-44-41-99-00. Fax: 01-43-25-64-81.* www.l-hotel.com.

Montalembert

$$$$$ **St-Germain-des-Prés (7e)** Montalembert is one of Paris's top hotels, with a unique meld of contemporary design, Art Deco fashion, and French tradition (and amenities such as in-room VCRs, fax machines, and modem lines). "Traditionelle" bedrooms are Louis-Phillipe style with heavily lacquered chestnut and gold Art Deco furnishings; "moderne" rooms incorporate dark sycamore and hand-crafted leather molded along clean,

simple, elegant lines. *See map p. 230. 3 rue de Montelembert (off rue de Bac, behind the church of St Thomas d'Aquin).* ☎ *800-447-7462 in the United States or 01-45-49-68-68 in Paris. Fax: 01-45-49-69-49.* www.montalembert.com.

Quai Voltaire

$$ **St-Germain-des-Prés (7e)** The Quai Voltaire has midsized rooms with a dreamy Parisian view that overlooks the Seine to the Louvre across the way. That view comes with a price, though: traffic noise from the quai that even the double-glazed windows don't quite drown out. *See map p. 230. 19 quai Voltaire.* ☎ *01-42-61-50-91. Fax: 01-42-61-62-26.* www.quaivoltaire.fr.

Timhôtel Louvre

$$ **Louvre (1er)** Two blocks from the Louvre, Timhôtel Louvre was once a writers' and artists' crash pad, but has been relentlessly renovated into cookie-cutter blandness by a chain selling itself to the business set. Good value, though. *See map p. 230. 4 rue Croix-des-Petits-Champs (off rue St-Honoré, 2 blocks east of the Palais Royal).* ☎ *01-42-60-34-86. Fax: 01-42-60-10-39.* www.timhotel.fr.

Dining in Paris

For the French, food is close to a religion, and they gladly worship at the altars of their award-winning celebrity chefs. Traditional haute cuisine — a delicate balance of flavors, sauces, and ingredients blended with a studied technique — includes such classics as *blanquette de veau* (veal in an eggy cream sauce), *pot-au-feu* (an excellent stew of fatty beef and vegetables), *coq au vin* (chicken braised in red wine with onions and mushrooms), *bouillabaisse* (seafood soup), and that hearty staple *boeuf bourguignon* (beef stew with red wine).

But when people started thinking healthy a few decades back, buttery, creamy, saucy French cuisine quickly found itself on the outs. So the French invented *nouvelle cuisine,* which gave chefs an excuse to concoct new dishes — still French, mind you, but less fattening because they use fewer heavy creams and less butter and serve smaller portions.

When the nouvelle trend lost steam, people began spinning off more-healthful and/or more-creative cooking styles. Add to these styles the mix of French regional restaurants and the many ethnic dining rooms, and you'll never want for variety.

Eating dinner in Paris is cheaper these days. A French economic crisis in the 1990s forced many restaurants to lower their prices, and some top chefs found opportunity in the downturn by opening up *baby bistros,* small, relaxed eateries whose menus are designed by the biggest names in the business but the prices are up to 75 percent below what you'd pay in these chefs' flagship restaurants.

French cheese is justifiably famous, with softies brie and Camembert and blue-veined Roquefort topping the list. There's no way I can fully cover French wines here, but your waiter or the restaurant's wine steward should be able to pair your meal with an appropriate vintage. Better yet, check out *Wine For Dummies,* 3rd Edition, by Ed McCarthy and Mary Ewing-Mulligan (Wiley Publishing). Ordering wine by the bottle can jack up the cost of your meal in no time, so be careful. Table wine by the liter carafe or *demi* (half a liter) is always cheaper. The top reds are produced in Bordeaux, Burgundy, Beaujolais, and the Loire and Rhone valleys (*Red Wine For Dummies* [Wiley] is a great reference). Great whites hail from Alsace, the Loire, Burgundy, and Bordeaux (consult *White Wine For Dummies* [Wiley] for more information). And don't forget that sparkling white wine from the vineyards east of Paris called Champagne; for more, check out *Champagne For Dummies* by Ed McCarthy (Wiley).

Some people may be intimidated by the idea of sitting down to what many consider the most refined food on the planet. Don't sweat it. The only people with a need to impress anyone are the chef and kitchen staff. Have your waiter suggest some dishes, and then just sit back and enjoy the flavors.

 If you're looking for a meal in a hurry, try Paris's greatest street food, crêpes, sold at sidewalk stands and from store windows. They're best when cooked fresh on the spot for you, but in touristy areas, crêpe stands often make up stacks in advance and merely reheat them on the griddle when you approach. The cheapest, and in my opinion best, is *au beurre et sucre* (with butter and sugar), although you may prefer Nutella (a hazelnut-chocolate spread) and banana, or ham and cheese.

You can visit a supermarket or gourmet store for your picnic supplies, but shopping at the little local food stores and street markets is more fun. Pick up a baguette at the *boulangerie* (bakery), cured meats and the like at a *charcuterie,* and other groceries at an *épicerie.* Top it all off with some fruit, pastries from a pâtisserie, a bottle of wine, and you're set.

Paris's top restaurants

Au Bascou
$$ Le Marais (3e)   BASQUE

In a simple and softly lit rustic interior, Jean-Guy Loustau serves up perhaps the best Basque dishes in the capital. (The Basque are a people from southern France/northern Spain known for their distinct dialect and excellent culinary skills.) Consider starting with a piperade basquaise (a light terrine of eggs, tomatoes, and spices) before moving on to roast wild duck or rabbit in a red-wine sauce. The light, flavorful Basque wines are a perfect accompaniment. Service is snappy, so you may want to save this place for a night when you don't want to linger over dinner.

See map p. 230. 38 rue Réaumur (between rue du Temple and rue de Turbigo). ☎ *01-42-72-69-25. Reservations recommended. Métro: Artes et Metiers. Main courses: 15€ ($17). AE, MC, V. Open: Lunch and dinner Mon–Fri, dinner Sat.*

Bofinger
$ The Marais (4e)   ALSATIAN

A brasserie is somewhere between a cafe and a restaurant, with great low prices and a cuisine usually based on the Franco-Germanic cooking of the Alsace region — lots of *choucroute* (sauerkraut, usually served with sausages or salamis). They're also good for off-hours dining, tending to stay open until 1 a.m. The first, and still the best, is Bofinger, opened in 1864 and sporting a restored 1919 Art Deco décor. Service can be whirlwind.

See map p. 230. 5–7 rue de la Bastille (just off place de la Bastille). ☎ *01-42-72-87-82.* www.bofingerparis.com. *Reservations recommended. Métro: Bastille. Fixed-price menus: 32€ ($37), with half-bottle of wine, dinner daily and lunch Sat–Sun; 22€ ($25) lunch weekdays. AE, DC, MC, V. Open: Lunch and dinner daily.*

La Taverne du Sergent Recruteur
$$ Ile St-Louis (4e)   FRENCH

Supposedly, unscrupulous army sergeants would get potential young recruits drunk at this popular 17th-century eatery, and the saps would wake up in the barracks the next day as conscripts. These days the only danger is overeating, because the fixed-price menu gets you all you can eat from a huge basket of veggies and cured meats, bottomless glasses of wine, a selection of basic main dishes, and a cheese board. Kids tend to like the simple fare.

See map p. 230. 41 rue St-Louis-en-l'Isle (on the main drag of the Ile St-Louis, just off rue des Deux Ponts). ☎ *01-43-54-75-42.* www.lesergentrecruteur.com. *Reservations recommended. Métro: Pont-Marie. Fixed-price menu: 38€ ($44), with wine. AE, MC, V. Open: Lunch Sun, dinner daily.*

L'Epi Dupin
$ St-Germain-des-Prés (7e)   FRENCH

Seeing the success of established chefs' "baby bistros" (see the dining introduction), many young and up-and-coming chefs decided to forgo the opening-a-fancy-restaurant part of their careers and start right off with a small, informal, relatively inexpensive trendy bistro. L'Epi Dupin is still perhaps the best, with fine modern bistro cuisine in an antique French setting of hewn beams and stone walls. The food runs to ultratraditional rural French, with lighter, modern alternatives like salmon carpaccio or spit-roasted grouse. Service, though friendly, can be seriously inattentive.

See map p. 230. 11 rue de Dupin (between rue de Sèvres and rue du Cherche Midi). ☎ *01-42-22-64-56. Reservations recommended. Métro: Sèvres Babylone. Fixed-price menus: 20€ ($23) lunch, 30€ ($35) dinner. AE, MC, V. Open: Lunch Tues–Fri, dinner Mon–Fri.*

Les Bouquinistes
$$ St-Germain-des-Prés (6e) FRENCH

About a decade ago, a tired haute scene and French recession teamed up to inspire top chefs to branch out into what have become known as baby bistros (see the dining introduction for more info). Renowned chef Guy Savoy spun off several successful little spots, the best of which is this Seine-side contemporary dining room with a constantly changing menu that hints at a Mediterranean touch.

See map p. 230. 53 quai des Grands-Augustins (at rue des Grands-Augustins). ☎ 01-43-25-45-94. www.lesbouquinistes.com. *Reservations required. Métro: Saint-Michel. Main courses: 18€–30€ ($21–$35). Fixed-price menus: 24€–27€ ($28–$31). AE, MC, V. Open: Lunch Mon–Fri, dinner Mon–Sat.*

Restaurant Plaza Athénée (Alain Ducasse)
$$$$$ Champs-Elysées (8e) FRENCH (MODERN/TRADITIONAL)

Few other chefs in the history of French cuisine enjoy the international fame of Alain Ducasse. This 5-star Michelin chef divides his time between Paris and Monaco. He seeds his dishes with produce from every corner of France — rare local vegetables, fish from the coasts, and dishes incorporating cardoons, turnips, celery, turbot, cuttlefish, and Bresse fowl. His French cuisine is contemporary and Mediterranean, yet not nouvelle cuisine. Although many dishes are light, Ducasse isn't afraid of lard, as he proves with his thick, oozing slabs of pork grilled to a crisp.

See map p. 230. In the Hotel Plaza Athénée, 25 av. Montaigne. ☎ 01-53-67-65-00. www.alain-ducasse.com. *Métro: FDR or Alma-Marceau. Reservations required. Main courses 70€–115€ ($81–$132); fixed-price menus 190€–300€ ($219–$345). AE, DC, MC, V. Open: Lunch Thurs–Fri, dinner Mon–Fri. Closed mid-July to mid-Aug and Dec 21–31.*

Taillevent
$$$$$ Champs-Elysées (8e) FRENCH

For tradition and a cuisine so scrupulously haute it belongs in a museum, you can do no better than Taillevent, named after France's first great chef and cookbook author (a 14th-century alchemist). The refined atmosphere is unobtrusive, so you can devote all your attentions to the creations of Jean-Claude Vrinat, who runs one of the foremost kitchens in town and is constantly incorporating the best of new trends into his art. Monsieur Vrinat was the restaurant's sommelier when his father was chef, and Taillevent's wine list is perhaps the best in Paris.

See map p. 230. 15 rue Lamennais (4 blocks form the Arc de Triomphe off av. de Friedland). ☎ 01-44-95-15-01. www.taillevent.com. *Reservations required weeks in advance, months if you can swing it. Métro: George-V. Main courses: 42€–88€ ($48–$101); fixed-price menus 70€–180€ ($81–$207). AE, DC, MC, V. Open: Lunch and dinner Mon–Fri. Closed last week in July and first three weeks of Aug.*

Thoumieux

$$$$ Les Invalides (7e) SOUTHWESTERN FRENCH

The star attraction here is the stunning Art Deco interior, its mirrors, wood, red banquettes, and white linen forming an elegant setting for a lively mix of tourists, neighborhood yuppies, and French families from the provinces. The excellent-value 14€ ($16) lunch menu offers dishes only the French can stomach, like *boudin* (blood sausage) and *tripes* (intestines), as well as more palatable lamb curry. On the à la carte menu, the duck dishes are the best, especially the *cassoulet*. Cozy **Café Thomieux**, next door, offers a mixture of French and Spanish tapas.

See map p. 230. 79 rue St-Dominique. ☎ *01-47-05-49-75.* www.thoumieux.com. *Métro: Invalides or Latour Maubourg. Reservations recommended. Main courses: 17€–48€ ($20–$55); fixed-price lunch menu 14€ ($16), fixed-price dinner menu 28€ ($32). AE, MC, V. Open lunch and dinner daily.*

Paris's runner-up restaurants

Brasserie Balzar

$ Latin Quarter (5e) Brasserie Balzar is the place to go for French comfort food at reasonable prices in the same worn, century-old environment enjoyed by the likes of Sartre, Camus, and James Thurber. *See map p. 230. 49 rue des Écoles (at rue d'Ulm).* ☎ *01-43-54-13-67.* www.brasseriebalzar.com.

Brasserie Lipp

$$ St-Germain-des-Prés (6e) Brasserie Lipp is Paris's most famous brasserie, opened in 1880 and a haven for intellectuals, artists, writers, politicos, and American expatriates who try to relive the times Hemingway sat at Lipp's dreaming up stories. It's very popular with Parisian businesspeople at lunch, so come around noon to secure a table. *See map p. 230. 151 bd. St-Germain (near the corner with rue de Rennes).* ☎ *01-45-48-53-91.* www.brasserie-lipp.fr.

Buddha Bar

$$$ Champs-Elysées (8e) Although no longer the hottest ticket in town, the funky Buddha Bar is still a see-and-be-seen joint, with good people-watching to accompany its French–Pacific Rim fusion cuisine. *See map p. 230. 8 rue Boissy d'Anglais.* ☎ *01-53-05-90-00.* www.buddha-bar.com.

Chantairelle

$$ Latin Quarter (5e) The Chantairelle is a quirky spot to sample the cooking of the wild Auvergne region, with piped-in bird song and a boutique of regional products; book ahead for a table on the pretty little flagstone garden out back. *See map p. 230. 17 rue Laplace.* ☎ *01-46-33-18-59.* www.chantairelle.com.

Man Ray

$$$ **Champs-Elysées (8e)**   Trendy Man Ray, co-owned by a Paris night-club impresario, Sean Penn, and Johnny Depp, offers a varied menu that borrows heavily from Asian and Mediterranean kitchens. *See map p. 230. 34 rue Marbeuf.* ☎ *01-56-88-36-36.* www.manray.info.

Restaurant Perraudin

$ **Latin Quarter (5e)**   This restaurant fills up early with hungry travelers and locals who come for the inexpensive classic bistro fare served in a convivial, wood-beamed atmosphere. *See map p. 230. 157 rue St-Jacques.* ☎ *01-46-33-15-75.*

Exploring Paris

By far Paris's best buy is the **Carte Musées et Monuments (**☎ **01-44-61-96-60)**, a pass that lets you into most Parisian sights free (the only notable exceptions are the **Eiffel and Montparnasse towers** and the **Marmottan** museum). The pass costs 18€ ($20) for one day — you save money if you visit just the **Louvre,** the **Musée d'Orsay,** and one other museum. You can also get a three-day/36€ ($41) or five-day/54€ ($62) version. The biggest benefit is that you don't have to wait in line! You just saunter up to a sep-arate window, and they wave you through. You can buy the pass at any train station, tourist office, main Métro station, or participating sights. For more info, visit the InterMusées Web site at www.intermusees.com — though sometimes that site doesn't work (in which case you can get much of the information at the Paris transport site www.ratp.fr).

Paris's top sights

Cathédrale de Notre-Dame (Notre-Dame Cathedral)
Ile de la Cité (4e)

"Our Lady of Paris" is the heart and soul of the city, a monument to Paris's past slung in the cradle of its origins. The 12th- to 14th-century cathedral is a study in gothic beauty and gargoyles, at once solid with squat, square facade towers and graceful with flying buttresses around the sides. It's been remodeled, embellished, ransacked, and restored so often that it's a wonder it still has any architectural integrity at all (during the Revolution, it was even stripped of its religion and rechristened the Temple of Reason).

Visiting Notre-Dame takes a good hour to 90 minutes out of your day. The lines are long to get in, but at least while you wait you have time to admire the Bible stories played out in intricate stone relief around the three great portals on the facade. Much of the facade was (poorly) restored once in the 18th century and then again (as well as could be done) in the 19th. If you're keen to see some medieval originals, the upper tier of the central portal is ancient, and much of the sculpture on the right-hand portal has also survived from 1165 to 1175.

The main draw, however, is the three enormous rose windows, especially the 69-foot diameter north window (left transept), which has retained almost all its original 13th-century stained glass. Save Notre-Dame for a sunny day to see the best light effects.

No visit to Notre-Dame is complete without tackling the 387 steps up the north tower (give it at least 45 minutes) to examine those grotesque, amusing, or sometimes downright frightening gargoyles — a safe thrill for kids who can manage the walk. One last thing you shouldn't forget to do is to walk around the building. Those famous flying buttresses at the very back, holding up the apse with 50-foot spans of stone strength, are particularly impressive. Cross the Seine to admire the entire effect from the quay on the Left Bank. Free (donation appreciated) guided tours in English depart on Wednesday and Thursday at noon, and on Saturday at 2:30 p.m.

At the opposite end of the square from the cathedral, a flight of steps leads down to the **Archaeological Crypt** (☎ 01-43-29-83-51 or 01-55-42-50-10; www.paris.fr/musees/musee_carnavalet), a 260-foot gallery extending under Notre-Dame's square. This excavation includes the jumbled foundations, streets, and walls of a series of Parises, including the medieval and Roman cities. You can even see a house from *Lutèce* — the town built by the Celtic *Parisii* tribe that flourished on the Ile de la Cité over 2,000 years ago. The crypt is open Tuesday to Sunday from 10 a.m. to 6 p.m. (to 5 p.m. in winter); admission is 3.30€ ($3.80).

See map p. 230. Place du Parvis de Notre-Dame, on Ile de la Cité. ☎ *01-42-34-56-10. www.cathedralenotredamedeparis.com. Métro: Cité. Admission: Cathedral is free; towers are 5.50€ ($6.30) adults, 4.50€ ($5.20) students 12–25, free for children under 12; the crypt rates are the same as the towers. Open: Cathedral, Mon–Fri 8 a.m.–6:45 p.m., Sat–Sun 8 a.m.–7:45 p.m. (closed Sat 12:30–2 p.m.; Sun, open for Mass only 9:30 a.m.–2 p.m.); treasury, Mon–Sat 9:30–11:30 a.m. and 1–5:45 p.m.; towers, Apr–June and Sept 9:30 a.m.–7:30 p.m., Oct–Mar 10 a.m.–5:30 p.m., and July–Aug 9 a.m.–7:30 p.m.; crypt, Apr–Sept daily 9:30–11:30 a.m. and 1–6:30 p.m., Oct–Mar daily 10 a.m.–5 p.m.; museum, Wed and Sat–Sun 2:30–6 p.m.*

Centre Pompidou
The Marais (4e)

The Pompidou is Paris's homage to 20th-century creativity. Aside from the gallery of modern art, you find exhibits on industrial design, music research, photography, and the history of film. The cafeteria on the top floor has some fantastic views.

Even if you don't want to spend an hour or two with the exhibits inside, come by to shake your head at the wildly colorful and controversial transparent inside-out architecture — which was outrageously avant-garde in the 1970s, but by 1998 had deteriorated so badly they had to shut it down for 18 months of repairs — and to enjoy Paris's best street performers on the sloping square out front.

See map p. 230. Place Georges Pompidou. ☎ *01-44-78-12-33. www.centre pompidou.fr. Métro: Rambuteau. Admission: Free admission to main level; museum only 7€ ($8.05) adults, 5€ ($5.75) students ages 18–25, free for ages 17 and under;*

entire center 10€ ($12) adults, 8€ ($9.20) students ages 18–25, free for ages 17 and under; or free with the Carte Musées et Monuments (see "Exploring Paris"). Open: Wed–Mon 11 a.m.–9 p.m. Public areas of the center (not the museum) stay open until 10 p.m. Last admission 8 p.m.

Musée d'Orsay
St-Germain-des-Prés (7e)

In 1986, Paris consolidated most of its collections of French art from 1848 to World War I in the most unlikely of spots: an old converted train station. Although the Orsay has earlier works by the likes of Ingres and Delacroix, its biggest draw is undoubtedly those crowd-pleasing Impressionists.

Many of the works are so widely reproduced that you may wander through with an eerie feeling of déjà vu. Degas's ballet dancers and *l'Absinthe;* Monet's women in a poppy field, his *Rouen Cathedral* painted under five different lighting conditions, and his giant *Blue Waterlilies;* van Gogh's *Restaurant de la Siréne,* self-portraits, peasants napping against a haystack, and *Bedroom at Arles; Whistler's Mother;* and Manet's groundbreaking *Picnic on the Grass* and *Olympia,* which together helped throw off the shackles of artistic conservatism and gave Impressionism room to take root.

Add in a generous helping of Cézanne, Gauguin, Rodin, Toulouse-Lautrec, Pissaro, and Seurat, and you could easily spend a full day exploring this museum, although a *quick* run through the highlights would only take around two hours.

See map p. 230. 1 rue Bellechasse or 62 rue de Lille. ☎ *01-40-49-48-14.* www.musee-orsay.fr. *Métro: Solférino. RER: Musée-d'Orsay. Admission: 7€ ($8.05) adults, 5€ ($5.75) ages 18–24 and for everyone after 6:15 p.m. Sun; free for ages 17 and under, for everyone on the first Sun of each month, or with the Carte Musées et Monuments (see "Exploring Paris"). Open: Tues–Wed and Fri–Sat 10 a.m.–6 p.m., Thurs 10 a.m.–9:45 p.m., Sun 9 a.m.–6 p.m. June 21–Sept 30, museum opens at 9 a.m. Last admission is 30 minutes before close.*

Musée du Louvre (Louvre Museum)
Louvre (1er)

The Grand Louvre — a former royal palace opened to the public as an art gallery when the French Revolution struck — has 195,000 square feet of galleries, 5 million visitors annually, and more than 30,000 works on display spanning three millennia. Besides one of the world's top painting galleries, the Louvre also houses a remarkable collection of antiquities from Greece, Etruria, Rome, Egypt, and the Orient; a sculpture section that boasts two of Michelangelo's *Slaves;* and a fine decorative-arts division.

A massive reorganization has opened up even more display space than ever before. It would take about three days to properly scratch the surface of all seven departments. Heck, it takes at least half a day merely to walk through the halls to see da Vinci's enigmatically smiling *Mona Lisa,* that armless beauty *Venus de Milo,* and the dramatic *Winged Victory of Samothrace* — just the three most famous of many instantly recognizable artistic icons that call the Louvre home.

 The floor plans and information desks on site can help you get a handle on the basic layout and plan your visit. The Louvre's problem — not a bad one to have — is that too many masterpieces fill the galleries. On a first visit, you may need to ignore most of the works you're passing — pieces that could be the pride of a lesser museum — in order to devote your art-appreciation energies to the greatest hits.

The highlights include an incredible five more da Vinci paintings (the *Virgin of the Rocks* is stupendous), fragments from the Parthenon, Ingres's *The Turkish Bath*, Veronese's enormous *Wedding Feast at Cana*, Vermeer's delicate *Lacemaker*, self-portraits by Dürer and Rembrandt, Uccello's odd *Battle of San Romano*, Géricault's dramatic *Raft of the Medusa*, and David's ceremonious *Coronation of Napoléon I*. If you have the time, try to take in the Louvre over several visits.

In November 2005, *Mona Lisa* will be moved to a gallery of her own, part of a $4.5-million refurbishment. At that time, officials will begin conducting tests, including X-rays, to check the condition of the painting (the poplar wood on which it is painted has become more warped over time and a brace on the back of the painting prevents a small crack from worsening). The work should occur when the museum is closed, allowing *Mona Lisa* to remain on display throughout the tests.

See map p. 230. You enter the Louvre through the glass pyramid in the Cour Napoléon courtyard, between the qaui du Louvre and rue de Rivoli. ☎ 01-40-20-53-17 for the information desk, or 08-92-68-46-94 to order tickets. www.louvre.fr. *Métro: Palais-Royal-Musée du Louvre. Admission: 8.50€ ($9.80) before 6 p.m., 6€ ($6.90) after 6 p.m.; free for ages 17 and under. Free for everyone (but crowded) the first Sun of each month, for 25 and under after 6 p.m. on Mon, or with the Carte Musées et Monuments (see "Exploring Paris"). Open: Thurs–Sun 9 a.m.–6 p.m.; Wed 9 a.m.–9:45 p.m., Mon 9 a.m.–6 p.m., plus main galleries until 9:45 p.m. The entrance/entresol, with its information desks, medieval Louvre exhibit, cafes, post office, and shops, stays open daily until 9:45 p.m.*

Musée Picasso *(Picasso Museum)*
The Marais (3e)

Picasso left some $50 million in French inheritance taxes when he died. The state instead accepted 203 paintings, 177 sculptures, and thousands of sketches and engravings. The good news is that this is one of the most representative collections of Picasso's works in the world, spanning his entire career. The bad news is that the space is much smaller than the collection (hence only a 30- to 45-minute diversion), and with the constant rotation of works, you never know whether you'll get to see masterpieces such as *Le Baiser, Pan Flute, Two Women Running Along the Beach, The Crucifixion,* or *Nude in a Red Armchair.*

See map p. 230. 5 rue de Thorigny (in the Hôtel Salé). ☎ 01-42-71-25-21. www.museepicasso.fr. *Métro: Chemin-Vert, St-Paul, or Filles du Calvaire. Admission: 5.50€ ($6.30) adults, 4€ ($4.60) ages 18–25 and for everyone Sun, free for ages 18 and under* *or with the Carte Musées et Monuments (see "Exploring Paris"). Admission during special exhibitions may be slightly higher. Open: Apr–Sept Wed–Mon 9:30 a.m.– 6 p.m.; Oct–Mar Wed–Mon 9:30 a.m.–5:30 p.m.*

Musée Rodin (Rodin Museum)
Les Invalides (7e)

After the critics stopped assailing Rodin's art, they realized he had been the greatest sculptor since Michelangelo, and the studio where Rodin worked from 1908 until his death in 1917 was opened as a museum to house some of the artist's greatest works. In the rose gardens you find *The Thinker, The Gate of Hell, The Burghers of Calais,* and *Balzac.* Inside are many famed sculptures — *The Kiss, The Three Shades, The Hand of God, Iris* — along with some of Rodin's drawings and works by his friends and contemporaries. You can see the whole place in 45 minutes.

See map p. 230. 77 rue de Varenne (in the Hôtel Biron). ☎ *01-44-18-61-10.* www. musee-rodin.fr. *Métro: Varenne or St François Xavier. Admission: 5€ ($5.75) adults, 3€ ($3.45) ages 18–26 and for everyone Sun; free for ages 17 and under or with the Carte Musées et Monuments (see "Exploring Paris"). Open: Apr–Sept Tues–Sun 9:30 a.m.–5:45 p.m.; Oct–Mar Tues–Sun 9:30 a.m.–4:45 p.m. Last admission 30 minutes before close.*

Sainte-Chapelle
Ile de la Cité (4e)

The interior of this tiny Gothic chapel, almost entirely hidden by the bulk of the Palace of Justice surrounding it, is a sculpture of light and color. The thin bits of stone that hold the tall stained-glass windows and brace the roof seem to dissolve in the diffuse and dappled brightness glowing through the 13th-century windows. Stopping here provides the most ethereal 20 minutes you can spend in Paris. The chapel was built in 1246 to house the Crown of Thorns.

See map p. 230. 4 bd. du Palais (in the Palais de Justice on the Ile de la Cité). ☎ *01-53-40-60-80.* www.monum.fr. *Métro: Cité, Châtelet–Les-Halles, or St-Michel. RER: St-Michel. Admission: 5.50€ ($6.30) adults, 3.50€ ($4) ages 18–25; free for children 17 and under and with the Carte Musées et Monuments (see "Exploring Paris"). Open: Daily 9:30 a.m.–6 p.m. Closed major holidays.*

Tour Eiffel (Eiffel Tower)
Les Invalides (7e)

Looking like two sets of train tracks that crashed into each other, Gustave Alexandre Eiffel's tower rises 1,056 feet above the banks of the Seine. The man who gave the Statue of Liberty a backbone designed this quintessential Parisian symbol merely as a temporary exhibit for the Exhibition of 1899 and managed to rivet together all 7,000 tons of it (with 2.5 million rivets) in under two years. Fortunately for the French postcard industry, the tower's usefulness as a transmitter of telegraph — and later, radio and TV — signals saved it from demolition.

Critics of the day assailed its aesthetics, but no one could deny the feat of engineering. The tower remained the tallest man-made structure in the world until the Chrysler Building stole the title in 1930, and its engineering advances paved the way for the soaring skyscraper architecture of the 20th century. The restaurants and bars on the first level are pricey, but not bad. The view from the second level is an intimate bird's-eye view of Paris; from the fourth level, you can see the entire city spread out below and, on a good day, as far out as 42 miles. Visibility is usually best near sunset; pausing for vistas at all levels takes about 90 minutes.

See map p. 230. Champs-de-Mars. ☎ *01-44-11-23-23.* www.tour-eiffel.fr. *Métro: Trocadéro, Ecole-Militaire, Bir-Hakeim. RER: Champ-de-Mars–Tour Eiffel. Admission: First landing, 4€ ($4.60) adults, 2.20€ ($2.50) children under 12; second landing, 7.30€ ($8.40) adults, 4€ ($4.60) children under 12; to highest level 10.40€ ($12) adults, 5.70€ ($6.55) children under 12; stairs to second floor, 3.50€ ($4). Open: June 19–Aug 29 daily 9:30 a.m. to midnight; Aug 30–June 18 9:30 a.m.–11 p.m (but stairs close at 6:30 p.m.).*

More cool things to see and do

✔ **Squandering the day away in a cafe:** Many European cultures have a third place, between home and work, where citizens play out their lives. In Paris, it's the cafe, a sort of public extension of the living room. In the cafe, you can sit all day over a single cup of coffee or order a light meal or a flute of champagne. Ensconce yourself indoors or stand at the bar, but most people choose to sit outside — in a glassed-in porch in winter or on the sidewalk in summer — because one of the cafe's biggest attractions is the people-watching. Here are some classic cafes: **Les Deux Magots** (☎ 01-45-48-55-25; www.lesdeuxmagots.fr), 6 place St-Germain-des-Prés, established in 1885, was the haunt of Picasso, Hemingway, and Sartre. Sartre wrote a whole trilogy holed up at a table in **Café de Flore** (☎ 01-45-48-55-26; www.cafe-de-flore.com), 172 bd. St-Germain-des-Pres, a Left Bank cafe frequented by Camus and Picasso and featured in Gore Vidal novels. The Champs-Elysées may no longer be Paris's hot spot, but **Fouquet's** (☎ 01-47-23-70-60) at no. 99 is still going strong based on its reputation, good food, and favorable reviews by Chaplin, Churchill, FDR, and Jacqueline Kennedy Onassis.

Henry Miller had his morning porridge at **La Coupole** (☎ 01-43-20-14-20; www.coupoleparis.com), 102 bd. du Montparnasse, a brasserie that also hosted the likes of Josephine Baker, John Dos Passos, Dalí, and F. Scott Fitzgerald. Finally, you can make a pilgrimage to the Art Nouveau interiors of the new **La Rotonde** (☎ 01-43-26-68-84), 105 bd. du Montparnasse, risen like a phoenix from the ashes of its namesake that once stood here. In *The Sun Also Rises,* Hemingway writes of the original, "No matter what cafe in Montparnasse you ask a taxi driver to bring you to . . . they always take you to the Rotonde."

✔ **Paying homage to the cultural giants at Cimetière du Père-Lachaise (Père-Lachaise Cemetery):** Chopin, Gertrude Stein, Delacroix, Proust, Rossini, Oscar Wilde, Georges Bizet, Ingres, Isadora Duncan, Pissaro, Molière, Edith Piaf, Modigliani, and The Doors' Jim Morrison — you couldn't imagine most of these people getting together in life, but they fit well together in death. Pick up the map of the graves and spend a morning under the trees of this vast and romantic cemetery of rolling hills and historic tombs. To get there, take the Métro to Père-Lachaise.

✔ **Strolling through Montmartre, the original bohemian 'hood:** Although inundated by tourists these days, Montmartre, an old artists' neighborhood crowning a hill at Paris's northern edge (the 18e), still has an intriguing village flavor. The Abbesses Métro stop is in Montmartre itself, but get off one stop early at Pigalle.

Here you're on the northwest edge of Paris's red-light district centered on the sex shop–lined boulevard de Clichy, which features such hangers-on as the **Moulin Rouge** at no. 87 (☎ **01-53-09-82-82;** www.moulinrouge.com) with its can-can shows celebrated in the 2001 movie of the same name, and the surprisingly quasitasteful **Musée de l'Erotisme** (Museum of the Erotic) at no. 72 (☎ **01-42-58-28-73**), which is open from 10 a.m. to 2 a.m.; admission is 7€ ($8.05).

Work your way uphill to the **Basilique du Sacré-Coeur** (☎ 01-53-41-89-00; www.sacre-coeur-montmartre.com), a frosty white neo-Byzantine basilica built from 1876 to 1919 and towering over the city. Climb the dome for a vista that on clear days extends 35 miles.

Some of Montmartre's quirkiest sights include a pair of windmills, visible from rue Lepic and rue Girardon, and Paris's only vineyard, on rue des Saules. Next door to the latter, at rue Saint-Vincent 12, is the **Musée de Vieux Montmartre** (Museum of Old Montmartre; ☎ 01-46-06-61-11), dedicated to the neighborhood in a house that was at times occupied by van Gogh, Renoir, and Utrillo.

Pay your respects to the writers Stendhal and Dumas, the composers Offenbach and Berlioz, and the painter Degas at their graves in the **Cimetière de Montmartre** on avenue Rachel. Finish the evening at 22 rue des Saules in **Au Lapin Agile** (☎ 01-46-06-85-87; www.au-lapin-agile.com) — in Picasso and Utrillo's day called *Café des Assassins*. The cover, including first drink, is a steep 24€ ($28).

✔ **Window-shopping with the best of them:** Paris is a world shopping capital. On boulevard Haussmann rise Paris's two flagships of shopping, the department stores **Au Printemps** (no. 64) and **Galeries Lafayette** (no. 40). Au Printemps is a bit more modern and American-styled, and Galeries Lafayette is more Old World French, but both are very upscale and carry the ready-to-wear collections of all the major French designers and labels.

If you prefer to shop boutiques, the best concentrations of stores are in the adjoining 1er and 8e. No single street offers more shops than the long rue du Faubourg St-Honoré/rue St-Honoré and its tributaries. Even if you can't afford the prices, having a look is fun. Big fashion houses such as **Hermès** (no. 24) hawk ties and scarves, **Au Nain Blue** (no. 406) has one of the fanciest toy emporiums in the world, and the prices at **La Maison du Chocolat** (no. 225) are as rich as the confections.

Window-shop for leather at **Didier Lamarthe** (no. 219) or **Longchamp** (no. 390) or for cutting-edge fashion at **Hervé Léger** (no. 29). At **Anna Lowe** (no. 104), women can find runway samples and slightly worn creations of the big names at a discount. **Réciproque,** 89–123 rue de la Pompe, 16e, has bargains on a remarkably wide range of the big labels and top designers.

Some of the best food shopping is concentrated on place de la Madeleine, 26e, home to **Fauchon,** Paris's homage to the finest edibles money can buy (although it faces serious competition from neighbor **Hediard,** at no. 21). Don't forget your Paris outlet for caviar, truffles, foie gras, and other pâtés: **Maison de la Truffe.** Jewels glitter on place **Vendôme,** 1er, at **Cartier** (no. 23), **Chaumet** (no. 12), and **Van Cleef & Arpels** (no. 22). Stink like the best of them with discounts on French perfumes at **Parfumerie de la Madeleine,** 9 place de la Madeleine, 8e, or **Michel Swiss,** upstairs at 16 rue de la Paix, 2e.

✔ **Having a flea market fling:** If the prices at **Cartier, Hermès,** and the like set your head to spinning, you may have more luck at the **Marché aux Puces de Saint-Ouen/Clignancourt,** the city's most famous flea market (open Sat–Mon). It's a group of several markets comprising almost 3,000 stalls, all along avenue de la Porte de Clignancourt.

Usually Monday is the best day to get a bargain, because the crowds are fewer and vendors are anxious for the dough. Keep in mind, though, that you can get a better price if you speak French and show that you're serious about and respectful of the merchandise.

Hours vary with the weather and the crowds, but stalls are usually up and running between 7:30 a.m. and 6:00 p.m. Take the Métro to Porte de Clignancourt; from there, turn left and cross boulevard Ney, and then walk north on avenue de la Porte de Clignancourt.

✔ **Cruising the Seine:** Is there anything more romantic than slipping down the current of one of the world's great rivers past 18th-century palaces? Well, perhaps killing the canned P.A. sightseeing commentary and getting rid of all the other camera-clicking tourists would help the romantic mood, but if it's mood you're after you can always take a more refined dinner cruise.

The classic *Bateaux-Mouches* float down the Seine is offered by several companies, the biggest being **Bateaux Parisiens** (☎ 01-44-11-33-44; www.bateauxparisiens.com), which departs from quai

Montebello or from pont d'Iena at the foot of the Eiffel Tower, and **Les Vedette du Pont-Neuf** (☎ 01-46-33-98-38), which leaves from Pont Neuf on the Ile de la Cité. Vessels depart every half hour (fewer in winter). Regular one-hour trips with multilingual commentary cost 9.50€ ($11) per adult, 4.50€ ($5.20) children ages 3 to 12; children under 3 ride free.

After dark, the boats sweep both banks with mega-powered flood-lights — illuminating everything very well, but sort of spoiling the romance. These tend to be touristy, too, unless you opt for a more refined and romantic luncheon or dinner cruise, which are more expensive — 50€ to 70€ ($58–$81) for lunch cruises and 90€ to 125€ ($104–$144) for jacket-and-tie dinner cruises, and the food is only so-so. The setting, however, can't be beat.

A cheaper, and less-contrived, alternative to the daytime tour is the **Batobus** (☎ 01-44-11-33-99; www.batobus.com), a kind of water taxi (no piped-in commentary) that stops every 25 minutes at eight major points of interest: the **Eiffel Tower**, the **Musée d'Orsay**, **St-Germain-des-Prés**, **Notre-Dame**, the **Jardin des Plantes**, **Hôtel de Ville**, **Louvre**, and the **Champs-Élysées**. A day ticket costs 11€ ($13) per adult or 5€ ($5.75) for ages 3 to 11; "short-trip" tickets with a maximum of four stops cost 7.50€ ($8.60) each for adults and 3.50€ ($4) for children. Batobus runs every 15 to 25 minutes April to November from 10 a.m. to 7 p.m. and until 9 p.m. May through August. In winter, Batobus runs every half hour from 10:30 a.m. to 4:40 p.m.

✔ **Paying a visit to le Mickey:** Contrary to popular belief, **Disneyland Paris** (☎ 407-934-7639 in the United States, 01-60-30-60-53 in Paris; www.disneylandparis.com) has been a fantastic success. More visitors head here than to the Louvre. The theme park, a slightly Europeanized version of California's Disneyland with both familiar and new versions of rides and those contrived cultural areas, has been inundated with guests since its opening day. Early financial troubles occurred when more people than expected stayed in Paris rather than in the Disney hotels.

To get there, take the A line RER from Gare de Lyon to Marne-la-Vallée/Chessy, within walking distance of the park. The RER station is in Zone 5 of the public-transport system, so the cheapest way there (and back again) is to buy a single-day Mobilis pass good through Zone 5, which costs 12€ ($14). Admission to the park is a whomping 40€ ($46) adults and 30€ ($35) children 3 to 11; children under 3 are admitted free. From January 6 to April 4, fees are 27€ ($31) adults and 23€ ($26) children 4 to 11; free for children 3 and under. The hours of Disneyland Paris vary with the weather and season, so call before setting out. In general, however, the park is open from 9 a.m. to 8 p.m. daily. It sometimes opens an hour later in mid-May, mid-June, and September and October.

Guided tours

The top tour-bus company in town is Grayline's **Cityrama** (☎ 01-44-55-61-00; www.cityrama.com), which does a two-hour, top sights tour daily at 10 and 11 a.m. and 2 and 3 p.m.; the cost is 24€ ($28) adults, free for children under 12 riding with two accompanying parents. Cityrama also offers a full-day "Paris Artistic/Historic" tour of **Notre-Dame** and the **Louvre** for 74€ ($85), 37€ ($43) ages 4 to 11, free for children 3 and under. Tours are available Monday and Wednesday through Saturday at 9:15 a.m. The "Seinorama" tour (daily at 2 p.m.) lasts four hours and includes a drive up the **Champs-Élysées,** a one-hour Seine cruise, and a hot drink on the second-floor restaurant of the **Eiffel Tower.** It costs 53€ ($61) for adults and 26.50€ ($30) for children.

Cityrama also offers a variety of "Paris by Night" tours with bus trips around the illuminated city and perhaps a Seine Cruise; many throw in a show at the **Moulin Rouge** or dinner in the **Eiffel Tower.** Cityrama offers free pickup from some hotels, or you can meet at their office at 4 Place des Pyramids, between rue Saint-Honoré and rue de Rivoli (across from the **Louvre**).

L'Open Tour (www.ratp.fr) offers three hop-on/hop-off routes. Use your Paris Visite card to get a discount off the 24€ ($28) one-day ticket or the 26€ ($30) two-day ticket.

If you prefer a more romantic tour of the city, try a cruise along the Seine. See "More cool things to see and do," earlier in this chapter.

Finally, **Paris Walking Tours** (☎ 01-48-09-21-40; www.pariswalking tours.com) offers two-hour guided walks along such mouthwatering themes as **Hemingway's Paris,** historic **Marais,** the **Village of Montmartre, Revolutionary Paris, Art Deco Paris,** the **Latin Quarter** to the **Sorbonne,** or Masterpieces of the **Musée d'Orsay.** Consult *Time Out Paris* for the tours being offered during your visit and for where and when to meet — usually at a Métro station entrance at 10:30 a.m., and again at 2:30 p.m. They cost 10€ ($12) adults, 7€ ($8.05) students under 25, and 5€ ($5.75) children. They also offer weekend jaunts to places such as **Fontainebleau** or **Monet's Garden** at Giverny.

Suggested itineraries

If you'd rather organize your own tour and you have a limited amount of time to sample the sights of Paris, try my recommendations for hitting the highlights.

If you have one day

Paris in a day? Better start out as early as possible: Be at **Cathédrale de Notre-Dame** when it opens at 8 a.m. Spend an hour poking around inside and climbing its tower before hustling across the river to visit the **Musée du Louvre** at a dead trot. You only have time for the top stuff here; pay your respects to *Mona Lisa* and the *Venus de Milo* and have lunch in the cafeteria. Cross the Seine again to pop into the **Musée d'Orsay** and spend two hours or so admiring its horde of Impressionists and other French greats. As the sun sets over your full day in Paris, head to the **Eiffel Tower** to toast the City of Light from its heights. Descend and treat yourself to a first-class dinner to celebrate your day in one of the world capitals of cuisine.

If you have two days

Plunge right in on the morning of **Day 1** with the **Musée du Louvre.** Lunch in the cafeteria, and by midafternoon, give up on trying to see it all and hustle on over to the **Eiffel Tower** before sunset to get your requisite picture and drink in the panorama of Paris. Have a classy dinner in a fine Parisian restaurant, or dine intimately at a tiny bistro.

Be at **Cathédrale de Notre-Dame** early (8 a.m.) on **Day 2** to beat the crowds, and then clamber up the cathedral towers after they open to examine the famed gargoyles up close. Notre-Dame affords a much more intimate view across Paris than the Eiffel Tower does. When you get back to ground level, cross the square in front of the cathedral and descend into the **Archaeological Crypt** to puzzle out Paris's earliest origins.

Continue to the far end of the square for the jewel-box chapel of **Sainte-Chapelle,** hidden amidst the government buildings. Grab some lunch on your way to the **Musée Picasso.** Don't stay too long with the works of this 20th-century master (leave by no later than 2:30 p.m.) because one of Paris's biggies lies ahead: the Impressionist treasure trove of the **Musée d'Orsay.** Stay there as long as possible before heading off to dinner.

If you have three days

Spend **Day 1** and **Day 2** as I describe in the preceding section. **Day Three** is daytrip time. Catch the RER out to **Versailles** to spend a day exploring the palace to end all palaces, where a string of kings Louis held court in the powdered-wig exuberance of the 17th century. Take at least one guided tour, and save time to wander the acres of gardens.

Return to Paris by late afternoon so you can take the Métro out to the original Bohemian quarter of **Montmartre** to watch the sun set from the steps of **Sacré-Coeur.** Wander the streets, peek at windmills and vineyards, or people-watch and write postcards at a classic Parisian cafe where you can rustle up some dinner.

Traveling Beyond Paris

The daytrips from Paris are as impressive as the in-town attractions. Among the many nearby destinations, following are two that exhibit the France of old in royal and religious splendor — the palaces at **Versailles** and the marvelous cathedral at **Chartres.**

Versailles: Palace of the Sun King

Versailles, with its extravagant 17th-century palace and gardens, is Paris's best and easiest daytrip. Versailles takes up at least a whole morning and in summer is packed by 10 a.m. Either go seriously early (the grounds open at 9 a.m.), or go late — after 3:30 p.m. you pay a reduced fare, and the tour buses have cleared out. In summer especially, this strategy gives you plenty of time to tour the emptying palace and, because the grounds are open until sunset, the extensive gardens as well.

Getting there

You can zip out here in half an hour on the C RER line (you want the C5 heading to Versailles–Rive Gauche station). Versailles is in Zone 4 of the public-transport system, so the Mobilis one-day pass will run you 8.75€ ($10) — covering not just there and back but also your Métro ride to Rive Gauche. Keep in mind that it's free if you have a Eurail pass. From the train station to the palace is a 15-minute stroll, or you can take a shuttle bus.

Across avenue Charles de Gaulle from the station and to the right a smidgen is a sunken shopping center with a branch of the tourist-information office on the right-hand side (no. 10). The main tourist office, 7 rue des Réservoirs (☎ **01-39-50-36-22;** www.chateau versailles.fr), is a five-minute walk to the right of the palace's main entrance.

Seeing the sights

What started in 1624 as a hunting lodge for Louis XIII was turned by Louis XIV into a palace of truly monumental proportions and appointments over his 72-year reign (1643–1715). The Sun King made himself into an absolute monarch, the likes of which hadn't been seen since the Caesars, and he created a palace befitting his stature.

You can wander the **State Apartments, Hall of Mirrors** (where the Treaty of Versailles ending World War I was signed), and **Royal Chapel** on your own (or with an audio tour), but taking one of the guided tours is much more informative and gets you into many parts of the palace not open to the casual visitor. These tours are popular and fill up fast, so your first order of business should be to head to the tour reservations office and sign up for one. You may have to wait an hour or more, so book an even later tour and use the intervening time to explore the magnificent gardens.

Le Nôtre (who designed Greenwich Park in London and the Vatican Gardens in Rome) laid out the hundreds of acres of palace grounds in the most exacting 17th-century standards of decorative gardening. The highlights are the **Grand Canal,** two-thirds of a mile long and once plied by a small warship and Venetian gondolas; the **Grand Trianon,** a sort of palace away from home for when the king wanted a break from the main chateau; and the **Petit Trianon,** a jewel of a mansion done in fine neoclassical style.

Nearby is Marie Antoinette's fairy-tale **Hameau,** or hamlet, created so Her Majesty could enjoy a cleaned-up version of peasant life. Here the Queen fished, milked the occasional cow, and watched hired peasants lightly toil at the everyday tasks she imagined they did in the country — she even had a little "house in the faux country" built here, sort of a thatched mansion.

Versailles has complicated hours and admissions. The **château** (☎ **01-30-84-76-18**) is open Tuesday to Sunday, May through September from 9:00 a.m. to 6:30 p.m.; and October through April on the same days, but only until 5:30 p.m. Entrance to the château is 7.50€ ($8.60) adults, 5.30€ ($6.10) students. The **Grand and Petit Trianon** are open daily November through March from noon to 5:30 p.m.; and April through October from noon to 6:30 p.m. Entrance to both is 5€ ($5.75) for adults and 3€ ($3.45) for students.

The **park** and **gardens** are open year-round, from 7 a.m. in summer and 8 a.m. in winter until sunset. Although admission to the park is generally free, there is a 3€ ($3.45) fee for entry to the gardens. On Sundays in May through October, there is a weekly fountain water show accompanied by classical music that costs 5€ ($5.75) to attend. Also in summer, special nighttime displays of fireworks and illuminated fountains take place, usually on Sundays. Call ☎ **01-39-50-36-22** for more information on both summertime spectacles.

You can buy your tickets online at www.chateauversailles.fr; e-ticket holders can use a special express line and skip the long wait for tickets.

There are five to nine **guided visits** offered (a few are in French only and the tour of the garden's groves runs only in summer). Standard tours of the chateau book early; go directly to entrance D upon your arrival to book a space. If you're interested in a more in-depth and themed tour, call ☎ 01-30-83-77-89 or visit www.chateauversailles.fr to see what's scheduled. The straightforward tours cost an additional 4€ to 6€ ($4.60–$6.90); themed tours vary in price.

Chartres Cathedral: A Gothic masterpiece

The French sculptor Rodin dubbed this building "The Acropolis of France." "Chartres is no place for an atheist," declared Napoléon upon laying eyes on this greatest of High Gothic cathedrals (still the fourth largest church in the world). Perhaps the would-be emperor had been moved by the ethereal world of colored light that fills the cathedral on a sunny day, streaming through an awe-inspiring 3,000 square yards of 12th- and 13th-century stained glass, turning the church walls into quasi-mystical portals to heaven. Budget three-quarters of a day for Chartres, returning to Paris for dinner.

Getting there

You can see all this for a 23.60€ ($27) round-trip train ticket from Paris's Gare Montparnasse, less than an hour's ride away. The tourism office (☎ 02-37-18-26-26) is right on the place de la Cathédral.

Seeing the sights

The first **cathedral** (☎ 02-37-21-75-02; www.diocese-chartres.com) was built in the fourth century atop a Roman temple. Many historians hold that the site was religious even before the Romans invaded Gaul (Celtic France), and there's evidence that Druids worshipped in a sacred grove here centuries before Christ.

You can spend hours just scrutinizing the charismatic 12th-century sculptures adorning the main **Royal Portal,** and their 13th-century cousins around to the north and south sides of the church as well. The Royal Portal is part of the west facade, which, along with the base of the south tower, is the only part of the Romanesque church to survive an 1194 fire.

The cathedral was quickly rebuilt in the 13th century, and the rest remains an inspiring tribute to High Gothic architecture. Tear your eyes from the stained-glass inside for at least long enough to admire the 16th- to 18th-century choir screen, whose niches are filled with statuettes playing out the Life of the Virgin.

You can take an excellent guided tour in English for 6€ ($6.90) Monday through Saturday at noon or at 2:45 p.m. with Malcolm Miller, who has been doing this for more than 40 years, and has even written a book on the cathedral. Meet just inside the cathedral on the left side. Call ☎ 02-37-28-15-58 for more information. The cathedral is open daily from 8:30 a.m. to 6:45 p.m.

You can climb the tower for gargoyle close-ups Monday through Saturday from 7:30 a.m. to noon and from 2 to 7 p.m., and also on Sunday from 8:30 a.m. to noon and from 2 to 7 p.m.; admission is 4€ ($4.60) adults and 2.50€ ($2.90) ages 18 to 25; free under 18. Make time to explore the cobbled medieval streets in the *Vieux Quartiers* (old town) and visit the 16th- to 19th-century paintings in the **Musée des Beaux-Arts de Chartres** (☎ 02-37-36-41-39) at 29 Cloître Notre-Dame.

Where to stay and dine

When hunger strikes, head to the second floor of 10 rue au Lait for the tasty bistro food of **Le Buisson Ardent** (☎ 02-37-34-04-66). If you decide to make a night of it, rest your weary head for 72€ to 83€ ($83–$95) per double at the **Hôtel Châtlet,** 6–8 Jehan-de-Beauce (☎ 02-37-21-78-00; Fax: 02-37-36-23-01; www.hotelchatelet.com), where many of the antique-styled rooms have panoramic views of the cathedral.

Fast Facts: Paris

Area Code

France's country code is **33**. Calling anywhere within the country's borders requires dialing a ten-digit phone number (it already includes the city code) even if you're calling another number from within Paris. To call Paris from the United States, dial 011-33, and then drop the initial zero of the French number and dial just the remaining nine digits.

American Express

The full-service office at 11 rue Scribe (☎ 01-47-77-79-28) is open Monday through Friday from 9 a.m. to 6:30 p.m. October to April; from May to September, it's open until 7:30 p.m. The bank is also open Saturday from 9 a.m. to 5:30 p.m., but the mail-pickup window is closed.

Currency

The French franc gave way to the euro (€) in 2002. The euro is divided into 100 cents, and there are coins of .01, .02, .05, .10, .20, .50, 1, and 2. Paper-note denominations are 5, 10, 20, 50, 100, 200, and 500. The exchange rate used in this chapter is 1€ = $1.15. Amounts over $10 have been rounded to the nearest dollar.

Doctors and Dentists

SOS Médecins (☎ 01-47-07-77-77) recommends physicians. SOS Dentaire (☎ 01-43-37-51-00 or 01-42-61-12-00) will locate a dentist for you. The U.S. Embassy also provides a list of doctors.

Embassies and Consulates

The embassy of the United States, 2 av. Gabriel, 8e (☎ 01-43-12-22-22; www.amb-usa.fr; Métro: Concorde), is open Monday through Friday from 9 a.m. to 6 p.m. Passports are issued at its consulate at 2 rue St-Florentin, 1er (☎ 01-43-12-22-22 or 08-36-70-14-88; Métro: Concorde). The consulate is open Monday to Friday from 9 a.m. to 12:30 p.m. and 1 to 3 p.m.

Emergency

Dial ☎ **17** for the police. To report a fire, call ☎ **18**. If you need an ambulance, call the paramedics at the Sapeurs-Pompiers (fire department) at ☎ **18**, or ☎ **15** for SAMU (Service d'Aide Medicale d'Urgence), a private ambulance company.

Hospitals

Both the American Hospital of Paris, 63 bd. Victor-Hugo in Neuilly-sur-Seine (☎ 01-46-41-25-25; Métro: Porte Maillot), and the Hertford British Hospital, 3 rue Barbes in Levallois-Perret (☎ 01-46-39-22-22; Métro: Anatole France), are staffed by English-speaking physicians.

Information

The city's tourist-information office, Office de Tourisme de Paris, maintains two full-service welcome centers. Both offer basic information about attractions in the city, help with last-minute hotel reservations, make bookings for daytrips, and sell transportation and museum passes — but for a small fee. The first, in Gare du Nord (Métro: Gare du Nord) beneath the glass roof, is open daily from 8 a.m. to 6 p.m. The second, at 11 rue Scribe (Métro: Opéra or Chaussée d'Antin) is open Monday to Saturday from 9 a.m. to 6:30 p.m.

Several auxiliary offices are scattered throughout the city. The Eiffel Tower office (Métro: Bir Hakeim or Trocadéro) is open daily from 11 a.m. to 6 p.m., daily May to September. The office in Gare de Lyon (Métro: Gare de Lyon) is open Monday to Saturday from 8 a.m. to 6 p.m. Both the office in Montmartre, 21 place du Tertre (Métro: Abbesses), and the office in the Louvre (Métro: Palais Royal or Musée du Louvre) are open daily from 10 a.m. to 7 p.m.

To reserve tickets for shows, exhibitions, or theme parks, visit www.ticketnet.fr or call ☎ 01-46-91-58-40.

Internet Access and Cybercafes

To surf the Net or check your e-mail for free, try Le Rendez-vous Toyota, 79 av. des Champs-Elysées (☎ 01-56-89-29-79; www.lrv.toyota.fr; Métro: George-V), open Monday through Thursday from 10:30 a.m. to 9 p.m. and Friday and Saturday from 10:30 a.m. to midnight. You may face long lines at both locations, so avoid weekends and lunchtimes.

The central cybercafe Baguenaude, 30 rue de la Grande-Truanderie (☎ 01-40-26-27-74; www.labaguenaude.com), is open Monday to Friday 11 a.m. to 9:45 p.m. and Saturday 2 to 9:45 p.m. Access costs 1.50€ ($1.75) for 10 minutes 2.30€ ($2.65) for 30 minutes, and 3.80 € ($4.35) for an hour.

Maps

Actually, the map the tourist office hands out isn't half bad.

Newspapers/Magazines

Paris is home to one of Europe's greatest events/nightlife/sightseeing weeklies, called *Pariscope* (www.pariscope.fr), sold at every newsstand for 0.40€ (45¢). A competitor is *L'Officiel des Spectacles,* costing a mere 0.35€ (40¢). You may also

want to pick up the free English-language *Paris Voice* (http://parisvoice.com), which comes out every two months and is widely available at hotels.

Pharmacies

One pharmacy in each neighborhood remains open all night. One to try is the 24-hour Pharmacie Dhery, 84 av. des Champs-Elysées, 8e (☎ 01-45-62-02-41; Métro: George-V), in the Galerie des Champs-Elysées shopping center. A Left Bank option is Pharmacie des Arts, 106 bd. du Montparnasse, 14e (☎ 01-43-35-44-88; Métro: Vavin), which is open until midnight Monday to Saturday; on Sunday it closes at 9 p.m. You can also check the door of the nearest pharmacy, which posts a list of the pharmacies open at night.

Police

Dial ☎ 17 for the police.

Post Office

The most convenient post office (www.laposte.fr) is at the Louvre, 52 rue du Louvre (☎ 01-40-28-20-00), open 24 hours (all other Paris post offices are open Mon–Fri 8 a.m.–7 p.m., Sat 9 a.m. to noon).

Safety

Paris is a relatively safe city with little violent crime, but there is plenty of petty theft. Around popular tourist sites, on the Métro, and in the station corridors lurk pickpockets — often children — who aren't afraid to gang up on you, distract you by holding or waving an item near your face, and then make off with your wallet. It only takes seconds, so hold on to your wallet or purse and yell at or push away your attackers — don't hold back just because they're children. Look out for thieves around the Eiffel Tower, the Louvre, Notre-Dame, Montmartre, and other popular tourist sites.

Taxes

In France a 19.6 percent value-added tax (VAT) is figured into the price of most items. Foreign visitors can reclaim a percentage of the VAT on major purchases of consumer goods (see Chapter 4 for more on this).

Taxis

See "Getting Around Paris," earlier in this chapter.

Telephone

Public phone booths are in cafes, restaurants, Métro stations, post offices, airports, train stations, and on the streets. The only coin-operated phones, however, are in cafes and restaurants. Most public phones are now equipped to take credit cards, and most Parisians find this method the most convenient. Or you can buy a *télécarte,* a prepaid calling card priced at 3.70€ ($4.25) for a 25-*unités* card, or 7.50€ ($8.60) for 50 *unités* and available at post offices and *tabacs.* Just insert the *télécarte* and dial. For directory assistance, dial ☎ 12. To make international calls, dial ☎ 00 (double zero) to access international lines.

To charge your call to a calling card or call collect, dial AT&T at ☎ 0-800-99-0011; MCI at ☎ 0-800-99-0019; or Sprint at ☎ 0-800-99-0087. To call the United States direct from Paris, dial 00 (wait for the dial tone), and then dial 1 followed by the area code and number.

Transit Info

See "Getting Around Paris," earlier in this chapter, or call ☎ 08-92-68-41-14 (0.34€/40¢ per minute) for information in English, or consult www.ratp.fr.

Chapter 14

Amsterdam and Environs

● ●

In This Chapter

▶ Getting to Amsterdam
▶ Checking out the neighborhoods
▶ Discovering the best places to sleep and eat
▶ Exploring the city's highlights
▶ Side-tripping to Haarlem and the tulip-filled bulb belt
▶ Searching out windmills and Europe's largest sculpture garden

● ●

Considering the ages of all the great European cities, Amsterdam is rather young. Founded in 1200 as a fishing village at the mouth of the Amstel River, the city rapidly grew into the western world's trading power-house. The 17th century ushered in the Dutch Golden Age, marked by a vast trade network and the American colony of Nieuw Amsterdam (later New York), which filled its coffers while painters such as Rembrandt colored its cultural life.

Elegant, 17th-century row houses that often look impossibly tall and skinny line the canals of Amsterdam, a city of 7,000 gables. For many years, property was taxed on the width of the frontage, so people built their houses as narrowly as possible. To get more square footage out of their property, Amsterdammers extended their structures high and deep.

Following a bout with strict Protestant laws, Amsterdam became an exceedingly tolerant city within a continent of prejudice. This made it attractive to religious and other dissidents from Europe, such as the Jews and the English Puritan Pilgrims, who eventually sailed from here to Massachusetts. Wealthy, 17th-century Amsterdam dug a slew of new canals, built stacks of town houses, and welcomed the artists with its beckoning atmosphere of tolerance and cultural interest.

The traditions of encouraging high art and tolerance while discouraging prudish morality laws have endowed the city with some of its greatest attractions. Amsterdam has some of the world's most famous museums; besides Rembrandt, the Dutch arts claim native masters such as Frans Hals, Jan Vermeer, Jan Steen, Vincent van Gogh, and Piet Mondrian. Its cityscape is one of the most beautiful anywhere, with 250-year-old town houses lining well-planned and scrupulously manicured canals.

The Dutch leniency toward drugs and prostitution has grown into a huge tourism industry that lures students and other hip, mellow types to the city's "smoking coffeehouses" and visitors of all stripes who giggle and gawk at the legal brothels in the (in)famous Red-Light District. In 2004, some Dutch legislators introduced a bill banning all marijuana use. Given the Netherlands' history of tolerance, it's unlikely to pass — though EU pressures to conform to continent-wide standards may change all this.

Nazi occupation during World War II threw the bright light of Dutch tolerance into sharp, shadowed relief with its anti-Semitism. Despite the best efforts of many locals, thousands of Amsterdam Jews were seized and deported. Among them was Anne Frank, a teenager whose hiding place still stands and whose diary remains one of the most powerful and enduring pieces of Holocaust literature.

No other city has such an eclectic mix of sights, from the basest of pleasures to the most somber reflections on human cruelty. Spanning from the Renaissance to the modern period, the Dutch presence and strength in the fine arts is an obvious tourist draw. Visitors also come to shop for diamonds, to drink Amsterdam beers such as Heineken and Amstel in *brown cafes* (so-called because the best of them are stained brown from years of smoke), or to see the tulip fields and the windmills. To really appreciate Amsterdam, you should plan on spending at least two full days there — for many, the museums alone may take that long.

Getting There

Thanks to Amsterdam's continuing popularity with visitors who are eager to sample its free-for-all lifestyle, getting to Amsterdam by air or rail couldn't be easier.

Arriving by air

Amsterdam's ultramodern **Schiphol Airport** (☎ 900-724-4746, www. schiphol.nl) is serviced by KLM, the national Dutch carrier (tightly allied with Northwest Airlines), as well as many other international airlines.

The VVV Holland Tourist Information office (☎ 020-2018-800), located in Arrivals Hall Two, is open daily from 7 a.m. to 10 p.m. There you can get help making last-minute accommodation reservations. You can also buy train tickets for Centraal Station. Also in the arrivals hall is a communications point for Internet and e-mail and 15 ATMs.

Regular trains provide a connection from Schiphol Airport to the Centraal train station in about 20 minutes for 3.10€ ($3.55). Or ask your hotel if it's part of the consortium that is serviced by the KLM shuttle bus that can whisk you straight to your hotel — for three times the cost of the

Holland (The Netherlands)

train. If convenience is your priority, the easiest way to transport yourself and your luggage from the airport to your hotel is to hail a taxi for a steep 35€ ($40).

Arriving by rail

Trains from Brussels, Paris, several German cities, Italy, Switzerland, and Eastern Europe arrive in Amsterdam at **Centraal Station,** built on an artificial island in the Ij River bounding the city's north edge. The square in front of the station has the city's main tourist office and tram terminal. You can take a tram to your hotel, or pick up a taxi from the taxi stand outside the station.

Orienting Yourself in Amsterdam

Infiltrated by canals of water, Amsterdam is like Venice. On a map, it looks like half of a spider web, with the canals as the threads radiating out from the center in tight, concentric arcs. Here, you must think in terms of the canals and six major squares as opposed to addresses, compass directions, and streets.

Introducing the neighborhoods

Try to remember a few street names, starting with Damrak. Think of the Damrak as the backbone of the **City Center,** a neighborhood made up of a few straight canals and a tangle of medieval streets. Damrak runs from the Centraal Station at the north end of town straight down to **Dam Square,** the heart of the city and where the first dam was built across the Amstel River (hence the name **Amstelledamme,** later to become Amsterdam).

Out the other end of Dam Square, the name of Damrak changes to **Rokin,** which curves down to the square and transportation hub of Muntplein. East of Muntplein, on the City Center's southeast corner, is **Waterlooplein,** home to one of the city's premier music halls and a flea market.

Next is the **Canal Zone,** wrapped around the City Center in a big arc. This zone is a series of six concentric canals laid out with 17th-century regularity. The irregular canal Singelgracht bounds this neighborhood. To the south lies the **Museumplein,** where you find the city's greatest art museums, the finest shopping, and some of the best small hotels.

On the other side of the Canal Zone southwest of Muntplein is **Leidseplein,** the bustling, throbbing center of Amsterdam's liveliest quarter of restaurants, nightclubs, and theaters. Nearby is **P. C. Hoofstraat,** Amsterdam's most fashionable shopping area.

The arc of the Singel Canal/Amstel River/Oude Schans surrounds the city and runs from the Centraal Station south to Muntplein, with Dam Square in the middle. This is where you can find the **Red-Light District.**

The most upscale residential district (of interest to upwardly mobile Amsterdammers but not to visitors) is **Amsterdam South.** The **Jordaan,** a grid of small streets between two canals at the northeastern end of the Canal Zone, is a neighborhood that is growing increasingly fashionable with several good restaurants. **Amsterdam East,** east of the City Center, is the fairly pleasant, residential, working-class and immigrant neighborhood with attractions such as the zoo and the tropical museum.

Finding information after you arrive

In the Netherlands, tourist offices are indicated by VVV (usually in a blue-and-white triangle). Amsterdam's most comprehensive VVV office is just outside the Centraal train station at Stationsplein 10. You also find a small desk in the station itself at platform 2b, and a branch in the heart of town at Leidseplein 1. Call for tourist info at ☎ **020-201-8800**, or use the Web site www.visitamsterdam.nl. You can find an information desk covering all the Netherlands in Schiphol Plaza at the airport.

Getting Around Amsterdam

Amsterdam's efficient trains, trams, and buses make getting around the city exceedingly simple.

Don't drive in Amsterdam, for several reasons. The city is a jumble of one-way streets, narrow bridges, and trams and cyclists darting every which way. Tough measures are in place to make driving as difficult as possible. No-parking zones are rigorously enforced and the limited parking spaces are expensive. And if all that's not bad enough, car break-ins are common. Outside the city, however, driving is a different story; you may want to rent a car to see the nearby countryside.

By bus

The public-transport **tickets** in the Netherlands work differently from the ticket systems in the rest of Europe. For one thing, a single type of ticket works in every city in the country, making it supremely easy to daytrip (see the last section of this chapter) out to, say Haarlem, because you'll be able to use the same ticket on its buses and trams that you're already using in Amsterdam. For another thing, in a strict sense there are no single-ride tickets available — just day-passes and the long, skinny multiuse *strippenkaart* (strip card). Strippenkaarts are priced based on how many strips appear on each long ticket, each strip corresponding to a zone in the transport system. You can buy a 2-strippenkaart for 1.60€ ($1.85), a 3-strippenkaart for 2.40€ ($2.75), or an 8-strippenkaart for 6.40€ ($7.35), from drivers and conductors. The 15-strippenkaart for 6.40€ ($7.35) and the 45-strippenkaart for 18.90€ ($22) you can get only from ticket dispensers, the GVB/Amsterdam Municipal Transportation ticket booths, VVV tourist offices (see "Fast Facts: Amsterdam," at the end of this chapter), and many newsstands and bookstores. (Obviously, the 15-strippenkaart is a far better deal than the 8-strippenkaart — they cost exactly the same — so it pays to go out of your way to pick up a 15-strippenkaart.) Each of the strips on this multiple-use ticket is good for one zone (and can be used in Amsterdam, Rotterdam, or Utrecht). Children ages 4 to 11 and adults over 65 can get a reduced-price 15-strippenkaart for 4.20€ ($4.85).

Before boarding a tram or bus, determine how many zones you need to traverse (virtually everything of interest to visitors is within Zone 1). Fold your strip card so that the total number of zones you are "using up" *plus one extra zone* is facing up and stick this end into the yellow box near the door as you enter. The machine stamps your card (some trams have a conductor who stamps the card). On buses, have the driver stamp your card. That **"plus one"** rule confuses most visitors. In other words, if you're going three zones, skip the first three strips and fold back the ticket so that the strip numbered 4 is at the physical end of the strip of paper and then stamp that fourth strip; if you're going just one zone, stamp the second strip. Everyone in your group can travel on the same strippenkart, but each person uses up his own set of strips (so, say a couple is traveling three zones together; fold over and stamp strip no. 4 then fold again to stamp strip no. 8). You can transfer as often as you like (between trams, buses, and Metro lines) for the next hour, as long as you stay within the number of zones you've stamped.

If all this stripping drives you batty, and you plan to ride a lot, just buy a regular 6.40€ ($7.35), 8-strippenkaart and have any bus driver stamp it as a **dagkaart (day ticket).** This way you don't have to bother with the folding and the stamping each ride, and it'll be valid for unlimited travel all day. You can save yourself a whopping 0.10€ (12¢) if, instead, you buy a regular 24-hour day-pass (6.30€/$7.25) at the GVB office on Stationsplein or from the machines in Metro stations; there are also 48-hour (10€/$12) and 72-hour (13€/$15) versions available.

The doors on trams and buses don't open automatically; you have to punch the *deur open* button. All the lines operate as explained here, except lines 4 and 13, where you board the back of the bus and deal with the conductor, not the driver; and line 5, where you have to get a ticket from a machine ahead of time. If all else fails, keep in mind that Amsterdam, with all its canals, is a city made for walking.

For **public-transit info,** call ☎ **0900-9292,** which charges 0.50€ (60¢) per minute. The Web site (www.gvb.nl), though, is free.

By taxi

The best way to see Amsterdam is to travel on foot, by tram, or on a bicycle. However, upon your arrival and your departure, getting yourself and your bags to and from the airport is easiest by taxi. Taxis are easy to find at the stands in front of most major hotels or at Leidseplein, Rembrandtplein, or Centraal Station. To call for a taxi, dial ☎ **020-6777-7777** or ☎ **020-7777-7777.** Initially, the charge is anywhere up to 5.12€ ($5.90) — depending on which company you use and how far you are from the nearest taxi when you call — and then anywhere up to 1.94€ ($2.25) per kilometer.

By tram

Ten of Amsterdam's 16 trolley, or tram, lines begin and end at Centraal Station. Dam Square, Muntplein, and Museumplein are the other main tram connection points. This is also true for buses.

By foot

The ring of canals making up the city center are not only easy to get around on foot, they also make for some of the most lovely walking in all of Europe — but watch out for those bikes! Amsterdammers really tear down those bike lanes, and tourists unused to this system are constantly getting knocked over. Just pretend the bike lane is the same as a street filled with cars, and look both ways before you cross. The museums and parks of the Museumplein are quite a hike from the Damrak; you'll probably want to take a tram (or, more scenically, a canal boat) to get there.

By bike

So you'd rather see Amsterdam as an Amsterdammer would? Why not rent a bike and tool around the canals? See "More cool things to see and do," later in this chapter for information.

Staying in Amsterdam

 Many of those picturesquely tall, gabled houses lining canals and historic streets have been converted into inns, but be forewarned: Dutch staircases give new meaning to the word *steep*. The older the building, the more difficult it is for a hotel to get permission to install an elevator, so if stairs present a problem for you, be sure to ask before booking.

A room with a canal view costs more, but it's often worth it for the atmosphere; plus, these rooms are often better outfitted and sometimes larger than the rooms without views.

All the places that I suggest are located in pleasant, safe neighborhoods. For July and August, you want to make hotel reservations in advance — especially for the budget places, which fill up with students eager to test Amsterdam's legendary lenient drug policy.

 For help finding accommodations anywhere in the Netherlands, contact the free **Netherlands Reservations Centre** (☎ **02-9968-9144;** www.hotel res.nl). The VVV tourist office (see "Fast Facts: Amsterdam," at the end of this chapter) will also reserve a room for you on the spot for a 3€ ($3.45) fee and a deposit; call them ahead of time at ☎ **020-2018-800.**

Amsterdam's top hotels and B&Bs

Avenue Hotel
$$$ City Center

The Avenue has all the bland, standardized charm of any international chain. But for solid, reliable comfort (if smallish rooms), American-style amenities at a great price, and a safe location near the rail station, you can do no better. The full Dutch breakfast adds local color.

See map p. 264. Nieuwezijds Voorburgwal 33 (one street east of Spuistraat, just a few minutes from the Centraal Station). ☎ *020-530-9530. Fax: 020-530-9599.* www. embhotels.nl. *Tram: 1, 2, 5, 11, 13, or 17. Rates: 158€–194€ ($182–$223) double. Rates include breakfast. AE, DC, MC, V.*

Bilderberg Hotel Jan Luyken
$$$$ Near the Museumplein

Nestled in a trio of 19th-century buildings between the city's top museums and P. C. Hooftstraat's shops, this boutique hotel, boasting refined amenities and personalized service, is a good splurge option. You get the best of both worlds here: an intimate inn with comfortably furnished bedrooms and complimentary afternoon tea in the lounge — and a pricey hotel with business services, modern baths, and several bars, patios, and dining spaces for relaxing. Sunday night specials bring the double room rate down to 100€ ($115)

See map p. 264. Jan Luykenstraat 54–58 (between Van de Veldestraat and Van Baerlestraat). ☎ *800-641-0300 in the U.S., 020-573-0730 in the Netherlands. Fax: 020-676-3841.* www.bilderberg.nl. *Tram: 2, 3, 5, 12, 16. Rates: 143€–282€ ($164–$324) double. Rates include breakfast. AE, DC, MC, V.*

Hotel Acro
$ Near the Museumplein

One of Amsterdam's not-so-secret bargains, the Acro has bright, clean, and well-kept small rooms close to the city's major museums and P. C. Hooftstraat's shops. With a shower in every room, a full Dutch breakfast included in the rates, and the hopping Leidseplein restaurant quarter just across the canal, what more could you ask for?

See map p. 264. Jan Luykenstraat 44 (near the corner with Honthorststraat). ☎ *020-662-5538. Fax: 020-675-0811.* www.acro-hotel.nl. *Tram: 2, 3, 5, 6, 7, 10, 12, 16, 24, or 25. Rates: 70€–115€ ($81–$132) double, including breakfast. AE, DC, MC, V (though there's a 5 percent surcharge if you pay by credit card).*

Hotel Toren
$$$$ Canal Zone

The Toren has medium-sized rooms in two buildings on a posh stretch of canal and is one of the best values in canalside accommodations. The furnishings are worn, but the staff is helpful, and you can even rent a cute

Accommodations, Dining, and Attractions in Central Amsterdam

HOTELS ■
Ambassade Hotel **13**
Amstel Botel **25**
Avenue Hotel **22**
Bilderberg Hotel
Jan Luyken **18**
Bridge Hotel **30**
Grand Hotel
Krasnapolsky **8**
Hotel Acro **17**
Hotel Toren **7**
Owl Hotel **16**
Rembrandt Residence **9**
RHO Hotel **29**

RESTAURANTS ◆
Bordewijk **2**
Café Luxembourg **14**
Christophe **5**
De Prins **4**
De Silveren Spiegel **21**
D'Vijff Vlieghen **10**
Haesje Claes **11**
Kam Yin **24**
Kantjil en de Tijger **12**
Pancake Bakery **3**
Toscanini **1**

ATTRACTIONS ●
Amsterdam
Sex Museum **23**
Anne Frankhuis **6**
Erotic Museum **27**
Museum Amstelkring **15**
Red Light District **28**
Rijksmuseum **20**
Stedelijk Museum
of Modern Art
(temporary home) **26**
Tropenmuseum **31**
Vincent van Gogh
Museum **19**

✝ Church
ⓘ Information
✉ Post office
— Railway

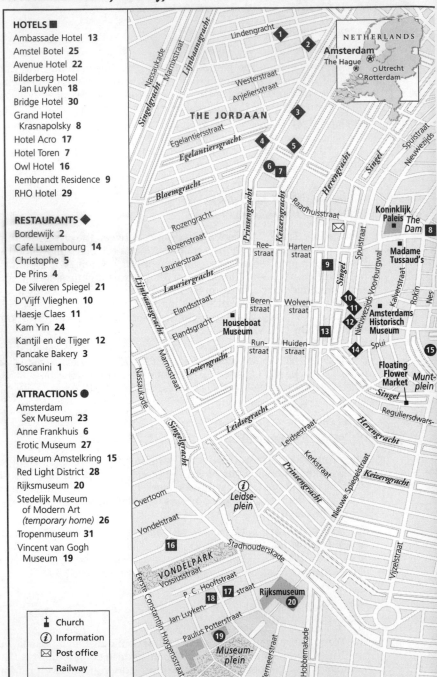

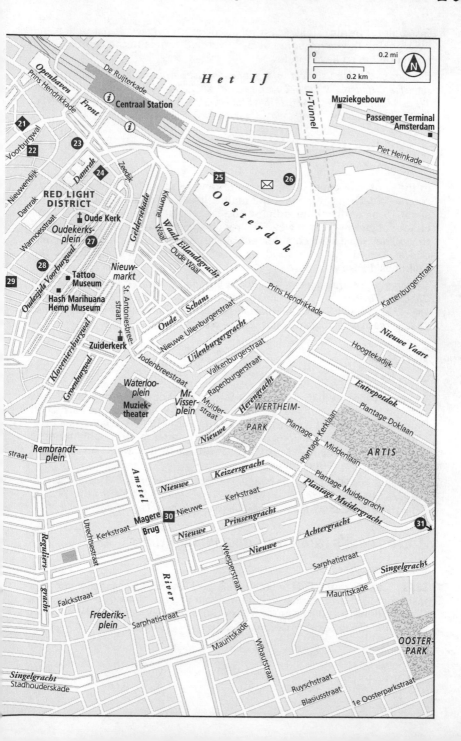

(read: floral prints) small guesthouse for extra privacy. Insist on a room overlooking the canal; some of the cramped rooms in the center of the hotel don't even have windows.

See map p. 264. Keizersgracht 164 (near Raadhuisstraat, close to the Westerkerk and Anne Frank House). ☎ *020-622-6352. Fax: 020-626-9705.* www.toren.nl. *Tram: 6, 13, 14, or 17. Rates: 136€–147€ ($156–$169) double without bathroom, 173€–242€ ($199–$278) double with bathroom. Breakfast 12€ ($14). AE, DC, MC, V.*

Rembrandt Residence
$$ Canal Zone

In the center of canal land, the Rembrandt Karena has many canalside rooms. Whether you stay in the main 18th-century house or one of the small 16th-century homes lining the Singel out back, you have a good chance of getting a canal view. The rooms are more modern than their settings: They have a full complement of amenities, almost all are of a generous size, and the odd wood beam or fireplace is a reminder of the buildings' history.

See map p. 264. Herengracht 255 (above Raadhuisstraat). ☎ *020-623-6638. Fax: 020-625-0630.* www.rembrandtresidence.nl. *Tram: 1, 2, 5, 6, 13, 14, or 17. Rates: 75€–175€ ($86–$201) double; lowest rates available via the Web site. Children under 12 stay free in parent's room. Rates include breakfast. AE, DC, MC, V.*

RHO Hotel
$$ City Center

Recently renovated, this hotel in a former gold-company building is one of the most conveniently located in Amsterdam — on a quiet side street off Dam Square. The Art Nouveau lobby hints at the hotel's origins as a turn-of-the-century theater. Unfortunately, the rooms are thoroughly modern and functional. The hotel provides all the amenities and is an excellent price for this level of comfort.

See map p. 264. Nes 5–23 (just off the southeast corner of Dam Square). ☎ *020-620-7371. Fax: 020-620-7826.* www.rhohotel.com. *Tram: 1, 2, 4, 5, 6, 9, 13, 16, 24, or 25. Rates: 120€–135€ ($138–$155) double. Rates include breakfast. AE, MC, V.*

Amsterdam's runner-up accommodations

Ambassade Hotel
$$$$ Canal Zone   This hotel fills out ten 17th-century canal houses with fashionable charm at relatively affordable prices. Almost all rooms look through floor-to-ceiling windows over the canal. *See map p. 264. Herengracht 341.* ☎ *020-555-0222. Fax: 020-555-0277.* www.ambassade-hotel.nl.

Amstel Botel

$ City Center   Amstel Botel is nothing if not unique and cheap: a huge houseboat with 176 bare-bones cabins. The botel is moored in front of a Le Corbusier–designed post office on the Amsterdam harbor (the best cabins feature water views), very near the temporary home of the Stedelijk Museum. Kids enjoy the novelty of staying on a boat. *See map p. 264. Oosterdokskade 2–4 just east of Centraal Station.* ☎ *020-626-4247. Fax: 020-639-1952.*

Bridge Hotel

$$ On Amstel River   This place has huge rooms and modern amenities overlooking the skinniest bridge over the Amstel River. *See map p. 264. Amstel 107–111, near Magere Brug.* ☎ *020-623-7068. Fax: 020-624-1565.* www.the bridgehotel.nl.

Grand Hotel Krasnapolsky

$$$$$ Red-Light District   This hotel faces the Royal Palace and has modern, posh rooms and a Victorian feel emanating from its famed, genteel restaurant. You pay for the style and central location, though. *See map p. 264. Dam 9.* ☎ *020-554-9111. Fax: 020-622-8607.* www.krasnapolsky.nl.

 ### Owl Hotel

$$ Near the Museumplein   The Owl is a neat little hotel on the Vondelpark just a few short blocks from the Museumplein. *See map p. 264. Roemer Visscherstraat 1, off Eerste Constantijn Huygensstraat.* ☎ *020-618-9484. Fax: 020-618-9441.* www.owl-hotel.nl.

Dining in Amsterdam

As the capital of a trading nation and former imperial power in the Near and Far East, Amsterdam has a good selection of restaurants serving all sorts of cuisines, from Dutch to Indonesian. Traditional Dutch cuisine tends to be hearty and rather uninventive, but it's still good and filling.

Specialties include *Hutspot* (beef rib stew) and *pannekoeken,* massive pancakes that can be eaten topped with sugar or fruit as a dessert or with meats and cheeses as a main course. Consider a Dutch beer such as Heineken, Grolsch, or Amstel (all light *pils* brews), or a dark Belgian beer to complement your main dish.

If you're looking for something a little more exotic, the dish to try is the Indonesian feast called *rijsttafel.* This "rice table" smorgasbord of Southeast Asian specialties consists of 17 to 30 tiny dishes, offering you a taste of some of the best food the former Dutch colony has to offer — Amsterdam is famous for its excellent Indonesian restaurants.

Small sandwiches called *broodjes* are the traditional snack of Amsterdam. They're available everywhere, but the best are at the specialty *broodjeswinkel* **Eetsalon Van Dobben,** at Korte Reguliersdwarsstraat 5–9, off

Rembrandtplein (☎ 020-624-4200; www.vandobben.com), or **Broodje van Kootje,** at Leidseplein 20 (☎ 020-623-2036). You can buy ultra-fresh picnic supplies at the market on Albert Cuypstraat, at the health-foody Boerenmarkt Farmer's Market at Noodermarkt, or in Albert Heijn supermarkets (there's one at the corner of Leidstraat and Koningsplein).

Amsterdam's top restaurants

Bordewijk
$$$$$ The Jordaan FRENCH

Against a starkly modern setting, the food is richly textured and tastefully French, with modern accents and Italian and Asian twists. The food is accompanied by attentive, but not overbearing, service. The constantly changing menu may include rib roast in a Bordelais sauce or red mullet with wild spinach. An outdoor terrace on the canal makes dining alfresco even more attractive.

See map p. 264. Noordermarkt 7 (at the north end of Prinsengracht). ☎ *020-624-3899. Reservations required. Tram: 3, 6, 10, 13, 14, or 17. Main courses: 24€–31€ ($28–$36). AE, MC, V. Open: Dinner Tues–Sun.*

Christophe
$$$$$ Canal Zone FRENCH/MEDITERRANEAN

For 15 years, Amsterdam's Michelin-starred restaurant has been a bastion of elegance and classic French cuisine with a Mediterranean twist and North African touch. All this is courtesy of the French-Algerian owner-chef Jean Christophe Royer, who trained at the Ritz in Paris and several top-notch Manhattan kitchens. The elegant rooms contain floral arrangements and displays of pricey vintage after-dinner ports, armagnacs, and sherries. Dress up for this one.

See map p. 264. Leliegracht 46 (between Prinsengracht and Keizersgracht). ☎ *020-625-0807.* www.christophe.nl. *Reservations practically required. Tram: 6, 13, 14, 17. Set-price menus: 55€–75€ ($63–$86). AE, DC, MC, V. Open: Dinner Tues–Sat.*

De Prins
$$ Canal Zone DUTCH/FRENCH

One of the best deals in the city, this tiny neighborhood place is so popular for its inexpensive brown cafe–style food that tables fill up fast, so call ahead. In a 17th-century canal-side house, Dutch and French dishes are expertly prepared at remarkably low prices. This is one of your best bets for an opportunity to mix with the locals. It's also open late — though the kitchen closes at 10 p.m., the cafe stays open until 1 a.m.

See map p. 264. Prinsengracht 124 (near the Anne Frank House). ☎ *020-624-9382. Reservations not accepted. Tram: 13, 14, 17, or 20. Main courses 2.60€–14.60€ ($3–$17). AE, DC, MC, V. Open: Lunch and dinner daily.*

D'Vijff Vlieghen
$$$$ Canal Zone DUTCH

An Amsterdam institution for 350 years, "The Five Fliers" resides in a string of five canal-front buildings. The place offers a variety of historic décors and an excellent cuisine prepared by a chef determined to prove that traditional recipes can be exquisite. Try the wild boar with stuffed apples or smoked turkey filet with cranberry. If gin is your drink of choice, check out the list of Dutch gins with more than 40 selections. You can often sit outdoors here in summer.

See map p. 264. Spuistraat 294–302 (below Raadhuisstraat). ☎ *020-530-4060.* www. d-vijffvlieghen.com. *Reservations recommended on weekends. Tram: 1, 2, 4, 5, 6, 9, 13, 16, 24, or 25. Main courses: 21.95€–27.95€ ($25–$32); fixed-price menus 32.50€–51€ ($37–$59). AE, DC, MC, V. Open: Dinner daily.*

Kantjil en de Tijger
$$$$ Canal Zone JAVANESE/INDONESIAN

This large and popular restaurant features a good *rijsttafel* for two and a tasty *nasi goreng Kantjil* (fried rice with pork kebabs and stewed beef). Southeast Asian specialties such as shrimp in coconut dressing complete the menu. The multilayered cinnamon cake is worth saving room for.

See map p. 264. Spuistraat 291–293 (beside Spui). ☎ *020-620-0994.* www.kantjil. nl. *Tram: 1, 2, or 5. Main courses: 11.25€–14.50€ ($13–$17); rijsttafel for two people 40€–50€ ($46–$58). AE, DC, MC, V. Open: Dinner daily.*

Pancake Bakery
$ Canal Zone DUTCH/PANCAKES

The name says it all: This canal-side joint does one thing only — *pannekoeken* — and it does it great. One of these disks topped with Cajun chicken or curried turkey and pineapple may be your dinner. For dessert, fruit compotes, syrups, and ice cream are typical pancake stuffings. Its décor is simple and slightly rustic, but in summer join the crowds (and the syrup-seeking bees) at the long tables outside with a canal view.

See map p. 264. Prinsengracht 191 (one block from the Anne Frank House). ☎ *020-625-1333.* www.pancake.nl. *Reservations suggested. Tram: 6, 13, 14, 17, 20, or 21. Main courses: 4.70€–10.50€ ($5.40–$12). AE, MC, V. Open: Lunch and dinner daily.*

Amsterdam's runner-up restaurants

Café Luxembourg
$$$ Canal Zone his large, stylish cafe draws an international crowd and serves huge portions of everything from soup and sandwiches to dim sum. *See map p. 264. Spuistraat 24, near Spui.* ☎ *020-620-6264.* www.cafe luxembourg.nl.

De Silveren Spiegel

$$$$$ City Center   Another old-school Dutch eatery that serves refined versions of Holland staples in an old merchant's house from 1614. You find a small garden out back. *See map p. 264. Kattengat 4–6, off Singel.* ☎ *020-624-6589.* www.desilverenspiegel.com.

Haesje Claes

$$$$ Canal Zone   Dutch to the core, from the Delftware and hanging lamps to the hutspot (beef rib stew) and Ijsselmeer paling (eel). *See map p. 264. Spuistraat 273–275, near Spui.* ☎ *020- 624-9998.* www.haesjeclaes.nl.

Kam Yin

$$ City Center   Constant turnover at this popular spot keeps the cooks busy all day, ensuring your meal is freshly prepared. The Suriname cuisines means heaping mounds of rice and noodles are topped with fish, meat, or vegetables blending Chinese, Indonesian, and South American flavors. *See map p. 264. Warmoesstraat 6 (off Damrak).* ☎ *020-625-3115.*

Toscanini

$$$ The Jordaan   Toscanini does excellent southern Italian cooking in a simple, laid-back (read: for long dinners only) atmosphere. *See map p. 264. Lindengracht 75, off Brouwersgracht.* ☎ *020-623-2813.*

Exploring Amsterdam

The **Amsterdam Pass** gets you into most Amsterdam museums, including all listed here except the Anne Frank House, plus a free canal cruise and free rides on public transportation. It costs 31€ ($36) for 24 hours, 41€ ($47) for 48 hours, or 51€ ($59) for 72 hours, and you can buy the card at any tourist office. If you're under 26, you can buy a **Cultureel Jongeren Pas (CJP — Cultural Youth Passport)** entitling you to discounts at 1,500 places (museums, movie theaters, concerts, record stores, and so on) across the Netherlands. The pass costs 12.50€ ($14) and is good for a year; for more info, surf to www.cjp.nl.

Amsterdam's top sights

Anne Frankhuis (Anne Frank House)

Canal Zone

As 13-year-old Anne Frank began her diary in July 1942, she dealt with the usual problems of adolescence, including feelings about her family and the boy next door. She also included the defining fact of her life: She was Jewish and had just moved into a hidden attic apartment with seven other people, comprising two families, as the Nazis occupied Amsterdam. Anne lived here for two years, with only a crack in the window and some pictures of movie stars on the wall to remind her of the outside world.

The Franks and their companions were betrayed eventually, and they all were deported to concentration camps. Anne went first to Auschwitz, and then was moved to Bergen-Belsen when the Nazis retreated. She died of typhus just weeks before the camp was liberated. Of the eight people who lived in the attic, only her father, Otto, survived. His model of the rooms as they looked in those years of concealment and Anne's photos on the walls are all that adorn the small apartment hidden behind a swinging bookcase. A photograph downstairs details the Holocaust in Amsterdam, and the bookshop carries copies of Anne's remarkable diary in dozens of languages. Half a million people come to pay their respects here every year, so expect crowds and arrive early.

To dig deeper into the history of Amsterdam's Jewish population, visit the **Joods Historisch Museum,** Jonas Daniël Meijerplein 2–4, near Waterlooplein (☎ 020-626-9945; www.jhm.nl), which was the heart of the Jewish district. This vast museum chronicles the 350 years of Jewish history and culture in the city; renovations though November 2004 will close parts of the museum, and until then admission prices will be 1€ to 3€ lower than usual (the exact discount varies month to month). Open daily from 11 a.m. to 5 p.m., admission is 6.50€ ($7.50) adults, 3€ ($3.45) ages 13 to 18, 2€ ($2.30) ages 6 to 12, free ages 5 and under. Ever a tolerant country, the Netherlands welcomed hundreds of mainly Sephardic Jews fleeing persecution in Spain and Portugal in the 15th and 16th centuries. **The Portuguese Synagogue** at Mr. Visserplein 3, built in 1665, is the only still-functioning temple to survive from that period. Although at first restricted to certain trades such as diamond-cutting, by 1796 Jews in Amsterdam were granted full civil rights (unheard of in that era in Europe), a position they enjoyed until the Nazi occupation.

See map p. 264. Prinsengracht 263 (just below Westermarkt). ☎ *020-556-7100.* www.annefrank.nl. *Tram: 6, 13, 14, 17, 20, or 21. Admission: 7.50€ ($8.60) adults, 3.50€ ($4) ages 10–17; free ages 9 and under. Open: Apr–Aug daily 9 a.m.–9 p.m.; Sept–Mar daily 9 a.m.–7 p.m.*

Museum Amstelkring (Our Lord in the Attic)
City Center

The giant **Gothic Oude Kirk** (Old Church; www.oudekerk.nl) is just down the block, but this tiny, well-preserved baroque church is much more interesting. In the heart of the Red-Light District, the church spreads across the connected third floors of three 17th-century homes. Now Amsterdam is famed for its tolerance, but in the 16th and 17th centuries, the practice of any religion except for the official Dutch Reformed Calvinism was forbidden. To worship, Jews, Mennonites, Lutherans, and, in this instance, Catholics, had to go underground — or aboveground, as the case may be — and hold services in secret. One of the houses below the church has been restored for visitors — it's the oldest house in Amsterdam open to the public.

See map p. 264. Oudezijds Voorburgwal 40 (about 3 blocks from Centraal Station, on the far side of the Damrak's canal). ☎ *020-624-6604.* www.museumamstelkring.nl. *Tram: 1, 2, 4, 5, 9, 13, 14, 16, 17, 21, 24, or 25 (any to Dam Square). Admission: 7€ ($8.05) adults, 5€ ($5.75) students, 1€ ($1.15) ages 5–18. Open: Mon–Sat 10 a.m.–5 p.m., Sun 1–5 p.m.*

Red-Light District

Dutch pragmatism and tolerance has led to the establishment of the best-known, safest, and cleanest prostitution zone of any Western city. Its sheer openness has made the district one of Amsterdam's major sightseeing attractions. Amsterdam never presumed to have the capability to stop the world's oldest profession, so it decided to regulate prostitution and confine the licensed brothels to the old city streets surrounding the Oude Kirk, or Old Church.

These houses of ill repute display their wares behind plate-glass windows. The storefronts of some of the prettiest 17th-century homes in Amsterdam are occupied by women half-naked or wrapped in leather watching TV, darning socks, reading books, and otherwise occupying themselves until a customer comes along. At such time, they either close the blinds or abandon the window for the privacy of an inner room.

Prostitutes pay their taxes, and the state ensures that they have regular medical checkups and health coverage. However, this didn't stop 60 percent of them from contracting HIV in the days before the spread of the disease was understood.

 The district is mostly frequented by five types of people. Three are harmless: lots of giggling, gawking tourists, darty-eyed career guys in suits, and the age-old sailors. Two other types can be scary and tragic: unlicensed prostitutes strung out on heroin and trolling the streets, and packs of shifty, seedy men who look like all they do is indulge in drugs and brothels.

Come prepared to be provoked or saddened by the sight of scantily clad women behind glass, who manage to look bored and provocative at the same time — and be even more careful and aware than usual. Don't take any pictures — they don't want their faces recorded, so you could find your Nikon being pitched into one of the canals. I've always felt pretty safe here during the day, but by night I'd either steer clear entirely or stick only to the main streets — and leave my valuables at the hotel.

See map p. 264. The Red-Light District fills the streets around the canals Oudezijds Achterburgwal and Oudezijds Voorburgwal. Tram: 1, 2, 4, 5, 9, 13, 14, 16, 17, 21, 24, or 25 to Dam Square, and then duck behind the Grand Hotel Krasnapolsky.

Rijksmuseum
Museumplein

Although it doesn't get as much publicity as the Louvre or the Uffizi, Amsterdam's Rijksmuseum is one of the top museums in Europe. Not surprisingly, it houses the largest collection of Dutch masters in the world. Rembrandt is the star of the show, with a couple of self-portraits, the gruesome *Anatomy Lesson,* the racy *The Jewish Bride,* and his masterpiece, *The Night Watch,* which is the defining work for the Golden Age of Dutch painting.

Frans Hals is well represented, with *The Merry Drinker* being one of his best portraits. You find party scenes courtesy of Jan Steen, de Hooch's intimate interiors, still-lifes by Bollengier, and four Vermeer paintings, including the famed *Woman Reading a Letter* and *The Kitchen Maid.* Note that the Rijksmuseum will be partly closed through 2008 for massive renovations. In the meantime, a "mini-Rijksmuseum" will remain open in the main buidling, comprising some 400 masterpieces, while the rest of the collections will be split up amongst temporary exhibits all over the Netherlands (including ten masterpieces, by the likes of Jan Steen and Rembrandt, at Schiphol Airport) or lent out to traveling shows.

See map p. 264. Stadhouderskade 42 (at Museumplein). ☎ *020-674-7047.* www.rijks museum.nl. *Tram: 2, 3, 5, 6, 7, 10, 12, 16, 24, or 25. Admission: 9€ ($10) adults, free under 18. Open: Daily 9 a.m.–6 p.m.*

Stedelijk Museum of Modern Art
Near Centraal Station

For modern art from Impressionism to the present, spend a morning at the Stedelijk. The permanent collections and regularly staged exhibitions highlight many movements and styles of the past century. Picasso, Chagall, Cézanne, Monet, Calder, Oldenburg, Warhol, Jasper Johns, and Man Ray are featured artists. Of particular interest are Gerrit Rietveld's *Red Blue Chair* and paintings by Mondrian — two major forces in the Dutch abstract De Stijl movement, which prefaced the Bauhaus and modernist schools. You also find a large collection by the Russian Kazimir Malevich, who experimented with supersaturated color in a style he called *Suprematism.* As of May 2004, the Stedelijk is being housed in a modern business highrise on the east end of the same island as Centraal Station, but its real home — closed for major renovations until sometime in 2008 — is a 1895 northern neo-Renaissance structure at Museumplein.

See map p. 264. Oosterdokskade 3–5 (just east of Centraal Station). ☎ *020-573-2911.* www.stedelijkmuseum.nl. *Tram: Any to Centraal Station. Admission: 8€ ($9.20) adults, 4€ ($4.60) children 7–16, children under 7 free. Open: Daily 10 a.m.–6 p.m. (Thurs to 9 p.m.).*

Vincent van Gogh Museum
Near Museumplein

The most famous modern artist of the Netherlands died an underappreciated, tormented genius who sold only one painting in his lifetime — to his brother. Bouts of depression landed him in an asylum at one point and at another led him to hack off his own ear after an argument with the painter Gauguin. Yet even while the artistic establishment was virtually ignoring him, van Gogh managed to carry the freedom of Impressionism to new heights, and he created an intensely expressive style all his own.

This monument to the artist offers a chronological progression of his works, including 200 paintings and 500 drawings, alongside letters and personal effects (some of which are featured in the paintings on display). A few of his more famous canvases here include *The Potato Eaters, Sunflowers, The Bedroom at Arles, Gauguin's Chair, Self Portrait with a Straw Hat,* and

The Garden of Daubigny. At the end of the exhibit hangs the powerful *Crows over the Cornfield,* one of the last paintings van Gogh completed in 1890 prior to committing suicide at the age of 37.

See map p. 264. Paulus Potterstraat 7 (at Museumplein). ☎ *020-570-5200.* www. vangoghmuseum.nl. *Tram: 2, 3, 5, 12, or 16. Admission: 9€ ($10) adults, 2.50€ ($2.90) children 13–18, children under 13 free. Open: Daily 10 a.m.–6 p.m.(Fri to 10 p.m.).*

More cool things to see and do

✔ **Cruising the canals:** Amsterdam has 165 canals spanned by more than 1,280 bridges, so your trip won't be complete until you take a canal cruise on a glass-roofed boat with multilingual commentary (recorded or live). This is the best way to get a feel for the city and see its gabled houses, lithe bridges, busy harbor, and some unforgettable sights. Some of these sights include the unlikely **Cat Boat,** home to about 150 furry felines who are *supposed* to detest being anywhere near water. Most tours depart from the Damrak or near the Rijksmuseum or Muntplein and last an hour. Tours run every 15 to 30 minutes in summer (9 a.m.–9:30 p.m.), every 45 minutes in winter (10 a.m.–4 p.m.), and cost around 8.50€ ($9.80) adults, 5€ ($5.75) children.

Similar tours are operated by more companies than you can shake an oar at, though two of the biggest are **Holland International** (☎ 020-622-7788) and **Meyers Rondvaarten** (☎ 020-623-4208). Romantics should try the two-hour night cruise with wine and cheese or a two- or three-hour dinner. The former run nightly year-round for 25€ ($29); dinner cruises run nightly April through November, around twice per week in winter for 69€ ($79). Contact Holland International or **Keytours** (☎ 020-623-5051; www.keytours. nl) for reservations, which are required.

✔ **Tramping to the sex museums:** These places are as squeaky clean as their subject matter allows and are full of giggling tourists. Of the two, the **Amsterdam Sex Museum,** Damrak 18 (☎ 020-622-8376), has more of a carnival-like atmosphere, with a section of antique porn photographs that border on being of historical interest and a room of everything you don't want to know about deviant sexual practices. Open daily from 10 a.m. to 11:30 p.m. The **Erotic Museum,** Oudezijds Achterburgwal 54 (☎ 020-624-7303), is more clinical and adds some mock-ups of an S&M "playroom" and a re-created alley from the Red-Light District in the good old days. Hours are daily from noon to midnight.

✔ **Drinking beer in a brown cafe, gin in a *proflokaal:*** When the Dutch want to go to the proverbial place where everybody knows their name, they head to the neighborhood *brown cafe* (so-called because they're stained from decades of smoke). This is the best place to try Dutch beer, where glasses drawn extra frothy from the tap are beheaded by a knife-wielding bartender. You can find hundreds of these cafes throughout the city, but here are a few of the best: **Café Chris,** Bloemstraat 42 (☎ 020-624-5942), has been around since 1642 and plays opera music on Sunday nights; **Gollem,** Raamsteeg 4 (☎ 020-626-6645 or 020-330-2890), has over 200 beers to offer; **Hoppe,** Spui 18–20 (☎ 020-420-4420), is an always-crowded classic from 1670; touristy **Reijnders** has some great people-watching on the Leidseplein at no. 6 (☎ 020-623-4419); and **De Vergulde Gaper,** Prinsengracht 30 (☎ 020-624-8975), is another good place for people-watching, with terrace tables and an atmospheric interior.

After you've become familiar with the local beer, try the hard liquor the Dutch made famous. Visit a gin-tasting house, or a *proflokaal,* which looks like a brown cafe but is usually owned by the distillery itself. It's customary to take the first sip no-hands, slurping it from the brim-filled shot glass as you lean over it. Try **Brouwerij't IJ,** Funenkade 7 (☎ 020-320-1786 or 020-622-8325; www.brouwerijhetij.nl), in a now-defunct windmill near the harbor (good beers from its own brewery, too); minscule **Café 't Doktortje,** Rozenboomsteeg 4 near Spui Square (☎ 020-626-4427), which has lots of antiques and tasty fruit brandies; or the **1679 Wijnand Fockink,** Pijlsteeg 31 (☎ 020-639-2695), where they've already heard all the English jokes about their name. They also display a series of liqueur bottles painted with portraits of all the city's mayors since 1591.

✔ **Lighting up:** I officially can't condone this, but I also can't write about Amsterdam without mentioning the special class of "coffee-houses" in town where the drug of choice isn't caffeine. Under pressure from the European Union, the Netherlands is cracking down on drugs, but the country is still lenient with marijuana. Contrary to popular belief, weed *is* illegal here, but police unofficially tolerate possession of a small amount for personal use — less than 5 grams (it used to be 30). These venerable establishments are allowed to sell small amounts of grass and hash — they even have marijuana menus! They can also sell joints (rolled with tobacco) and various hash products, coffee, tea, and juice, but no food. The most famous smoking coffee shop is **Bulldog,** whose main branch is at Leidseplein 17 in — get this — a former police station (☎ 020-625-6278; www.bulldog.nl).

✔ **Spending an afternoon in the tropics:** The **Tropenmuseum** (☎ 020-568-8215; www.kit.nl/tropenmuseum) investigates the indigenous cultures of the country's former colonies in India, Indonesia, and the Caribbean. The best exhibits are set up as typical villages you can wander through. They're so realistic that you almost wonder where all the inhabitants went. This place may be a good bet when the kids' (or your own) interest in Dutch Old Masters starts flagging and you need a change of pace. The address is East Amsterdam on Linnaesstraat 2 at Mauritskade; take tram 9. Admission is 7.50€ ($8.60) adults, 3.75€ ($4.30) ages 6 to 17, or 5€ ($5.75) over 65. Hours are daily from 10 a.m. to 5 p.m.

✔ **Cycling around Amsterdam on two wheels:** The Dutch are avid bicyclists: The country holds 15 million people . . . and 12 million bikes. The streets are divided into lanes for cars, lanes for pedestrians, and lanes for bikes (each even has its own stoplights). Renting a bike is one of the best ways to explore Amsterdam away from the tram routes and major sights (quiet Sundays are best). The only hills are the humps of the bridges over scenic canals. For rentals, try **Macbike,** Stationsplein 12–33 (☎ **020-620-0985**). Prices average 6.50€ to 9.75€ ($7.50–$11) per day or 30€ to 45€ ($35–$52) per week.

Guided tours

For a quick overview of town, take a bus tour from **Key Tours** (☎ **020-623-5051**), Dam 19; or **Holland International Excursions** (☎ **020-622-7788**), Dam 6. A three-hour tour costs around 28€ ($32) and usually includes either a canal cruise or a visit to the Rijksmuseum.

 Mike's Bike Tours (☎ **020-622-7970;** www.mikesbiketours.com) offers half-day tours around the canals in town, and a ride outside the city to see windmills and a cheese farm and clog factory (touristy, but fun). The price is 24€ ($28) adult, 22€ ($25) students, 15€ ($17) kids under 12. Meet daily at 12:30 p.m. (except May 16–Aug 31, when there are 2 tours, at 11:30 a.m. and 4 p.m.) near the reflecting pool behind the Rijksmuseum (tram: 2, 3, 5). December through February, you have to book in advance (minimum 3 people).

And don't forget about touring Amsterdam from the canals' point of view; see "Cruising the canals," under "More cool things to see and do," earlier in this chapter. Amsterdam's most innovative tour has to be the **Canal Bus** (☎ **020-622-2181;** www.canal.nl), a trio of color-coded boats that stop near most of the city's museums and attractions, including all those mentioned in this chapter. The full-day fare — valid until noon the next day — is 16€ ($18) for adults, 11€ ($13) under age 14 and includes discounts on admissions for some museums. The boats leave every half hour from Centraal Station.

Suggested itineraries

If you're pressed for time and prefer to organize your own tour, this section offers tips for building your own Amsterdam itinerary.

If you have one day

Start off the day early with a canal cruise at 9 a.m. Get to the **Rijksmuseum** when it opens and spend about 90 minutes enjoying the Rembrandts and Vermeers. Then pop down the block for another 45 minutes in the company of Holland's towering master modernist at the **Vincent van Gogh Museum.** Head to the **Pancake Bakery** for a quick canalside lunch, then stroll up the street to pay your respects at the **Anne Frankhuis.**

Because Amsterdam attracts all types, I leave the late afternoon up to you: Explore the town by bike, titillate at one of the sex museums, stroll the canals, or make the rounds of the brown cafes (or the other kind of cafe). In the early evening, take the requisite shocked spin through the Red-Light District — before sunset if possible (that is, before the seedy night elements come out, but while the ladies are putting their best, er, foot forward for the businessmen who stop by on their way home). Cap the day off with an Indonesian feast at **Kantjil en de Tiger.**

If you have two days

Start off **Day 1** with the ol' canal cruise — the best intro to the charming side of Amsterdam that money can buy. Head to the masterpieces in the **Rijksmuseum** next and spend two hours or so perusing the Old Masters. After lunch, pay homage to The Earless One at the nearby **Vincent van Gogh Museum.** Head back up to the Centraal Station neighborhood to check out the **Stedelijk Museum of Modern Art** before wandering back down to the Damrak so you can spend the early evening visiting the **Red-Light District.** Settle in for a thoroughly Dutch dinner at **Restaurant d'Vijff Vlieghen.**

Begin **Day 2** indulging in a favorite Dutch pastime: Rent a bike and tool around on your own, or take one of Mike's excellent guided bike tours. Lunch at the **Pancake Bakery** before seeing the **Anne Frankhuis,** and then head across to the old part of town to see the Oude Kirk and the bizarre **Museum Amstelkring,** also known as "Our Lord in the Attic." Spend the early evening hopping between brown and gin cafes, and then poke around the Leidseplein district for the best little Indonesian restaurant you can find for dinner.

If you have three days

Spend **Day 1** and **Day 2** as outlined in the preceding section, and take **Day 3** to visit either the re-created folk village of **Zaanse Schans** in the morning and **Haarlem** in the afternoon, or — especially if you're in town for the spring flower season — Haarlem in the morning followed by a drive, bike ride, or train trip through the flower-bedecked **Bloembollenstreek.** I cover all these sights in the next section.

Traveling Beyond Amsterdam

Several interesting destinations are an easy daytrip from Amsterdam — among them the tulip region near Haarlem, the traditional village of Zaanse Schans, and the Vincent van Gogh Museum in Hoge Veluwe national park.

Discovering the other Haarlem

Haarlem makes perhaps the most pleasant daytrip from Amsterdam, offering a much more laid-back and less hectic version of a tidy Dutch city. Haarlem boasts a great museum, too.

Getting there

Every half-hour or so, a train makes the 20-minute jaunt to Haarlem from Amsterdam. The local **VVV tourist office** (☎ **0900-616-1600** or 023-616-1600; www.vvvzk.nl) is outside the station at Stationplein 1.

Seeing the sights

The town's pretty central square, Grote Markt, is anchored by the late Gothic–style church St. Bavokerk, better known as the **Grote Kerk.** Inside are artist Frans Hals's tombstone and a cannonball embedded in the wall during the Spanish siege of 1572 to 1573. The church also houses one of the world's great organs, a 68-stop 5,068-pipe beauty built by Christian Müller from 1735 to 1738 — both Handel and a 10-year-old Mozart once came to play it. Late April to late September, you can enjoy free organ recitals Saturdays from 3 to 4 p.m. On the church's south side, 17th-century shops and houses nestle together like barnacles. These were built so they could be rented for additional income to help with the church's upkeep.

Haarlem's biggest attraction is the **Frans Hals Museum,** Groot Heiligeland 62 (☎ 023-511-5775; www.franshalsmuseum.nl), set up in the pensioner's home where the painter spent his last days in 1666. Frans Hals's works make up the bulk of the collections, but many Dutch painters from the 16th century to the present are represented as well. The works are all displayed in 17th-century-style rooms that often bear a striking resemblance to the settings in the works themselves. Admission is 5.40€ ($6.20) adults, 4€ ($4.60) over 65, and free under age 19. It's open Tuesday through Saturday from 11 a.m. to 5 p.m. and Sunday from noon to 5 p.m.

Where to stay and dine

The **Hotel Carillon** (☎ 023-531-0591; www.hotelcarillon.com) has clean 76€ ($87) doubles in the heart of town at Grote Markt 27. The boisterous tavern **Stadscafe,** Zijlstraat 57 (☎ 023-531-5533), serves hearty Dutch food at great prices.

Stopping to admire the tulips

Believe it or not, tulips aren't even Dutch! They came to the Netherlands from Turkey in the 1590s. By 1620, tulips gained popularity and growers couldn't keep up with the demand. By the year 1636, rare tulip bulbs were being sold for their weight in gold. Bulbs have come down in price since then, but the Netherlands is still one of the world's largest producers of flowers.

The **Bloembollenstreek** is Amsterdam's bulb belt, home of the tulip. It's located between Haarlem and Leiden and stretches across a 19-mile strip of land. These lowlands along the North Sea are fields of gladioli, hyacinths, lilies, narcissi, daffodils, crocuses, irises, dahlias, and the mighty tulip for miles as far as the eye can see. January is when the earliest blooms burst into color, and the floral show doesn't slow down until the end of May. Mid-April, though, is the Time of the Tulip.

Getting there

Haarlem is just a quick 20-minute ride by train from Amsterdam. Buses run between Haarlem and Leiden to service the region. Bus 172 heads to Aalsmeer from Amsterdam's Centraal train station.

Seeing the sights

While you're traveling through the countryside, which is rewarding in itself, you may want to make a few stops. **The Frans Roozen Nursery** (☎ 023-584-7245) in Vogelenzang is one of the first sights as you head south from Haarlem on the N206. Established in 1789, the nursery offers free, guided tours that give you an excellent introduction to the fine art of tulip husbandry. Open daily from 8 a.m. to 6 p.m.

If you're here from around March 20 to around May 20, rush to the **Keukenhof Gardens** in Lisse (☎ 0252-465-555; www.keukenhof.nl), to see their 7,000,000-plus bulbs in full bloom over 80 acres. These are perhaps the top floral gardens on Earth. Open daily from 8:00 a.m. to 7:30 p.m., there are cafeterias on-site so you don't have to miss any of the surrounding chromatic spectacle. Admission is a steep 12€ ($14) adults, 11€ ($13) over 65, and 5.50€ ($6.30) ages 4 to 11. Take bus 54 from Leiden.

One of the bulb-field region's chief attractions is just 6 miles south of Amsterdam at the **flower auction** in Aalsmeer (☎ 0297-393-939; www.aalsmeer.com). Nineteen million cut flowers daily (and 2 million other plants) are auctioned at a speedy pace. As you watch from the visitors gallery, giant dials tick down rapidly from 100 to 1 — as the numbers count down, the price drops — and the first bidder to buzz in on that lot stops the clock at that price and gets the bouquet. Because only one bid gets the goods, it's like a huge game of chicken. The auction runs Monday through Friday from 7:30 to 11:00 a.m. (try to show up before 9 a.m. for the best action).

Tilting at windmills

Luckily, when the Dutch pave the way for progress, they also set aside space for preservation. As industrialization of the countryside north of Amsterdam started during the first half of the 20th century, people realized that a way of life and mode of architecture was rapidly disappearing. In the late 1950s, dozens of local farms, houses, and windmills dating from that ever-popular 17th century were broken down, carted off, and reassembled into a kind of archetypal "traditional" village called **Zaanse Schans,** where the Dutch 17th century lives on.

Getting there

Zaanse Schans is about 10 miles northwest of Amsterdam, just above the town of Zaandam, to which there are numerous daily trains from Amsterdam (a 12-minute ride). The **tourist office** (☎ 075-616-8218; www.zaanseschans.nl) is at Schansend 1.

Seeing the sights

Although **Zaanse Schans** (☎ 075-628-8958; www.zaansemolen.nl) is a little bit of a tourist trap, it's not just a sightseeing attraction — people actually live in most of the cottages and houses, doing their daily tasks in as much an early 18th-century way as possible. The grocery stores and the like are truly from a different era, and a few of the buildings are museums for the public, including the four working windmills. A half dozen of the town's windmills are open to visitors for 2.50€ ($2.90) each, but keep widely varying hours — roughly 9 or 10 a.m. to 4 or 5 p.m., with shorter hours November through March (see the Web site for details). Short cruises on the river Zaan are also popular. The little museum in the village is open Tuesday to Friday 11 a.m. to 5 p.m. (Oct–May, hours change to 10 a.m. to noon and 1–5 p.m.), Saturday 2 to 5 p.m., Sunday 1 to 5 p.m. Admission is 3.50€ ($4) adults, 2.50€ ($2.90) over 65 and under 13.

If you'd like to see some more impressive windmills, head 66 miles south of Amsterdam to the **Kinderdijk** region below Rotterdam (☎ 078-691-5179; www.kinderdijk.org). Nineteen functioning, old-fashioned windmills built from 1722 to 1761 dot the landscape like sailboats, turning their 42-foot-long sails slowly in the wind on Saturdays from 1:30 to 5:30 p.m. in July and August. For the rest of the year, they just sit there looking picturesque. The visitor's mill is open to the public April through September, Tuesday through Saturday from 10 a.m. to 6 p.m. Take the train from Amsterdam's Centraal Station to Rotterdam, and then the metro to Zuidplein, and then bus 154.

Biking to the Kröller-Müller Museum

One of the Netherlands's top modern-art museums and Europe's largest sculpture garden is the **Kröller-Müller Museum,** set in the middle of **Hoge Veluwe,** a 13,750-acre national park of heath, woods, and sand dunes. This is my favorite Dutch excursion and can easily be done as a daytrip from Amsterdam.

Getting there

Trains scheduled twice hourly run from Amsterdam to Arnhem in 65 minutes. From Arnhem's station, hop on the no. 12 bus, which stops in the park both at the museum and at the visitor center/cafeteria (☎ 0318-591-627), where you can pick up maps of the park.

Before taking that bus in Arnhem, do some advance reconnoitering by popping into the city's **VVV tourist office** (☎ 0900-202-4075 or 026-442-6767) at Stationsplein 45 outside the station to pick up park info and maps.

Seeing the sights

Biking is the primary form of transportation in **Hoge Veluwe National Park** (☎ 0900-464-3835; www.hogeveluwe.nl); grab a free white bike by any entrance or at the visitors' center — just drop it off before you leave. As you bike through the calm, lush greenery of the park, you may catch glimpses of red deer, foxes, wild boar, or badgers. Under the visitor center lies the **Museonder,** a series of displays and tunnels dedicated to underground ecology, open daily 10 a.m. to 5 p.m. (as is the visitor center). The park itself is open daily November to March from 9 a.m. to 5:30 p.m., April 8 a.m. to 8 p.m., May and August 8 a.m. to 9 p.m., June and July 8 a.m. to 10 p.m., and September and October 9 a.m. to 8 p.m. Admission to the park is 6€ ($6.90) adults, 3€ ($3.45) ages 6 to 12.

The **Kröller-Müller Museum** (☎ 0318-591-241; www.kmm.nl), within the park, displays paintings from radically different artists and eras all side-by-side like wallpaper. The museum displays a rotating selection of their 278 (!) works by van Gogh. Other featured artists include Picasso, Mondrian, Seurat, Monet, and Braque.

The 27-acre **sculpture garden** behind the museum features work by Rodin, Oldenburg, Henry Moore, Barbara Hepworth, Mark di Suvero, and Lipchitz. My favorite is Jean Dubuffet's enormous *Jardin d'Emaille,* an interactive artscape of the sculptor's patented white-with-black-lines raised above ground level, so you have to climb a set of stairs. This enables you to wander around on the art (which, when I was 11 years old, I thought was a fantastic concept). The museum is open Tuesday through Sunday from 10 a.m. to 5 p.m. The sculpture garden closes a half-hour earlier. Admission to the museum is another 6€ ($6.90) adults, 3€ ($3.45) ages 6 to 12 on top of the park fee.

Fast Facts: Amsterdam

Area Code

The country code for the Netherlands is **31.** Amsterdam's city code is **020,** but drop the initial zero if you're calling from outside the Netherlands. To call Amsterdam from the United States, dial 011-31-20, then the number.

American Express

American Express is at Damrak 66 (☎ 020-504-8770) and provides currency exchange. It's open Monday to Friday from 9 a.m. to 5 p.m. and Saturday from 9 a.m. to noon.

Currency

The euro (€) has replaced the guilder in the Netherlands. The euro is divided into 100¢, and there are coins of .01, .02, .05, .10, .20, .50, 1, and 2. Paper-note denominations are 5, 10, 20, 50, 100, 200, and 500. The exchange rate used in this chapter is 1€ = $1.15. Amounts over $10 have been rounded to the nearest dollar.

Doctors

For 24-hour doctor and dentist referrals, contact the Central Medical Service (☎ 0900-503-2042). For 24-hour first-aid service, head to Onze Lieve Vrouwe Gasthuis, at Eerste Oosterparkstraat 279 (☎ 020-599-9111; tram 3, 6, or 10). Also see "Hospitals," later in this section.

Embassies and Consulates

The U.S. Consulate is at Museumplein 19 (☎ 020-575-5309; www.usemb.nl/consul.htm; Tram: 3, 5, 12, 16, or 20), open Monday to Friday from 8:30 to 11:30 a.m.

Emergency

For police assistance, an ambulance, or the fire department, call ☎ 112.

Hospitals

You can reach the Academisch Medisch Centrum at Meibergdreef 9 (☎ 020-566-9111; www.amc.uva.nl) from the center of Amsterdam on buses 29, 59, or 60. Also see "Doctors," earlier in this section.

Information

In the Netherlands, tourist offices are indicated by VVV (usually in a blue-and-white triangle). Amsterdam's most comprehensive VVV office is just outside the Centraal train station at Stationsplein 10. You also find a small desk in the station itself, a branch in the heart of town at Leidseplein 1, and another at the corner of Stadionplein and Van Tuyll van Serooskerkenweg. Call for tourist info on ☎ 020-201-8800, or go to the Web site www.visitamsterdam.nl. You can find an information desk covering all the Netherlands in Schiphol Plaza at the airport.

For transportation information, call ☎ 0900-9292.

Internet Access and Cybercafes

EasyInternetcafé has locations at Damrak 33 (open daily 9 a.m.–10 p.m.), and Leidestraat 24 (open Tues–Sat 9:30 a.m.–7p.m., Mon 11 a.m.–7 p.m.,

Sun 11 a.m.–6 p.m.). Charges start at 2.50€ ($2.90) per hour.

Maps

Though the tourist office hands out a decent enough freebie map, it pays to pick up a more detailed one from any newsstand or bookstore.

Newspapers/Magazines

The tourist office publishes a 1.50€ ($1.70) magazine called *Day by Day* (in English) covering events and exhibitions alongside the usual attractions, museums, shopping, and restaurant info.

Pharmacies

An *apotheek* is a pharmacy that fills prescriptions; a *drogerji* sells toiletries. The most central apotheek is called simply Dam at Damstraat 2 (☎ 020-624-4331). For a list of the local pharmacies whose turn it is to stay open at night or on weekends, check the door of any *apotheek;* a sign will direct you to the nearest late-night pharmacy.

Police

Call ☎ 112 for the police.

Post Office

The main post office, Singel 250 (☎ 020-556-3311), is open Monday through Wednesday and Friday from 9 a.m. to 6 p.m., Thursday from 9 a.m. to 8 p.m., and Saturday from 10:00 a.m. to 1:30 p.m. A second location, Centraal Station, Oosterdokskade 3–5 (☎ 020-622-8272), is open Monday through Friday from 8:30 a.m. to 9:00 p.m., and Saturday from 9 a.m. to noon.

Safety

Although violent crime is rare, the Dutch tolerance of drugs invites drug-related crime. Protect yourself against pickpockets in all tourist areas, on public transportation, and around Damrak, Dam Square, and the Red-Light District. The Red-Light District becomes less than savory after dark, particularly as the evening wears on and tourists have returned to their hotels. Avoid this area at night; I do not recommend that you wander the district alone or call attention to yourself. If you simply must walk through this area late at night, at least make sure you're in a group of people.

Taxes

In Amsterdam, a value-added tax (VAT) is figured into the price of most items. As a foreign visitor, you can reclaim about 13 percent of the VAT on consumer goods as long as you spend at least 137€ ($158) in a single store in a single day (see Chapter 4 for more on this).

Taxis

See "Getting Around Amsterdam," earlier in this chapter.

Telephone

A local call in Amsterdam costs 0.10€ (12¢) to connect plus 0.10€ (12¢) per minute. Almost all pay phones in the Netherlands accept only phone cards, which are sold at newsstands, post offices, tobacconists, and train stations — confusingly, different types of cards are required for the orange-and-gray phones in train stations than for the green phones everywhere else. While talking, watch the digital reading: It tracks your decreasing deposit, so you know when your card is out. For directory assistance, call ☎ 0900-8008.

To charge a call to your calling card, dial AT&T (☎ 0-800-022-9111), MCI (☎ 0-800-023-5103, not accessible from mobile phones), or Sprint (☎ 0-800-022-9119). To call the United States from the Netherlands direct, dial 001 followed by the area code and number.

Transit Info

See "Getting Around Amsterdam," earlier in this chapter.

Chapter 15

Munich and Bavaria

. . . .

In This Chapter

▶ Getting to Munich

▶ Checking out Munich's neighborhoods

▶ Discovering the best places to sleep and eat

▶ Exploring the city's highlights

▶ Heading into Bavaria with stops at Neuschwanstein and Dachau

. . . .

Munich is Germany's center of intellect and industry, a lively European arts-and-culture hub, and the world capital of beer and classy cars (but don't mix those last two). The city is equally comfortable as a vibrant university town, where the Nobel Prize winners Thomas Mann and Albert Einstein rank among the famed intelligentsia, and as an economic powerhouse surrounded by cutting-edge industry. Munich is also the gateway to the rustic, folklore-saturated Bavarian region.

Each autumn, Munich is home to beer and food bashes during a month-long celebration called Oktoberfest. Munich's cultural events, theatres, and museums are sure to keep you busy for several days.

Getting There

With one of the most modern airports in the world and one of the largest train stations in Europe, Munich's status as a major travel hub means that you'll have no trouble finding your way there.

Arriving by air

The ultramodern **Munich Airport International** (☎ **089-97-500;** www. munich-airport.de) is 18 miles northeast of Munich. At the information desks on levels 3 and 4 of the main concourse, you can make hotel reservations for Munich and the surrounding area. The desks are open 6 a.m. to 11 p.m. daily. A 24-hour Internet point is in the airport's center area, and ATMs are located throughout the airport.

You can catch the S8 S-Bahn (light-rail train), which leaves the airport every 20 minutes, for the 45-minute trip to Munich (8€/$9.20).

Germany

Arriving by train

Trains to Munich arrive at the high-tech **Hauptbahnhof train station** on the city's western edge. From here, the S-Bahn runs into the center of town.

For help or tickets, skip the lines and head to the private **EurAide** agency (www.euraide.de), staffed by English-speakers and geared toward helping rail-pass holders by selling tickets and supplements and helping you plan rail journeys from Munich (Room 3 next to Track 11). The office is open June to October 3, daily from 7:45 a.m. to noon and 1 to 6 p.m.; in winter, hours vary.

Orienting Yourself in Munich

Munich's sights are not confined to its **Altstadt,** or old center — as in many European cities. Munich's cultural attractions are spread across town. The tangled streets of the Altstadt are at the core of the city, bearing a combination of medieval and contemporary structures that have been restored or replaced after World War II bombings.

Introducing the neighborhoods

Marienplatz is the heart of the city, with its bustling square and a light-rail juncture underneath. **Neuhauserstrasse** is one of the city's main east-west routes and begins at **Karlsplatz** (a few blocks east of **Hauptbahnhof** station). This street changes names to **Kaufingerstrasse** and beyond Marienplatz, it becomes **Im Tal.** This street leads east into **Isartorplatz,** on the Altstadt's eastern edge. Just a few blocks away is the **Isar River,** which borders the eastern edge of the city.

Art galleries and designer boutiques fill **Maximilianstrasse,** the other main east-west route. This fashionable street runs from the Isar River west into the Altstadt and ends at **Max Joseph Platz** — the location of the **Residenz** royal palace — just a few blocks north of Marienplatz. **Residenzstrasse** runs from Max Joseph Platz to **Odeonsplatz.** Odeonsplatz is an elegant, if heavily trafficked, square surrounded by neo-Renaissance buildings; it marks the Altstadt's northern edge.

From Odeonsplatz, **Ludwigstrasse/Leopoldstrasse** heads due north toward the University district and **Schwabing,** a trendy quarter filled with restaurants and cafes. **Prinzregentenstrasse** runs east-west just north of the city center. This street passes along the southern border of the **Englischer Garten** park and is lined with several museums (including the Bavarian National Museum). An area of neoclassical buildings houses more museums (including both the **Neue and Alte Pinakotheks**) to the northwest corner of the Altstadt. You can reach this area via **Briennerstrasse,** which heads west out of Odeonsplatz.

Finding information after you arrive

The main tourist office, **Fremdenverkehrsamt** (☎ **089-233-0300** or 089-2339-6500; www.munich-tourist.de), is at the Hauptbahnhof at the south exit opening onto Bayerstrasse. Open Monday through Saturday from 9:00 a.m. to 6:30 p.m. and Sunday from 10 a.m. to 6 p.m., it offers a free map of Munich and can **reserve hotel rooms** (☎ **089-2339-6555**). Tourist information can also be obtained in the town center on Marienplatz inside the Rathaus Monday through Friday from 10 a.m. to 8 p.m., Saturday from 10 a.m. to 4 p.m.

Getting Around Munich

Munich was one of the first cities to close many of the streets in its Altstadt (old center) to cars, making getting around the inner city by foot both enjoyable and a necessity (not even trams are allowed). But buses, trams, and two light-rail systems (the **U-Bahn** and **S-Bahn**) are available to help you get around Greater Munich.

Buses, trams, S-Bahns, and U-Bahns all use the same **tickets,** which you buy at machines in S-Bahn/U-Bahn stations. The longer your trip, the more zones you have to cross, and the more you'll pay. One zone covers about two S-Bahn or U-Bahn stops or four bus or tram stops. If you have a Eurail pass, you can use it on the S-Bahn, so don't buy a separate ticket.

A **single-journey ticket** for a ride within the city's central Zone 1 — a large area that few tourists ever leave — costs 2.10€ ($2.40). However, if you're traveling four stops or fewer, you can buy a **"short trip" ticket** for just 1.10€ ($1.25). If you go to the outermost zones of the subway system, your ride could cost as much as 8.40€ ($9.65).

 You can save money by purchasing a *Streifenkarte* **(strip card),** which gives you ten strips to use over several rides for 9.50€ ($11). Fold over the ticket to the number of strips your journey "costs." Brief trips of up to four stations cost one strip, but each full zone costs two strips. Each time you stamp a set of strips, those are good for three hours (one hour for a "short trip" of four stops) and unlimited transfers, as long as you're headed in the same direction (in other words, it doesn't cover your return trip). You can also use the strip card for multiple passengers — for two people to ride two zones, simply stamp four strips.

The *Tageskarte* **(day ticket)** is an even better deal. For 4.50€ ($5.20), you have unlimited access within the central zone for a full day (11€/$13 for three days). For 9€ ($10), you can have access to all of Greater Munich — a 50-mile radius. Partner versions of the tickets are valid for two adults and cost 8€ ($9.20) for the inner district (18.50€/$21 for the three-day variety), or 16€ ($18) for Greater Munich.

Your other option is the **Munich Welcome Card;** see the introduction of the "Exploring Munich" section, later in this chapter.

By U-Bahn and S-Bahn (subway and light rail)

The **S-Bahn** is a state-run commuter train line that covers a wider area than the U-Bahn (and is often aboveground); the **U-Bahn** runs mostly underground as a city subway. In the center of Munich, they're both, effectively, subways providing visitors with an overlapping, interchangeable set of networks. The most important difference between the S-Bahn and the U-Bahn is that you can use your **rail pass** on the S-Bahn, but not on the U-Bahn. The major central junctures of multiple lines are Hauptbahnhof, Karlsplatz, Marienplatz, Sendlingertor, and Odeonsplatz.

Most S-Bahn lines discussed in this chapter (S1 through S8) run the same east-west route through the city, and stop at Hauptbahnhof, Karlsplatz, Marienplatz, and Isartorplatz. The most useful of the U-Bahn lines (**U3** and **U6**) run north-south through the city center, and stop at Sendlingertor, Marienplatz, and Odeonsplatz before going to Schwabing.

By tram and bus

Trams and buses are great for getting to a few areas within the Altstadt and for traveling out into Greater Munich, but they're less effective at getting you where you want to go in the center of town. The 19 tram runs along Maximilianstrasse and the northern part of the Altstadt before heading to Hauptbahnhof. The 18 tram trundles from Hauptbahnhof through Sendlinger Top and Isartor right to the Deutsches Museum.

By taxi

With Munich's efficient public-transportation system, you don't need to take taxis — and at their steep prices, you probably won't want to. The initial charge is 2.50€ ($2.90) and then 1.45€ ($1.65) for each kilometer up to 5; 1.30€ ($1.50) per kilometer for kilometers 5 through 10, then 1.20€ ($1.40) for each kilometer over 10. You're charged an extra 0.50€ (60¢) per bag for luggage. You can call a taxi to pick you up by dialing ☎ 089-21-610 or 089-19-410 or 089-450-540, but you'll pay 1€ ($1.15) more for the convenience.

Staying in Munich

Munich has a healthy supply of hotel rooms that serve a large tourist population, as well as a commercial and industrial trade. Unfortunately, year-round demand keeps prices high.

Rates in Munich rise when a trade fair is in town, during the summer tourist season, and during Oktoberfest. You'll want to book a room well in advance for the city's big keg party, or you'll pay high prices or end up a long way from the center — or both.

If you arrive in town without a hotel, the tourist office can land a room for you. Call them at ☎ 089-2339-6555, or see "Finding information after you arrive," earlier in this chapter, for locations.

Munich's top hotels

An der Oper
$$$ Near the Residenz

An der Oper is a great value right in the heart of town, near major sights, shopping, theater, and the Hofbräuhaus. Rooms are modern and basic, with sitting areas and little touches like mini-chandeliers instead of bed-side lamps. Most rooms are midsized to large. The restaurant serves a mix of Bavarian and French cuisine.

See map p. 290. Falkenturmstrasse 11 (just off Maximilianstrasse, near the Residenz end). ☎ 089-290-0270. Fax: 089-2900-2729. www.hotelanderoper.com. Tram: 19. Rates: 150€–235€ ($173–$270) double. Rates include breakfast. AE, MC, V.

Bayerischer Hof
$$$$ Near the Residenz

A Bavarian version of New York's Waldorf-Astoria, this hotel is in a swank location, opening onto a little tree-filled square. Rooms range from medium size to extremely spacious, each with plush duvets; many beds are four-posters. Décor ranges from Bavarian provincial to British country house chintz. The large bathrooms have tub/shower combos, private phones, and state-of-the-art luxuries.

See map p. 290. Promenadeplatz 2–6. ☎ 800-223-6800 in the U.S., or 089-21-200. Fax 089-212-0906. www.bayerischerhof.de. *Tram: 19. Rates: 205€–416€ ($236–$478) double. Rates include breakfast. AE, DC, MC, V.*

Hotel Am Markt
$ Near Marienplatz

You may have to hunt to find this budget favorite near Munich's outdoor market. The owner keeps the place spotless, welcoming all sorts of visitors from families to students to stars of stage and opera. Rooms are sparse but functional, small but comfortable. This is one place that doesn't raise prices for Oktoberfest.

See map p. 290. Heiliggeistrasse 6 (a tiny alley between the Tal and the Viktualienmarkt). ☎ 089- 225-014. Fax: 089-224-017. www.hotelinmunich.de. *U-Bahn or S-Bahn: Marienplatz. Walk under the arches of the Altes Rathaus; the hotel is down the first right turn off the Tal. Rates: 66€–68€ ($76–$78) double without bathroom, 87€–92€ ($100–$106) double with bathroom. Rates include breakfast. MC, V.*

Kempinski Hotel Vier Jahreszeiten
$$$$$ Near the Residenz

You may have to splurge at this grand old hotel, built in 1858 for Maximilian II to accommodate the overflow of guests from his nearby Residenz. But the extra cash is worth it if you appreciate discreet service, constantly renovated rooms, a rooftop pool, a bevy of fine restaurants, boutique shops, posh accommodations, and the proximity of shopping, theatre, and galleries. The least expensive rooms are in the uninteresting 1972 wing (although the rooms themselves are vintage 2002); if you're splurging anyway, go for the modern rooms in the original building.

See map p. 290. Maximilianstrasse 17 (3 blocks from the Residenz and hard to miss). ☎ 800-426-3135 in the United States; 089-21-250 in Germany. Fax: 089-2125-2000. www.kempinski-vierjahreszeiten.de. *Tram: 19. Rates: 345€–495€ ($397–$569) double. Rates include breakfast. AE, DC, MC, V.*

Splendid-Dollmann
$$$ Near the Isar

This Old World hotel offers great value. Oriental carpets, chandeliers, and antiques fill public rooms; bedrooms are outfitted in neo-Bavarian baroque

Accommodations, Dining, and Attractions in Munich

HOTELS ■
Adria **22**
Advokat Hotel **33**
An der Oper **25**
Bayerischer Hof **9**
Hotel Am Markt **29**
Hotel Carlton **15**
Kempinski Hotel
Vier Jahreszeiten **23**
Pension Westfalia **7**
Splendid **31**
Torbräu **30**

RESTAURANTS ◆
Boettner's **24**
Der Tisch **10**
Donisl **27**
Ederer **20**
Halali **16**
Löwenbräukeller **10**
Mama's Kebap Haus **13**
Nürnberger Bratwurst
Glöckl Am Dom **26**
Restaurant Königshof **8**
Straubinger Hof **32**
Zum Koreaner **14**

ATTRACTIONS ●
Alte Pinakothek **11**
Bayerisches
Nationalmuseum **18**
Cuvilliés Theater **19**
Deutsches Museum **34**
Englischer Garten **17**
Marienplatz **28**
Neue Pinakothek **12**
Residenz Palace **21**

**SCHLOSS
NYMPHENBURG INSET**
Amalienburg **4**
Badenburg **3**
Magdalenenklause **6**
Marstallmuseum **5**
Pagodenburg **1**
Schlosspark **2**

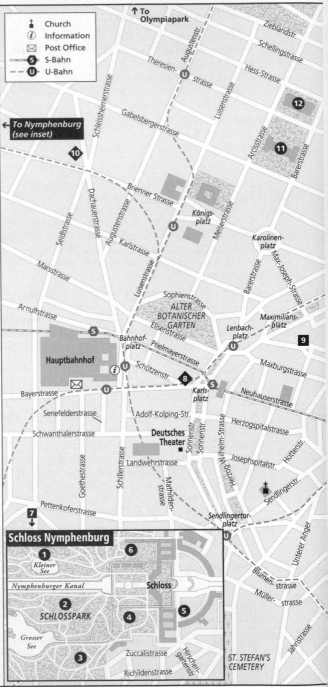

‡ Church
ⓘ Information
✉ Post Office
Ⓢ S-Bahn
Ⓤ U-Bahn

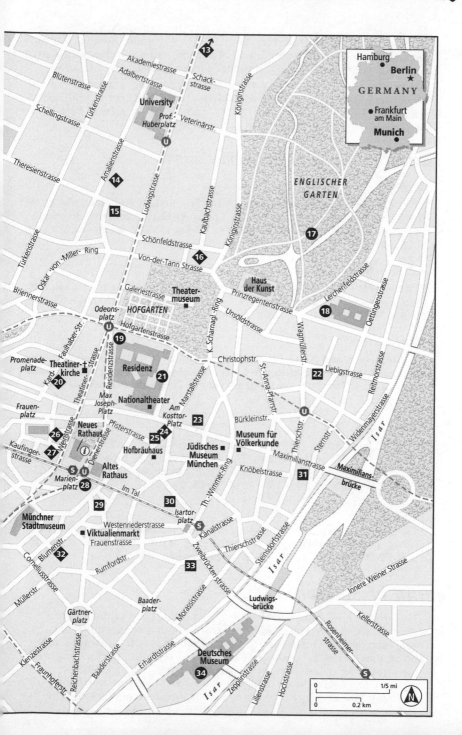

country style. Splendid is located just outside of the Altstadt (with free parking, no less), near the river, and close to several museums. You can get an inexpensive room without a bath (there's one just down the hall), and enjoy your breakfast on the trellised patio in summer.

See map p. 290. Thierschstrasse 49 (at Maximilianstrasse, 1 block before the Maximilian Bridge over the Isar). ☎ *089-296-606 or 089-238-080. Fax: 089-291-3176 or 089-2380-8365.* www.hotel-splendid-dollmann.de. *U-Bahn: Lehel. Tram: 17, 19. Rates: 115€–170€ ($132–$196) double. Breakfast 10.50€ ($12). AE, DC, MC, V.*

Munich's runner-up accommodations

Adria

$$ Near the Englischer Garten   Adria is a stylishly modern place triangulated between the Isar River, the Englisher Garten, and the old center. *See map p. 290. Liebigstrasse 8a.* ☎ *089-242-1170. Fax: 089-2421-17999.* www.adria-muenchen.de.

Advokat Hotel

$$$ Near the Isar   This minimalist contemporary hotel sits comfortably between Isartorplatz and the river. *See map p. 290. Baaderstrasse 1.* ☎ *089-216-310. Fax: 089-216-3190.* www.hotel-advokat.de.

Hotel Carlton

$$ Near Alte and Neue Pinakotheks   Visitors enjoy the neo-baroque comfort of this hotel on the edge of trendy Schwabing, very near Munich's art museums. *See map p. 290. Fürstenstrasse 12.* ☎ *089-282-061. Fax: 089-284-391.* www.renner-hotel-ag.de.

Pension Westfalia

$ Near Goetheplatz   This four-story town house, originally built in 1895, is one of Munich's best pensions. The location faces the meadow where the annual Oktoberfest takes place. *See map p. 290. Mozartstrasse 23.* ☎ *089-530-377. Fax: 089-543-9120.* www.pension-westfalia.de.

Torbräu

$$$ Near Isartorplatz   This place has basic, modern rooms with a 15th-century pedigree, and it's just inside the edge of the Altstadt. *See map p. 290. Tal 41.* ☎ *089-242-340. Fax: 089-234-235.* www.torbraeu.de.

Dining in Munich

The primary food groups in Munich are sausage, beer, salted white radishes, and pretzels, so don't even think about dieting while you're here. Sausages (or *wurstel,* to the natives) come in many shapes, sizes, and stuffings. Look for *bratwurst* (finger-sized seasoned pork), *frankfurter* (the forerunner of hot dogs, but more appetizing), *blütwurst* (blood sausage), *leberwurst* (liver), and, Munich's specialty, *weisswurst* (veal, calf brains, and spleen, spiced to mild deliciousness and boiled). The proper way to eat weisswurst is to cut it in half, dip the cut end in mustard, and suck the filling out of the casing in one fell slurp.

Another word you may see on menus is *knödel*, which means "dumpling." Knödel may be made of *semmel* (bread), *leber* (liver), or *kartoffel* (potato). You can usually get these specialties in a beer hall tavern, where people sit communally at big tables. The outdoor *biergarten* is a wonderful Munich tradition. For more on this, see "More cool things to see and do," later in this chapter.

Now about that beer. Munich is one of the world's beer capitals, and you'll want to raise toast after toast of light beer (*light* refers to the color, not the calories). You can get light beer in a giant liter-sized mug called *ein Mass*. At Oktoberfest tents, if you order *ein Bier*, you usually get a half-liter; if you want the giant one, you need to order it by name.

Munich beer types include: *weissbier* (made with wheat); *pils* (ale); *dunklesbier, bock,* or *dopplebock* (all dark beers); and the beer-and-lemonade spritzer called *radlermass*. All beers are made under the strictest quality guidelines and almost never contain preservatives. *Helles* means light-colored beer; *dunkles* is dark beer.

Munich's top restaurants

Boettner's

$$$$$ Near the Residenz   INTERNATIONAL

Boettner's remains the hottest restaurant in town, despite its recent move to a Renaissance palace — though it did pack up its famous old woody interior and refined service and take those along in the move. Its inspired international cuisine has a bit lighter but richer touch, mixing seafood and truffles into the general Franco-Bavarian mélange of ingredients. It'll be difficult, but try to save room for dessert; your taste buds will thank you.

See map p. 290. Boettnerstrasse 9 (off Platzl square just north of the Hofbräuhaus). ☎ *089-221-210. Reservations strongly recommended. U-Bahn or S-Bahn: Marienplatz. Main courses: 25€–45€ ($29–$52). AE, DC, MC, V. Open: June–Sept, lunch and dinner Mon–Fri; Oct–May, dinner only Mon–Sat.*

Donisl

$$ On Marienplatz   BAVARIAN/INTERNATIONAL

Munich's oldest beer hall has summer tables outside and skylit, pine-paneled galleries inside. The Bavarian cuisine menu features the traditional weisswurst; but the restaurant also serves specials that draw from many culinary traditions (when the chef offers duck, dive for it). An accordion player makes the atmosphere feel that much more Bavarian.

See map p. 290. Weinstrasse 1 (just above Marienplatz). ☎ *089-220-184.* www. bayerischer-donisl.de. *Reservations recommended. U-Bahn or S-Bahn: Marienplatz. Main courses: 6€–12€ ($6.90–$14). AE, DC, MC, V. Open: Lunch and dinner daily.*

Halali

$$$ North of the Residenz FINE BAVARIAN

Refined, but still traditionally Bavarian, Halali features a candlelit dining room with a few dozen trophy antlers. The restaurant serves traditional Bavarian dishes — blütwurst, venison, and other game — but with delicate flavors and attractive presentations. Red wine, not beer, is the beverage of choice in this upscale eatery.

See map p. 290. Schönfeldstrasse 22 (3 long blocks north of Odeonsplatz). ☎ *089-285-909. Reservations required. U-Bahn: Odeonsplatz. Main courses: 15€–22€ ($17–$25). Fixed-price menus 21€–46€ ($24–$53). AE, MC, V. Open: Lunch and dinner Mon–Fri, dinner Sat.*

Nürnberger Bratwurst Glöckl Am Dom

$$ Near Marienplatz BAVARIAN

This place is my choice for best traditional Munich beer-hall grub. You can't get any more Bavarian than rustic dark-wood tables and carved chairs and tin plates full of wurstel. Since 1893, this place has served up the finger-sized sausage specialty of nearby Nürnburg. A platter of assorted wursts, a pretzel, and a tankard of Augustiner Bollbier or Tucher Weissbier make the perfect meal.

See map p. 290. Frauenplatz 9 (off the back end of the cathedral). ☎ *089-291-945.* www.bratwurst-gloeckl.de. *Reservations recommended. U-Bahn or S-Bahn: Marienplatz. Main courses: 5€–19€ ($5.75–$22). No credit cards. Open: Lunch and dinner daily.*

Restaurant Königshof

$$$$$ Near Hauptbahnhof INTERNATIONAL

On the top floor of the Hotel Königshof, you're rewarded not only with fine cuisine, but with a view of the city. Appetizers are sometimes pleasantly startling, like the delicately diminutive rib and loin chops, liver, and rolled duck in a sweet-and-sour ice wine, the flavor enhanced by a pumpkin vinaigrette. The wine list is one of the finest in Germany.

See map p. 290. In the Hotel Königshof, Karlsplatz 25 (Am Stachus). ☎ *089-551-360.* www.koenigshof-muenchen.de. *Reservations required. S-Bahn: Karlsplatz. Tram: 19, 20, or 21. Main courses 29€–44€ ($33–$51); fixed-price menus 85€–118€ ($98–$136). AE, DC, MC, V. Open: Lunch and dinner daily.*

Munich's runner-up restaurants

Ederer

$$$$ Northwest Corner of City Center One of Munich's hottest celebrity chefs has opened a new restaurant in a baronial old building, setting his culinary skills to turning out a creative modern cuisine fusing Asian,

European, and Bavarian styles. Cheapskates can sample the sumptuous fare at lunch, when the set-price menu goes for just 20€ ($23) — at dinner it's 70€ ($81)! *See map p. 290. Kardinal-Faulhaberstrasse 10, 1 block west of Theatinerstrasse (near the Residenz).* ☎ *089-2423-1310.*

Löwenbräukeller

$ West of City Center   This fine beer hall is far enough from the center to keep away most of the tourists (which means the locals still patronize it in droves). The beer garden along the side is perfect on a warm day. *See map p. 290. Nymphenburgerstrasse 2.* ☎ *089-526-021.* www.loewenbraeukeller.com.

Mama's Kebap Haus

$ Schwabing   This small and simple self-service restaurant with a friendly staff in the heart of Schwabing's nightlife district is always crowded with young diners, who enjoy the pizza, kebabs, and daily specials. *See map p. 290. Feilitzschstrasse 7.* ☎ *089-392-642.* www.mamas-kebaphaus.de.

Straubinger Hof

$$ South of Marienplatz   This Paulaner-brand brew hall serves up platters of würstel, cheese, and even a mean Tafelspitz. *See map p. 290. Blumenstrasse 5.* ☎ *089-260-8444.*

Zum Koreaner

$ North of Odeonsplatz   You'll find this excellent and devastatingly cheap Korean spot in a residential neighborhood. *See map p. 290. Amalienstrasse 46.* ☎ *089-283-115.* www.zum-koreaner.de.

Exploring Munich

The **Munich Welcome Card** costs 6.50€ ($7.50) for one day (or 11€/$13 for the "Partner Card" version good for two people), 16€ ($18) for three days (or 23.50€/$27 for a Partner Card). It allows you unlimited transportation on train, bus, and tram routes within the city center, plus small discounts (usually around 25 percent, but sometimes as much as 50 percent) on sightseeing tours and at some sights, including the Residenz Museum and Schatzkammer, the Deutsches Museum, and Schloss Nymphenburg. The three-day version covering transport throughout Greater Munich isn't worth the 28€ ($32). You can buy the card at tourist offices or most hotels.

You can get a two-day **combined ticket** for 12€ ($14) adults, 4.60€ ($5.30) students and seniors, that gets you into both the **Alte and Neue Pinakothek,** as well as the **Pinakothek der Moderne** of 20th-century art (Barerstrasse 40; ☎ **089-2380-5360;** www.pinakothek-der-modern.de), which otherwise charges 9€ ($10) admission.

Munich's top sights

Alte Pinakothek (Old Art Museum)

The Alte Pinakothek is no Louvre or Uffizi, but its rich collection of 14th-to 19th-century works is well worth an hour or three of your time. You find paintings by Italian Renaissance artists Giotto, Filippo Lippi, Botticelli, Perugino, Signorelli, Leonardo da Vinci *(Madonna and Child)*, Raphael *(Holy Family* and a couple of versions of *Madonna and Child)*, Titian *(Christ with the Crown of Thorns* is one of his most mature works), and Tintoretto. The museum also has several works by Rubens and some Spanish pieces by El Greco, Ribera, Velasquez, and Murillo.

The Dutch and Germans are well represented here. Roger van de Weyden's works are numerous, including the huge *St. Colombia Altarpiece;* loads of Rembrandts and Van Dycks grace the walls; and there are a host of good Germanic altarpiece paintings by maestros of the mid-15th to mid-16th centuries.

Albrecht Dürer's *Self Portrait* (from around 1500) is the centerpiece of the collection. Many artists before Dürer painted themselves into the background or crowds in large works as a kind of signature, but Dürer was the first to make himself, the artist, the star of the show. Full frontal portraiture had been used only to portray Christ prior to this self-portrait.

See map p. 290. Barerstrasse 27 (off Theresienstrasse, several long blocks northwest of city center). ☎ *089-2380-5216.* www.pinakothek.de. *U-Bahn: U2 to Königsplatz. Tram: 27. Bus: 53. Admission: 5€ ($5.75) adults, 3.50€ ($4) students ages 15–18, disabled, and senior citizens; free ages 14 and under when accompanied by a parent. Free admission Sundays. Open: Wed –Sun 10 a.m.–5 p.m., Tues 10 a.m.–8 p.m.*

Bayerisches Nationalmuseum (Bavarian National Museum)

The National Museum has an impressive collection of medieval church art, including statuary, altarpieces, and carved ivories (look for the A.D. 400 Munich Ivory showing the Lamentation and Christ ascending into Heaven). The Bavarian sculptor Tilman Riemenschneider, who worked in the early 16th century, often managed to fashion the most eloquent, expressive figures out of plain, unpainted wood.

This museum's hodgepodge collection features armor from the 16th to 18th centuries, baroque porcelain confections, delicate stained-glass panels, and elaborate Christmas crèches from Germany, Austria, Italy, and Moravia. The Weaver's Guild Room is painted with stories from the Bible and the life of Alexander the Great.

See map p. 290. Prinzregentenstrasse 3 (off the southeast corner of the Englischer Garten, northeast of the city center). ☎ *089-211-2401.* www.bayerisches-nationalmuseum.de. *U-Bahn: U4, U5 to Lehel. Tram: 20. Bus: 53. Admission: 3€ ($3.45) adults, 2€ ($2.30) students and seniors, free for ages 18 and under. Free admission Sundays. Open: Tues–Wed and Fri–Sun 10 a.m.–5 p.m., Thurs 10 a.m.–8 p.m.*

Deutsches Museum (German Museum of Science and Technology)

If you have kids, don't miss this fantastic see-and-touch science museum. The placards are in German and English, and the rooms cover industrial machinery, the digging of tunnels, astronautics, computers and micro-electronics, textiles, mining, and electricity in wonderful detail.

You may especially enjoy the High Voltage demonstrations (11 a.m., 2 p.m., and 4 p.m. daily) — they actually produce lightning. A hangar filled with historic aircraft and a collection of venerable cars, including the very first automobile (an 1886 Benz), are not to be missed if you're interested in transportation. You also find the first diesel engine (1897) and the lab bench at which Hahn and Strassmann first split the atom (1938).

The Deutsches Museum is one of the few museums in Munich that is open on Monday.

See map p. 290. Museuminsel 1 (on an island in the Isar river). ☎ *089-21-791.* www. deutsches-museum.de. *U-Bahn: U1, U2 to Fraunhoferstrasse. S-Bahn: Isartorplatz. Tram: 18. Admission: 7.50€ ($8.65) adults, 4.10€ ($4.70) seniors, 3€ ($3.45) students aged 6–15; free ages 6 and under. A Family Ticket for parents and up to two kids costs 15€ ($17). Open: Daily 9 a.m.–5 p.m. (on Wed certain exhibits remain open until 8 p.m. — and admission is only 3€/$3.45 if you enter Wed after 4 p.m.).*

Marienplatz

In the center of Munich is the lively, cafe-lined Marienplatz (see map p. 290), home to street performers and the daily bustle of the city. This city square is bounded along its long north side by the pinnacles and tracery of the 19th-century Neues Rathaus, done in neo-Gothic style. The clock on this town hall is equipped with a bilevel *glockenspiel* (a percussion instrument that produces bell-like tones), the fourth largest in Europe, whose mechanical jousting show plays out daily at 11 a.m. and noon (and at 5 p.m. in summer).

St. Peter's Church is on the southeast corner of the square, with a 300-foot tower that you can climb for a small fee. At the top, you're rewarded with excellent city views that reach the Alps on clear days.

Neue Pinakothek (New Art Museum)

Across from the Altes Pinakothek, the Neue Pinakothek covers the late-18th through mid-20th centuries with the likes of Gainsborough, Goya, Delacroix, Manet, Monet, Degas, Cézanne, van Gogh, Klimt, Beckmann, and Munch. An amusing section displays works by the Nazarenes, a group of early-19th-century German artists trying their darndest to paint like 15th-century Italian artists (the older set of paintings is a better choice if you're on a tight schedule). Visit the Alte Pinakothek first, and then see if you have an hour or so left for these galleries.

See map p. 290. Barerstrasse 29 (off Theresienstrasse, several long blocks northwest of city center). ☎ *089-2380-5195.* www.pinakothek.de. *U-Bahn: U2 to Königsplatz. Tram: 27. Bus: 53. Admission: 5€ ($5.75) adults, 3.50€ ($4) students ages 15–18, disabled, and senior citizens; free ages 14 and under when accompanied by a parent. Free admission Sundays. Open: Tues and Thurs–Sun 10 a.m.–5 p.m., Wed 10 a.m.–8 p.m.*

Residenz Palace

The official residence of Bavarian royalty is a rambling palace that was started in 1385 and added on to until World War I. A medieval merchant family, the Wittlesbachs, rose to power in Bavaria in 1180 and didn't relinquish power until revolutionaries came banging at the Residenz front door in 1918 — making them Europe's longest-lasting dynasty.

Must-see highlights include the Residenz Museum, the Treasure House, and the Cuvilliés Theater. To see all the details, you have to take both a morning and an afternoon tour, but you can enjoy the ornate splendors on your own in just a couple of hours.

In the **Residenz Museum,** 120 rooms of Wittlesbach history and furnishings, check out the Ancestor's Gallery (1728–1730), a royal photo album of oil portraits set into the gilded stucco walls of a long hallway, and the huge Renaissance Hall of Antiquities, covered with 16th- and 17th-century frescoes. Don't miss Maximilian I's Reiche Kappelle, a closet-sized chapel featuring inlaid marble, gilding, and ivory carvings. The Residenz is so big that they open separate sets of rooms in the morning (10 a.m.–2:30 p.m. for Circular Tour I) and the afternoon (12:30–4 p.m. for Circular Tour II).

The Bavarian crown jewels, some dating back to A.D. 1000, are kept in the **Schatzkammer (Treasure House),** but the greatest treasure is the gold St. George Slaying the Dragon (1590). It's a wonder the saint, encumbered by all those diamonds, rubies, sapphires, and other gems, ever managed to slay the emerald beast.

Around the corner is the beautiful **Cuvilliés Theater,** named after its architect, a former court jester who overcame 18th-century prejudices about his dwarfism, won the patronage of the Wittlesbachs, and became one of southern Germany's most important architects. Enjoy concerts and opera here in summer; Mozart's *Idomeneo* premiered here in 1781.

See map p. 290. Max Joseph Platz 3. ☎ 089-290-671. www.schloesser.bayern.de. *U-Bahn: U3, U5, U6 to Odeonsplatz. Admission: Combination museum and Treasure House, 9€ ($10) adults, 8€ ($9.20) students/seniors; museum or Treasure House individually, 6€ ($6.90) adults, 5€ ($5.75) seniors/students; Cuvilliés Theater, 3€ ($3.45) adults, 2€ ($2.30) students and seniors; all free for ages 15 and under. Open: All three are open daily 9 a.m.–6 p.m. (10 a.m.–4 p.m. Oct 16–Mar), although Cuvilliés Theater sometimes shortens hours when rehearsing or setting the stage for a production.*

Schloss Nymphenburg

The Wittelsbachs spent summers in a sophisticated countryside palace, named Schloss Nymphenburg after the nymphs frescoed in its main entrance hall (concerts are presented here in summer). This place started as a modest Italianate villa in 1664 and was changed radically over the next 150 years, including a change of face to French baroque.

A network of pavilions at the palace provides interesting architecture and artwork. The south pavilion (where Queen Caroline resides) features Ludwig I's Gallery of Beauties — portraits commissioned by the king of the 36 most beautiful women in the realm. In the **Mastrallmuseum**, you find a collection of royal coaches including King Ludwig II's wedding coach, entirely gilded and encrusted with rococo stucco swirls.

The **Schlosspark** has more than 500 acres of grassy lawns, English-style gardens, canals, and pavilions. Visit Electress Amalia's **Amalienburg** pavilion, which features extravagant rococo inside, and the **Badenburg** on the lake, with its frescoed-ceilinged bath in the basement. The pseudo-Chinese **Pagodenburg** and the religious retreat **Magdalenenklause** also offer an enjoyable visit.

See map p. 290. Schloss Nymphenburg 1 (3 miles west of the city center). ☎ 089-179-080. www.schloesser.bayern.de. U-Bahn: U1 to Rotkreuzplatz, then tram 12 toward Amalienburgstrasse. Bus: 41. Admission: Combined ticket to all attractions, 10€ ($12) Apr–Oct 15, 8€ ($9.20) Oct16–Mar; separate admissions, 5€ ($5.75) to Schloss Nymphenburg, 4€ ($4.60) each to Marstallmuseum and Porcelain Collection or Amalienburg complex. Open: Apr 15–Oct 15 daily 9 a.m.–6 p.m.; Oct 16–Mar daily 10 a.m.–4 p.m.

More cool things to see and do

✔ **Eating lunch at a biergarten:** Bring your own food, and order huge mugs of beer. Biergartens are generally open from 10 a.m. to 10 p.m. or midnight. They usually offer simple sandwiches, and pretzels and other snacks are always available. Try these biergartens: the **Biergarten Chinesischer Turm** (☎ 089-383-8730; www.chinaturm.de) in the heart of the Englischer Garten Park under the shade of a Chinese pagoda; the **Augustinerkeller** (☎ 089-594-393; www.augustinerkeller.de) at Arnulfstrasse 52, several long blocks past Hauptbahnhof; and the **Hirschgarten** (☎ 089-172-591; www.hirschgarten.de), in Nymphenburg Park, the world's largest beer garden with room for 8,000 guzzlers.

✔ **Watching an entire city drink itself into a stupor at Oktoberfest:** For the better part of a month, tens of thousands of people do nothing but party medieval-style, listening to oompah bands, roasting whole oxen on spits, and drinking more than 5 million liters of beer. Oktoberfest (there's a direct link on www.muenchen.de) is the world's ultimate keg party. The event started with the celebrations for Prince Ludwig's marriage to Princess Therese in 1810, and the locals enjoyed themselves so much that they made it an annual event. The name is a bit misleading, because the first weekend in October is the *end* of the festivities — the fun starts a few weeks earlier.

The action centers on the Theresienwiese park fairgrounds, southwest of Hauptbahnhof, but the whole city has a distinct party air (just follow the smell of the beer). You must reserve a hotel room months in advance; call the tourist office to determine the exact dates of this year's festival.

✔ **Spending an afternoon in the Englischer Garten:** Munich's Englischer Garten (named after a British ex-pat who first devised the park) stretches for 3 miles along the west bank of the Isar River. The park features beer gardens, trees, grassy lawns, bicycle paths, and streams and lakes where you can swim. Around the Eisbach, some people (mostly men) sunbathe in the nude, and near the park's southern entrance, just behind the Haus der Kunst on Prinzregentenstrasse, you find a Japanese teahouse in the middle of a small lake. Traditional Japanese tea service is available the second and fourth weekends of each month from April through October at 3 p.m., 4 p.m., and 5 p.m. (Sunday also at 2 p.m.).

Guided tours

You have two choices for orientation bus tours. The **Stadtrundfahrt** run by **Panorama Tours** (☎ 089-5490-7560; www.autobusoberbayern.de/panorama) is a straightforward affair — just hop on in front of Hauptbahnhof and buy your 11€ ($13) ticket onboard. The hour-long tour is delivered in eight languages; departures are at 10 a.m., 11 a.m., noon, 1 p.m., 2 p.m., 2:30 p.m., 3 p.m., and 4 p.m. daily (Apr–Oct also at 11:30 a.m. and 5 p.m.).

Panorama also offers two-and-a-half-hour, 19€ ($22) city tours that, in addition to the city orientation tour, spend some time exploring a single site. One visits the Olympic Area where you can climb its 960-foot Olympic Tower (daily at 2:30 p.m., plus another at 10 a.m. Apr–Oct); another spends time in the Alte Pinakothek (Tues–Sun at 10 a.m. — costs an extra 2€/$2.30); and a third heads to the Schloss Nymphenburg (daily at 2:30 p.m.).

But perhaps the most popular way to see town is with the English-speaking ex-pats at **Mike's Bike Tours** (☎ 089-2554-3988 or 0172-852-0660; www.mikesbiketours.com). Mike's offers four-hour, 22€ ($25) spins around the sights of central Munich (including 45 minutes in a beer garden). The daily tours leave at 2:30 p.m. September to November 10 and March to April 15; at 11:30 a.m. and 4 p.m. April 16 through August. In June and July, there's also a 5:15 p.m. tour, plus they run an extended, seven-hour, 33€ ($38) tour that leaves at 10:30 a.m. and hits Schloss Nymphenburg and the Olympic Park. All tours meet 15 minutes before setting off, under the tower of the Altes Rathaus on Marienplatz.

Despite the name, Mike's also does three-hour **walking tours,** which cost 9€ ($10) and meet daily April 15 through August 31 at 3:30 p.m. at the main entrance to the Hauptbahnhof train station.

Suggested itineraries

If you're the type who likes to strike out on your own, this section offers tips for building your own Munich itinerary.

If you have one day

Start the day off with a tour of the **Residenz Palace,** the most impressive downtown palace in Europe. Take in the old masters paintings in the **Alte Pinakothek** before moseying on down to **Marienplatz** around noon to take in the clock-tower show and grab a late lunch in a beer hall or (if it's summer) the biergarten in the middle of the Viktualienmarkt.

Enjoy the displays in the **Bayerisches Nationalmuseum** after lunch, and then set off for what everyone really comes to Munich for: drinking enormous tankards of beer. Have dinner downstairs in **Nürnberger Bratwurst Glöckl Am Dom** — or just nibble on würstel as you crawl from beer hall to beer hall.

If you have two days

Spend Day 1 as described in the preceding section, and then on the morning of Day 2, head out to **Schloss Nymphenburg** for more royal splendor. In the late afternoon, stroll the **Englischer Garten** (look for the modern art galleries that ring its southern edge), or investigate the scientific wonders of the **Deutsches Museum.**

If you have three days

Spend Days 1 and 2 as described in the previous sections. On the morning of Day 3, head out of town, either to the somber concentration-camp museum at **Dachau** or, if you get an early start, to see Mad King Ludwig's fantastical **Neuschwanstein.** Depending on what time you get back into town, wind down with one last stein of beer at one of the biergartens mentioned earlier in this chapter.

Traveling Beyond Munich

The Bavarian Alps is a region of spectacular scenery; any trip from Munich into the surrounding countryside is bound to be unforgettable. In addition to the excursions mentioned here, Munich is just two to three hours away from **Innsbruck** by train. Innsbruck is covered as an excursion from Vienna, Austria, in Chapter 16.

Neuschwanstein: Mad King Ludwig's fairy-tale castle

Ever wonder where Walt Disney got the idea for the Cinderella castle at his theme parks? He drew direct inspiration — and even some blueprints — right from Bavaria's storybook castle, Neuschwanstein.

King Ludwig II — in many ways the epitome of a 19th-century romantic — built or renovated many a castle for himself. But the only thing that would completely satisfy him would be to create a castle that looked like something from a story by the Brothers Grimm.

Neuschwanstein was the result and is still a stunning, dreamlike sight, perched halfway up a forested mountain near a waterfall. The structure features slender towers, ramparts, and pointy turrets done in pale gray. Sadly, the castle was never quite finished, and the king got to live in his half-completed fantasy for only 170 days before his death.

You can take a bus or make a strenuous 25-minute downhill walk from Neuschwanstein to **Hohenschwangau,** to find the much more practical castle created by Ludwig II's father. Between these two fortresses and Munich, off a side road, hides the pilgrimage church of **Wieskirche,** one of the most glorious examples of the late baroque period in Germany.

Getting there

Although you can do all this in a day, you may find it more relaxing to stay a night in Füssen and trek to Neuschwanstein from there. As Bavaria's biggest tourist draw, Neuschwanstein is packed by 9 a.m., and the crowd doesn't thin out until 4 p.m. or so. (You can wait hours just to take the 35-minute tour.) You can't avoid the crowds, but you can take a late train into Füssen the night before in order to arrive at Neuschwanstein with the first tourist wave.

You really need a car for this trip, but you can use **public transportation** from Munich in a pinch. Take one of the nearly hourly trains to Füssen (a two-hour trip), from which hourly buses make the ten-minute trip to the castle parking lot. The sister castles of Neuschwanstein and Hohenschwangau are usually referred to collectively on road signs as *Königsschlösser* (king's castles).

When driving into this castle complex, you have your choice of **parking lots** in Schwangau, that little tourist center by the lake. Park in Lot D for the quickest (but steepest) walk up to Neuschwanstein (20–30 minutes). Go farther down the road to the big lot on the right if you want to take the longer (but less steep) paved road up (30–45 minutes). It's a fairly strenuous hike either way. Horse-drawn carriages leaving from the Müller Hotel (5€/$5.75 uphill, 2.50€/$2.90 downhill) can take you to the ticket office, two-thirds of the way up.

For the easiest route, take the **shuttle bus** that leaves from near Hotel Lisl, overshoots the castle, and stops at Marienbrücke, a bridge across the gorge above Neuschwanstein (1.80€/$2.05 uphill, 1€/$1.15 downhill, or 2.60€/$3 round-trip). This lets you walk (steeply) back downhill in ten minutes to the castle and gives you a great view of the castle with Alpsee Lake in the background.

If you prefer an **escorted bus tour** here direct from Munich, **Mike's Bike Tours** (☎ 089-2554-3987; www.mikesbiketours.com) can hook you up with a 49€ ($56), all-day trip that includes a bike ride around Swan Lake and a hike to the castle in addition to the castle tour (though admission is not included). Meet at the Discover Bavaria Shop on Hochbrückenstrasse at 8:45 a.m. Tours run Monday and Tuesday and Thursday through Saturday in June and July. From May 15 to May 31 and in August, there are full tours Mondays, Fridays, and Saturdays; Wednesdays you can pay 39€ ($45) for a "train tour" that includes a rail ticket to the castle, the bike ride and hike, and castle admission. You can get the same "train tour" deal Mondays, Wednesdays, Fridays, and Saturdays from April 15 to May 14 and September 1 to October 2.

You can get information on Neuschwanstein at the tourist office in Munich. The local **tourist office** (☎ 083-628-1980; www.schwangau.de) in the tiny village/parking lot of Schwangau is closed mid-November to mid-December.

Note that you can get a **combined "Kings Ticket"** to visit both Hohenschwangau (first) and Neuschwanstein (second) for 17€ ($20) adults, 15€ ($17) students and seniors over 65 (children under 18 can get in free if traveling with their parents — though you have to request the free ticket).

Seeing the sights

The tour of **Neuschwanstein** (☎ 08362-939-880; www.neuschwanstein.de) shows you some of the castle's most theatrical details, including the king's bedroom — almost every inch covered in intricately carved wood — his near-finished neo-Byzantine-Romanesque Throne Room, and the huge Singers Hall, covered with paintings that refer to the work of composer Richard Wagner.

The king was enthralled by Wagner's music; he supposedly convulsed and writhed in such bliss to the strains of the composer's operas that his aides feared he was having an epileptic fit. Ludwig bailed Wagner out of debt and poured money into whatever project the composer desired.

This was the sort of thing that earned Ludwig II the moniker "Mad King Ludwig," but the monarch probably wasn't certifiable. Although beloved by his subjects as a genial and well-meaning ruler, Ludwig's withdrawal into his fantasies caused him to lose touch with his court and the political machinations in Munich. In 1886, he was deposed in absentia, and a few days later his body was found drowned, under suspicious circumstances, in a few feet of water at the edge of a lake.

You can visit the interior of Neuschwanstein by **guided tour only,** April through September daily from 9 a.m. to 6 p.m., the rest of the year from 10 a.m. to 4 p.m. (The ticket booth closes one hour before closing time.) Tickets are 9€ ($10) adults, 8€ ($9.20) students and seniors over 65, free under 18. The 35-minute tour is available in English.

At the bottom of Neuschwanstein's hill is the tiny village/parking lot of Schwangau, which serves as a lunch stop for tour-bus crowds. Across the road and up a short hill is **Hohenschwangau** (☎ 08362-930-830; www.hohenschwangau.de), a sandy-colored castle restored in neo-Gothic style by Ludwig's father (Maximilian II). By comparison to Neuschwanstein, it's almost ordinary, but tours (usually in German, unless enough English speakers show up) can prove interesting. Ludwig made his home in Hohenschwangau for 17 years.

The castle is open daily, April through September from 8:00 a.m. to 5:30 p.m., the rest of the year from 9:00 a.m. to 3:30 p.m. Admission is 9€ ($10) adults; 8€ ($9.20) students and seniors over 65, free under 18.

The Nazi concentration camp at Dachau

In 1933, in a little town outside Munich called Dachau, SS leader Heinrich Himmler set up Nazi Germany's first concentration camp. Between 1933 and 1945, 206,000 prisoners were officially registered here, and countless thousands more were interned without record.

Getting there

To spend an hour or two here remembering the darkest days of modern history, take a 20-minute ride on the S2 **S-Bahn train** from Marienplatz. From Dachau station, bus 724 or 726 takes you to the camp. For information on the town, visit www.dachau.info; for information on the concentration-camp memorial site, contact ☎ 08131-669-970 or visit www. kz-gedenkstaette-dachau.de. **Panorama Tours** (☎ 089-5490-7560; www.autobusoberbayern.de/panorama) in Munich leaves from the Bahnhofplatz at Herties Department Store for a four-and-a-half-hour tour of Dachau (22€/$25) from May 15 to October 16 on Saturdays at 1:30 p.m.

Seeing the sights

The taunting Nazi slogan *Arbeit Macht Frei* (Work Brings Freedom) is inscribed on the gate where you enter. Allied troops razed the 32 prisoners' barracks to the ground when they liberated the camp in 1945, but two have been reconstructed to illustrate the squalid living conditions. Each barrack was built to house 208 people; by 1936, they accommodated up to 1,600 each.

The former kitchen is now a museum with photographs documenting the rise of the Nazis and the persecution of Jews, communists, gypsies, homosexuals, and others. You can watch a short documentary film (the English version usually shows at 11:30 a.m. and 3:30 p.m.).

The ovens of the crematorium and a gas chamber disguised as showers are at the back of the camp. No prisoners were gassed at Dachau (though more than 3,000 Dachau inmates were sent to an Austrian camp to be gassed); this room was used for beatings and cruel interrogations. Although Dachau, unlike other camps such as Auschwitz in Poland, was primarily for political prisoners and not expressly a death camp, more than 32,000 people died here, and thousands more were executed. The camp is scattered with Jewish, Catholic, and Protestant memorials.

The camp is open Tuesday through Sunday from 9 a.m. to 5 p.m.; admission is free, and free tours are conducted in English from June through August at 12:30 p.m.

Fast Facts: Munich

Area Code

Germany's country code is **49**. The city code for Munich is **089**. If you're calling Munich from outside Germany, you can drop the city code's initial zero. In other words, to call Munich from the United States, dial 011-49-89 and the number.

American Express

American Express has Munich offices at Promenadeplatz 6 (☎ 089-2280-1465) open Monday through Friday from 9 a.m. to 6 p.m. and Saturday from 9:30 a.m. to 12:30 p.m.; at Neuhauserstrasse 47 and the corner of Herzog-Wilhemstrasse (☎ 089-2280-1387) open Monday through Friday from 9:30 a.m. to 6 p.m. and Saturday from 10 a.m. to 1 p.m.; and in the Munich Airport (☎ 089-9758-4408) open daily from 7 a.m. to 9 p.m.

Currency

The Deutsche Mark gave way to the euro in 2002. The euro is divided into 100 cents, and there are coins of .01, .02, .05, .10, .20, .50, 1, and 2. Paper-note denominations are 5, 10, 20, 50, 100, 200, and 500. The exchange rate used in this chapter is 1€ = $1.15. Amounts over $10 have been rounded to the nearest dollar.

Doctors and Dentists

The American, British, and Canadian consulates keep a list of recommended English-speaking physicians. For emergency doctor service, phone ☎ 089-551-771 or 01805-191-212. For an English-speaking dentist, try the Gemeinschaftspraxis (Partnership Practice for Dentistry) at Rosenkavalierplatz 18 (☎ 089-928-7840).

Embassies and Consulates

U.S. Consulate at Königstrasse 5 (☎ 089-28-880; www.usembassy.de) is open Monday through Friday from 8 a.m. to 1 p.m.

Emergency

For an ambulance, call ☎ **112**. For emergency doctor service, phone ☎ 089-551-771 or 01805-191-212. Call the police at ☎ **110**. Report a fire at ☎ **112**.

Hospitals

Munich's main hospitals are the Red Cross Hospital in Neuhausen (Ärztliche Bereitschaftspraxis im Rotkreuz Krankenhaus) at Nymphenburger Strasse 163 (☎ 089-1278-9790); and the Schwabing Hospital (Ärztliche Bereitschaftspraxis im Krankenhaus Schwabing) at Kölner Platz 1 (☎ 089-3304-0302).

Information

The main tourist office, Fremdenverkehrsamt (☎ 089-233-0300 or 089-2339-6500; www.munich-tourist.de), is at the Hauptbahnhof at the south exit opening onto Bayerstrasse. For specifics on it, and on other offices, see "Finding information after you arrive," near the beginning of this chapter.

Internet Access and Cybercafes

You can send e-mails or check your messages at the Times Square Online Bistro, BayerStrasse 10A (☎ 089-550-8800), open daily from 7 a.m. to 1 a.m. There's an easyInternetcafé (☎ 089-260-0230) with more than 450 terminals across from the main train station at Banhofplatz 1. It's open daily from 6 a.m. to 1.a.m.

Maps

The center of Munich is pretty small, so the map the tourist office gives out should serve you just fine.

Newspapers/Magazines

The tourist office hands out a monthly events calendar called *Monatsprogramm.* You may also want to pick up the ex-pat magazine *Munich Found* (www.munich found.de) — full of events, news, and articles of interest to foreigners in Munich — on newsstands.

Pharmacies

Apotheke (pharmacies) in Munich rotate the duty of staying open nights and weekends. For the location of the nearest 24-hour pharmacy, check the sign in the window of any pharmacy. The International Ludwigs-Apotheke, Neuhauser Strasse 11 (☎ 089-1894-0300), is open Monday through Friday from 9 a.m. to 8 p.m. and Saturday from 9 a.m. to 4 p.m.

Police

Call the police at ☎ 110.

Post Office

A large post office is at Bahnhofplatz 1 (☎ 089-599-0870; www.deutschepost. de), across from the train station, and is open Monday through Friday from 7 a.m. to 8 p.m., Saturday from 9 a.m. to 4 p.m., and Sun from 9 a.m. to 3 p.m.

Safety

While visiting Munich, you may be targeted for petty crimes such as purse-snatching and pickpocketing. You probably don't have to worry about violent crime, but you should be careful in popular areas such as the Marienplatz and around the Hauptbahnhof, especially at night.

Taxes

In Germany, a 16 percent value-added tax (VAT) is figured into the price of most items. Foreign visitors can reclaim a percentage of the VAT on purchases of 25€ ($29) or more in a single store (see Chapter 4 for more on this).

Taxis

See "Getting Around Munich," earlier in this chapter.

Telephone

Pay phones in Munich take phone cards, which are available from newsstands in 6.15€ ($7.05) and 26€ ($30) denominations. To charge your call to a calling card, you can call AT&T (☎ 0800-225-5288), MCI (☎ 0800-888- 8000), or Sprint (☎ 0800-888-0013). To call the United States direct, dial 001 followed by the area code and phone number.

Transit Info

For public-transportation information, visit www.mvv-muenchen.de. For train info, visit www.bahn.de. For more, see "Getting Around Munich," earlier in this chapter.

Chapter 16

Vienna and the Best of Austria

. . . .

In This Chapter

▶ Getting to Vienna

▶ Exploring the neighborhoods of Vienna

▶ Discovering Vienna's top hotels, restaurants, and attractions

▶ Side-tripping to charming Innsbruck

. . . .

*M*ore than any other European city, Vienna maintains a link with the past. In attitude, architecture, and interior décor, Vienna still reverberates with the stately elegance of the Hapsburg dynasty, which ruled the Austro-Hungarian Empire in the 18th and 19th centuries. The city on the Danube is pure refinement: Its imperial palaces and art museums delight, its rococo churches and ornate beer taverns excite, and its charming cafes and awe-inspiring concert halls thrill.

Vienna lays claim to one of Europe's richest and most varied musical heritages. The birthplace of the waltz, it's home to the likes of Mozart, Haydn, Beethoven, Schubert, the Strauss family, Brahms, Mahler, and the Vienna Boys Choir. Plan for at least two or three days in Vienna — or slightly longer to take in all the sights and give yourself time just to walk, sample more delectable pastries, and people-watch in a fantastic European capital.

Getting There

Vienna is a relatively brief five-hour train ride from both Munich and Prague, making the city a convenient destination to reach by either air or rail. Once there, you find that most tourist sights are concentrated in a small part of the city center.

Arriving by air

Wien Schwechat airport (☎ 01-70-070; www.viennaairport.com) is
12 miles southeast of the city. If you're traveling with your own laptop,
you'll be able to take advantage of several wireless LAN zones throughout
the airport. The information desk is located in the arrivals hall, where
there are also two ATMs.

The City Airport Train (☎ 01-25-250; www.cityairporttrain.at) connects the terminal with Wien Mitte train station in just 16 minutes for 8€
($9.20). Buses cost 6€ ($6.90) (☎ 01-930-000; www.oebb.at), leave every
20 minutes, and stop downtown at Südtiroler Platz (20 min.), Südbahnhof
(25 min.), and Westbanhof (35 min.). The S7 S-Bahn service is the cheapest
(3€/$3.45) but also the slowest (35 min. or more). It leaves every 30 min-
utes for stops at Wien Mitte and Wien Nord.

Arriving by rail

By train, you arrive in Vienna at **Westbahnhof** from northern Europe,
or **Südbahnhof** from southern Europe (central Europe arrivals are split
between the two). Trains from Prague and Berlin occasionally arrive at
the northerly **Franz-Josef Bahnhof,** and if you're coming from Prague or
the airport, you may disembark at **Wien Mitte/Landstrasse** on the eastern edge of the city.

The **U-Bahn** (subway) and tram system runs between these stations and
the center of town — except Südbahnhof, from which you can catch the
D tram to downtown (look for the tram in a terminal on the station's east
side, not right out in front near the other tram stop).

Orienting Yourself in Vienna

Vienna's inner city is the oldest part of town and home to the most spectacular sights and almost all the hotels and restaurants recommended in
this chapter.

When you're trying to figure out a **Viennese address,** remember that the
building number comes *after* the street name. A number before the name,
especially a Roman numeral, indicates the *bezirk* (city district) in which
the address resides. (The inner city is "I bezirk.")

Introducing the neighborhoods

The **Ringstrasse,** or Ring Road, encircles the inner city with an elegant,
tree-lined thoroughfare. This boulevard follows the outline of the medieval
city walls of yesteryear. The road is studded with many of Vienna's most
prized gems: churches, palaces, and museums. Although the Ring is a
continuous stretch of road, its name changes often. Just remember this:
Any road whose name ends in *-ring* (such as Opern Ring or Kärntner Ring)
is part of this avenue.

Austria

Forming the northeast border of the old city is the **Danube Canal** (the actual famed river, which isn't really blue, is farther northeast). The northward-running shopping boulevard **Kärntnerstrasse** begins where Kärntner Ring becomes Opern Ring at the Staatsoper opera house. This avenue bisects the inner city to **Stephansplatz,** the epicenter of town and home of St. Stephan's Cathedral.

The only place you're likely to venture outside of Vienna's Ring is the refined neighborhood of **Karlsplatz** (just southeast of the Staatsoper) with its namesake church, history museum, and major U-Bahn (subway) junction. You may also head west of the Ring a bit to the **Naschmarkt,** a fresh produce market, and maybe a touch farther beyond that to **Mariahilferstrasse,** the wide shopping street that runs from the Opern Ring to **Westbahnhof** train station.

Finding information after you arrive

Vienna's tourist office is an excellent resource. You'll find it behind the Staatsoper, at Kärntnerstrasse 38 (☎ 01-24-555; Fax: 01-2455-5666; www.wien.info). Hours are daily from 9 a.m. to 7 p.m.

Getting Around Vienna

You use the same ticket for all Viennese public transportation. Tickets are available at *Tabak-Trafiks* (tobacco/newsstands), automated machines at major stops and U-Bahn stations, and on trams (though they cost 0.50€/60¢ more onboard). A single (one-ride) ticket costs 1.50€ ($1.75), which is also the price of two rides for a child. Children under 6 ride free. A one-day pass for 5€ ($5.75) and a three-day pass for 12€ ($14) are also available.

A potential cost-saving option, if you're going to be doing lots of sightseeing, is the 17€ ($20), 72-hour **Vienna Card** (see the introduction to "Exploring Vienna," later in this chapter, for details).

By U-Bahn (subway)

Although inner-city Vienna is great for hoofing it, you need public transportation for some of the longer hauls. To get where you want to go as quickly as possible, I recommend the **U-Bahn** (subway). The U3 heads from Westbahnhof station through the center of town, stops at Stephansplatz, and then proceeds on to Wien Mitte/Landstrasse station. The U1 cuts through the center of town north-south, stopping at Karlsplatz, Stephansplatz, Swedenplatz (near the Danube Canal), and Praterstern/Wien Nord (at the Prater city park). The U2 curves around the Ring's west side to Karlsplatz, where it ends, and the U4 continues circling around the Ring's eastern half before heading north to the Friedensbrücke stop (the closest to Franz-Josef Bahnhof).

By tram or bus

For a more scenic way to get about town, try the tram. Lines include: 18 (Südbahnhof to Westbahnhof), D (hedging around much of the Ring before veering off to Südbahnhof), and 1 and 2 (circling along the Ring — 1 goes clockwise, 2 goes counterclockwise).

You can also take buses that crisscross the center of town (1A, 2A, and 3A) or head out to the 'burbs.

By taxi

Although you can see most of the touristy sites in Vienna on foot, you may prefer the comforts of a taxi for trips from the airport or train station to your hotel. Be aware that taxis won't cruise the streets of Vienna looking for you. Instead, you need to hire taxis at stands located throughout the city, or call ☎ 31-300, 60-160, 81-400, or 40-100 (a 2€/$2.30 charge is added onto your fare when you call a cab).

The basic fare for one passenger is 2.50€ ($2.90), plus 1.09€ ($1.25) per kilometer for the first 4km, then 0.87€ ($1) for each kilometer after that. You pay a 1€ ($1.15) surcharge for luggage, and a 0.10€ (12¢) surcharge between 11 p.m. and 6 a.m. and on Sundays and holidays (and the per-kilometer rate goes up to 1.31€/$1.50). Each additional passenger costs

1€ ($1.15) more. Rides to the airport (☎ 676-380-5797; www.airport service.at) also cost extra, or you can get a taxi for a flat rate, around 23€ to 27€ ($26–$31).

Staying in Vienna

If you're on a shoestring budget, you can find a concentration of cheap, plain hotels around Westbahnhof, a short tram ride from the center of town. This area is usually safe at night, except as you near Karlsplatz, a pretty plaza that junkies claim after dark. Vienna's popularity booms in late spring and late summer, and rooms can get scarce, so reserve ahead.

The **tourist office** (see "Finding information after you arrive," earlier in this chapter) can help you find lodging in a hotel or private home.

Vienna's top hotels

Hotel Astoria
$$$$$ Near the Staatsoper

Recapturing the twilight days of the Austro-Hungarian Empire, this classic hotel has a frayed but cared-for elegance. Its location is prime for shopping and visiting the opera house and the cathedral. Avoid the dark and cramped interior rooms, and try your luck at getting one of the front rooms (outside, Kärntnerstrasse is pedestrian-only, so you won't be disturbed much at night). Although hard to snag, the large, light-filled "superior" corner rooms, featuring lovely marble fireplaces, stucco wall decorations, and 19th-century furnishings, are definitely worth asking about (however, as the staff laments, "we only have so many corners"). Check the hotel's Web site for the cheapest rates and special packages; lower rates are available for stays of two nights or more.

See map p. 312. Kärntnerstrasse 32–34 (entrance actually on side road Führichgasse, 4 blocks north of Kärntnerring). ☎ 01-51-577. Fax: 01-515-7782. www.austria-trend.at/asw. *U-Bahn: Stephansplatz. Rates: 152€–211€ ($175–$243) double. Rates include breakfast. AE, DC, MC, V.*

Hotel Kärntnerhof
$$$ North of Stephansdom

Take just a few minutes' walk north of the cathedral to find this comfortable hotel, modest but not spare, with pricing right for any bracket. The near-modern accommodations are a bit worn and frayed at the edges (an overhaul of some of the older baths would be welcome), but the facilities are sparkling clean. If you're traveling with a group or family, ask about the three roomier apartments, each of which has two bedrooms joined by a short hall.

See map p. 312. Grashofgasse 4 (near the corner of Kollnerhof and Fleischmarkt). ☎ 01-512-1923. Fax: 01-513-222-833. www.karntnerhof.com. *U-Bahn: Stephansplatz. Rates: 80€–146€ ($92–$168) double. Rates include breakfast. AE, DC, MC, V.*

Accommodations, Dining, and Attractions in Vienna

HOTELS ■
Hotel Am Stephanplatz **23**
Hotel Astoria **16**
Hotel Austria **33**
Hotel Kärntnerhof **31**
Hotel Mercure
  Secession Wien **5**
Hotel Neuer Markt **18**
Hotel Post **34**
Hotel Royal **25**
Hotel Wandl **22**
Pension Altstadt Vienna **3**
Pension Nossek **21**
Pension Pertschy **19**

RESTAURANTS ◆
Augustinerkeller **17**
Buffet Trzesniewski **20**
Drei Husaren **26**
Figlmüller **30**
Griechenbeisl **32**
Gulaschmuseum **29**
Kardos **36**
Novelli Osteria **28**
Plachutta **35**
Rathauskeller **2**
Ristorante Firenze
  Enoteca **27**

ATTRACTIONS ●
Akademie der Bildenden
  Kunste-Gemäldegalerie **6**
Burgkapelle **11**
Grinzing **1**
Hofburg Palace **10**
Kaiserappartments **13**
Kunsthistorisches Museum **7**
Museum für Völkerkunde **8**
Neue Burg **9**
Prater **37**
Schatzkammer **12**
Schloss Schönbrunn **4**
Spanische Reitschule **14**
Staatsoper **15**
Stephansdom **24**

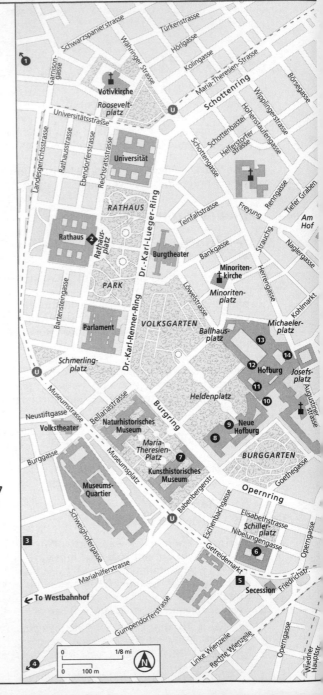

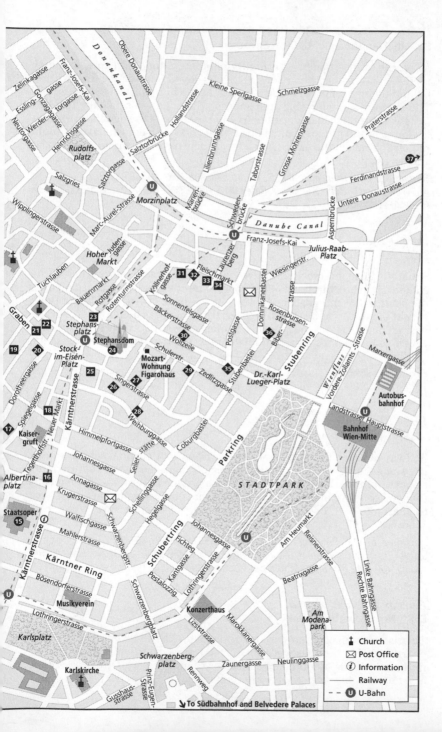

Zelinkagasse
Franz-Josefs-Kai
Gonzagagasse
Essling gasse
Neutorgasse
Werdertorgasse
Heinrichsgasse
Rudolfs-platz
Salzgries
Wipplingerstrasse
Salztorgasse
Marc-Aurel-Strasse
Obere Donaustrasse
Donaukanal
Kleine Sperlgasse
Schmelzgasse
Hollandstrasse
Lilienbrunngasse
Taborstrasse
Grosse Mohrengasse
Praterstrasse
Ferdinandstrasse
Marien-brücke
Salztorbrücke
Morzinplatz
Schwedenbrücke
Aspernbrücke
Untere Donaustrasse
Danube Canal
Franz-Josefs-Kai
Julius-Raab-Platz
Wiesingerstr.
Hoher Markt
Judengasse
Tuchlauben
Bauernmarkt
Rotgasse
Rotenturmstrasse
Köllnerhof-gasse
Fleischmarkt
Lautenzer berg
31 **32**
33 **34**
Sonnenfelsgasse
Bäckerstrasse
Postgasse
Dominikanerbastei
Rosenbursen-strasse
Stubenring
Graben
22
21
23
Stephans-platz
Stephansdom
24
20
19
Dorotheergasse
Stock-im-Eisen-Platz
25
Wollzeile
30
Schulerstr.
Mozart-Wohnung Figarohaus
29
Zedlitzgasse
Stubenbastei
35
36
Biber
Dr.-Karl-Lueger-Platz
Marxergasse
Vordere Zollamts-Strasse
Autobus-bahnhof
Singerstrasse
27
26
Kärntnerstrasse
28
Weihburggasse
Himmelpfortgasse
Coburgbastei
18
Spiegelgasse
Neuer Markt
Tegetthoffstr.
Seilerstätte
17
Kaiser-gruft
Johannesgasse
Landstrasser Hauptstrasse
Bahnhof Wien-Mitte
Albertina-platz
16
Annagasse
Krugerstrasse
Schellinggasse
Hegelgasse
Parkring
STADTPARK
Am Heumarkt
Reisnerstrasse
Staatsoper
15
Walfischgasse
Schwarzenbergstr.
Mahlerstrasse
Schubertring
Johannesgasse
Fichteg
Kantgasse
Lothringerstrasse
Beatrixgasse
Kärntner Ring
Kärntner Strasse
Bösendorferstrasse
Pestalozzig
Linke Bahngasse
Rechte Bahngasse
Musikverein
Lothringerstrasse
Konzerthaus
Lisztstrasse
Marokkanergasse
Am Modena-park
Karlsplatz
Schwarzenberg-platz
Zaunergasse
Neulinggasse
Karlskirche
Prinz-Eugen-Strasse
Rennweg
Guschaus-strasse
↘**To Südbahnhof and Belvedere Palaces**

Wirnfluss

37➛

Legend:
† Church
✉ Post Office
ⓘ Information
— Railway
--Ⓤ U-Bahn

Hotel Mercure Secession Wien (formerly Hotel Schneider)
$$ Just southeast of the Ringstrasse

A favorite of entertainers, this modern hotel is redone with contemporary modular furnishings every few years. Art lovers appreciate the location behind the Academy of Fine Arts and near the Kunsthistoriches Museum. The Mercure's comfortable apartments, which feature small kitchenettes (a nearby produce market can help you take care of the details), are great for families and groups. The main street is noisy, so light sleepers should request a room in the back. Only a few rooms have air-conditioning, so be sure to ask for it.

See map p. 312. Getreidemarkt 5. ☎ *01-588-380. Fax: 01-5883-8212.* www.accor hotels.com. *U-Bahn: Karlsplatz. Rates: 84€–175€ ($97–$201) double; breakfast 13€ ($15). AE, DC, MC, V.*

Hotel Royal
$$$$ Near Stephansdom

Situated at the intersection of two prestigious streets on a corner of the cathedral square, this hotel offers good value at a great location. Don't miss the piano in the antique-filled lobby — it was once owned by Wagner. Don't stay at the Royal for history, however; this place was built in 1960. For the best accommodations the hotel has to offer, choose one of the corner rooms, which have spacious foyers and balconies overlooking the Stephansdom.

See map p. 312. Singerstrasse 3 (at the corner with Kärntnerstrasse). ☎ *01-515-680. Fax: 01-513-9698.* www.kremslehnerhotels.at. *U-Bahn: Stephansplatz. Rates: 136€–190€ ($156–$219) double. Rates include breakfast. AE, DC, MC, V.*

Hotel Wandl
$$$$ Near Stephansdom

Halfway between the cathedral and the Hofburg, this inn has been run by the same family for generations. Pleasant, nice-size rooms feature functional furniture. Only one doesn't have a private bathroom, which means that you can save big-time if you choose that one, and you don't even have to share the bath down the hall — it's yours alone. Be sure to ask for a room with a view of St. Stephan's steeple.

See map p. 312. Petersplatz 9. ☎ *01-534-550. Fax: 01-534-5577.* www.hotel-wandl.com. *U-Bahn: Stephansplatz. Rates: 142€–182€ ($163–$209) double with bathroom; 110€ ($127) double without bathroom. Rates include breakfast. AE, DC, MC, V.*

Pension Altstadt Vienna
$$$ Near Kärntnerstrasse

This is an undiscovered gem for those who like their hotels small and charming. The premises were converted from a century-old private home in the mid-1990s by noted connoisseur of modern art, Otto Wiesenthal. The comfortable, cozy rooms are reminiscent of a stately English home.

See map p. 312. Kirchengasse 41. ☎ *01-522-6666. Fax: 01-523-4901.* www.altstadt. at. *U-Bahn: Volkstheater. Rates: 129€–149€ ($148–$171) double. Rates include breakfast. AE, DC, MC, V.*

Pension Pertschy
$$ Near Stephansdom

One of Vienna's most atmospheric hotels — and a bargain to boot — Pension Pertschy sits smack-dab in the middle of town. This family-owned and -operated hotel is situated in a gorgeous baroque building (dating back to 1723). Rooms are decorated in old-fashioned Biedermeir style and include lovely chandeliers (a few even have 200-year-old ceramic heaters). Take advantage of one of the hotel's larger, homey rooms, which have sofas or easy chairs.

See map p. 312. Habsburgergasse 5 (just off the Graben). ☎ *01-534-490. Fax: 01-534-4949.* www.pertschy.com. *U-Bahn: Stephansplatz. Rates: 97€–165€ ($112–$190) double. Rates include breakfast. DC, MC, V.*

Vienna's runner-up accommodations

Hotel Am Stephansplatz

$$$$$ Near Stephansdom   This hotel may be mostly modern (although some rooms have rococo stylings), but its location, right on the cathedral square, can't be beat. *See map p. 312. Stephansplatz 9.* ☎ *01-534-050. Fax: 01-5340-5711.* www.hotelamstephansplatz.at.

Hotel Austria

$ North of Stephansdom   Hotel Austria lies in all its functional glory just a few blocks north of the cathedral, in a quiet residential neighborhood just a few minutes' stroll from the tourist sights. The cheapest rooms don't have a private bath. *See map p. 312. Am Fleischmarkt 20.* ☎ *01-51-523. Fax: 01-5152-3506.* www.hotelaustria-wien.at.

Hotel Neuer Markt

$$ Near Kärntnerstrasse   Hotel Neuer Markt occupies a baroque building on a fountain-blessed square, in the perfect location, halfway between the cathedral and the opera house. *See map p. 312. Seilergasse 9.* ☎ *01-512-2316. Fax: 01-513-9105.*

Hotel Post

$ North of Stephansdom   Hotel Post is another ancient hotel that once hosted the likes of Mozart and Hayden; today, below the comfy, modern bedrooms, a cafe/wine bar still pipes in their music. Rooms without a bath are the true bargain. *See map p. 312. Fleischmarkt 24.* ☎ *01-515-830. Fax: 01-5158-3808.* www.hotel-post-wien.at.

Pension Nossek

$ **Near Stephansdom** Pension Nossek was once home to Mozart and has been a simple, sensible inn on the main shopping drag near the royal palace since 1909. *See map p. 312. Graben 17.* ☎ *01-5337-0410. Fax: 01-535-2646.*

Dining in Vienna

Viennese cooking is varied and palate-pleasing — with German, Swiss, and Italian influences, as well as more eastern-tinged Turkish, Hungarian, and Balkan flavors. Far and away, Vienna is most famous for being the birthplace of *wiener schnitzel,* a simple, flat cutlet of pork or veal breaded and fried (traditionally in lard), which is then tucked into a roll as a sandwich or served on a plate that can barely contain it.

Tafelspitz is another delicious (and dyed-in-the-wool) Viennese dinnertime meal. This boiled beef dish served with applesauce topped with horseradish shavings has been popular for centuries — in fact, Emperor Franz Joseph was noted for eating it daily. From Hungary (the other half of the Austro-Hungarian Empire), the Viennese pantry has several spicy influences; look for paprika popping up in a variety of dishes, especially in the flavorful pork or beef stew called *gulasch.*

The Ottoman Turks besieged Vienna frequently throughout the 16th and 17th centuries and in the process introduced the city to a beverage that would eventually become one of Vienna's passions — *kaffee* (coffee). (For the skinny on the best Viennese cafes, head to the section "More cool things to see and do," later in this chapter.) And of course, mouthwatering pastries are a necessity with any cup of kaffee. Vienna's world-renowned baked goods include *strudel,* which comes with numerous tempting fillings (*apfelstrudel* with apple is still the reigning pastry king). Other irresistible choices include *gugelhupf* (cream-filled horns) and *rehrucken* (chocolate cake encrusted with almonds).

Ready to overload on chocolate? Set your sights on sampling some *sachertorte,* the original chocolate lover's delight (made unique by a touch of apricot jam). The **Hotel Sacher,** Philharmonikerstrasse 4 (☎ 01-514-560; cafes.sacher.com), was the birthplace of this tempting creation in 1832, but found itself engaged in a long legal battle with **Café Demel,** Kohlmarkt 14 (☎ 01-535-1717; www.demel.at), during the 1960s over the right to call its dessert delight the "Original Sachertorte." Although the Hotel Sacher won, your taste buds will be hard-pressed to tell the difference, so sample the sweets at both!

Top Austrian beers include lighter fare such as Gold Fassl, Kaiser, and Weizengold (a wheat beer). Or, if you prefer richer brews, try Gösser Spezial and Eggenberger Urbock (the latter dates back to the 17th century and is considered one of the world's most powerful beers).

When it comes to enjoying the best of Austria's wines, you'll find that whites dominate. Although the pinnacle white is the fruity Grüner Veltiner, the country's dry Rieslings are also quite celebrated, along with several fine Chardonnays and Pinot Blancs. Also, keep your palate open to sample some Eiswein, a special Austrian dessert wine made from grapes that are allowed to ripen on the vine until after the first frost hits. This unusual growing process freezes water in the grapes and concentrates the fruit's alcohol level and taste. And don't forget about schnapps, delightfully flavored liqueurs distilled from various fruits.

Vienna's top restaurants

 ### Augustinerkeller
$$ Near the Staatsoper   AUSTRIAN

Serving simple meals such as schnitzel, spit-roasted chicken, and tafelspitz since 1954, this restaurant in a vaulted brick cellar under the Hofburg Palace features long communal tables and a good selection of Viennese beer and wine. Touristy elements — including wandering accordion players in the evenings — tend to drive away the locals, but coming here is a fun dining experience, with ample, palette-pleasing food.

See map p. 312. Augustinerstrasse 1 (a little way off Albertinaplatz, across from Augustinia church). ☎ *01-533-1026. Reservations not necessary. U-Bahn: Stephansplatz. Main courses: 7€–19€ ($8.05–$22). AE, DC, MC, V. Open: Lunch and dinner daily.*

Drei Husaren
$$$$$ Near Stephansdom   VIENNESE/INTERNATIONAL

Decorated with Gobelin tapestries and antiques, this fine establishment has been regarded as Vienna's top eatery since World War I. You can sample both traditional and more inventive Viennese cuisine, including an hors d'oeuvres table filled to the brim with more than 35 goodies, *kalbsbrücken Metternich* (the chef's specialty veal dish), and cheese-filled crêpes topped with chocolate topping.

See map p. 312. Weihburggasse 4 (off Kärtnerstrasse, 2 blocks south of Stephansplatz). ☎ *01-512-1092.* www.drei-husaren.at. *Reservations required. U-Bahn: Stephansplatz. Main courses: 18€–36€ ($21–$41); tastings menu (6 courses): 68€ ($78); fixed-price lunches: 33€–40€ ($38–$46). AE, DC, MC, V. Open: Lunch and dinner daily. Closed mid-July to mid-Aug.*

Figlmüller
$$$ Near Stephansdom   VIENNESE

This perennially popular Viennese *beisel* (tavern) is home to wiener schnitzel so colossal it overflows the plate. The dining room (dating back over 500 years) has an aged glow from thousands of delighted diners who've settled down to generous helpings of salads, sausages, tafelspitz, and goblets of exceptional wine.

See map p. 312. Wollzelle 5 (go 1 block north on Rotenturmstrasse from Stephansplatz and turn right; the restaurant is up an alley half a block down on the left). ☎ *01-512-6177.* www.figlmueller.at. *Reservations recommended. U-Bahn: Stephansplatz. Main courses: 11€–19€ ($13–$22). No credit cards. Open: Dinner daily. Closed Jan 7– Mar 31.*

Griechenbeisl
$$$ North of Stephansdom   AUSTRIAN

Beethoven and Mark Twain (among other fans) certainly can't be wrong! This 550-year-old restaurant with its iron chandeliers and low vaulted ceilings has been a favorite for centuries. Taste buds thrill to hearty dishes such as venison steak, Hungarian goulash, and an excellently prepared tafelspitz. Plus, the accordion and zither music gets the feet tapping.

See map p. 312. Fleischmarkt 11 (from Swedenplatz, take Laurenzerberg away from the Canalto Fleischmarkt and turn right). ☎ *01-533-1977 or 01-533-1941.* www. griechenbeisl.at. *Reservations required. Tram: N or Z. Main courses:14€–19€ ($16–$22). AE, DC, MC, V. Open: Lunch and dinner daily.*

Kardos
$$ East of Stephansdom   HUNGARIAN/BALKAN

Huge portions and elements of Vienna's eastern heritage await you at Kardos. From its Gypsy-rustic accents and deep wooden booths to its exotic fare that includes such tasty treats as rolls stuffed with spiced pork, Balkan fish soup, and grilled meats, Kardos highlights the days when Austria's influence extended far and wide. Be sure to get the ball rolling with the Hungarian apricot aperitif *barack*.

See map p. 312. Dominikanerbastei 8 (take Wollzeile several long blocks east of Stephansdom and turn left up Stuben Bastei, which becomes Dominikaner Bastei). ☎ *01-512-6949.* www.restaurantkardos.com. *Reservations recommended. U-Bahn: Schwedenplatz. Main courses: 6€–16€ ($6.90–$18). AE, MC, V. Open: Lunch and dinner Tues–Sat. Closed Aug.*

Ristorante Firenze Enoteca
$$$$ Near Stephansdom   TUSCAN/ITALIAN

If you're experiencing schnitzel overdose, head over to the premier Italian eatery in Vienna. The delightful décor with reproduced frescoes recalls the Italian Renaissance, while the cuisine highlights central Italian staples such as spaghetti with seafood, penne with salmon, and veal cutlets. Take a break from beer and get yourself a bottle of smooth Chianti.

See map p. 312. Singerstrasse 3 (1 short block south of Stephansplatz, Singerstrasse branches off to the left/east; the restaurant is 2 blocks down). ☎ *01-513-4374.* www. kremslehnerhotels.at. *Reservations recommended. U-Bahn: Stephansplatz. Main courses: 13€–25€ ($15–$29). AE, DC, MC, V. Open: Lunch and dinner daily.*

Vienna's runner-up restaurants

Novelli Osteria

$$$ **Near Stephansdom** A decent — and remarkably cheap — Tuscan (really, a bit pan-Italian) restaurant in the heart of the Austrian capital. *See map p. 312. Weihburggasse 3–5.* ☎ *01-512-7955.* www.haslauer.at.

Buffet Trzesniewski

$ **Near Stephansdom** This was neighbor Franz Kafka's favorite spot for a wide selection of scrumptious finger sandwiches and beer. *See map p. 312. Dorotheergasse 1.* ☎ *01-512-3291.* www.trzesniewski.at.

Gulaschmuseum

$$ **Near Stephansdom** A laid-back beisel with a few tables on the sidewalk and 16 types of goulash on the menu, along with grills and other paprika-inspired Hungarian dishes. *See map p. 312. Schulerstrasse 20.* ☎ *01-512-1017.* www.gulasch.at.

Plachutta

$$$$ **Near Stadtpark** Plachutta is famed for its dozen different preparations of tafelspitz in a halfway rustic, halfway refined ambience. *See map p. 312. Wollzeile 10.* ☎ *01-512-1577.* www.plachutta.at.

Rathauskeller

$$$ **In the Rathaus** Vienna's 100-years-plus beer hall–style restaurant under the town hall (common to most German and Austrian towns), with vaulted ceilings and a killer Rathauskellerplatte (an assorted platter of meat dishes made for two). *See map p. 312. Rathausplatz 1.* ☎ *01-405-1210.* www.wiener-rathauskeller.at.

Exploring Vienna

If you're going to be in town for few days, consider picking up the **Vienna Card,** which gives you 3 days of unlimited public transportation plus discounts at 30 city sights and museums (as well as on a load of restaurants, shops, bars, nightlife venues, tours, and other attractions). The card costs 17€ ($20) and is available at the tourist office, hotel desks, or U-Bahn stations.

Because several museums fall under the purview of the Kunsthistoriches Museum, you can get several combination tickets. The 19€ ($22) Bronze-ticket covers the main Kunsthistoriches Museum and the Schatzkammer and Neue Berg at the Hofburg (all reviewed in this section). The 21€ ($24) Silberticket covers those plus the Austrian Theater Museum. The 23€ ($26) Goldtickets covers all that, plus the Lippizzaner Museum and Wagenburg.

Vienna's top sights

Akademie der Bildenden Kunste-Gemäldegalerie (Academy of Fine Arts)

If time permits, try to make at least a quick stop at this small but choice gallery with a fine painting collection that covers the 14th to 17th centuries. The collection features a 1504 *Last Judgment* by Hieronymus Bosch (a major influence on the Surrealists), a *Self Portrait* by Van Dyck, and works by Rubens, Guardi, Rembrandt, and Cranach the Elder.

See map p. 312. Schillerplatz 3 (just south of the Staatsoper). ☎ *01-5881-6225.* www.akademiegalerie.at. *U-Bahn: Karlsplatz. Admission: 5€ ($5.75) adults, 3€ ($3.45) students and seniors. Open: Tues–Sun 10 a.m.–4 p.m.*

Hofburg Palace

A wonder of connective architecture, the palace of Hofburg (actually the Hapsburgs' winter home) is a jumbled complex that was added on to from 1279 to 1913. It spreads out over several blocks and features numerous entrances, but the main entrance on Michaelerplatz ushers you into the majestic courtyard that leads to the Imperial Apartments, or **Kaiserappartments** (☎ 01-533-7570; www.hofburg-wien.at). Here you'll also find the Imperial Silver and Porcelain Collection containing 18th- and 19th-century Hapsburg table settings, and the Sissi Museum dedicated to the beloved 19th-century empress Elisabeth.

The **Schatzkammer** (Imperial Treasury) is another must-see attraction at the Hofburg (☎ 01-533-7931; www.khm.at). Head left from the In der Burg courtyard and enter through the Swiss Court. The treasury, Europe's greatest, houses a collection of historic gems and jewelry likely to impress even the most jaded of tourists.

The **Neue Burg** (New Castle) is yet another section of the palatial estate worth visiting (☎ 01-5252-44471; www.khm.at). Constructed in the early 20th century, the building's elegantly curving exterior houses several collections. Collections include (in descending order of interest): historical musical instruments (many used by famous composers; try the audio tour even though it's in German — it features wonderful snippets of period music); arms and armor; and classical statues (mainly from the Greco-Turkish site of Ephesus). An entrance next door (closer to the Ringstrasse) leads to the **Museum für Völkerkunde** (Museum of Ethnology), featuring the only intact Aztec feather headdresses in the world — though this collection will be closed until 2006 for renovations (☎ 01-5252-4403; www.ethno-museum.ac.at).

See map p. 312. The palace takes up many square city blocks, but the main entrance is on Michaelerplatz. Each section has its own phone number and Web site, which are listed in the preceding description. U-Bahn: Herrengasse or Stephansplatz (walk down Graben, then left onto Kohlmarkt). Tram: 1, 2, D, or J. Admission: **Kaiserappartments** *7.50€ ($8.65) adults, 5.90€ ($6.80) students under 25, 3.90€ ($4.50) children 6–15, free for children 5 and under;* **Schatzkammer** *8€ ($9.20) adults; 6€ ($6.90) children, senior* citizens, and students; free for children 5 and under; **Neue Burg** (including the Museum für Völkerkunde) 8€ ($9.20) adults, 6€ ($6.90) children. Open: **Kaiserappartments** daily 9 a.m.–5 p.m.; **Schatzkammer and Neue Burg** (including the Museum für Völkerkunde) Wed–Mon 10 a.m.–6 p.m.

Kunsthistoriches Museum (Museum of Fine Arts)

An amazingly diverse art collection awaits you in this 100-room museum. Start with ancient Egyptian and Greco-Roman art and work your way through the Renaissance and then on to the Flemish, Dutch, and German masters like Memling, Van Dyck, Rembrandt, and especially Breughel the Elder (the majority of his known works are here).

Must-see pieces include Dürer's *Blue Madonna,* Vermeer's *The Artist's Studio,* and works by Italian masters Titian, Raphael, Veronese, Caravaggio, and Giorgione. Top ancient works consist of a Roman onyx cameo of the *Gemma Augustea,* and a roly-poly blue hippopotamus from 2000 B.C. Egypt (which also serves as the museum's mascot). Also check out Archimboldo's idiosyncratic and allegorical still lifes–cum–portraits, in which the artist cobbles together everyday objects to look like a face from afar. Craggy, wooden-faced *Winter* is really Francis I of France, and flame-haired *Fire* may be Emperor Maximillian II himself.

See map p. 312. Maria Theresien Platz (across the Burgring from the Neue Burg). ☎ **01-525-240.** www.khm.at. U-Bahn: Mariahilferstrasse. Tram: 52, 58, D, or J. Admission: 10€ ($12) adults, 7.50€ ($8.65) students and seniors, free for children 5 and under. Guided tours in English at 11 a.m. and 3 p.m., 2€ ($2.30). Open: Daily 10 a.m.–6 p.m.; Thurs 10 a.m.–9 p.m.

Schloss Schönbrunn (Schönbrunn Palace)

You have to travel about 4 miles from Vienna's center to experience this palace — but it's definitely worth the effort. Scloss Schönbrunn was the baroque playground of Empress Maria Theresa and served as the Hapsburgs' summer palace after its completion in the mid-18th century. Only 40 of the sprawling palace's 1,441 rooms are open to visitors.

Two different self-guided tours lead the way through state apartments that brim with gorgeous chandeliers and old-world detail. The basic "Imperial Tour" guides you through 22 rooms and costs 8€ ($9.20) adults, 7.40€ ($8.50) students, or 4.30€ ($5) for children under 15; but for just 2.50€ ($2.90) more — 1.20€ ($1.40) more for students, 1.10€ ($1.25) for kids — the "Grand Tour" gives you all 40 viewable rooms. Play your cards right, and you can also enjoy a guided Grand Tour for an additional 2.50€ ($2.90) adults or students, 1€ ($1.15) kids. (Be sure to call ahead for tour costs and times; summertime tours leave as frequently as every 30 minutes.)

Your visit is not compete without a jaunt through the extravagant roccoco gardens, complete with faux "Roman ruins" and a baroque coffeehouse that overlooks the gardens (a fantastic photo op). If imperial coaches are your thing, don't miss the Wagenburg carriage museum.

See map p. 312. Schönbrunner Schlossstrasse. ☎ *01-8111-3333.* www.schoenbrunn.at. *U-Bahn: U4. Admission: Palace, see descriptions of tours earlier; gardens, 2.60€ ($3) adults, 2.20€ ($2.55) students and seniors, 1.50€ ($1.75) ages 6 to 15. Open: Palace, daily Apr–June and Sept–Oct 8:30 a.m.–5 p.m., July–Aug 8:30 a.m.–6 p.m., and Nov–Mar 8:30 a.m.–4:30 p.m.; gardens, daily 9 a.m. to sunset.*

Staatsoper (State Opera House)

One of the world's greatest opera meccas, the regal Staatsoper has a marvelous musical heritage dating all the way back to its 1869 opening with a performance of Mozart's *Don Giovanni*. Mahler and Strauss — among other classical musical titans — have served as its musical directors. Take a short 40-minute tour during the day or, even better, catch a thrilling performance in the evening (see "More cool things to see and do," later in this chapter).

See map p. 312. Opern Ring 2. ☎ *01-514-442-606.* www.wiener-staatsoper.at. *U-Bahn: Oper or Karlsplatz. Tram: 1, 2, D, J, 62, or 65. Admission: Tours 4.50€ ($5.20) adults, 3.50€ ($4.05) seniors, 2€ ($2.30) students, and 1.50€ ($1.75) children up to age 14. Open: The ever-changing schedule of tours (2–5 English-language tours offered daily, usually between 1 and 3 p.m.) is posted at an entrance on the right (east) side.*

Stephansdom (St. Stephan's Cathedral)

The heart of Vienna lies in this visual and cultural landmark from the 12th to 14th centuries. (Mozart's 1791 pauper funeral was held here.) Visit the fanciful tombs, an impressive 15th-century carved wooden altar, and a crypt filled with urns containing the entrails of the Hapsburgs. See the quintessential Viennese vista with its colorful pattern of mosaic-like tiling from atop the 450-foot, 343-stepped *Steffl* (south tower). The unfinished north tower (named for its *Pummerin* bell) offers a less impressive view, but you can catch a glimpse of the Danube.

See map p. 312. Stephansplatz 1. ☎ *01-51-552.* www.stephansdom.at *or* www.st.stephan.at. *U-Bahn: Stephansplatz. Admission:* **Church** *is free, but the towers require admission;* **north tower** *4€ ($4.60) adults, 1.50€ ($1.75) children 15 and under;* **south tower** *3€ ($3.45) adults, 1€ ($1.15) children 14 and under;* **church tours** *4€ ($4.60) adults, 1.50€ ($1.75) children 14 and under; evening tours, including tour of the roof, 10€ ($12) adults, 3.65€ ($4.20) children 14 and under. Open:* **Church** *daily 6 a.m.–10 p.m., except during services;* **north tower** *Nov–Mar daily 8:30 a.m.–5 p.m., Apr–Oct daily 8:30 a.m.–5:30 p.m. (July–Aug to 6 p.m.);* **south tower** *daily 9 a.m.–5:30 p.m.;* **church tours** *in English daily Apr–Oct 3:45 p.m.*

More cool things to see and do

✔ **Spending a night at the opera:** Vienna's Staatsoper is a truly world-class theatrical venue, and you don't want to miss experiencing a performance, even if you don't consider yourself an opera aficionado. The season runs September through June, and you can get tickets at a variety of prices (5€–254€/$5.75–$292) at the box office one month in advance (☎ **01-514-442-960**), the day after the season opens by calling ☎ **01-5144-47810,** or on the Web at www.wiener-staatsoper.at.

You can save a few bucks and try your luck by purchasing last-minute tickets the day of a performance. Or you can show up at least three hours before the performance to get in line for standing-room-only space — it costs only 2€ ($2.30), or 3.50€ ($4.05) for the Parterre. Bring a scarf and tie it around the railing at your standing spot — that's all you need to do to save your place. Then wander through the glittery rooms and circulate among the black-tie crowd until the performance begins.

When the summer heat chases the company out of the State Opera House, get your opera fix at **open-air concerts** — from Mozart and the Vienna Boys Choir to Lenny Kravitz and David Bowie — at Schloss Schönbrunn (☎ www.schoenbrunn.at). The Schloss itself also stages musical concerts year-round; call for info (☎ **01-8125-0040;** www.imagevienna.com).

✔ **Drinking java, eating strudel, and people-watching at a Kaffeehaus:** Legend has it that Vienna's first coffeehouse was established in 1683 — and certainly, they've been a vibrant part of Viennese culture ever since. One of the grandest places, the chandeliered **Café Landtmann** at Dr. Karl Lueger Ring 4 (☎ **01-241-000;** www.landtmann.at), was once a fav of Freud's.

The granddaddy of all Viennese cafes is **Café Demel** (☎ **01-535-1717;** www.demel.at), which moved to Kohlmarkt 14 in 1888 and hasn't changed its ornate décor since. You can enjoy your kaffee in a variety of ways, the most popular being *schwarzer* (black), *melange* (mixed with hot milk), or *mit schlagobers* (topped with whipped cream).

✔ **Seeing the Vienna Boys Choir:** Dating all the way back to 1498, this Viennese institution has been the training ground for many talented musicians, including Joseph Hayden and Franz Schubert. Catch a sonorous Sunday or holiday Mass (Jan–June and mid-Sept–Christmas) at 9:15 a.m. in the **Hofburg's Burgkapelle,** with accompanying members of the Staatsoper chorus and orchestra. You can pick up tickets at the box office the preceding Friday from 5 to 6 p.m. Get in line early — this is one of the few times you find people shelling out $4.55 to $25 to go to church. The boys also warble at a weekly afternoon concert somewhere in town (the venue and times vary), and in summer often put on evening concerts at the Schloss Schönbrunn (for info on that last one, visit www.theviennaboyschoir.com). Contact them at ☎ **01-216-3942** or go to www.wsk.at to see their upcoming concert schedule (these kids travel *a lot!*).

✔ **Riding the Riesenrad in the Prater:** Courtesy of Johann Strauss, Sr., in 1820, this former imperial hunting ground on the Danube Canal is the true birthplace of the waltz. Aside from the lovely grounds, visit the Prater Park (www.wiener-prater.at) to experience its year-round amusement park/fair that's bursting with restaurants, food stands, and a beer garden. Also, take a spin on the Riesenrad — at 220 feet and 100 years, one of the world's oldest (and slowest) operating Ferris wheels (www.wienerriesenrad.com), open daily from

10 a.m. until at least 8 p.m. (to 10 p.m. Mar, Apr, and Oct; until midnight May–Sept). Admission is 7.50€ ($8.65) adults, 3€ ($3.45) ages 3 to 14, or 19€ ($22) for a Family Ticket (two adults, two kids).

✔ **Watching the horse ballet at the Spanische Reitschule (Spanish Riding School):** You don't have to attend a show to see the world-famous Lippizaner horses strut their stuff. The Hofburg's school teaches complicated baroque horse choreography, based on 16th-century battle maneuvers. The horses and riders practice regularly (10 a.m.–1 p.m.Tues–Sat Feb–June 19, Aug 30–Oct 16, and Dec 2–29). You can purchase training session tickets from your travel agent or at the door for 12€ ($14) adults, 8.50€ ($9.80) seniors, or 5€ ($5.75) children. Get them in advance at the visitors center on Michaelerplatz 1, or at the door at Josefsplatz, gate 2.

However, if only the full, 1-hour-20-minute show will do (Mar–June and Sept–mid-December most Sun 11 a.m.; plus Sat 11 a.m. Apr–May; and Fri 6 p.m. May and Sept), reserve a ticket as far in advance as possible by visiting www.spanische-reitschule.com. Tickets run 40€ to 145€ ($46–$167) for seats, 24€ to 27€ ($28–$39) for standing room. (Children 2 and under not admitted, but children 3 to 6 attend free with adults.) Hour-long dressage training sessions to classical music sometimes take place during the show season Fridays at 10 a.m., and you can observe for 20€ ($23), though tickets are limited and tend to sell out quickly.

✔ **Taking a heuriger crawl in Grinzing:** *Heuriger* is the name of both Viennese new wines and the country taverns that serve them. Most heuriger are centered around the fringes of the famous Vienna Woods, just a 15-minute tram ride northwest of the city center. The tradition's capital is Grinzing, home to about 20 taverns (take Tram 38 from the underground station at Schottentor, a stop on the U2 U-Bahn and trams 1, 2, and D).

Due to the rising popularity of heuriger crawling, the village works hard to maintain its medieval look. Stroll down Cobenzigasse and sample the wine at heuriger along the way while you enjoy the sounds of accordion and zither music.

Guided tours

You find plenty of **city orientation tours,** but why pay $20 when a tram ticket and a good map gets you the same thing minus the stilted commentary? Buy an all-day ticket, step onto the **no. 1 or 2 tram,** and ride it all the way around the Ring, hopping on and off at sights where you want to spend time. The whole ride only takes half an hour if you don't get off. After you're oriented, you can abandon the tram to visit the sights off the Ring, such as the Hofburg Palace and Stephansdom. The tourist office has a brochure called **Walks in Vienna** that can fill you in on other, more organized guided tours.

Suggested itineraries

If you're the type who'd rather organize your own tours, this section offers some tips for building your own Vienna itineraries.

If you have one day

Be at the **Hofburg Palace** and in the **Kaiserappartments** at 9:15 a.m. to admire the excesses of the Hapsburgs, and in the **Schatzkammer** around 10 a.m. for its impressive medieval crown jewels and other royal artifacts.

Exit the Hofburg by the main Michaelerplatz entrance and start strolling up Kohlmarkt, pausing to indulge in a coffee and snack/early lunch amid the 19th-century elegance of **Cafe Demel.** Turn right on the Graben to arrive at **Stephansdom.** Tour the cathedral, climb its south tower for a city panorama, and then start waltzing your way down the main pedestrian drag, Kärtnerstrasse. Settle into the ground-floor cafe of the **Hotel Sacher** for a sinfully delicious Sachertorte.

Continue to the end of Kärtnerstrasse where it hits the Ring. Admire the **Staatsoper** exterior and, unless you'll be getting standing-room-only tickets (for which you'll return here shortly), stop into the box office to pick up discounted day-of-performance tickets for tonight's opera. Then hop tram 1, 2, or D heading west/clockwise (left) around the Ring one stop and get off at Burgring for the **Kunsthistorishes Museum** and an hour and a half to two hours of exquisite paintings and ancient statues.

If you got tickets to the opera, get right back on tram 1 or 2 and ride it clockwise halfway around the Ring road, past the greatest glories of Viennese architecture. Get off at Schwedenplatz and transfer to the U1; go two stops north, getting off at Praterstern. Enjoy the city park–cum-carnival of Prater by taking a late-afternoon spin on the **Reisenrad** (Ferris wheel) and tossing back a few tall cold ones in the **Biergarten** before returning to the **Staatsoper** half an hour before the performance begins. You can also stop for dinner along the way, or just have some schnitzel in the Prater. If you have plenty of time to make it to the opera at your leisure, get off the U1 at Schwedenplatz again and simply get back on tram 1 or 2 to continue all the way around the Ring to the opera house. If you dallied too long in the Prater, stay on the U1 all the way to Karlsplatz, 2 blocks south of the Staatsoper. If you're still hungry after the proverbial fat lady sings, stop at nearby **Augustinerkeller,** which stays open until midnight.

Fans of standing-room-only tickets need to plan their evening like so: Depending on the hour when you get out of the museum, you either have time (half an hour) to ride tram 1 or 2 clockwise almost all the way around the Ring Road (getting off back at the Staatsoper), or you can just mosey the two long blocks back (counterclockwise) to the opera house. You need to pick up a snack to eat while waiting in line at the opera house — be there by 5 p.m. for the best spots. Have dinner late at **Augustinerkeller,** after the performance is over.

If you have two days

Spend Day 1 as outlined in the preceding section. That's a pretty packed day, so take Day 2 to relax at Vienna's suburban sights. Head out in the morning to **Schloss Schönbrunn** for even more imperial excess than you saw at the Hofburg. After marveling at Hapsburgian opulence and taking a spin through the gardens, return downtown on the U4, transferring at Karlsplatz to the U2 toward Schotten Ring. Get off at the Schottentor stop and hop Tram 38 out to Grinzing for an afternoon of *heuriger* (country tavern) crawling, snacking, and drinking your way through Vienna's specialty foods and white wines. If you're in town during the season (and booked tickets long before you left on this trip), get back to town by 6:30 p.m. so you can take in the 7 p.m. show of the Lippizaner horses at the famed **Spanische Reitschule.**

If you have three days

Days 1 and 2 in the preceding sections give you all the best Vienna has to offer. Take Day 3 for a big daytrip out to the lovely Austrian village of **Innsbruck,** which I cover in the next section.

Traveling Beyond Vienna: Innsbruck

Although Innsbruck is technically in Austria, traveling there from Munich, Germany (see Chapter 15), is much faster and more convenient. This section provides directions from both Munich and Vienna, and it's a perfect excursion to do en route from one to the other.

Innsbruck, famous for hosting the Winter Olympics as well as the imperial family of the Austro-Hungarian Empire, is a sleepy little gem of a town, bordered by the stupendous Alps and a milky white river. The village is a great starting point for hiking, skiing, and scenic driving.

Getting there

Ten daily trains arrive at Hauptbahnhof from Vienna (5 hours away), passing through Salzburg (2 hours away). 14 trains arrive from Munich daily (1½ to 2 hours away).

The **tourist office** is at Burggraben 3, a road which rings the Altstadt at the end of Maria Theresien Strasse (☎ **0512-598-500;** Fax: 0512-598-507; www.innsbruck.info and www.tiscover.com/innsbruck). It's open Monday to Friday 8 a.m. to 6 p.m., Saturday 8 a.m. to noon.

 If you'll be doing heavy-duty sightseeing, purchase the **Innsbruck Card** to get free access to all city sights and free public transportation. The tourist office sells cards for 21€ ($24) for one day, 26€ ($30) for two days, or 31€ ($36) for three days. Children receive a 50 percent discount.

Seeing the sights

Walking the Maria Theresien Strasse, you pass through a triumphal arch and reach the rustic, souvenir shop–lined **Herzog Friedrich Strasse**. The **Stadtturm** tower (☎ **0512-587-1133;** www.innsbruck marketing.at) is at the end of the street, offering gorgeous views of the surrounding Alps. The tower is open daily June through September from 10 a.m. to 8 p.m.; October through May from 10 a.m. to 5 p.m. Admission is 2.50€ ($2.90) adults, 2€ ($2.30) students and seniors, or 1€ ($1.15) kids under 15.

The street ends in a wide spot, which the **Goldenes Dachl** (☎ **0512-581-111**) overlooks. The structure is basically an overblown imperial balcony erected and gilded for Emperor Maximillian I in the 16th century as a box seat for the festivities on the square below. Admiring it from below is enough, although its Maximillian-oriented museum is open Tuesday through Sunday from 10:00 a.m. to 12:30 p.m. and 2 to 5 p.m. (daily 10 a.m. to 6 p.m. May through September). Admission is 3.60€ ($4.15) adults, 1.80€ ($2.05) children.

Turn right on Universitätsstrasse, then left on Rennweg for a half-hour tour of the exuberant, curving, baroque stylings of Maria Theresa's **Hofburg Palace** (☎ **0512-587-186**), open daily from 9 a.m. to 5 p.m.; admission 5.45€ ($6.25) adults, 4€ ($4.60) seniors, 3.63€ ($4.15) students, 1.09€ ($1.25) children under 15. Next-door is the equally rococo **Dom** (cathedral). Across from the Hofburg at no. 2 Universitätsstrasse is the **Hofkirche** (☎ **0512-584-302;** www.hofkirche.at), containing a massive, statue-ridden monument to Maximillian I. It's open Monday through Saturday from 9 a.m. to 5 p.m. (to 5:30 p.m. in July and Aug), Sunday 1 to 5 p.m. Admission is 3€ ($3.45) adults, 2€ ($2.30) students, or 1.50€ ($1.75) children under 15. Its neighbor is the **Tiroler Volkskunst-Museum** (☎ **0512-584-302;** www.tiroler-volkskunst museum.at), a folk museum celebrating everyday life in the history of the Tyrol district. The museum is open daily from 9 a.m. to 5 p.m. (to 5:30 p.m. in July and Aug), but closed noon to 1 p.m. Sundays. Admission is 5€ ($5.75) adults, 3.50€ ($4.05) students, 1.50€ ($1.75) children under 15. The 6.50€ ($7.50) "Combi card" covers adult admission to both the Hofkirche and museum.

Outside the Alstadt is the **Alpenzoo** (☎ **0512-292-323;** www.alpenzoo. at) at Weiherburggasse 37, which clings to the Alpine cliffs and features regional wildlife. The zoo is open daily from 9 a.m. to 6 p.m. (until 5 p.m. in winter). Admission is 7€ ($8.05) adults, 5€ ($5.75) students, 3.50€ ($4.05) children 6 to 15, 2€ ($2.30) children ages 4 to 5. From the center, cross the Inn River, turn right, and follow the signs a long way; you can also take bus N, D, E, or 4 from the Altes Landhaus on Maria-Theresien Strasse.

The zoo sits at the base of the **Hungerburg plateau** (☎ 0512-586-158), which offers magnificent city views. In summer, the hungerburgbahn cog railway ascends from the corner of Rennweg and Kettenbrücke at 15-minute intervals daily from 9 a.m. to 8 p.m., and then runs at 30-minute intervals until 10:30 p.m. The rest of the year, the railway operates at hourly intervals daily from 8:30 a.m. to dusk (5–6 p.m.). Round-trip fares on the cog railway cost 4.30€ ($4.95) adults and 2.70€ ($3.10) children.

Where to stay and dine

Please your palate at the inexpensive **Restaurant Ottoburg** (☎ 0512-574-652) at Herzog Friedrich Strasse 1, an Austrian tradition since 1745. The **City-Hotel Goldene Krone,** Maria Theresien Strasse 46 (☎ **0512-586-160;** Fax: 0512-580-1896; www.touringhotels.at), features modern comforts and baroque touches, in a lovely house just outside the Altstadt. Doubles run 74€ to 126€ ($85–$145) and include breakfast.

Fast Facts: Vienna

Area Code

Austria's country code is **43**; Vienna's city code is **01**. Drop the zero if calling from outside Austria. To call Vienna from the United States, dial ☎ 011-43-1 followed by the phone number; to call Vienna from another Austrian city, dial 01 and then the number.

American Express

Vienna's American Express office is located at Kärntnerstrasse 21–23 (☎ 01-51-540). Hours are Monday through Friday, from 9 a.m. to 5:30 p.m. and Saturday from 9 a.m. to noon.

Currency

The Austrian schilling gave way to the euro (€) in 2002. The euro is divided into 100 cents, and there are coins of .01, .02, .05, .10, .20, .50, 1, and 2. Paper-note denominations are 5, 10, 20, 50, 100, 200, and 500. The exchange rate used in this chapter is 1€ = $1.15.Amounts over $10 have been rounded to the nearest dollar.

Doctors and Dentists

For a list of English-speaking doctors, call the Vienna Medical Association at ☎ 01-1771 (or, during the nighttime in an emergency, at ☎ 40-144). Dr. Woflgang Molnar at the Ambulatorium Augarten (☎ 01-330-3468; www.ambulatorium. com) is the panel physician for the U.S. Embassy — and you can always contact the consulate for a list of English-speaking physicians. For dental emergencies, call Dr. Lydia Hgofmann, Breitenfurterstrasse 360–368 (☎ 01-333-6796).

Embassies and Consulates

The U.S. Embassy's consulate (☎ 01-31-339; www.usembassy.at) is located at Gartenbaupromenade 2–4, A-1010 Vienna. It handles lost passports, tourist emergencies, and other matters, and is open from Monday through Friday from 8:30 a.m. to noon (and after-hours for emergency service through 5 p.m.).

Emergency

Dial ☎ **144** for an ambulance; call the police at ☎ **133**; or report a fire by calling ☎ **122.**

Hospitals

For emergency medical care, go to the Neue Allgemeine Krankenhaus at Währinger Gürtel 18–20 (☎ 01-4040-001501; www.akh.wien.gv.at); take tram 5 or 33 to the entrance at Spitalgasse 23 (at night, the N6 and N64 buses stop at the main entrance).

Information

The helpful Vienna Tourist Board office is behind the Staatsoper, at Kärntnerstrasse 38 (☎ 01-24-555; Fax: 01-2455-5666; www.wien.info). Hours are daily from 9 a.m. to 7 p.m.

Internet Access and Cybercafes

Mediencafe im Amadeus, Kärntnerstrasse 19, on the fifth floor of Steffl (☎ 01-5131-45017; www.amadeusbuch.co.at), offers free Web surfing Monday through Friday from 9:30 a.m. to 7:00 p.m., Saturday from 9:30 a.m. to 5:30 p.m.

Located at Rathausplatz 4 (☎ 01-405-2626; www.einstein.at/engl), Cafe Einstein is a cool cafe with a historic-looking pub and lots of atmosphere. Hours are Monday through Friday from 7 a.m. to 2 a.m., Saturday from 9 a.m. to 2 a.m., Sunday from 9 a.m. to midnight.

Cafe Stein Wahringerstrasse 6–8 (☎ 01-319-7241; www.cafe-stein.com), is open daily from 10 a.m. to 11 p.m.

Maps

The tourist office hands out a decent city map — and because the center is pretty small, it's easy to navigate with it.

Newspapers/Magazines

The tourist office (see "Information," earlier in this section) has a series of informative pamphlets on a variety of Viennese tourist activities, as well as free copies of the events rag *Wien Monatsprogramm.*

Pharmacies

Vienna's pharmacies are generally open Monday through Friday from 8 a.m. to noon and 2 to 6 p.m., Saturday from 8 a.m. to noon. Look for signs outside each pharmacy that list which drugstores are open during the off-hours.

Police

Call the police at ☎ **133.**

Post Office

The main post office is at Fleischmarkt 19 (☎ 01-5138-3500; www.post.at), open Monday through Friday from 8 a.m. to 5 p.m.

Safety

Vienna has its share of purse-snatchers and pickpockets, so be especially cautious in crowded, touristy areas, especially Kärntnerstrasse between Stephansplatz and Karlsplatz. Be careful when taking out your wallet or opening your purse in public areas; many pitiable children who beg for money are accompanied by adult thieves who snatch wallets and run. The only central area that can become somewhat scary after dark is Karlsplatz, which is frequented by heroin addicts.

Taxes

In Austria, a value-added tax (VAT) is figured into the price of most items. Luxury items such as jewelry are taxed 34 percent, while clothing and souvenirs are taxed 20 percent. As a foreign visitor, you can reclaim a percentage of the VAT if you spend more than 75.01€ ($86) in a single shop (see Chapter 4 for more on this).

Taxis

See "Getting Around Vienna," earlier in this chapter.

Telephone

All public phones take coins. Some phones take prepaid phone cards called *Wertkarte,* which you can purchase from post offices, newsstands, and tobacconists.

To charge a call to your calling card or credit card, insert a nominal fee into the pay phone and dial ☎ 0-800-200-288 for AT&T, ☎ 0-800-999-762 for MCI, or

☎ 0-800-200-236 for Sprint. To call the United States direct from Austria, dial 001 and then the area code and phone number. For an international operator, dial 09. For Austrian directory assistance, dial ☎ 11811; for international directory assistance, call ☎ 11813.

Transit Info

See "Getting Around Vienna," earlier in this chapter. For transportation information, call ☎ 01-790-9100 or go to www. wienerlinien.at.

Chapter 17

Bern and the Swiss Alps

● ●

In This Chapter

▶ Finding your way to Bern and the Swiss Alps

▶ Exploring the neighborhoods of Bern

▶ Discovering Bern's best hotels, restaurants, and attractions

▶ Finding the best of Switzerland's other great cultural capitals: Zurich and Basel

▶ Heading into the Alpine countryside and the Bernese Oberland

● ●

*A*lthough the Swiss capital of Bern is a fine place to visit — and, unlike Switzerland's larger cities, still has an almost medieval, Swiss-village feel — the real attractions of this country are those mighty, snow-covered Swiss Alps. In this chapter, I cover Bern fully, hit the cultural highlights of Basel and Zurich, and then head south into the Bernese Oberland, a region that encompasses the legendary 13,642-foot peak of the Jungfrau, Queen of the Alps.

Getting There

Bern has direct rail connections to the surrounding countries. This includes service via a high-speed rail line from France, making the train a quick, and quite scenic, option. The city itself is compact enough that after you're there, navigation is a breeze.

Arriving by air

The tiny **Berne-Belp Airport** (☎ **031-960-2111;** www.flughafenbern.ch), about 6 miles south of the city, receives flights from several major European cities. A shuttle bus runs from the airport to the city's train station, where you can find the tourist office. The 20-minute trip costs 14SF ($11). A taxi from the airport to the city costs about 50SF ($40). Most European and transatlantic passengers fly into **Zurich's Kloten Airport** (www.zurich-airport.com), from which one to two trains per hour (47SF/$37) make the 90-minute trip direct to Bern.

Arriving by rail

Bern's **Hauptbahnhof train station** (☎ 031-328-1212) is at the west end of the **Altstadt** (Old Town). Ticketing, track access, and lockers are in the basement. Luggage storage and train and tourist info are on the ground floor. For national rail information, visit www.sbb.ch, call ☎ 0900-300-300 (1.19SF/95¢ per minute), or use the computers in the **SBB train info office** (across from the tourist office) to look up and print out your itinerary.

If you leave the train station from the most obvious exit, at the tourist office, you'll be facing south; turn left to head into the **Altstadt.**

Orienting Yourself in Bern

The **Aare River** is Bern's defining geological feature. It makes a sharp, U-shaped bend around the Altstadt, with the **Hauptbahnhof** train station at the open (western) end of the U. From there, you can follow the **Spitalgasse** east into the heart of the Altstadt. The street's name soon changes to **Marktgasse,** the main road of the Old City.

Introducing the neighborhoods

Bern's most interesting section, the **Altstadt** (Old City), is very small and easily navigable on foot. Tucked into a sharp, U-shaped bend of the Aare River, the Altstadt is made up of five long, arcaded streets (whose names change at every block), two large squares (**Bärenplatz Waisenhausplatz/ Bundesplatz** and **Kornhausplatz/Casinoplatz**), and a dozen cross streets. Lots of shop-lined passageways, not shown on most maps, cut through buildings from one main drag to another. Just south of the Altstadt, across the Aare, are several museums and the embassy district (take the Kirchenfeldbrücke Bridge to get there).

Finding information after you arrive

The Bern Tourist Office (☎ 031-328-1212; Fax: 031-312-1233; www.bern etourism.ch) is in the **Hauptbahnhof** (train station). June through September hours are daily from 9:00 a.m. to 8:30 p.m.; October through May, it's open Monday through Saturday from 9:00 a.m. to 6:30 p.m. and Sunday from 10 a.m. to 5 p.m. A smaller info station is inside the building at the Bear Pits (offering a free 20-minute multimedia show called *Bern Past and Present*), open June through September daily from 9 a.m. to 6 p.m.; October and March through May, daily from 10 a.m. to 4 p.m.; and November through February, Friday through Sunday from 11 a.m. to 4 p.m.

Getting Around Bern

You can buy two types of public-transit tickets (good for both buses and trams): the 1.70SF ($1.35) version, which is good to travel up to

Switzerland

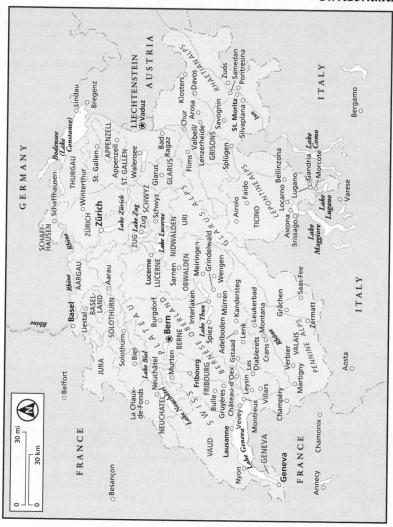

six stops and valid for 45 minutes, and the 2.60SF ($2.05) version for longer rides over six stops and for up to 90 minutes. You won't need more than six stops to get to any of the hotels, restaurants, or attractions in this chapter, so always get the cheaper ticket. Buy your ticket from the machine at each stop. You can buy a daily ticket for 7SF ($5.50), but you'd have to make five or more trips a day (unlikely) to save any money.

By tram and bus

Bern's **bus and tram system** (☎ 031-321-8888; www.bernmobil.ch) is extensive, but the Altstadt (Old City) is small enough to cover on foot. However, if you're visiting the **Bear Pits,** you may want to take Bus 12 on the way back uphill toward the city center and station. Most buses and trams begin and end their routes around the **Hauptbahnhof,** and many on **Bubenbergplatz** just to the station's south.

"Moonliner" night buses (www.moonliner.ch) run Thursday through Saturday three or four times between midnight and 4 a.m. (Thursdays usually just at 12:30 a.m.), and cost 5SF ($3.95). The most useful is the M3, which runs from the train station through the Altstadt, across the river past the Bear Pits, and returns via the casino. Several others are designed specifically to get partiers from outlying clubs and discotheques back to the central train station.

By taxi

If you're only sightseeing in Altstadt, you can see it all on foot. If, however, you want to taxi to your hotel, you can catch a cab at the train station, Casinoplatz, or Waisenhausplatz, or you can call ☎ **031-371-1111,** ☎ 031-331-3313, ☎ 031-311-1818, or ☎ 031-301-5353.

By foot

The historic center of Bern is very compact — only a few blocks wide — and a joy to wander, and most of the sights listed here won't take you too far from that walkable center.

Staying in Bern

Bern is small for a national capital, and conventions and international meetings overbook it regularly. For this reason, I chose some of the town's larger hotels to try to maximize your chances of finding a room. No matter when you plan to visit, make reservations far in advance.

The folks at the Bern tourist office (☎ **031-328-1212;** Fax: 031-312-1233; www.bernetourism.ch) will book you a room for free, or you can use the big hotel board and free phone just outside the tourist office (at the top of the escalators down to the train tracks).

Bern's top hotels

Hotel Bern

$$$$ Altstadt

This massive hotel is popular with diplomats and business travelers who are drawn to its modern rooms and large selection of in-house restaurants. Rooms facing the streets are bigger and brighter than those opening onto the small inner courtyard. The cheaper rates apply during weekends and

Accommodations, Dining, and Attractions in Bern

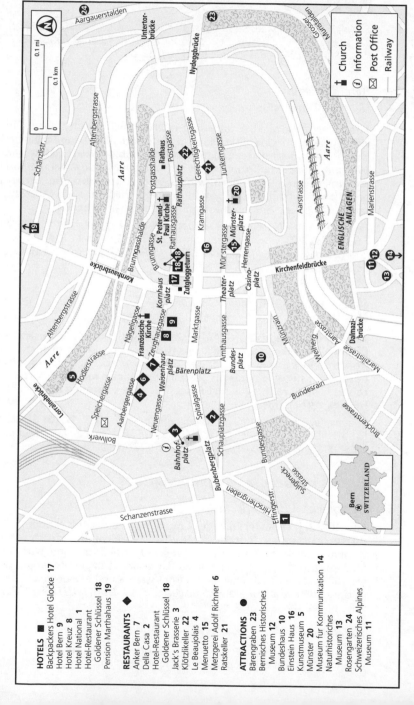

HOTELS ■
Backpackers Hotel Glocke **17**
Hotel Bern **9**
Hotel Kreuz **8**
Hotel National **1**
Hotel-Restaurant
Goldener Schlüssel **18**
Pension Marthahaus **19**

RESTAURANTS ◆
Anker Bern **7**
Della Casa **2**
Hotel-Restaurant
Goldener Schlüssel **18**
Jack's Brasserie **3**
Klötzlikeller **22**
Le Beaujolais **4**
Menuetto **15**
Metzgerei Adolf Richner **6**
Ratskeller **21**

ATTRACTIONS ●
Bärengraben **23**
Bernisches Historisches
Museum **12**
Bundeshaus **10**
Einstein Haus **16**
Kunstmuseum **5**
Münster **20**
Museum für Kommunikation **14**
Naturhistoriches
Museum **13**
Rosengarten **24**
Schweizerisches Alpines
Museum **11**

holidays. Children under 16 stay free in their parents' room (or at a 20 per-cent discount in a separate one).

See map p. 335. Zeughausgasse 9 (just off Kornhausplatz). ☎ *031-329-2222. Fax: 031-329-2299.* www.hotelbern.ch. *Bus/Tram: 3, 5, 9, 10, 12, or 30. Rates: 235SF–300SF ($186–$237) double. Rates include breakfast. AE, DC, MC, V.*

Hotel National

$$ Near Hauptbahnhof

The prices are low at this imposing 1908 castle-in-the-city, but it's a bit life-less. The elevator doesn't make it up to the fifth floor, where the bathrooms and furnishings are newer and the modern double-glazed windows more effi-cient at blocking traffic noise from the boulevard below. Accommodations are larger than most in Bern, with patterned rugs atop the carpet and a hodgepodge of faux antique and modular furnishings. The hotel incorpo-rates the popular South American–themed Shakira bar.

See map p. 335. Hirschengraben 24 (just south of the train station). ☎ *031-381-1988. Fax: 031-381-6878.* www.nationalbern.ch. *Bus: 9, 10, or 16. Rates: 100SF–120SF ($79–$95) double without bathroom, 130SF–150SF ($103–$119) double with bathroom. Rates include breakfast. AE, DC, MC, V.*

Hotel-Restaurant Goldener Schlüssel

$$ Altstadt

Jost Troxler runs his hotel and restaurant with care (see the next section for a review of the latter), and keeps the prices low for an inn just "99 steps" from the clock tower. The modular furnishings are beginning to show wear but remain sturdy. Rooms on the back overlook a medieval Bern sweep of rooftops and are the quietest (except for the charming hourly chimes of the nearby bell tower).

See map p. 335. Rathausgasse 72 (just off Kornhausplatz). ☎ *031-311-0216. Fax: 031-311-5688.* www.goldener-schluessel.ch. *Bus/Tram: 3, 5, 9, 10, 12, or 30. Rates: 130SF ($103) double without bathroom, 155SF ($122) double with bathroom. AE, MC, V.*

Bern's runner-up accommodations

Backpackers Hotel Glocke

$ Altstadt   Though I don't go in much for hostels, this former hotel right on the main square in town (a bit noisy, but located perfectly) improved dramatically when it was taken over and turned into one, with a shared kitchen and cheap laundry facilities. There are even private rooms available for 100SF ($79) per double if you don't want a bed in a dorm at 29SF ($23) per person. *See map p. 335. Rathausgasse 75.* ☎ *031-311-3771. Fax: 031-311-1008.* www.bernbackpackers.com.

Hotel Kreuz

$$$ Altstadt   The Hotel Kreuz is another large, amenitied, business-oriented hotel, like its neighbor the Hotel Bern. Many rooms hide foldaway beds for families. *See map p. 335. Zeughausgasse 39–41.* ☎ *031-329-9595. Fax: 031-329-9596.* www.hotelkreuz-bern.ch.

Pension Marthahaus

$$ **North of the Alstadt**   The Marthahaus is Bern's only pension, with cheap rates and rooms a bit larger than those of the central hotels — plus the lady who runs it is a sweetheart. Rooms with private bathrooms (30SF/$24 more) also come with TVs and phones and have slightly nicer furnishings. *See map p. 335. Wyttenbachstrasse 22a (north of the Aare River).* ☎ *031-332-4135. Fax: 031-333-3386.* www.marthahaus.ch.

Dining in Bern

Switzerland has taken culinary influences from the surrounding countries of Germany, France, and Italy, giving Swiss cooking a very international flavor. Cheese is a holey Swiss ingredient. There are about 100 varieties besides the sour, hole-riddled Emmentaler we generically refer to as "Swiss cheese." Emmentaler and Gruyère, along with white wine, garlic, and lemon, often get thrown together in a melting crock and carried to your table — fondue, one of the country's specialties.

Another national specialty is *raclette,* created when half a wheel of cheese is held over an open fire; when the exposed surface begins to melt, the wheel is rushed over to you, and a melted layer is scraped off on your plate. You should eat the dish with hunks of brown bread.

To go with your cheese, the Swiss offer the omnipresent and delicious *rösti* (a sort of hash brown), lake fish, or sausages. Another typical Bernese dish is the *Bernerplatte,* a plate of sauerkraut or beans, piled with sausages, ham, pig's feet, bacon, or pork chops.

An excellent way to wash all this down is with one of Switzerland's fine white or light red wines or a handcrafted local beer. Swiss chocolates are some of the world's finest (Nestlé is a Swiss company). Although some locals eat chocolate at breakfast, many Americans find that a bit too rich so early in the morning.

Cheap cafes and restaurants line Bern's two main squares, **Bärenplatz and Kornhausplatz.** Lining the arcaded streets of the city you find kiosks selling *donner kebab* (pita stuffed with spicy lamb and a hot sauce), various Asian nibblers, pizzas, pretzel sandwiches, and *Gschnätzltes* (a Bern specialty of fried veal, beef, or pork; order yours *sur chabis,* with sauerkraut).

For a variety of quick-bite options, head to the indoor marketplace **Markthalle,** Bundesplatz 11, which features lots of small food booths hawking prepared specialty foods to take away or to enjoy at a small table. The hours are Monday through Friday from 8 a.m. to 7 p.m. (until 9 p.m. Thurs), and Saturday from 8 a.m. to 4 p.m. The supermarkets **Migros** (Marktgasse 46/Zeughausgasse 31) and **Coop** (in the Ryfflihof department store on Neuengasse) sell fresh picnic ingredients, and both have inexpensive cafeterias where meals generally cost less than 20SF ($16). They're open Monday from 9:00 a.m. to 6:30 p.m.; Tuesday, Wednesday, and Friday from 8:00 a.m. to 6:30 p.m.; Thursday from 8 a.m. to 9 p.m.; and Saturday from 7 a.m. to 4 p.m.

Bern's top restaurants

Della Casa
$$$ Altstadt SWISS

This creaky local legend, housed in a building from the 1500s, has been around for more than a century. The low-ceilinged, wood-paneled rooms are slathered with off-green paint, and the service is friendly and furious. The staff weaves expertly among the large crowded tables to bring the abundant portions of ravioli and *lamm-médaillons* (tender lamb medallions in a rich sauce) with Swiss efficiency. If you feel like loosening your wallet straps (and your belt), splurge on the local specialty *Bernerplatte*, an enormous platter of grilled meats served over beans and kraut — it'll cost 40SF ($32) but will probably tide you over for two meals. Most regulars prefer the jovial tavern atmosphere on the ground floor to the fancier, more sedate dining room upstairs.

See map p. 335. Schauplatzgasse 16. ☎ *031-311-2142. Reservations recommended. Tram/Bus: 9, 10, 12, or 16. Main courses: 22SF–40SF ($17–$32); 20SF–25SF ($16–$20) at lunch. AE, DC, MC, V. Open: Lunch Mon–Sat, dinner Mon–Fri.*

Hotel-Restaurant Goldener Schlüssel
$$ Altstadt SWISS

You can tuck into hearty Swiss peasant cooking such as *Bauern Bratwurst erlebnis* (a 200-gram sausage under an onion sauce with rösti), or one of several vegetarian dishes of Indian or Mexican inspiration in this converted stone and wood 16th-century stable. Wash it all down with a half-liter bottle of a local Bern brew, *Mutzenbügler*.

See map p. 335. Rathausgasse 72 (just off Kornhausplatz). ☎ *031-311-0216. Reservations recommended. Bus/Tram: 9, 10, or 12. Main courses: 20SF–35SF ($16–$28); fixed-price lunch 20SF–24SF ($16–$19). Open: Lunch and dinner daily.*

Jack's Brasserie (Stadt Restaurant)
$$$$$ Altstadt FRENCH/CONTINENTAL

Nostalgically outfitted in a style that evokes a Lyonnais bistro, Jack's bustles in a way that's chic, convivial, and matter-of-fact, all at the same time. The best dishes on the menu include the kind of Wiener schnitzels that hang over the sides of the plate, a succulent sea bass, veal head vinaigrette for real regional flavor, tender pepper steaks, and smaller platters piled high with salads, risottos, and pastas.

See map p. 335. In the Hotel Schweizerhof, Bahnhofplatz 11. ☎ 031-326-8080. Tram: 3, 9, or 12. Reservations recommended. Main courses 25SF–65SF ($20–$51); fixed-price menu 85SF ($67). AE, DC, MC, V. Open: Breakfast, lunch, and dinner daily.

Ratskeller
$$$$ Altstadt SWISS

This starched-tablecloth restaurant is a bit pricey (the laid-back, brick vaulted *keller* [cellar] underneath is cheaper), but for professional service and excellent meat dishes, this is one of the best splurge deals in town for a quiet, understated dinner. The *Oberlander rösti* are a house specialty, the cheesy rösti layered with bacon and topped by a fried egg.

See map p. 335. Gerechtigkeitsgasse 81. ☎ 031-311-1771. Reservations recommended. Bus: 12. Main courses: 20SF–50SF ($16–$40); fixed-price lunch menu: 22SF ($17). AE, DC, MC, V. Open: Lunch and dinner daily (cellar open only at lunch).

Bern's runner-up restaurants

Anker Bern
$ Altstadt The Anker Bern ain't fine dining, but this dark-wood locals' tavern does offer low-cost hearty meals — 15 types of pizzas, nine rösti — in a convivial atmosphere. *See map p. 335. Kornhausplatz/Zeughausgasse 1. ☎ 031-311-1113.* www.roeschti.ch.

Klötzlikeller
$$ Altstadt Since 1635, Klötzlikeller has been the best and most authentic of Bern's old-fashioned brick-vaulted keller (cellar joints), serving big glasses of wine and beer alongside a limited menu of excellent Swiss specialties — and hosting live music some evenings. *See map p. 335. Gerectigkeitsgasse 62. ☎ 031-311-7456.*

Le Beaujolais
$$$ Altstadt Le Beaujolais is a candlelit-yet-comfy French bistro with refined food at reasonable prices. *See map p. 335. Aarbergergasse 50–52. ☎ 031-311-4886.*

Menuetto
$$ Altstadt This vegetarian spot serves dishes such as samurai rice (a fancy permutation of tofu) and nasi goring (the well-accessorized national rice dish of Indonesia). The all-vegetable broth is superb. *See map p. 335. Münstergasse 47 at the Herrengasse. ☎ 031-311-14-48.*

Metzgerei Adolf Richner
$ Altstadt This butcher hand carves meat for a sandwich or stuffs a roll with a hot dog for as little as 5SF ($3.95), sauerkraut included. *See map p. 335. Aarbergergasse 3. ☎ 031-311-02-11.*

Exploring Bern

Bern's historic center is comfortably scenic and walkable, with low-key sights like a dozen statue-topped fountains dating back to the 1500s and the **Zytgloggeturm (Clock Tower),** on Kramgasse at the corner with Bärenplatz, which for over 460 years has treated Bern to a simple mechanical puppet show four minutes before every hour. May through October, there's a 45-minute tour of the clock's inner workings daily at 11:30 a.m. (in July and Aug, also at 4:30 p.m.); admission is 9SF ($7.10) adults and 4.50SF ($3.55) children.

In 2004, the city started selling a **BernCard** good for unlimited travel on the local trams and buses, 20 percent discounts on city and clock tower tours, and 1SF to 4SF off the price of admission to most city sights and museums. It costs 10SF ($7.90) for one day, 14SF ($11) for two days, or 17SF ($13) for three days, and is sold at the tourist offices and major museums.

Bern's top sights

Bernisches Historisches Museum (Bern Historical Museum)
South of the Alstadt

Switzerland's second-largest historical museum is housed in a fanciful faux-medieval castle from 1894 and contains a rich collection of artifacts. Here you find a bit of everything, from Burgundian suits of armor, furnishings and decorative arts, and Flemish tapestries to the original 15th-century carvings from the cathedral's *Last Judgment* portal and dioramas of everyday life in Bern over the past three centuries. Don't miss the Oriental collection (mostly Islamic), rendered all the more fascinating by its post-industrial display cases.

See map p. 335. Helvetiaplatz 5. ☎ *031-350-7711.* www.bhm.ch. *Tram: 3 or 5. Admission: 13SF ($10) adults, 8SF ($6.30) students and seniors. Open: Tues and Thurs–Sun 10 a.m.–5 p.m., Wed 10 a.m.–8 p.m.*

Einstein Haus (Einstein House)
Alstadt

A young German dreamer named Albert Einstein was working in the Bern patent office in 1905 when he came up with $E = mc^2$. He devised his famous "Special Theory of Relativity," which revolutionized 20th-century science, while living in this house. The modest museum consists mainly of photos and photocopied letters, most translated into English.

See map p. 335. Kramgasse 49. ☎ *031-312-0091.* www.einstein-bern.ch. *Bus: 12. Admission: 3SF ($2.35) adults, 2SF ($1.60) students/children; free for children 5 and under. Open: Feb–Apr 10 Tues–Fri 1–5 p.m., Sat noon to 4 p.m.; Apr 13–Oct 31 Tues–Fri 10 a.m.–5 p.m., Sat 10 a.m.–4 p.m.*

Kunstmuseum (Fine Arts Museum)
Alstadt

This museum preserves the world's largest collection of paintings and drawings by Bern native Paul Klee, offering a unique insight into this early-20th-century master's skill with color and expression. Although the museum also has a smattering of pieces by the likes of Fra' Angelico, Duccio, and Delacroix, the museum's particular strength is late 19th- and early-20th-century art: a few works each by the best Impressionists and Surrealists along with paintings by Kandinsky, Modigliani, Matisse, Picasso, Léger, Pollock, and Rothko.

See map p. 335. Hodlerstrasse 12. ☎ 031-328-0944. www.kunstmuseumbern.ch. Bus: 20 or 21 (or five-minute walk from train station). Admission: 7SF ($5.55) adults, 5SF ($3.95) students; special exhibitions 18SF ($14). Open: Tues 10 a.m.–9 p.m., Wed–Sun 10 a.m.–5 p.m.

Münster (Cathedral)
Alstadt

On Münsterplatz, with its 16th-century Moses fountain, is Bern's Gothic cathedral from 1421, with enormous stained-glass windows and an elaborate *Last Judgment* carved over the main door (most of it is reproduction; the originals are in the Bernisches Historisches Museum). The biggest draw of the cathedral is its 300-foot belfry, the highest in Switzerland, which offers a great panoramic view across Bern and its river with the Alps in the distance.

See map p. 335. Münsterplatz. No phone. Bus: 12. Admission: Cathedral, free; belfry 3SF ($2.35) adults, 1SF (80¢) ages 7 to 16. Open: Easter Sun–Oct Tues–Sat 10 a.m.–5 p.m. and Sun 11:30 a.m.–5 p.m.; Nov through the day before Easter Tues–Fri 10 a.m. to noon and 2–4 p.m., Sat 10 a.m. to noon and 2–5 p.m., and Sun 11:30 a.m.–2 p.m. The belfry closes 30 minutes before the church.

More cool things to see and do

- ✔ **Floating down the Aare:** Unlike most capital cities, Bern has a river so unpolluted the locals actually swim in it regularly. In warm weather, join the Bernese for a short hike up the river and then a leisurely float down the Aare to a free public beach just below the Altstadt (make sure you get out at the beach, because a dam/waterfall is the river's next stop).

- ✔ **Feeding the bears:** Bern's most unique sight has to be the **Bärengraben** (Bear Pits), just on the other side of Nydeggbrücke bridge from the Altstadt. Here you find up to 12 very well-fed live examples of Bern's civic symbol roaming around. Bern has had bear pits since at least 1441 — formerly on the square still named Bärenplatz, here since 1875. The bears are out daily from 9 a.m. to 4 p.m. (until 5:30 p.m. in summer); the keeper sells 3SF ($2.35) baggies of fruit to feed them — these hairy fellows ham it up to get you to drop them a piece of apple or carrot. *Remember:* They're strict vegetarians. To the Bear Pits' left, a long path leads up the hillside to a ridge planted with Bern's fragrant **Rosengarten** (Rose Garden), with killer views over medieval Bern.

✔ **Observing how a federal government can operate on just $5 per citizen per year:** Switzerland began as a confederation of three forest *cantons* (states) in 1291. Today's 23 cantons retain a remarkable degree of autonomy and governmental powers, making this one of the West's least centralized democracies. The federal chambers meet only four times a year for three-week sessions to debate legislative issues and foreign treaties. If you'd like a glimpse into such a lean federal machine, you can tour the 1902 **Bundeshaus (Parliament),** Bundesplatz (☎ 031-322-8522; www.parliament. ch), the dome of which was modeled loosely on that of Florence's cathedral. Free tours are given Monday through Saturday at 9 a.m., 10 a.m., 11 a.m., 2 p.m., 3 p.m., and 4 p.m. (except when Parliament is in session, at which time you can observe from the galleries).

✔ **Shopping till you drop (chocolates, watches, and Swiss army knives):** Bern has almost 4 miles of virtually continuous shopping arcade running down its three parallel main streets, with even more shops crowding the alleys and corridors connecting them.

Switzerland is home to **Nestlé, Lindt,** and those triangular **Toblerone** chocolates. You can get these famous factory-made chockies at **Merkur,** Spitalgasse 2 (☎ 031-311-0425; www.merkur. ch). If you want handmade sweets from a traditional confectioner, head to **Confiserie Abegglen,** Spitalgasse 36 (☎ 031-311-2111; www.confiserie-abegglen.ch), or **Confiserie Tschirren,** Kramgasse 73 (☎ 031-311-1717; www.swiss-chocolate.ch) and in the Markthalle at Bubenbergplatz 9.

If you're in the market for a fine watch, the shop with the most reasonable prices is **Columna,** Spitalgasse 4 (☎ 031-311-0975). If you're using this guide mainly to save enough to afford that 3,750SF ($2,963) Rolex (that's the cheapest model), put on your best and head to the burnished wood shrine of **Bucherer,** Marktgasse 38 (☎ 031-328-9090; www.bucherer.ch).

The **Hullinger Swiss Knife Shop,** Aarbergergasse 11 (☎ 031-311-1992), carries cutlery in addition to Swiss Army knives, but you find the best prices from the locksmith's shop **Schlüssel Bern,** Neuengasse 5 (☎ 031-312-1315). You can also find knives, watches, cuckoo clocks, and a little bit of everything Swiss (or imagined to be Swiss) at general souvenir shops like **Swiss Plaza,** Kramgasse 75 (☎ 031-311-5616); **Edelweiss,** Gerechtigkeitgasse 21 (no phone); or **Boutique Regina,** Gerechtigkeitgasse 75 (☎ 031-311-5616).

More Bern museums

Bern's only truly great museum is the **Kunstmuseum,** although the **Bernisches Historisches Museum** is also worth a visit. (You find listings for both of these museums under "Bern's top sights," earlier in this chapter.)

The best of the rest is the **Schweizerisches Alpines Museum (Swiss Alpine Museum),** Helvetiaplatz 4 (☎ **031-350-0440;** www.alpinesmuseum.ch), explaining all you ever wanted to know about the Alps via maps, do-it-yourself slide shows, and a whole collection of scale relief models of Alpine regions, some dating from 1800. Admission is 11SF ($8.70) adults, 7SF ($5.55) students/seniors; hours are Monday from 2 to 5 p.m. and Tuesday through Sunday from 10 a.m. to 5 p.m. (mid-Oct through May closed from noon to 2 p.m.).

Others that may pique your interest are the **Naturhistoriches Museum (Natural History Museum),** Bernastrasse 15 (☎ **031-350-7111;** www.nmbe.unibe.ch), not the best of its kind, but you can pay your respects to Barry (1800–1814), the most famous of the old rescue Saint Bernards (he saved more than 40 people before retiring to Bern at age 12), and the **Museum fur Kommunikation (Museum of Communication),** Helvetiastrasse 16 (☎ **031-357-5555;** www.mfk.ch), covering everything from stamps to cellphones. The admission for the Communication Museum is 9SF ($7.10) for all comers; the Natural History Museum charges 7SF ($5.55) adults and 5SF ($3.95) students. Both keep hours roughly Tuesday through Sunday from 10 a.m. to 5 p.m. (the Natural History Museum opens 9 a.m. weekdays, and is also open Mon 2–5 p.m.).

Guided tours

The **Bern Tourist Office,** in the Hauptbahnhof (☎ **031-328-1212;** Fax: 031-312-1233; www.bernetourism.ch), sponsors a **two-hour bus tour** of the center and major sights with a multilingual guide. The tour costs 29SF ($23) adults and 10SF ($7.90) children under 17 and runs daily at 11 a.m. May through November 1, Saturdays only November 2 though April 30.

A **90-minute walking tour** of the Altstadt costs 15SF ($12) adults, 7.50SF ($5.90) kids under 17, and leaves at 11 a.m. daily June through September (plus daily in Apr at 2:30 p.m.). June through September, you can also see the city from below via a 90-minute raft tour daily (45SF/$36 adults; 25SF/$20 children under 17) — this is a genuine rubber-raft deal, not a cruise-type river boat, meaning you help paddle and need to bring a swimsuit. You have to contact the tourist office to see when these are running — they require a minimum of four people to sign up before it's a go — but they tend to float around 5 p.m.

Suggested itineraries

If you're the type who'd rather organize your own tours, this section offers some tips for building your own Bern-centered itineraries.

If you have one day

You can do the best of Bern easily in a day. First thing, head to the **Kunstmuseum** to commune with the works of Paul Klee and other old and modern masters. At 11 a.m., take a tour of **Bundeshaus.** Then just head up to **Marktgasse** and start strolling downhill toward the far end of the **Altstadt,** taking in the ambience of the city, with its soft gray stone buildings with their coats of arms and red-tiled roofs and the cobbled streets with their statue-topped fountains. Pop into the **Einstein Haus** before having lunch at **Klötzlikeller.**

After lunch, mosey across the river to visit the bears at the **Bärengraben** and climb up to the **Rosengarten** for a beautiful vista across Bern. Head back into the Altstadt and detour left up Junkerngasse to visit the **Münster** after the cathedral reopens at 2 p.m. and climb its tower for another great cityscape. If you have time left, cross the river to the south to check out the **Bernisches Historisches Museum** before it closes at 5 p.m. End with a traditional Swiss dinner at **Della Casa.**

If you have two days

Spend **Day 1** as the one-day itinerary, only save the **Bernisches Historisches Museum** for the morning of the second day. After the historical museum and before lunch, check out the **Schweizerisches Alpines Museum,** plus any of the others that catch your fancy. After lunch, head up to Bern's mini-mountain, the **Gurtenkulm,** or spend the afternoon shopping downtown. If you have only two days for all Switzerland, forget all that and spend **Day 2** in the Alps (see "Visiting the Bernese Oberland," later in this chapter).

If you have three days

You've covered all of Bern's major sites (see the preceding section), so on **Day 3,** get up early and splurge 217SF ($171) on a round-trip to the **Jungfraujoch,** Europe's highest train station slung 11,333 feet up between two of the mightiest Alps (see "Visiting the Bernese Oberland," later in this chapter).

Traveling Beyond Bern

The two excursions in this section take you to nearby urban destinations — Zurich, the banking capital of Europe, and Basel, a college town with an amazing repository of art. For trips into the countryside, see "Visiting the Bernese Oberland," later in this chapter.

Zurich: Swiss counterculture meets high finance

Switzerland's largest city and banking capital, Zurich is the prettiest of the country's big cities. Its oldest quarter is spread over the steep banks on either side of the swan-filled **Limmat River,** which flows out of the Zürichsee (Lake Zurich).

Zurich has always been a hotbed of radicalism and liberal thought. The Swiss Protestant Reformation started here in the 16th century, and the 20th century has drawn the likes of Carl Jung, Lenin (who spent World War I here, planning his revolution), Thomas Mann, and James Joyce, who worked on *Ulysses* in Zurich and returned a month before his death in 1941. Joyce's grave in **Friedhof Fluntern cemetery** (take Tram 2) is near those of Nobelist Elias Canetti and *Heidi* author Joanna Spyri.

I recommend spending a relaxing 48 hours in Zurich, but you can get a surprisingly good feel for the city in just a day.

Getting there

Zurich is well connected with Europe's major cities and is only 75 to 120 minutes from Bern by train. Trains arrive at **Hauptbahnhof** (the main train station) on the riverbank at the north end of town. The tourist office (☎ **01-215-4000;** Fax: 01-215-4044; www.zuerich.ch) is at the train station, Bahnhofplatz 15.

From the station, the tree-shaded shopping street of **Bahnhofstrasse** runs south, paralleling the **Limmat** a few blocks away, all the way to the shores of the **Zürichsee.** Running off to the left of this street are a series of medieval alleys that lead down to the river. Several bridges cross the river to the wide **Limmatquai Street.** Narrow side streets lined with shops lead to the other half of the old city.

You need to hop a **tram or bus** (www.vbz.ch) for some of the outlying sights and hotels, even though you can get to most of central Zurich on foot. The cost is 3.60SF ($2.85) for rides up to one hour, and 7.20SF ($5.70) for a **Tageskarte,** a 24-hour ticket.

The **ZürichCARD** (www.zvv.ch) costs 15SF ($12) for 24 hours, 30SF ($24) for 72 hours, and covers all public transport and free admission to 43 museums (plus a free "welcome drink" at two dozen local restaurants).

Seeing the sights

The 13th-century **St. Peter's Church** at St. Petershofstaat 6 has the largest clock face in Europe — 28½ feet across with a 12-foot minute hand. Nearby is one of Zurich's top sights, the Gothic **Fraumünster** church, with five 1970 stained-glass windows by artist Marc Chagall.

From here, cross the Münsterbrücke over the Limmat River to reach Zurich's cathedral, the twin-towered **Grossmünster.** Founded on a site said to have been chosen by Charlemagne's horse (he bowed his head on the spot where a trio of 3rd-century martyrs were buried), its construction ran from 1090 through the 14th century. Swiss artist Alberto Giacometti designed the stained glass in 1933. Climb the tower (3SF/$4) from March 15 through October 31 for a great city view.

A long walk up Kirchgasse from the church and a left on Seiler Granben/ Zeltweg takes you to Heimplatz and the **Kunsthaus** (☎ 01-253-8484; www.kunsthaus.ch), Zurich's fine-arts museum. The main collection starts with the Impressionists of the late 19th century and runs to contemporary times, featuring works by Monet, Degas, Cézanne, Chagall, Rodin, Picasso, Mondrian, Marini, and especially the Swiss-born Giacometti. Admission is 6SF ($4.75) for adults, 4SF ($3.15) for students (free under age 17) — more when one of the frequent special exhibits is on — and it's closed Monday (you can also take Tram 3 here). Wednesdays, admission is free to all.

Zurich's cheapest sight is the park lining the mouth of the Zürichsee. You can stroll the west bank of the lake up and down the **General Guisan quai** (at the end of Bahnhofstrasse), which leads to an arboretum. Also at the base of Bahnhofstrasse are the piers from which dozens of steamers embark for tours of the lake. A full-length tour of the lake costs 20SF ($16) in second class and 33SF ($26) in first class. A shorter boat ride on the northern third of the lake costs 5.40SF ($4.25). For more information, contact the **Zürichsee Schiffahrtsgesellschaft** (☎ 01-487-1333; www.zsg.ch).

Where to stay and dine

Zur Oepfelchammer, Rindermarkt 12, just off the Limmat (☎ 01-251-2336), serves up reasonably priced Swiss and French cuisine in a friendly, atmospheric setting. Although pricey at 520SF to 680SF ($411–$537) double, the romantic **Hotel Zum Storchen,** Am Weinplatz 2 (☎ 01-227-2727; Fax: 01-227-2700; www.storchen.ch), is the best bet in town — a 640-year-old inn right on the river in the center of Zurich's Altstadt. The tourist office can help you find someplace cheaper or other rooms if you can't find a room here.

Basel: Three, three, three countries in one!

The Swiss answer to Four Corners, USA, is Basel, a university city that features a pylon on the **Rhine River** where you can walk in a circle and move from Switzerland into Germany, then France, and back into Switzerland (the spot's called **Dreiländereck**). Basel's number of museums (27) makes it an art capital of Switzerland, and the city claims Hans Holbein the Younger (along with thinker Friedrich Nietzsche) among its famous past residents. Non–art lovers needn't bother visiting, but give the city at least a day or two if you're a fan of modern and contemporary art.

Getting there

Half-hourly trains make the 60- to 75-minute trip from **Bern** and arrive at **SBB Hauptbahnhof.** A small branch of the tourist office can be found in the train station, but the main office (☎ 061-268-6868; Fax: 061-268-6870; www.baseltourismus.ch) is on the Rhine at Schifflände 5, just past the Mittlere Bridge (take Tram 1). Basel's compact, historic center lies mainly on the south bank of the Rhine River.

Seeing the sights

Although the elaborately carved face of the impressive 14th-century **Münster** (cathedral) is the pride of Basel, this city is really about museums. Top honors go to the eclectic collections of the **Kunstmuseum (Fine Arts Museum)**, St. Alban Graben 16 (☎ 061-206-6262; www. kunstmuseumbasel.ch). This museum has everything from Holbein the Younger and Konrad Witz to van Gogh, Picasso, Klee, Chagall, Rodin, and Alexander Calder.

Next door is the **Museum für Gegenwartskunst (Museum for Contemporary Art)** (☎ 061-272-8183), with contemporary art ranging from the 1960s to the present day by the likes of Bruce Nauman, Joseph Beuys, and Donald Judd. Nearby you can also find the **Kunsthalle,** Steinenberg 7 (☎ 061-272-4833), whose changing installations by contemporary artists are advertised on banners throughout town. Admission (covering both museums) is 10SF ($7.90), or free the first Sunday of each month. Most Basel museums are closed on Monday.

The city also has the **Basler Zoologischer Garten,** Binningerstrasse 40 (☎ 061-295-3535; www.zoobasel.ch), a world-renowned zoo just a seven-minute stroll from the train station, with 600 species represented.

Where to stay and dine

The restaurant **Zum Goldenen Sternen,** St. Alban-rheinweg 70, at the Rhine's edge (☎ 061-272-1666; www.sternen-basel.ch), has served up a good, inexpensive medley of French-accented Swiss and continental dishes since 1421. Art aficionados with shallow pockets will want to stay just across the river from the main part of town at the **Hotel Krafft am Rhein,** Rheingasse 12 (☎ 061-690-9130; Fax: 061-690-9131; www.hotel krafft.ch), overlooking the Rhine. The setting is 19th century, and the rooms are modern and comfy. Rates are 170SF to 250SF ($134–$198) double.

Visiting the Bernese Oberland

The triple peaks of the **Eiger** (13,025 feet), **Mönch** (13,450 feet), and **Jungfrau** (13,642 feet) dominate the Jungfrau region. A trip through the area can be a thrilling, scenic ride on trains that hug (or punch through) cliff sides and ski-lift gondolas that dangle high above mountain glaciers.

The gateway to the Bernese Oberland is **Interlaken,** a bustling resort town in the foothills of the Alps that is flanked by a pair of lakes and is just a one-hour train ride from Bern. Interlaken itself doesn't have too much to hold your interest, but it makes an optimal base for forays into the Bernese Oberland.

The Bernese Oberland

The Alps are scattered with tiny villages and quaint resort towns. One of the most visitor-friendly of these is **Mürren,** where I recommend a few restaurants and hotels. Although I think you should visit the region at least three or four days, on the tightest of schedules you can take an overnight train to Interlaken, switch for a train up to **Jungfraujoch** to spend the day, and make it back to Interlaken by evening for another overnight train out — but that's pushing it.

Getting there

Two trains per hour run between Bern and Interlaken (a 50- to 60-minute ride), some requiring a change in Spiez. Get off at Interlaken's

Westbahnhof station for the main part of town; get off at **Ostbahnhof station** to transfer to trains into the Jungfrau region.

Finding information

For information on the Bernese Oberland and the Alps, the **Tourist Office of Interlaken** (☎ **033-826-5300;** Fax: 033-826-5375; www.interlaken tourism.ch) is the unofficial central information bureau, with maps and advice on getting around the region. It's a seven-minute walk from Westbahnhof train station, in the Hotel Metropole at Höheweg 37. The tourist office is open May to October Monday through Friday from 8 a.m. to noon and 1:30 to 6:00 p.m., Saturday from 9 a.m. to noon (open through the midday break in May, June, and Oct); July through September, hours are Monday through Friday 8:00 a.m. to 6:30 p.m., Saturday 8 a.m. to 5 p.m., and Sunday 10 a.m. to noon and 5 to 7 p.m. You find **Mürren's Tourist Office** in the Sportszentrum (☎ **033-856-8686;** Fax: 033-856-8696; www.muerren.ch).

General info on the Bernese Oberland is available at www.berner oberland.ch. Timetables for the major trains and cable cars are supplied in English at www.jungfraubahn.ch.

Learning the lay of the land

Interlaken lies on the brief stretch of the Aare River (the same river that runs through Bern) that connects two lakes, **Lake Thun** and **Lake Brienz** — hence the city's name, which means "between the lakes." Its busiest tourist area stretches between the two train stations along the Aare. The road that connects the stations is **Bahnhof Strasse,** which becomes the parklike **Höheweg.**

Now about the **Alps:** The Bernese Oberland is large, but this chapter stays within the western half — it's the most popular and the easiest to reach from Interlaken. Imagine you're standing in Interlaken and looking south toward the Alps. Low mountains lie directly in front of you. Behind them, to the east, is a trio of enormous peaks called **Eiger, Mönch,** and, the most famous, **Jungfrau.**

Farther off to the west (right) is the slightly more modest peak of the **Schilthorn.** Running south from Interlaken between the Jungfrau and Schilthorn is a wide valley called the **Lauterbrunnen;** this is where the area's main train line leads to various Alpine destinations (halfway up the valley in the town of Lauterbrunnen is a station where you may transfer trains frequently).

Scattered throughout the upper reaches of this valley are many small resorts and alpine towns, such as **Mürren** (at the base of the **Schilthorn**) and **Wengen** (halfway to the **Jungfrau**). Between Interlaken and Lauterbrunnen town, a valley that branches off to the east from Lauterbrunnen Valley interrupts the Alpine foothills. Train tracks lead through here to the village of **Grindelwald.**

Getting around the Bernese Oberland

Unfortunately, the various scenic and private rail lines — not to mention funiculars, ski lifts, and cable cars — that connect the peaks and towns are ridiculously expensive. Rail passes such as Swissrail or Eurail only get you a 25 percent discount at most. Always ask about discounts for children, seniors, students, and so on. For each of the sights in this chapter, I give directions and some idea of the frequency of trains and connections.

Traveling around the Bernese Oberland means plenty of train changes, but this usually turns out to be kind of fun (if pricey). The wait between connections is usually five to ten minutes. Because trains tend to run hourly, it's fairly easy to hop off at any station, go see whatever town you're in, and pick up the transfer an hour or two later.

The tourist office in Interlaken has Bernese Oberland transportation maps (get one if you plan to explore) and schedules of the whole system. The staff is usually very good at helping you work out an itinerary. A summer **Bernese Oberland Regional Pass** (www.regiopass-berneroberland. ch) gets you 7 days of travel (3 days for free, 4 at 50 percent off) for 220SF ($174), or 15 days (5 days free, 10 at 50 percent off) for 265SF ($209), but again the pass gets you only a discount on the **Jungfraujoch and Schilthorn rides.**

Staying in the Bernese Oberland

At Interlaken and Bernese Oberland resorts, you receive a "guest card" from your hotel for significant discounts on everything from the **Jungfrau train** to adventure outfitters. If your hotel doesn't give you one, be sure to ask for it.

Interlaken certainly doesn't lack hotels, but it also doesn't lack visitors to fill them. If you're having trouble finding a room, check out the hotel billboards at each train station, or visit the tourist office (at the Hotel Metropole), which can book you a room for free. The tourist offices of **Mürren** and other Bernese Oberland towns can help you find rooms as well, but these burgs are so small that you can do just as well following one of the many hotel signs as you exit the station.

The Bernese Oberland's top hotels

Alpenruh
$$$$ Mürren

One of Mürren's top choices is this Alpine-cozy but fully amenitied hotel next to the cable-car station with an excellent restaurant and private sauna. Best of all, they give you a free voucher for a morning ride up to the Schilthorn where you can breakfast in style — already a 48SF ($38) per-person savings. The hotel stays open year-round, although the excellent restaurant closes in November.

Mürren. ☎ *033-856-8800. Fax: 033-856-8888.* http://www.muerren.ch/
alpenruh/. *Rates: 180SF–260SF ($142–$205) double. Rates include breakfast. AE, DC, MC, V.*

Hotel Weisses Kreuz
$$$ Interlaken

On the classiest drag in town, which is basically a city park, this year-round hotel has functionally spartan rooms. The comfort is good, the price is right, and the people-watching from its terrace is unparalleled.
Höheweg (at the corner with Jungfraustrasse). ☎ *033-822-5951. Fax: 033-823-3555.*
www.weisseskreuz.ch. *Rates: 170SF–220SF ($134–$174) double. Rates include breakfast. AE, DC, MC, V.*

Victoria-Jungfrau Grand Hotel
$$$$$ Interlaken

If you can swing the price tag, you can join a long list of dignitaries and royalty by checking into this massive 1865 landmark of over-the-top Alpine architecture. Antiques fill the rooms, the most expensive of which overlook the park of Höheweg and the Alps beyond.
Höheweg 41 (several blocks from Interlaken West station). ☎ *033-828-2828. Fax: 033-828-2880.* www.victoria-jungfrau.ch. *Rates: 530SF–720SF ($419–$569) double. Breakfast 30SF–37SF ($24–$29). AE, DC, MC, V.*

The Bernese Oberland's runner-up accommodations

Alpina Hotel
$$ **Mürren**   The Alpina offers lower prices than the Alpenruh and great clifftop vistas across the Lauterbrunnen Valley. ☎ *033-855-1361. Fax: 033-855-1049.* www.muerren.ch/alpina.

Chalet-Hotel Oberland
$$$ **Interlaken**   The Chalet-Hotel Oberland is another modernish hotel offering somewhat nicer, newer, and roomier accommodations at similar prices to the Splendid (no views, though). *Postgasse 1 (just off Interlaken's main drag).* ☎ *033-827-8787. Fax: 033-827-8770;* www.chalet-oberland.ch.

Splendid
$$$ **Interlaken**   The Splendid is a nondescript modern hotel with comfy rooms, all the amenities, glimpses of the mountains, and a popular corner pub featuring Interlaken's only Internet access. Rooms without a bath are cheaper. *Höheweg 33 (in the center of Interlaken).* ☎ *033-822-7612. Fax: 033-822-7679.* www.splendid.ch.

Dining in the Bernese Oberland

Most hotels in Bernese Oberland resort towns either require or offer some meals in their own restaurants — and, in fact, there aren't enough nonhotel restaurants to go around. But don't despair. The hotel food is usually quite good. However, I recommend that you don't sign up for full board; that way, at least one meal a day you can try the food at *other* hotel dining rooms in town!

For a primer on Swiss foods, see "Dining in Bern," earlier in this chapter.

In Interlaken, you can fill your daypack for picnics and hikes at Migros supermarket, just to the right of the Westbahnhof, or at the huge co-op supermarket center across from the Ostbahnhof. You also find a co-op market in Mürren.

The Bernese Oberland's top restaurants

Hirschen
$$$ Matten SWISS

There has been a Gasthaus Hirschen here since 1666, an oasis of old-fashioned flavors and Alpine hospitality in touristy Interlaken. The low wood-paneled ceilings and overdressed tables strike an odd balance somewhere between rustic and fussy, but you'll be glad the fussiness spreads to their exacting standards in the kitchen — this is by far the best Swiss dining in town. Try the *Hirschen Platte* for two, a platter of grilled meats with rösti and a salad.

Hauptstrasse 11 (in Matten, the southerly neighborhood of Interlaken). ☎ *033-822-1545. Reservations recommended. Main courses: 18SF–47SF ($14–$37). DC, MC, V. Open: Dinner daily, lunch Sat and Sun. Closed mid-Apr to May and Nov 1–Dec 15.*

Restaurant im Gruebi
$$$ Mürren SWISS

This restaurant excels in both mountain views (from its outdoor terrace or the glassed-in hexagonal dining room) and local cuisine, from herb-flavored rack of lamb for two to fondue bourguignonne.

In the Hotel Jungfrau (follow signs from the station). ☎ *033-855-4545.* www.hotel jungfrau.ch. *Reservations recommended. Main courses: 18SF–45SF ($14–$36). AE, DC, MC, V. Open: Lunch and dinner daily.*

Restaurant Piz Gloria
$$$ Schilthorn SWISS

To cap off an idyllic trip to the Swiss Alps, dine in Europe's most stratospheric restaurant — it slowly rotates atop a 9,804-foot mountain. If you can tear your eyes away from the view for a moment, sample the hearty Hungarian goulash or sirloin steak. This place is also a good place to have a high-altitude breakfast if you catch the first cable car up.

Atop Schilthorn mountain, above Mürren. ☎ *033-855-2141. Reservations suggested, but not required. For directions, see "A bit of Bond history atop the Schilthorn," later in this chapter. Main courses: 17SF–44SF ($13–$35). AE, DC, MC, V. Open: Daily from the first cable car's arrival until the last one's departure. Closed Nov 15–Dec 15, one week in May, and during blizzards.*

The Bernese Oberland's runner-up restaurants

Il Bellini

$$$$ **Interlaken** Il Bellini is one of the best Italian restaurants in Switzerland and a worthy splurge. Even on a budget, though, you can ride the skyscraping Metropole's elevator to the 18th floor and the Top o' Met cafe, where just 4SF ($3.15) buys a hot cocoa against a backdrop of Interlaken's best *Alpine panorama. Höheweg 37 (in Hotel Metropole).* ☎ *033-828-6666.* www.metropole-interlaken.ch.

Steigerstübli

$ **Mürren** Steigerstübli is a rough-and-ready locals' joint in the center of Mürren offering the cheapest nonhotel eats in town. ☎ *033-855-1316.*

Goldener Anker

$$$ **Interlaken** The Goldener Anker serves cheap, hearty, and surprisingly good food in an unassuming modern tavern atmosphere. *Marktgasse 57 (between the train tracks and the river).* ☎ *033-822-1672.* www.anker.ch.

Exploring the Bernese Oberland

Prepare for the unique climate of the skyscraping Alps before you get on that train to the top of the world. A warm sunny day in Interlaken may still be sunny atop the Jungfrau, but the wind can bring temperatures deep into negative territory, so bring a heavy jacket. The sun reflects strongly off all that snow, and UV rays are more concentrated, so be sure to wear sunglasses and sunscreen. The highest peaks poke into a very thin atmosphere (about 30 percent less oxygen than at sea level), so overexerting yourself into dizziness and hyperventilation is easy.

Check the weather conditions and forecasts before you set off into the mountains. An overcast day can make an excursion to the panoramic terraces of Jungfrau or Schilthorn a moot point, and avalanche warnings may crimp your skiing or hiking plans. Displayed on TVs at train stations, tourist offices, and hotel rooms are the live Webcam video feeds of the **Jungfraujoch,** the **Schilthorn,** and the **Männlichen** peaks — which are also live-linked at www.swisspanorama.com. In addition, the Web site for Interlaken (www.interlakentourism.ch) links to several local weather-forecasting sites — most in German, but pretty easy to figure out. Real-time forecasts are also available by phone at ☎ **033-855-1022** for the Jungfraujoch, ☎ **033-856-2655** for the Mürren/Schilthorn area, ☎ **033-855-4433** for the Männlichen/Kleine Scheidegg area, or ☎ **033-854-5054** for the first ski area above Grindelwald.

The queen peak at Jungfraujoch

The most spectacular and rewarding excursion in the region is to **Jungfraujoch,** where at 11,333 feet — the highest rail station in Europe — your breath quickens from the stupendous views and the extremely thin air. An elevator takes you up from the station to the even higher **Sphinx Terrace** viewpoint to look out over Europe's longest glacier, the 25km (15½-mile) **Great Aletsch,** whose melt-off eventually makes its way to the Mediterranean.

The view goes on seemingly forever — on a clear day, you can even see as far as Germany's **Black Forest.** One of the popular attractions is the **Eispalast (Ice Palace),** a warren of tunnels carved into a living glacier and filled with whimsical ice sculptures, including a family of penguins and a sumo wrestler. You can eat at a mediocre restaurant (22SF/$17 fondue) or a cafeteria up top if you didn't pack a lunch.

Trains run half-hourly from **Interlaken's Ostbahnhof** (two-and-a-half hours; 169SF/$134). You change once in **Lauterbrunnen** (☎ 033-855-1261), pause in **Wengen,** and change again in **Kleine Scheidegg** (☎ 033-855-1417) before making the final run to **Jungfraujoch station** (☎ 033-855-2405). This popular route has run since 1894, so the transfers are smooth.

Four of the last 6 miles of track are in tunnels, but the train pauses a few times to let you peer out through windows in the rock at the glaciated surroundings. On your way back down, you can change trains at **Kleine Scheidegg** to detour west through **Grindelwald.** For more information, contact the Jungfraubahnen directly at ☎ **033-828-7233** or on the Web at www.jungfraubahn.ch.

A bit of Bond history atop the Schilthorn

A favorite excursion of mine is to take a ride from **Mürren** — home to a fabulous **Sportzentrum** sports complex, with an indoor pool, outdoor skating rink, squash, tennis, curling facilities, and more — up the dizzying cable car to the 9,804-foot peak of the **Schilthorn.** The trip takes you across the Lauterbrunnen Valley with views of the **Big Three peaks,** so you get a great panorama of the Alps' poster children. The summit shares its scenic terrace with the **Restaurant Piz Gloria** (see "The Bernese Oberland's top restaurants," earlier in this chapter).

When the financiers building Europe's most spectacularly sighted restaurant atop the Schilthorn went over budget, James Bond came to the rescue. A film company used the half-finished structure to play the role of "Piz Gloria," headquarters of evil SPECTRE leader Telly Sevalas in *On Her Majesty's Secret Service.* George Lazenby (filling in for 007 between Sean Connery and Roger Moore), fought bad guys while hanging from the cable-car lines (and on skis, and in a bobsled . . .). After shooting wrapped, the film company helped pay for the restaurant's completion and, because the movie provided such great advance publicity, the restaurant decided to take its stage name.

Trains run every half-hour to **Mürren** from **Interlaken's Ostbahnhof,** with a change at Lauterbrunnen (60 minutes; 16SF/$13). When the funicular-train line from Lauterbrunnen to Mürren is snowed in, take the hourly Postbus (15 minutes; 4SF/$3.15) to Stechelberg and the half-hourly **Schilthornbahn cable car** (☎ 033-826-0007; www.schilthorn.ch) up to Gimmelwald (first stop) and thence on to Mürren (10 minutes; 15SF/$12). Half-hourly cable cars from Mürren get you to the top of the **Schilthorn** in 20 minutes (94SF/$74 round-trip total from Stechelberg — 64SF/$51 round-trip from Mürren — with a 25 percent discount if you take the "early-bird" run before 7:30 a.m.; discounts for various rail- and ski-pass holders). If you're up for a workout, you can hike up in a rather demanding, but exhilarating, five hours (a 4,363-foot climb).

Mürren's **Tourist Office** is in the Sportszentrum (☎ 033-856-8686; Fax: 033-856-8696; www.muerren.ch).

Skiing and other outdoorsy stuff

If you came to Switzerland hoping to log a few miles of **Alpine skiing,** you can't do better than **Wengen,** a resort under the looming **Jungfrau trio** and near the **Lauterbrunnen Valley** with some 23 lifts (from cable car to T-bar) and access to most of the region's major ski areas (Wengen, Männlichen, and Kleine Scheidegg). There are half-hourly trains here from **Interlaken's Ostbahnhof,** with a change in Lauterbrunnen (45 to 55 minutes; 12SF/$9.50). Those arriving by car have to leave their wheels in the garage down in Lauterbrunnen (☎ 033-855-3244) and take the train up to car-free Wengen.

The tourist office (☎ 033-855-1414; Fax: 033-855-3060; www.wengen.com) can help you make sense of the multitude of trails, some 20 lifts (both cable car and chair), and more than 7 miles of cross-country terrain. They can also point you toward rental outfitters and the local branch of the famous **Swiss Ski School** (☎ 033-855-2022; www.wengen.com/sss). Less intrepid sports enthusiasts can skate or curl in town.

When there isn't much snow, Wengen sports more than 310 miles of hiking trails (most open in summer only, but 31 miles open in winter, too). One of the most popular is a fairly flat jaunt along the wide ridge of the Männlichen massif, from the top of the Männlichen cable-car station (☎ 033-854-8080; www.maennlichen.ch) to Kleine Scheidegg (one-and-a-half hours; descending gradually about 555 feet). A bit more of a workout, but wonderfully scenic, is the steady uphill walk from **Wengen** to **Kleine Scheidegg,** with a terrific panorama of the **Jungfrau** group (two-and-a-half to three hours; 2,594-foot climb).

Even more spectacular hikes are available down in **Lauterbrunnen Valley** (Lauterbrunnen town is 15 minutes by train or 90 minutes by foot below Wengen). From Lauterbrunnen, take the hourly postal bus or walk in 45 minutes to **Trümmelbach Falls** (☎ 033-855-3232; www.truemmelbach.ch), actually ten stair-stepped waterfalls in one created by glacial melt-off from the surrounding mountains thundering down the deep crevice of a gorge at 20,000 liters per second. April through

November, you can ride an elevator up the inside of the cliff to stroll behind the cascades daily from 9 a.m. to 5 p.m. (July and Aug, from 8 a.m. to 6 p.m.); bring a raincoat. Admission is 10SF ($7.90) adults and 4SF ($3.15) children ages 6 to 16. Also near Lauterbrunnen, **Staubbach Falls** is a 1,000-foot ribbon of water plunging straight down the valley's cliff side at the edge of Lauterbrunnen town.

Hikes in the hills from Grindelwald

Cars can reach **Grindelwald**, so this resorty village in the eastern alpine foothills gets more crowded than its less-accessible neighbors. However, the village is also one of the best bases for hiking. Half-hourly trains from **Interlaken's Ostbahnhof** take 36 minutes and cost 9.80SF ($7.75); be sure you're on the right car; the train splits in half at Lauterbrunnen

The **Tourist Office** (☎ 033-854-1212; Fax: 033-854-1210; www. grindelwald.com) has trail maps covering everything from easy scenic rambles to rock climbing up the sheer eastern face of **Mount Eiger.** Or **Grindelwald Sports** (☎ 033-854-1290; www.grindelwald sports.ch) can organize guided hikes of all degrees of difficulty, from glacier-climbing lessons to an easy, three-hour guided romp along the foot of Mount Eiger.

An hour's hike up to **Milchbach** brings you to the base of the **Obere Gletscher** glacier, whose milky white runoff gives the spot its name. If you continue 45 minutes up the side of the glacier, you're treated to the **Blue Ice Grotte.** Glacial ice turns a deep, resonant blue as you get down into it, and you can take a spin inside a slowly creeping glacier here for 6SF ($4.75) mid-May through October, 9 a.m. to 6 p.m. daily. A postal bus can run you back down to town in 15 minutes.

Fast Facts: Bern

Area Code

Switzerland's country code is **41.** Bern's city code is **031.** If you're calling Bern (or any other Swiss desitnation) from beyond Switzerland's borders, drop the city code's initial zero. To call Bern from the United States, dial ☎ 011-41-31 followed by the phone number.

American Express

Bern no longer has a full-time American Express representative, so you have to change your traveler's checks at a bank. However, American Express travel and mail services are handled by the local travel agency 7-Seas Travel, Kramgasse 83, 3000 Bern 7, Switzerland (☎ 031-327-7777). Amex cardholders can have their post sent to "Your Name/Amex Cardholder" at the preceding address and 7-Seas will hold it for you at no charge.

Currency

Switzerland has so far opted out of adopting the euro. The basic unit of currency is the Swiss franc (I abbreviate it SF, though sometimes you'll see it as CHF), which is composed of 100 centimes. At press time, the rate of exchange, and the one used throughout this chapter, was $1 = 1.27SF, or 1SF = 79¢.

Doctors and Dentists

For a list of doctors and dentists, visit the U.S. consulate (see the following listing) or call the national English-speaking tourist hotline ☎ 157-5014 (2.13SF/$1.70 per minute).

Embassies and Consulates

The U.S. Embassy, Jubiläumsstrasse 93 (☎ 031-357-7234; www.us-embassy.ch; Bus: 19), is open Monday through Friday from 8:30 a.m. to 12:30 p.m. and 1:30 to 5:30 p.m.

Emergency

Dial ☎ 117 for the police; ☎ 144 for an ambulance; ☎ 118 to report a fire; and ☎ 140 (not a free call) for car breakdown.

Hospitals

For emergency care, go to the 650-year-old Insel Hospital, Freiburgstrasse (☎ 031-632-2707; www.insel.ch).

Information

The Bern Tourist Office (☎ 031-328-1212) is in the Hauptbahnhof (train station). For specifics on it, and on other offices, see "Finding information after you arrive," near the beginning of this chapter.

Internet Access and Cybercafes

The traveler's best bud in Bern is the BZ Café, Zeughausstrasse 14 (☎ 031-327-1188). Run by *Berner Zeitung,* the local daily paper, the cafe lets you use the half-dozen computers with lightning ISDN access for free (yes, it's popular, but they even have some Sega game systems for you to play while you wait).

Maps

The map handed out for free by the tourist office is more than good enough for ambling about the tiny town center.

Newspapers/Magazines

Aside from the local daily *Berner Zeitung* (German only), there's no particular magazine or newspaper for visitors in the city, but the tourist office has scads of pamphlets and announcements on current events, shows, concerts, and the like.

Pharmacies

Central-Apotheke Volz & Co., Zeitglockenlaub 2 (☎ 031-311-1094; www.central-apotheke-volz.ch), staffs English-speaking attendants. Located near the Clock Tower, it's open Monday from 9 a.m. to 6:30 p.m., Tuesday through Friday from 7:45 a.m. to 6:30 p.m., and Saturday from 7:45 a.m. to 4 p.m.

Police

Dial ☎ 117 for the police.

Post Office

Bern's main post office (☎ 031-386-6552; www.post.ch) is at Schanzenpost 1 (behind the train station), open Monday through Friday from 7:30 a.m. to 9 p.m., Saturday from 8 to 4 a.m., and Sunday from 4 to 9 p.m. There are several branches throughout the Altstadt.

Safety

With the exception of the park that surrounds Parliament, where heroin addicts roam after dark, you should feel comfortable on the streets of central Bern day or night. But take the same precautions you'd take in any city to protect yourself against crime.

Taxes

Switzerland's value-added tax (VAT) on consumer goods is 7.6 percent. Foreigners who spend more than 400SF ($316) at one store can reclaim it by requesting the necessary forms at the store.

Taxis

See "Getting Around Bern," earlier in this chapter.

Telephone

A local call in Bern costs 0.60SF (50¢). Switzerland's phone system is highly advanced — most booths contain digital, multilingual phone books — and few phones accept coins anymore. You can use your major credit cards in most pay phones, or buy a *Taxcard* (prepaid phone card) in denominations of 5SF ($3.95), 10SF ($7.90), and 20SF ($16) from the train station or any newsstand, gas station, or post office. For direct dialing internationally, you may want the *Value Card* versions for 20SF ($16) or 50SF ($40). Dial ☎ 111 (not free) for directory assistance.

To charge your call to a calling card (or make an operator-assisted call), dial the appropriate number: AT&T (☎ 0-800-890-011), MCI (☎ 0-800-890-222), or Sprint (☎ 0800-899-777). To call direct from Bern abroad, dial 00 followed by the country code (1 for the United States), the area code, and the number.

Transit Info

See "Getting Around Bern," earlier in this chapter.

Chapter 18

Prague and Environs

• •

In This Chapter

▶ Getting to Prague
▶ Checking out the neighborhoods
▶ Discovering the best hotels, restaurants, and attractions
▶ Exploring beyond Prague

• •

*P*rague emerged from behind the Iron Curtain in 1989 to shine once again as a world-class city. Cobbled streets weave past baroque palaces, lively beer halls, glowering castles, and light-infused cathedrals. In summer, some of the best street musicians in Europe play on elegant bridges spanning the swan-filled river.

When the Communist Bloc disintegrated with the Soviet Union's breakup, a group of Czech activist writers and artists led by Vaclav Havel encouraged Czechoslovakia to make a peaceful transition from communism to democracy. The movement, which many called the "Velvet Revolution," also peaceably redrew the ancient dividing line between the Czech and Slovak republics. Prague became the hot new destination, a "Paris of the '90s" for Gen-Xers imitating Hemingway's ex-pat routine. But because of rapid expansion, the city's magic was doused by skyrocketing prices and tainted by the influx of Western culture. But Prague has finally revived itself.

In summer, backpackers and bus-tour groups flock to the city — if you're looking for a romantic setting, pick another season. And you may hear more English than Czech spoken on the streets of the Old Town. In the fall and winter, the crowds are gone, and Prague is all yours. Look for the magic, and spend several days of your trip here to fully capture the city's dreamy flavor. The skyline is dotted with spires, steeples, and towers, and Prague becomes a fairy-tale place at sunrise and sunset.

With a little practice, you can pronounce tongue-twisting Czech words with ease. Vowels are usually short, but any accent makes them long. Consonants are pronounced more or less as in English, except slightly roll your r's, and c sounds like *ts*, c sounds like *ch*, ch sounds like *k, j* sounds like *y*, r sounds like *rsh*, s sounds like *sh*, w sounds like *v,* and z sounds like the slurred *zh* sound in *azure* or *pleasure*. Pronounce consonants followed by an apostrophe (d, n, t) as if there were a *y* following them. For example, *deêkuji* (thank you) is pronounced dyeh-*koo*-ee; *chci* (I would like . . .) is spoken ktsee; and *namêstî* (square) is pronounced nay-mee-*stee*.

To get to your hotel, you can pick up a bus or taxi at the airport; train stations are connected to the subway lines. Although subway stations abound in central Prague, the best way to explore the city is on foot.

Arriving by air

Prague's small **Ruzyne airport** (☎ 02-2011-1111; www.csl.cz), is 12 miles west of the city center. Inside the manageable arrivals hall is an information desk that doesn't hand out city maps but will tell you how to get downtown. Several ATMs are located throughout the hall.

From the airport, a half-hourly ČEDAZ (☎ 02-2011-4296) shuttle bus runs every 30 minutes to namêstí Republiky, for 90Kč ($3.60). City bus 100 is an express heading right from the airport to the Zlicín Metro stop (west end of the B line) in 15 minutes; buses 119 and 254 zip to the Dejvická stop (western terminus of the A Metro line) in 20 minutes. A ticket on any technically costs 8Kč (30¢), but because you'll want to hop on the Metro after you get there, buy the transfer ticket, which costs 12Kč (50¢) — annoyingly, you'll also have to buy a 6Kč (25¢) ticket for each piece of luggage.

A taxi from the airport downtown should cost around 650Kč ($26). You can line up for a taxi at the curb, but you're more likely to get a fair deal and a lower rate if you call one of the radio taxi companies listed under "By taxi," later in this chapter (though you'll have to wait ten minutes or more).

Arriving by rail

Trains arrive in Prague either at the **Hlavní Nádrazí (Main Station)** on the east edge of Nové Mêsto, or, from Berlin and other northerly points, at the smaller **Nádrazí Holesovice (Holesovice Station)** across the river to the north of the city center.

Both train stations, especially the main one, are seedy and chaotic. Dozens of hoteliers practically assault you the instant you step off the train, trying to sell you a hotel room — very annoying. Just ignore them and push ahead. If you want a reputable accommodation agency in the station, see the section on hotels in this chapter.

Orienting Yourself in Prague

Central Prague is divided into four main neighborhoods that straddle both sides of the **Vltava River,** which flows through the city from the south and then curves off to the east. **Staré Mêsto** (Old Town) is tucked into a bend of the river (on the east bank), hemmed in by the Vltava on

The Czech Republic

the north and west and by the continuous arc of streets **Národní/Ríjna/
Napríkopé/Revolucni** on the south and east.

Introducing the neighborhoods

Staré Mĕsto, which means Old Town, is Prague's center. You find mean-
dering streets dating back to the Middle Ages and wide boulevards from
more-recent centuries. Filled with restaurants, cafes, and gorgeous
Gothic and baroque architecture, the area is a great place to spend most
of your time. Within Staré Mĕsto is **Josefov,** the famed old Jewish quarter. The focal point of the Old Town is **Staromĕstské námĕstí,** or Old
Town Square.

Surrounding the Old Town on all but the riverside is the **Nové Mĕsto**
(New Town). Much less interesting than the Old City or the Malá Strana
district (described later in this section), New Town is comprised mostly
of office and apartment buildings. Still, you may enjoy the National
Theater here, and the hotels are generally less expensive than those in
Old Town.

In the center of Nové Mĕsto is **Václavské namĕstí** (Wenceslas Square), a
4-block-long divided boulevard sloping gradually up to the dramatic neo-
Renaissance National Museum. The strip down the middle (for pedestrian traffic) is lined on both sides with sausage stands and neoclassical
and Art Nouveau buildings. (This area has been called New Town since
its 1348 founding; the fact that much of that medieval neighborhood was
replaced in the 19th and 20th centuries by an even newer New Town is
just a coincidence.)

You cross a statue-lined **Karlův most** (Charles Bridge) from the Old Town into the **Malá Strana,** the "Little Quarter" on the west bank of the Vltava River. Above the Malá Strana is the small **Hradcany,** the "Castle District," which houses **Prazsk; Hrad** (Prague Castle), the city's major sight. Over the centuries, many palaces (several now housing museums) and monasteries have gathered around this traditional seat of government.

Beyond Prague's four traditional neighborhoods, the city has sprawled outward in every direction. One outlying neighborhood that you may want to visit is on the eastern edge of New Town. **Vinohrady** was named after the vineyards (owned by the king) that once filled this upscale residential zone. If Prague has a modern trendy district, Vinohrady is it — clean, full of shops and restaurants, and just a short hop from the city center on the Metro line A.

Finding information after you arrive

Prague Information Service (PIS), at Na Príkope 20 (☎ 12-444; www. prague-info.cz), is the main information office in town. PIS is open Monday 11 a.m. to 6 p.m., Tuesday to Sunday 9 a.m. to 6 p.m. (Nov–Mar, it closes at 5 p.m.). There are other branches in the Old Town Hall at Staroměstské nám 1, in the train station, and (summer only) in the tower over the Malá Strana end of Charles Bridge.

Getting Around Prague

You can use the same tickets for all of Prague's public transportation. The 8Kč (32¢) nepřestupní ("no change") version is good for 15 minutes or 4 metro stops, but you cannot change to another bus/tram (you can transfer within the Metro). With the 12Kč (48¢) přestupní ("change") version, you can make unlimited bus, tram, or Metro transfers within the 60-minute time limit (90 minutes from 8 p.m. to 5 a.m. and on weekends). There are also 1-day (70Kč/$2.80), 3-day (200Kč/$8), 7-day (250Kč/$10), and 15-day (280Kč/$11) passes available.

You can buy tickets from machines at Metro stations, newsstands marked Tabak or Tafika, and DP ticket kiosks.

By Metro (subway)

Prague's Metro (subway) system does a good job of covering the town with only three lines: A, B, and C. Each line intersects the other two only once: A and B at Můstek (the north end of Václavské namêstí), A and C at Muzeum (the south end of Václavské namêstí), and B and C at Florenc (a regional bus station).

By tram and bus

The tram system, supplemented by buses, is a more complete network that effectively covers much of central Prague. In winter, the tram seats are heated. Beware of Tram 22: Many people call it the "pickpocket tram" because of the pickpockets who prey on its riders. The line passes by the National Theater and heads through the Malá Strana up to Prague Castle. Staré Mêsto has only a few public trams and buses following its boundary roads. Several lines skirt the riverbank (especially Tram 17) to hit Staromêstské namêstí, which also has a Metro line A station.

By taxi

You probably don't want to use a taxi unless your hotel is a great distance from Prague's center. The taxi drivers are notorious for ripping off unsuspecting tourists. If you must take a taxi, call a radio cab. In a pinch, hail one on the street, but be careful — you may end up with an unlicensed mafia cab (*mafia* here means that you're likely to be taken for a ride — financially, that is).

Wherever you get the cab, keep an eye on the meter. The display window on the left shows your fare; the window on the right should read 1, 2, 3, or 4, indicating the rate you're being charged. (The higher the number, the higher the rate.) Unless you venture far out from the center of town, the window on the right shouldn't read anything but 1 (although the parking lot of the main railway station is zoned 2). The initial charge should be 30Kč ($1.20) and then 22Kč (90¢) per kilometer. If the rate is increasing by more than that, question it.

Don't let a taxi driver cover the meter's displays or change the rate as he changes gears. Let the cabbie see you making a note of the taxi number and any other identifying info as you get into the cab, and sit in the front seat to keep an eye on the driver.

Your chances of getting an honest cabbie are better if you call a radio cab company (most Praguers tell you *never* to hail a cab, especially ones waiting around tourist sights). Because a radio cab's trip is logged in an office, inflating the fare is more difficult for the driver. Companies with English-speaking dispatchers include **AAA Taxi** (☎ 14-014) or **ProfiTaxi** (☎ 261-314-151).

Staying in Prague

Prague is an expensive city, probably the most expensive in Eastern Europe. Prices soared in the years after the fall of the Iron Curtain but have since stabilized and, in some cases, gone down as competition has increased. The priciest rooms are in the most desirable neighborhoods: Staré Mêsto and Mála Strana.

On May 1, 2004, the Czech Republic joined the European Union (EU). Although Czechs welcomed the invitation, it is not yet clear how prices will change. As of this writing, economists predicted a 1 percent increase in inflation over the course of the first year, but a decrease in some

Accommodations, Dining, and Attractions in Prague

HOTELS ■
Betlem Club 12
Flathotel Orion 30
Hotel Cloister Inn 15
Hotel Evropa 28
Hotel Kampa 8
Hotel Paříž 25
Residence Nosticova 9
U Karlova mostu 10

RESTAURANTS ◆
Bellevue 11
Klub Architektů 13
La Provence 24
Obchod Cerstvých
   Uzenin 29
Pizzeria Rugantino 20
U Medvídků 14
U modré kachnicky 7
U třech modrých Koulí 27
Vinárna U Maltézských
   Rytířů (Knights of Malta) 6

ATTRACTIONS ●
Karlův most 16
Ceremonial Hall 18
Jewish Museum 18
Klausen Synagogue 18
Maisel Synagogue 21
Old Jewish Cemetery 18
Old-New Synagogue 18
Old Town Hall &
   Astronomical Clock 22
Staroměstské náměstí 23
Pinkas Synagogue 17
Prazský Hrad 3
Spanish Synagogue 19
St. George's Basilica 5
St. Vitus Cathedral 4
Stavovské divadio 26
Sternberský palác 2
Strahovský Kláster 1
Church of Our Lady
   Before Týn 23

Prague
THE CZECH REPUBLIC

--- Ⓜ Metro
ⓘ Information

0   0.1 mi
0   0.1 km

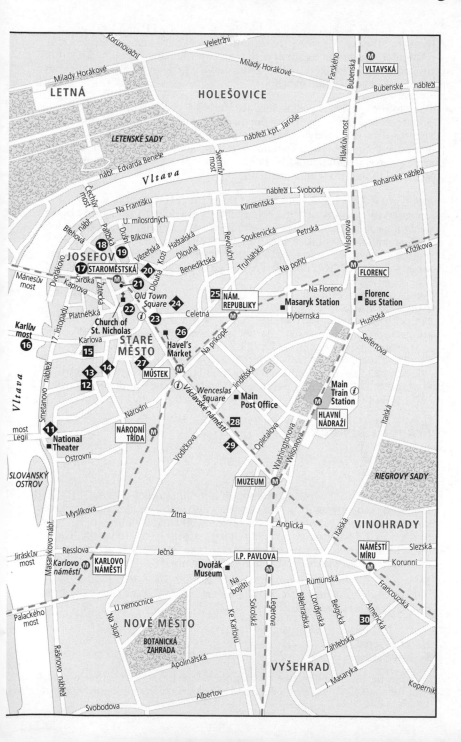

prices of other items, such as wine, because of the EU and VAT regulations. In other words, the prices in this chapter are being compiled at a particularly tumultuous time, economically speaking, and it's likely that they may have changed by the time you visit Prague. The euro currency is at least several years away.

The rapid capitalist invasion has also led to some dubious business practices. Many hotels charge one price for Czechs and another for foreign tourists. It's annoying but unavoidable. Hotels won't give you a good exchange rate from koruna to dollars, so don't pay your bill in dollars or euros (though most business-oriented hotels still tie their rates to one of those two stable currencies).

Remember: As soon as you step off the train at the station, you're accosted by an army of hotel representatives trying to sell you a good deal on a room. These deals are almost always a scam. Either the hotels have an inconvenient location, don't look anything like the "creative" photos suggest, or charge hidden extra fees not included in the quoted rates. If you need help finding a room, go to a legitimate agency instead.

Plenty of these agencies can help you find a hotel room, a pension, or even a full apartment. The most reputable is **AVE Ltd.** (www.avetravel.cz), with desks at the two main PIS offices (for open hours see "Finding information after you arrive" earlier in this chapter) — in the Old Town Hall at Staroměstské nám 2 (☎ 224-223-613) and at Na Prikope 18 (☎ 226-226-087) — as well as in the arrival halls of the main rail station (☎ 224-223-226; open daily 6 a.m. to 11:30 p.m.), the Nádraží Holešovice station (☎ 266-710-514; open daily 7 a.m.–8:30 p.m.), and the airport (☎ 220-114-650; open daily 7 a.m.–10 p.m. — 9 p.m. in winter).

Prague's top hotels

Betlem Club
$$ Staré Město

The Betlem Club is a pleasant enough hotel in a quiet corner of the Old City across the street from the church where Jan Hus started his protestant revolution. Most of the rooms are done in shades of brown, tan, gray, brass, and the odd orange splash, but they are immaculately kept. They're oddly shaped, but most are of a good size (except for some of the top-floor mansard rooms, which can be comically cramped).

See map p. 364. Betlémské Námcčstí 9. ☎ 222-221-574. Fax: 222-220-580. www.betlemclub.cz. *Metro: Národní Třída. Rates: 2,300Kč–3,900Kč ($92–$156) double. Rates include breakfast. MC, V.*

Hotel Evropa
$ Nové Město

You may be impressed by the remarkable, statue-topped Art Nouveau facade (from around 1903–1905) and classy sidewalk cafe of Prague's prettiest hotel.

Unfortunately, the rooms seem to belong to a different hotel entirely. They vary widely in size and décor. Most are merely adequate, and some verge on dingy, but many also have a bit of faded low-rent, turn-of-the-20th-century style hanging about. The rooms on the high-ceilinged first two floors make for quite an enjoyable stay.

See map p. 364. Václavské nám 25. ☎ 234-125-229. Fax: 777-251-106. www.prague holiday.cz/evropa.html. *Metro: Můstek. Rates: 1,950Kč–2,600Kč ($78–$104) double without bath, 2,900Kč–3,800Kč ($116–$152) double with bath. Rates include breakfast. AE, MC, V.*

Hotel Kampa
$$$ Malá Strana

The Kampa is a Best Western affiliate inhabiting a 17th-century armory on a quiet side street across the river, about a five-minute walk from the Charles Bridge. The simple, whitewashed, somewhat large rooms are boringly institutional, but comfy enough. Try to get one overlooking the river or nearby park. The restaurant is a trippy cellar joint outfitted in that faux-medieval crossed-swords-on-the-wall style.

See map p. 364. Všehrdova 16 (just off Újezd). ☎ 257-404-444. Fax: 257-404-333. www. bestwestern.com. *Metro: Malostranská. Rates: 140€–210€ ($161–$242) double. Rates include breakfast. AE, DC, MC, V.*

Hotel Paříž
$$$$$ Staré Město

This whimsically fantastic Czech Art Nouveau behemoth was built in 1904 at the edge of the Old Town. It is, hands-down, my choice for luxury in town, with far more character than most Prague business hotels. The large rooms were overhauled in 1998 and fitted with a modern interpretation of Deco — soft sofas and chairs in a sitting corner and contemporary prints on the walls. The lobby is flanked by the Café de Paris and the Sarah Bernhardt, serving French and international delicacies, the ceilings feature Art Nouveau chandeliers, and the walls are wrapped with aqua and gold mosaics.

See map p. 364. U Obecního domu 1 (off Náměstí Republicky). ☎ 222-195-195. Fax: 224-225-475. www.hotel-pariz.cz. *Metro: Můstek. Rates: 320€–350€ ($368–$403) double (the Paříž only quotes its rates in euros). AE, DC, MC, V.*

Prague's runner-up accommodations

Flathotel Orion

$ Vysehrad This apartment hotel is Prague's best family value. All rooms are one- or two-bedroom flats, sleep up to six, and have well-equipped kitchens. Comfortable, but not imaginative. *See map p. 364. Americká 9. ☎ 222-521-700. Fax: 222-521-701.* www.hotel.cz/orion.

Hotel Cloister Inn

$$ **Staré Město** Stylish simplicity defines this moderate hotel right in the Old City. The spacious rooms are fitted with modern furnishings and bright colors, and there's even free Internet, tea, and coffee in the lobby. *See map p. 364. Konviktská 14.* ☎ *224-211-020. Fax: 224-210-800.* www.cloister-inn.com.

Residence Nosticova

$$$$ **Mala Strana** This baroque palace tucked into Mala Strana's back streets retains its stone staircase and Imperial style. All ten units are sumptuously decorated suites, and all are worthy of a visiting dignitary. *See map p. 364. Nosticova 1.* ☎ *257-312-513. Fax: 257-312-517.* www.nosticova.com.

U Karlova mostu

$$$ **Mala Strana** This former brewery on Na Kampê Island has been turned into a lovely inn complete with beamed ceilings in many rooms. Your choices of view are a quiet cobbled square or the river and Charles Bridge. *See map p. 364. Na Kampě 15.* ☎ *257-531-430. Fax: 257-533-168.* www.archibald.cz.

Dining in Prague

Traditional Czech cuisine is usually simple and hearty. Soups are meaty and frequently flavored with garlic. A favorite is *hovězí polévkas játrov; m̃asi knedlícky* (liver dumplings in beef stock). Praguers are fond of dumplings, called *knedlícky,* made of *bramborové* (potatoes) or *houskové* (bread) and sliced into discs. Dumplings are side dishes to such favorites as *svíčková na smetane*, a beef pot roast sliced and served with a creamy and rich vegetable sauce and a sour cranberry chutney.

Also check out *pecená kachna,* roast duck with bacon dumplings and sauerkraut. Game dishes, such as *zvêrina* (venison), *zajíc* (hare), *bazant* (pheasant), and *hus* (goose), are usually roasted. Popular freshwater fish are *pstruh* (trout) and *kapr* (carp). Hungarian *guláš* (beef goulash) is a good, cheap standby for quick lunches. The best desserts are *ovocné knedlíky* (fruit dumplings), *vdolek* (jam tarts), and chocolate- or fruit-filled *palicinky* (crêpes).

Czech *pivo* (beer) is a great brew. Light-colored beer is *svétlé* (*svyet*-lay); dark beer is *cerné* (*cher*-nay). This is the home of **Pilsner Urquell,** the country's famed lager (the brewery also makes a smooth, for-local-consumption-only beer, **Gambrinus**). If you're a beer-drinker, you may also want to try **Staropramen** (the most common Prague suds), **Velkopopovick;** (a wonderful dark beer), and **Kozel** (a spicy, but not bitter, brew).

By far, the most renowned Czech beer is **Budvar,** the original Budweiser — although it's nothing like the watery, mass-produced American beverage. (Budvar and Anheuser-Busch have been fighting for years over the name rights.)

 With the exception of some of the better restaurants and the tourist-trap places nearest the sights, meals in Prague can be very inexpensive. One of the trade-offs is remarkably poor service, a relic of the Communist era, when restaurant patrons received their meals only at the extreme convenience of the server. When service is haughty, ignore it and don't tip; when service is scarce, just chalk it up to economic growing pains. As investors start finer restaurants in Prague, their attention to service and food presentation should raise the bar for the rest of the industry.

 Watch out for these restaurant rip-offs:

✔ **Every item brought to your table may be charged to your bill, including bread, bowls of nuts, and so on.** Often, these small items turn out to be ridiculously expensive. Make sure that you know the price of everything before you eat it.

✔ **Examine your bill closely at the end of the meal to make sure it isn't padded with items that you didn't order.** Also, some restaurants doctor the amount written on a credit-card slip, so you may want to write the total, in words, somewhere on the slip.

For quick eats, tasty, tiny, open-faced sandwiches called *chelbícky* are all the rage at **U Bakaláre** (Celetná 12). Sidewalk stands hawk *klobásy* (grilled sausages) and *párky* (boiled frankfurters) served with bread and *horcice* (mustard).

Prague's top restaurants

Bellevue
$$$$$ Staré Město   INTERNATIONAL

At Bellevue, one of the city's finest restaurants, you can enjoy your food surrounded by live music and, if you scam a window seat, a view of Prague Castle. The international menu varies from spinach tagliatelle in a salmon cream sauce to braised rabbit, always well prepared and presented. But the veggie dishes are less than thrilling. Sunday brunch features live jazz. Incidentally, the restaurant name can get confusing: This was once the location of a famed restaurant called Parnas, which is now located down the street. Stick with Bellevue; the food is far better.

See map p. 364. Smetanovo nábřezí 2 (at the foot of Legli Bridge). ☎ *222-221-443.* www.pfd.cz. *Reservations highly recommended. Metro: Staroměstská. Main courses: 590Kč–1,190Kč ($24–$48); fixed-price menu 1,090Kč–1,190Kč ($44–$48). AE, DC, MC, V. Open: Lunch and dinner daily.*

U modré kachničky
$$$ Malá Strana   CZECH/GAME

This very private and relaxing Art Nouveau–styled space is renowned for its traditional Czech game dishes. The interior contains a series of small dining rooms with vaulted ceilings and playfully frescoed walls. Service is professional and friendly, and the refined cookery manages to rise above most "Bohemian cuisine" in town, while still remaining adamantly Czech — lots of duck and venison alongside salmon, trout, and rabbit (but you can get beef, pork, and chicken as well).

See map p. 364. Nebodviská 6 (a small street parallel to Karmelitská, south of the castle). ☎ *257-320-308.* www.umodrekachnicky.cz. *Reservations recommended. Tram: 12 or 22. Main courses: 280Kč–420Kč ($11–$17). AE, MC, V. Open: Lunch and dinner daily.*

U třech modrých koulí
$$ Staré Město   REFINED CZECH

If you'd like to sample the best of fine Czech cuisine but don't quite have the scratch to pay for U modré (preceding listing) or the Vinárna (following listing), make reservations at "The Three Blue Balls," another of Prague's excellent, candle-lit, cellar restaurants — but one without the airs (or high prices) of its culinary compatriots. The cooking, though, is top-notch, as it has been since 1816. The duck breast in cabernet is tender, and the beef medallions in a honey-wine sauce are absolutely delicious.

See map p. 364. Havelská 8 (just off Uhelný trh). ☎ *224-238-130.* www.trikoule.cz. *Reservations recommended. Metro: Mustek. Main courses: 155Kč–310Kč ($6–$12). AE, MC, V. Open: Lunch and dinner daily.*

Vinárna U Maltézských Rytířů (Knights of Malta)
$$$ Malá Strana   REFINED CZECH

This is one of Prague's most beloved eateries, a bastion of Czech food, good flavors, and warm welcomes. Seating is limited (especially in the atmospheric, candlelit basement), so reserve ahead to enjoy duck breast with cranberry sauce, a lamb cutlet, or pasta with fresh vegetables. The apple strudel with ice cream and eggnog is a must for dessert.

See map p. 364. Prokopská 10 (off Karmelitská). ☎ *257-520-075 or 257-533-666.* www. umaltezskychrytiru.cz. *Reservations recommended. Metro: Malostranská. Main courses: 280Kč–500Kč ($11–$20). AE, MC, V. Open: Lunch and dinner daily.*

Prague's runner-up restaurants

Klub Architektů
$$ Staré Město   This little place occupies a series of hot vaulted cellar rooms under Jan Hus's old church; the food can be uneven, but the con-vivial atmosphere is catching and the prices are low. *See map p. 364. Betlémské náměstí 5.* ☎ *224-401-214.*

La Provence

$$$$ Staré Město La Provence serves sometimes uneven Provençal-inspired cuisine (although coq au vin and roasted duck are both winners), but it's set below one of the city's trendier bars, so an amiable atmosphere is guaranteed. *See map p. 364. Štupartská 9 (1 long block off the east side of Staroměstské náměstí).* ☎ *257-535-050.* www.laprovence.cz.

Obchod Čerstvých Uzenin

$ Nové Město Here's a great Czech deli that has goulash and other stand-up hot foods available at the back. *See map p. 364. Václavské náměstí 36.* ☎ *222-243-236.*

Pizzeria Rugantino

$ Staré Město You find excellent wood-oven pizzas, and a few pasta dishes, in boisterous rooms here. It even has a nonsmoking section. *See map p. 364. Dušní 4.* ☎ *222-318-172.*

U Medvídků

$$ Staré Město This beer hall dates from 1466. The beer on tap is the original Budvar, and the Czech food is hearty and filling. *See map p. 364. Na Perštýne.* ☎ *224-211-916.* www.umedvidku.cz.

Exploring Prague

Although Prague's classical music and the Czech Republic's unmatched beer are reasons to visit, the primary draw for many is simply walking along the winding cobblestone streets and enjoying the unique atmosphere. This section points out highlights to look for along the way.

Prague's top sights

Jewish Prague
Josefov

The **Jewish Museum** in Prague is the organization managing all the Jewish landmarks in Josefov, which forms the northwest quarter of Old Town. Jews lived in Prague before the 10th century, but by the 12th century, they were confined to a small part of town. At the time, this area was walled off. Ironically, even though 88,000 of the country's 118,000 Jews died during the Holocaust, Nazi occupiers spared this center of Jewish culture. Hitler planned to put all the scrolls, torahs, and other artifacts he collected while exterminating Jews across Europe on display in Prague, turning Josefov into a "museum to a vanished race."

Most of those seized items were returned in 1994 to the diaspora from which they had been taken, but more than 39,000 local items (and more than 100,000 books) from Bohemia and Moravia stayed here in Prague as part of the Jewish Museum, its collections split among several synagogues.

You can see Josefov's highlights in 45 minutes to an hour, but I recommend spending a morning here.

The area has become so insanely popular that it now operates a bit disconcertingly like a theme park: you go to a central ticketing office to pick up you multi-admission ticket, which has timed entries to each of the neighborhood's sights, in order.

Your first stop is right next to the ticketing office window at the **Klausen Synagogue** (on U Starého Hřbitova), now deconsecrated and containing the first half of a collection that illustrates the fascinating socio-cultural history of the Czech Jews. The exhibits continue in the nearby **Ceremonial Hall**, the cemetery's former mortuary hall, highlighting the customs and traditions surrounding illness and death, including a fascinating series of small paintings depicting all the steps in funeral ceremonies (which, for some frustrating reason, are no longer hung all together in one room, nor are they presented in chronological order, rendering it a bit difficult to make sense of it all).

Next up, behind these buildings, is one of Prague's most evocative sights: the **Old Jewish Cemetery**, off U Starého Hřbitova, behind a high wall. This Jewish burial ground dates back to the 15th century — when Jews couldn't bury their dead outside of the ghetto. Within this one-block plot, they had to find final resting places for some 20,000 to 80,000 deceased (the exact number is unknown). Consequently, they stacked the bodies 12 deep in some places. The shady, overgrown, undulating ground is blanketed with some 12,000 time-worn tombstones lurching and tilting in varying degrees of disrepair. The air is melancholy yet serene. This is one sight in Jewish Prague that you don't want to miss. The somewhat elaborate sarcophagus is of the holy man Rabbi Loew, who died in 1609.

Josefov's most moving sight is next door, the **Pinkas Synagogue** on Široká, built in the flamboyant high Gothic style of the 16th century. From 1950 to 1958, Holocaust survivors painted on the inside walls the names of 77,297 Czech Jews who died under the Nazi regime. The Communist regime closed the synagogue and, claiming that dampness was leading to the deterioration of the walls, had the place replastered. As soon as communism ended and the synagogue was reopened, the Jews began the meticulous, four-year task of inscribing those names back on the walls. After Prague's disastrous summer 2002 floods filled this low-lying area with water and mud, they had to break out the paintbrushes yet again and start relettering all the names on the lower few feet of the walls — a project still ongoing as this book went to press. Upstairs are drawings (from a collection of 4,000) made by Jewish children while interned at the nearby Terezín Nazi camp (see "Traveling Beyond Prague," later in this chapter). Of the 8,000 children who passed through there on the way to concentration camps, only 242 survived.

Two blocks over and down sits the next stop, the 16th-century **Maisel Synagogue**, on Maiselova, a renovated space that contains an exhibit of historical Jewish objects from the 10th to the 18th centuries. Part II of this collection (18th century to present) resides several blocks to the east up

Široká in the gorgeous neo-Renaissance/Iberian-styled 1868 **Spanish Synagogue,** on Dušní, and reopened in late 1998 after a decades-long restoration of its lush, Moorish-inspired decorations.

There's one other sight in Jewish Prague that's still an active temple and, therefore, not part of the Jewish Museum group: the **Old-New Synagogue,** at Cervaná 2, built in 1270 and the only Gothic temple of its kind remaining. The small interior is beautiful, with high ceilings crisscrossed with five-ribbed fan vaulting. (Gothic church vaulting uses four ribs, but because those ribs represent the cross, the Jews decided five would be a bit more appropriate.) Admission to this one is a ridiculous extra 200Kč ($8), paid at a shop across the street from the entrance.

See map p. 364. The ticket window is at U Starého Hřbitova 3a (right in the crook of an elbow-shaped street between Břehová and Pařížská). ☎ *222-317-191* www. jewishmuseum.cz. *Metro: A to Staroměstská. Tram: 17, 18, 51, or 54. Bus: 135 or 207. Admission: 300Kč ($12) adults, 200Kč ($8) students and seniors. Open: Sun–Fri Nov–Mar 9 a.m.–4:30 p.m.; Apr–Oct 9 a.m.–6 p.m.*

Karlův most (Charles Bridge)
Between Malá Strana and Staré Město

This may be the loveliest and liveliest bridge anywhere in Europe. The statue-lined Charles Bridge is bustling with people throughout the day and evening — tourists, musicians, street performers, caricature artists, and crafts peddlers. The 1,700-foot span was constructed in the 14th century, but the majority of statues date from the early 18th century. (Actually, what you see on the bridge are copies; most of the originals have been moved inside for protection from the weather.)

Two of the earliest statues include the 1629 crucifix near the Old Town end (great effects during sunrise or sunset) and, halfway across, the haloed statue of St. John Nepomuk (1683), which honors the holy man tortured to death by King Wenceslas IV and then tossed off the bridge. A bronze plaque under the statue describes the event; rub the shiny, worn figure of the plummeting saint for good luck.

Climb the towers at either end for great bridge and city spire panoramas. The climb will cost you 40Kč ($1.60). Both are open daily from 10 a.m. to 6 p.m. (sometimes hours change Nov–Mar).

Prazský Hrad (Prague Castle)
Hradcany

Prague Castle, sternly overlooking Prague, is its own tiny city. Work began in the ninth century and seems never to stop, with constant renovations taking place. Massive fortifications enclose the castle, which spills over with churches, palaces, buildings, shops, and alleys that take a full day to explore properly. (You may be able to make a *quick* run-through in two to three hours.) This is Prague's only truly must-see sight. The massive cathedral is one of Europe's grandest Gothic churches.

Construction on **St. Vitus Cathedral,** the castle's centerpiece, began under Emperor Charles IV in 1344. After a long interruption, it was finished in the 19th and 20th centuries in a neo-Gothic style that tried to follow the original plans closely. The mosaic over the door dates from 1370. The light-filled interior of the cathedral contains the sumptuously decorated **Chapel of St. Wenceslas** (built in the 14th to 16th centuries). The sarcophagi of Bohemian kings are stored in the crypt.

The **Royal Palace** was the home to kings since the ninth century. The vaulted Vladislav Hall is still used for state occasions such as the inauguration of the Czech president, but the Czechs don't celebrate like they used to. In the Middle Ages, knights on horseback entered through the Rider's Staircase for indoor jousting competitions.

St. George's Basilica was built in the tenth century and is the oldest Romanesque structure in Prague. Its adjacent **convent** houses a museum of Gothic and baroque Bohemian art (☎ **257-320-536;** www.ngprague.cz), part of the National Gallery museums system and hence subject to a separate admission fee of 50Kč ($2) adults, 20Kv (80¢) students and seniors; it is open Tuesday through Sunday from 10 a.m. to 6 p.m.

The row of tiny houses clinging to the inside base of the castle ramparts was known as **Golden Lane,** because they were once home to goldsmiths and shopkeepers; today the area houses souvenir stands and cafes. Franz Kafka worked, and perhaps lived, for a time at No. 22. Whether alchemists practiced their craft of trying to turn lead into gold on this "golden" lane is a point of debate. Some say yes, but others point to a similar lane off the left flank of St. Vitus Cathedral as "Alchemy Central."

See map p. 364. Main entrance at Hradčanské námêstí. ☎ 224-373-368. www.hrad.cz. *Metro: A to Malostranská or Hradčanská. Tram: 22 or 23. Admission: Grounds, free; three-day combination ticket to main castle attractions (St. Vitus Cathedral, Royal Palace, St. George's Basilica, Powder Tower), 200Kč ($8) adults, 100Kč ($4) students; admisison to just St. Vitus Cathedral and Royal Palace 160Kč ($6) adults, 80Kč ($3.20) students. Open: Everything open daily (everything closes 1 hour earlier in winter): information/ticket office 9 a.m.–4 p.m.; grounds 6 a.m. to midnight; individual buildings 9 a.m.–5 p.m.*

Staroměstské námêstí (Old Town Square)
Staré Mêsto

A massive memorial to the 15th-century religious reformer and martyr Jan Hus graces Prague's most gorgeous baroque square, Staroměstské. Beautiful buildings surround the square, which is perpetually crowded with street performers, tourists, and the general bustle of the city. Sit at an outdoor cafe table, and just watch it all for a while.

You can climb the tower in the **Old Town Hall** (☎ 224-228-456) for views across the rooftops, but its most popular feature is the **Astronomical**

Clock. Rather than tell the hour, this 15th-century timepiece keeps track of moon phases, equinoxes, and various Christian holidays tied to them. On every hour from 8 a.m. to 8 p.m., the clock puts on a glockenspiel-style show of marching apostles and dancing embodiments of evil.

Here's a grisly tale for you: The architect of the clock, Master Hanus, did such a good job that the city council feared he might one day build a better one elsewhere. To ensure that their clock remained superior, they had him blinded. As the legend goes, Master Hanus, in despair and hoping for revenge, jumped into the clock's mechanism, crushing himself and throwing the works off-kilter for a century.

The **Church of Our Lady Before T; n** stands out with its twin multi-steepled towers. The structure is mainly Gothic, dating from 1380, and is the seat of Prague's Protestant congregation.

See map p. 364. Staroměstské náměstí. Metro: A to Staroměstská. Tram: 17, 18, 51, or 54. Bus: 135 or 207. Admission: Old Town Hall 30Kč ($1.20) adults, 20Kč (80¢) students and seniors; plus another 30Kč ($1.20) adults, 20Kč (80¢) students or seniors to climb the tower. Open: Old Town Hall, Apr–Oct Mon 11 a.m.–6 p.m., Tues–Sun 9 a.m.–6 p.m.; Nov–Mar Mon 11 a.m.–5 p.m., Tues–Sun 9 a.m.–5 p.m.

Sternberský palác (National Gallery at Sternberk Palace)
Hradcany

Prague's main art gallery is housed in a gorgeous late-17th-century palace near the Castle. The collection spans the 15th to 20th centuries, including paintings by Rembrandt, Brueghel the Elder, Klee, and Munch. The finest piece is Dürer's huge *Feast of the Rosary,* painted in 1506.

See map p. 364. Hradčanské náměstí 15 (across from the main entrance to Prague Castle). ☎ 02-2051-4599. Metro: A to Malostranská or Hradčanská. Tram: 22, 23. Admission: 60Kč ($2.40) adults, 30Kč ($1.20) students and children. Open: Tues–Sun 10 a.m.–6 p.m.

Strahovský Klášter (Strahov Monastery)
Malá Strana

Founded in 1140 by the Premonstratensian monks (an order that still lives here), this monastery was rebuilt in the Gothic style of the 13th century. It's renowned for its libraries, both the collections — more than 125,000 volumes, many of them priceless illuminated manuscripts — and for the long baroque hall that houses the philosophy and theology books. The ceiling fresco of the *Struggle of Mankind to Know Real Wisdom* is not to be missed. Also check out the baroque Church of Our Lady.

See map p. 364. Strahovské nádvoří 132. ☎ 220-516-671. www.strahovsky klaster.cz. *Tram: 22, 23. Admission: 70Kč ($2.80); 50Kč ($2) students under 27. Open: Daily 9 a.m. to noon and 1–5 p.m.*

More cool things to see and do

✔ **Going concert-hopping:** As my first visit to Prague ended, I seriously considered abandoning the planned next leg of my journey to stay here. I had seen plenty of sights, but I had truly fallen in love with the dozens of classical concerts offered every evening throughout town — in churches and concert halls, in intimate private chambers and large public halls, under street arches, and in the squares. Many estimate that more musicians per capita live in the Czech Republic than anywhere else. The **Prague Information Service** (see "Fast Facts: Prague," later in the chapter) sells tickets at all its offices via the agency **Ticketpro** (☎ 02-2481-4020; www.ticketpro.cz), or you can contact **Bohemia Ticket** at Malé nám. 13 (☎ 224-227-832; www.bohemiaticket.cz).

In the city that gave the world the composers Smetana and Dvořák, and where Mozart wrote *Don Giovanni* and found greater acclaim than in his native Austria, you find a smorgasbord of offerings to choose from: an organ concert in the Týn Church, a chamber ensemble in a defunct monastery, or the Czech Philharmonic in the 19th-century **Dům umělců (Rudolfinum)**, Alšovo nábřeží 12 (☎ 227-059-352; www.czechphilharmonic.cz).

The *Prague Post* lists most events around town, or you can just wander the Old City, especially around Staroměstské Square, where you find the highest concentration of posters proclaiming the week's concerts and venues. If it's playing, attend Mozart's *Don Giovanni* in the venue where it premiered, the restored 1783 **Stavovské divadlo (Estate´s Theater)**, Ovocnýthr 1 (☎ 224-215-001; www.narodni-divadlo.cz). This theater is the only baroque performance space preserved just as it appeared in Mozart's day.

✔ **Making friends in a beer hall:** "Wherever beer is brewed, all is well. Whenever beer is drunk, life is good." So goes the Czech proverb. Praguers love their *pivo* (beer) — they consume 320 pints per year per Czech — and they love their local *hospoda* (pub or beer hall). Beer halls serve as gathering places for almost everyone.

Refer to the restaurant section for information about the different types of Czech beer. Also note this beer-hall etiquette:

• Share tables. Always ask *Je tu volno* ("Is this spot taken?").

• Put a coaster in front of you if you want beer. Never wave down the waiter — he'll ignore you entirely.

• Nod at the waiter and hold up your fingers for how many beers you want. He'll leave a marked slip of paper at your table with the drinks.

The waiter visits you twice (at the most), so when he comes around again, order all the beer you'll want for the rest of your stay. Pay him when he drops off your drinks, or you may have to wait for hours.

Check out the famous beer hall, U **Flekû,** Křemencova 11 (☎ 224-934-019; www.ufleku.cz), a brewery from 1459 — rather touristy, but great brewskis, plus there's a cheesy-but-fun brass band in the courtyard garden. Or go to the 1466 U **Medvídků,** na Perstýne 7 (see "Prague's runner-up restaurants" earlier), for real Budvar on tap and good Czech pub grub. For a real, albeit famous, Praguer's bar, hit **U Zlatého tygra,** Husova 17 (☎ 224-229-020), a smoky haunt of writers and politicians.

✔ **Visiting a park along the river:** Letná Park (Letenské sady) is a wide, flat swath of trees and shrubs on the western bank of the Vltava River, north of Malá Strana. It has plenty of picnic spots, lots of paths winding through the trees and along the river, and even a beer garden in summer on the park's north side. Walk along the river tossing bread to, and making friends with, Prague's famed mute swans. Tram 1, 8, 25, or 26 gets you there.

✔ **Renting a paddle boat:** The Vltava is a beautiful river, filled with graceful swans and spanned by dramatic bridges. You may feel compelled to become a part of it — but don't. It's so polluted that swimming is out of the question. From March through September, you can rent paddle boats (80Kč/$3.20 per hour) and rowboats (40Kč/$1.60 per hour) from **Půojcovna Romana Holana** at the docks of Slovanskýostrov, an island 2 blocks south of the National Theater.

Next door, at **Rent-A-Boat,** you can rent a rowboat with a lantern at the bow in the evenings (until 11 p.m.) and row around the river under the romantic moonlight and floodlit spires of the city. This boat costs you 80Kč ($3.20) per hour. Rent-A-Boat also stays open until October (Nov if the weather holds).

Guided tours

Plenty of outfits run **bus tours** of the city. Try these for the best reputation and prices:

✔ **Martin Tour** (☎ 224-212-473; www.martintour.cz) runs a variety of city tours (general, Jewish Prague, historical, river cruises) lasting from 75 minutes to 3½ hours. Tours cost from 250Kč to 670Kč ($10–$27). You can hop on at Staroměstské náměstí, Náměstí Republiky, Melantrichova, or Na Příkopé.

✔ **Premiant City Tour** (☎ 0606-600-123 or 296-246-070; www.premiant.cz) also runs city intro, historical/Jewish Prague, and river cruises lasting two to three-and-a-half hours. The cost is 380Kč to 750Kč ($15–$30). Hour-long bus tourists cost 220Kč ($9). All tours leave from Na Příkopé 23.

If you're interested in a walking tour, try **City Walks** (☎ 222-244-531 or 608-200-912; www.praguewalkingtours.com). Tours meet under the Astronomical Clock on Staroměstské náměstí (look for the person with the ID badge holding a yellow umbrella). Most tours — Prague Intro (daily 9:45 a.m. and 1:30 p.m.), Prague Castle (daily 11 a.m.), Jewish Quarter (daily 2:30 p.m.), Legends & Mysteries (Tues–Fri 4 p.m.), Revolution Walks (Sat and Sun 11:30 a.m.), Kafka Walks (Sat–Mon 4 p.m.), Old Town & Architecture Walk (Sat and Sun 2 p.m.), and the Ghost Trail (daily 7 p.m. and 8:30 p.m.) — last about one-and-a-half hours each and cost 300Kč ($12) adults, 250Kč ($10) students. Specialty tours — by bike (Sat and Sun noon), scooter (daily noon), boat (daily 10:30 a.m.), or historic tram (Sat and Sun 11:45 a.m.); Old Town pubs (Tues, Thurs, Sat, and Sun 7:30 p.m.), literary pubs (daily noon), or the "all-in-one" Insider Tour (daily 9:45 a.m. and 1:30 p.m.) — last two to three hours (four hours for the Insider Tour) and cost 450Kč ($18) adults, 350Kč ($14) students.

Suggested itineraries

If you're the type who'd rather organize your own tours, read this section for tips on building your own Prague itineraries.

If you have one day

Spend a full morning exploring **Prazsk; Hrad** (Prague Castle) — the **Cathedral, the Royal Palace, St. George's Basilica,** and other sights nearby. Make your way down to the river, grab an eat-as-you-go lunch along the way, and cross the remarkable **Karlův most** (Charles Bridge) into the **Staré Město** (Old Town). Take your first left to walk up into **Josefov,** and spend the afternoon in the museums, synagogues, and cemetery of the Jewish quarter.

When evening falls, make your way to the lovely heart of Prague, the baroque building–lined square **Staroměstské nám,** where dozens of billboards, posters, and ticket hawkers allow you to browse for the best classical concert to suit your tastes. If you don't want to leave things to chance, stop by a Prague Information Service (PIS) office when you get to town and book tickets in the morning — the best concerts do sometimes sell out. If it's summer, you can pick up tickets when you're crossing the Charles Bridge around lunchtime — a PIS office/ticket booking center is in the base of the tower at the **Malá Strana** end of the bridge.

If you have two days

Spend all of **Day 1** in the **Malá Strana.** Start off at **Prazsk; Hrad,** but take a bit more time after seeing the big sights to enjoy some of the temporary exhibits that rotate through its galleries and halls. Pop into **Sternbersk; palác** (National Gallery at Sternberk Palace) afterward for a dip into Renaissance and baroque art. Then make your way down to **Malostranské nám,** exit it on **Karmelitská** street, and take the first left down **Prokopská,** which becomes **Nebodviská,** to have a Czech lunch at **U Modré Kichnicky.**

After lunch, continue down Nebodviská to **Hellichova,** take a right, cross Karmelitská, and wind your way up through the **Seminárská Zahrada** (Seminary Gardens) to the library and frescoes inside the **Strahovsk;**

Kláster (Strahov Monastery) at the western edge of the gardens. Hop on Tram 22 and ride it all the way around to the back side of Prague Castle to **Malostranské nám** again, where you can get off and mosey on down to **Karlův most,** crossing back into the **Staré Město** to rustle up some dinner and a concert.

Start off **Day 2** in **Josefov,** exploring the sights, synagogues, and culture of Jewish Prague. If Prague's Jewish history intrigues you, leave early enough (by 1 p.m.) to get to Florenc station and grab a bus for the hour's ride outside town to the Nazi internment camp at **Terezín** (see "Traveling Beyond Prague," later in this chapter). If you've had your fill at Josefov, spend your afternoon wandering the **Staré Město,** popping into its baroque churches, relaxing with the locals in Staroměstské nám, and browsing for the evening's concert. Dine at **U trech modr; ch koulí,** or just get some goulash at a pub.

If you have three days

Spend **Day 1** and **Day 2** as outlined in the preceding section, and on **Day 3** head out to imposing **Karlstejn Castle.** If you plan to visit **Terezín,** definitely do it on the afternoon of Day 2, because on Day 3, you want to be back in Prague early enough to engage in a rewarding wander around the **Staré Město** in the late afternoon (be sure to catch the sunset over the **Karlův most**).

Traveling Beyond Prague

Several fascinating destinations lie just a short bus or train ride from the city center. You can explore a 14th-century castle and a "model" Nazi internment camp that was designed to mask Hitler's true motives.

Medieval Karlštejn Castle

This highly picturesque, 14th-century castle perched scenically above the river is Prague's most popular daytrip. (Tour companies love coming here, where more than 350,000 people visit annually.)

It takes only a few hours to get here, see the castle, and return to Prague, but you can stick around for lunch and enjoy Karlštejn's small-town setting. (But be aware that it's usually quite crowded.)

Getting there

You can get to the castle by train in about 45 minutes. The trains leave from Prague's Smíchov Station (take Metro line B to Smichovské nádrazí).

Martin Tour (refer to "Guided tours," earlier in this chapter) does five-hour trips to Karlštejn Castle Tuesday to Sunday for 950Kč ($38), leaving at 10 a.m. and including lunch; **Premiant** does it in four hours Tuesday to Sunday (at 10 a.m. and again at 2:15 p.m.) for 800Kč ($32) adults, 750Kč ($30) students. From April through September, you may want to ride

Side Trips from Prague

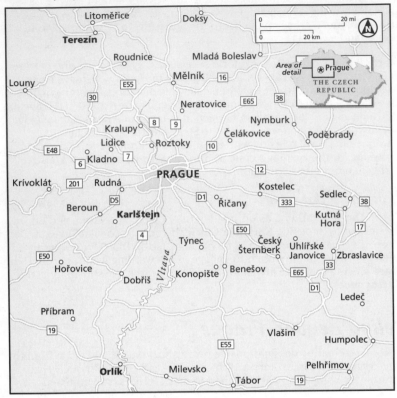

instead with **Central European Adventures** (☎ 222-328-879; members. tripod.com/cea51), whose 680Kč ($27) price includes transportation from Prague (8:30 a.m. at the Astronomical Clock) to the castle, a guide, plus an 18-mile round-trip bike excursion to a nearby cave — but not castle admission. (All tours run Tues–Sun only.)

This is a one-trick town, so you won't find a tourism office; just hike up to the castle and the admissions office for information.

Seeing the castle

The walk uphill to **Karlstejn Castle** (☎ 311-681-617; www.hrad karlstejn.cz) from the train station is a rigorous mile, but the view from the castle across the fertile river valley makes the climb worth it. (Unfortunately, no buses are available for those who can't manage the walk.) Charles IV built the fortress (between 1348 and 1357) to protect the crown jewels, which have been moved.

A 19th-century restoration stripped the place of later additions and rebuilt the castle in line with how folks from the Romantic Era thought a medieval castle should look (close to the original, but a bit fanciful in places). You can get inside only by guided tour, which takes you through parts of the South Palace to see the Audience Hall and Imperial Bedroom — both impressive in an austere, medieval way.

The castle's most spectacular room, the famed Holy Rood Chapel with its ceiling of glass "stars," is only visible on the longer version of the tour — and because that is limited to 12 visitors per hour, it's worth calling ahead to reserve (☎ 274-008-154) and paying the 40Kč ($1.60) booking fee.

Admission for a 50-minute tour is 200Kč ($8) adults and 100Kč ($4) students, a 70-minute tour is 300Kč ($12) adults, 100Kč ($5) students. The castle is open Tuesday through Sunday, in May, June, and September from 9 a.m. to noon and 12:30 to 5:00 p.m.; July and August from 9 a.m. to noon and 12:30 to 6:00 p.m.; April and October from 9 a.m. to noon and 12:30 to 4:00 p.m.; and November through March from 9 a.m. to noon and 1 to 3 p.m. (closed Jan 12 to the end of Feb and Nov 22–Dec 25).

Where to dine

The main road leading up to the castle is littered with souvenir shops and restaurants. The best food is at **Restaurace Blanky z Valois,** a cozy place serving good Czech food with a French twist.

The Nazi camp at Terezín

Terezín was built as a city/fortress in the 19th century. The Nazi camp here served mainly as a transfer station in the despicable traffic of human cargo — sending Jews, homosexuals, Gypsies, and political dissidents on to other, more deadly destinations. At least half of the 140,000 people who passed through Terezín ended up in the death mills of Auschwitz and Treblinka.

Terezín's infamy is that it was the site of one of the most effective public-relations deceptions perpetrated by SS leader Heinrich Himmler. In 1944, the Nazis allowed three Red Cross workers to visit the camp to see whether the horrible rumors about SS methods were true. Instead, they found a self-governed modern ghetto with children studying at school, stores stocked with goods, internees apparently healthy — and none of the overcrowding that they had suspected. The Red Cross had no idea that all this was elaborately staged.

Getting there

Terezín is an hour's bus ride from Florenc station. You need a full morning to fully explore the camp. **Wittmann Tours**, Manesova 8, Praha 2 (☎ 222-252-472; www.wittmann-tours.com), has by far the best Terezin tour available; all guides are either survivors of the camp or experts on it. This seven-hour tour leaves Prague at 10 a.m. (daily

May–Oct; Tues, Thurs, Sat, and Sun Mar 15 through Apr and Nov through Dec), includes lunch, and costs 1,150Kč ($46) adults, 1,000Kč ($40) students. **Martin Tour** tours Terezín in five hours and costs 1,100Kč ($44); **Premiant's** visit also lasts five hours and costs 1,050Kč ($42). For details on both companies, refer to "Guided tours," earlier in this chapter.

The **information office** (☎ 416-782-225; www.pamatnik-terezin.cz) is on the town's main square, Náměstí cs. Armady 84.

Seeing the camp

The **Main Fortress** (Hlavní Pevnsot) houses a **Ghetto Museum,** detailing life in this camp and the rise of Nazism. The museum is open daily from 9 a.m. to 6 p.m. (5:30 p.m. in winter) The prison barracks, execution grounds, and isolation cells are in the **Lesser Fortress,** a ten-minute walk away, open daily from 8 a.m. to 6 p.m. (4:30 p.m. in winter). In front is the **Jewish Cemetery,** where bodies exhumed from Nazi mass graves were properly reburied. The cemetery is open Sunday through Friday from 10 a.m. to 5 p.m. (4 p.m. in winter). The **Magdeburg Barracks** re-create a Ghetto dormitory. Here you see displays on Ghetto art and music. The barracks is open daily from 9 a.m. to 6 p.m. (5:30 p.m. in winter).

Admission to the either Ghetto Museum or Lesser Fortress alone is 160Kč ($6) adults, 130Kč ($5) children. A combined ticket for all attractions costs 180Kč ($7) adults, 140Kč ($6) children.

Where to dine

As you may expect, Terezín doesn't offer many places to eat. However, in the main parking lot you can buy snacks and drinks at a small stand. Inside the Main Fortress, near the museum, is a decent, inexpensive restaurant with Czech fare.

Fast Facts: Prague

Area Code

The country code for the Czech Republic is **420**. Prague no longer has a separate city code. Instead, old numbers have had the former city code (2) grafted onto the front of them — if you see any number in outdated literature presented as "02-213 . . ." just drop the zero. In other words, to call Prague from the United States, dial 011-420 followed by the number.

American Express

Prague has two American Express offices. The main one is at Václavské nám 56, Praha 1 (☎ 02-2280-0237), is open daily from 9 a.m. to 7 p.m. There's another office at Staroměstské náměstí 5 (☎ 02-2481-8388) open daily 9 a.m. to 7:30 p.m.

Currency

The Czech unit of currency is called the koruna (Kč) and is divided into 100 hellers.

Roughly, $1 equals 25Kč, or 10Kč equals 40¢. Czech coins include 10, 20, and 50 hellers and 1, 2, 5, 10, 20, and 50 koruna. Bills come in denominations of 20, 50, 100, 200, 500, 1,000, and 5,000 koruna.

Doctors and Dentists

Unicare Medeical Center, Na dlouhém láne 11 (☎ 235-356-553 — or 601-201-040 after hours; www.unicare.cz), has physicians in most specialities, as well as dentists, open Mon–Fri 8 a.m.–8 p.m., Sat 9 a.m.–1 p.m. See also "Hospitals," later in this section.

Embassies and Consulates

The Consulate services of the U.S. Embassy, Tržiště 15, Praha 1 (☎ 257-530-663; www.usembassy.cz), are open daily from 9 a.m. to noon.

Emergency

In a general emergency, dial ☎ 112. Dial ☎ 158 to call the police, or ☎ 150 to report a fire. For an ambulance, call ☎ 155.

Hospitals

In a medical emergency, head to Motol Hospital's 24-hour Center for Foreigners, U Uvalu 84 (☎ 224-433-681). If it's between 7:30 a.m and 4:30 p.m., try the Foreigner's Medical Clinic at Na Homolce Hospital, Roentgenova 2, Praha 5 (☎ 257-272-174; www.homolka.cz).

Information

Prague Information Service (PIS), at Na Príkope 20 (☎ 12-444; www.prague-info.cz), is the main information office in town. For specifics on it, and on other offices, see "Finding information after you arrive," near the beginning of this chapter.

Internet Access and Cybercafes

Bohemia Bagel, Újezd 16 (☎ 257-310-694; www.bohemiabagel.cz) has dozens of terminals open daily 7 a.m. to midnight — plus, great bagels. To surf for free (three computers; no time limit; long waits) or get your wi-fi on, head to the pubby restaurant Jáma, V jámê 7 (☎ 224-222-383; www.jamapub.cz).

Maps

The maps printed in some of the tourist-office handouts aren't bad, but you really should pick up a better one at a newsstand or bookstore.

Newspapers/Magazines

Newsstands carry an English-language weekly newspaper, the *Prague Post* (www.praguepost.com), packed with useful information and events calendars. You can also pick up *Culture In Prague*, a monthly bilingual events calendar.

Pharmacies

A Czech pharmacy is called a *lékárna*. Several pharmacies remain open 24 hours a day, including Palackého 5, Praha 1 (☎ 224-946-982), and Lékárna U Andêla, Stefánikova 6, Praha 5 (☎ 257-320-918).

Police

Dial ☎ 158 to call the police.

Post Office

The main post office is at Jindřišská, just off Václavské námêstí (☎ 221-131-111; www.cpost.cz), open 24 hours.

Safety

Walking or taking the Metro or trams alone at night is safe, but always be on the lookout for pickpockets, especially on Charles

Bridge, around parts of Old Town, and on public transportation. Wenceslas Square is a little seedy during the day and is traveled mainly by prostitutes at night.

Taxes

A 16 percent value-added tax (VAT) is built into the price of most goods and services. You can get a refund on the VAT so long as you spend more than 2,500Kč ($100) in a single shop. See Chapter 4 for more details.

Taxis

See "Getting Around Prague," earlier in this chapter.

Telephone

A local call in Prague costs at least 4Kč (15¢) for 104 seconds of local time or 35 seconds of long distance (longer after 7 p.m.). Pay phones accept either coins or phone cards, sold at post offices, tobacconists, or newsstands in denominations ranging from 150Kč to 600Kč ($6–$24). Coin-operated phones do not make change, so insert money as needed, but use smaller coins. Here's something to confuse you: A Czech dial tone sounds like

a busy signal in the United States; the Czech busy signal sounds like a U.S. dial tone. For Czech directory assistance, call ☎ 1180; for international directory assistance, dial ☎ 1181. To dial direct internationally, press 052, the country code, and the number.

To charge a call to your calling card, dial AT&T (☎ 00-4200-0101), MCI (☎ 00-4200-0112, not accessible from mobile phones), or Sprint (☎ 00-4208-7187). To call the United States direct from Prague, dial 001 followed by the area code and number.

Transit Info

Call ☎ 221-111-122 for train info, or go online to the Czech Railways site at www.cdrail.cz or see the timetable at www.vlak.cz. For intercity buses call ☎ 900-149-144 or go to www.vlak-bus.cz. For the city transport system, call ☎ 296-191-817 or go to www.dpp.cz or www.dp-praha.cz (same site, but given the frequency with which Czech Web addresses change, I figured it was best to provide both). For more, see "Getting Around Prague," earlier in this chapter.

Part V
Mediterranean Europe

The 5th Wave   By Rich Tennant

"He had it made after our trip to Italy. I give you Fontana di Clifford."

In this part . . .

*A*h, bright and sunny Mediterranean Europe. You can enjoy winding, coastal drives and long, moonlit dinners; gemlike islands and afternoon siestas; and ripe olives and fine wine. The Mediterranean life runs at a slower pace and is more laid-back than that of Northern and Central Europe.

Here you can discover the ruins of ancient Greece and Rome. But a few dusty rocks and chipped columns do not make a Western civilization. I also guide you to the treasures — masterpieces by Michelangelo, Raphael, Donatello, da Vinci, Botticelli, and many, many others — that fill the museums and churches of Rome, Florence, and Venice.

From there, you head to Spain. Madrid boasts its own share of artistic treasures, but excursions to Toledo and Segovia give you a taste of the country's stunning landscape. Barcelona awaits with its distinctively whimsical architecture and a vibrant, happening nightlife. And finally, it's off to the warm simplicity and sunshine of Santoríni in the Greek islands.

Chapter 19

Rome and Southern Italy

● ●

In This Chapter

▶ Getting to Rome

▶ Checking out the neighborhoods

▶ Discovering the best hotels, restaurants, and attractions

▶ Side-tripping to Tivoli and Ostia Antica

● ●

*A*s the center of the ancient Roman Empire and then the vibrant Christian empire, Rome is appropriately titled the "Eternal City." The city's 2,000-year-old ruins, which include major sights such as the Roman Forum, the Pantheon, and, of course, the Colosseum, hint at Rome's glorious past. And Rome wasn't just togas and Caesars — the culture also produced sculptures in abundance. You can view the cream of the crop in the Vatican, Capitoline, and Roman National museums.

Following the Roman Empire, the Christian empire added more than 900 churches to the city. Actually, *church* doesn't begin to describe fully these amazing houses of worship — they're more like magnificent museums filled to the brim with the greatest art from the Renaissance and baroque eras (the best of the churches being St. Peter's Basilica). Rome also contains many of the greatest sculptures and paintings of the artistic masters — Michelangelo, Raphael, Borromini, Bernini, Botticelli, and Caravaggio.

Although history abounds, modern Rome hasn't sat on its laurels. Between visiting ruins and browsing magnificent museums, sample a few of this bustling city's simpler joys: a morning cappuccino, the hum of motor scooters, deliciously hearty meals. Find time for leisurely evening strolls past Renaissance palaces and fountains or just sitting in one of the many Roman *piazze* (squares).

As a saying goes, it would take a lifetime to see all of Rome, but that seems a little off to me — I'd wager the figure is more like 100 lifetimes. You can, however, get a good sampling of its wonderful flavors in three or four days. Because you won't see everything before you depart, be sure to toss a coin into the Trevi Fountain — legend has it that, if you do, you're destined to return someday.

Getting There

Rome is a perennially popular destination, with plenty of flights available on a wide variety of international airlines. Rome is also easily accessible by train from most major European cities.

Arriving by air

Most international flights land at **Leonardo da Vinci International Airport,** also called **Fiumicino** (☎ **06-6595-3640** or 06-65-951; www.adr.it), 18 miles west of the city. Touch-screen "totems" (marked with an *i*) throughout the terminals direct passengers to ATMs and information desks in the airport.

To get downtown, follow the *treni* signs for half-hourly nonstop trains to the main rail station, Stazione Termini (30 minutes; 8.80€/$10). You can also take a local train every 20 minutes to the Tiburtina station (45 minutes; 4.70€/$5.40) from the same tracks (get off at Ostiense and walk to the Piramide Metro stop to catch the B line to Termini; 1€/$1.15).

Many charter and continental flights land at the smaller **Ciampino Airport** (☎ **06-7934-0297** or 06-794-941), 9 miles south of the city. Outside the terminal, a COTRAL bus (☎ **800-150-008;** www.cotralspa.it; 1€/$1.15) leaves about twice an hour for the 20-minute trip to Anagnina, the terminus of Metro line A, where you can grab a subway to Stazione Termini (1€/$1.15).

Taxis to and from either airport cost about 40€ ($46), plus another 2€ ($2.30) for each suitcase.

Arriving by rail

The majority of trains headed for Rome stop at **Termini,** the main station on Piazza dei Cinquecento (☎ **800-888-088,** 06-4730-6599, or 1478-88-088; train info: www.trenitalia.com; station info: www.roma termini.it). A few long-haul trains may stop only at the Tiburtina station northeast of the center, from which you can hop on the Metro (subway) and head for Termini.

Orienting Yourself in Rome

The curving **Tevere (Tiber River)** forms an S-shaped dividing line through Rome. East of the Tevere lies most of the city's *centro storico* (historic center). Although Rome has numerous official "administrative districts," locals usually orient themselves based on their location relative to such-and-such major monument or *piazza* (square), so this chapter tries to do the same. However, Rome is nearly bursting at its seams with monuments and piazze (which essentially break the city into little neighborhoods). That said, finding your way in Rome can be a tad complicated. Using a good map will help you figure out the lay of the land.

Italy

Introducing the neighborhoods

If you arrive at **Termini,** Rome's main train station, the first neighborhood you encounter is just east of the city center in a grid of 19th-century streets. This part of town offers a few sights and some churches of note but is, generally, duller than the rest of Rome. Scads of cheap hotels are here, but despite the recent cleanup of the neighborhood, it's still not the most savory area.

The northern tip of the city center features the oval **Piazza del Popolo,** from which three major thoroughfares radiate south: Via del Babuino, Via del Corso, and Via di Ripetta. **Via del Corso** (usually just called the **Corso**) cuts the center of town into halves.

From the Corso, head east to reach the popular **Trevi Fountain** and **Spanish Steps.** Rome's ritziest hotels — as well as stylish shopping on boutique-lined **Via dei Condotti** — border these touristy sights.

West of the Corso you find the medieval **Tiber Bend area,** home to many of the great Roman sights, including the **Pantheon,** the vibrant **Piazza Navona,** the market square of **Campo de' Fiori,** and the medieval **Jewish Ghetto** (which continues to be home to Europe's oldest Jewish population, numerous houses of worship, and a few small museums). Lovely for walking and people-watching, the Tiber Bend area, much of it pedestrianized, offers some of Rome's best restaurants.

The **Piazza Venezia** serves as a rather abrupt end to the Corso. The famous (and enormous) **Vittorio Emanuele Monument** dominates this major traffic circle and bus juncture. Head west from Piazza Venezia and you reach Via Plebescito, which becomes **Corso Vittorio Emanuele II,** a broad boulevard that chops the Tiber Bend area in half before proceeding across the river and to the Vatican (Piazza Navona and the Pantheon lie to the north of it; Campo de' Fiori and the Jewish Ghetto to the south).

At Piazza Venezia, you can take stairs up to **Capitoline Hill,** the seat of Roman government dating all the way back to before the Empire. From the piazza, the expansive **Via dei Fori Imperiali** beelines to the **Colosseum,** passing two famous forums: the Roman and the Imperial. The monuments in this area are often referred to collectively as **Ancient Rome.** The residential area of **Aventine Hill** lies south of the monuments, and beyond that another hill is home to the trendy dinner and dancing environ **Testaccio.**

Although the preceding neighborhoods are most popular with tourists, a few others deserve mention. The area northwest of the train station (east of the Spanish Steps area) is home to numerous embassies and the famous main drag known as **Via Veneto.** As the setting for Federico Fellini's 1960 film, *La Dolce Vita* ("The Sweet Life"), Via Veneto still brims with cafe life — although today's version is overpriced and pretty darn touristy. Via Veneto butts up against the southern portion of a large park, **Villa Borghese,** which is located northeast of the *centro storico* and is accessible from Piazza del Popolo.

On the other side of the Tevere, you find two other major neighborhoods of interest: **Vatican City and St. Peter's** and **Trastevere.** The Vatican and surrounding areas are tourist magnets, complete with shops, eateries, and lodging that cater to visitors. (Generally, hotels in Vatican City are modestly priced but bland and modern; to really experience Rome, try staying elsewhere.) South of the Vatican and parklike **Gianicolo** hill, you encounter Trastevere. At one time Bohemian, then fashionable, and now touristy, this medieval district still maintains many authentic restaurants and shops.

Finding information after you arrive

Rome has established about a dozen tourist-information kiosks near popular sights. See "Fast Facts: Rome" at the end of this chapter for addresses.

Getting Around Rome

You purchase a 1€ ($1.15) *biglietto* (ticket) to ride any public transportation within Rome. Tickets are good for 75 minutes, during which you may board the Metro system one time and transfer buses as frequently as you need — just stamp your ticket on the first bus and the final bus. You can also buy daily (4.10€/$4.70), three-day (11€/$13), or weekly (16€/$18) passes. Look for passes and tickets at *tabacchi* (tobacconist shops indicated by a brown-and-white *T* sign), Metro stations, newsstands, and machines near major bus stops. Keep your ticket with you as you travel in order to avoid paying a fine.

By subway

Because of Rome's rich ancient heritage, its Metro system is small and not especially developed (seems that whenever the city attempts to add a new leg to the subway, it encounters ruins that archaeologists must examine). The Metro's two lines, the orange A line and the blue B line, intersect at Termini. Line A runs from the recently constructed Battistini through such stops as Flaminia (near Piazza del Popolo), Piazza Spagna (Spanish Steps), Termini, and San Giovanni (Rome's cathedral). You'll find the B line great for hitching rides from Termini to popular destinations like Circo Massimo (the Circus Maximus) and the Colosseo (Colosseum).

By bus

Thankfully, Rome has a much more developed bus and tram system, so you can avoid walking for miles. There is no free official bus map; buy a *mappa degli autobus* at a newsstand for 6€ ($6.90) or simply scan the list of stops at your *fermata* (stop) to determine which line to ride. One of the most useful lines is Bus 40, which originates at Termini, passes through Piazza Venezia in central Rome, and ends at Castel Sant'Angelo. There you can switch to the 62, which shuttles to and from the Vatican. You may also use buses 116, 117, and 119, petite electric buses that scurry the streets of the *centro storico*. For bus information, call ☎ 800-431-784 or visit www.atac.roma.it.

Many bus routes originate in the large Piazza dei Cinquecento right outside Termini. Additionally, the *centro storico*'s three major squares are major hubs for converging and transferring. These include: Largo di

Tritone (east of the Trevi Fountain), Largo di Torre Argentina (south of the Pantheon), and Piazza San Silvestro (just off the Corso, between the Spanish Steps and Trevi Fountain).

By taxi

Although Rome is a wonderful town for walking or taking the bus, you may prefer a taxi for the ride from the train station or airport to your hotel. Look for taxi stands in major piazze, including **Largo Argentina**, **Piazza Venezia**, at the **Pantheon**, and in front of **Termini**.

You can also call for a taxi (☎ **06-3570** or 06-4994). However, be aware that the meter begins running from the moment the driver answers your call, not when he picks you up. Taxis charge an initial fee of 2.33€ ($2.70), plus .78€ (90¢) per kilometer. You pay extra for luggage (1.04€/1.20 per bag), and can expect supplements to the initial charge for nighttime travel (2.33€/$2.70) and Sunday rides (1.03€/$1.20).

By foot

Any of the neighborhoods described in "Introducing the neighborhoods," earlier in this chapter, will make for a memorable walk — especially the *centro storico* (historic center) or the Roman Forum. Or join the evening *passegiata* along Via del Corso as Romans head out to see and be seen.

Staying in Rome

Break out of the boring hotels that crowd the gridlike streets around Termini train station and try some of Rome's more interesting accommodations in the historic center. Of course, if all the rooms in the historic center are taken, or you just don't have the cash, settle for hotels in the northern area around Termini. (The area south of the station can be somewhat dicey; I don't recommend spending a lot of time there at night.)

For general tips on booking and what to expect from European accommodations, see Chapter 7.

Rome's top hotels

Abruzzi

$$$ **Near Piazza Navona**

In April 2003, new owners took what had been an utterly basic comfortable old shoe of a cheap *pensione* with no amenities and turned it into a full-bore, 3-star (moderate) hotel. Although most rooms here have a stellar view of the Pantheon — one of the greatest views in all of Rome — the renovation means that prices have more than doubled. All rooms now have private bathrooms as well as telephones, air-conditioning, TVs, and minibars. The furnishings are all new, as are the doubled-paned windows (the piazza is lively both day and night). Corner rooms are still the best in the house. The renovation left no space for a breakfast room, so you take the included continental breakfast in a cafe on the piazza.

See map p. 394. Piazza della Rotunda 69. ☎ *06-9784-1351 or 06-679-2021. Fax: 06-6978-8076.* www.hotelabruzzi.it. *Bus: 116, 116T, or one of the many to Largo Argentina, then walk 4 blocks north. Rates: 165€–195€ ($190–$224) double. Rates include breakfast. DC, MC, V.*

Albergo Cesàri
$$$ Near Piazza Navona

Location, location, location — this one has it for sure! Albergo Cesari is just off the Corso, right in the heart of popular attractions such as the Pantheon, the Spanish Steps, the Trevi Fountain, and the Roman Forum. Notable guests during the hotel's two-century-old history include French author Stendhal and Italian statesman Giuseppe Garibaldi. The rooms today are modern and comfortable, with a few antiques thrown in here or there for effect. To get the lowest rates, plan on sharing a bath.

See map p. 394. Via di Pietra 89A (just off the Corso, a block south of Piazza Colonna). ☎ *06-674-9701. Fax: 06-6749-7030.* www.albergocesari.it. *Bus: 62, 63, 81, 85, 95, 116, 116T, 117, 204, 119, 160, 175, 492, 628, 630, 850, N25, or N99. Rates: 150€–200€ ($173–$230) double. Rates include breakfast. AE, DC, MC, V.*

Casa Kolbe
$ Near the Forum

If you love archaeology but don't need too many amenities, this monastically quiet converted convent may be perfect. It's as hidden as you can get in the heart of Rome, around the corner from the Roman Forum's "back door" on the little-traveled side street hugging the west flank of the Palatine Hill. Most of the large, basic, institutional rooms overlook palm-filled gardens, but the street-side rooms on the second floor enjoy a low panorama of Palatine ruins.

See map p. 394. Via S. Teodoro 44 (bordering the west side of the Palatine archaeological zone). ☎ *06-679-4974. Fax: 06-6994-1550. Bus: H, 30, 44, 63, 81, 95, 160, 170, 204, 271, 628, 630, 715, 716, 780, 781, N44, N72, N91, or N96. Rates: 84€ ($97) double. Continental breakfast 6€ ($6.90). AE, MC, V.*

Hotel Campo de' Fiori
$$ Near Campo de' Fiori

A gem for the budget-conscious traveler, the rooms here vary greatly: Some are carpeted and modern, while others have rustic touches like beamed ceilings, frescoed ceilings, or brickwork. Some are large, but a few are about the size of the beds. The killer room is no. 602 (sorry, no elevator), which offers a choice vista of Rome's domes and rooftops (all visitors can enjoy the view from the roof terrace). Most bathrooms are shared and clean, but private baths are available at the higher price listed here. The hotel also rents four nearby apartments for longer stays that sleep up to seven people.

Accommodations, Dining, and Attractions in Rome

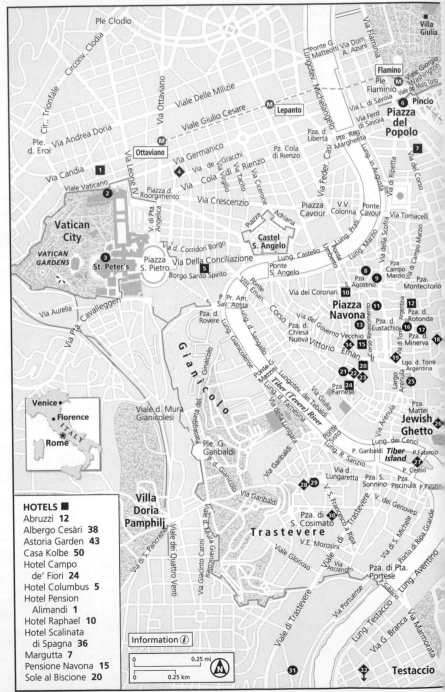

HOTELS ■

Abruzzi **12**
Albergo Cesàri **38**
Astoria Garden **43**
Casa Kolbe **50**
Hotel Campo
  de' Fiori **24**
Hotel Columbus **5**
Hotel Pension
  Alimandi **1**
Hotel Raphael **10**
Hotel Scalinata
  di Spagna **36**
Margutta **7**
Pensione Navona **15**
Sole al Biscione **20**

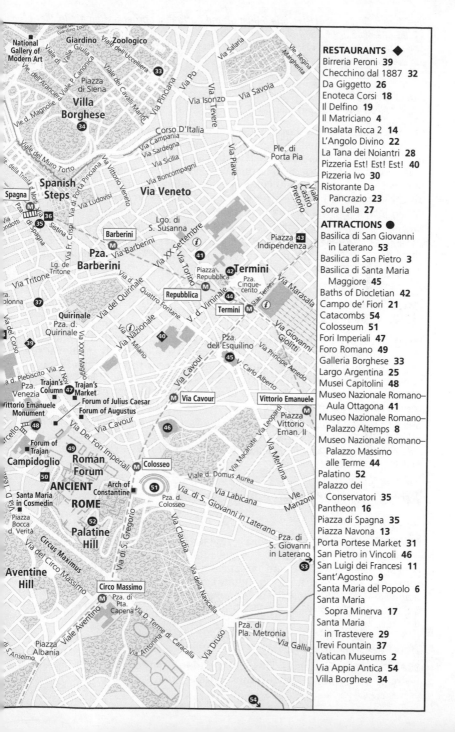

RESTAURANTS ◆
Birreria Peroni **39**
Checchino dal 1887 **32**
Da Giggetto **26**
Enoteca Corsi **18**
Il Delfino **19**
Il Matriciano **4**
Insalata Ricca 2 **14**
L'Angolo Divino **22**
La Tana dei Noiantri **28**
Pizzeria Est! Est! Est! **40**
Pizzeria Ivo **30**
Ristorante Da
  Pancrazio **23**
Sora Lella **27**

ATTRACTIONS ●
Basilica di San Giovanni
  in Laterano **53**
Basilica di San Pietro **3**
Basilica di Santa Maria
  Maggiore **45**
Baths of Diocletian **42**
Campo de' Fiori **21**
Catacombs **54**
Colosseum **51**
Fori Imperiali **47**
Foro Romano **49**
Galleria Borghese **33**
Largo Argentina **25**
Musei Capitolini **48**
Museo Nazionale Romano–
  Aula Ottagona **41**
Museo Nazionale Romano–
  Palazzo Altemps **8**
Museo Nazionale Romano–
  Palazzo Massimo
  alle Terme **44**
Palatino **52**
Palazzo dei
  Conservatori **35**
Pantheon **16**
Piazza di Spagna **35**
Piazza Navona **13**
Porta Portese Market **31**
San Pietro in Vincoli **46**
San Luigi dei Francesi **11**
Sant'Agostino **9**
Santa Maria del Popolo **6**
Santa Maria
  Sopra Minerva **17**
Santa Maria
  in Trastevere **29**
Trevi Fountain **37**
Vatican Museums **2**
Via Appia Antica **54**
Villa Borghese **34**

See map p. 394. Via del Biscione 6 (just off the northeast corner of Campo de' Fiori). ☎ *06-687-4886 or 06-6880-6865. Fax: 06-687-6003.* www.hotelcampodeifiori. com. *Bus: 40, 46, 62, 64, 116, 116T, 571, 916, N45, or N98. Rates: 100€–150€ ($115–$173) double. Rates include breakfast. MC, V.*

Hotel Columbus
$$$$ **Near the Vatican**

Michelangelo's patron, Pope Julius II, once owned this lovely 15th-century *palazzo* — located just blocks from the entrance to St. Peter's — and certainly the place feels like a Renaissance castle, complete with oil paintings and tapestries. Most bedrooms are fairly simple yet comfortable, but a few choice rooms have remnants of decorated ceilings and frescoes. You'll find all the amenities here — air-conditioning and room service, plus high-speed Internet access in many of the rooms.

See map p. 394. Via della Conciliazione 33 (on the wide boulevard leading to St. Peter's). ☎ *06-686-5435. Fax: 06-686-4874.* www.hotelcolumbus.net. *Bus: 23, 34, 40, 62, 64, 271, 982, N29, or N30. Rates: 160€–320€ ($184–$368) double. Rates include breakfast. AE, DC, MC, V.*

Hotel Raphael
$$$$$ **Near Piazza Navona**

For plush accomodations, look no farther than the Raphael. Just pull back the ivy curtains on this elegant hotel located in a distinctly medieval setting, and you'll find well-appointed, contemporary rooms and a fantastic view from the roof terrace. With facilities and amenities aplenty (even a fitness room), you can kick back in style. But heads up: A couple of the rooms are surprisingly small.

See map p. 394. Largo Febo 2 (just off the northwest corner of Piazza Navona). ☎ *06-682-831. Fax: 06-687-8993.* www.raphaelhotel.com. *Bus: 30, 70, 81, 87, 116, 116T, 186, 204, 492, 628, N78, or N99. Rates: 390€–420€ ($449–$483) double. Buffet breakfast 30€ ($35). AE, DC, MC, V.*

Rome's runner-up accommodations

Astoria Garden
$$$ **Near Piazza Indipendenza** This hotel has fantastic prices (because it's near Termini) for what you get: comfort and style in a late-19th-century palazzo with private garden. Renovated in 2001, the rooms feature reproductions and soft carpets; some even have jacuzzis. A/C is extra. *See map p. 394. Via V. Bachelet 8 (the 1-block stretch of Via Varese just before Piazza Indipendenza).* ☎ *06-446-9908 or 06-491-097. Fax: 06-445-3329.* www.hotelastoria garden.it.

Hotel Pension Alimandi
$$$ **Near the Vatican** This is a standard, modern, tour group–style hotel, but one of the better ones, with a great location 3 blocks from

Rome's best daily food market and just a staircase away from the Vatican Museums. As this book went to press, the Alimandi had plans to open a 25-room, 4-star annex nearby. *See map p. 394. Via Tunisi 8, at Via Veniero and the base of the steps up to Viale Vaticano.* ☎ *06-3972-3941. Fax: 06-3972-3943.* www.alimandi.org.

Hotel Scalinata di Spagna

$$$$ **Top of Spanish Steps** This is always a top choice and considered a "steal," given all the pricey hotels in the neighborhood. Aside from a few boring rooms, many of the hotel's rooms feature antique furniture and low wood ceilings. Reserve early. *See map p. 394. Piazza Trinità dei Monti 17.* ☎ *06-679-3006 or 06-6994-0896. Fax: 06-6994-0598.* www.hotelscalinata.com.

Margutta

$$ **Near Piazza del Popolo** Margutta rooms are a bit cramped, but offer a touch of style for an inexpensive central choice on a tranquil side street. The hard-working management is friendly, and the bed frames are beautiful, but the mattresses are lumpy. In 2003 — following a brutal summer heat wave — the Margutta installed air-conditioning along with TVs. The pricier rooms have terraces. *See map p. 394. Via Laurina 34, 2 blocks from Piazza del Popolo between Via Babuino and Via del Corso.* ☎ *06-322-3674. Fax: 06-320-0395.*

Pensione Navona

$$ **Near Piazza Navona** Run by a very friendly family, the Navona offers decent accommodations, many of which have been renovated and some of which open to views of the central courtyard. A/C is extra. *See map p. 394. Via dei Sedari 8 (off Corso del Rinascimento, between Piazza Navona and the Pantheon).* ☎ *06-686-4203. Fax: 06-6880-3802.* www.hotelnavona.com.

Sole al Biscione

$$ **Near Campo de' Fiori** In a great location, Sole al Biscione is Rome's oldest hotel (founded in 1462) — the age shows in some corners, with peeling linoleum and sway-backed cots. But most of the sizeable rooms are in decent shape. Rooms on the fourth floor even get a Roman rooftop view. And unlike prices in the rest of Rome, rates here have risen only slightly, making it a good deal. *See map p. 394. Via del Biscione 76 (half a block north of Campo de' Fiori).* ☎ *06-6880-6873. Fax: 06-689-3787.* www.solealbiscione.it.

Dining in Rome

Typically, evening meals in Rome are events: gigantic, multicourse affairs that last for hours. Although you may suspect that this conga line of courses is just a trick to make you spend more money, Italians actually often eat meals this huge (although in today's faster-paced world, less frequently).

Dining out Italian style means ordering at least two courses — preferably stretching out the meal even longer with some tasty wine and spirited conversation. If you're not looking for a mega-meal, just ask for *mezza* (half) portions for your selected courses.

Roman taste temptations begin with *antipasti* (appetizers), and the best local choice is simple *bruschetta* (peasant bread grilled, rubbed with garlic, drizzled with olive oil, and sprinkled with salt; order it *al pomodoro* and it comes with a heap of cubed tomatoes). Another specialty meal starter that is especially popular is *carciofi* (artichokes), done *alla giudea* (lightly fried in olive oil) or otherwise.

The first course (called the *primo*) can go a variety of ways: Try a soup like *stracciatella,* egg-drop and Parmesan in broth, or a pasta like *spaghetti all'Amatriciana* (spicy tomato sauce dappled with pancetta bacon), *alla carbonara* (with eggs, *pancetta* [flavored pork, rolled and sliced], and cracked pepper), or *al pomodoro* (in a regular ol' tomato sauce); *penne all'arrabbiata* ("hopping mad" pasta quills in a spicy tomato sauce); or *gnocchi* (potato-based pasta dumplings).

During the main course *(secondo),* you may choose to get adventurous with some traditional local cuisine. Popular dishes include *coda alla vaccinara* (braised oxtail with tomatoes) and surprisingly appetizing *pajata* (made with calves' intestines still clotted with mother's milk). For something a little more familiar, order *pollo* (chicken), *scallopine* (veal cutlets, cooked in various ways), *involtini* (veal rolled with veggies and stewed in its own juices), or *bocconcini di vitello* (nuggets of veal, typically stewed with potatoes and sage). One of the best Roman secondi is *saltimbocca,* or "jumps-in-the-mouth," a veal cutlet cooked until tender in white wine with sage leaves and served with a slice of prosciutto ham draped over it.

For a finale, sample *tiramisù* (espresso-soaked ladyfingers layered with sweetened, creamy mascarpone cheese and dusted with cocoa) or *tartufo* (vanilla and chocolate ice cream, both dusted with cocoa and containing a fudge center).

Although Florence is more famous for its ice cream, the gelato in Rome is still a treat. For the ultimate in sinfully sweet snacking, visit the 19th-century **Giolitti** (☎ **06-699-1234**), a few long blocks north of the Pantheon at Via Uffici del Vicario 40. Of course, you can find plenty of other ice-cream parlors about town; just be sure that the one you choose has a sign advertising *produzione propria* (homemade).

Roman table wine is most often fruity, light, and white and originates in the hills to the south. Look for **Frascati, Castelli Romane,** and **Orvieto Classico** (an excellent white from a town north of Rome). Most restaurants in town have nicely stocked cellars that feature the best wines Italy has to offer.

Restaurants throughout Italy tack on the unavoidable "bread and cover" charge *(pane e coperto)* that runs anywhere from 1€ to 10€ ($1.15–$12). Keep in mind that most meals include much more than just a first and second course — water and wine, an appetizer, coffee, dessert, and a *digestivo* (after-dinner drink) all add to your total bill.

The finest in Roman "fast food" has to be *pizza rustica* or *pizza a taglio,* which you can buy from tiny shops where they cut the pizza of your choice from big, steaming sheets. For 2€ ($2.30) you can get a healthy portion of "plain" *margherita* pizza — topped with tomato sauce, basil, and mozzarella. Expand your palate with a buffet of *napolitana* (with anchovies), *patate* (with julienned potatoes, but no sauce), *rosso* (just the sauce), or *bianca* (just the dough, brushed with olive oil and salt, sometimes with rosemary).

For picnic supplies, you can try a variety of little shops, including *alimentari* (small grocery stores), *forno* (bakery), and *fruttivendolo* (fruit and vegetable stand), or head to a *Standa* department store basement which doubles as a supermarket (Viale Trastevere 60 or Via Cola di Rienzo 173, near the Vatican).

Rome's top restaurants

Checchino dal 1887
$$$$$ In Testaccio (south of Ancient Rome)   ROMAN

Started by the Mariani family as a blue-collar wine shop more than a century ago, this establishment is now a Roman temple of refinement and classic cuisine. Savor such local sensations as *pajata* and *coda alla vaccinara,* which evolved because the only ingredients available to slaughterhouse workers a hundred years ago were undesirable "fifth-fourth" — the feet, tails, and other offal. Cecchino has menu items for the less adventurous, too. And don't miss the wine cellars carved into the "hill" (a really old pile of discarded jars).

See map p. 394. Via di Monte Testaccio 30 (in trendy Testaccio, just south of the Aventine Hill). ☎ *06-574-3816.* www.checchino-dal-1887.com. *Reservations required. Metro: Piramide. Bus: 95, 673, 719, N29, N30, or N91. Main courses: 9€–22€ ($10–$25). AE, DC, MC, V. Open: Lunch and dinner Tues–Sat. Closed Aug and one week around Christmas.*

Da Giggetto
$$$$ Near Campo de' Fiori   ROMAN/JEWISH

For Roman Jewish cuisine, look no farther than this popular eatery in the Jewish Ghetto among columns of still-standing ruins. Enjoy the house specialty *carciofi alla giudia* (lightly fried artichokes). Other flavorful fare includes *fiori di zucca* (stuffed zucchini flowers), *fettucine all'amatriciana,* and *saltimbocca.*

See map p. 394. Via de Portico d'Ottavia 21–22 (1 block up from Lungotevere d. Cenci). ☎ *06-686-1105. Reservations recommended. Tram: 8. Bus: H, 23, 63, 271, 280, 630, 780, N29, N72, N96. Main courses: 7.50€–15€ ($8.65–$17). AE, MC, V. Open: Lunch and dinner Tues–Sun. Closed Aug.*

Enoteca Corsi
$$ Near Piazza Navona   ROMAN

This dirt-cheap, old-fashioned spot has kept up with the times — but not the prices — so although the wine shop looks every inch the *vini olii* of 1937, behind it and next door are large, fan-cooled rooms with long tables to accommodate the lunchtime crowds of local workers. The chalkboard menu changes daily but may run the mill from *penne all'arrabbiata* to delectable specials like *zucchine ripiene* (baked zucchini flowers stuffed with minced meats).

See map p. 394. Via del Gesù 87–88 (off Via d. Plebescito). ☎ *06-679-0821. Reservations not accepted. Bus: 30, 40, 46, 62, 63, 64, 70, 81, 87, 186, 492, 571, 628, 630, 780, 810, 916, N45, N98. Main courses: 5€–8€ ($5.75–$9.20). AE, DC, MC, V. Open: Lunch Mon–Sat.*

Il Matriciano
$$$$ Near the Vatican   ROMAN

Join the politicians and movie stars at Il Matriciano for a country-style meal that's both refined and relaxed. From a sidewalk table, sample the restaurant's namesake pasta: *bucatini* (thick, hollow spaghetti) *all'amatriciana*. Other typical Roman dishes include *trippa* (tripe) and *abbacchio* (succulent roasted lamb).

See map p. 394. Via dei Gracchi 55 (from the north side of Piazza del Risorgimento, head up Via Ottaviano and turn right onto Via dei Gracchi). ☎ *06-321-3040. Reservations highly recommended. Metro: Ottaviano–San Pietro. Bus: 19, 23, 32, 49, 271, 492, 590, 982, 990, N29, N30. Main courses: 8.50€–17€ ($9.80–$20). AE, DC, MC, V. Open: May–Oct lunch and dinner Sun–Fri; Nov–Apr lunch and dinner Thurs–Tues. Closed Aug 6–21 and Dec 24–Jan 2.*

La Tana dei Noiantri
$$$$ Trastevere   ROMAN/ITALIAN/PIZZA

Everybody comes to this Trastevere spot for the romance of dining out on the cobblestones, under the tent-like umbrellas of a pocket-sized piazza. The interior is more formal, with wood ceilings and painted coats of arms hanging above baronial fireplaces. The crisply bow-tied waiters serve a wonderfully hot *penne all'arrabbiata*. The best among the secondi are *abbacchio arrosto con patate* and *fritto cervello di abbacchio* (fried lambs brains and zucchini).

See map p. 394. Via della Paglia 1–3 (the street leading west out of Piazza Santa Maria in Trastevere). ☎ *06-580-6404. Reservations highly recommended. Tram: 8. Bus: H, 23, 115, 271, 280, 780, N30, N72, N96. Main courses: 7.50€–16€ ($8.65–$18). AE, MC, V. Open: Lunch and dinner Wed–Mon. Closed Jan 8–Feb 2.*

Pizzeria Ivo
$$ In Trastevere PIZZA ROMAN

You find this beloved pizza parlor packed with equal parts locals and tourists just about any time of the day or night. But don't let the crowds scare you off — popularity has kept quality high and prices low. Pizzeria Ivo is a wonderful place to have your first date with genuine, wood-oven Italian pizza. Favorites include the "plain" *margherita* (tomato sauce, mozzarella, and basil), *al prosciutto,* and the *capricciosa* (which can include whatever the chef wants but is likely to feature olives, anchovies, prosciutto, and a fried egg).

See map p. 394. Via San Francesco a Ripa 158 (from Viale di Trastevere, take a right onto Via Fratte di Trastevere, then left on Via San Francesco a Ripa). ☎ *06-581-7082. Reservations not usually necessary. Tram: 8. Bus: H, 23, 44, 75, 115, 271, 280, 780, N30, N44, N72, N96. Pizza: 5€–9€ ($5.75–$10). Main courses: 6.20€–13€ ($7.15–$15). AE, DC, MC, V. Open: Dinner Wed–Mon.*

Sora Lella
$$$$ On Tiber Island ROMAN/INVENTIVE ITALIAN

This refined rustic classic on Tiber Island sports rough-hewn beams, cozy rooms, elegant service, a great wine list, and a menu ranging from traditional favorites to innovative lighter fare. The specialty is *tonnarelli alla cuccagna* (pasta with sausage, eggs, walnuts, cream, and a dozen other ingredients), and for *secondo,* try the rarely found *abbacchio brodettato* (veal pieces sautéed with eggs, lemon, parmigiano reggiano, and parsley).

See map p. 394. Via Ponte Quattro Capi 16 (on Tiber Island, at the foot of Ponte Fabricio). ☎ *06-686-1601. Reservations highly recommended. Bus: H, 23, 63, 115, 271, 280, 630, 780, N29, N72, N96. Main courses 10€–21€ ($12–$24). AE, DC, MC, V. Open: Lunch and dinner Mon–Sat.*

Rome's runner-up restaurants

Birreria Peroni

$$ Near Plaza da Quirinale This German-style beer hall (owned by Italy's leading brewery) has served Italian and Teutonic specialties since 1906. The buffet is popular at lunch with the local business set, so show up early. *See map p. 394. Via San Marcello 10.* ☎ *06-679-5310.*

Il Delfino

$ Near Campo de' Fiori Il Delfino offers fast, cheap, and reliable service to visitors determinedly tramping about the heart of the centro storico. Delicious self-service hot foods and pizza are at this fantastically convenient location 2 blocks south of the Pantheon. *See map p. 394. Corso Vittorio Emanuele 67, at the corner of Largo Argentina.* ☎ *06-686-4053.*

Everyday's a Roman holiday

As in most of Italy, almost all shops and offices, most churches, and many museums in Rome observe a siesta-like midafternoon shutdown called *riposo,* roughly from noon or 1 p.m. to 3 or 4 p.m. Figure out the few sights in town that remain open during *riposo* so you can save them — and a leisurely lunch — to fill this time. Most shops are open Monday from 3 or 4 p.m. to 8 p.m., and Tuesday through Saturday from 8 a.m. to noon or 1 p.m. and again from 3 or 4 p.m. to 8 p.m. Food shops are generally open Monday mornings but closed Thursday afternoons. However, more and more stores are posting *orario continuato* ("no-stop") signs and staying open through *riposo.*

Insalata Ricca 2

$$$ Near Piazza Navona   The best-located of Rome's popular mini-chain of excellent vegetarian restaurants, offering lighter, low-fat fare, over-sized salads at outdoor tables. *See map p. 394. Piazza Pasquino 72, southwest of Piazza Navona.* ☎ *06-6830-7881.*

L'Angolo Divino

$$ Near Campo de' Fiori   A former wine shop and now one of Rome's modern wine bars, old-fashioned in style but contemporary in the kitchen, L'Angolo Divino serves platters of cheeses, salamis, and smoked fish along-side vegetable terrines and quiches — and, of course, dozens of wines by the glass. *See map p. 394. Via dei Balestrari 12 (a block southeast of Campo de' Fiori).* ☎ *06-686-4413.*

Pizzeria Est! Est! Est!

$$ Off Via Nazionale   This century-old pizza joint is patronized by local police and shopkeeps alike. Join the diners outside and order an appetizer of supplì (gooey fried balls of rice and mozzarella) and olive ascolane (green olives stuffed with minced meat, breaded, and fried) before your excellent pizza. *See map p. 394. Via Genova 32.* ☎ *06-488-1107.*

Ristorante Da Pancrazio

$$$$$ Campo de' Fiori   Da Pancrazio has fine food and one major sell-ing point: The basement rooms are set into the restored arcades of Pompey's 55 B.C. theater. It's like dining in a museum — plus the cooking is surprisingly excellent. *See map p. 394. Piazza del Biscione 92 (just off the north-east corner of Campo de' Fiori).* ☎ *06-686-1246.*

Exploring Rome

You can purchase either of two **cumulative tickets** good for admission to many of **Ancient Rome's sights.** The **Museum Card** (9€/$10) gives you seven days in which to visit all the branches of the Museo Nazionale Romano, which includes Palazzo Altemps, Palazzo Massimo, and the

Baths of Diocletian. With the 20€ ($23) **Roma Archeologia Card,** you get all those sights plus the Colosseum, Palatine Hill, the Baths of Caracalla, and the Appian Way, as well as some minor sights not covered by this guide. You can purchase the passes at all participating sights except the Palatine.

If you're visiting Rome during the high season — or if you want to ensure admission to a particular attraction — make advance reservations. **Pierreci** (www.pierreci.it; telephone number varies, so see the individual listings in the following section) handles reservations at the following: Palazzo Massimo, Palazzo Altemps, Baths of Diocletian, Capitoline Museums, Colosseo, Foro Romano, Palatine and Palatine Museum, Hadrian's Villa at Tivoli, and other sights not covered in this guide. Pierreci charges a 1.50€ ($1.75) fee per ticket. The reservations office is open Monday to Saturday, 9:00 a.m. to 1:30 p.m. and 2:30 to 5:00 p.m.

Rome's top attractions

Basilica di San Pietro (St. Peter's Basilica)

St. Peter's is one of the grandest creations of Rome's Renaissance and baroque eras, and Europe's biggest church. St. Peter's takes at least an hour — not because there's so much to see, but because it takes that long to walk from one end to the other and back. (St. Peter's is longer than two football fields.) More comprehensive visits take two to three hours and include a climb up Michelangelo's dome (offering a gorgeous view), a trek into the crypt and papal tombs, and a visit to the treasury to view a fine collection of silver chalices, embellished robes, and fragments of statuary.

You must observe St. Peter's strict dress code — you won't be allowed to enter if you aren't dressed appropriately. Proper dress means no skirts above the knee, no shorts, and no bare shoulders. If your dress isn't quite up to code, gents and ladies alike can purchase big, inexpensive scarves from a nearby souvenir stand and wrap them around their legs as a long skirt or throw them over their shoulders as a shawl. In summer, some vendors sell paper pants to shorts-wearing tourists.

Approach the church by means of the Bernini's oval colonnade, the string of columns that encases the **Piazza San Pietro.** As you enter, look right and be awestruck by the church's single greatest sight, **Michelangelo's Pietà,** carved by the artist when he was only in his early 20s. Unfortunately, the sculpture has been behind protective glass since the 1970s (due to the efforts of a hammer-wielding lunatic). Under the central dome is **Bernini's** *Baldacchino,* all twists and columns, which serves as the altar canopy.

See map p. 394. Piazza San Pietro (an information office/bookshop is on the square to the south/left of the steps up to the church). ☎ *06-6988-1662 or 06-6988-4466. Metro: Ottaviano–San Pietro. Bus: 23, 32, 34, 40, 62, 64, 81, 271, 492, 590, 982, or 990. Tram: 19. Admission: Church, sacristy, and crypt free; dome, 5€ ($5.75); treasury, 4€ ($4.60). Ask about the 10€ ($12) guided tour of the subcrypt around St. Peter's tomb* *at the information office or call the Ufficio Scavi at ☎ 06-6988-5318. Open: **Church**, daily 7 a.m.–7 p.m.; **crypt**, daily 7 a.m.–6 p.m.; **dome**, daily 8 a.m.–6 p.m.; **treasury**, daily 9 a.m.–6:30 p.m. Everything closes about an hour earlier Oct–Mar.*

Colosseo (Colosseum)

Blood and gore and sport — who could ask for anything more? The world's most famous sports arena, with its large, stately oval shape and broken-tooth profile, is a top sight for any visitor. Started in A.D. 70, this grand amphitheater hosted fights between gladiators, as well as exotic animals, to a crowd of 50,000, while onlooking emperors decided whether the loser got the thumbs-up signal to live or thumbs-down to be finished off.

As the empire slipped away, so did the Colosseum. Earthquakes shook its foundations, and folks many years later took its stones and marble to construct other buildings. The original seats and wooden floors are gone, and the central area is now a maze of walls, which were once holding pens and corridors for equipment, animals, and gladiators. A visit here has become vastly more interesting in recent years since they started allowing visitors to roam at will throughout most of the complex (for decades, tourists were limited to one small viewing terrace).

See map p. 394. Piazza del Colosseo. ☎ 06-700-4261. For reservations ☎ 06-3996-7700 or www.pierreci.it. Metro: Colosseo. Bus: 60, 75, 81, 85, 87, 117, 175, 186, 204, 271, 571, 673, 810, 850. Tram: 3. Combined admission with Palatine Hill (see listing later in this section): 8€ ($9.20). Open: Daily 9 a.m. to 1 hour before sunset (generally 7:15 p.m. in summer, 4:30 p.m. in winter).

Foro Romano (Roman Forum), Palatino (Palatine Hill), Fori Imperiali (Imperial Forums), and More

The Forum, nestled snugly between the Capitoline and Palatine Hills, was the birthplace of the Roman Republic. And the Palatine Hill is where Rome began in the eighth century B.C. as just a wee Latin village. Be sure to bring along your imagination when you visit. With all the broken arches and crumbling columns, some visitors have a hard time picturing the glory of Ancient Rome, but this archaeological zone is certainly a joy to discover, nevertheless.

You can explore the Forum and surrounding areas in about an hour or two, but many visitors choose to pack a lunch and spend four or five hours touring. Do keep in mind that the area gets dusty and hot (especially in August), so visit early in the day, bring along lots of water, and wear a protective hat.

Under republican rule, this patch of drained swampland became Rome's public "forum" of temples, administrative halls, podiums for speakers, markets, and law courts. The forum today is a collection of columns and debris sprinkled about that designates where important buildings once stood. Their names mean almost nothing if you're not a fan of ancient history, so the following touches on the more visually stunning sights.

As you enter on the eastern side, you see the triumphal **Arch of Septimius Severus** (A.D. 203), which lists the emperor's military victories in what are today Iran and Iraq. As you stroll east among the ruins, find your way back against the south side of the grounds to explore the partially rebuilt **House of the Vestal Virgins** (third to fourth centuries). The building was home to the consecrated young women who tended the sacred flame in the nearby Temple of Vesta. Head back to the Forum's north side and check out the massive brick remains and ceilings of the **Basilica of Constantine and Maxentius** (fourth century), which once served as the public law courts. (Early Christians adopted this architectural style for their houses of worship, which is why so many ancient churches are called basilicas.) Trot back south and east, and discover yet another triumphal arch, this time the **Arch of Titus** (A.D. 81), which illustrates scenes from the war that ended with the expulsion of Jews from Judea, thus beginning the Jewish diaspora throughout Europe (look for the menorah).

Next, take a hike up the **Palatine Hill,** home to that original Latin village and later to the dwelling of wealthy families and the the first emperors. The hilltop is overgrown and tree-shaded, and features gardens and fragments of ancient villas. Despite its fine little museum and lovely view, most visitors don't climb the hill — and now that the Forum below is free but the Palatine charges, that's even more true. Use this fact to your advantage and have a romantic, scenic escape from the crowds. Stroll among the passageways of the mansion of ancient Rome's rich and famous. From Palatine Hill's southern portion, you can look out over the long grassy oval that was the **Circus Maximus,** where Ben Hur–types used to race chariots (joggers are the only athletes you find today).

Across Via dei Fori Imperiali from the Roman Forum, you can see many other small forums, collectively known as the **Imperial Forums.** These were partly unearthed in the 1930s, but recently the digging started up again as part of a long-awaited, ambitious project to create a vast archaeological park extending from the Capitoline Hill, across the Roman and Imperial Fori, to the Colosseum. Broad boulevard Via dei Fori Imperiali will be reduced to a raised viaduct for buses and taxis.

At the western foot of the Palatine Hill, on Piazza della Bocca della Verità, sit two small temples from the second century B.C. and the church **Santa Maria in Cosmedin,** with its early-12th-century bell tower and marble inlay floors. Crowds flock to the front porch of this church to stick their hands inside the **Mouth of Truth,** a fourth-century B.C. sewer cover with a gaping maw. Medieval legend says that if you stick in your hand and tell a lie, the Mouth will clamp down on your fingers (apparently, a priest once added some sting to this belief by hiding behind the Mouth with a scorpion, dispensing justice as he saw fit). You may remember seeing the Mouth of Truth in the Audrey Hepburn/Gregory Peck movie *Roman Holiday.*

See map p. 394. Via dei Fori Imperiali (Forum entrance across from where Via Cavour ends; Palatine entrance from within Forum or at Via di San Gregorio 30). ☎ *06-699-0110. For reservations* ☎ *06-3996-7700 or* www.pierreci.it. *Metro: Colosseo. Bus: 60, 63, 70, 75, 81, 84, 85, 87, 95, 117, 160, 170, 175, 186, 628, 630, 715, 716,*

810, or 850. Admission: Forum, free; Palatine Hill, 8€ ($9.20), which includes admission to the Colosseum (see listing earlier in this section). Open: Daily 9 a.m. to 1 hour before sunset (generally 7:15 p.m. in summer, 4:30 p.m. in winter).

Galleria Borghese

My choice for the finest small museum in the world goes to this collection. This frescoed early-17th-century villa contains the finest marble sculptures the baroque period has to offer. See masterpieces by the rococo genius Gianlorenzo Bernini, including his *Aeneas and Anchises* (which he finished when he was only 15), *Hades and Persephone, Apollo and Daphne,* and the vibrant *David* — which serves as the baroque response to Michelangelo's Renaissance creation in Florence. The Renaissance David is contemplative, all about proportion and philosophy. This baroque *David* is all action, with a twisting body about to let a stone fly from his sling. While you're on the ground floor, be sure to see the room with six Caravaggio paintings. The second floor houses the rest of the painting collection, with works by Andrea del Sarto, Titian, Corregio, and a large masterpiece by a young Raphael, *The Deposition.*

The new *mandatory* ticket reservations policy is annoying, but in summer especially, the museum can sell out days — sometimes even weeks — ahead of time, so book well ahead of your visit to ensure you get the entry time you want. You must pick up your tickets a half-hour prior to the entry time or risk losing the reservation. The price listed here includes the required 2€ ($2.30) reservations fee. Audioguides are available for rent (5€/$5.75).

See map p. 394. In the northeast corner of Villa Borghese Park, off Via Pinciana. ☎ *06-841-7645 (information);* ☎ *06-32-810 (mandatory reservations) or* www. ticketeria.it. *Metro: Spagna. Bus: M, 52, 53, 63, 86, 88, 92, 95, 116, 116T, 204, 217, 360, 490, 491, 495, 630, 910. Admission: 8.50€ ($9.80), free 17 and under and over 65. Open: Summer Tues–Sat 9 a.m.–10 p.m., Sun 9 a.m.–8 p.m.; winter Tues–Sun 9 a.m.–7 p.m.*

Musei Capitolini (Capitoline Museums)

On the Piazza del Campidoglio, behind Piazza Venezia's Vittorio Emanuele monument, a reproduction bronze statue of Marcus Aurelius stands proud and almost seems to bless Rome and the two nearby musuems. To the left of the statue is the **Palazzo Nuovo,** housing ancient sculpture, such as busts of philosophers past.

If your trip allows you time for just one museum, make your stop the **Palazzo dei Conservatori.** Its entrance courtyard brims with oversized marble body parts — a head, hands, foot, arm, and kneecap — from what was once a 40-foot-tall statue of Constantine II. The in-house collection includes the first-century A.D. *Spinario,* a little bronze child plucking a thorn from his foot, and the Etruscan bronze *She-Wolf,* crafted in the late sixth century B.C. (the suckling toddlers were added in the 16th century).

But the real gems of the museum are its paintings — wonderful works by Guercino, Titian, Veronese, Pietro da Cortona, Rubens, and two by Caravaggio: the *Gypsy Fortune Teller* and the surpringly sensual *St. John the Baptist.*

The two wings of the mueum are now connected by an undergound passage that affords views out over the Roman Forum, but for really great Forum vistas, make sure you stop by the cafe with its roof terrace.

See map p. 394. Piazza del Campidoglio 1 (behind Piazza Venezia's Vittorio Emanuele monument). ☎ *06-6710-2475;* www.museicapitolini.org. *Reservations:* ☎ *06-3996-7700 or* www.pierreci.it. *Bus: H, 30, 40, 44, 46, 62, 63, 70, 75, 81, 84, 87, 95, 160, 170, 271, 204, 271, 628, 630, 715, 716, 780, 781, 810, or 916. Museum admission: 6.20€ ($7.15); exhibition only: 4.20€ ($4.85). Open: Tues–Sun 9 a.m.–8 p.m. (in summer may stay open to 9 p.m.; call ahead). Last admission 1 hour before close.*

Museo Nazionale Romano (National Roman Museum)

In 1998, Rome took what was once a single museum — one that languished for decades in a quasi-mythical state inside the eternally closed Baths of Diocletian — and split it up across the city in four incredible "Museo Nazionale Romano" collections, together boasting the best ancient Roman statuary, mosaics, and frescoes you can possibly see, a where-have-you-been-all-my-life experience for antiquities buffs.

The Ludovisi, Mattei, and Altemps Collections of Classical statuary are now displayed in the 16th- to 18th-century **Palazzo Altemps** near Piazza Navona (Piazza di Sant'Apollinare 44; ☎ **06-683-3759**), itself a gorgeous space, with a grand central courtyard and many original frescoed and painted wood ceilings.

More statues, plus exquisite ancient Roman mosaics, bronzes, incredible frescoes, coins, and jewelry, are packed into the **Palazzo Massimo alle Terme** near Termini train station (Largo di Villa Peretti 1, where Piazza del Cinquecento meets Via Viminale; ☎ **06-4890-3500**).

Bathhouse art and colossal statuary fill the echoey ancient brick chamber of the **Aula Ottagona,** an original part of Diocletian's baths just off Piazza della Repubblica (Via G. Romita 3; ☎ **06-488-0530**), and they are also putting the finishing touches on a collection installed in the original **Baths of Diocletian** space (Via E. De Nicola 78; call Aula Ottagona for info) with its massive cloisters designed by Michelangelo.

See map p. 394. For addresses and phone numbers, see the preceding text; www. archeorm.arti.beniculturali.it. *For reservations* ☎ *06-3996-7400, 06-3996-7700, or* www.pierreci.it. *Metro: Termini or Repubblica for all but Palazzo Altemps. Bus: For all but Palazzo Altemps, take any bus to Termini; for Palazzo Altemps, by bus: 30, 70, 81, 87, 116, 116T, 186, 492, or 628. Admission included with 9€ ($10)* **Museum Card** *(see the tips under "Exploring Rome," earlier in this chapter). Individual admission:* **Palazzo Altemps,** *5€ ($5.75) adults, free 17 and under and over 60;* **Palazzo Massimo alle Terme,** *6€ ($6.90);* **Aula Ottagona,** *free. Open:* **Palazzo Altemps,** *Tues–Sun 9 a.m.–7:45 p.m. (last admission 1 hour before close);* **Palazzo**

Massimo alle Terme, Tues–Sun 9 a.m.–7:45 p.m. (may close Sun at 2 p.m. in winter); Aula Ottagona, Tues–Sat 9 a.m.–2 p.m.; Sun 9 a.m.–1 p.m.

Pantheon

In the poetic words of Byron, the Pantheon is "simple, erect, severe, austere, sublime." And, as you'll find, this lovely description doesn't even begin to capture the power and magic that this best-preserved of Rome's ancient buildings holds. Emperor Hadrian designed the Pantheon in the second century, A.D. and his skilled eye was instrumental in creating the mathematically exact, almost gravity-defying space inside.

Some amazing factoids await: The 1,800-year-old bronze entrance doors weigh 20 tons each. The interior and ceiling create a perfect hemisphere, and the 18-foot *oculus,* or hole, in the center of the ceiling lets rain and light in. The dome is exactly 140 feet across, and the building is 140 feet high.

This marvel of engineering remained unduplicated until the Renaissance — and only recently have scholars actually figured out all the building's architectural secrets. For starters, the roof is poured concrete (a Roman invention) made of light pumice stone, and the weight of it is distributed by brick arches embedded sideways into the walls and channeled into a ring of tension around the lip of the oculus (25-foot thick walls also come in handy here).

Although the décor is spare, the building houses the tombs of the painter Raphael as well as Italy's short-lived 19th-century monarchy (two of the total three kings lie here). Fortunately, the Pantheon has survived for centuries, because people — barbarians, overzealous Christians, and others — have recognized its classic beauty and left the building alone for the most part.

See map p. 394. Piazza della Rotunda. ☎ *06-6830-0230. Tram: 8. Bus: 30, 40, 46, 62, 63, 64, 70, 81, 87, 116, 116T, 186, 492, 571, 628, 810, 916, N45, N78, N98, N99. Admission: Free. Open: Mon–Sat 8:30 a.m.–7:30 p.m., Sun 9 a.m.–6 p.m.*

 ## Vatican Museums

Not only is the Vatican the center of the Catholic faith, it's also home to one of the greatest museum complexes in the world, with 12 apartments and collections, all worth viewing (including the wonderful Raphael Rooms and the amazing Sistine Chapel). In other words, this one may take more than one visit.

 To avoid waiting in line with busloads of tourists, I recommend arriving at the Vatican early — in the summer, about 30 minutes before it opens, if possible. After you take in the museums, head on over to St. Peter's, which is immense enough to hold tens of thousands of people, no problem.

Your first stop is most likely the **Pinacoteca (Picture Gallery),** which houses Leonardo da Vinci's unfinished *St. Jerome,* Giotto's *Stefaneschi Triptych,* and Caravaggio's *Deposition from the Cross.* The most famous work here is certainly Raphael's masterpiece, the huge study in colors and light called the *Transfiguration,* which Raphael had not quite completed by the time of his sudden death at the age of 37.

The pinnacle of Renaissance painting fills the ceiling and end wall of the **Sistine Chapel.** Originally, Pope Julius II hired Michelangelo to create a magnificent burial site for him, but then he switched the artist to another job — painting the chapel ceiling. Michelangelo at first balked at the request, saying that he was a sculptor, not a frescoist, but eventually he agreed to work on the ceiling.

After four years of arduous work, the frescoes were unveiled. Michelangelo had transformed the barrel-vaulted ceiling of the chapel into a blueprint for the continuing development of Renaissance art, developing new means of depicting the human form, new methods of arranging frescoes, and new uses of light and color that painters would embrace for generations to come. He covered the Sistine ceiling with nine scenes from Genesis (the fingers-almost-touching *God Creating Adam* is the most famous) and ringed these with figures of the ancient prophets and sybils, with nudes in contorted positions that show off brilliant attention to human musculature.

The walls of the chapel are covered by wonderful frescoes from earlier Renaissance biggies including Signorelli, Botticelli, Pinturicchio, Perugino, Ghirlandaio — all works that would command attention if they weren't under such a fabulous ceiling. In 1545, at the age of 60, Michelangelo returned to the chapel to paint the entire end wall with the *Last Judgment* — a masterwork of color, despair, and psychology.

If I had to choose the other top sight in the Vatican, it would be the **Pio-Clementino Museum,** which houses ancient Greek and Roman sculpture. Look here for the famed *Laocoön* group (first century B.C.), the *Apollo Belvedere* (ancient Roman copy of a fourth-century B.C. Greek original), and the muscular *Belvedere Torso,* a first-century B.C. fragment of a Hercules statue that served as inspiration to Renaissance artists such as Michelangelo.

The Vatican has numerous other museums, but you need months to get through all of them. Some of the best include a collection of **Egyptian** and **Etruscan** artifacts, a **Modern Religious Art** gallery with robes by Matisse, an **Ethnological Museum** covering 3,000 years of history across all continents (the stuff from China is particularly good), an outstanding **Library,** and a museum devoted to the **History of the Vatican.**

See map p. 394. Viale Vaticano (on the north side of the Vatican City walls, between where Via Santamaura and the Via Tunisi staircase hit Viale Vaticano; about a 5- to 10-minute walk around the walls from St. Peter's). ☎ *06-6988-4466.* www. vaticano.va. *Metro: Cipro–Musei Vaticani. Bus: 23, 32, 49, 62, 81, 271, 490, 492, 982, or 990. Admission: 12€ ($14) adults, 8€ ($9.20) students under 26; free last Sun of each month (8:45 a.m.–1:45 p.m.) and crowded like you wouldn't believe. Open: Mar–Oct and Dec 20–30 Mon–Fri 8:45 a.m.–4:45 p.m., Sat 8:45 a.m.–1:45 p.m.; Nov–Feb Mon–Sat 8:45 a.m.–1:45 p.m. Last admission 75 minutes before closing. Closed Jan 1 and 6, Feb 11, Mar 19, Easter Mon, May 1 and 20, June 10 and 29, Aug 14, Nov 1, Dec 8 and 25, and many religious holidays; check the Web site or call ahead.*

Via Appia Antica (Appian Way) and the Catacombs

The Via Appia Antica was built in 312 B.C. but is still a major Roman road-way that is bordered with ancient tombs of Roman families and miles of catacombs chiseled out of the soft tufa stone below. The catacombs, of course, are the famous burial site for thousands of early Christians. Wander in awe through miles of musty, dusty tunnels with tens of thousands of burial niches (which each hold two to three bodies). Most of the niches are still capped with headstones, but many others are open, so skulls and bones are plentiful — macabre, yes, but also quite interesting. Take a tour lead by a priest and monk, but be prepared for a bit of Christian-centric history and a heavy dose of sermonizing. You can spend all day at the catacombs, but a one- to two-hour visit is probably enough if you can get a spot in one of the popular English-language tours. Sundays, when the Appian Way is closed to traffic, the road fills with Romans strolling, bicycling, and picnicking.

Although the **Catacombe di San Sebastiano** has tunnels that go on for 7 miles and the esteemed bones of Sts. Paul and Peter were once hidden here, the tour is one of shortest and least satisfying of all the catacombs visits. (However, you *do* get to see some well-preserved stuccoes and frescoes in several pagan tombs that were once part of an above-ground cemetery). The **Catacombe di San Domitilla** is the oldest of the catacombs and, hands-down, the winner for most enjoyable catacomb experience. Groups are small, and most guides are genuinely entertaining. There are fewer "sights" than in the other catacombs — although the second-century fresco of the *Last Supper* is impressive.

The **Catacombe di San Callisto** offers a huge parking lot — as well as huge crowds from the tour buses. The tour is the cheesiest of the catacomb tours, full of canned commentary and stilted jokes. Some of the tunnels, however, are phenomenal, 70 feet high and less than 6 feet wide, with elon-gated tomb niches pigeon-holed all the way up to the top. Of all the cata-combs, these are among the oldest and certainly the largest (12 miles of tunnels spread over 33 acres and five levels that house the remains of half a million Christians). You also get to ogle some of the earliest Christian frescoes and carvings.

See map p. 394. Via Appia Antica 136 (San Sebastiano) and 110 (San Callisto), or Via delle Sette Chiese 283 (San Domitilla). ☎ *06-5130-1580 or 06-513-0151.* www. catacombe.roma.it. *Bus: 118 from Piramide Metro stop. Admission: 5€ ($5.75) adults, 3€ ($3.45) ages 6–14. Open: Thurs–Tues 8:30 a.m. to noon, 2:30–5 p.m. (to 5:30 p.m. in summer).*

More cool things to see and do

- ✔ **Sampling cafe life in Piazza Navona:** Rome is bursting with charming public squares, but the oblong and lively Piazza Navona is one of the premiere hangouts. Okay, so you do pay a pretty penny for food and drink at the cafes that border the piazza (particularly if you order from the cute exterior tables). But don't think of it as buying a $6 cappuccino— think of it as admission for a front-row seat to an energetic circus of color, sight, smell, and sound. And for the perfect snack, visit **Tre Scalini** (☎ 06-6880-1996) and check out its legendary tartufo ice-cream balls.

✔ **Flexing your shopping muscles around Piazza di Spagna (Spanish Steps):** Italy's artistic heritage is not only housed in its museums and churches. Italy, like Paris, is a world center for high fashion and design. Although most of the big-name designers are centered in Florence and Milan, they all have boutiques in Rome. You can find the most famous shops in a triangle of couture formed by the streets between Piazza del Popolo, the Spanish Steps, and the Corso. On Via de' Condotti, experience the fashions of **Gucci** (no. 68A) and **Valentino** (no. 13); shoes from **Fragiacomo** (no. 35) and **Ferragamo** (nos. 65, 73–74); jewelry and silver from **Bulgari** (no. 10); and some of the finest men's shirts in the world at **Battistoni** (no. 61A). The ever-popular **Benetton** has locations throughout Rome but also on Piazza di Spagna (nos. 67–69).

Via Frattina is home to **Max Mara** fashions (no. 28), fine lingerie at **Brighenti** (no. 7–8), and antique and modern silver at **Anatriello del Regalo** (no. 123) and **Fornari** (no. 133). Via Borgognona boasts fashions from **Givenchy** (no. 21), **Fendi** (no. 36–40), and **Gianfranco Ferré** (no. 42B). Via del Babuino offers the relatively affordable "Emporio" division of fashion giant **Armani** (no. 140), sportswear at **Oliver** (no. 61), historic prints at **Olivi** (no. 136), and paintings of Italian scenes — no Renaissance masterpieces — but good prices and fine quality control at **Alberto di Castro** (no. 71) and **Fava** (no. 180). A bit farther south, where Via Tritone hits the Corso at no. 189, is **La Rinascente,** Rome's biggest and finest upscale department store.

Truth be told, the big fashion names aren't much cheaper in Rome than they are in the United States. So if you plan to splurge, check out the prices back home before you buy in Rome so you know what kind of deal you're actually getting. But if you're like many shop-a-holics, price isn't even an issue — it's just the thrill of purchasing Ferragamo pumps in Italy.

✔ **Squaring off:** Rome is as much about squares and fountains as about museums and monuments. Take the time to visit the lively, oval **Piazza Navona.** Hit the morning flower and veggie market on **Campo de' Fiori,** Rome's public execution ground in the Middle Ages. The center of **Largo Argentina** sits a good 15 feet below street level (what was ground level in ancient Roman times). Trees shade the remains of three small temples and, along the west edge, a bit of Pompey's Curia, the building Julius Caesar was leaving when he was assassinated.

The off-center, yet graceful curves of **Piazza di Spagna (Spanish Steps)** are covered with bright azaleas in spring and teem with visitors year-round; they're flanked by the twin-towered Trinità dei Monti church at the top and by the beloved "Ugly Boat" fountain at the bottom.

A few blocks to the south sits an even more famous set of water-works, the huge baroque confection called the **Trevi Fountain,** presided over by a muscular Neptune. Legend (and a host of American movies) holds that if you toss a coin into this fountain, you will one day return to Rome. Some say you should toss it backward over your shoulder. Others insist you use three coins for it to work. City authorities don't want you throwing any coins, because they rust at the bottom, irreparably damaging the fountain.

✔ **Peeking in churches:** Stepping into Rome's churches is one of my favorite pastimes. And because Rome has well over 900 churches, you can keep yourself entertained for quite a while.

Rome has several top houses of worship. First built in the fourth century, the mammoth **Basilica di San Giovanni in Laterano** has been robbed and reworked so often that almost nothing original remains. The great pilgrimage church of **Basilica di Santa Maria Maggiore** sparkles with scintillating mosaics, many of which date back to the fifth century. **San Luigi dei Francesi** features three paintings on St. Matthew by Caravaggio, and his *Adoration of the Shepherds* adorns the nearby church of **Sant'Agostino.**

You can see Michelangelo's muscular *Christ* and frescoes by Filippo Lippi in **Santa Maria Sopra Minerva,** Rome's only Gothic church. **Santa Maria del Popolo** has frescoes by Pinturicchio, two of Caravaggio's most famous paintings *(The Conversion of St. Paul* and *The Crucifixion of St. Peter),* and the Raphael-designed Chigi Chapel. Join the crowds at **San Pietro in Vincoli** who gather to see Michelangelo's restored *Moses* statue. Over a millennium old, **Santa Maria in Trastevere** has an elaborate floor of 12th-century marble inlay and gorgeous medieval mosaics in the apse.

✔ **Getting funky in Trastevere:** Trastevere is equal parts working-class and modern trendiness, which makes it a popular hangout for Brits and Americans. The neighborhood is fairly busting at the seams with eateries (both casual and sophisticated). Its web of tight ancient streets and peppy piazze offer fun shopping, bars, clubs, galleries, and even an English-language movie house (the Pasquino, on Piazza S. Egidio).

✔ **Pedaling your way through the Villa Borghese or the Via Appia Antica:** Hop on a bike and see all that Villa Borghese park has to offer — fountains, monuments, groomed gardens, a nice zoo, and three museums (the Galleria Borghese, a big ol' museum of Etruscan antiquities called the Villa Giulia, and the city's modern-art gallery).

Sundays are great for biking because traffic is light and many roads are closed to cars — essentially the city is yours. Bike Via de Fori Imperiali (which heads for the Colosseum, passing the Roman and Imperial Forums) and Via Appia Antica (lined with tombs, picnickers, and early Christian catacombs).

Rent bikes or scooters at **Treno e Scooter** (☎ 06-4890-5823), at track 1 inside Termini station; **I Bike Rome,** Via Veneto 156, in section three of the underground parking lot (☎ 06-322-5240); or **Roma Solutions Rent A Scooter,** locations at Via F. Turati 50 near Termini (☎ 06-446-9222) and Corso V. Emanuele II 204 near Piazza Navona (☎ 06-687-6922).

✔ **Bargaining and dealing at Rome's Porta Portese flea market:** Every Sunday, from 7 a.m. to 1 p.m., the tranquil streets in the southwest corner of Trastevere come alive with Rome's biggest, most chaotic flea market, **Porta Portese.** The fun, frenetic gathering began as a black market after World War II but now features such varied goodies as secondhand appliances, bootleg pop music, slightly used clothing, antiques, furniture, paintings, car parts, underwear, grilled corn cobs, birds, religious icons, and comic books. Take tram 3 or 8 or buses H, 44, 75; get off with the crowd halfway down Viale Trastevere; and watch out for pickpockets.

Guided tours

What kind of **guided bus tour** you get depends on how much you spend. City-run **ATAC bus 110** (☎ 06-4695-2252) runs on a three-hour circuit on a giant silver bus where your only "guide" is an information leaflet. The bus leaves from outside Stazione Termini daily at 45-minute intervals from 9:00 a.m. to 10:30 p.m. Tickets cost 12.91€ ($15) if purchased from the kiosk opposite the taxi stand on Piazza dei Cinquecento, or 13.94€ ($16) if purchased onboard.

Green Line Tours, Via Farini 5A (☎ 06-482-7480 or 06-482-7017; www. greenlinetours.com; Metro: Termini; Bus: 16, 70, 71, 75, 105, 204, 360, 590, 649, or 714 to Via Cavour, or any to Termini; Tram: 5 or 14), gives you an audioguide in the language of your choice for their hop-on/hop-off bus tour costing 18€ ($21) for a 24-hour ticket. They also do eight live-commentary, guided, themed half- and full-day tours costing from 31.50€ to 45€ ($36–$52).

A **walking tour** may be more your style. **Enjoy Rome,** Via Marghera 8a (☎ 06-445-1843; www.enjoyrome.com; Metro: Termini; Bus: any to Termini), has a young staff from various English-speaking countries who run three-hour walking tours for up to 20 people. Tours of Ancient Rome and Rome at Night run daily. Tours of the Vatican and the Jewish Ghetto/Trastevere are offered several times a week. They cost 21€ ($24) or 15€ ($17) for those under 26.

Suggested itineraries

If you're short on time and you prefer to organize your own tour of Rome, this section offers some recommendations for hitting the highlights. Keep in mind that, if you're following the two- or three-day itinerary, you may want to switch the order of the days (doing the Day 2 itinerary first, for example) depending on what days of the week you're in town and, therefore, when you can best visit various museums.

If you have one day

Rome wasn't built in a day, so don't expect to see it all in one day either. Spend the early morning at the **Vatican Museums** (you'll have time only for the highlights: the Pinacoteca, Raphael Rooms, and Sistine Chapel) and St. Peter's, having lunch on the run to see the **Roman Forum.** After taking a gander at the **Colosseum,** check out the **Pantheon** and then wander the churches and piazze of the Tiber Bend area, making sure to stop by the **Spanish Steps.** After dinner, swing past the **Trevi Fountain** to toss in a few coins and ensure your return to the Eternal City.

If you have two days

Spend more time at the **Vatican Museums** and St. Peter's from **Day 1,** and add to the Day 1 experience the churches and museums of the Tiber Bend, including the **Pantheon** and the **Palazzo Altemps.** Make the earliest reservation possible at the **Galleria Borghese** for **Day 2,** then see the **Palazzo Massimo alle Terme** on your way down to the **Forum/Colosseum,** taking a *passeggiata* past the **Spanish Steps** at dusk and the **Trevi Fountain** after dinner. On such a tight schedule, you'll want to make advance reservations at both Palazzo Altemps and Palazzo Massimo alle Terme.

If you have three days

What should you not miss after you've glimpsed Rome's best-known areas? You may want to start with the **Capitoline Museums.** You can also plan to spend more time at the Forum on Day 1, and leave all the museums and churches of the Tiber Bend to **Day 3.**

Traveling Beyond Rome

If you can tear yourself away from Rome, consider exploring the splendor of Tivoli and the ancient Roman ghost town of Ostia Antica, both just a short hop away.

Tivoli: The villas of Roman emperors, princes, and popes

Welcome to the good life! Since the dawn of Rome, Tivoli (just 19 miles east of Rome) has served as home away from home for the wealthy and powerful. Emperor Hadrian started things in the second century by building a gorgeous vacation home here, and others, including a Renaissance cardinal and 19th-century pope, followed suit.

Getting there

Take Rome's B Metro to Ponte Mammolo stop, where you catch the COTRAL bus to Tivoli-Villa d'Este (1.80€/$2.05; every 30 minutes) or Tivoli-Villa Adriana (every hour). **Green Line Tours** (☎ 06-482-7480 or

06-482-7017; www.greenlinetours.com) — described under "Guided tours" earlier in this chapter — runs half-day Tivoli trips for 49€ ($56).

The best way to see Tivoli is to take a picnic, spend the day, and return to Rome in time for dinner. Tivoli's **tourist office** (☎ 0774-311-249 or 0774-21-249) is on Largo Garibaldi.

Seeing the sights

Hadrian served the ancient Roman Empire as a general and later as Emperor, traveling much of the known world during his lifetime. He also tried his hand at being an architect when he designed Villa Adriana, or **Hadrian's Villa** (Information: ☎ 0774-530-203; Reservations: ☎ 06-3996-7800 or www.pierreci.it), which brims with international influences — Egyptian, Greek, and Asian. Although much of the estate is still being unearthed, look for the Canopus (a sacred Egyptian canal 225 feet long and lined with statues); the Lyceum (the ancient school where Aristotle taught), the Maritime Theatre (a pool featuring an island retreat); and several baths. Plan on two to four hours to fully explore the grounds and perhaps enjoy a picnic lunch under the cypress and olive groves that mingle with the remains of ancient columns. Admission is 6.50€ ($7.50), and the villa is open daily from 9 a.m. to 7 p.m. (to 5 p.m. in winter).

During the 16th century, Cardinal Ippolito d'Este, whose mother was the infamous Lucrezia Borgia, took a 13th-century convent and renovated it into the extravagant **Villa d'Este** (☎ 0774-312-070). However, the real draw here is the spectacular gardens and nearly 100 fountains, including spacious pools, spurting jets, stair-stepping cascades, wall fountains covered with mossy gargoyles, and even one that once played an organ with the force of its water. The fountains are most spectacular when water is pumping through them at full force. To get the best effect, call ahead and find out when the fountains will be at full blast (sunny weekend days are your safest bet). Admission is 6.50€ ($7.50); the villa is open Tuesday through Sunday from 8:30 a.m. to 6:30 p.m. (to 4 p.m. in winter).

Where to dine

Since the 1950s, **Le Cinque Statue,** Via Quintillio Varo 1 (☎ 0774-335-366), has been offering Tivoli visitors honest home cookin', Roman style.

Ostia Antica: Not quite Pompeii, but much closer

The ancient Roman republic constructed Ostia to serve as Rome's port (the Tiber River wasn't ever deep enough to be useful for trade). The city flourished and at one point had nearly 100,000 inhabitants. In the fourth century, the river's mouth began to fill with silt. Eventually, the empire fell, disease set in, and Ostia became a marshy bog. The city was rediscovered in the early 20th century but has never gained a popular following. Even though the scenery is gloriously reminiscent of a long-lost era, you don't have to fight the crowds here. More good news: The city is just a fast ride via public transportation from the heart of Rome.

Visit Ostia bright and early in the morning, explore the site for two to three hours, and trot on back to Rome for lunch (or picnic in the ruins, if you prefer).

Getting there

Take the **Metro line B** to **Magliana station,** transfer to the Lido train (you need another Metro ticket), and ride it 20 minutes to the Ostia Antica stop.

You won't find a **tourist office.** Just beeline to the site's entrance (☎ 06-5635-2830 or 06-32-810) for a map and more info.

Seeing the sight

Solitude is usually yours at Ostia Antica. You can simply stroll this ancient town and imagine what life must have been like here. Walk the dusty streets, relax on the forum, and imagine attending a Greek tragedy in the theater. Roam among the columns of a raised temple, savor a picnic in the company of a solitary, armless, nameless statue, or get an intimate look at the crumbling mosaic floor of what must have been a wealthy citizen's home. Ostia Antica is open Tuesday through Sunday from 9 a.m. to 6 p.m. (until 4 p.m. in winter); the small on-site museum is open from 9:00 a.m. to 1:30 p.m. Admission is 4.13€ ($4.75) adults, free for ages 16 and under or over 60.

Fast Facts: Rome

Area Code

The country code for Italy is **39**. Rome — along with the rest of Italy — no longer has a seperate city code, though you'll notice almost all numbers in town still start with 06 (the old city code). As they run out of new numbers, that will be changing . And, unlike in the past, you must dial that initial zero.

American Express

The office, Piazza di Spagna 38, to the right of the Spanish Steps (☎ 06-67-641) is open Monday through Friday from 9:00 a.m. to 5:30 p.m. and Saturday from 9:00 a.m. to 12:30 p.m.

Currency

In 2002, the euro became the legal tender in Italy, replacing the lira. The exchange rate used to calculate the dollar value given in this chapter is 1€ equals $1.15. Amounts over $10 are rounded to the nearest dollar.

Doctors and Dentists

Call the U.S. Embassy (☎ 06-46-741) for a list of English-speaking doctors and dentists.

There's a special H bus that connects Rome's municipal hospitals. It takes the usual 1€ ($1.15) ticket.

Embassies and Consulates

The U.S. Embassy, Via Vittorio Veneto 121 (☎ 06-46-741; www.usembassy.it), is open Monday through Friday from 8:30 a.m. to 12:30 p.m. For passport and consular services, head to the consulate, left of the Embassy's main gate.

Emergency

Dial ☎ **113** in any emergency, ☎ **112** for the *carabinieri* (the military-trained and more useful of the two police forces); ☎ **118** or **06-5100** to summon an ambulance, or ☎ **115** for the fire department. *Pronto Soccorso* is Italian for "first aid," but you can also use the phrase to get to an emergency room. Call ☎ **116** for roadside assistance (not free).

Hospitals

First aid is available 24 hours a day in the emergency room *(pronto soccorso)* of major hospitals. English-speaking doctors are always on duty at the Rome American Hospital, Via Emilio Longoni 69; (☎ 06-22-551), and at the privately run Salvator Mundi International Hospital, Viale delle Mura Gianicolensi 67 (☎ 06-588-961). With Italy's partially socialized medical system, you can usually pop into an emergency room and get taken care of speedily without dealing with any forms.

In the center of town is San Giacomo, Via Canova 29, off Via del Corso 2 blocks from Piazza del Popolo (☎ 06-3626-6354 or 06-36-261).

Information

The main tourist office, Via Parigi 5 (☎ 06-3600-4399; Fax: 06-481-9316; www.roma turismo.com; Metro: Reppublica), is about a five-minute walk straight out from the Termini station and across several piazze and traffic circles. The office is open Monday through Saturday from 9 a.m. to 7 p.m. The new large information office at Termini station (☎ 06-4890-6300) is usually crowded and sparse of information, making it useful only on Sundays, when the main office is closed.

Helpful information kiosks are at the following locations: Largo Goldoni/Via del Corso, across from the end of Vie de' Condotti (☎ 06-6813-6061); Via Nazionale in front of the Palazzo delle Esposizioni (☎ 06-4782-4525); Via dei Fori Imperiali, near the Roman Forum (☎ 06-6992-4307); Piazza di Cinque Lune, off Piazza Navona (☎ 06-6880-9240); Lungotevere Castel Sant'Angelo (☎ 06-6880-9707); Via del Tritone, at La Rinascente department store (☎ 06-6920-0435); Piazza San Giovanni in Laterano (☎ 06-7720-3535); and Piazza Sonnino in Trastevere (☎ 06-5833-3457).

Visit any newsstand for a copy of *Roma C'è*, which lists events (in Italian), or purchase Thursday's *La Reppublica* newspaper and dive into the pullout Trovaroma section. For events info in English, look for the monthly *Wanted in Rome*.

For info on city buses, contact ATAC (☎ 800-431-784;www.atac.roma.it), and for suburban buses, contact COTRAL (☎ 800-150-008; www.cotralspa.it).

Internet Access and Cybercafes

The best spot to surf the Net is the gargantuan 24-hour easyInternetcafé, Via Barberini 2 (no phone; www.easy internetcafe.com; Metro: Barberini). You can also log on at Thenetgate (www.thenetgate.it), with locations in Termini's underground mall (☎ 06-8740-6008) open daily from 6 a.m. to midnight, at Piazza Firenze 25 (☎ 06-687-9098; bus: 116), and in Termini train station (☎ 06-8740-6008), both open Monday through Saturday from 10:30 a.m. to 9:00 p.m.

Maps

The tourist office hands out a free map. You can buy more detailed ones at any newsstand or bookstore.

Newspapers/Magazines

If you want to try your hand at Italian, the Thursday edition of the newspaper *La Repubblica* contains the magazine insert "TrovaRoma" (www.repubblica.it), with entertainment, event, gallery, and show listings. One other prime resource is the weekly magazine *Roma C'è* (1€/ $1.15; www.romace.it), which has a "This Week in Rome" section in English. You'll find all of these at most newsstands. Less complete, but free, is the tourist office's bimonthly events pamphlet *L'Evento.*

Pharmacies

You find a 24-hour *farmacie* (pharmacy) at: Piazza Barberini 49 (☎ 06-487-1195; Metro: Barberini; Bus: 52, 53, 61, 62, 63, 80, 95, 116, 116T, 117, 119, 175, 204, 492, 590, 630, N25, N45, N55, or N60); Piazza Risorgimento 44 (☎ 06-3973-8166; Bus: 23, 32, 49, 81, 271, 492, 590, 982, 990, 991, N29, or N30); Via Arenula 73 (☎ 06-6880-3278; Tram: 8; Bus: H, 63, 115, 271, 280, 630, 780, N29, or N72). A pharmacy at Termini on Piazza del Cinquecento 49–51 (☎ 06-488-0776; Metro: Termini; bus: any to Termini) stays open until 10 p.m.

Police

Dial ☎ **113** in any emergency or ☎ **112** for the *carabinieri,* a division of the Italian army.

Post Office

The Italian mail system is notoriously slow, and friends back home may not receive your postcards for anywhere from one to eight weeks (sometimes longer). The main post office is at Piazza San Silvestro 19, 00187 Roma, Italia (off Via del Corso, south of the Spanish Steps; Bus: 52, 53, 61, 62, 63, 71, 80, 81, 85, 95, 116, 116T, 117, 119, 160, 175, 204, 492, 590, 628, 630, 850). Hours are Sunday through Friday from 9 a.m. to 6 p.m.,

Saturday from 9 a.m. to 2 p.m. You can pick up stamps at any *tabacchi* (tobacconists).

If you want your letters to get home before you do, use the Vatican post office. It costs the same and is much quicker and more reliable — but you must use Vatican stamps, available only at their post offices. You can visit three different offices: to the left of the basilica steps, just past the information office; behind the right-hand colonnade of Piazza San Pietro (where the alley ends beyond souvenir stands); and in the Vatican Museums.

Safety

Random violent crime in Rome is very rare, but petty thieves — particularly pickpockets — seek out travelers.

Most pickpockets frequent the buses running from Termini to other biggie tourist traps (be extra careful on buses 40 and 62, which travel between Termini and the Vatican). Women should be aware of occasional drive-by purse snatchings by young Vespa-riding thieves. Men should keep their wallets in their front pockets. Also, protect your personals at the following top attractions: Termini, Piazza del Popolo, the Forums, the Colosseum, and around the Vatican.

Be wary of groups of gypsy kids dressed in colorful but filthy rags, often seen roaming around tourist areas and subway tunnels, sometimes waving bits of cardboard. They aren't physically dangerous but are masterful pickpockets. Do your best to give them a wide berth, forcefully yell *"Va via!"* ("Scram!"), or loudly invoke the *polizia,* if necessary. Also watch out for a scam in which a baby — often thrown at you — is used to distract your attention while pickpockets steal your money.

Taxes

The value-added tax in Italy (called IVA) varies with the item or service, up to 19 percent, and is already included in the sticker price of any item (except, oddly, in the most expensive luxury hotels). Non-EU citizens who spend more than 154.94€ ($178) in a single store are entitled to a refund. See Chapter 9 for details on receiving one.

Taxis

See "Getting Around Rome," earlier in this chapter.

Telephone

To call one city from another within Italy, dial the entire number, complete with that initial zero (which, in the past, was dropped in some cases). To dial direct internationally, dial 00, then the country code for the country you're calling, then the area or city code, and then the local number. Direct-dial calls from the United States to Italy are usually cheaper than calls placed from an Italian hotel to most phones in North America, so if possible, try to arrange for friends and acquaintances to call you at your hotel at prearranged times.

Local calls in Italy cost .10€ (12¢). There are two types of public pay phones: those that take both coins and phone cards and those that take only phone cards (*carta telefonica* or *scheda telefonica*). You can buy these prepaid phone cards at any *tabacchi* (tobacconists) or most newsstands. Break off the corner before inserting it and don't forget to take the card with you when you hang up!

To call free national telephone information (in Italian) in Italy, dial ☎ 12. European information is available by calling ☎ 176, but costs .60€ (70¢) per request.

To make calling-card calls, insert a phone card or .10€ (12¢) — the amount is refunded at the end of your call (the new green-and-white Infostrada pay phones don't require the deposit) — and dial the local number for your service: AT&T at ☎ 800-172-444, MCI at ☎ 800-90-5825, or Sprint at ☎ 800-172-405. You can use any one of these numbers to place a collect call even if you don't carry that particular phone company's card.

Transit Info

See "Getting Around Rome," earlier in this chapter.

Chapter 20

Florence and the Tuscany Region

. . . .

In This Chapter

▶ Getting to and around Florence

▶ Learning the lay of the land

▶ Discovering the best hotels, restaurants, and attractions

▶ Side-tripping to Pisa, Siena, and San Gimignano

. . . .

*I*f you're an art or history buff or have even a modest interest in the Renaissance, Florence is a must-see destination on your trip to Europe. For more than two centuries beginning in the late 1300s, artists, writers, musicians, philosophers, and scientists sparked a creative movement in Florence that essentially killed the Middle Ages throughout Europe and came to be called the Renaissance, or "rebirth."

The Florentine Renaissance was an era of spirited artistic and intellectual activity, and symbols of that period are still very much in evidence today. Your exploration of the Renaissance in Florence may include Michelangelo's *David,* Giotto's frescoes in Santa Croce, Brunelleschi's ingenious cathedral dome, and the Uffizi Galleries — the world's most esteemed collection of Renaissance artwork, from da Vinci's *Annunciation* to Botticelli's *Birth of Venus.*

But Florence has much more to offer than just centuries-old art. You can enjoy a sumptuous Tuscan meal with plenty of Chianti wine from the countryside. Or you can test the durability of embossed plastic at the high-fashion and fine-leather boutiques in the city that brought the world Gucci, Pucci, Ferragamo, and Beltrami.

The Leaning Tower of Pisa and the quaint hill towns of the Tuscany region are all close enough for easy daytrips from Florence. Or you can stay in Florence and let the lush greenery and warm sunshine of the Boboli Gardens inspire you to write or paint your own masterpiece. Spend at least two days here, three if you can swing it.

Getting There

Although it's a good-sized city, Florence is by no means the mega-metropolis that many European travelers are used to tackling. This can make getting there a little more difficult — most flights from outside Italy land at an airport that's 60 miles away — but getting around town is comparatively easy.

Arriving by air

Amerigo Vespucci Airport (☎ 055-30-615; www.aeroporto.firenze.it) is about 4km (3 miles) northwest of Florence, but most of the flights that land there come from within Italy. A **tourist information office** (☎ 055-315-874) in the arrivals terminal can provide information on getting into Florence.

From the airport, visitors can take **Vola in Bus** (☎ 800-424-500 within Italy; www.ataf.net) to Stazione Santa Maria Novella, Florence's main terminal, located on the western edge of the city's historic center. The ride takes about 30 minutes and costs 4€ ($4.60); buy your ticket onboard. For the same price — but without the local stops — is the half-hourly **SITA bus** (☎ 800-373-760 within Italy or 055-219-383; www.sita-on-line.it) to Florence's bus station at Via Santa Caterina 15r. For around 13€ ($15), you can take a metered taxi from the airport directly to your hotel — about a 15-minute ride.

Most flights from elsewhere in Europe land at **Galileo Galilei Airport** (☎ 050-849-111; www.pisa-airport.it) in Pisa, 60 miles from Florence. Frequent one-hour train service (www.trenitalia.it), which costs 4.95€ to 5.80€ ($5.70–$6.65), connects the airport to Stazione Santa Maria Novella.

Arriving by rail

Trains to Florence pull into **Stazione Santa Maria Novella** (☎ 055-288-765), which is often abbreviated as S.M.N. The station is on the western edge of the city's compact historic center, and is a 10- to 20-minute walk to most hotels and major attractions. If your hotel is not within a reasonable walking distance, or if you simply don't want to haul your luggage through the streets, you can get a taxi at a stand outside the station in the Piazza Stazione.

Orienting Yourself in Florence

Two focal points lie at the core of Florence's *centro storico* (old center): **Piazza di San Giovanni/Piazza del Duomo** around the famous Cathedral and, several blocks to the south, **Piazza della Signoria**, a statue-filled square lined with cafes, the medieval Palazzo Vecchio, and the art-packed Uffizi Galleries. **Via dei Calzaiuoli,** a wide, pedestrian-choked promenade, links the two *piazze* (squares), and the center of medieval Florence takes shape in the maze of cobblestone streets between them.

Introducing the neighborhoods

West of central Florence and in the middle of **Via Roma** is Florence's primary shopping district, the 19th-century **Piazza della Repubblica.** Nearby is the main artery of Florence's high-fashion industry, **Via de' Tornabuoni.** As it heads south, Via Roma changes names — first becoming **Via Calimata,** and then **Via Por Santa Maria.** Farther south along this road you come to **Ponte Vecchio,** a famous bridge over the Arno River, lined with jewelry shops. In the middle of the bridge, some extra space between buildings creates a small piazza with wonderful river views.

Northwest of Piazza del Duomo is **Piazza Santa Maria Novella,** on which sits a church by the same name. The piazza marks the western edge of the historic city. Just north of the church is the train station, which is surrounded by streets full of cheap hotels. Between the station and the Duomo are **Piazza San Lorenzo** and **Piazza del Mercato Centrale** (indoor Central Market). Stalls of leather merchants fill the streets around them.

Three main streets head north from Piazza del Duomo: **Via de' Martelli/ Via Cavour** leads straight up to **Piazza San Marco,** site of the San Marco monastery; **Via Ricasoli** heads to the Accademia, home of Michelangelo's *David;* and **Via dei Servi** runs into the gorgeous **Piazza SS. Annunziata,** bordered on three sides by porticoes designed by Brunelleschi. **Borgo de' Greci** wanders east from Piazza della Signoria to **Piazza Santa Croce,** home to a major church, the center of a neighborhood that has many of Florence's best restaurants, and the eastern edge of the visitor's city.

The **Arno River** flows through the southern end of the city; most of Florence is north of the Arno. South of the river is an old artisan's quarter called the **Oltrarno,** which features the famed Pitti Palace and excellent restaurants and shopping. In the middle of the Oltrarno is **Piazza Santo Spirito,** which contains a fine early Renaissance church interior courtesy of Brunelleschi.

 Florence uses two different systems for numbering addresses. Shops, businesses, and restaurants have plaques with red numbers, but homes, offices, and hotels have plaques numbered *independently* in black (and sometimes blue). Red addresses show an *r* after the number; black ones may have a *b,* but more often have nothing after the number. The two systems overlap but don't affect each other. So this means that a street with a row of buildings designated shop, restaurant, hotel, shop, and home could have address plaques that read, in order, "1r, 3r, 1, 5r, 3." So if nothing appears to be at the address you wrote down, try looking for a plaque with the same number but in a different color.

Finding information after you arrive

The city's largest **tourist office** is at Via Cavour 1r (☎ **055-290-832**; Fax: 055-276-0383; www.firenzeturismo.it), about 3 blocks north of the Duomo. Outrageously, they now charge for basic, useful info: 0.50€ (60¢) for a city map (although there's still a free one that differs only in that it lacks relatively inane brief descriptions of the museums and sights), 2€ ($2.30) for a little guide to museums, and 1€ ($1.15) each for pamphlets on the bridges and the piazza of Florence. The monthly Informacittà pamphlet on events, exhibits, and concerts is still free. Hours are Monday through Saturday from 8:30 a.m. to 6:30 p.m. and Sunday from 8:30 a.m. to 1:30 p.m.

The tourist office at Stazione Santa Maria Novella (☎ **055-212-245**) is outside at Piazza della Stazione 4. This office is usually open Monday through Saturday from 8:30 a.m. to 7:00 p.m. (often until 1:30 p.m. in winter) and Sunday from 8:30 a.m. to 1:30 p.m.

Getting Around Florence

Florence has no subway system, and most of the sights in the central historic district are best seen on foot, but buses and taxis are available as well.

By bus

Even though Florence is pedestrian-friendly, the bus system can help you get your bags from the train station to your hotel or visit the sights farthest outside the central city. Almost all bus routes begin, stop, or end at the train station, and many also pass through Piazza San Marco (near the Accademia, where *David* is housed). Most routes make only three or four stops before heading out of Florence and to the hills. The bus system does not serve the historic center of the city very well, although the new electric minibuses A, B, C, and D do dip into it.

Bus tickets good for 60 minutes cost 1€ ($1.15). You can take as many different rides as you want within the time limit; just stamp one end of your ticket in the orange box on the first bus you board. You can also get a 4.50€ ($5.20) 24-hour ticket and two-, three-, or seven-day tickets for 7.60€ ($8.75), 9.60€ ($11), or 16€ ($18), respectively. Tickets are available at newsstands and in *tabacchi* (tobacconists, marked by a white *T* against a brown background). Stop by the tourist office to pick up a bus map.

By taxi

Taxis are not an economical way to get around town. Their rates are not cheap, and the one-way street system forces the drivers to take convoluted routes; you're usually better off on foot. But taxis are useful when you need to get your luggage between your hotel and the train station in the *centro storico,* where a bus is a rare sight. The station isn't too far from most *centro storico* hotels and shouldn't cost more than 8€ ($9.20).

The standard rate for taxis is .80€ (90¢) per kilometer, with a whopping minimum fare of 2.38€ ($2.75) to start the meter (that rises to 4.03€/$4.65 on Sun; 5.16€/$5.95 10 p.m.–6 a.m.), plus 0.57€ (.65¢) per bag. You can't hail a cab, but you can find one at a **taxi stand** in or near a major piazza; otherwise, you have to call for a radio taxi; try ☎ **055-4242,** 055-4798, or 055-4390.

By foot

Florence's *centro storico* (old center) is small and reserved for pedestrians, so getting around on foot is extremely easy. Walking from one end of this tourist area to the other takes only about 30 minutes. In the evening, join the Florentines for the *passeggiata* on Via dei Calzaiuoli and Via Roma/Via Calimala.

Staying in Florence

You can find any kind of sleeping accommodations in Florence, from crash pads for the economically challenged to restored Renaissance palaces for those with money to burn. Florence is so small that staying anywhere in the *centro storico* puts you within easy walking distance of almost every attraction.

 Keep in mind that the area around the train station (especially immediately to the east) is a boring part of town. Yes, it's packed to the gills with hotels, but these places are more often than not cramped budget joints favored by students. As a last resort, you can almost certainly find a place to sleep just by walking up Via Faenza (the area's main hotel strip) and inquiring at every inn.

If you need help finding a room, the **Consorzio Informazioni Turistiche Alberghiere (ITA)** (near Track 9 in the train station) or the tourism office (near Track 16) can make reservations for you. Both charge a small commission for their services. Or go to the official tourist office's Web site subsection on accommodations at www.toscanaeturismo. net/dovedormire.

Because Florence's *centro storico* is too small to break up into neighborhoods, I describe the location of the hotels and restaurants in this chapter in relation to the closest landmarks.

Florence's top hotels

Grand Hotel Cavour
$$$ Near the Bargello

In the 1860s, this comfortable, centrally located 3-star hotel was made out of a medieval *palazzo* (palace) and has since been outfitted with modern conveniences and standard comforts, all in contemporary good taste. You can take in a breathtaking view of the city's landmarks from the roof terrace, and the front and side rooms look out to the Bargello and Badia towers. The elegant hotel restaurant serves excellent traditional cuisine.

See map p. 426. Via del Proconsolo 3 (next to the Badia). ☎ *055-266-271. Fax: 055-218-955.* www.hotelcavour.com. *Bus: 14, 23, or 71. Rates:186€–218€ ($214–$251) double. Rates include breakfast. AE, DC, MC, V.*

Hotel Bellettini
$$$ Just northwest of the Duomo

Two cordial sisters run this comfortable hotel that sits on a quiet street between the Duomo and the outdoor leather market. The rooms have mostly modern décor, with a few antique pieces and a hint of 19th-century style. The breakfast spread is ample. The place stays busy all year with many repeat guests. In 2000, they added a lovely six-room annex with frescoes, marble bathrooms, minibars, and coffeemakers; doubles there run a bit more, about 170€ ($213).

See map p. 426. Via dei Conti 7 (just off Via dei Cerretani). ☎ *055-213-561. Fax: 055-283-551.* www.hotelbellettini.com. *Bus: A, 1, 6, 7, 10, 11, 14, 17, 22, 23, 36, or 37. Rates: 130€–160€ ($150–$184) double. Rates include breakfast. AE, DC, MC, V.*

Hotel Firenze
$$ Between the Duomo and Palazzo Vecchio

A recent renovation has transformed the Firenze from bare-bones student hangout to a 2-star hotel. Rooms are still simple but will soon have air-conditioning. Although the hotel lacks the warmth and ambience of other hotels in Florence, it's just a few steps away from Florence's major sights.

See map p. 426. Piazza Donati 4 (on Via del Corso, just off Via dei Calzaiuoli). ☎ *055-268-301 or 055-214-203. Fax: 055-212-370. Bus: A, 14, or 23. Rates: 94€ ($108) double. Rates include breakfast. No credit cards.*

Hotel Hermitage
$$$$ Near the Ponte Vecchio and Uffizi

Located on a small piazza near the foot of the Ponte Vecchio, the Hotel Hermitage overlooks the Arno River and its famous old bridge. But the roof terrace has the best view; from there, you can see the nearby Palazzo

Accommodations, Dining, and Attractions in Florence

HOTELS ■
Albergo Mia Cara **12**
Grand Hotel Cavour **10**
Hotel Alessandra **18**
Hotel Bellettini **14**
Hotel Brunelleschi **5**
Hotel Casci **22**
Hotel Firenze **8**
Hotel Hermitage **30**
Hotel Monna Lisa **24**
Hotel Pensione
  Pendini **17**
Hotel Ritz **33**
Hotel Silla **34**

RESTAURANTS ◆
Caffè Cibrèo/
  Trattoria Cibreo **26**
Continetta Antinori **15**
Il Latini **16**
Il Pizzaiolo **25**
Paoli **6**
Ristorante
  Acqua Al 2 **28**
Ristorante Casa di
  Dante (Da Pennello) **7**
Trattoria Antellesi **13**
Trattoria Casalinga **19**
Trattoria Le Mossacce **9**
Trattoria Zà-Zà **21**
Vivoli **29**

ATTRACTIONS ●
Badia **11**
Baptistry **1**
Bargello **27**
Campanile di
  Giotto **3**
The Duomo **2**
Galleria dell'
  Accademia **23**
Museo dell'Opera
  del Duomo **4**
Palazzo Pitti **20**
Piazzale
  Michelangiolo **35**
Santa Croce **32**
The Uffizi
  Galleries **31**

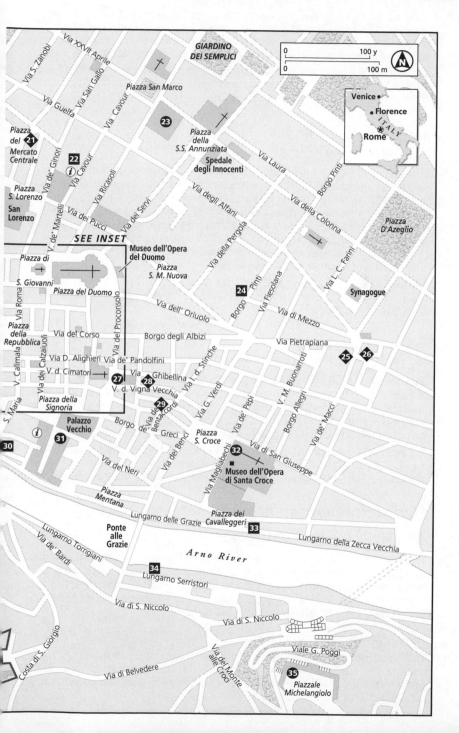

Vecchio. The friendly management serves a filling breakfast, and a 1997 renovation gave most rooms Jacuzzis and wood floors. If you want to step out the door and into the Uffizi in the morning, this is the place to stay.

See map p. 426. Vicolo Marzio 1/Piazza del Pesce (left of the Ponte Vecchio). ☎ 055-287-216. Fax: 055-212-208. www.hermitagehotel.com. *Bus: 23 or 71. Rates: 245€ ($282) double. Rates include breakfast. MC, V.*

Hotel Monna Lisa
$$$$ North of Santa Croce

This eclectic hotel is my splurge choice among Florence's opulent accommodations, most of which look pretty much the same. Oil paintings, sculptures, and lush potted plants fill this hotel, set up like the villa of a wealthy Florentine family. Room décor varies widely, in keeping with the private home atmosphere; you may have a coffered wood ceiling, antique furnishings, or a Jacuzzi gracing your room. In 2002, the owners restructured 15 additional rooms in another, recently acquired building bordering the courtyard and dubbed it "La Limonaia."

See map p. 426. Borgo Pinti 27. ☎ 055-247-9751. Fax: 055-247-9755. www.monnalisa.it. *Bus: B, 14, 23, or 71. Rates: 182€–350€ ($209–$403) double. Rates include breakfast. AE, DC, MC, V.*

Hotel Pensione Pendini
$$ Between the Duomo and Palazzo Vecchio

For more than 100 years, this classic Italian *pensione* has been a favorite of travelers. The devoted regulars appreciate the mix of antiques and modern conveniences in the usually spacious rooms. The hotel rises above the storefronts and cafes of Piazza della Repubblica, is near the major sights, and is right in the middle of Florence's best shopping area.

See map p. 426. Via Strozzi 2 (just through the grand arch of Piazza della Repubblica on the right). ☎ 055-211-170. Fax: 055-281-807. www.hotelpendini.net. *Bus: 22, 36, or 37. Rates: 110€–150€ ($127–$173) double. Rates include breakfast. AE, DC, MC, V.*

Florence's runner-up accommodations

Albergo Mia Cara/Archi Rossi Hostel
$ Near Stazione Santa Maria Novella   This hotel has double-paned windows, spacious no-frills rooms, renovated plumbing, and attractive iron headboards. A hostel (☎ 055-290-804; Fax: 055-230-2601; www.hostelarchirossi.com) is on the hotel's main floor. *See map p. 426. Via Faenza 58 (off Via Nazionale). ☎ 055-216-053. Fax: 055-230-2601.*

Hotel Alessandra
$$ Near the river and Ponte Vecchio   This hotel has spacious high-ceilinged rooms in a 16th-century palazzo. Most rooms have private bath, but it's unlikely you'll have to wait for a shared bathroom. Air-conditioning

is free, but you must request it when you make reservations. *See map p. 426. Borgo SS. Apostoli 17 (between Via dei Tornabuoni and Via Por Santa Maria).* ☎ *055-283-438. Fax: 055-210-619.* www.hotelalessandra.com.

Hotel Brunelleschi

$$$$$ **Near Duomo** This posh property is tucked away within the restored remains of a medieval church and a sixth-century Byzantine tower in the heart of town. The rooms are spacious and very comfortable, with large baths, but they're disappointingly modern. *See map p. 426. Piazza Sant'Elisabetta 3 (off Via de' Calzioli).* ☎ *055-27-370. Fax: 055-219-653.* www.hotel brunelleschi.it.

Hotel Casci

$$ **Near San Lorenzo** Run by the exceedingly helpful Lombardi family, Hotel Casci has a frescoed breakfast room (composer Rossini used to live here). The double-paned windows can't quite block out the traffic from busy Via Cavour, so ask for a room facing the inner courtyard's magnolia tree. The hotel welcomes families. *See map p. 426. Via Cavour 13 (between Via de' Gori and Via Guelfa).* ☎ *055-211-686. Fax: 055-239-6461.* www.hotelcasci. com.

Hotel Ritz

$$$ **Between Santa Croce and the river** The Hotel Ritz is one of the more intimate hotels on the Arno River, with modern, mix-and-match furniture and iron-ornamented bed frames. Two rooms on the front of the hotel have balconies to better enjoy the Arno view, and two on the back (numbers 37 and 38) have small private terraces. *See map p. 426. Lungarno della Zecca Vecchia 24.* ☎ *055-234-0650. Fax: 055-240-863.* www.hotelritz.net.

Hotel Silla

$$$ **South of the river** Every room is unique in this 15th-century palazzo on a shaded riverside piazza. Some rooms have beamed ceilings and parquet floors, while others have floral wallpaper and stylish furnishings. Many rooms overlook the Arno. *See map p. 426. Via dei Renai 5 (on Piazza Demidoff, east of Ponte delle Grazie).* ☎ *055-234-2888. Fax: 055-234-1437.* www.hotelsilla.it.

Dining in Florence

If enjoyed in traditional fashion, a Florentine meal can take a few hours to finish. The multiple courses begin with an appetizer, traditionally *affettati misti* (assorted salami) and *crostini misti* (round toast and toppings such as liver pâté, mushrooms, tomatoes, and cheese). Your first course (called the *primo*) could be a soup — try the stewlike *ribollita* (vegetables, beans, and bread). You may get one of these pastas as your *primo* instead: *spaghetti alla carrettiera* (in a spicy tomato sauce) or *al pomodoro* (in a plain tomato sauce), *pappardelle al cinghiale* (wide noodles in a wild boar sauce), or *crespelle Fiorentine* (pasta layered with cheese and béchamel sauce).

The main course *(secondo)* could be a *pollo* (chicken) dish, *scallopine* (veal cutlets, cooked in one of several ways), *lombatina di vitello* (veal chop), *involtini* (veal rolled with veggies and stewed in its own juices), or *bistecca Fiorentina* (steak grilled and brushed with olive oil and pepper). The waiter will expect you to order a side dish (a *contorno*) to go with this main dish, and *fagioli* — white Tuscan cannellini beans (sometimes served *all'uccelleto,* stewed with sage and tomatoes) — are the tastiest choice.

Florence makes some of the world's best ice cream, called *gelato,* and no visit is complete without indulging. The city's most renowned purveyor of the cool, creamy snack is **Vivoli** (☎ 055-292-334) at Via Isole delle Stinche 7r, off Via Ghibellina west of Santa Croce. Other ice-cream parlors around town are good, too; just look for a sign saying it is *produzione propria* (homemade).

The countryside around Florence is famous across the globe for its wines — especially red Chianti classico, which is generally the house table wine at a Florentine restaurant. You may also want to try the more complex (and expensive) reds from southern Tuscany: Vino Nobile di Montepulciano and Brunello di Montalcino (perfect for a *bistecca alla fiorentina*).

Restaurants in Florence universally add a mandatory "bread and cover" charge *(pane e coperto)* to your bill of about 1€ to 10€ (1.15€–$12).

For great take-out food, go to any *tavola calda* (literally "hot table") or *rosticceria* (a *tavola calda* restaurant that also serves spit-roasted chicken), where delicious, pre-prepared hot meals are sold by weight. Try **Giuliano's** (☎ 055-238-2723) at Via dei Neri 74. For a true Florentine experience, try the boiled tripe sandwich called *lampredotto* at the street stand in front of the American Express office on Piazza de' Cimatori. For a quick bite, don't buy slices of pizza in Florence; you'll get the wrong impression of Italian pizza, which is only good if it comes from Rome or southernmost Italy. For picnic supplies, try any of the *alimentari* (grocery stores) or *forno* (bakeries).

Florence's top restaurants

Caffè Cibrèo/Trattoria Cibreo
$$$ North of Santa Croce FLORENTINE

This is two restaurants in one: a rustically elegant *ristorante* on one side of the kitchen and a less-expensive trattoria on the other (with an abridged selection of the same dishes). This famous haven for food aficionados changes its menu daily, depending on what was freshest that morning at the market next door. The menu does not have any typically Tuscan pastas or grilled meat, but the kitchen's savory creations are still based on traditional Florentine recipes (with an occasional modern touch).

See map p. 426. Via A. del Verrocchio 5r (at San Ambrogio Market, off Via de' Macchi). ☎ **055-234-5853.** *Reservations recommended for the restaurant (☎ **055-234-1100**), not accepted at the trattoria (come early). Bus: A, C, or 14. Main courses: 6€–13€ ($6.90–$15) at restaurant; 10€ ($12) at trattoria. AE, DC, MC, V restaurant only. No credits cards in trattoria. Open: Lunch and dinner Tues–Sat. Closed late July to early Sept.*

Il Latini

$ **Near Santa Maria Novella** **TUSCAN**

This traditional trattoria has managed to keep its food authentic despite becoming a tourist favorite. Join the throng at the door at 7:30 p.m. and wait to be seated at communal tables under wood beams with hanging prosciuttos. The restaurant has a menu, but most people choose the unofficial set meal, which includes a *primo* (soup or pasta), a choice from an overflowing platter of roasted meats for your main course, dessert, and all the house wine you can drink.

See map p. 426. Via del Palchetti 6r (off Via d. Vigna Nuova). ☎ **055-210-916.** *Reservations highly recommended (but show up early). Bus: A, B, 6, 11, 36, or 37. Main courses: 6€–16€ ($6.90–$18); fixed-price meal 30€–35€ ($35–$40). AE, DC, MC, V. Open: Lunch and dinner Tues–Sun. Closed 15 days in Aug and Dec 24.*

Ristorante Acqua Al 2

$$$ **Just behind the Bargello** **TUSCAN/ITALIAN**

Some of the best pasta in Florence is served under the barrel-vaulted ceilings of this popular restaurant. Sample the *assaggio dei primi,* a tasty platter of five flavorful first courses. And if you still have room for a main course, try the poor Tuscan's steak: a perfectly grilled giant portobello mushroom.

See map p. 426. Via della Vigna Vecchia 40r. ☎ **055-284-170.** www.acquaal2.com. *Reservations required. Bus: A, 14, or 23. Main courses: 7€–17€ ($8.05–$20). AE, MC, V. Open: Dinner daily. Closed one week in Aug.*

Ristorante Casa di Dante (Da Pennello)

$$ **Between the Duomo and Palazzo Vecchio** **FLORENTINE**

This classic Florentine restaurant is descended from a 16th-century *osteria* (the term once used for a place with a limited menu of basic fare, most likely simple pastas and wine). One of the keys to Da Pennello's success is its famed antipasto table, a buffet of vegetables, fish, and other delicacies. Prices vary, but you can expect to spend 5€ to 9€ ($5.75–$10) for a sampling. The rest of the meal here is good, too, with spaghetti in a spicy tomato sauce, grilled sea bass, and the Florentine sponge-cake-and-mousse *zucotto* dessert heading up the list.

See map p. 426. Via Dante Alghieri 4r. ☎ **055-294-848.** *Reservations recommended. Bus: A, 14, or 23. Main courses: 5.50€–13€ ($6.35–$15); fixed-price menu 20€ ($23). AE, MC, V. Open: Lunch and dinner Tues–Sat. Closed Aug.*

Trattoria Antellesi
$$$ Near the Medici Chapels   ITALIAN

The young Florence/Arizona combination of chef Enrico and manager/ sommelier Janice Verrecchia run this attractive spot in a converted Renaissance *palazzo*. The smiling staff will talk you through a memorable dinner that should start with their signature antipasto of pecorino cheese and pears. Follow with *crespelle alla fiorentina* (crepes stuffed with ricotta and spinach and baked) or spaghetti *alla chiantigiana* (pasta with Chianti-marinated beef cooked in tomato sauce).

See map p. 426. Via Faenza 9r. ☎ *055-216-990. Reservations required. Main courses 10€–13€ ($12–$15). AE, DC, MC, V. Open: Lunch and dinner Mon–Sat.*

Trattoria Le Mossacce
$$ Near the Bargello   FLORENTINE

The best Italian meals are usually served in simple, small trattorie such as this one, where businessmen, farmers, and a few in-the-know tourists have been lining up to take their turn at the hearty Tuscan dishes since 1942. The *ribollita* (a stew-like mix of vegetables, beans, and bread) is bested only by the *crespelle* (pasta layered with cheese and béchamel sauce), and the *involtini* (veal rolled with veggies) are splendid.

See map p. 426. Via del Proconsolo 55r (near the Bargello). ☎ *055-294-361. Reservations suggested for dinner. Bus: A, 14, or 23. Main courses: 4.20€–14€ ($4.85–$16). AE, MC, V. Open: Lunch and dinner Mon– Fri.*

Florence's runner-up restaurants

Cantinetta Antinori
$$$$$ At the top of Via Tornabuoni   The Antinori marchesi started their wine empire 26 generations ago, and, taking their cue from an ancient vintner tradition, installed a wine bar in their 15th-century palazzo 30 years ago. Today, it maks the msot refined shopping stop on Via Tornabuoni, and a fabulous place to dine on refined cuisine and award-winning wines. *See map p. 426. Palazzo Antinori, Piazza Antinori 3.* ☎ *055-292-234.* www.antinori.it.

Il Pizzaiolo
$$ Near Santa Croce   Here you find Florence's only decent pizzeria — probably because the cook is from Naples, where the stuff was invented. Even with a reservation, expect a wait. Without one on weekends, forget it: Locals love this place. *See map p. 426. Via de' Macci 113r (at the corner of Via Pietrapiana).* ☎ *055-241-171.*

Paoli
$$$$ Between the Duomo and Piazza della Signoria Paoli   More popular with visitors than locals, this is still one of the city's finest restaurants. Paoli turns out a host of specialties but could be recommended almost

solely for its medieval-tavern atmosphere. All pastas are homemade, and the fettuccine alla Paoli is served piping hot and full of flavor. *See map p. 426. Via dei Tavolini 12r.* ☎ *055-216-215.*

Trattoria Casalinga

$ Between Via Maggio and Piazza Santo Spirito It's a bit noisy and service can be surly, but the heaping platters of home cooking are delicious and the prices can't be beat. *See map p. 426. Via Michelozzi 9r.* ☎ *055-267-9243.*

Trattoria Zà-Zà

$$$$ Near Piazza del Mercato Centrale This trattoria sits across from the central food market and is patronized by its stall owners, so you know the ingredients are prime. Picture lots of wood benches, Chianti bottles, and thick steaks. *See map p. 426. Piazza Mercato Centrale 26r.* ☎ *055-215-411.* www.trattoriazaza.it.

Exploring Florence

The art and architecture of Florence attracts an overwhelming number of visitors. In summer, you can wait in line for two hours just to buy a ticket for the Uffizi Galleries — no joke. I highly recommend that you reserve your Uffizi ticket ahead of time by calling **Firenze Musei** at ☎ **055-294-883** or visiting them on the Web at www.firenzemusei.it. This is one thing I always book even before I leave the United States. At Firenze Musei, you can also reserve tickets for the Accademia Gallery (avoiding another interminable line to see the *David*), as well as the Galleria Palatina in the Pitti Palace and the Bargello (although you don't really need reservations for those last two). There is a 1.55€ ($1.80) fee — worth every penny.

For a note about museum and business hours in Italy, see the sidebar "Everyday's a Roman holiday," in Chapter 19.

Florence's top attractions

Bargello (Sculpture Gallery)

What the Uffizi is to Renaissance painting, the Bargello is to sculpture from the same era. You can spend 45 minutes here or, if you get really engrossed, two hours. The collection includes early works by Michelangelo, including a tipsy *Bacchus*, the *Madonna of the Stairs*, and a *Bust of Brutus* that may be a semi-self-portrait. Be sure to see the works by Donatello, the first great sculptor of the Renaissance. A huge second-floor room contains some of his masterpieces, including a mischievous bronze *Cupid* and two versions of a *David* — an early marble work and a bronze that depicts the Biblical hero as a young boy.

See map p. 426. Via del Proconsolo 4. ☎ *055-238-8606.* www.sbas.firenze.it. *Ticket reservations: 055-294-883* or www.firenzemusei.it. *Bus: A, 14, or 23.*

Admission: 4€ ($4.60). Open: Tues–Sat 8:15 a.m.–1:50 p.m. Also open first, third, and fifth Mon of every month and second and fourth Sun.

The Duomo (Cathedral), Battistero (Baptistery), and Campanile di Giotto (Giotto's Bell Tower)

The Duomo of Florence is decorated in festive white, green, and pink marble, with an extravagant neo-Gothic facade from the 18th century, all capped by a huge brick-red dome that extends nobly into the skyline. The cathedral is joined on its bustling square by the Baptistery, Giotto's Bell Tower, and a museum — a group of buildings that together take about three hours to see.

If you're pressed for time and want to see all three buildings in one visit, keep in mind that the Baptistery is only open in the afternoon. The cathedral closes first, so make that the initial stop. Climbing either Brunelleschi's dome (463 steps) or Giotto's Bell Tower (414 steps) takes about an hour.

Florence's cathedral appears to be inside out — nicely decorated on the outside but rather drab inside. I recommend that you enjoy it in front on the little piazza, where visitors gather and musicians and artists display their talents. Inside, you can see some interesting early Renaissance frescoes that are colorful but not particularly good. In the crypt are the remains of an earlier church, Santa Reparata, on the same site. Be sure to wander to the back-left corner of the cathedral to admire the bronze doors (by Luca della Robbia).

Climb the cathedral's 348-foot-high dome both for its panoramic view and to see Brunelleschi's architectural marvel up close. At the time, experts told him he could never build a dome that big without using scaffolding and supports that would be too costly to build. Brunelleschi proved them wrong by using the secrets of Rome's Pantheon (distributing the weight on embedded stone ribs and building the dome with two shells, which both get thinner nearing the top and center).

To the right of the cathedral is what's known as Giotto's Bell Tower, even though that early Renaissance painter designed and built only the first two levels. Several architects finished it (using their own styles), and the tower became "The Lily of Florence," a 277-foot-high marble pillar with slender windows. If climbing the Duomo's dome didn't tire you out, try clambering up this monument, too — and without the crowds found at the dome. The view's not quite so sweeping, but you get a great close-up of the neighboring dome.

The Baptistery, across from the Duomo, is the oldest building of the group, dating back to between the fourth and seventh centuries. Its bronze doors covered with relief panels are famous; Michelangelo once called them "The Gates of Paradise," and the name stuck. The grandest are the ones facing the Duomo, which were cast by Ghiberti from 1425 to 1453 (although they have since been replaced by replicas). These large panels show the artist's skill in using perspective and composition to tell complicated stories. Inside, glittering 13th-century mosaics cover the Baptistery, and a cone-shaped ceiling contains a highly detailed *Last Judgment* scene presided over by an enormous Christ.

The Museo dell'Opera Del Duomo (Museum of Cathedral Works) is right behind the cathedral at Piazza del Duomo 9. The museum holds all the statues removed from the outside of the cathedral in order to save them from the elements. The rooms are also filled with early works by Andrea Pisano, Arnolfo di Cambio, and Luca della Robbia, as well as the expressive statues of Donatello, including a wooden *Mary Magdalen* and the leering bald prophet *Habbakuk* (called "Pumpkinhead" by locals). The original panels from Ghiberti's *Gates of Paradise* are gradually being brought out for display as they're cleaned. One of Michelangelo's *Pietà* sculptures, depicting Mary and the dying Jesus (there's another at St. Peter's Basilica in Rome), is on the landing between the first and second floors; the figure of Nicodemus in the back is a self-portrait.

See map p. 426. Piazza del Duomo/Piazza di San Giovanni. ☎ 055-230-2885. www. peraduomo.firenze.it. Bus: A, 1, 6, 7, 10, 11, 14, 17, 22, 23, 36, or 37. Admissions: **Duomo**, free; **Santa Reparata excavations**, 3€ ($3.45) adults, 5 and under free; **dome**, 6€ ($6.90) adults, 5 and under free. **Baptistery**, 3€ ($3.45), 5 and under free. **Giotto's Bell Tower**, 6€ ($6.90). **Museo dell'Opera**, 6€ ($6.90), 5 and under free. Open: **Duomo, Santa Reparata excavations**, and **dome**, Mon–Wed and Fri 10 a.m.–5 p.m.; Thurs 10 a.m.–3:30 p.m.; first Sat of month 10 a.m. to noon and 3–4:20 p.m.; other Sat 10 a.m.– 4:45 p.m.; Sun 1:30–4:45 p.m. (open Sun morning for services only); free tours Mon–Sat every 40 minutes 10:30 a.m. to noon and 3–4:20 p.m. **Baptistery**, Mon–Sat noon to 7 p.m., Sun 8:30 a.m.–2 p.m. (last admission 30 minutes before close). **Giotto's Bell Tower**, daily 8:30 a.m.–7:30 p.m. (last admission 30 minutes before close). **Museo dell'Opera**, Mon–Sat 9 a.m.–7:30 p.m., Sun 9 a.m.–1:40 p.m. (last admission 40 minutes before close).

Galleria dell'Accademia (Michelangelo's David)

Many visitors come to Florence with one question on their lips: "Which way to the *David?*" The Accademia contains many magnificent paintings (by Perugino, Botticelli, Pontormo, and others) plus Giambologna's plaster study for the *Rape of the Sabines,* but most people come for one thing only.

In 1501, Michelangelo took a huge piece of marble that a previous sculptor had declared unusable and by 1504 had carved a Goliath-sized *David,* a masterpiece of the male nude. The sculpture is so realistic — the weight shifted onto one leg, the sling held nonchalantly on the shoulder — that it changed how people thought about sculpting the human body. *David* stood in front of the Palazzo Vecchio until 1873 (a replica is there now); the location inside this gallery makes the sculpture look a little oversized, giving it an awkward feel.

The hall leading to the *David* is lined with Michelangelo's *nonfiniti* (unfinished) *Slaves.* Many people find these statues more compelling than the oversized nude in the next room. These *Slaves* are in varying stages of completion and shed light on how Michelangelo approached his craft — fully finishing the abdomen before moving on to rough out limbs and faces. The title of the work is rather fitting because these muscular figures seem to be struggling to emerge from their stony prisons.

At the peak of the summer season, lines start forming early outside the Accademia and can stretch for blocks. Bypass the lines by reserving ahead at the number listed here. If you show up when the museum first opens and don't have a long wait, you can pop in and admire *David* in about 20 minutes, but it takes at least 45 minutes to wander through the rest of the Accademia's collection.

See map p. 426. Via Ricasoli 58–60. ☎ 055-238-8609 or 055-238-8612. www.sbas. firenze.it/accademia. *Reservations at ☎ 055-294-883 or* www.firenze musei.it. *Bus: C, 1, 6, 7, 11, 17, 20, 25, 31, 32, 33. Admission: 6.50€ ($7.50). Open: Tues–Sun 8:15 a.m.–6:50 p.m (last admission ½ hour before close).*

Palazzo Pitti (Pitti Palace)

On the south side of the Arno River, this huge palace, once home to the Medici grand dukes, now houses several museums and an impressive painting gallery. You'd be hard-pressed to visit all six of the museums *and* the Boboli Gardens in one day, but one and a half to two hours should be enough for you to run through the main paintings collection, the **Galleria Palatina** (☎ 055-238-8614). These lavish rooms are appointed to look much the way they did in the 1700s, with works by a mind-boggling list of late-Renaissance and baroque geniuses such as Caravaggio, Rubens, Perugino, Giorgione, Guido Reni, Fra Bartolomeo, Tintoretto, Botticelli, and many more. The selection of works by Raphael, Titian, and Andrea del Sarto is particularly good. Admission is 6.50€ ($7.50). Hours are Tuesday to Sunday from 8:15 a.m. to 6:50 p.m. (may stay open later daily in summer).

Your ticket to the Galleria Palatina also allows for admission to the **Apartamenti Reali,** or Royal Apartments (which shares a telephone number with Galleria Palatina). The Italian royal family lived in the Pitti Palace itself during the brief time that Florence was the capital of a newly unified Italy in the 1870s. Although they aren't nearly as nice as those at Versailles or other northern European palaces, they are still a sight to behold with their rich fabrics, frescoes, and oil paintings. The apartments are open the same hours as the Palatina but are closed in January.

If you can only see two parts of the Pitti Palace, make them the Galleria Palatina, described earlier, and the **Boboli Gardens** (☎ 055-265-1816), one of the finest Renaissance gardens anywhere. Designed between 1549 and 1656, and located behind the Pitti Palace, the gardens feature statues, fountains, grottoes, a rococo *kaffehaus* for summer refreshment, and some nice wooded areas to walk in. In 1589, the Medici held a wedding reception in the Boboli Gardens and hired Jacopo Peri and Ottavio Rinuccini to provide musical entertainment. The composers came up with the idea of setting a classical story to music and having actors sing the whole thing — the birth of opera. Admission is 4€ ($4.60) for adults, free under 18 and over 60. The park is open daily from 8:15 a.m. to dusk. ("Dusk" is 5 p.m. Nov–Feb; 6 p.m. in Mar and Oct; 7 p.m. Apr, May, and Sept; and 8 p.m. in June and Aug.) The gardens are closed the first and last Monday of each month.

As for other sites in the Pitti Palace, the **Galleria d'Arte Moderna,** or Modern Art Gallery (☎ 055-238-8601), has some good works by the *Macchiaioli* school, the Tuscan version of Impressionism. The **Galleria del Costume,** or Costume Gallery (☎ 055-238-8713), has some wonderful dresses that date back to the 1500s. The **Museo degli Argenti,** or Silver Museum (☎ 055-238-8709), is a decorative arts collection that shows off the grand duke's consistently bad taste but does have kitsch appeal. The Galleria d'Arte Moderna and the The Galleria del Costume charges 5€ ($5.75), and the Museo degli Argenti charges 2€ ($2.30). All are open daily from 8:30 a.m. to 1:50 p.m. (closed the first, third, and fifth Mondays and the second and fourth Sundays of each month).

See map p. 426. Piazza dei Pitti (cross the Ponte Vecchio and follow Via Guicciardini). ☎ *055-294-883 for all or individual numbers listed earlier.* www.sbas.firenze.it. *For reservations:* ☎ *055-294-883 or* www.firenzemusei.it *(3€/$3.45 fee). See descriptions earlier for open hours. Bus: D, 11, 36, or 37. Admission: See earlier for individual fees; shared ticket for Galleria Palatina, Boboli Gardens, Galleria d'Arte Moderna, and Museo degli Argenti: 11€ ($13).*

Santa Croce

This large Franciscan church on the city's western edge is the Westminster Abbey of the Renaissance. The church houses the tombs of several household names: Michelangelo, composer Rossini (*Barber of Seville* and the *William Tell Overture*), political thinker/writer Machiavelli, and astronomer and physicist Galileo.

The church also has a monument to poetic giant Dante Alighieri, who was exiled from his beloved Florence on trumped-up charges during a period of political turmoil and whose bones rest in the city of Ravenna, where he died just after completing his masterpiece, the *Divine Comedy* (of which the famed *Inferno* is but one-third).

Inside you can also see two chapels covered by the frescoes of Giotto, an ex-shepherd who became the forefather of the Renaissance in the early 14th century. Near the chapels, a corridor leads through the gift shop to the famed leather school (pricey, but very high quality).

Admission to the church also gets you into the **Museo dell'Opera di Santa Croce.** This museum houses many of the artistic victims of the 1966 Arno flood, including Cimabue's *Crucifix,* as well as the Cappella de' Pazzi, designed by Brunelleschi. Enter through a door to the right of the church facade. The church and museum share the same open hours.

See map p. 426. Piazza Santa Croce. ☎ *055-244-619. Bus: B, 13, 23, or 71. Admission: 4€ ($4.60). Open: Mon–Sat 9:30 a.m.–5:30 p.m., Sun 1–5:30 p.m.*

The Uffizi Galleries

The Uffizi Galleries are a visual primer on the growth of the Renaissance from the 13th to the 18th centuries. Although it's not nearly as big as other famous galleries, such as the Louvre or the Vatican, the Uffizi still ranks among the world's best. Come here for quality, not quantity, with room after room of recognized masterpieces. You can easily spend all day here, but the super-fast visit takes about three hours.

Your exploration of the Uffizi gets off to a fast start in the first room with a trio of giant *Maestà* paintings tracing the birth of the Renaissance — from the rigid, Byzantine style of Cimabue, through Gothic elements from Sienese great Duccio, to the innovative work by Giotto, who broke painting out of its static mold and gave it life, movement, depth, and emotion. From there, you move through rooms featuring the work of early Sienese masters, such as Pietro Lorenzetti and Simone Martini, and then continue on to Florentine and other Tuscan virtuosos such as Fra' Angelico, Masaccio, Piero della Francesca, Paolo Uccello, and Filippo Lippi.

Next, you enter a huge room dedicated to Botticelli and focused on his two most famous works, *The Birth of Venus* (the woman rising out of a seashell) and *The Allegory of Spring*. Visitors tend to crowd in front of these for 20 minutes at a time, so you may have to wait to get a good view. In the meantime, you can enjoy lesser-known works by Boticelli and his contemporary Ghirlandaio, who taught a young Michelangelo how to fresco. After this, you can see works by Signorelli and Perugino; a young Leonardo da Vinci's *Annunciation;* and rooms filled with northern European art from the pre- and early-Renaissance eras (Dürer, Cranach, Hans Holbein the Younger) and Venetian masters such as Correggio, Bellini, and Giorgione.

After you move to the second corridor, Michelangelo's colorful *Holy Family* signals your entry into the High Renaissance. Michelangelo's use of startling colors and his attention to detail in the twisting bodies influenced a generation of artists called *mannerists,* whose paintings are on display in the next few rooms. Works by mannerist artists (Rosso Fiorentino, Pontormo, Andrea del Sarto, and Parmigianino) are mixed with paintings by such famous names as Raphael, Titian, and Caravaggio.

In the spring of 2004, Italy's minister of culture announced plans to open the first floor of the Uffizi for exhibition space, doubling its size and allowing for the display of as many as 800 works of art. At press time, reports suggested that work, which should begin in the summer of 2004, could be completed in 2006. The expansion is intended to make the Uffizi one of Europe's premier art museums, on a par with museums the size of Paris's Louvre or Madrid's Prado (although in terms of quality of art, the Uffizi already is). In the mean time, though, it's not clear what effect — if any — the renovation work will have on vistors to the Uffizi.

See map p. 426. Piazzale degli Uffizi 6 (off Piazza della Signoria). ☎ *055-238-8651.* www.uffizi.firenze.it. *Reservations:* ☎ *055-294-883 or* www.firenze musei.it. *Bus: A, B, 23, or 71. Admission: 8€ ($9.20), free under 18 and over 60. Open: Tues–Sun 8:15 a.m.–7 p.m. Ticket window closes 45 minutes before museum.*

More cool things to see and do

✔ **Striking a bargain at the outdoor leather market:** How are your negotiation skills? Around San Lorenzo church, stalls peddling imitation Gucci merchandise, souvenir T-shirts, jewelry, wallets, and lots of leather fill the streets. Many stalls are just extensions of the stores behind them. Every owner seems to speak fluent English, so be ready for the hard sell.

If you're tough and patient, you can buy goods at a reasonable price. If not, at least you get to experience a carnival of colors and noise, a welcome, down-to-earth break from all that art. Just be alert to pickpockets. The stalls stay open from 8 a.m. to 8 p.m. (later if business is booming) daily March through October, and Tuesday to Saturday November through February.

✔ **Visiting Dante's stomping grounds:** The labyrinth of narrow, cobbled streets between the Duomo and Piazza della Signoria still look a lot like they did in the 13th century when statesman and poet Dante Alghieri lived in the neighborhood. **Dante's house (Casa di Dante),** located appropriately on Via Dante Alghieri, is typical of the era (actually, nobody is sure which building Dante lived in, so a representative one was chosen). Inside is a museum (☎ 055-219-416) that traces the poet's life. Around the corner, at the **Badia Fiorentina** church, Dante first laid eyes on Beatrice, the woman he loved from afar and the inspiration for his best poems. The museum is open Monday and Wednesday through Saturday from 10 a.m. to 6 p.m. (to 4 p.m. in winter) and Sunday from 10 a.m. to 2 p.m. Admission has skyrocketed to 6.50€ ($7.50), so only die-hard fans should bother.

✔ **Shopping on Via de' Tornabuoni:** Florence shares the top spot on the hill of Italian high fashion with Milan. Pucci, Gucci, Beltrami, and Ferragamo all established themselves in Florence, and their flagship stores make for some interesting browsing even if you didn't bring your gold card. Florence has several shopping districts, but the best concentration lies along **Via de' Tornabuoni,** Florence's Fifth Avenue, and its side streets. On Via de' Tornabuoni itself, you can stroll past Ferragamo (4r–14r), Beltrami (48r), and Gucci (73r). Buccellati (71r) specializes in jewelry and silver.

Along nearby **Via della Vigna Nuova,** you find styles from Italy's fashion guru Armani (51r) and Tuscan Enrico Coveri (25r to 29r), as well as stylish women's clothes at Alex (19r). Italy also has more than its share of industrial design gurus. Stop by Controluce (89r) to see some beautifully designed light fixtures.

✔ **Catching the view from Piazzale Michelangiolo:** Bus number 13 snakes up the hills of the artisan's quarter called Oltrarno to Piazzale Michelangiolo, a plateau packed with visitors snapping photos of the Florentine panorama spread before them. Just up the road is a Romanesque church called **San Miniato,** which contains some good medieval art and has a lovely, geometrically precise facade. (Incidentally, this facade made up the original view from the hotel window in E. M. Forster's *A Room with a View*.)

✔ **Spending an afternoon in Fiesole:** You can experience a bit of Tuscan village life with a ride on Florence's number 7 bus. Older than Florence and overlooking it from above, the hilltop Etruscan village of Fiesole has a few sights, cafes on the main square, and best of all, a cool mountain breeze on even the hottest summer days.

A tourism office (☎ 055-598-720; www.comune.fiesole.fi.it), Piazza Mino 37, is on your right as you step off the bus. Stop by the 11th-century cathedral, which contains some delicate Mino da Fiesole carvings, and then go up (*way* up) Via San Francesco to the panoramic gardens overlooking a picture-perfect view of Florence down in the valley.

Perhaps the most popular sight in Feisole is the ruins of the Roman theater and baths (☎ 055-59-118; www.fiesolemusei.it), an excavation that has a temple from the fourth century B.C., a theater from the first century B.C. (which now hosts summertime concerts under the stars), and a few arches still standing from some first century A.D. baths.

Guided tours

American Express, Via Dante Alighieri 22r (☎ 055-50-981), teams with venerable **CAF Tours,** Via Roma 4 (☎ 055-283-200; www.caftours.com), to offer two half-day bus tours of town (39€/$45), including visits to the Uffizi, the Medici Chapels, and Piazzale Michelangiolo. Call for departure times and other specifics.

Suggested itineraries

If you don't like tour buses and would prefer to discover Florence and the surrounding region on your own, this section provides some suggested plans of attack.

If you have one day

If you want to see Florence in a day, you won't have time to pace yourself. It's art-on-the-run time. To help keep up the pace, make advance reservations at both the Accademia and the Uffizi (see listings for details). By 8:15 a.m., be at the **Accademia** to see *David*. Spend no more than 30 minutes here so you can be admiring Ghiberti's *Gates of Paradise* in front of the **Duomo** by 10 a.m. Seeing the inside of the Duomo itself takes only 15 minutes, but you may want to give yourself another hour to make it up to the top of Brunelleschi's dome.

After lunch, make your way to **Santa Croce** to pay your respects to the earthly remains of Michelangelo and Galileo and to see Giotto's frescoes.

You may also want to pop into the famous leather school. Exit the piazza on the north end. Take a right on Via Verdi and an immediate left onto Via dei Lavatoi, which spills out onto Via Isola delle Stinche right above the **Vivoli ice cream parlor,** home of the best gelato in the city. Enjoy your midafternoon snack.

Next, head west to get in line at the **Uffizi.** Peruse some of the greatest art Italy has to offer, until they kick you out just before 7 p.m. In the twilight, wander amid the statues of **Piazza della Signoria** and get an eyeful of the **Palazzo Vecchio.** Stroll across the Ponte Vecchio before dinner and wander back through the medieval heart of Florence between Piazza della Signoria and the Duomo after a dinner with plenty of good wine.

If you have two days

On **Day 1,** be in line at the **Accademia** when it opens; spend about 45 minutes, then move on to **San Marco** and its Fra' Angelico frescoes, which will gobble up an hour or so. Stop in the **Palazzo Medici-Riccardi** to see the frescoed Magi Chapel, then visit **San Lorenzo** and its Medici Tombs by Michelangelo. Now it's time for some lunch, perhaps including some haggling at the outdoor leather stalls in this district. After lunch, head to the **Duomo** and the **Baptistery.** Don't spend more than one and a half hours here, including climbing the dome for its spectacular view. Make your way to the **Uffizi** and spend the rest of the afternoon looking around until it closes.

On **Day 2,** start off at the frescoed church of **Santa Maria Novella** and its museum. Next, head over to the **Bargello** sculpture museum and admire all its Donatello and Michelangelo statues. Have a lunch on the go so you don't miss anything, and spend the *riposo* hours (1–4 p.m.) visiting the tombs of famous Florentines, Giotto frescoes, and the leather school in **Santa Croce.** Next, head across the **Ponte Vecchio** into the Oltrarno district and make your way to **Santa Maria del Carmine** to see Masaccio's groundbreaking frescoes in the Brancacci Chapel. Stop by **Santo Spirito** when it opens at 4 p.m., but then hightail it over to the **Pitti Palace** and get into the painting gallery.

If you have three days

Spend **Day 1** and **Day 2** as indicated in the preceding section. On the morning of **Day 3,** take the bus up to **Fiesole** to enjoy the city's cool pleasures and Roman ruins. Get back to Florence for lunch, and afterward go back to **Palazzo Pitti,** this time to stroll amid the Boboli Gardens. Later in the afternoon, take in a few of the churches you've missed — **Santa Trínita, Ognissanti,** the **Badia** — or just wander the medieval streets. Shoppers may want to revisit the leather market or hit the fashion strip of Via de' Tornabuoni. Art lovers can head back to the Uffizi.

Traveling Beyond Florence

Several worthwhile sites make easy daytrips from Florence. My favorites are Pisa, Siena, and San Gimignano. Each one has its own unique allure.

Pisa: The Leaning Tower and more

When Pisa was one of the maritime commerce centers of the world from the 11th to the 13th centuries, it used its wealth to develop a new religious center for the city. This Campo dei Miracoli, or "Field of Miracles," is a series of simple but beautiful marble buildings with an Eastern-influenced design that became known as Pisan Romanesque. The listing *campanile,* or bell tower, attracts hordes of visitors to Pisa each year to pose for snapshots of themselves holding up the Leaning Tower.

You can see Pisa's main sights comfortably in two to three hours, which makes it a good half-day trip from Florence (consider picnicking on the grass in front of the Leaning Tower before heading back).

Getting there

Trains leave Florence for Pisa every half-hour; the trip takes 60 to 75 minutes. From the Pisa train station, bus number 1 (or a 15-minute walk) takes you to the Piazza del Duomo (also known as Campo dei Miracoli).

A tiny tourism office sits to the left of the train station exit (☎ **050-42-291**), but the main **tourism office** is just outside the Porta Santa Maria gate on the west end of the Campo dei Miracoli at Via C. Cammeo 2 (☎ **050-560-464**; www.pisa.turismo.toscana.it).

Seeing the sights

The **Campo dei Miracoli** is one of the most picturesque squares in Italy. Gleaming white-and-gray-striped Romanesque and Gothic buildings deck the huge, grassy area. The cathedral bell tower, better known as the **Leaning Tower,** is attractive enough to draw attention even if it didn't tilt so curiously. This long cylinder of white marble threaded with colonnade arches is one of the prettiest towers you may ever see.

Because all that marble is too heavy for the sandy soil to support, the tower started tilting right away in the 12th century. When builders tried to correct the tilt during construction, they inadvertently gave the tower a slight banana-like curve. In 1990, engineers determined that the tower's slant — 15 feet from center — made it too dangerous for visitors, and the tower was closed. For years it sat with steel bands belted around it to keep the masonry from falling apart and ugly lead weights stacked on one side to slow further tipping. In 1997, engineers removed 70 tons of soil from the foundation's high side so the tower could gradually tip back. When, in December 2001, the tower was deemed safe (now only 13½ feet off-center), it was reopened to the public — but with a new and highly restricted admissions policy. Guided visits last 30 minutes, are limited to

Tuscany

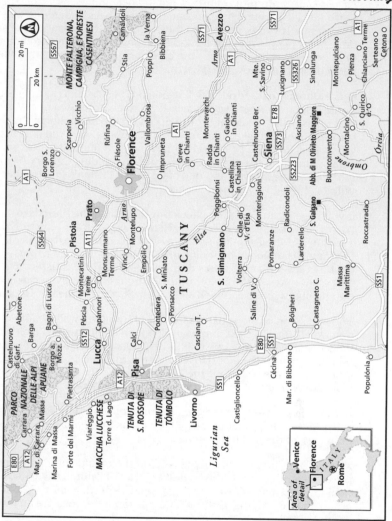

20 people (book well in advance at ☎ **050-560-547** or www.opapisa.it/boxoffice), and cost 17€ ($20) per person (that includes the reservations fee). When I checked ticket availability in April (not even high season, mind you), tours were sold out more than two weeks in advance. If you just show up in Pisa without reservations you will *not* be able to tour the tower.

Galileo Galilei earned his status as one of the fathers of modern physics in Pisa. He spent the 16th century watching pendulums, asserting that the Earth revolved around the sun, and dropping balls of differing weights off the Leaning Tower to prove that they would hit the ground at the same time. Many people thought he was nuts, and the Church excommunicated (and nearly executed) him for the blasphemy of suggesting that the universe did not revolve around Earth.

Pisa's **Duomo (cathedral)** (☎ 050-560-547; www.opapisa.it) is a huge Romanesque structure with a facade of stacked colonnades. Make sure that you see the medieval bronze doors on the back side of the right transept, facing the Leaning Tower; these doors were the only set to survive a 1595 fire. The cathedral's interior was rebuilt after the fire, but some items from the earlier era remain — including Cimabue's 1302 mosaic *Christ Pancrator* and one of Giovanni Pisano's greatest carved pulpits (1302–1311), a masterpiece of Gothic sculpture.

If you liked Pisano's pulpit, check out the one in the **Battistero** (Baptistery) sculpted by his dad, Nicola Pisano, from 1255 to 1260. This huge, drumlike building has a Romanesque base, but Nicola and Giovanni Pisano finished it off with a Gothic skullcap of a roof, which contains several small spires and statues. Ask the Baptistery's guard to sing a few notes at the center of the structure so that you can hear the outstanding acoustics (when a choir sings, you can hear it for miles).

The north end of the square is bordered by a long wall of Gothic marble that quietly marks the **Camposanto,** a kind of cloister/mausoleum whose halls contain ancient stone coffins and Renaissance tombs. Allied firebombs in World War II destroyed most of the dazzling medieval frescoes that covered the walls, but the few that were salvaged — including the macabre *Triumph of Death* — are on display in a side room.

Across the square from the Camposanto, obscured by souvenir stands, is the **Museo delle Sinopie,** which contains the *sinopie,* or preparatory drawings, of the ill-fated frescoes.

Many statues and other works taken off the outside of the Duomo for preservation are in the **Museo dell'Opera del Duomo** (☎ 050-561-820), behind the Leaning Tower. Among them is an 11th-century Islamic bronze griffin. Etchings of the destroyed Camposanto frescoes are on the second floor.

Admission charges for the group of monuments and museums on Campo dei Miracoli are tied together and are quite confusing. The Duomo (cathedral) alone costs 2€ ($2.30). A ticket including the Duomo and Battistero is 6€ ($6.90). Any other single sight is 5€ ($5.75); any two of the other sights are 6€ ($6.90). The Duomo plus any two other monuments is 8€ ($9.20). An 8.50€ ($9.80) ticket gets you into the Baptistery, Camposanto, Museo dell'Opera del Duomo, and Museo delle Sinopie, and a 10.50€ ($12) version throws in the Duomo as well.

Open hours for all (except the Duomo) are the same: April through September, daily from 8:00 a.m. to 7:30 p.m.; March and October, daily from 9:00 a.m. to 5:30 p.m.; and November through February, daily from 9:00 a.m. to 4:30 p.m. (Last admission to Museo dell'Opera del Duomo is ten minutes before close.) Duomo hours are as follows: April to September, Monday through Saturday from 10:00 a.m. to 7:30 p.m. and Sunday, 1:00 to 7:30 p.m.; March and October, Monday through Saturday from 10 a.m. to 5 p.m. and Sunday 1 to 5:30 p.m.; November to February Monday through Saturday 10:00 a.m. to 12:45 p.m. and 3:00 to 4:30 p.m., and Sunday 3:00 to 4:30 p.m.

Where to stay and dine

For terrific Pisan cuisine in a traditional trattoria setting, head just north of the city walls to **Da Bruno** (☎ 050-560-818; www.pisaonline.it/ trattoriadabruno), Via Luigi Bianchi. The **Villa Kinzica** (☎ 050-560-419; Fax: 050-551-204; www.hotelvillakinzica.it), Piazza Arcivescovado 2, is not very attractive, but it's just a few steps from the Campo dei Miracoli and has doubles for 108€ ($124). Ask for a room with a view of the Leaning Tower.

Siena: A departure from the Renaissance

Siena is a city of the Gothic Middle Ages rather than the Renaissance. In this overgrown medieval hill town, you find brick-and-marble palaces and cafes, not museums and boutiques. Siena has its own proud artistic tradition, which relies on emotion, elegance of line, and rich color — a shift from Florence's precise, formula-driven, exacting classical painting.

Siena's decorated cathedral is a huge artistic jewel box. But Siena is also a good place to sit back on the bricks of the sloping Il Campo, the town's unusual main piazza, and simply enjoy a bottle of Chianti and a good book or take a nap under the Tuscan sun.

Many people spend only half a day in Siena, but I recommend spending at least one night so that you have a good day and a half to absorb its medieval atmosphere and see its scattered sights.

 Siena has a plethora of reduced-price ticket combos you can pick up at any of the participating museums or sights. They range from a 13€ ($15) ticket that includes the Libreria Piccolomini (inside the Duomo), Museo dell'Opera Metropolitana, and the Baptistery, to the 16€ ($18) ticket that gets you into five additional sights and is valid for a week. Both tickets are valid for a week. For more information, visit www.santamaria. comune.siena.it.

Getting there

Nineteen trains make the 90- to 135-minute trip from Florence daily, but Siena's train station is 2 miles from town (frequent buses connect the station with the historic center, or grab a taxi). On a daytrip, you can save time and hassle by taking advantage of these bus companies' offerings: TRAIN offers an express bus (46 daily; 75 to 95 minutes; ☎ 0577-204-245; www.trainspa.it), and SITA offers a slower bus (10 daily, 2 to 2½ hours; ☎ 055-483-651; www.sita-on-line.it) directly from Florence to Piazza San Domenico in Siena, a five-minute stroll from the main square.

A **tourism office** (☎ 0577-280-551; www.siena.turismo.toscana.it) is at Piazza del Campo 56 in Siena.

American Express (☎ 055-50-981) teams with **CAF Tours,** Via Roma 4 (☎ 055-283-200; www.caftours.com), for an all-day excursion from Florence that includes both Siena and San Gimignano, described later in this chapter, for 49€ ($56).

Seeing the sights

At the center of the city is **Il Campo,** a beautiful, fan-shaped brick area that slopes down to the **Palazzo Pubblico** (1297–1310). You can climb the 503 steps of its bell tower, the **Torre di Mangia,** for 5.15€ ($5.90), to get an unforgettable view over the city's burnt sienna rooftops out to the green countryside beyond.

Inside the *palazzo* is the **Museo Civico** (☎ 0577-292-226), the best art museum in town. Several paintings done just for this town hall are the museum's most famous. Simone Martini's 1315 *Maestà* — a Mary in majesty surrounded by her court of saints under a canopy — was the artist's first and best work. Across the room is one of his later frescoes, *Guidoriccio da Foligno,* which depicts a gracious knight on horseback with a fabulously checkered cloak.

In the next room is the greatest secular fresco to survive from medieval Europe, the *Allegory of Good and Bad Government and Its Effect on the Town and Countryside.* The length of Ambrogio Lorenzetti's 1338 masterpiece rivals that of its name, wrapping around three walls and depicting the medieval ideal of civic life.

Admission to the Museo Civico is 6.50€ ($7.50), for adults without a reservation, 6€ ($6.90) for adults with a reservation. A 9€ ($10) cumulative ticket with the Torre Mangia is also available (9.50€/$11 without reservations). The museum is open daily from 10 a.m. to 7 p.m. (open to 6:30 p.m. Nov–Mar 15).

Siena's other grand sight, the **Duomo (cathedral)** (☎ 0577-283-048; www.operaduomo.it), is a huge zebra-striped Gothic structure with a facade by Giovanni Pisano and an interior whose floor is a combination of inlaid, carved, and mosaic marble panels (1372–1547). At the right transept is the Chigi Chapel, designed by the baroque master Bernini. Nicola Pisano's best pulpit is at the start of the left transept; the intricately carved Gothic panels (which his son, Giovanni, helped create) depict the life of Christ in great detail. Off the left aisle is the entrance to the Libreria Piccolomini, which Umbrian master Pinturicchio filled with frescoed scenes from the life of Pope Pius II. Just outside this room is a large marble altar that holds statuettes of Sts. Peter, Paul, and Gregory carved by a 26-year-old Michelangelo. Admission to the cathedral is free, except in September and October, when the floor is uncovered and admission is 5.50€ ($6.35). The **Libreria Piccolomini** costs 1.50€ ($1.75), or can be visited on Siena's cumulative tickets. The cathedral is open daily November to March 15 from 10 a.m. to 1 p.m. and 2:30 to 5:00 p.m., and March 16 through October from 9:00 a.m. to 7:30 p.m.

If you walk down the steep stairs around the Duomo's right side and turn around at the bottom, you see the **Baptistery,** which was built under the cathedral. Inside is a font with bronze panels by some of the early Renaissance's greatest sculptors: Donatello, Ghiberti, and Siena's Jacopo della Quercia. Creative frescoes from the 15th century (look for the alligator) cover the walls and ceiling. March 15 to September, the Baptistery is open 9:00 a.m. to 7:30 p.m.; October to March 14, it's open 10 a.m. to 5 p.m. Admission is 2€ ($2.30) or on the cumulative ticket.

About 700 years ago, Siena planned an ambitious expansion of its cathedral that would have turned the present Duomo into just a portion of the grand new structure. Builders finished one thick nave wall and started on the new facade wall before the Black Death hit in 1348, killing three-fourths of the town's population. The **Museo dell'Opera Metropolitana** (☎ 0577-283-048; www.operaduomo.siena.it) now fills the interior (enter across from the back-right corner of the Duomo's exterior). This museum was set up to hold the sculptures removed from the Duomo for preservation.

In the museum, you can climb several worn staircases up onto the wall of the unfinished nave for great views across the city. Admission to the museum is 5.50€ ($6.35) or on the cumulative ticket. The museum is open daily March 15 through September from 9:00 a.m. to 7:30 p.m., October from 9 a.m. to 6 p.m., and November to March 14 from 9 a.m. to 1 p.m.

If you're eager for a respite from history and art, visit the **Enoteca Italiana Permanente** (☎ 0577-288-497; www.enoteca-italiana.it), Italy's official wine-tasting bar (774 labels in stock). It fills the echoing brick halls and cellars of the 16th-century **Fortezza Medicea** fortress in Siena's northwest corner. Glasses range from 2€ to 5€ ($2.30–$5.75), and it's open Monday from noon to 8 p.m., and Tuesday through Saturday from noon to 1 a.m.

Where to stay and dine

Good, solid Sienese food is available at **Antica Trattoria Papei,** Piazza del Mercato 6 (☎ 0577-280-894), on a piazza behind the Palazzo Pubblico. For economical sleeping accommodations, try **Cannon d'Oro,** Via Montanini 28 (☎ 0577-44-321; Fax: 0577-280-868; www.cannondoro.it), a northerly extension of Via Banchi di Spora. The hotel is only a few minutes from the Campo on the main street in town. Rooms are nowhere near fancy, but they're big and cost only 70€ ($81) per double.

San Gimignano: Hills and towers

Perhaps the most famous of Tuscany's hill towns, San Gimignano bristles with 14 medieval towers that are remnants of the days when tiny city-states such as this were full of feuding families that sometimes went to war right in the middle of town. Although no other city in Italy has saved so many of its towers, what you see today is only a fraction of what used to be there; San Gimignano sported at least 70 towers in the 13th and 14th centuries. Although this little town is often packed with day-trippers, you won't find any other spot with such a profound Middle Ages flavor.

 You can see San Gimignano in two to three hours or so, but smart travelers know that all the day-trippers head for their tour buses at dusk, leaving wonderful medieval towns like this virtually untouched. Those who spend the night can absorb the ancient village atmosphere and get to know the locals.

Getting there

The only way to get to San Gimignano is by bus, and you must almost always transfer in the village of Poggibonsi. From Florence, SITA (Via Santa Caterina 17, just west of the train station) sends 26 buses daily on the 50- to 90-minute trip to Poggibonsi, 13 of which meet the connection to San Gimignano with no time to spare. From Siena, TRAIN (Piazza San Domenico) runs about 33 daily buses to Poggibonsi in 35 to 45 minutes. From Poggibonsi, 19 buses make the 20-minute trek to San Gimignano Monday through Saturday, but only two buses run on Sunday (at 7:20 a.m. and 12:55 p.m.).

The **tourism office** (☎ 0577-940-008; www.sangimignano.com) is at Piazza del Duomo 1.

Seeing the sights

 The small town center consists of two interlocked, irregularly shaped squares, with a 13th-century well in the center of one and the Collegiata (main church) taking up one end of the other. If you can't resist climbing up one of the looming towers, go to the **Museo Civico/Torre Grossa** (☎ 0577-940-340). After you admire paintings in the gallery by artists such as Pinturicchio, Gozzoli, and Lippo Memmi (and secular 14th-century frescoes in an anteroom that show the racier side of medieval courtship), you can climb the tallest remaining tower in town (178 feet), which provides a 360-degree view of the town and the rolling green countryside just outside its walls. The Museo Civico/Torre Grossa is open March through October daily from 9:30 a.m. to 7:20 p.m., and November through February daily from 10:00 a.m. to 5:50 p.m.

The **Collegiata** (☎ 0577-940-316) has no bishop's seat and therefore technically is no longer a *duomo* (cathedral), but it sure is decorated to look like one. The interior walls are completely covered with a colorful collage of 14th- and 15th-century frescoes. The ones down the left wall tell Old Testament stories; the right wall features the New Testament. A *St. Sebastian* thick with arrows is against the entrance wall, and near the entrance — high on the interior nave wall — spreads a gruesomely colorful *Last Judgment* scene. Off the right aisle is the tiny **Chapel of St. Fina,** which Ghirlandaio frescoed with two scenes from the young saint's brief life.

From April through October, the church is open Sunday through Friday from 9:30 a.m. to 7:30 p.m. and Saturday from 9:30 a.m. to 5:00 p.m.; November through January 26, hours are Monday through Saturday from 9:30 a.m. to 5:00 p.m. and Sunday from 1 to 5 p.m. Closed January 27 to February 28. Admission is 3.50€ ($4.05) or on Siena's cumulative ticket.

Where to stay and dine

La Mangiatoia, Via Mainardi 5 (☎ **0577-941-528**), has an intimate atmosphere and a hearty Tuscan menu, and its more imaginative dishes are the best. **La Cisterna,** Piazza della Cisterna 23–24 (☎ **0577-940-328;** Fax: 0577-942-080; www.hotelcisterna.it), is located in the remains of two centrally located towers and has one of the best restaurants in town. Doubles cost 82€ to 120€ ($94–$138); rates include breakfast.

Fast Facts: Florence

Area Code

The country code for Italy is **39**. Florence — along with the rest of Italy — no longer has a separate city code, though you'll notice almost all numbers in town still start with 055 (the old city code). As they run out of new numbers, that will change . And, unlike in the past, you must dial that initial zero.

American Express

The Florence American Express office, Via Dante Alighieri 22r (☎ 055-50-981), is open Monday through Friday from 9:00 a.m. to 5:30 p.m., and Saturday from 9:00 a.m. to 12:30 p.m. The office cashes all traveler's checks (not just American Express checks) without a fee.

Currency

In 2002, the euro became the legal tender in Italy, replacing the lira. The exchange rate used to calculate the dollar value

given in this chapter is 1€ equals $1.15. Amounts over $10 are rounded to the nearest dollar.

Doctors and Dentists

For a list of English-speaking dentists and doctors, contact the U.S. Consulate, Lungarno Amerigo Vespucci 38 (☎ 055-239-8276). Visitors who need emergency care can call Volunteer Hospital Interpreters at ☎ 055-234-4567; the interpreters are always on call and offer their services free.

Embassies and Consulates

The consulate of the United States is at Lungarno Amerigo Vespucci 38 (☎ 055-266-951), near its intersection with Via Palestro. Drop-ins are welcome Monday through Friday from 9:00 a.m. to 12:30 p.m. Appointments are taken Monday through Friday from and 2:00 to 4:30 p.m.

Emergency

Dial ☎ 113 in any emergency, ☎ 112 for the *carabinieri* (the military-trained and more useful of the two police forces); ☎ 118 or 06-5100 to summon an ambulance, or ☎ 115 for the fire department. *Pronto Soccorso* is Italian for "first aid," but you can also use the phrase to get to an emergency room. Call ☎ 116 for roadside assistance (not free).

Hospitals

First aid is available 24 hours a day in the emergency room *(pronto soccorso)* of major hospitals.

There's a special Tourist Medical Service, Via Lorenzo il Magnifico 59, north of the city center between the Fortezza del Basso and Piazza della Libertà (☎ 055-475-411), open 24 hours; take bus 8 or 80 to Viale Lavagnini or buses 4, 12, or 20 to Via Poliziano.

The most central hospitals are the Arcispedale di Santa Maria Nuova, a block northeast of the Duomo on Piazza Santa Maria Nuova (☎ 055-27-581), and the Misericordia Ambulance Service, on Piazza del Duomo across from Giotto's bell tower (☎ 055-212-222 for ambulance).

Information

The city's largest tourist office is at Via Cavour 1r (☎ 055-290-832; Fax: 055-276-0383; www.firenzeturismo.it), about 3 blocks north of the Duomo. For specifics on it, and on other offices, see "Finding information after you arrive," near the beginning of this chapter.

For transit Information, call ☎ 055-565-0222.

Internet Access and Cybercafes

To check or send e-mail, head to the Internet Train (www.internettrain.it), with 15 locations including Via dell'Oriuolo 25r, 3 blocks from the Duomo (☎ 055-263-8968); Via Guelfa 24a, near the train station (☎ 055-214-794); and Borgo San Jacopo 30r in the Oltrarno (☎ 055-265-7935). Open hours vary but run at least daily from 9:00 a.m. to 8:30 p.m., often later.

Maps

The tourist office hands out a free map. You can buy more-detailed ones at any newsstand or bookstore.

Newspapers/Magazines

The monthly *Informacittà* pamphlet on events, exhibits, and concerts is free; pick it up at any tourist office.

Pharmacies

For pharmacy information, dial ☎ 110. Three places offering English-speaking service and 24-hour schedules are the Farmacia Communale, at the head of track 16 in the train station (☎ 055-216-761); Molteni, Via dei Calzaiuoli 7r, just north of Piazza della Signoria (☎ 055-289-490); and All'Insegno del Moro, at the Duomo square, Piazza di San Giovanni 20r (☎ 055-211-343).

Police

Dial ☎ 113 in any emergency or ☎ 112 for the *carabinieri,* a division of the Italian army.

Post Office

Florence's main post office is at Via Pellicceria 3, off the southwest corner of Piazza della Repubblica. You can buy stamps *(francobolli)* and pick up letters sent General Delivery *(Fermo Posta)* after showing some ID. The post office is open Monday through Friday from 8:15 a.m. to 7:00 p.m., and Saturday from 8:15 a.m. to 12:30 p.m.

Safety

You can feel very safe in all of central Italy, which has practically no random violent crime. Florence, like any city, has plenty of petty thieves looking to pick your pocket, plus a few light-fingered children (especially near the train station). Use common sense, try to avoid them, and yell *"Polizia!"* if they come too close.

Otherwise, there aren't any dangers that are hard to avoid. You should stay out of the Cascine park at night, when you may risk getting mugged, and you probably won't want to hang out with the heroin addicts shooting up on the Arno mudflats below the Lungarno embankments on the edges of town.

Taxes

The value-added tax in Italy (called IVA) varies with the item or service, up to 19 percent, and is already included in the sticker price of any item (except, oddly, in the most expensive luxury hotels). Non-EU citizens who spend more than 154.94€ ($178) in a single store are entitled to a refund. See Chapter 4 for details on receiving one.

Taxis

See "Getting Around Florence," earlier in this chapter.

Telephone

See "Fast Facts: Rome," in Chapter 19 for information on making calls and calling-card access codes.

Transit Info

See "Getting Around Florence," earlier in this chapter.

Chapter 21

Venice and Environs

- -

In This Chapter

▶ Getting to Venice

▶ Exploring the city by neighborhood

▶ Discovering the city's best hotels, restaurants, and attractions

▶ Side-tripping to the Venetian islands and Padova

- -

*B*uilt on water and marshland, Venice is not just an amazing city —
it's also a feat of engineering and determination. The city's famous
canals serve as its main streets, traveled by a variety of boats, including
the famous gondolas.

Venice's canals and boats hint at the city's seafaring past. During the fifth
century, barbarians overran Italy's peninsula, prompting some in the
region to flee to where no sane barbarian could attack: the middle of the
water. Although the Venetian lagoon was populated with fishing communities, Venice rapidly built itself up as a commercial seafaring powerhouse. Through the power and volume of its shipping and trading, Venice
became the Queen of the Adriatic by the 16th century, controlling most
of the Mediterranean region. Centuries of political stability and wealth
allowed Venice to create a rich urban and cultural landscape (including
hundreds of churches such as the Basilica de San Marco) and to nurture
such great late-Renaissance artists as Titian and Tintoretto.

Modern-day Venice experiences invasions of another sort — every year,
up to 1.5 million tourists join the city's 70,000 residents, making the
town called *La Serenissima* (the Most Serene) anything but calm. During
peak times (June, July, Sept, and Carnevale), hotels are booked solid,
and the crowds can be overwhelming. Venice gets more attention than
it wants or can handle; the city government is debating the passage of
quota laws to curb the number of tourists. Someday soon, Venice may
become the first European city that you need a ticket to enter.

Getting There

Water surrounds Venice, threading its way through every neighborhood —
so arriving in town without hopping on a boat of some sort is nearly
impossible. While in the city, your feet are your best means of
transportation.

Arriving by air

Flights land at the **Aeroporto Marco Polo,** 4½ miles north of the city on the mainland (☎ 041-260-9260 for flight info, 041-260-9240 for general information; www.veniceairport.it). You'll find ATMs and a tourist-information desk on the ground floor in the arrivals hall.

Two buses travel from the airport to the city (well, almost to the city): The special **ATVO airport shuttle bus** (☎ 041-520-5530; www.atvo.it) connects with Piazzale Roma not far from Venice's Santa Lucia train station — the closest point to Venice's attractions accessible by land. Buses leave to and from the airport every 20 minutes, cost 3€ ($3.45), and make the trip in about 30 minutes. The twice-hourly local **public ACTV bus no. 5** (☎ 041-528-7886; www.actv.it) costs 1.50€ ($1.75) and takes 30 to 45 minutes. Buy tickets for either option at the news-stand just inside the terminal from the sign-posted bus stop. For both buses, you have to walk to/from the final stop at Piazzale Roma to the nearby *vaporetto* (water bus) stop for the final connection to your hotel. You rarely see porters around to help with luggage, so remember to pack light.

A land taxi from the airport to the Piazzale Roma to pick up your vaporetto runs about 30€ ($35).

Arriving by boat

The most fashionable and traditional way to arrive in Piazza San Marco is by sea. For 10€ ($12), the **Cooperative San Marco/Alilaguna** (☎ 041-523-5775; www.alilaguna.it) operates a large *motoscafo* (shuttle boat) service from the airport with two stops at Murano and the Lido before arriving (after about one hour's ride) in Piazza San Marco. Call for the daily schedule of a dozen or so trips from about 6 a.m. to midnight, which changes with the season and is coordinated with the principal arrivals/departures of the major airlines (most hotels have the schedule). If your hotel isn't in the Piazza San Marco area, you have to make a connection at the *vaporetto* (water bus) launches (your hotel can help you with the specifics).

A private *taxi acquei* (water taxi) is convenient and takes 20 to 30 minutes to travel to or from the airport, but it's costly — a legal minimum of 55€ ($63) but usually more around 75€ ($86) for two passengers with bags. However, it's worth considering if you're pressed for time, have an early flight, have a lot of luggage (a Venice no-no), or can split the cost with a friend or two. A water taxi may be able to drop you off at the front (or side) door of your hotel or as close as it can maneuver given your hotel's location (check with the hotel before arriving). Your taxi captain should be able to tell you before boarding just how close he can get you. Try **Corsorzio Motoscafi Venezia** (☎ 041-522-2303; www.motoscafi venezia.it).

Arriving by rail

Stazione Santa Lucia (☎ 800-888-088 toll-free from anywhere in Italy; www.trenitalia.it) is the train station in Venice itself. However, don't worry if your ticket is to "Venezia-Mestre" — Mestre is merely a landlubbing industrial suburb that's one stop short of Venice. Shuttle trains leave Mestre every few minutes for the 10-minute, 5-mile ride across the lagoon into Venice proper.

Orienting Yourself in Venice

Consider this fair warning: Venice has one of the most confusing, frustrating, and unfathomable layouts of any city. Ever. At first glance, the city seems simple: The palace-lined *Canale Grande* (Grand Canal), a sweeping backward-S curve, wraps around a few big islands while numerous smaller canals snake in and out through the blocks of land. Well, sort of. Being able to find anything you're looking for in Venice is much more complicated. Your best defense: Arm yourself with the best map you can buy, take a deep breath, and prepare to get lost repeatedly.

Venice has two transportation networks: one of narrow streets, the other of canals. These infrastructures work together occasionally, and sometimes they interfere with each other. Narrow alleyways that run you in circles, dead end, or drop off abruptly into a canal are all too common. Often you find yourself backtracking.

Sometimes, an alleyway that leads you from one place to another suddenly opens up into a large *campo* (square), or crosses over a canal on one of Venice's tiny arched marble bridges (the most magnificent of these bridges is the **Rialto Bridge** over the Grand Canal).

If your vision is keen, you can follow the numerous tiny signs that point hither and yon to various major sights. These paths are often convoluted and take three times as long as you'd think. However, don't fret about being late. Simply treat any trek through the city as an adventure — getting lost can actually be a truly enjoyable activity.

Introducing the neighborhoods

Centuries ago, someone tried to bring some order to Venice's chaos by dividing the city into six *sestieri,* or districts (which don't include the some 168 outlying islands). The central Venetian district is **San Marco,** filled to the brim with visitors these days. This district features the amazing *Piazza San Marco* (St. Mark's Square) with its cathedral and *Palazzo Ducale* (Doge's Palace). The Piazzetta San Marco extends from the Piazza San Marco and runs along the Palazzo Ducale to the Grand Canal. The San Marco is famous for having hundreds of souvenir shops, the ritziest (and most costly) hotels, the world-renowned La Scala opera house, and many (again, generally expensive) restaurants.

Street smarts: Venetian addresses

Venice doesn't label its streets and squares like the rest of Italy does. A *calle, ruga,* or *ramo* is a street; a *rio terrà* is a street made from a filled-in canal; and a *fondamenta* or *riva* is a sidewalk along the edge of a canal. A *canale* or *rio* is a canal. A *campo* or *campiello* is a square (but you see exceptions here, including Piazza San Marco, Piazzetta San Marco, and Piazzale Roma).

Although a street or *campo* name can be used only once within a Venetian neighborhood, no rule exists against another *sestiere* using the exact same label. As a result, the most popular names (such as Calle della Madonna) are recycled three or four times in Venice, yet refer to streets half a city apart. Because of the confusing naming conventions, save yourself a headache and know the *sestiere* along with any address. (By the way, don't even try to figure out the street-numbering system in Venice — it's devoid of any logic whatsoever.)

East of San Marco you find the large neighborhood of **Castello,** which offers the *Riva degli Schiavoni,* a classy stretch of lagoon-front property with upscale hotels aplenty. Much of the activity in Castello is centered around the old ship-building sector of the city, the *Arsenale.* This sector with its working navy yard is mostly closed to the tourists.

The northernmost Venetian neighborhood that greets you as you enter Venice by train or car is the **Cannaregio.** Cannaregio also has the dubious honor of being home to Europe's first incorporated Jewish Ghetto. Cheap lodging exists near the train station, but the neighborhood is largely residential. Unless you're stopping by to see a specific sight, you probably won't spend much time here.

San Polo (or San Paolo) takes up a huge chunk of the side of the city west of the Grand Canal. This commercial district is known for its moderately priced hotels, shopping, and trattorias, as well as some impressive churches that are popular with sightseers. Just a bit north, you find the very untouristy *sestiere* of **Santa Croce,** which is half industrial and half traditional, with a lovely ancient cathedral.

On the opposite side of the Grand Canal from San Marco is the trendy southern district of **Dorsoduro.** Although Venice's Carnevale is reputed to rival New Orleans's Mardi Gras, the rest of the year the town's only nightlife is in this neighborhood. The sparsely populated area, with its smattering of bars and cafes, some good trattorias and cheap hotels, and Venice's two great art museums, the Accademia and the Peggy Guggenheim, is popular with younger travelers.

Finding information after you arrive

The main tourist office, **Venice Pavilion/Palazzina dei Santi** (☎ 041-529-8711 or 041-522-5150; www.turismovenezia.it; Vaporetto: San

Marco), is located right when you get off the vaporetto at the San Marco stop, in a stone pavilion wedged between the small green park on the Grand Canal and the famous Harry's Bar. Frankly, it's more interested in running its gift shop than in helping tourists. Hours are daily from 10 a.m. to 6 p.m. Another office (smaller, but equally indifferent) is under the arcade at the west end of Piazza San Marco at no. 71F, on the left of the tunnel-like street leading to Calle dell'Ascensione (☎ 041-520-8964; Fax: 041-523-0399; Vaporetto: San Marco). Hours are Monday through Friday from 9:00 a.m. to 3:30 p.m. During peak season, a small info booth operates in the arrivals hall at the **Marco Polo Airport.** It's open daily from 9:00 a.m. to 7:30 p.m. You also find a small office in the train station, **Stazione Santa Lucia,** open daily from 8:00 a.m. to 6:30 p.m.

Getting Around Venice

Venice has no motorized traffic, so your only options for getting around are by foot or by boat.

By foot

Venice is a walking city. There really isn't any other way to get around. The only time you won't be walking is when you take the *vaporetto* (water bus) between the train station and Piazza San Marco, go on long hauls to outlying islands, or shell out big bucks for a private *taxi acquei* (water taxi).

By vaporetto (water bus)

The vaporetto, Venice's public ferry service, takes the place of a bus network. The **Azienda del Consorzio Trasporti Veneziano (ACTV)** operates the system (☎ 041-528-7886; www.actv.it). The maps that the tourist office hands out can help you plan your route. The vaporetto most visitors use is Line 82, which chugs regularly from the train station down the Grand Canal, stopping five times (including at the Rialto Bridge and the Accademia) en route to the San Marco stop, which is just off Piazzetta San Marco in the Giardinetti Reali. (At night, the N follows the same route.) Line 1 is a commuter line that follows a similar route but takes longer and makes more stops. Lines 51 and 52 run from the station to S. Zaccaria, which is just past the Doge's Palace off the other side of Piazzetta San Marco, but bypass the Grand Canal, going the long way around the Dorsoduro. A **one-way** vaporetto *biglietto* (ticket) is a steep 3.50€ ($4.05); a **round-trip** ticket is 6€ ($6.90). You can also purchase a **24-hour ticket** for 10.50€ ($12), a **three-day pass** for 22€ ($25), or a **seven-day pass** for 31.50 ($36). Most lines run every 10 to 15 minutes, 7 a.m. to midnight, and then hourly until morning. Most vaporetto docks (the only place you can buy tickets) have timetables posted. Note that not all stations sell tickets after dark; if you haven't bought a pass or extra tickets beforehand, you have to settle up with the conductor on board (you have to find him — he won't come looking for you) for an extra .50€ (60¢) per ticket. If you try for a free ride, you risk a 21€ ($24) fine, no excuses accepted.

By traghetto (ferry skiff)

Just three bridges span the Grand Canal. To fill in the gaps, *traghetti* skiffs (oversized gondolas rowed by two standing gondoliers) cross the Grand Canal at eight intermediate points. You can find stations at the end of any street named Calle del Traghetto on your map and indicated by a yellow sign with the black gondola symbol. The fare is .50€ (60¢), which you hand to the gondolier when boarding.

By taxi

Taxi acquei (water taxis) are convenient but expensive. For journeys up to seven minutes (which are highly unlikely), the rate is 14€ ($16). Add .25€ (30¢) for each 15 seconds thereafter. Each bag more than 19 inches long costs 1.15€ ($1.30), plus there's an additional 4.40€ ($5.05) charge for service between 10 p.m. and 7 a.m. and a 4.65€ ($5.35) surcharge on Sunday and holidays (these last two can't be applied simultaneously). If you call ahead for a *taxi acquei,* tack on another 4.15€ ($4.75). The preceding rates cover up to four passengers; you pay another 1.60€ ($1.85) per extra passenger.

Six water-taxi stations serve key points in the city: the **Ferrovia** (☎ 041-716-286), **Piazzale Roma** (☎ 041-716-922), the **Rialto Bridge** (☎ 041-523-0575), **Piazza San Marco** (☎ 041-522-9750), the **Lido** (☎ 041-526-0059), and **Marco Polo Airport** (☎ 041-541-5084). **Radio Taxi** (☎ 041-522-2303 or 041-723-112) can pick you up from any place in the city.

By gondola

What's sleek, black, slightly crooked, and looks like a cross between a coffin and a canoe? A gondola, of course — the most popular mode of transportation in Venice until speedboats began roaring down the canals in recent decades. No visit to Venice is complete without taking at least one of these time-honored water taxis for a spin. The average ride lasts about an hour. Before you take any gondola rides, make absolutely certain that you and the gondolier agree to the trip's price and duration. To get your money's worth, write down the agreement and time the ride yourself. (Strangely, the gondoliers' watches often run fast.)

Officially, gondola rides (if you're using the gondola as a taxi) are 62€ ($71) for the first 50 minutes (for up to six people) and then 31€ ($36) for each 25 minutes after that. (Rides also cost more after 8 p.m.) You can find cut-rate, brief trips that follow only the Grand Canal (from the Dogana docks, off Piazza San Marco, to San Toma) for 19€ ($22; ☎ 041-528-5075; www.gondolavenezia.it). However, a reasonably priced gondola ride is a Venetian rarity. If you encounter a gondolier who even remotely follows the "official" rates, write down his name and tell everyone (including me!) about it.

Staying in Venice

Get ready to shell out some clams: Venice is a pricey destination in just about every respect, but especially in terms of lodging. Summer prices soar, and your lodging choices can be pretty slim if you haven't reserved months in advance.

Savvy travelers often take advantage of an easier (and cheaper) stay in Padova, just a half-hour's train ride from Venice (see "Suggested itineraries," later in this chapter). As always in Italy, bargaining for a discount doesn't hurt — especially in the slower winter season (just don't get your hopes up for more than 10 to 15 percent off).

If you don't want to hotel-hunt on your own, visit an **AVA hotel association reservations booth** at the train station (☎ **800-843-006** within Italy or 041-522-2264; www.veneziasi.it). Simply state the price range you want to book and they'll confirm a hotel while you wait. There's no fee for the service.

Venice's top hotels

Albergo Royal San Marco
$$$ San Marco

The cozy rooms of the Albergo Royal (formerly Boston Hotel) feature 18th-century reproduction Venetian décor and are just steps away from Piazza San Marco. The best accommodations have small balconies that overlook a canal. TVs are free upon request. Only 20 rooms have A/C, so request one when booking if you need it.

See map p. 460. San Marco, Ponte de Dai 848 (halfway down the north colonnade of Piazza San Marco, a street leads north across a canal; the hotel is just over the bridge on the right). ☎ *041-528-7665. Fax: 041-522-6628.* www.sanmarcohotels.com. *Vaporetto: San Marco or San Zaccaria. Rates: 106€–300€ ($122–$345) double. Rates include breakfast. AE, DC, MC, V.*

Hotel Gallini
$$ San Marco

A family operation, the immaculate Gallini features big, modern rooms with marble and parquet floors and friendly service. Some rooms have air-conditioning. Rooms on the back side of the hotel that lack baths cost the least; more expensive options overlook the charming Rio della Verona canal. Off-season rates are about 10 percent lower.

See map p. 460. San Marco 3673 (on Calle della Verona; from La Fenice opera house on Campo San Fantin, head up the main street going north, over a bridge, and the hotel is on the right). ☎ *041-520-4515. Fax: 041-520-9103.* www.hotelgallini.it. *Vaporetto: Sant'Angelo. Rates: 100€–154€ ($115–$177) double. Rates include breakfast. AE, DC, MC, V.*

Hotel San Cassiano Ca'Favretto
$$$ San Polo

Try this place for a moderate splurge. About half the rooms look across the Grand Canal to the gorgeous Ca d'Oro (accounting for the highest rates below); most of the others open onto a side canal. This 14th-century palace is steeped in dusty Old World elegance, with rooms outfitted with antiques and reproductions. A dining room porch overlooks the Grand Canal.

See map p. 460. Santa Croce 2232 (on Calle della Rosa; after you step off the vaporetto, turn left to cross in front of the church, take the bridge over the side canal and turn right. Then turn left, cross another canal and turn right, then left again. Cross yet another canal and turn right, then immediately left and then left again toward the Grand Canal and the hotel). ☎ **041-524-1768.** *Fax: 041-721-033.* www.sancassiano. it. *Vaporetto: San Stae. Rates: 70€–325€ ($81–$375) double. Rates include breakfast. AE, DC, MC, V.*

Hotel Londra Palace
$$$$$ Castello

Tchaikovsky wrote his Fourth Symphony in room 108 of this 19th-century neo-Gothic palace, one of the best values on the prime real estate of the Riva degli Schiavoni. The cushy accommodations include lacquered furniture and romantic attic rooms. With 100 windows overlooking the San Marco basin, you spend an hour or two just watching people strolling below, as well as distant vistas of the lagoon. Quieter, cheaper rooms look out to the inner courtyard. The onsite Do Leoni is one of the city's best hotel dining rooms.

See map p. 460. Riva degli Schiavoni 4171 (on the canal right at the San Zaccaria vaporetto stop). ☎ **041-520-0533.** *Fax: 041-522-5032.* www.hotelondra.it. *Vaporetto: San Zaccaria. Rates: 275€–485€ ($316–$558) double. Rates include breakfast. AE, DC, MC, V.*

Pensione Accademia
$$$ Dorsoduro

Venice regulars simply adore this pension. Set up your reservation well in advance to get any room here, but especially one overlooking the breakfast garden, a terrace nestled between two canals. Period antiques decorate the "superior" rooms on the first floor of this 17th-century villa, and the atmosphere is decidedly old-fashioned and elegant. (Fans of the movie *Summertime* may remember that Katharine Hepburn's character lived here.)

See map p. 460. Dorsoduro 1058 (Fondamenta Bollani; step off the vaporetto and turn right down Calle Gambara, which doglegs first left and then right. It becomes Calle Corfu, which ends at a side canal; walk left for a few feet to cross over the bridge, and then head to the right back up toward the Grand Canal and the hotel). ☎ **041-521-0188.** *Fax: 041-520-4172.* www.pensioneaccademia.it. *Vaporetto: Accademia. Rates: 130€–275€ ($150–$316) double. Off-season discounts available. Rates include breakfast. AE, DC, MC, V.*

Accommodations, Dining, and Attractions in Venice

HOTELS ■
Albergo al Gambero **11**
Albergo Royal
  San Marco **16**
Hotel Dolomiti **1**
Hotel Gallini **12**
Hotel San Cassiano
  Ca'Favretto **7**
Hotel San Geremia **2**
Hotel Londra Palace **23**
Pensione Accademia **4**
Pensione alla Salute
  (Da Cici) **22**
Pensione la Calcina **6**
Westin Hotel Europa
  & Regina **15**

RESTAURANTS ◆
Antico Martini **13**
Arcimboldo **25**
Bistrot de Venise **11**
Da Sandro **8**
Do Forni **17**
Ristorante Corte Sconta **26**
Rosticceria San
  Bartolomeo **10**
Trattoria alla Madonna **9**
Trattoria da Remigio **24**
Vino Vino **14**

ATTRACTIONS ●
Galleria dell'Accademia **5**
Basilica di San Marco **19**
Collezione Peggy
  Guggenheim **21**
Palazzo Ducale **20**
Piazza San Marco **18**
Scuola Grande di
  San Rocco **3**

• Venice
• Florence
ITALY
Rome

Decollato

To the Stazione FS.S. Lucia
(see inset)

San
Giacomo
dell' Orio

Santa Maria
Mater Domini

Campo S.
Giacomo
dell' Orio

Casa
Zane

Rio della S.

Rio di S. Agostino

Scuola di San
Giovanni Evangelista

Rio di S. Polo

Rio terra S. Toma

Campo di
San Polo

Palazzo Corner
Mocenigo

San Polo

† San
■ Rocco

Campo
dei
Frari

Frari

Rio di San Polo

Scuola Grande
di S. Rocco

Palazzo Centani
(Museo Goldoni)

Palazzo
Grimani

Rio della Frescada

S. Angelo

Palazzo Corner-
Spinelli

S. Toma

Rio Ca' Foscari

Ca' Mocenigo

Ca' Foscari

Palazzo
Grassi

Saliz S. Samuele

C. Crosera

S.
Samuele

Ca' Rezzonico

Campo
S. Stefano/
F. Morosini

Rio di S. Barnaba

Canal Grande

Near the Stazione FS. S. Lucia

Rio Malpaga

Ca' d'
Duca

Rio del Duca

C. Vetturi

Rio di S. Vidal

Campo
San Vidal

Palazzo Loredan

Fondamenta Venier

C. d. Ghetto Vecchio

C. d. Procuratie

R. t. S.
Leonardo

C. della Misericordia

Campo S.
Geremia

Rio della Crea

C. Priuli detta dei Cavaletti

C. Carmelitani

Rio della Toletta

Palazzo Contarini
D. Scrigni

Ponte dell'
Accademia

Rio del

Rio Terra Lista di Spagna

Stazione FS.
S. Lucia

Canal Grande

*F. S. Simeon
Piccolo*

San
Trovaso

Rio di S. Trovaso

Accademia

Palazzo
Brandolin Rota

Palazzo
Loredan

Rio di S.

Vio

Squero di
San Trovaso

Church † Information ⓘ

ⓘ

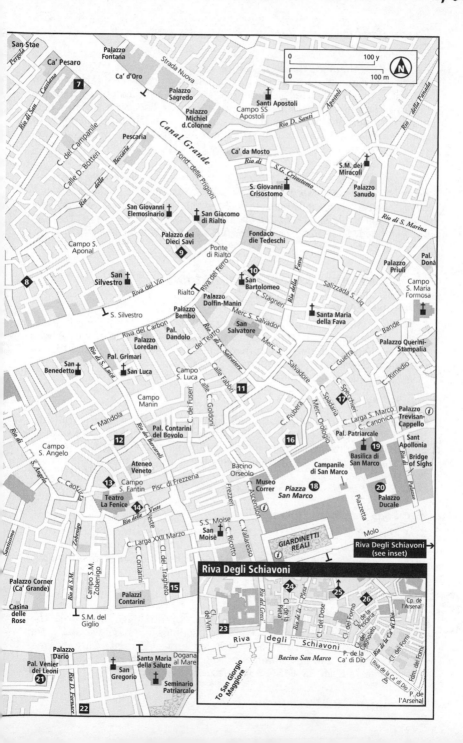

Westin Hotel Europa & Regina
$$$$$ **San Marco**

Recently overhauled, this hotel once again ranks among Venice's top hotels. Just a minute or two from Piazza San Marco, down a quaint, hidden side alley, this hotel's Tiepolo and Regina wings sport eclectic turn-of-the-century European furnishings and modern fabrics. The Europa wing is decorated in traditional Venetian style. A cozy bar with tables opens out onto the Grand Canal, and a new open-kitchen restaurant has received good reviews. Room rates vary with season and view (Canale Grande rooms are priciest).

See map p. 460. San Marco 2159 (off Via XXII Marzo; head west out of the southwest corner of Piazza San Marco down Saliz San Mose; cross the bridge to continue straight on Calle Larga XXII Marzo; you'll see hotel signs directing you down the alleyways to the left). ☎ **041-240-0001.** *Fax: 041-523-1533.* www.westin.com. *Vaporetto: San Marco. Rates: 667€–932€ ($767–$1,072) double. Buffet breakfast 55€ ($63). AE, DC, MC, V.*

Venice's runner-up accommodations

Albergo al Gambero
$–$$ **San Marco** You find this 3-star hotel at 2-star prices halfway between San Marco and the Rialto bridge, with 14 canalside rooms. Guests receive a 10 percent discount in the lively ground-floor restaurant, Bistrot de Venise. *See map p. 460. San Marco 4687 (on Calle dei Fabbri).* ☎ **041-522-4384** *or 041-520-1420. Fax: 041-520-0431.* www.locandaalgambero.com.

Hotel Dolomiti
$ **Cannaregio** This old-fashioned but reliable choice near the train station has large, clean, ordinary rooms spread over four floors (no elevator). Sergio and Lorenzo and their efficient multilingual staff supply umbrellas, restaurant suggestions, and a big smile after a long day of sightseeing. *See map p. 460. Cannaregio 73 to 74 (on Calle Priuli ai Cavalletti).* ☎ **041-715-113** *or 041-719-983. Fax: 041-716-635.* www.hoteldolomiti-ve.it.

Hotel San Geremia
$ **Cannaregio** Seven of the tastefully renovated rooms at this inn overlook the little square (better yet, one of two top-floor rooms has a small private terrace). *See map p. 460. Cannaregio 290A (on Campo San Geremia).* ☎ **041-716-245.** *Fax: 041-524-2342.* www.sangeremia.com.

Pensione alla Salute (Da Cici)
$–$$ **Dorsoduro** One of the best choices in the Guggenheim area, this converted 17th-century palazzo has high ceilings and huge windows. Ten rooms have canal views; four face the lovely terrace garden. Many are large enough to accommodate families of four. *See map p. 460. Dorsoduro 222 (on Fondamenta Cá Balà).* ☎ **041-523-5404.** *Fax: 041-522-2271.* www.hotelsalute.com.

Pensione La Calcina

$$ Dorsoduro Half the unfussy but luminous rooms at this 3-star hotel overlook the sunny Zattere and Giudecca Canal toward architect Palladio's 16th-century Redentore. The outdoor floating terrace or the rooftop terrace are glorious places to begin or end any day. *See map p. 460. Dorsoduro 780 (on Zattere al Gesuati).* ☎ *041-520-6466. Fax: 041-522-7045.* www.lacalcina.com.

Dining in Venice

It can take a few hours to work your way through the numerous courses of a Venetian meal. This much eating isn't just for tourists; Italians actually eat long, rich meals accompanied by fine wine and lively banter. A Venetian meal begins with an appetizer, usually a seafood dish. The popular *frutti di mare,* or "fruits of the sea," includes a tasty array of shellfish, crustaceans, and tentacled sea creatures.

Another classic starting point is *sarde in saor,* sardines prepared in a sweet-and-sour sauce on slices of grilled *polenta* (cornbread's wetter, denser cousin). For the first course (called the *primo*), sink your spoon into *zuppa di cozze* (mussel soup) or savor a rice dish such as *risotto alle seppie* (rice stained with squid ink) or *risi e bisi* (a creamy blend of rice and fresh peas, sometimes with bacon). For pasta dishes, sample *spaghetti alle vongole* (with clams) or *al pomodoro* (in a plain tomato sauce).

Many main courses *(secondo)* utilize Venice's coastal setting, so try some fish. Most seafood entrees are priced by weight and grilled or otherwise simply prepared, and served on a bed of bitter red radicchio lettuce. Other popular *secondi* include *anguille in umido* (eels stewed with tomatoes, garlic, and white wine) and the staple *fegato alla Veneziana* (tender calf's liver cooked with onions). Cap off the perfect meal with your choice of *formaggi* (cheeses) or *tiramisù* (espresso-soaked lady fingers layered with sweetened, creamy mascarpone cheese and dusted with cocoa).

Italy is famed for its wines, and the vineyards around Venice produce some great ones, including the white Soave and reds Bardolino and Valpolicello. The best table wines tend to be whites.

Although dining in Italy is relatively inexpensive, remember that meal costs include much more than just your first and second course. Italian restaurants add to your bill an unavoidable "bread and cover" charge *(pane e coperto)* of about 1€ to 6€ ($1.15–$6.90). This *coperto* plus water and wine, an appetizer, coffee, dessert, and a *digestivo* (after-dinner drink) can quickly add up.

Tasty Italian take-out comes in the form of *tavola calda* and *rosticceria,* which sell prepared hot dishes by weight. Most bars sell *tramezzini,* which are like giant tea sandwiches without crusts, packed with tuna, ham, tomatoes, mozzarella, and other deli delicacies. For picnic supplies, stop by *alimentari* (grocery stores), *forno* (bakeries), and *fruttivendolo* (fruit and vegetable stands).

Don't waste your time with the take-out pizza slices in Venice. Italian pizza is only worth eating in Rome and in Rome's southern region.

Venice's top restaurants

Antico Martini
$$$$ San Marco   VENETIAN/INTERNATIONAL

Founded as a simple cafe in 1720, this eatery is now one of Venice's top restaurants. Since 1921, the Baldi family has maintained the restaurant's airy, clubby atmosphere, especially its outdoor summer dining terrace. Local taste temptations such as *risotto di frutti di mare* and *fegato alla Veneziana* are prepared to perfection. However, the food comes at a stiff price due to the establishment's reputation and proximity to La Fenice opera house.

See map p. 460. Campo San Fantin (on the edge of the square occupied by La Fenice opera house). ☎ *041-523-7027 or 041-522-4121.* www.anticomartini.com. *Reservations required. Vaporetto: San Marco or Santa Maria del Giglio. Main courses: 17€–36€ ($20–$41); 4-course fixed-price menus 46€ ($53); 6-course menu degustazione 79€ ($91). AE, DC, MC, V. Open: Lunch Wed–Mon, dinner Thurs–Mon.*

Arcimboldo
$$$ Castello   VENETIAN/ITALIAN

Archimboldo is always popular and is fast becoming one of Venice's leading restaurants. In the summer, grab yourself an outdoor table to watch action on the canal while sampling the restaurant's meticulously prepared Venetian cuisine. And you don't have to stick with Venetian specialties like seafood and liver — enjoy cuisines from the rest of Italy. The ingredients are bought fresh daily, and the wines are heavenly.

See map p. 460. Calle dei Furlani (a little street leading east from San Giorgio degli Schiavoni; when you reserve, ask about its boat service from San Marco). ☎ *041-528-6569.* www.arcimboldovenice.com. *Reservations recommended. Vaporetto: Arsenale or San Zaccaria. Main courses: 12€–18€ ($14–$21). AE, DC, MC, V. Open: Lunch and dinner Wed–Mon.*

Do Forni
$$$$ San Marco   VENETIAN/INTERNATIONAL

The dining rooms here are like two sides of a coin: One is decorated country style, and the other does its best imitation of an *Orient Express* dining car. Whichever atmosphere you choose, the food remains delicious and purely Venetian. The ample menu features many examples of the sea's bounty, along with a few choice world-cuisine dishes. Do Forni isn't cheap, though, and its bustling energy sometimes detracts from the posh atmosphere.

See map p. 460. Calle dei Specchieri (on the street leading north from Piazzetta dei Leoncini, which is around on the left flank of San Marco basilica). ☎ **041-523-2148.** www.doforni.it. *Reservations required. Vaporetto: San Marco. Main courses: 13€–23€ ($15–$26). AE, DC, MC, V. Open: Lunch and dinner daily.*

Ristorante Corte Sconta
$$$ Castello   **VENETIAN SEAFOOD**

Don't let the spare décor fool you: This trendy, out-of-the-way trattoria has a surprisingly high-quality, all-seafood menu, with an emphasis on freshness (they toss the shrimp live on the grill). Seafood fans should make reservations here for their very first night. At this hidden gem you can hang out with artists, foodies, and writers. In nice weather, you can dine under a canopy of grapevines in the courtyard.

See map p. 460. Calle del Pestrin 3886 (from San Marco, walk east along Riva degli Schiavoni; you eventually pass the church of La Pietà and then over a canal named for it; turn left onto Calle del Dose, which leads into Campo Bandiera e Moro; turn right to exit this square on Calle dei Preti; where this road turns right, Calle del Pestrin branches to the left). ☎ **041-522-7024.** http://ristoranti.ombra.net/ cortesconta. *Reservations recommended. Vaporetto: Arsenale. Main courses: 12€–20€ ($14–$23). MC, V. Open: Lunch and dinner Tues–Sat. Closed Jan 7–Feb 7 and July 15–Aug 15.*

Trattoria alla Madonna
$$$ San Polo   **VENETIAN**

This veritable seafood mecca sometimes verges on chaotic. The service here is friendly but occasionally brusque as waiters constantly rush to satisfy diners. You won't be able to linger over your meals here — so only visit if you're looking for fast, delicious, traditional food. If they're offering a mixed fish fry, dig in. Otherwise, check out the Venetian specialties enjoyed by local families, Italian businessmen, and travelers.

See map p. 460. Calle della Madonna (cross the Rialto Bridge and immediately turn left to walk down the Grand Canal's embankment; turn right down the second side street and the restaurant is 100 yards down on the left). ☎ **041-522-3824.** www. ristoranteallamadonna.com. *Reservations not accepted for parties fewer than 8. Vaporetto: Rialto. Main courses: 9€–15€ ($10–$17). AE, DC, MC, V. Open: Lunch and dinner Thurs–Tues. Closed Dec 24–Jan 31 and Aug 4–17.*

Vino Vino
$ San Marco   **VENETIAN/WINE BAR**

The owner of the exclusive, pricey Antico Martini restaurant also owns this relaxed, affordable little joint, which specializes in excellent staple dishes coupled with an impressive wine list featuring more than 350 Italian and foreign vintages (all for sale by the glass as well as by the bottle).

Taking care of business

Standard business hours for shops in Venice are Monday through Saturday from 9:00 a.m. to 12:30 p.m. and 3:00 to 7:30 p.m.; shops close Monday mornings in summer and Saturday afternoons in winter. Most grocers close Wednesday afternoon throughout the year. Restaurants are required to close at least one day per week (*il giorno di riposo*), but the particular day varies. Many are open for Sunday lunch but close for Sunday dinner and close Monday when the fish market is closed. Restaurants close one to two weeks for holidays (*chiuso per ferie*), sometimes in July or August, frequently over Christmas, and sometimes in January or February before the Carnevale rush.

Order at the counter, then find a free seat at the simple tables in one of two cramped rooms. Servers bring your meal out to you as you sit back and enjoy a self-guided wine tasting.

See map p. 460. San Marco 2007 (on Ponte della Veste; head west out of the southwest corner of Piazza San Marco down Saliz San Mose; cross the bridge to continue straight on Calle Larga XXII Marzo, from which you'll turn right up Calle delle Veste; the restaurant is at the opposite end of a short bridge, just before La Fenice opera house). ☎ *041-241-7688.* www.vinovino.co.it. *Reservations suggested. Vaporetto: San Marco. Main courses: 5€–12€ ($5.75–$14). AE, DC, MC, V. Open: Lunch and dinner Wed–Mon.*

Venice's runner-up restaurants

Bistrot de Venise

$$–$$$ **San Marco** This artists' hangout with a bistro style offers an eclectic menu of Italian, French, and historic 15th-century Venetian recipes. Peek in the back room (or check out the Web site) to see what's going on in the evening — art exhibits, live music, poetry readings, and so on. *See map p. 460. San Marco 4687 (on Calle dei Fabbri below the Albergo al Gambero).* ☎ *041-523-6651.* www.bistrotdevenise.com.

Da Sandro

$–$$ **San Polo** A good choice if you're looking for an inexpensive pizza-and-beer meal. Like most pizzerias/trattorias, Da Sandro offers a dozen varieties of pizza as well as a full trattoria menu of pastas and entrees. *See map p. 460. San Polo 1473 (on Campiello dei Meloni on the main drag linking the Rialto to Campo San Polo).* ☎ *041-523-4894.*

Rosticceria San Bartolomeo

$–$$ **Near Rialto Bridge** A popular tavola calda offering ready-made hot dishes and pizza with no cover charge right in the heart of the action. Short on atmosphere, long on budget value. The dining hall upstairs costs

20 percent more. See map p. 460. San Marco 5424 (on Calle della Bissa).
☎ *041-522-3569.*

Trattoria da Remigio

$–$$ **Castello** Famous for its straightforward renditions of Adriatic
classics, this spot bucks the current Venetian trends by continuing to offer
exquisite food and excellent service at reasonable prices. Locals love it
for a night of semi-refinement, so book ahead. *See map p. 460. Castello 3416
(on Calle Bosello near Scuola San Giorgio dei Greci).* ☎ *041-523-0089.* http://
ristoranti.ombra.net/remigio.

Exploring Venice

Even though the city of Venice has been working fiercely on hydraulic
dams, each winter the tides force the Adriatic Sea to rush into Venice's
lagoon and the lagoon to rush into the streets. These *acque alte,* or high
waters, can raise in-town water levels up to 3 feet for brief spells (usually
one to five hours). When the *acque alte* strike, usually between October
and March, low-lying Piazza San Marco is the first area to flood. As the
waters rise, you may find yourself having the peculiarly Venetian experience of walking about the packed city street atop long, jerry-rigged
bridges of wooden planks. The system of dams won't be in operation
until the end of this decade.

In addition to the attractions mentioned in this chapter, keep in mind that
if you come to the city during Carnevale, you're in for one nonstop party
(see "Europe's Calendar of Events" in Chapter 2 for more information).

If you're between ages 16 and 29, pick up a **Rolling Venice Card,** which
offers discounts on selected hotels (mostly hostel-type accommodations),
restaurants, sights, and public transportation. The pass, good for a year,
is 3€ ($3.45). In summer, you can stop by the special Rolling Venice office
set up in the train station, Stazione Santa Lucia, open daily from 8 a.m. to
8 p.m.; in winter, you can get the pass at the Transalpino travel agency
just outside the station's front doors and to the right, at the top of the
steps. It's open Monday through Friday from 8:30 a.m. to 12:30 p.m. and
3 to 7 p.m., and Saturday from 8:30 a.m. to 12:30 p.m.

The **VeniceCard** (☎ **899-909-090** in Italy, or 041-271-4747 or 041-2424
outside of Italy; www.venicecard.com) offers discounts on a wide range
of services and sights. The "blu" version will get you free passage on
buses and *vaporetti,* usage of public toilets, and a reduced daily rate —
and a reserved spot — at the public ASM parking garage. The "orange"
version adds to these services admission to all the sights covered under
the expanded version of the Musei di Piazza San Marco cumulative ticket
(see "Piazza San Marco," later in this section), plus the card lets you
bypass the often long lines.

For adults over 30, the "blu" card costs 14€ ($16) for one day, 29€ ($33) for three days, or 51€ ($59) for seven days; for ages 4 to 29, the "blu" card costs 9€ ($10) for one day, 22€ ($25) for three days, or 49€ ($56) for seven days. For adults, the "orange" card costs 28€ ($32) for one day, 47€ ($54) for three days, or 68€ ($78) for seven days; for ages 4 to 29, the "orange" card costs 18€ ($21) for one day, 35€ ($40) for three days, or 61€ ($70) for seven days. You can order it in advance by phone or online, and they'll tell you where to pick it up. (There are versions that also include a ride into town from the airport, but it doesn't save you any money in the long run, so skip it.)

Venice's top attractions

Galleria dell'Accademia
Dorsoduro

If you only have time for only one museum in Venice, take in the Accademia. Set aside a good one and a half to three hours to peruse the vast collections of masterpieces by Venice's color-loving artists. The museum covers the biggies in Venetian painting, from Paolo Veneziano's 14th-century *Coronation of the Virgin* altarpiece to Giorgione's strange *The Tempest* and Giovanni Bellini's numerous *Madonna and Childs*.

Also on display are Carpaccio's intricate *Cycle of St. Ursula,* Titian's late *Pietà,* and Tintoretto's *The Stealing of St. Mark,* commemorating the Venetian merchants who, in A.D. 828, spirited the body of the saint away from Alexandria during an era when acquiring bona fide saints was the order of the day for relic hunters.

When Paolo Veronese unveiled his *Last Supper,* the puritanical leaders of the Inqusition nearly had a conniption. They threatened him with charges of blasphemy for portraying this feast as a drunken banquet more in keeping with a Roman orgy than the holiest of moments. The painting was unaltered but retitled *Feast in the House of Levi* (certainly a more safely secular title), and the censors let it pass.

The new reservations service costs an additional 1€ ($1.15) per ticket but ought to cut down on your wait.

See map p. 460. Dorsoduro (at the foot of Accademia Bridge, on Campo della Carità). ☎ *041-522-2247 or* www.gallerieaccademia.org. *Reservations:* ☎ *041-520-0345. Vaporetto: Accademia. Open: Mon 8:15 a.m.–2 p.m.; Tues–Sun 8:15 a.m.–7:15 p.m. Last admission 30 minutes before close (winter hours may be shorter). Admission: 9€ ($10).*

Basilica di San Marco (St. Mark's Basilica)
San Marco

No church in Europe is more lavishly decorated, more exquisitely mosaicked, more glittering with gold than Venice's San Marco. Dating to the 11th century, the originally Byzantine architecture and decoration now includes Romanesque and Gothic touches, too.

A few basic do's and don'ts when visiting here:

  ✔ Dress appropriately — that means no bare shoulders or knees (no shorts, short skirts, or sleeveless shirts).

  ✔ Keep silent.

  ✔ Do not take pictures.

More than 40,000 square feet of gold-backed mosaics crafted between the 12th and 17th centuries cover the church's atrium, ceilings, walls, and multiple domes. The oldest were created by Eastern masters, and later ones were based on works by Tintoretto, Veronese, and Titian. The floor carries on a mosaic feel with its wonderfully spiraling marble tiles. The only disappointing aspect of this wonder of architecture? Its immense popularity. Visitors are often pushed through the site like cattle. Still, the 20 to 60 minutes you spend inside (depending on how many of the church's side attractions you visit) will be truly unforgettable.

Don't miss checking out the baptistery alcove, which features a font carved by Sansovino, or taking a peek at the presbytery with its *Pala d'Oro,* a golden trophy studded with gems from Constantinople. The Marciano Museum (also known as *Logia dei Cavalli*) can be entered through an atrium. The Museum offers you a close-up look at some of the building's mosaics and houses the original *Triumphal Quadriga* of four horses, life-size bronze sculptures that are truly one of Venice's cultural treasures. Taken in 1204 from Constantinople during the crusades, the sculptures' exact origin is unclear, but they're certainly ancient (the best guess is second century A.D., and either Roman or Hellenistic in origin). The cathedral runs free guided tours in summer, usually around 10:30 a.m. Monday through Saturday (check in the atrium for specifics).

Large bags are no longer allowed inside the basilica, and a left-luggage office has been established at Ateneo San Basso in Calle San Basso 315A. It's open Monday through Saturday from 10 a.m. to 4 p.m. and Sundays from 2 to 4 p.m. Please note that the basilica is experimenting with this service, and its location, hours, or other conditions may have changed by the time you visit Venice.

See map p. 460. Piazza San Marco. ☎ *041-522-5205. Vaporetto: San Marco or San Zaccaria. Admission:* **Basilica,** *free;* **treasury,** *2€ ($2.30);* **Marciano Museum,** *1.50€ ($1.75). Open:* **Basilica and treasury,** *Apr–Oct Mon–Sat 9:45 a.m.–5 p.m., Sun 2–5 p.m.; Nov–Mar Mon–Sat 9:45 a.m.–4 p.m.* **Marciano Museum,** *daily 9:45 a.m.–5 p.m. (winter hours may be shorter).*

Collezione Peggy Guggenheim
Dorsoduro

Peggy Guggenheim's former residence in Venice is now one of the world's top modern-art museums. The uncompleted (only the first floor was built) 18th-century Palazzo Venier dei Leoni sits on the Grand Canal and is filled with the late, great art collector's personal favorites. The museum offers a comprehensive survey of avant-garde modern art.

You find works by her short-lived hubby Max Ernst and her discovery, Jackson Pollock, as well as pieces by some of her favorites: Picasso (notably, his 1911 *The Poet*), Miró, Mondrian, Brancusi, Duchamp, Kadinsky, Chagall, Dalí, and Giacometti. A racy version of Tuscan sculptor Marino Marini's patented man-on-horseback bronzes stands at attention in the small garden.

See map p. 460. Calle San Cristoforo, San Gregorio 701. ☎ *041-240-5411.* www.guggenheim-venice.it. *Vaporetto: Accademia. Admission: 10€ ($12) adults, 8€ ($9.20) over 65, free children under 12 and holders of the Rolling Venice card. Open: Wed–Mon 10 a.m.–6 p.m. (Apr–Oct until 10 p.m. Sat).*

Palazzo Ducale (Doge's Palace)
San Marco

One of Italy's grandest and most history-saturated town halls is a confection of Gothic-Renaissance design. Raised in 1309 and rebuilt after a 1577 fire, the palace features public halls with canvases and frescoes by Venice's greatest artists, including lovely works by Veronese and Tintoretto. The guided tour leads you through the palace in about 45 to 100 minutes, depending on your pace.

Even with an informative audio guide and English placards describing the artworks and the civic purpose of each room, you may find wandering the public halls a bit cold and distancing. Your experience may be enhanced by knowing that the real governing of Venice was never done in these public areas but rather in a series of low-ceilinged corridors and tiny offices that wrapped around the building like a governmental cocoon (the entrances were hidden behind secret doors set into the gorgeous paintings and carved woodwork in the public rooms).

 You can see this inner sanctum — and get a great primer on Venetian politics and intrigue — by taking the 90-minute "Secret Itineraries" tour. Among the stops on the tour are the inquisition room and the "leads," the prison cells in the roof rafters where guides recount the tale of Casanova's famous escape. After the tour, you can visit the public palace on your own.

Off the back of the palace, you cross over the famous, enclosed Bridge of Sighs *(Ponte dei Sospiri),* named by romantic-era writers who imagined condemned prisoners letting out a lament as they crossed it and got their final glimpse of Venice and its lagoon through tiny windows in the center. The cells on the other side preserve the scrawls and graffiti of ancient prisoners.

See map p. 460. Piazzetta San Marco. ☎ *041-271-5911.* www.museicivici veneziani.it. *Vaporetto: San Marco or San Zaccaria. Admission: 11€ ($13) adults, 5.50€ ($6.35) students ages 15–29, 3€ ($3.45) ages 6–14; the ticket also gets you into the Museo Civico Correr (see the next listing). "Secret Itineraries" tour (with ticket to Museo Civico Correr): 12.50€ ($14) adults, 7€ ($8.05) students, 4€ ($4.60) ages 6–14. Open: Apr–Oct daily 9 a.m.–7 p.m.; Nov–Mar daily 9 a.m.–5 p.m. Last admission 1 hour before close.*

Piazza San Marco (St. Mark's Square)
San Marco

A year-round carnival is the best way to describe Piazza San Marco, a gathering place filled to the brim with milling visitors, swarms of hungry pigeons, locals enjoying espresso at outdoor cafes, and couples dancing on the cobblestones to the strains of live piano music. The living room of Venice, San Marco is surrounded on three sides by a 16th-century arcade and anchored by one of Italy's most gorgeous mosaic-covered cathedrals, Basilica di San Marco. Visitors and locals mob the site at midday, so try a late-night or early-morning visit when the space is virtually deserted and has a magical emptiness all its own.

On July 14, 1902, the too-tall **Campanile,** or bell tower (☎ 041-522-4064), crumbled to the ground almost instantly. Because every Italian city feels compelled to have a dome, tower, or some other high edifice for tourists to climb (just kidding!), Venice quickly built a new tower. The new structure resembles the old, but with two major differences: This one is architecturally sound, and, even better, has an elevator. From atop the tower, take in the many domes and spires of the cathedral's rooftop, along with a sweeping vista of the city and the Grand Canal. Admission is 6€ ($6.90); the tower is open from April to June and from September to October daily from 9:00 a.m. to 7:45 p.m.; July and August it's open from 9 a.m. to 9 p.m.; November through March it's open 9:30 a.m. to 4:15 p.m. Year-round, the last admission is one hour before closing.

The **Torre dell'Orolorgio** (☎ 041-522-4951; www.museicivicivenezian i.it), a late-15th-century clock tower, enlivens the square and chimes out the hour. The clock tower features two hammer-wielding statues called the Moors of Venice. (Actually, the statues were supposed to represent European shepherds, but time and environmental conditions have darkened the bronze figures to the point where the locals decided they looked more Moorish.) The tower has been under restoration for years, with various — and increasingly delayed — reopening dates given. At press time the tower was set to open late in 2004. You may be able to visit it, but don't count on it.

The core collections of the **Museo Civico Correr** (☎ 041-240-5211; www.museicivicivenezian i.it), in the square's southwest corner, take visitors through Venetian painting from the 14th to 16th centuries, highlighting the works of Tintoretto, Veronese, Carpaccio, and the Bellini family (Jacopo and sons Gentile and Giovanni, the greatest of the three) along the way. But some of the strongest works in the collection are by non-Venetians such as Antonello da Messina and Cosmé Tura. Admission is by joint ticket (see the next paragraph or the listing earlier for Palazzo Ducale). The museum is open April through October daily from 9 a.m. to 7 p.m. and November through March daily from 9 a.m. to 5 p.m. Last entrance is one hour before closing.

The **Musei di Piazza San Marco** joint ticket grants admission to all the piazza's museums — the Palazzo Ducale (see listing earlier), Museo Civico Correr, Museo Archeologico Nazionale, and Biblioteca Nazionale Marciana — for 11€ ($13) adults, 5.50€ ($6.35) students.

See map p. 460. Piazza San Marco. Vaporetto: San Marco or San Zaccaria.

Scuola Grande di San Rocco
San Polo

A *scuola* was a lay fraternity whose members worked diligently for various charitable causes. Because these private gentlemen's clubs were also places to show off, many *scuole* were decorated by commissioned artists. In 1564, the Scuola di San Rocco held an art competition to choose its decorator. Renaissance master Tintoretto outdid his rivals by completing an entire painting and secretly installing it in the ceiling of the Sala dell'Albero off the second-floor hall.

The judges were duly impressed, and Tintoretto got the job, eventually filling the *scuola*'s two floors with dozens of works over the next quarter century. Be sure to check out the *Rest on the Flight into Egypt* on the ground floor, as well as a huge *Crucifixion* that ranks among the greatest and most moving works in the history of Venetian art. The San Rocco baroque orchestra holds excellent regular chamber concerts in this fantastic setting; for info call ☎ 041-962-999 or go online to www.musicinvenice.com.

See map p. 460. San Polo 3058 (on Campo San Rocco adjacent to Campo dei Frari). ☎ 041-523-4864. www.sanrocco.it (under construction). Vaporetto: San Tomà. Open: Mar 28–Nov 30 daily 9 a.m.–5:30 p.m.; Dec–Mar 27 daily 10 a.m.–4 p.m. Last admission 30 minutes before close. Closed Easter and Dec 25–Jan 1. Admission: 5.50€ ($6.35) adults, 4€ ($4.60) students.

More cool things to see and do

✔ **Getting lost:** So you've found a great map of Venice? Well, stick it in your traveling bags and forget about it. Hey, if you get lost in Venice (and you probably will), why not make a day of it? Forget about those "helpful" signposts that dot the cityscape and avoid the crowded squares and attractions. Whenever things start to feel a little too touristy, just walk a block or so away from the action. Doing so enables you to explore Venice's private side — its ancient sounds, its classic energy, its distinctive rhythms. Stop for a meal in a little cafe that seems popular with locals, or purchase some picnic supplies and enjoy a meal at a tiny campo or canalside *riva*.

✔ **Cruising the Grand Canal:** Think of the Grand Canal as the watery Champs-Elysées of Venice. Hundreds of boats of all shapes and sizes — ferries, gondolas, garbage scows, speedboats, and small commercial craft — fill the canal to capacity. Buildings and palaces that face the Grand Canal display a variety of styles — from the intricate Byzantine-Romanesque to the classically proportioned Renaissance and neoclassical.

Take a relaxing ride on the no. 1 or 82 vaporetto line. Don't get all flustered about which *palazzo* was built when by whom. Instead, open your eyes (or your camera lens) and explore the rich details of the ride — a mysterious woman clothed in black, workmen tinkering with water-rotted moorings, lazy cats resting precariously on high open windowsills.

✔ **Shopping for fine glass, lace, and Carnevale masks:** This trio of Venetian craft specialties is everywhere about town, in little hole-in-the-wall shops and big, crowded boutiques (estimates put the number of glass shops in the San Marco district alone at 1,000).

Be aware of quality. Many items are machine-produced or crafted elsewhere — sometimes Eastern Europe or Taiwan. Your best guide is not to worry about pedigree and simply purchase things you like. However, if you're looking for the real deal or you're buying to build a formal collection, resign yourself to the fact that prices for quality items are high.

The following are some of the top emporia for the most popular crafts. (Every piece on display in these shops is guaranteed hand-crafted by Venetian artisans.)

- For glass, visit **Venini,** Piazzetta dei Leoncini (off the left flank of Basilica di San Marco); **Pauly & Co,** Ponte Consorzi (just behind the Doge's Palace, although they also have boutique shops on Piazza San Marco); or **Salviati,** on Piazza San Marco.

- For lace, go to **Jesurum,** on Mercerie del Capitello.

- For masks, visit the **Laboratorio Artigiano Maschere,** at Barbaria delle Tole, in the Castello district.

Incidentally, the most traditional craftsmen of Venetian glass are located on the island of Murano, and the ladies who tat the best lace are on the island of Burano, both described in "The Venetian lagoon: Island hopping and shopping," later in this chapter.

Or, take the easy route and simply stroll along one of Venice's premier (and priciest) avenues, Le Mercerie (head out of Piazza San Marco at the clock tower). This route's fancy boutiques and souvenir shops can give you a wonderful taste of the best of Venice. *Note:* The avenue is actually a series of different streets with constantly changing names — but don't fret, just realize that all streets begin with the word *mercerie*.

Guided tours

Most of the central travel agencies have posters in their windows advertising half- and full-day walking tours of the city's sights. Most of these tours are piggybacked onto those organized by **American Express** (☎ **041-520-0844**) and should cost the same: about 21€ ($24) for a two-hour tour and 34€ ($39) for a full day, per person. **Free tours** of the

Basilica di San Marco and some of the other churches are often offered, but on erratic schedules because they're given by volunteers.

Suggested itineraries

If you're the type who'd rather organize your own tours, this section offers some tips for building your own Venice itineraries.

If you have one day

The first order of business is wandering through the glittering mosaic wonderland of the **Basilica di San Marco.** Then head next door and take the "Secret Itineraries" tour (in English at 10:30 a.m.) of the **Palazzo Ducale** for an insider's glimpse into the hidden offices, courtrooms, archives, and prisons from which the true Venetian Republic ruled for 900 years.

After a light lunch, tour the **Scuola Grande di San Rocco** for its festival of Tintorettos and the **Accademia,** Venice's top painting gallery. Spend the evening simply wandering the spellbinding Venetian labyrinth of streets and passages. At some point, either when you arrive or prepare to leave, ride the **No. 1 vaporetto** line its full length between Piazza San Marco and the Ferrovia — about 45 minutes each way. This vaporetto cruises by the hundreds of proud *palazzi* lining the principal aquatic boulevard.

If you have two days

Spend the morning of **Day 1** as described in the preceding section, in **San Marco** and touring the **Doge's Palace,** but also take time to ride the elevator to the top of the **Campanile di San Marco** for a terrific panorama across the city. After lunch, head to the **Ca' d'Oro** (north of the Rialto Bridge), Venice's most famous private palace and today a museum providing a look at one of the great *palazzi* gracing the Grand Canal as well as a small but fine art collection. Cross the Rialto Bridge into San Polo to see the **Scuola Grande di San Rocco,** and then round off the day with a crawl through the bars serving *cicchetti* (munchie food) around the **Rialto Market.**

Although the city has plenty of official "sights," one of Venice's greatest attractions is the city itself, so spend the morning of **Day 2** simply lost in the city's back alleyways. For its way of life and Eastern/Western fusion of architecture and wealth of history, Venice has no match. Some of the residential neighborhoods off the beaten path are eastern Castello near the **Arsenale,** the **Ghetto** (once the Jewish quarter) in northern Cannaregio, and the island of **La Giudecca.**

Suitably refreshed and recharged, cross into the **Dorsoduro** neighborhood in the afternoon for some hardcore art appreciation. Visit the **Accademia** for a look at the city's Renaissance heritage and the nearby **Collezione Peggy Guggenheim** for one of Europe's best galleries of international 20th-century works. If you have the time and energy, fit in the **Ca' Rezzonico** as well (like the **Ca' d'Oro,** another restored historic patrician palace with a small painting gallery).

If you have three days

On **Day 1** and **Day 2,** follow the previous section. Use **Day 3** to take a circle tour of the best outlying islands in the **Venetian lagoon:** Murano with its glass factories; Burano with its colorful fishing houses and lace school; and Torcello, a glimpse into what Venice looked like in its early days with a gloriously mosaicked Byzantine church in the middle.

Traveling Beyond Venice

For a change of pace, consider leaving Venice for a day in search of quieter (and less touristy) pleasures. A quick boat ride can lead you to various islands in the Venetian lagoon (although low-key, the islands offer some great shopping). Or take a short train ride to Padova, a college town with stunning architecture and art galore.

The Venetian lagoon: Island hopping and shopping

Want to see what Venice looked like before it became a tourist mecca of *palazzi* and museums? If so, you need to go no farther than the fishing-village islands of the northern Venetian lagoon. A 1½-mile vaporetto ride takes you to **Murano** with its rich glass-blowing heritage, **Burano** with its old-fashioned lace works, and **Torcello** with its remarkable medieval church.

Getting there

Most vaporetto ferries to the islands leave from Fondamente Nove in Venice, which is on the far north side of the Castello district. However, you can also ride line 71 to Murano from San Zaccaria (on Riva degli Schiavoni near Piazzetta San Marco). Otherwise, from Fondamente Nove, get on line 12, 13, 41, or 42 to Murano. Line 12 continues from Murano to Burano, and then from Burano to Torcello. From Torcello, you can return to Venice only on Line 12 (to Fondamente Nove, where you can catch the 52 back to San Marco).

 If you plan to visit the islands of the Venetian lagoon, get up early in the morning and plan to be out of town all day (at least five to seven hours). Because the ferries between the islands leave hourly, plan your time on the islands in hour increments. One hour is usually enough for Burano and Torcello; allow two hours or more for Murano. Additionally, figure the following travel times: 35 minutes for the ride from Venice to Murano, 20 minutes from Murano to Burano, 5 minutes from Burano to Torcello, and 50 minutes from Torcello to Venice.

Seeing the sights

Murano is the largest of the three islands. This active island is home to numerous fishermen and several age-old glass factories. If you're interested in shopping for fine examples of this outstanding craft, head to the island's outlet stores (most stores on Murano take quality seriously). Never pay the sticker price at these stores; instead, bargain for at least 30 percent off the asking price. If you're looking for a one-of-kind glass item, talk with any of the glassblowers in the workshops. Most can create original items, especially trinkets, for you on the spot.

If you're interested in the history behind glass craft, stop by the **Museo del Vetro** (☎ 041-739-586), which offers a large collection of glass objects from ancient Roman times through the 19th century as well as displays that explore the history and practice of the craft itself.

For a change of pace, the **church of San Pietro Martire** has unexpected riches in the form of oil paintings by Tintoretto, Veronese, and Giovanni Bellini. For 1.50€ ($1.75), you can see the sacristy's carved paneling. Also, check out another truly ancient church, **Santa Maria e Donato,** with its gorgeous exterior that features stacked colonnades, dog-tooth molding, and inlaid Byzantine details. Rebuilt in the 12th century, the current structure features Corinthian columns dating from Roman times, a pulpit from the sixth century, a patterned floor from 1141 that is reminiscent of those in San Marco, and 15th-century frescoes.

Note that Murano has six vaporetto docks. You usually land at Colonna or Faro from Venice, but you should continue on to the island of Burano from the Faro dock.

Lacemaking is the highlight of your visit to the tiny island of **Burano.** Although lace from Burano fetches high prices in Venetian shops, prices on the island can be a bit more reasonable — beautiful edged hankies are available for around 2.60€ ($3). Learn a bit about lacemaking's history at the **Museo del Merletto** (☎ 041-730-034), a shop that keeps this ancient tradition vibrantly alive. Be sure to visit the second floor of the shop, where women still work on extremely delicate and beautiful lace items by hand. Admission is 4€ ($4.60) adults and 2.50€ ($2.90) students, or free with the cumulative San Marco ticket. The shop is usually open Wednesday through Monday from 10 a.m. to 5 p.m. (until 4 p.m. Nov–Mar). Burano also features a Tiepolo Crucifixion in the parish church of San Martino, streets of brightly painted houses, and a leisurely, seafaring pace that comes as a welcome respite from the frenzy of Venice.

An 11th-century Byzantine cathedral is the highlight of the grassy, semi-deserted island of **Torcello.** To reach the cathedral from the dock, walk along the island's only canal for about ten minutes. One wall of the cathedral features a remarkable mosaic of the Last Judgment and the apse has a massive Madonna mosaic. Admission is 3€ ($3.45), and it's open daily from 10 a.m. to 6 p.m. (until 5 p.m. in winter). Across the square is the tiny **Museo dell'Estuario** (☎ 041-730-761), whose collection includes archaeological fragments and the remains of some ten other churches that once stood on Torcello. Admission is 2€ ($2.30); it's open Tuesday through Sunday from 10:00 a.m. to 12:30 p.m. and 2 to 4 p.m.

Where to dine

For lunch, consider picking up supplies in Venice (Torcello is great for a relaxed picnic) or sitting down for a hearty meal at **Trattoria Al Corallo** (☎ 041-739-636; ristoranti.ombra.net/corallo), Fondamenta dei Vetrai 73 in Murano, or **Trattoria da Romano** (☎ 041-730-030; www.daromano.it), at Via Baldassare Galuppi 223 in Burano. Or pull out all the stops and splurge on **Locanda Cipriani** (☎ 041-730-150; www.locandacipriani.com), a refined restaurant in the middle of nowhere on Torcello that was one of Hemingway's favorite dining spots.

Padova: Outstanding art and architecture

For the best daytrip (in my opinion) in the Veneto region, make tracks for **Padova** (Padua) — a city of saints and scholars, Giotto frescoes, and arcaded piazze. Right on your way to Bologna, Florence, and Rome via rail, Padova makes a great stop en route to or from Venice. Allow four to five hours (and some hustling) to see the sites, or stay the night and take in the city at a more leisurely pace.

Getting there

Padova is only 32 minutes by half-hourly train from Venice. (For this reason, many savvy travelers choose to stay in Padova during peak tourist season and day-trip to crowded, expensive Venice.)

The **tourist office** (☎ 049-875-2077; www.padovanet.it) is at the train station.

Seeing the sights

The must-see site for Padova is on the northernmost edge of town (take bus 3 or 8, 10, or 12 at the Piazza Eremitani off Corso Garibaldi) — the **Cappella degli Scrovegni (Arena Chapel)** (☎ 049-201-0020; www.cappelladegliscrovegni.it), which Giotto, a master of emotion and artistic technique, adorned with gorgeous frescoes from 1303 to 1306. The chapel as a whole is breathtaking, depicting scenes from the life of Mary and Jesus in 38 panels including the awe-inspiring *Last Judgment,* the insightful *Arrest of Christ,* and the woe-filled *Lamentation of Christ.* Advance reservation is required; the admission prices listed here include the 1€ ($1.15) reservation fee. Admission (available at the Musei Civici di Eremitani) is 12€ ($14 adults), 1€ ($1.15) children under 6 and seniors over 65. It's open daily from 9 a.m. to 7 p.m. (in summer it may stay open until 10 p.m.). You must collect your tickets at the box office one hour prior to your admission.

The nearby **Musei Civici di Eremitani,** Piazza Eremitani 8 (☎ 049-820-4550), houses an archaeological collection on the ground floor, a Giotto *Crucifix,* and minor works by major 14th-century Venetian painters (including Giorgione, Jacopo Bellini, Veronese, and Tintoretto). Admission is combined with the Cappella degli Scrovegni (unless you choose to see the museum alone for 10€/$12) and the hours are February to October daily 9 a.m. to 7 p.m. and November to January 9 a.m. to 6 p.m.

Padova's other great sight is the eastern-looking **Basilica di Sant'Antonio,** Piazza del Santo 11 (☎ 049-878-9722). Outside, the basilica is all domes and mini-minarets, while altars inside feature Donatello bronzes. Be sure to see the north transept for the tomb of St. Anthony and the south transept for a 14th-century fresco of the *Crucifixion.* A beautiful bronze sculpture of a man on horseback called *Gattamelata,* also by Donatello, dominates the church's piazza. Admission is free, and the basilica is open daily from 6:20 a.m. to 7:45 p.m. in summer (until 7 p.m. in winter).

Where to stay

If you're looking for value in Paduan hotels, check out the bright, modernized rooms of family-run **Hotel al Fagiano,** Via Locatelli 45 (west of Piazza del Santo; ☎ 049-875-0073; www.alfagiano.it). Doubles with a bathroom cost 75€ to 81€ ($86–$93).

Where to dine

The extravagantly neoclassical **Caffé Pedrocchi,** Piazzetta Pedrocchi 15 (☎ 049-878-1231; www.caffepedrocchi.it), promises one of Italy's most elegant cafe experiences. Although drinks are pricey, the setting, with its colorful 19th-century décor and whimsical references to ancient Rome and Egypt, makes this establishment worth the splurge. In summer, get a table on the stone patio and experience the gentle ebb and flow of Paduan life.

Fast Facts: Venice

Area Code

The country code for Italy is **39.** Venice — along with the rest of Italy — no longer has a separate city code, though you'll notice almost all numbers in town still start with 041 (the old city code). As they run out of new numbers, that will be changing. And, unlike in the past, you must dial that initial zero.

American Express

American Express is at San Marco 1471, 30124 Venezia, on Salizzada San Moisè just west of Piazza San Marco (☎ 041-520-0844). May through October banking hours are Monday through Saturday from 8 a.m. to 8 p.m. (All other services are available 9 a.m.–5:30 p.m.) From November through April, hours are Monday through Friday from 9:00 a.m. to 5:30 p.m. and Saturday from 9:00 a.m. to 12:30 p.m.

Currency

In 2002, the euro became the legal tender in Italy, replacing the lira. The exchange rate used to calculate the dollar values given in this chapter is 1€ equals $1.15. Amounts over $10 are rounded to the nearest dollar.

Doctors and Dentists

Your best bet is to have your hotel call and set up an appointment with an English-speaking dentist or doctor. The American Express office also has a list.

Embassies and Consulates

The nearest U.S. Consulate is in Milan at Largo Donegani 1 (☎ 02-290-351), open Monday through Friday from 9 a.m. to noon for visas only. From Monday through Friday, it's also open for telephone service info from 2 to 4 p.m.

Emergency

Dial ☎ **113** in any emergency ☎ **112** for the *carabinieri* (the military-trained and more useful of the two police forces), ☎ **118** or **06-5100** to summon an ambulance, or ☎ **115** for the fire department. *Pronto soccorso* is Italian for "first aid," but you can also use the phrase to get to an emergency room. Call ☎ **116** for roadside assistance (not free).

Hospitals

First aid is available 24 hours a day in the emergency room *(pronto soccorso)* of major hospitals. Try the Ospedale Civile di Venezia (☎ 041-529-4111), Campo SS. Giovanni e Paolo or Fatebenefratelli di Venezia (☎ 041-783-111), Cannaregio 3458.

Information

The main tourist office, Venice Pavilion/ Palazzina dei Santi (☎ 041-529-8711 or

041-522-5150; www.turismovenezia. it; Vaporetto: San Marco), is located right when you get off the vaporetto at the San Marco stop, in a stone pavilion wedged between the small green park on the Grand Canal and the famous Harry's Bar. For more information on it and other offices, see "Finding information after you arrive," near the beginning of this chapter. The official site of the city government (also full of good resources) is www. comune.venezia.it. Several good privately maintained sites are Meeting Venice (www.meetingvenice.it), *Un Ospite di Venezia* (www.unospitedivenezia. it), and Doge of Venice (www.doge.it).

Internet Access and Cybercafes

Venetian Navigator, Castello 5269 on Calle delle Bande between San Marco and Campo Santa Maria Formosa (☎ 041-522-6084; www.venetiannavigator.com) is open daily 10 a.m. to 10 p.m. (Nov–Apr 10 a.m.–1 p.m. and 2:30–8:30 p.m.). The Internet Cafe, San Marco 2976–2958 on Campo San Stefano (☎ 041-520-8128; www.nethousecafes.com), is open 24 hours daily.

Maps

The tourist office hands out a free map, part of the *LEO Bussola* brochure, but it's good only for finding vaporetto lines and stops. Buy a more detailed map at any newsstand or bookstore.

Newspapers/Magazines

The tourist office's *LEO Bussola* brochure is useful for museum hours and events. Pick up a copy of the useful, info-packed monthly *Un Ospite di Venezia* (www. unospitedivenezia.it); most hotels have a handful of copies. Also keep an eye out for the ubiquitous posters around town with exhibit and concert schedules.

Pharmacies

Pharmacies take turns staying open late. International Pharmacy, Via XXII Marzo 2067 (☎ 041-5294111; Vaporetto: San Marco), is well recommended and centrally located. To find a pharmacy in your area, call ☎ 192 or 041-523-0573, or ask at your hotel.

Police

Dial ☎ 113 in any emergency or ☎ 112 for the *carabinieri,* a division of the Italian army.

Post Office

The main post office is at San Marco 5554, 30124 Venezia, on the San Marco side of the Rialto Bridge at Rialto Fontego dei Tedeschi (☎ 041-271-7111 or 041-528-5813). This office sells stamps at Window 12 Monday through Saturday 8:30 a.m. to 6:30 p.m. (for parcels, 8:10 a.m.–1:30 p.m.).

Safety

The worst Venetian criminal you'll encounter is the occasional pickpocket. Watch your wallet on crowded streets, near popular tourist sites, and on the vaporetti. One other tip: Don't even think of swimming in the canals. These things are used as sewers.

Taxes

The value-added tax in Italy (called IVA) varies with the item or service, up to 19 percent, and is already included in the sticker price of any item (except, oddly, in the most expensive luxury hotels). Non-EU citizens who spend more than 154.94€ ($178) in a single store are entitled to a refund. See Chapter 4 for details on receiving one.

Taxis

See "Getting Around Venice," earlier in this chapter.

Telephone

See "Fast Facts: Rome," in Chapter 19 for information on making calls and calling-card access codes.

Transit Info

See "Getting Around Venice," earlier in this chapter.

Chapter 22

Madrid and the Best of Castile

- -

In This Chapter

▶ Getting to Madrid

▶ Finding your way around the city

▶ Discovering the best hotels and Spanish cuisine

▶ Exploring an art-lover's paradise

▶ Side-tripping to Toledo, El Escorial, and Segovia

- -

Madrid is the capital city and center of all Spain. An art lover's paradise, the city boasts the outstanding Prado Museum with works by Picasso, Velázquez, Goya, El Greco, and hundreds of other European artists. But Madrid is more than just art.

Madrid buzzes around the clock. You can see the royal palace in the morning, an 18th-century art gallery in the early afternoon, and bullfights in the late afternoon. Take the evening pre-dinner stroll, called the *paseo*. Then, after dark, you can begin your evening with a fashionably late dinner, perhaps followed by a flamenco show or dancing until daybreak at a happenin' nightclub.

Art aficionados can easily spend four to five days in Madrid. If you're not into art, the city is still worth at least two days, plus two more for exploring the surrounding region of Castile on daytrips to Toledo and Segovia (see "Traveling Beyond Madrid," later in this chapter).

Getting There

Madrid is a long, 13-hour train ride from Paris, the closest non-Spanish city in this book — so unless you're arriving in Madrid from elsewhere in Spain, flying here is probably a good idea. After you arrive, you'll find that Madrid's local transportation system is efficient and relatively easy to use.

Arriving by air

Madrid's airport, **Barajas** (☎ 91-305-8343; www.aena.es), is about 10 miles outside town. In the arrivals hall, you'll find two banks at which you can change money and a post office.

The airport's **tourist information office** (Oficina de Información Turistica; ☎ 91-305-8656) is open daily from 8 a.m. to 8 p.m.

The Metro (subway) runs from the airport to the *Nuevos Ministerios* stop (12 minutes), and then another 15 minutes from there to downtown. Or you can take a shuttle bus to Plaza de Colón in the city center for 2.50€ ($2.90). A taxi into town is at least 17€ ($20), plus tip and airport and baggage-handling surcharges. Plan on 30 to 45 minutes travel time from the airport to downtown.

Arriving by rail

If you take the train to Madrid, you'll most likely arrive at the city's main station, **Chamartín** (☎ 91-323-2121), which is the hub for trains coming from eastern Spain and France (international train routes come through the France-Spain border). From Chamartín, which is in the northern suburbs, you can get downtown quickly on Metro line 10.

Madrid has two other train stations. Trains to and from southwest Spain and Portugal come into **Atocha** (☎ 91-563-0202). (Confusingly, two Metro stops also go by the name Atocha; the one marked Atocha RENFE is the one beneath Atocha train station; the Atocha Metro stop is one stop north of Atocha RENFE.) **Norte,** or Príncipe Pío, serves northwest Spain. **RENFE** is the name of the Spanish national train service; for information, call ☎ 90-224-0202 or visit www.renfe.es.

Orienting Yourself in Madrid

Thanks to Madrid's many major *plazas* (squares) and the splendid boulevards linking them, you can quickly master the city's layout. The most significant plazas are shown on the map in this chapter, but I describe some of the most important in this section.

Introducing the neighborhoods

Plaza del Sol marks the very center of Madrid (and all of Spain, for that matter; all distances within the country are measured from a 0km mark in the plaza's southwest corner). The nearby **Plaza Mayor** is more scenic and is flanked by cafes and colonnades; in the center sits an equestrian statue of Felipe III (by Italian mannerist Giambologna and his student Pietro Tacca). These two plazas constitute the heart of **Old Madrid,** an area filled with authentic Spanish restaurants and nightlife hot spots. Madrid's 17th-century district lies south of Plaza del Sol.

Spain

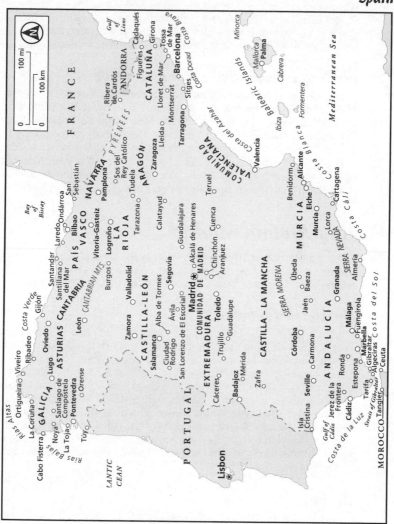

The wide, modern **Plaza de España** marks the northwest corner of the city. Calle de Bailén runs south from there, bordering the **Palacio Real** (royal palace) and marking the city's western edge. Madrid's main boulevard, Gran Vía, zigzags from Plaza de España across the northern Old City. Department stores, cafes, movie theaters, and office buildings line the grand boulevard. North of it are the **Malasana** and **Chueca** districts; they are rundown areas but have nonetheless retained their status as trendy nightlife zones.

Old Madrid's east side is bordered by the tree-planted Paseo del Prado, which runs from north to south from **Plaza de la Cibeles** through **Plaza C. del Castillo** to the Atocha train station square. Hotels, cafes, and the city's major museums line the street. The vast **Retiro Park,** center of the up-and-coming **Retiro** neighborhood, lies on the east side of the Paseo.

Finding information after you arrive

Barajas Airport has an **Oficina de Información Turística** (☎ 91-305-8656), open daily from 8 a.m. to 8 p.m. Primarily a distribution center for brochures and maps, the **Oficina Municipal de Turismo,** Plaza Mayor 3 (☎ **91-588-1636** or 588-2900; Metro: Sol) is open daily from 10 a.m. to 8 p.m. The regional government's tourism office in Madrid is at Duque de Medinaceli 2 (☎ 91-429-4951; Metro: Banco de España), open daily from 9 a.m. to 7 p.m. The general tourist information number is ☎ **90-210-0007,** but operators don't always speak English.

Getting Around Madrid

 Buying a **Metrobus 10-journey ticket** is the best choice for using the public-transport system. Each ticket costs 5.35€ ($6.15) and is good for ten trips on Metro or bus, and they can be used by one or more people.

By Metro (subway)

Madrid's Metro system (www.metromadrid.es) has 11 lines that intersect at the following major junctions: Puerta del Sol, Alonso Martinez, Ópera, and Avienda de América. Although slow and crowded at rush hour — name a big-city subway system that isn't — the Metro is otherwise very fast and efficient and is a good way for travelers to cover the hefty distances between Madrid's sights, which are dispersed throughout the city. The service runs from 6:30 a.m. to 1:30 a.m. A **one-way ticket** is 1.15€ ($1.30), or you can buy ten rides at a reduced rate (see the introduction to the "Getting Around Madrid" section"). You can buy tickets at machines within the Metro stations or from newsstands and tobacconists.

By bus

Madrid's bus service is pretty standard for a major-city bus system. But it may, in fact, be more efficient than most because the buses travel in special lanes and don't have to fight traffic. Still, most conductors don't speak English, so I recommend sticking to the Metro. Regular buses run from 6:00 a.m. to 11:30 p.m., with night buses going every 20 minutes from midnight to 6 a.m.

By taxi

When you hail a taxi in Madrid, make sure you get a legitimate taxi rather than a *gypsy cab* (which may charge higher fares because it's not metered). "Real" taxis are white with diagonal red bands. You can either hail one in the street (a green light on the roof means it's available) or pick one up where they're lined up (usually outside hotels).

Legitimate taxis charge 1.50€ ($1.75) plus 0.85€ ($1) per kilometer. A surcharge of 2€ ($2.30) applies when you take a taxi at night, on Sundays and holidays, or from a train station. The driver adds a surcharge of 4€ ($4.60) on trips to the airport. Drivers are allowed to double the fare on the meter for trips outside the city limits. To call a taxi, dial ☎ **91-447-5180,** 91-547-8200, or 91-371-3711.

By foot

Madrid is one of the few European cities where you won't want to spend much time strolling around on foot. The wide boulevards are great for getting from place to place, but most offer relatively little in the way of character. With a couple of notable exceptions, such as **Plaza Mayor,** you won't miss much by traveling underground on the Metro.

Staying in Madrid

Madrid offers three main types of sleeping accommodations: regular hotels, which can be anything from deluxe, elegant turn-of-the-last-century establishments to modern, moderately priced inns; *hostales,* bare-bones businesses where travelers usually get good value for their money; and *pensiones,* even simpler, less-expensive boarding houses, often requiring half or full *board* (meals taken on premises).

Many hotels are scattered along the Gran Vía, which is not a good place to be walking after dark, and near Atocha Station. The Old City also has a good selection of accommodations ringing Madrid's central squares, such as Plaza Mayor and Puerta del Sol. These areas attract their share of pickpockets because they're popular travel destinations, but due to their proximity to prime dining and sightseeing, they're also among the most exciting places to be in Madrid.

The tourism office maintains the hotel Tourist Line at ☎ **901-300-600.**

All accommodation rates in this section, including breakfast, are quoted including the 7 percent tax that most official price lists in Madrid exclude.

Madrid's top hotels

Anaco
$$$ **Near the Gran Vía**

Located on a tree-shaded plaza near a major crossroads, this budget-friendly hotel features built-in furnishings in its clean, contemporary rooms. The Anaco gets the nod over the Hostal-Residencia Continental

Accommodations, Dining, and Attractions in Madrid

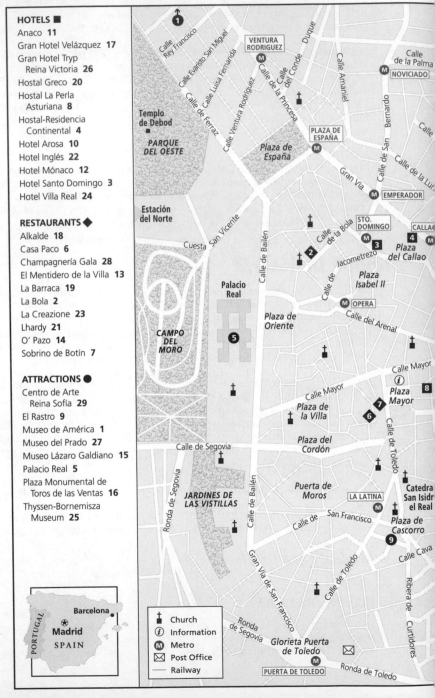

HOTELS ■
Anaco **11**
Gran Hotel Velázquez **17**
Gran Hotel Tryp
  Reina Victoria **26**
Hostal Greco **20**
Hostal La Perla
  Asturiana **8**
Hostal-Residencia
  Continental **4**
Hotel Arosa **10**
Hotel Inglés **22**
Hotel Mónaco **12**
Hotel Santo Domingo **3**
Hotel Villa Real **24**

RESTAURANTS ◆
Alkalde **18**
Casa Paco **6**
Champagnería Gala **28**
El Mentidero de la Villa **13**
La Barraca **19**
La Bola **2**
La Creazione **23**
Lhardy **21**
O' Pazo **14**
Sobrino de Botín **7**

ATTRACTIONS ●
Centro de Arte
  Reina Sofía **29**
El Rastro **9**
Museo de América **1**
Museo del Prado **27**
Museo Lázaro Galdiano **15**
Palacio Real **5**
Plaza Monumental de
  Toros de las Ventas **16**
Thyssen-Bornemisza
  Museum **25**

PORTUGAL

Barcelona ●
✱ **Madrid**
SPAIN

✝ Church
ⓘ Information
Ⓜ Metro
✉ Post Office
— Railway

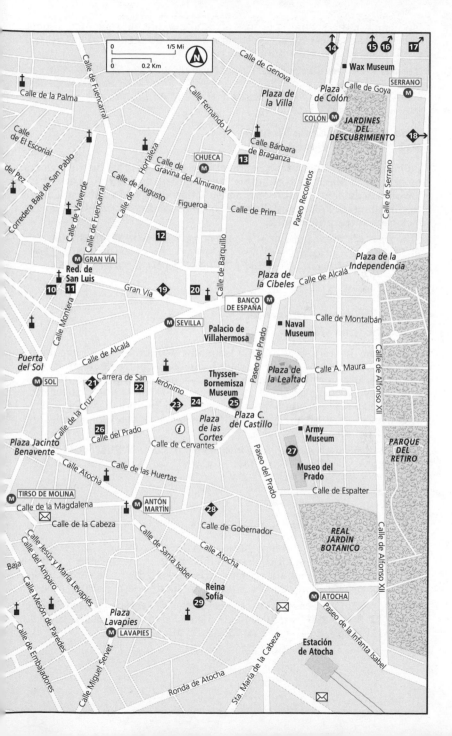

(see listing in this section) because of its air-conditioning and nicer rooms. The choicest, largest rooms (with terraces) are on the top floor. The connected tapas bar is open until 3 a.m.

See map p. 486. Tres Cruces 3 (just down from the Metro stop). ☎ *91-522-4604. Fax: 91-531-6484.* www.anacohotel.com. *Metro: Gran Vía. Rates: 98€–103€ ($113–$118) double. Continental breakfast 5€ ($5.75). AE, DC, MC, V.*

Gran Hotel Tryp Reina Victoria
$$$$ Near the Puerta del Sol

Bullfighting stars and discriminating travelers stay at this historic monument, one of Madrid's top hotels. An abundance of early-20th-century flavor is in evidence, and rooms are soundproofed against the sounds of this bustling neighborhood. If you want to relax after a busy day, you can kick back in the private plaza.

See map p. 486. Plaza Santa Ana 14 (on the Calle del Prado). ☎ *91-531-4500. Fax: 91-522-0307.* www.trypreinavictoria.solmelia.com. *Metro: Tirso de Molina or Puerta del Sol. Rates: 189€–233€ ($217–$268) double. Breakfast 17€ ($20). AE, DC, MC, V.*

Hostal-Residencia Continental
$ On the Gran Vía

This *hostal* (hostel), in a building brimming with other cheap accommodations, is the finest — clean, updated, and fairly comfy. Remember, *basic* is still the key word in this price range. Rooms are large, if institutional, and all have a TV, phone, and bath — but no air-conditioning. The location on the busy plaza is convenient for the Metro, but noisy. If you want to save even more, you can try one of the cheaper, less well-kept *hostales* and *pensiones* at this address.

See map p. 486. Gran Vía 44 (just up from the Metro stop). ☎ *91-521-4640. Fax: 91-521-4649.* www.hostalcontinental.com. *Metro: Callao. Rates: 51€ ($59) double. No breakfast offered. AE, MC, V.*

Hotel Inglés
$$$ Near the Puerta del Sol

If you like to mix food and fun, this may be the place for you. *Tavernas* and *tascas* (see "Dining in Madrid," later in this chapter) line the street, and the lobby TV is a magnet for soccer fans. Even though the rooms are boringly contemporary, all are in good condition and many feature sitting areas.

See map p. 486. Calle Echegaray 8 (between Carrera de San Jerónimo and Calle del Prado). ☎ *91-429-6551. Fax: 91-420-2423. Metro: Puerta del Sol or Sevilla. Rates: 107€ ($123) double. Breakfast 5€ ($5.75). AE, DC, MC, V.*

Hotel Mónaco
$$$ Chueca

This former deluxe brothel was remodeled in the late 1950s but tastefully retains some of the plush features. Past clients have included royalty, illustrious Fascists, and loads of hot-blooded bullfighters. Rooms 20, 123, and 127 are particularly lavish and historic. The *barrio* is one of the city's liveliest, originally an artisans' quarter and now a trendy, largely nightlife and gay district. Rooms do not have air-conditioning.

See map p. 486. Calle Barbieri 5 (just east of Plaza de Vazquez de Mella). ☎ *91-522-4630. Fax: 91-521-1601.* www.derbyhotels.es. *Metro: Chueca, Banco de España, or Gran Via. Rates: 80€ ($92) double. Breakfast to order 3.20€–5€ ($3.70–$5.75). AE, DC, MC, V.*

Hotel Villa Real
$$$$$ On Plaza de las Cortés

One of Madrid's poshest accommodations, this hotel features an unusual mix of neoclassical, modern, and Aztec design, with lots of nice extras — such as satellite TV, modem/fax lines, and built-in mahogany furnishings. They'll even provide guests with a free *Smart car* (an environmentaly-friendly compact) to putter around town in. Even "standard" rooms, although not large, are split-level with small sitting areas and marble baths with two sinks. The larger rooms feature a small terrace and two bathrooms (one with Jacuzzi). The central location of this comfortably plush hotel is excellent, and the staff is very helpful. Conference rooms are decorated with Greek vases and ancient Roman mosaics (the largest such private collection in the world).

See map p. 486. Plaza del las Cortés 10 (where the Carrera de San Jerónimo meets Calle del Prado, very near the Paseo del Prado). ☎ *91-420-3767. Fax: 91-420-2547.* www.derbyhotels.es. *Metro: Antón Martín. Rates: 160€–375€ ($184–$431) double. Breakfast 19€ ($22). AE, DC, MC, V.*

Madrid's runner-up accommodations

Gran Hotel Velázquez

$$$$ Retiro   This hotel with Art Deco charm and largish rooms is located in a classy, mainly residential neighborhood. *See map p. 486. Calle de Velázquez 62.* ☎ *91-575-2800. Fax: 91-575-2809.* www.hotelvelazquez.com.

Hostal la Perla Asturiana

$ Near Puerta del Sol   This clean, simple, family-run inn offers fantastically low prices. *See map p. 486. Plaza de Santa Cruz 3.* ☎ *91-366-4600. Fax: 91-366-4608.* www.perlaasturiana.com.

Hotel Arosa

$$$$ Near the Gran Vía   This hotel is about as central as you can get, offering standardized comforts and modern-art prints on the walls. Try to get one of the trapezoid-shaped corner rooms, where the bed is flanked by columns. *See map p. 486. Calle Salud 21 (at the Gran Vía).* ☎ *91-532-1600. Fax: 91-531-3127.*

Hostal Greco

$ **Chueca, just north of Gran Vía** A perfectly respectable place today, Hostal Greco, like the Mónaco, retains a bit of the faux-luxurious décor that hearkens back to its tenure as a high-class brothel. Erotic frescoes, plus a good story to put on your postcards ("Hey, guess where I'm staying . . ."). *See map p. 486. Calle Infantas 3.* ☎ *91-522-4632. Fax: 91-523-2361.*

Hotel Santo Domingo

$$$$ *Near Plaza de España* Although geared toward business travelers, Hotel Santo Domingo provides a good location, standardized amenities, and fifth-floor rooms with balconies overlooking Madrid that can be appreciated by any traveler — especially at the lower weekend rates. *See map p. 486. Plaza Santo Domingo 13.* ☎ *91-547-9800. Fax: 91-547-5995.* www.hotel santodomingo.com.

Dining in Madrid

The Basque region in the north of Spain is home to the country's best and most innovative cooking, hands down. This ever-changing cuisine is very sophisticated, particularly the Basque codfish recipes and incomparable baby eel dishes. Restaurants in Madrid, however, feature food from all Spain's regions, including two local styles of cuisine called *Madrileños* and *Castillian.* Spain's trademark dish is *paella,* a Mediterranean medley of seafood and rice usually eaten for lunch. On the heartier side of the menu are the roast meats, especially *cordero* (lamb) and *cochinillo* (suckling pig). Spain is the place to be if you like pork; at times it seems like you can't walk into a restaurant without tripping over some *chorizo* sausage and salty *jamón serrano* ham. The king of carnivorous pleasures in Madrid is *cocido madrileño,* a hearty stew of beef, chicken, pig's feet, sausage, garbanzo beans, veggies, pasta, and bread dumplings all cooked together for a long time.

Although Madrid is landlocked, a fleet of trucks and airplanes keeps the capital city well stocked with excellent fresh fish. But ironically, one of Madrid's most popular seafood dishes is *bacalao* — dried salt cod that is softened and served either by itself or *al ajoarriero* (flaked and stewed with tomatoes, potatoes, garlic, and peppers). While you're eating dinner, try to save some room for *flan,* a staple dessert in Spain that many say is even better than a similar French treat, crème caramel. Table wine is usually excellent in and around Madrid, especially the Castillian Valdepeñas and Rioja varieties. My favorite Spanish beverage is *sangria,* a punch made by filling a container with wine, ice, and pieces of fruit. And one of the greatest alcoholic treats in Europe is the sweet, powerful wine from the Spanish city Jerez — we call it *sherry* in English.

A traditional Spanish breakfast consists of thick hot chocolate and *churros,* which are made by forming a bready batter into long sticks and then deep frying them until a crisp crust forms on the outside. These chewy, hot morsels are then covered with oil and sugar. *Churros* are one of the world's heavenly delights, but your doctor may advise you to stick to coffee or tea and rolls for breakfast.

Madrileños maintain a different eating schedule than the rest of the Continent. So far, mostly, they've managed to ward off the infiltration into Europe of the hectic, Americanized daily schedule. Many still find time to eat their biggest meal between 1 and 4 p.m. After a siesta, at about 5 p.m., they go out to *paseo* — an evening stroll to see and be seen and, most importantly, to eat tapas.

Tapas are snacks of different kinds eaten in small portions at bars called *tascas.* (The word *tapas* is Spanish for "lid"; the morsels got their name because pieces of bread or slices of ham were once used to keep flies out of wine glasses.) Today, Spaniards turn out by the thousands in the afternoons and evenings to *tapeo* — walk from *tasca* to *tasca,* drink, chat, and chomp up those delicious *tapas.* (I mention some of the better *tascas* and describe some typical *tapas* in "More cool things to see and do," later in this chapter.)

Tasca-hopping is important because it keeps you from getting too hungry before dinnertime, which is about 10 p.m. Some restaurants that try to attract travelers serve dinner as early as 8 p.m., but few Spaniards would even think of eating that early. Most restaurants — in particular the better and more authentic ones — don't even open their doors until 9:00 or 9:30 p.m. This late supper is usually a light meal.

To gather food for a picnic, visit **Mallorca,** Velázquez 59 (☎ **91-431-9900**), for deluxe pickings; **Rodilla,** Preciados 25 (☎ **91-522-5701**), for carry-out sandwiches, pastries, and tapas; and the **Mercado de San Miguel,** on Plaza San Miguel, for produce.

Madrid's top restaurants

Alkalde
$$$$ **In Retiro BASQUE/INTERNATIONAL**

With its stony cellar dining rooms and ham hocks hanging from wood-beamed ceilings upstairs, Alkalde feels more like a Basque country inn than the fine metropolitan restaurant that it is. The combination of incredible cookery and great atmosphere is unbeatable. Be sure to try the *cigalas* (crayfish) and trout Alkalde.

See map p. 486. Jorge Juan 10 (off Calle de Serrano, behind the archaeological museum). ☎ 91-567-3359. www.alkalderestaurante.com. Reservations required. Metro: Serrano or Retiro. Main courses: 14€–25€ ($16–$29); fixed-price menus from 40€ ($46). AE, DC, MC, V. Open: Lunch and dinner daily.

La Barraca
$$ Near the Gran Vía   VALENCIAN

This Valencian country inn — just off the bustling Gran Vía — has two floors of dining rooms filled with paintings, ceramics, and other Spanish bric-a-brac. The house specialties include *paella à la Barraca* (made here with pork and chicken) and brochette of angler fish and prawns.

See map p. 486. Reina 29 (between Calle de Alcalá and Calle Clavel, just off the Gran Vía). ☎ 91-532-7154. www.interocio.es/labarraca. Reservations recommended. Metro: Gran Vía or Sevilla. Main courses: 11€–20€ ($13–$23). AE, DC, MC, V. Open: Lunch and dinner daily.

La Bola
$$ Between Ópera and Plaza de España   MADRILEÑA

This 1870s tavern offers an escape to Old Madrid — nothing has changed since the days when Ava Gardner and Ernest Hemingway were frequent customers. The lobster cocktail makes a good starter, but the thing to do here is order the delicious *cocido madrileño.*

See map p. 486. Calle del la Bola (just north of the Ópera). ☎ 91-547-6930. Metro: Santo Domingo or Ópera. Main courses: 10€–19€ ($12–$22); fixed-price menu 27€ ($31). No credit cards. Open: Mon–Sat, lunch and dinner. Closed Aug.

La Creazione
$ Near Plaza Santa Ana   ITALIAN

The main room is a brick-lined pizzeria where diners gather over table-clothed or glass-topped tables to assault pasta platters (gnocchi with sage-and-butter drizzle or five other sauces) and impressive pizzas. Both pastas and pizzas are made on the premises and prepared to order. Below the open kitchen is a more formal cellar, where dishes run to saltimbocca and sea bass with porcini and prices are significantly pricier. Most food is available *para llevar* — for takeout.

See map p. 486. Ventura de la Vega 9 (near Carrera de San Jerónimo). ☎ 91-429-0387. Metro: Sol. Main courses: 8€–13€ ($9.20–$15); pizzas and pastas: 7€–11€ ($8.05–$13). AE, DC, MC, V. Open: Lunch and dinner daily.

Lhardy
$$$$$ Near the Puerta del Sol   SPANISH/INTERNATIONAL

A Madrileño legend since it opened in 1839, this is a gathering place for the city's literati and political leaders. Its street level contains what may be the most elegant snack bar in Spain, where cups of steaming consommé are dispensed from silver samovars into delicate porcelain cups. Fish is a speciality, as is *cocido,* the chickpea stew of Castilla, made with sausage, pork, and vegetables.

See map p. 486. Carrera de San Jerónimo 8 (east of Puerta del Sol). ☎ 91-521-3385. Metro: Puerta del Sol or Sevilla. Reservations recommended in the upstairs dining *room. Main courses: 24€–48€ ($28–$55). AE, DC, MC, V. Open: Lunch and dinner daily. Closed Aug.*

Sobrino de Botín
$$$ Near Plaza Mayor   SEGOVIAN/SPANISH

The *Guinness Book of World Records* says Botín is the oldest continuously operating restaurant in the world — and I don't think much has changed since it opened in 1725. It has an 18th-century tile oven in its open kitchen, as well as hanging copper pots and painted plates on the walls. You can still order roast suckling pig, the house specialty that Hemingway's heroes ate in the final scene of *The Sun Also Rises*. A restaurant doesn't stay in business 275 years without being very popular, so expect the place to be busy.

See map p. 486. Calle de Cuchilleros 17 (off Calle de Toledo, a few steps down from Plaza Mayor). ☎ 91-366-4217. Reservations required. Metro: La Latina or Ópera. Main courses: 11€–36€ ($13–$41); fixed-price menu: 29€ ($33). AE, DC, MC, V. Open: Lunch and dinner daily.

Madrid's runner-up restaurants

Casa Paco
$$$ Near Plaza Mayor   The Madrid version of a classy barbecue, with mouth-watering steaks and a tapas bar out front to keep you company while you wait for a table. *See map p. 486. Plaza Puerta Cerrada 11 (just of Plaza Mayor). ☎ 91-366-3166.*

Champagnería Gala
$ **Near Paseo del Prado**   It's all about arroces (rice dishes) here. Italian risottos join the paellas and fideuàs (a similar dish with thin noodles instead of rice), and come with a choice of accompaniments, from cheese and bull's tail to rabbit and fish. *See map p. 486. Moratín 22 (west of Paseo del Prado). ☎ 91-429-2562.*

El Mentidero de la Villa
$$$$$ Chueca   A delicious study in multiculturalism, El Mentidero provides a sort of Spain-meets-Japan-in-France experience. You never know what the kitchen will turn out, but it's bound to be flavorful and good. *See map p. 486. Santo Tomé 6. ☎ 91-308-1285.*

O'Pazo
$$$$ Chamartín (a northern suburb)   This place may be a bit north of the action, but you won't find Galacian food done any better in Spain's capital — the fish is flown in daily from the country's Galacian coast. Try the zarzuela, a seafood casserole. *See map p. 486. Calle Reina Mercedes 20. ☎ 91-553-2333.*

Exploring Madrid

Madrid is an art lover's paradise for many reasons, and here's just one: The "Paseo del Arte" combination admission ticket to the Prado, Reina Sofia, and Thyssen-Bornemisza costs 7.66€ ($8.80) — that's a 25 percent savings — and is available at any of the museums.

Madrid's top sights

Centro de Arte Reina Sofía
Near Estación de Atocha

This is Madrid's leading modern-art museum, and works from Spain's 20th-century greats, such as Picasso, Miró, Dalí, and Gris, cover the walls. Picasso's *Guernica* (1937) overshadows them all; this massive black-and-white commentary on the horrors of war is the most moving, eloquent work in the collection. Picasso's painting is named after a Basque religious center. During Spain's bloody Civil War (1936–1939), German bombers working for the forces of fascist dictator Francisco Franco leveled the town, and 1,645 civilians died. The painting is surrounded by studies Picasso made before starting the main work. Allot a solid hour or two to visit the museum — perhaps more if Madrid's ambitious expansion plans to nearly double the size of its three main museums (Reina Sofia included) by the spring of 2005 goes forward.

See map p. 486. Calle de Santa Isabel 52 (parallel to Calle Atocha, 3 blocks from the station). ☎ *91-467-5062.* http://museoreinasofia.mcu.es. *Metro: Atocha. Bus: 6, 10, 14, 18, 19, 26, 27, 32, 34, 36, 37, 41, 45, 46, 55, 57, 59, 68, 86, 119, or C. Admission: 3€ ($3.45) adults, 1.50€ ($1.75) students; free for under 18 and over 65 and everyone Sat after 2:30 and Sun. Open: Mon and Wed–Sat 10 a.m.–9 p.m., Sun 10 a.m.–2:30 p.m.*

Museo de América (Museum of the Americas)
North of Parque del Oeste

Columbus may have been Italian, but Spain had a lot to do with his voyage to the New World. Spanish Queen Isabella and her husband, Ferdinand, bankrolled his little excursion to find a sea passage to India. Then, when the Spaniards learned that gold, silver, and lots of free land and cheap labor (Indian slaves) were there for the taking in the New World, explorers, conquistadors, and settlers went over in droves. Ignoring the protests of native inhabitants, they claimed the land for God and Spain and quickly conquered and colonized most of Central and South America (as well as what is today Florida, Texas, the American Southwest, and California).

Spain's colonial conquests brought vast treasures into royal and private collections. This museum preserves some of what wasn't melted down to make gold bricks and bouillon. You find one of the world's most remarkable collections of Native American artifacts, treasures, textiles, parchments, inscriptions, and jewelry from prehistoric times to the present. Spend an hour or two learning about the ancient cultures.

See map p. 486. Avienda de los Reyes Catolicos 6. ☎ 91-543-9437. http://museo deamerica.mcu.es. *Metro: Moncloa. Bus: 46, 62, 82, 83, A, D, or G. Admission: 3€ ($3.45) adults, 1.50€ ($1.75) students; free for under 18 and over 65; free to everyone on Sun. Open: Tues–Sat 9:30 a.m.–3 p.m., Sun and holidays 10 a.m.–2:30 p.m. Closes one hour earlier in Jul and Aug.*

Museo del Prado (Prado Museum)
Near Plaza C. del Castillo

Some experts consider the Prado to be the second-best art museum in Europe (after the Louvre in Paris). The Spaniards are finally realizing their flagship museum's vast potential and have embarked on a massive expansion project intended to nearly double the Prado's exhibition space by the spring of 2005. Until that time, more than 7,000 works are already on display in the core Prado — don't try to see them all in one day. Pace yourself by spending most of one day and at least half of another day here. Even if you're in Madrid just for a day, try to visit for at least three hours.

The lineup of masterpieces ranges from Fra' Angelico's *Annunciation* (1430) and El Greco's eerily lit *Adoration of the Shepherds* (1614) to José de Ribera's *The Martyrdom of St. Philip* (1630) and Rubens's fleshy *Three Graces* (1739). The museum is brimming with many more works by Spanish, Italian, Dutch, Flemish, and French painters. You can buy informative little guides describing nearby paintings from vending machines throughout the museum for 1€ ($1.15).

The supreme masterpiece of Spanish painting, Velázquez's *Las Meninas* (The Ladies-in-Waiting), represents the Prado better than any other work. It depicts a king (Felipe IV) and queen having their picture painted — the painting is not the portrait itself, but rather the royals'-eye view of Velázquez as he's painting their portrait. A mirror in the background reflects the image of the king and queen. Velázquez's masterful perspective is flawless; the scene is so real and the gazes so intense, you get the eerie feeling that their Royal Highnesses must be standing right next to you.

At the Prado you can also see the three-paneled painting *The Garden of Earthly Delights,* painted by Hieronymus Bosch ("El Bosco" to the Spanish) in 1516. It's a strange panorama of tiny nude figures, some half human/half bug, engaging in the oddest of activities. This early surreal vision of heaven and hell rivals anything dreamed up by Salvador Dalí or William Burroughs.

The Prado also displays works by Spanish painter Francisco Jose de Goya, who — after starting out as a tapestry designer — began painting playful, joyful scenes such as *Blind Man's Bluff* in the late 18th century. By 1800, he pushed the limits of nudity in art at that time by painting both a *Naked Maja* and a *Clothed Maja.* Goya ended his long career with a very dark expressionistic series called "The Black Paintings," the most disturbing and famous of which is *Saturn Devouring One of His Sons* (1823).

See map p. 486. Paseo del Prado. ☎ 91-330-2800. http://museoprado.mcu.es. *Metro: Banco de España or Atocha. Bus: 10, 14, 27, 34, 37, or 45. Admission: 3€ ($3.45)* *adults, 1.50€ ($1.75) students; free for seniors over 65 and children under 18; free to all on Sat after 2:30 p.m. and on Sun. Open: Tues–Sat 9 a.m.–7 p.m., Sun 9 a.m.–2 p.m.*

Museo Lázaro Galdiano
North of Jardines del Descubrimiento

Although not ranking among Madrid's elite museums, Museo Lázaro Galdiano is among the best in the second tier of the city's art displays. It's still set up as a private gallery in the 19th-century mansion of its founder, Señor Lázaro Galdiano, who collected large amounts of both decorative and fine arts. Of the former, the museum includes crystal and enamels from Limoges, royal daggers and swords, pocket watches (take a look at the cross-shaped timepiece that belonged to Carlos V), medieval armor, and ancient Roman bronzes.

The museum features paintings by El Greco, Velázquez, Goya, Bosch, and Ribera, along with Brits such as Constable, Reynolds, and Gainsborough, and Italian rococo master Tiepolo. Unfortunately, you have to know your artists pretty well because little more than half the works are labeled. The museum is worth a half-hour of your time, unless you detest portraits, which make up the majority of the collection.

See map p. 486. Serrano 122. ☎ 91-561-6084. www.flg.es. Metro: Rubén Darió or Gregorio Marañón. Bus: 9, 12, 16, 19, 27, 45, 51, or 150. Admission: 4€ ($4.60); 3€ ($3.45) students; free for seniors/children under 12; free for everyone Wed. Open: Wed–Mon 10 a.m.–4:30 p.m.; closed holidays and Aug.

Palacio Real (Royal Palace)
On Plaza de Oriente

Some of this palace's 2,000 rooms are closed to the public because the building is still used for official occasions (even though the royal family now lives outside town).

Construction of the palace began after Madrid's Alcazar fortress-palace burned down in 1734. The baroque and rococo styles preferred by the Bourbon monarchs (especially Carlos II and IV) decorate the interior. The palace's lavish air of muted dark blues, burgundies, shiny gold, and gleaming brass surrounds rich marbles, sumptuous tapestries, gilded stuccoes, frescoes, and chandeliers. In the aptly named Porcelain Room, the walls are sheathed in green-and-white ceramics from the royal Buen Retiro factory.

Palace tours last 50 minutes plus a 10- to 20-minute wait, during which you can check out the historical Pharmacy. You can breeze through the building on your own in half an hour. During those rare moments when I reach Museum Overload — when even palatial background art starts getting to me — I like to relax by wandering the gravel paths through the long, green slope of the palace's Campo del Moro gardens, with its fountains and ponds stocked with white and black swans.

See map p. 486. Plaza de Oriente, Calle de Bailén 2. ☎ 91-454-8800 or 91-454-8803 for guided tours. www.patrimonionacional.es. Metro: Ópera or Plaza de

España. Admission: 6€ ($6.90) adults, 3€ ($3.45) seniors/students/children 11 and under; 6.90€ ($7.95) for guided tours; additional fees for temporary exhibits. No credit cards. Open: Mon–Sat 9:30 a.m.–6 p.m., Sun 9 a.m.–3 p.m.

Thyssen-Bornemisza Museum
On Plaza C. del Castillo

Straight across the street from the Prado, you can find the newest addition to Madrid's art scene, opened in 1992 to hold a large collection that had outgrown its original home in Switzerland. The museum offers a unique survey of European art from the 13th century up to the 1960s. How large is the collection? This list of artists gives you some idea: Ghirlandaio, Caravaggio, Ribera, Bernini, Tintoretto, Memling, Rembrandt, Ruben, El Greco, Dürer, Velázquez, Goya, Manet, Monet, Degas, Picasso, Rodin, Homer, Frederick Church, Chagall, O'Keeffe, Hopper, Dalí, Mondrian, de Kooning, and Lucien Freud. You can easily spend one to three hours here. Like the Prado and Reina Sofía, the Thyssen is aiming to vastly expand its gallery space by early 2005 to put more of the family's incredible art collection on display.

See map p. 486. Paseo del Prado 8. ☎ 91-420-3944 or 91-369-0151. www.museo thyssen.org. *Metro: Banco de España. Bus: 1, 2, 5, 9, 10, 14, 15, 20, 27, 34, 37, 45, 51, 52, 53, 74, 146, or 150. Admission to permanent collection 6€ ($6.90) adults, 4€ ($4.60) seniors/students, under 12 free; to temporary exhibits, 3€ ($3.45) adults, 2€ ($2.30) seniors/students, under 12 free. Open: Tues–Sun 10 a.m.–7 p.m. Last admission 30 minutes before close.*

More cool things to see and do

- ✔ **Sifting through the hidden treasures of El Rastro's flea market:** This busy flea market is one of the biggest and most interesting in Europe. Here you can find almost anything — antiques, used car parts, paintings, assorted junk, secondhand clothes, and more. Stalls are open Sunday from dawn to 2 p.m. Take the Metro to La Latina; the market fills the streets around Ribera de Curtidores and Plaza Cascorro. Get ready to haggle over prices, and beware of pickpockets.

- ✔ **Seeing the spectacle of a bullfight:** Mixing barbarism with ballet and viewed as something between sport and art form, bullfighting draws the best and brightest young men (and a few women) from all corners of Spain. Bullfighters are the Spanish equivalents of movie stars or sports heroes, and their fame can be even more fleeting. One misjudgment, one stray into the bull's charge, and their midsections can literally take the bull by the horns.

  Their constant proximity to danger explains why matadors take every second in the bullring so seriously. The bullfight is a dance with death that's painstakingly choreographed, yet totally unpredictable. If the sight of blood sickens you, please stay away, but the spectacle of the *corridas* (bullfights) offers a uniquely Spanish slice of life.

The main season lasts from early spring to mid-October. **Plaza Monumental de Toros de las Ventas** (☎ 91-356-2200; Metro: Ventas) is the primary bullring in Madrid (and all of Spain); *corridas* are performed on Sundays and holidays. Seat prices range widely, from 3.50€ to 105€ ($4.05–$121), with the cheapest seats being up high and in the sun. Fights start a few hours before sundown, at about 7 p.m. in the summer and around 5 p.m. in fall and spring.

✔ **Sampling wines and snacks during** *paseo:* From 5 to 8 p.m., you can be part of the evening *paseo,* tiding yourself over until your 10 p.m. dinner by visiting several tapas bars and snacking on such Spanish specialties as *chorizo* (sausage), *jamón serrano* (salty ham), *tortilla española* (onion and potato omelet wedges), *albondigas* (tender meatballs), *calamares fritos* (fried squid), *gambas al la plancha* (grilled shrimp), and *queso manchego* (sheep's cheese). Eating at the bar is cheaper than grabbing a table.

At the **1827 Casa Alberto,** Huertas 18 (☎ 91-429-9356), where the Spanish author Cervantes once lived, snackers are surrounded by bullfighting memorabilia. **Antonio Sanchez,** Mesón de Parades 13 (☎ 91-539-7826), is another *tasca* (tapas bar) loaded with bullring paraphernalia. **Cervecería Alemania,** Plaza de Santa Ana 6 (☎ 91-429-7033), is a Hemingway haunt on a lively little square.

The local minichain jokingly named **Museo del Jamón** (Museum of Ham — slogan: "The tastiest museums in Madrid") serves great tapas, heavy on the pork, in semimodern crosses between cafes, *tascas,* and butcher shops at Avienda de Córdoba 7 (☎ 91-500-626), Carrera de San Jerónimo 6 (☎ 91-521-0346), Paseo del Prado 44 (☎ 91-420-2414), Plaza Mayor 18 (☎ 91-542-2632), and Capitán Haya 15 (☎ 91-555-3667).

✔ **Experiencing the flamenco rhythm:** Flamenco is the rhythmic music of suffering, of eroticism, of secret joy. Flamenco evolved from the murky histories of Spain's unwanted classes of Jews and Moors during the Middle Ages, and then was appropriated and interpreted through the gypsy culture of Andalusia. The best flamenco music and dancing breaks out spontaneously in bars in the wee hours of the morning, when revelers strum guitars, clap their hands, play castanets, and begin moving gracefully to the rhythm.

Although lacking in spontaneity, the scheduled flamenco club shows can be just as much of a spectacle. Shows usually start at 10:30 or 11 p.m. and last until 2 or 3 a.m., but many clubs open around 9 p.m. to serve dinner before the show. (I suggest eating at a regular restaurant and heading to the club just for the performance.) Among the more reliable clubs are **Casa Patas,** Calle Cañizares 10 (☎ 91-369-0496), which costs 23€ to 27€ ($26–$31) per show, and the slightly less authentic **Café de Chinitas,** Torija 7 (☎ 91-547-1502), which costs about 29€ ($33) for the show and a drink.

✔ **Dancing the night away — literally:** It may not be the city that never sleeps, but Madrid is the town that parties until sunrise. After a light snack of tapas, you can dance at a club from about 6 to 9 p.m. Then you can go eat dinner and return to the clubs around 11 p.m. or midnight. The clubs really heat up somewhere between 1 and 2 a.m., and people don't start leaving until the break of dawn. Most clubs have an admission charge of around $15, which includes your first drink.

The most popular nightclubs and discos change faster than a supermodel's wardrobe, but some of the current biggies include **Kathmandú,** Señores de Luzón 3 (☎ 91-6344201), an Asian fusion disco spinning hip-hop, funk, jungle, and other trendy tunes; the sprawling, anything-goes, cross-cultural **Kapital,** Atocha 125 (☎ 91-420-2906); the Latin inclined **Joy Eslava** (also known as Joy Madrid), Arenal 11 (☎ 91-366-5439), and **Pachá,** Barceló 11 (☎ 91-447-0128), the stylish Madrid incarnation of the national chain that first struck a chord in Ibiza.

Guided tours

One of the best bus-tour companies is the distinctive **Madrid Vision Bus** (☎ 91-779-1888; www.madridvision.es). For the 11€ ($13) ticket, you can get off and reboard as many times in a day as you want. Or you can go for two days at 14€ ($16). Children 7 to 16 and seniors receive a 50 percent discount; kids under 7 ride free. The air-conditioned buses carry multilingual guides who provide info over earphones. Daily departures from the starting point, Gran Vía 32, are every 45 minutes from 9:30 a.m. to midnight in high season (June 21–Sept 20).

Suggested itineraries

If you're the type who'd rather organize your own tours, this section offers some tips for building your own Madrid itineraries.

If you have one day

Begin your day exploring the artistic treasures of the **Prado Museum** — which should hold you for several hours, at least until lunchtime. Eat a light lunch at the **Museo del Jamón** on Paseo del Prado before jogging around the corner to pay homage to Picasso's *Guernica* in the **Centro de Arte Reina Sofía.** That and the other modern masters will keep your attention for an hour or more, after which it's time to head back to your hotel for a well-earned siesta from all this art.

Make sure you take the time to walk through the **Plaza Mayor** at the heart of town, perhaps just before setting off on your *tapeo* in the early evening. This stroll through the heart of Old Madrid — from tapas bar to tapas bar, nibbling and imbibing along the way — should last from around 5 to 8 p.m. Head back to your hotel to rest up until 9:30 p.m. or so, when you can safely venture out for dinner at **Sobrino de Botín.**

If you have two days

Spend **Day 1** pretty much as outlined in the preceding section. Start off **Day 2** touring the **Palacio Royal.** Afterward, head to the little **Museo Lázaro Galdiano** for a peek at what a private museum once looked like, and then over to the **Thyssen-Bornemisza Museum** to see how serious money and a penchant for art can grow a private collection.

If these two days in Madrid represent the full extent of your time in Spain — and if it's the proper season — try to take in a bullfight at 5 p.m. If it's not bullfighting season, *tapeo* again this evening. Either way, catch a flamenco show in the later evening (after dinner).

If you will be heading to Spain's Andalusia region at all, skip both the bullfight and the flamenco — you find better examples of both down south.

If you have three days

Spend **Day 1** and **Day 2** as outlined in the preceding sections, then head off on **Day 3** for a daytrip to Toledo, a commanding large hill town that was once the capital of Spain and also home to that weird Renaissance master El Greco.

Traveling Beyond Madrid

Strange as it may seem, one of the best things to do when you're visiting Madrid is to get out of town. Among the sights in the surrounding area are Toledo, the one-time Spanish capital; the imposing 16th-century palace/monastery El Escorial; and Segovia, which features a castle that's like something out of a fairy tale and an incredible cathedral.

Holy Toledo! Religious art and architecture

Toledo is easily the best daytrip from Madrid. The town and the surrounding area are designated as a national landmark, for good reason. Toledo was the capital of Castile until the 1500s, was home to the painter El Greco, and has always been the religious center of Spain — home to the Primate of Spain and a one-time host to a thriving Jewish community. You find Toledo worth the visit for its Gothic cathedral, its Renaissance paintings, and the famous views of the city captured on canvas.

If you kick into high gear, you can tour Toledo in just a few hours, making it a long half-day trip from Madrid. You can also spend the whole day there and return to Madrid in the evening. But your best bet is to spend the night in Toledo; that enables you to explore the city at a leisurely pace after the day-tripping crowds leave.

Don't visit on a Monday, when half the sights are closed.

Getting there

Ten trains make the journey from Madrid's Atocha Station to Toledo every day. The trip takes 60 to 80 minutes one way. When you're in the station just outside Toledo, bus number 5 takes you to Plaza de Zocodover in the heart of the old city (you find a visitor information kiosk there).

Pullmantur, in Madrid at Plaza de Oriente 8 (☎ **91-541-1805;** www. pullmantur.com), runs both half-day and full-day jaunts to Toledo. Prices start at 42€ ($48) for a half day and 63€ ($72) for a full day. An all-day tour that stops briefly in Toledo before hurrying on to El Escorial and the Valley of the Fallen (a memorial to Spain's Civil War dead) costs 89€ ($102).

The Toledo **tourist office** (☎ **92-522-0843**) is at Puerta de Bisagra, on the north end of town (turn right out of the station, go over the bridge, and walk along the city walls).

Seeing the sights

The **Gothic Cathedral** (☎ **92-522-2241**) is in the center of Toledo, on Arcos de Palacio. Built from 1226 to 1493, the cathedral features a gigantic carved and painted wooden *reredos* (screen) on the high altar, and behind it — illuminated by a skylight — the alabaster and marble baroque Transparente altar. Admission to the church is free, but entry to the treasury — with its 10-foot-high, 500-pound gilded 16th-century monstrance (made from gold brought back by Christopher Columbus) — costs 4.95€ ($5.70), students and seniors 4.35€ ($5). Summer hours are Monday through Saturday from 10:30 a.m. to 6:30 p.m. and Sunday and holidays from 2:00 to 6:30 p.m.; the cathedral closes an hour later in winter.

Although the cathedral contains works by El Greco, fans of his work find that the more important church in town is **Iglesia de Santo Tomé** (☎ **92-521-0209**), Plaza del Conde 2, Vía Santo Tomé. Here the Greek painter's masterpiece, the turbulent *Burial of Count Orgaz* (1586), dominates a tiny chapel. Admission is 1.25€ ($1.45); summer hours are daily from 10:00 a.m. to 6:45 p.m. (to 5:45 p.m. the rest of the year).

If you want to see more of El Greco, you can visit his Toledo home, **Casa y Museo de El Greco,** Calle Samuel Leví (☎ **92-522-4046**). (Actually, his house and studio were probably in the old Jewish quarter, but this is the place set up as an El Greco museum.) Nobody pretends that the works in the museum are his best stuff; the collection is primarily small portrait-style paintings of Christ and the apostles, along with one of his famous views of Toledo. Admission is 2.50€ ($2.90), and it's open Tuesday through Saturday from 10 a.m. to 2 p.m. and 4 to 6 p.m. (to 7 p.m. in summer); and Sunday from 10 a.m. to 2 p.m.

Some visitors find that the Renaissance-style entrance and stairs of the **Museo de Santa Cruz,** Miguel de Cervantes 3 (☎ 92-522-1036), are more impressive than the works inside this former 16th-century hospice. Amid 15th-century tapestries, jewelry, artifacts, and swords and armor made from Toledo's famous damascene steel (blackened and traced with gold wire), you find works by Goya, Ribera, and the omnipresent El Greco — who's represented by the 1613 *Assumption,* one of his last paintings. The artists are great, but these particular works are nothing more than mediocre. Admission is 1.25€ ($1.45) for adults and free for children. The museum is open Monday through Saturday from 10 a.m. to 6 p.m., and Sunday from 10 a.m. to 2 p.m.

What do you get when a thriving Jewish community is crushed by the Catholic Inquisition and the local diocese takes over the temples? The answer: a synagogue named for the Virgin Mary. The **Sínagoga de Santa María La Blanca,** Calle Reyes Católicos 2 (☎ 92-522-7257), has been restored to its Hebrew origins, which were heavily influenced by Islamic architecture. Built in the 1100s, it is the oldest of Toledo's eight remaining synagogues and features Moorish horseshoe arches atop the squat columns of the spare interior. Admission is 1.25€ ($1.45), and it's open July through September daily from 10:00 a.m. to 1:45 p.m. and 3:30 to 6:45 p.m.; from October to June, daily hours are from 10 a.m. to 2 p.m. and 3:30 to 5:45 p.m.

The 14th-century **Sínagoga del Tránsito,** Calle Samuel Leví (☎ 92-522-3665), also blends Gothic, Islamic, and traditional Hebrew motifs. This synagogue contains a frieze inscribed with Hebrew script and set with a coffered ceiling. The **Museo Sefardí,** connected to the synagogue, preserves ancient tombs, manuscripts, and sacred objects of Toledo's Sephardic (Spanish Jewish) community. Admission (temple and museum together) is 2.50€ ($2.90). Hours are Tuesday through Saturday from 10 a.m. to 2 p.m. and 4 to 6 p.m., and Sunday from 10 a.m. to 2 p.m.

The rebuilt **Alcázar,** Calle General Moscardó 4 (☎ 92-522-3038), which dominates the town's skyline, is not too much to look at now, but this fortress withstood many a siege. In 1936, it held up during 70 days of bombing during Spain's Civil War. A museum inside uses photographs, models, and a walking tour to remember those days of honor and horror. Admission is 1.25€ ($1.45) for adults and free for those under 10. It's open Tuesday to Sunday from 9:30 a.m. to 2:30 p.m.

Where to stay and dine

The **Hostal del Cardenal,** Paseo de Recaredo 24 (☎ 92-522-4900; Fax: 925-222-991; www.hostaldelcardenal.com), charges reasonable prices for terrific Spanish cuisine, such as roast suckling pig. It also rents double rooms for 80€ to 102€ ($92–$117). Otherwise, stay at **Hotel María Cristina,** Marqués de Mendigorría 1 (☎ 92-521-3202; Fax: 92-521-2650), which has uniquely beautiful double rooms and a historic setting for 93.50€ ($108).

El Escorial: A king-sized monastery

King Felipe II was nothing if not creative — and maybe a bit zealous. When he needed a new royal residence in the late 16th century, instead of following in the footsteps of his European peers and building a palace, he built himself a live-in monastery. But not your run-of-the-mill monastery. Fortress-thick walls enclose San Lorenzo de El Escorial, a frescoed and tapestried complex of royal apartments, with a giant basilica, terrific art gallery, opulent library, and Spain's royal tombs.

Other than the huge monastery, you don't find much else in the town of El Escorial; allow about two to three hours to tour the monastery.

Getting there

From Madrid, the bus and train trips to El Escorial both take about an hour. Buses from Madrid's Moncha Metro station (you can buy tickets at a kiosk in the station) drop you off right in front of the monastery. About 25 trains leave Madrid's Atocha Station daily for El Escorial; buses meet incoming trains to shuttle visitors the remaining mile to Plaza Virgen de Gracia, a block east of the monastery.

Pullmantur, in Madrid at Plaza de Oriente 8 (☎ 91-541-1805; www. |pullmantur.com), runs an all-day tour that stops briefly in Toledo before hurrying on to El Escorial and the Valley of the Fallen (a memorial to Spain's Civil War dead). The tour costs 89€ ($102).

The **tourist office** (☎ 91-890-5313) is at Grimaldi 2, north of the visitor entrance to the complex.

Seeing the monastery

Felipe II's royal apartments in the monastery/fortress of San Lorenzo de El Escorial (☎ 91-890-5902; www.patrimonionacional.es) are as stark and monastic as a king could get. He was such a devout Christian that he had his bedroom built to overlook the high altar of the impressive basilica, which has four organs and a dome based on Michelangelo's plans for St. Peter's in Rome. The basilica is also home to Cellini's *Crucifix.* Under the altar is the Royal Pantheon, a mausoleum containing the remains of every Spanish king from Charles I to Alfonso XII. The tapestried apartments of the Bourbon kings, Carlos III and Carlos IV, are more elaborate and in keeping with the tastes of most monarchs.

Paintings such as Titian's *Last Supper,* Velázquez's *The Tunic of Joseph,* El Greco's *Martyrdom of St. Maurice,* and works by Dürer, van Dyck, Tintoretto, and Rubens are the source of the New Museum's popularity. The Royal Library houses more than 40,000 antique volumes under a barrel-vaulted ceiling frescoed by Tibaldi in the 16th century.

El Escorial is open Tuesday to Sunday and holidays from 10 a.m. to 6 p.m. (until 5 p.m. in winter). Admission is 6€ ($6.90) adults and 3€ ($3.45) seniors/students.

Where to dine

 Even though El Escorial is an easy half-day trip from Madrid, you may want to eat lunch before you return, so try the heavenly fare at the cave-like **Mesón la Cueva,** San Antón 4 (☎ **91-890-1516;** www.mesonlacueva. com).

Segovia: A tour through history

Segovia brings to life a cross-section of Spain's history. Still standing here are a Roman aqueduct, a Moorish palace, and a Gothic cathedral. With its medieval streets, Romanesque churches, and 15th-century palaces, Segovia is an enjoyable place to stroll and get a sense of what it was like to live in a small Castilian city.

You can easily see Segovia in three to four hours, but if you're in need of a break from the big city, it makes a nice place to hang around for an overnight escape.

Getting there

Trains leave Madrid for Segovia every other hour (they depart Madrid from Atocha Station but also pause at Chamartín en route). The trip takes two hours. From Segovia's train station, bus number 3 runs to Plaza Mayor in the center of town.

Pullmantur, in Madrid at Plaza de Oriente 8 (☎ **91-541-1805;** www. pullmantur.com), runs an all-day tour to Segovia and Avila for 68€ to 79€ ($78–$91) depending on your lunch choice.

The **tourist office** (☎ **92-146-0334**) is at Plaza Mayor 10.

Seeing the sights

The majestic Roman **aqueduct** runs 895 yards along the Plaza del Azoguejo on the east side of town. The aqueduct, much of it two tiers high, contains 118 arches and is 96 feet at its highest point. Built in the first century A.D. using stone blocks with no mortar, the aqueduct was one of the city's major water sources all the way until the 19th century.

The last great Gothic **cathedral** (☎ **92-146-2205**) built in Spain is right in the middle of the city. Isabella I (of Ferdinand and Isabella fame) was named queen on this very spot in 1474. The cathedral, built from 1515 to 1558, is all buttresses and pinnacles. It has some beautiful stained-glass windows, which light the carved choir stalls, the 16th- and 17th-century paintings, and the grille-fronted chapels inside. The attached cloisters were originally part of an earlier church at the same location. Church admission is free, but entry to the cloisters, chapel room, and tiny museum (which holds paintings by Ribera, Flemish tapestries, jewelry, and manuscripts) costs 1.80€ ($2.05). April through September hours are daily from 9:00 a.m. to 6:30 p.m. (9:30 a.m. to 5:30 p.m. the rest of the year).

Segovia's commanding **Alcázar** (☎ **92-146-0759**; www.alcazarde segovia.com), anchors the west end of town. Originally raised between the 12th and 15th centuries, it was largely rebuilt after a disastrous 1862 fire destroyed many of its Moorish embellishments. Behind the formidable exterior are some sumptuous rooms, from the Gothic King's Room to the stuccoed Throne Room. Clamber up the Torre de Juan II, built as a dungeon, for panoramic views. Admission is 3€ ($3.45) adults and 2€ ($2.30) ages 8 to 14. Hours are daily from 10 a.m. to 7 p.m. (to 6 p.m. Oct–Mar).

Where to stay and dine

The tavern-like **El Bernardino**, Cervantes 2 (☎ **92-146-2477**; www.el bernardino.com), offers hearty Castilian specialties, including paella. You can get a double room for 45€ to 60€ ($52–$69) in the **Hostal Las Sirenas,** Juan Bravo 30 (☎ **92-146-2663**; Fax: 92-146-2657), a modern hotel on one of Segovia's nicest plazas.

Fast Facts: Madrid

Area Code

The country code for Spain is **34** and the city code for Madrid is **91**.

American Express

Madrid has two American Express offices. One is across from the Palace Hotel at Plaza de las Cortés 2 (☎ 91-322-5500). You can find the other office at Calle Francisco Gervás 10 (☎ 91-572-0320). The offices keep the same hours: Monday through Friday from 8:30 a.m. to 4:30 p.m. They replace cards and traveler's checks and hold mail for their customers for up to one month free.

Currency

In 2002, the euro, the new European currency, became the legal tender in Spain, replacing the peseta. The exchange rate used to calculate the dollar values given in this chapter is 1€ = $1.15. Amounts over $10 are rounded to the nearest dollar.

Doctors and Dentists

For bilingual dental and medical attention, call ☎ 061 or check with the U.S. embassy for its list of approved dentists and doctors.

Embassies and Consulates

The U.S. Embassy, Calle Serrano 75 (☎ 91-587-2200; Metro: Núñez Bilbao), is open Monday through Friday from 9 a.m. to 6 p.m. except for U.S. and local holidays.

Emergency

For street emergencies, call ☎ **061**. For an ambulance, call ☎ **112** or **092**.

Hospitals

Two major hospitals provide emergency care: Hospital General Gregorio Marañón, Calle Dr Esquerdo 46 (☎ 91-586-8000), and Hospital La Paz, Paseo de la Castellana 261 (☎ 91-727-7000). For help finding an English-speaking doctor, call the Anglo-American Medical Unit, Calle Conde de Aranda 1 (☎ 91-435-1823). All insurance is recognized, and emergencies will be seen to without bureaucratic red tape.

Information

Primarily a distribution center for brochures and maps, the Oficina Municipal de Turismo is at Plaza Mayor 3 (☎ 91-588-1636 or 588-2900). For details on it and other tourism offices, see "Finding information after you arrive," near the beginning of this chapter.

For bus information, call ☎ 91-530-4800 or 91-468-4200. For train information, call ☎ 90-224-0202 or 90-224-3402 or log on to www.renfe.es. For flight information, dial ☎ 91-305-8344.

Internet Access and Cybercafes

Check your e-mail or send messages at the big BBiGG, Alcalá 21 (☎ 91-521-9207; www.bbigg.com; Metro: Sevilla and Sol), which has 300 computers with flat-screen monitors. Another reliable option, with snacks for sale, too, is easyEverything, Calle Montera 10–12 (☎ 91-523-5563; www.easyeverything.com), open 24/7, with more than 200 computers.

Maps

Tourist offices and El Corte Inglés department stores provide free maps, which show most of the sights, major plazas, and thoroughfares serving as landmarks, as well as the all-important Metro stops.

Newspapers/Magazines

Free from Tourist Offices is *Madrid What's On,* a regularly updated monthly in both Spanish and English, listing special events as well as perennial favorites. Ditto the English-language monthly *InMadrid,* also to be found at various expat hangouts, including bars and cafes. At the airport, look for the free *Madrid Barajas,* bilingual and with lots of info.

Pharmacies

Finding a late-night pharmacy is no problem in Madrid. A list of area *farmacias* (pharmacies) that stay open late is posted on every pharmacy. You can also call ☎ 098. Farmacia Lastra, Calle Conde de Peñalver 27 (☎ 91-402-4363, Metro: Goya) is open 24/7 and accepts credit cards.

Police

Call ☎ 112 or 092.

Post Office

The main post office is the grand Palacio de Comunicaciones on Plaza de las Cibeles, 28014 Madrid (☎ 91-521-650 or 90-219-7197; Metro: Banco de España). It's open for stamps Monday through Friday from 8:30 a.m. to 9:30 p.m., Saturdays 9:30 a.m. to 9:30 p.m., and Sundays and holidays from 8:30 a.m. to 2:00 p.m. at Window H. Stamps are also sold at *estancos* (tabacco sellers). An airmail letter or postcard to the United States is .75€ (85¢).

Safety

Purse-snatchers and pickpockets are probably the worst criminals you'll find in Madrid, but they are crafty — often working in groups to separate you from your wallet. Even locking your car doesn't deter an experienced purse-snatcher. So take precautions: Carry only the money you need until you get back to your hotel, and be alert when riding the Metro. Areas where you should be especially attentive: around Sol, El Rastro, and Plaza Mayor, as well in the red-light zone north of Gran Via, where it is definitely not a good idea to venture after dark — and never if you're a woman alone. In all cases, walk with purpose and exude confidence. At night, parks are also best avoided.

Taxes

The government sales tax, known as IVA (value-added tax), is levied nationwide on all goods and services, and ranges from 7 to 33 percent.

Taxis

See "Getting Around Madrid," earlier in this chapter.

Telephone

The minimum charge for local telephone calls is .25€ (30¢). Be aware that many hotels and hostels tack on a hefty surcharge for long-distance calls. Most public phones have clear instructions in English, and some new high-tech phones provide on-screen instructions in four languages. Some phones accept phone cards available for 12€ ($14) at *estancos* (tobacco sellers), post offices, and the *locutorios telefónicas* (central phone offices) at Gran Vía 30 and Paseo de Recoletos 41 (open Mon–Sat 9 a.m. to midnight, Sun and holidays noon to midnight). Another *locutorio* is at the main post office on Plaza de las Cibeles (open Mon–Fri 8:30 a.m.–9:30 p.m., Sat 9:30 a.m.–9:30 p.m., and Sun and holidays 8:30 a.m.–2 p.m.).

To make collect or calling-card calls at more economical rates from a pay phone, dial ☎ 900-99-0011 to access AT&T, ☎ 800-099-357 to access MCI, or ☎ 900-99-0013 for Sprint. When calling from a hotel, check first to make sure there's no service charge or surcharge, or at least to find out how much it is. To make international calls to the United States and Canada, dial 00, wait for another tone, then dial 1, followed by the area code and number. The average cost of a three-minute call to the United States using the Tarjeta Telefónica is about $1 per minute but can get up to as much as $12 when calling from a hotel.

Transit Info

See "Getting Around Madrid," earlier in this chapter.

Chapter 23

The Best of Barcelona

In This Chapter

▶ Getting to Barcelona

▶ Finding out about the neighborhoods

▶ Taking advantage of Barcelona's best restaurants and hotels

▶ Seeing Barcelona's top sights

*B*arcelona is the capital of the proudly independent region of Catalonia. In the last decade, this Mediterranean city has transformed itself into a vibrant new capital of European commerce and tourism. This triumph is much to the advantage of the tourist anxious to experience local flavor.

A city of beauty and the arts, Barcelona is home to the whimsical architectural style of Antoni Gaudí. Picasso also studied in Barcelona, and the city's Picasso Museum is the best outside of Paris. Surrealist painters Salvador Dalí and Joan Miró are native sons.

So stroll down the shady Las Ramblas promenade, explore the Gothic Quarter around the cathedral, haggle over fruit at the Boquería market, and ride the funicular (cable car) up to the park on Montjuïc hill, with its museums and re-created Spanish village. Or perhaps just relax with a drink in a tapas bar and watch the world go by for an afternoon.

You may notice that Spanish is spoken a little differently in Barcelona. That's because it isn't Spanish — it's Catalán. As an autonomous region of Spain, Catalonia is slowly reasserting the native traditions that were squashed during Spain's Franco years, including the reemergence of its native language, a romance tongue closely related to that of the Provence region of France. Evidence of Catalán's comeback was visible during the 1992 Olympics, when all the signs and official news reports were printed in Catalán first and Castilian Spanish second.

Barcelona is a great town for just hanging out — the perfect place to schedule extra time to relax without all the usual sightseeing pressures. If you're just passing through, try to spend at least two full days here.

Getting There

Getting into the city from the airport is fairly simple, and the train station is connected to a subway line. When you're in town, getting around by public transportation is also easy.

Arriving by air

Barcelona's **El Prat** airport (☎ **93-478-5000;** www.aena.es) is 11km (7 miles) southeast of the city. In the arrivals hall are several ATMs and an information desk.

Trains run every 30 minutes from the airport to Estació Sants, Plaça Catalunya, and Arc de Triomf, or you can board an Aerobús every 15 minutes to Plaça de Catalunya, Passeig de Gracia, or Plaça Espanya. The trip takes 25 to 40 minutes and costs 3.45€ ($3.95). Tickets are sold on the bus. A taxi into town is about 15€ to 20€ ($17–$23), plus tip and supplements for luggage.

Arriving by train

Most trains bound for Barcelona arrive either at the **Estació Sants** on the western edge of the Eixample or the **Estació de Franca,** near the harbor at the base of the Ciutadella park. Both stations link to the Metro network.

Orienting Yourself in Barcelona

A split personality of the city is evident in the contrast between the old city and the new city. The **Ciutat Vella** (Old City) is a hexagon of narrow streets nudged up against the harbor. The massive grid of streets that makes up the new city surrounds the old one.

The famed street **Las Ramblas** (Les Rambles in Catalán) bisects the Ciutat Vella and runs from the harbor north to Plaça Catalunya. Las Ramblas is a wide, tree-shaded boulevard with street entertainers, flower stalls, cafes, and the bustle of the city. It's a tour in itself. (The street runs northwest, but all city maps are oriented with this street pointing straight up and down.) The street degenerated during the fascist Franco era early in the 20th century, as did much of old Barcelona, but has mostly regained its footing and respectability as new businesses revive the Ciutat Vella.

Introducing the neighborhoods

Barri Gòtic, the medieval heart of town around the cathedral, lies to the east of Las Ramblas. Site of the original Roman city, this is the most fun area for wandering. Lots of shops, museums, and restaurants fill its narrow streets with old buildings. The Barri Gòtic's eastern edge is Via Laietana, and from this wide street over to the Passeig de Picasso stretches the **Barri del la Ribera** and its vibrant adjunct **El Born.**

Formerly fallen on bad times as well, the Barri del la Ribera is now an up-and-coming district of art galleries, bars, clubs, and grand old mansions. South of these two districts is the scenic, lake-spotted **Parc de la Ciutadella.** On a triangular peninsula jutting into the harbor just south of that, the former fishing village of **Barceloneta** teems with activity, seafood restaurants, and tapas bars.

The **Barri Xinés** (officially know as the **Raval**), a historically seedy neighborhood of prostitutes, beggars, and thieves, is to the west of Las Ramblas, down near the harborfront. It has improved somewhat and makes an intriguing walk by day, but I wouldn't venture there after dark. Well beyond this, to the city's west, rises the hill of **Montjuïc,** site of the World's Fair and Olympic parks.

Dividing the old city from the new, the **Plaça de Catalunya** at Las Ramblas's north end is the center of Barcelona. The grid of streets spreading north from this plaza is known as the **Eixample,** and its grandest avenue is logically, if prosaically, named Avinguda Diagonal, as it crosses the grid diagonally. Beyond this, the thoroughly Catalán neighborhood of **Gràcia** expands to the north, where Castilian truly is a foreign language and plenty of colorful, local nightspots add glamour and excitement in the evenings.

Finding information after you arrive

The most central and helpful of the several information offices is the subterranean **Centre d'Informació,** at the southeast corner of Plaça Catalunya (☎ **93-368-9730;** www.barcelonaturisme.com; Metro: Catalunya), open Monday through Friday from 9 a.m. to 9 p.m., Saturday from 10 a.m. to 8 p.m., and Sundays and holidays from 10 a.m. to 2 p.m. The multilingual attendants can provide street maps, answer questions, change money, and make hotel reservations. The office also has two computers for Internet access.

The following tourist offices also offer maps, brochures, and schedules of cultural events: Estació Sants, open Monday through Friday from 8 a.m. to 8 p.m. and Saturday, Sunday, and holidays from 8 a.m. to 2 p.m.; Plaça Sant Jaume, open Monday through Friday from 9 a.m. to 8 p.m., Saturday from 10 a.m. to 8 p.m., and Sundays and holidays from 10 a.m. to 2 p.m.; and the airport information office, open Monday through Saturday from 9:30 a.m. to 8:00 p.m. and Sunday and holidays from 9:30 a.m. to 3:00 p.m.

Getting Around Barcelona

Tickets for the bus and Metro cost 1€ ($1.15). The 4.20€ ($4.85) T1 pass allows you unlimited rides for one day on the bus, Metro, and funicular. A three-day metro and bus pass costs 11€ ($13), and a five-day is 17€ ($20). You can also get free rides on all public transport with the Barcelona Card (see "Exploring Barcelona," later in this chapter).

For transit info call ☎ **010** or check online at www.tmb.net for city public transport. Call ☎ **93-478-5000** for flight info.

By public transportation

Barcelona's Metro system covers the city pretty well. Line 3 runs down Las Ramblas (and to the Sants-Estació train station), and Line 4 follows Via Laietana, bordering the eastern edge of the Ciutat Vella. Plaça de Catalunya is one of the main Metro junctions, with nearby Passeig de Gràcia as another main transfer station. You can hoof it from most Metro stations to wherever you're headed, but occasionally you may find that taking a bus is easier.

By taxi

Because of the 1992 Olympics, Barcelona's public-transportation system has been fully updated, so you probably won't need a taxi except for perhaps travel to and from the airport (although trains and buses run there frequently). In addition to the numerous taxi stands located throughout the city, cabs cruise the streets looking for fares. Available cars advertise with "Libre" or "Lliure" signs or with an illuminated green sign. If you want to call a taxi, try ☎ **93-357-7755**, 93-358-1111, or 93-300-3811.

The initial charge is 1.20€ ($1.40) and then .71€ (80¢) for each additional kilometer. After 10 p.m. and on weekends and holidays, the per-kilometer charge is slightly higher. You're charged an extra 2.10€ ($2.40) for rides to and from the airport, plus 1.05€ ($1.20) per suitcase.

By funicular

Funiculars (cable cars) run up some of the hills around the city, such as Montjuïc; other slopes are fitted with outdoor escalators to ease your way.

By foot

Unlike Madrid, Barcelona is a joy to wander — especially the medieval alleys of the Barri Gòtic and *most* especially along the wide pedestrian sidewalk that runs down the middle of Las Ramblas — though you'll want to take public transportation to get out to the Gaudí sights in the newer part of town.

Staying in Barcelona

Barcelona's hotels are relatively inexpensive for a big European city. Some guidebooks may disagree with this statement, because the city was dirt-cheap until the 1992 Olympics. Now it's merely on the low end of moderate.

Accommodations, Dining, and Attractions in Barcelona

HOTELS ■
Albinoni **16**
Ducs de Bergara **14**
Hotel Astoria **4**
Hotel Colón **22**
Hotel Condes
de Barcelona **7**
Hotel Cortes **18**
Hotel Granvía **13**
Hotel Regencia Colón **21**
Le Meridien
Barcelona **17**
Mesón Castilla **15**
Montecarlo **23**
Rialto **28**

RESTAURANTS ◆
Agua **33**
Beltxenea **8**
Can Ros **32**
Casa Leopoldo **26**
Els Quatre Gats **19**
Garduña **24**
L'Hostal de Rita **9**
Los Caracoles **30**
Pitarra **31**
Pollo Rico **25**

ATTRACTIONS ●
Casa Amatller **11**
Casa Batlló **10**
Casa Lleó Morera **12**
Casa Milà **5**
Catedral **27**
Museu Nacional
d'Art de Catalunya **2**
Museu Picasso **29**
Palau de la Musica
Catalana **20**
Park Güell/Casa-Museu
Gaudí **3**
Poble Espanyol **1**
Sagrada Familia **6**

Avinguda de Madrid
↑ Tibidabo
Carrer de Vallespir
Carrer de Berlin
Carrer de Numància
Carrer de la Infanta Carlota Joaquima
Carrer de Còrsega
Carrer de Rosselló
Carrer de Sant Antoni
Carrer de Provença
Carrer de Sants de la Creu Coberta
Avinguda de Roma
Estació Sans
Train Station
Carrer de Tarragona
PARC
JOAN
MIRÓ
Carrer d'Entença
Carrer de Rocafort
Carrer de Calàbria
Carrer de Viladomat
Carretera de la Bordeta
Plaça de
Espanya
Gran Vía de les Corts Catalanes
Carrer de Sant Fructuós
Carrer de Sepulveda
Av. de Marquès de Comillas
Av. de la Reina Maria Cristina
Carrer de Floridablanca
Avinguda de Paral·lel
Carrer de Tamarit
❶
Carrer de Manso
Carrer del
Parlament
❷
Avinguda de l'Estadi
Fundació
Joan Miró
Estadi
Olímpic
Avinguda de Miramar
PARC DE MONTJUÏC
PARC D'ATRACCIONS
DE MONTJUÏC
Passeig de Josep Carner

PORTUGAL
Barcelona
✪ Madrid
SPAIN

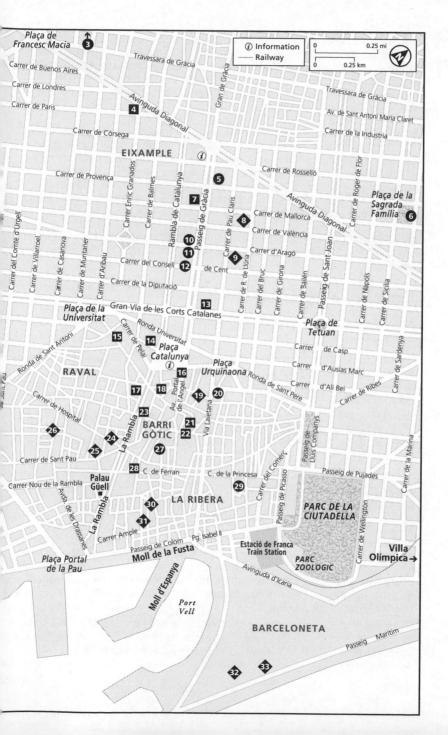

Plaça de Francesc Macià 3

Carrer de Buenos Aires

Carrer de Londres

Carrer de Paris

Travessara de Gràcia

Gran de Gràcia

Avinguda Diagonal 4

Carrer de Còrsega

Travessara de Gràcia

Av. de Sant Antoni Maria Claret

Carrer de la Industria

i Information
— Railway

0   0.25 mi
0   0.25 km

EIXAMPLE *i*

Carrer de Rosselló

Carrer de Provença

Carrer Enric Granados

Carrer de Balmes

Rambla de Catalunya

Passeig de Gràcia

Carrer de Pau Claris

5

7

8 Carrer de Mallorca

Carrer de València

Avinguda Diagonal

Carrer de Roger de Flor

Plaça de la Sagrada Família 6

Carrer del Comte d'Urgell

Carrer de Villarroel

Carrer de Casanova

Carrer de Muntaner

Carrer d'Aribau

Carrer del Consell

10

11

12

de Cent

9 Carrer de R. de Llúria

Carrer d'Aragó

Carrer del Bruc

Carrer de Girona

Carrer de Bailèn

Passeig de Sant Joan

Carrer de Nàpols

Carrer de Sicília

Carrer de la Diputació

Gran Via de les Corts Catalanes 13

Plaça de la Universitat

Ronda Universitat

Ronda de Sant Antoni

Carrer de Pelai

15

14 Plaça Catalunya *i*

Plaça Urquinaona

Ronda de Sant Pere

Plaça de Tetuan

Carrer   de Casp

Carrer   d'Ausias Marc

Carrer   d'Ali Bei

Carrer de Sardenya

RAVAL

Carrer de Hospital

17

16

18

Av. Portal de l'Angel

19

20

Via Laietana

Carrer de Ribes

Carrer de la Marina

26

23

BARRI GÒTIC

21

22

24

25

27

28 C. de Ferran

C. de la Princesa

29

Carrer del Comerç

Passeig de Lluís Companys

Passeig de Picasso

PARC DE LA CIUTADELLA

Passeig de Pujades

Carrer de Wellington

Carrer de Sant Pau

Palau Güell

La Rambla

30

31

LA RIBERA

Carrer Nou de la Rambla

Avda. de les Drassanes

Carrer Ample

Passeig de Colom

Moll de la Fusta

Pg. Isabel II

Estació de Franca Train Station

PARC ZOOLOGIC

Villa Olímpica →

Plaça Portal de la Pau

Avinguda d'Icaria

Moll d'Espanya

Port Vell

BARCELONETA

Passeig   Maritim

32

33

The only real concern in Barcelona is safety. Although it's not a seriously dangerous town, pickpockets and other thieves do work the night more brazenly here than in other comparable European cities. Although the situation is rapidly improving, much of the Ciutat Vella still has the slightly unsavory element acquired early in the 20th century. When you're looking for a room, definitely steer clear of the Barri Xinés (the Raval) and anywhere near it.

Most of the Barri Gòtic is pretty safe now, as long as you're watchful of pickpockets, and the part of the Ciutat Vella to the west of Las Ramblas up near the Plaça de Catalunya is just fine (full of hotels). I find the grid of the Eixample a bit boring, but it's certainly a safe neighborhood in which to base yourself, and often rooms are cheaper there than in the Old City. Additionally, the tourist office can help you find a room; call its special hotel line at ☎ 93-304-3232.

All accommodation rates in this section, including breakfast, are quoted including the 7 percent tax that most official price lists in Barcelona leave off.

Barcelona's top hotels and B&Bs

Hotel Astoria
$$ Sur Diagonal

Behind an Art Deco facade and common areas with high ceilings lies a midrange hotel offering good service and very-well-kept rooms. Older accommodations are done in exposed cedar; more recently renovated ones sport louvered closets, whitewashed walls, and checkerboard floors.

See map p. 512. Carrer de París 201 (at Carrer Granados, 1 block down from the Diagonal). ☎ *93-209-8311. Fax: 93-202-3008.* www.derbyhotels.es. *Metro: Diagonal. Rates: 118€–160€ ($136–$184) double; buffet breakfast 12€ ($14). AE, DC, MC, V.*

Hotel Condes de Barcelona
$$$$ Eixample

This late-19th-century villa is one of Barcelona's finest old-world hotels and is set within one of Barcelona's architectural wonderlands — the modernismo buildings of the Passeig de Gràcia. The facade is neo-medieval, and the interior is a mix of high-tech and traditional opulence. Rooms come with all the standard amenities, plus marble baths and reproduction Spanish paintings. The Art Deco piano bar off the lobby is a lovely place to wind down with a drink.

See map p. 512. Passeig de Gràcia 73–75 (at Carrer de Mallorca). ☎ *93-467-4786 or 93-467-4780. Fax: 93-467-4785.* www.condesdebarcelona.com. *Metro: Passeig de Gràcia. Rates: 214€–268€ ($246–$308) double; buffet breakfast 17€ ($20). AE, DC, MC, V.*

Hotel Regencia Colón
$$ Barri Gòtic

Just a few steps from the cathedral on the edge of the Barri Gòtic, the Regencia Colón is one of Barcelona's great central values. The rooms are bland but comfortably worn, although a 1999 overhaul added new furnishings and parquet floors. Most accommodations are plenty large, although the baths are small, and enjoy amenities from phones and TVs to air-conditioning and minibars.

See map p. 512. Sagristans 13–17 (just north of the cathedral). ☎ *93-318-9858. Fax: 93-317-2822.* www.hotelregenciacolon.com. *Metro: Jaume 1 or Urquinaona. Rates: 123–158€ ($141–$182) double; buffet breakfast 10€ ($12). AE, DC, MC, V.*

Le Meridien Barcelona
$$$$$ On Las Ramblas

This modernismo structure is Barcelona's top hotel, a thoroughly contemporary affair spilling over with amenities, such as heated bathroom floors and in-room VCRs. The location is superb, but even the double glazing can't keep out all the noise of Las Ramblas below.

See map p. 512. Ramblas 111. ☎ *800-543-4300 in the United States, 93-318-6200 in Spain. Fax: 93-301-7776.* www.lemeridien-barcelona.com. *Metro: Liceu or Plaça de Catalunya. Rates: 385€–471€ ($443–$542) doubles; buffet breakfast or continental in-room breakfast 21€ ($24). AE, DC, MC, V.*

Mesón Castilla
$ Ciutat Vella

A clean budget hotel with lots of amenities (phone, TV, minibar) and a huge breakfast buffet, the Mesón Castilla has a perfect location near Las Ramblas and is on the border between the New and Old Cities. Rooms are reliably comfortable, with interesting, ornate headboards; request one of the rooms with a large terrace. Each of the three rooms without bath en suite has a private bath next door.

See map p. 512. Valldoncella 5 (a few blocks west of Plaça de Catalunya). ☎ *93-318-2182. Fax: 93-412-4020.* www.husa.es. *Metro: Universitat. Rates: 131€ ($151) double. Rates include breakfast. AE, DC, MC, V.*

Montecarlo
$$$ On Las Ramblas

This is my frugal choice for a hotel in the heart of the action. Although the rooms are functionally modern, the public areas still have the chandeliers, fireplaces, and carved doors that hearken back to the private mansion it was 120 years ago. Rooms are standardized and modern; superior rooms differ mainly by being slightly longer with a small table and chairs and double sinks in the marble baths. You're right on Las Ramblas here, which is wonderful as far as location is concerned, but a bit noisy — request a room overlooking the palms of a quiet interior courtyard.

See map p. 512. Rambla dels Estudis 124. ☎ *93-412-0404. Fax: 93-318-7323.* www.mercure.com. *Metro: Plaça de Catalunya. Rates: 154€–332€ ($177–$382) double. Buffet breakfast 14€ ($16). AE, DC, MC, V.*

Barcelona's runner-up accommodations

Albinoni

$$$ **Ciutat Vella** Rooms in this stately 1886 neoclassical mansion are a decent size, with several rooms facing the courtyard or the street. Request one with a balcony. *See map p. 512. Av. Portal de l'Àngel 17 (south of Plaça de Catalunya).* ☎ *93-318-4141. Fax 93-301-2631.* www.hoteles-catalonia.es.

Ducs de Bergara

$$$$ **Edge of Ciutat Vella** This hotel may have been built in 1899, but most of the room décor (especially in the new tower annex) is modern. Public areas, though, retain the modernismo touch of architect Emilio Sala i Cortes. *See map p. 512. Bergara 11.* ☎ *93-301-5151. Fax: 93-317-3442.* www.hoteles-catalonia.es.

Hotel Colón

$$$$ **Barri Gòtic** Under the same management as its neighbor, the Hotel Regencia Colón (see "Barcelona's top hotels and B&Bs," earlier), this hotel offers classier digs — some of which open directly onto the cathedral facade — and a higher price. *See map p. 512. Avenida de la Catedral 7.* ☎ *93-301-1404. Fax: 93-317-2915.* www.hotelcolon.es.

Hotel Cortes

$ **Ciutat Vella** The Cortes has comfortable bedrooms, about half of which face a quiet courtyard, and a good, basic restaurant on the ground floor. The location, a mere block from Plaça de Catalunya, just off the Ramblas, is good — and rates are cheap. *See map p. 512. Santa Anna 25.* ☎ *93-317-9112. Fax: 93-302-7870.*

Hotel Granvía

$$ **Eixample** Hotel Granvía has a grand, skylit foyer and high-ceilinged, spacious rooms with antique dressers. The neighborhood offers chic shopping and is just a few blocks from Las Ramblas in the old quarter of town. *See map p. 512. Gran Vía de les Corts Catalanes 642 (between Passeig de Gràcia and Carrer Pau Claris).* ☎ *93-318-1900. Fax: 93-318-9997.*

Rialto

$$ **Barri Gòtic** The Rialto's modernized rooms have a touch of class, and the location is hard to beat at these prices. *See map p. 512. Ferran 40–42 (near Plaça de Saint Jaume).* ☎ *90-222-2240 (toll-free) or 93-318-5212. Fax: 93-318-5312.*

Dining in Barcelona

As the capital of Catalonia, Barcelona has plenty of traditional local restaurants that make the excellent casseroles that made this region famous. As a port city, Barcelona has incredible seafood. Make sure you try some of the interesting surf-'n'-turf combinations, such as the traditional *llagosta i pollastre* (chicken and lobster in a tomato-hazelnut sauce). *Suquet* is made of shellfish stewed with tomatoes, potatoes, saffron, and wine. Unattractive but tasty is *butifarra negra amb mongetes,* a fat, black sausage (pork bellies, blood, and spices) in a plate of white beans.

Nearby Valencia contributes to Barcelona's tables the mighty *paella,* saffron-tinged rice simmered with a medley of seafood, chicken, tomatoes, peppers, beans, pork, hare, and so on.

Don't leave Spain without sampling some Basque cuisine — although Catalonians are no slouches in the kitchen, supremacy for invention and refinement goes to the Basque (see the introduction to Madrid dining in Chapter 22). Spend at least one evening doing a *tapeo,* or tapas-bar crawl (see "More cool things to see and do," later in this chapter).

For a meal on the run, **L. Simo,** Passeig de Gràcia 46, makes good sandwiches and salads, and **Las Campanas,** Mercè 21 (behind the Port Vell and near the main post office), specializes in spicy *chorizo* (sausage) sandwiches, best washed down with ample beer and wine. The best picnic pickings by far are at the excellent La Boquería market on Las Ramblas — it's loaded with produce, meats, fish, and cheeses.

Barcelona's top restaurants

Beltxenea
$$$$$ **Eixample**   BASQUE

Some of Barcelona's finest Basque chefs hold court in this converted modernismo apartment building. Splurge for a special occasion here and sample succulent Basque cooking in dishes such as hake garnished with clams or grilled rabbit. In summer, you can dine in the formal garden.

See map p. 512. Carrer Mallorca 275 (between Passeig de Gràcia and Carrer de Pau Claris). ☎ *93-215-3024. Reservations recommended. Metro: Passeig de Gràcia. Main courses: 16€–45€ ($18–$52). Tasting menu: 50€ ($58). AE, DC, MC, V. Open: Lunch Mon–Fri, dinner Mon–Sat; closed Aug and two weeks at Christmas.*

Els Quatre Gats
$$ **Barri Gòtic**   CATALÁN

This turn-of-the-last-century cafe/restaurant was the legendary gathering place of Barcelona's bohemians and intellectuals, a place where Picasso once displayed his works. The set-price menu (served until 4 p.m.) is one of the city's best values, with dishes based on whatever is most fresh at the market that day. À la carte prices, though, are creeping up, and service can be quite scatterbrained. Some evenings, a live pianist pounds out standards.

See map p. 512. Carrer Montsió 3 (just off Av. Portal de l'Angel). ☎ *93-302-4140. Reservations suggested Sat–Sun. Metro: Plaça de Catalunya. Main courses: 10€–19€ ($12–$22). Fixed-price lunch: 11€ ($13). AE, MC, V. Open: Restaurant lunch and dinner daily; cafe all day daily.*

Los Caracoles
$$$ Barri Gòtic   CATALÁN/SPANISH

This colorful Barcelona institution of good, solid cooking patronized by Salvador Dalí and John Wayne lies near the port. Try the snails (its namesake) or the spit-roasted chicken. Its fame does draw the crowds, but the quality remains uncompromised.

See map p. 512. Carrer dels Escudellers 14 (turn east off Las Ramblas at Plaça del Teatre and just follow the curving street). ☎ *93-302-3185. Reservations suggested. Metro: Drassanes. Main courses: 9.05€–30€ ($10–$35). AE, DC, MC, V. Open: Lunch and dinner daily.*

Pitarra
$$ Barri Gòtic   CATALÁN

Named after the famous Catalán poet/playwright who once lived here, Pitarra has stuck to the staples — traditional dishes cooked just like Mama used to — since 1890. The Valencian paella is good, as is the grilled squid, but in winter go for a hearty game dish, such as hare with wild mushrooms.

See map p. 512. Carrer de Avinyó 56 (off Carrer de Ferran). ☎ *93-301-1647. Reservations recommended. Metro: Liceu. Main courses: 7€–23€ ($8.05–$26). MC, V. Open: Lunch and dinner, Mon–Sat; closed Aug.*

Pollo Rico
$ Ciutat Vella   SPANISH

Most frugal travelers eventually find their way to Pollo Rico, where you can eat rich with a poor man's purse. The ground floor sells scrumptious spit-roasted chicken and *tortillas* (omelettes), which you can carry out or eat at the scruffy tables. The comfortable upstairs dining room offers simple fixed-price menus.

See map p. 512. Carrer Sant Pau 31 (2 blocks west of Las Ramblas). ☎ *93-441-3184. Reservations suggested. Metro: Liceu. Main courses: 2.50€–18€ ($2.90–$21). Fixed-price menu: 6.30€ ($7.25). No credit cards. Open: Lunch and dinner Thurs–Tues.*

Barcelona's runner-up restaurants

Can Ros

$$$ Barcelonata   The place to head for an 9.50€ ($11) paella in Barcelonata if the prices at fancier Casa Leopoldo (see next listing) put you off your appetite. *See map p. 512. Almirall Aixada (off Passeig Joan de Borbó).* ☎ *93-221-4579.*

Casa Leopoldo

$$$$$ **Ciutat Vella** This surprisingly sophisticated restaurant offers some of the freshest seafood in town. There's a popular tapas bar in front and two dining rooms, one slightly more formal than the other. Take a taxi coming and going. *See map p. 512. Sant Rafael 24 (near Carrer de la Riereta).* ☎ *93-441-30-14.*

Garduña

$$ **Ciutat Vella** Garduña could very well be shut down by one well-timed visit from the health inspector, but this teensy eatery remains the classic restaurant among those who cling around the edges of La Boquería market. If not the best food in town, it's certainly among the most atmospheric places to eat, and the prices are pretty low. *See map p. 512. Jerusalem 18–19 (on the farside of La Boquería market, on the square behind it, off Rambla de Sant Josep).* ☎ *93-302-4323.*

L'Hostal de Rita

$$$ **Eixample** A welcoming, stylish little place that does a great rollito de pollo con jamon (chicken rolled with ham) and a fixed-price menu for 7.30€ ($8.40). *See map p. 512. Carrer d'Aragó 279 (at Carrer de Pau Claris, a block off Passeig de Gràcia).* ☎ *93-487-2376.*

 ### Agua

$$$ **Barcelonata** One of the most original and hip of the myriad choices along the seafront. Enter from the promenade above, but choose either terrace seating with a view, or indoors set off with excellent contemporary art. Signature dishes feature rice with seafood. Reservations a must. *See map p. 512. Paseo Marítim de la Barceloneta 30.* ☎ *93-225-1272.*

Exploring Barcelona

 The **Barcelona Card** (www.barcelonaturisme.com), available at tourist offices, grants you free rides on all public transportation, plus 30 to 50 percent off on admissions to most sights in town, and 12 to 25 percent off at certain shops, tours, and entertainment venues. The card costs 17€ ($20) for one day, 20€ ($23) for two days, and 23€ ($26) for three days. Rates for children between ages 4 and 12 are 3€ ($3.45) less at each level. Another bargain card, the **ArTicket** (www.articket.com; 15€/$17) gets you admission to six museums: the Museum of Catalan Art, the Gaudi Museum in La Pedrera, the Museum of Contemporary Art, the Joan Miró Foundation, the Museum of Contemporary Culture, and the Antoni Tápies Foundation.

Barcelona's top sights

Catedral (Cathedral)
Barri Gòtic

Behind an elaborate neo-Gothic facade and spire from the 19th century, you find Madrid's massive Gothic cathedral, a dark, cavernous space built between 1298 and 1450. There's not much to see inside besides the marvelously carved 15th-century choir stalls and ranks of glowing votive candles, but a visit including a stop in the shady cloisters takes a good 45 minutes. This tranquil oasis in the midst of the old city is surrounded by magnolias, palm trees, and ponds with geese.

Medieval Catalonian art stuffs the little Museu de la Catedral adjacent to the cathedral. The Plaça de San Jaume, in front of the cathedral, is a pleasant place to spend time people-watching; at noon on Sundays a troupe performs the complicated folk dance *sardana* here.

See map p. 512. Plaça de la Seu. ☎ *93-315-1554 or 93-310-2580. Metro: Jaume I, Liceu. Bus: 16, 17, 19, 22, or 45. Admission: Cathedral and cloister free; choir 1.50€ ($1.75); Museu de la Catedral 1€ ($1.15). Open: Church daily 8 a.m.–1:30 p.m. and 5–7:30 p.m.; museum daily 11 a.m.–1 p.m.; cloister 9 a.m.–1:15 p.m. and 4–7 p.m. daily.*

Museu Nacional d'Art de Catalunya
Montjuïc

In an enormous 1929 palace atop Montjuïc hill is one of the world's biggest and best collections of Romanesque art, centered around a series of gorgeous 12th-century frescoes removed from Catalonian churches in the Pyrenees. You also find a good store of Spanish Gothic art and sculpture. Outside the palace is a network of stair-stepping fountains that star in a sound and light show on summer nights (Thursday through Sunday).

See map p. 512. Palau Nacional, Parc de Montjuïc. ☎ *93-622-0375.* www.gencat. es/mnac. *Metro: Espanya. Bus: 61. Admission: 4.50€ ($5.20) adults, 2.10€ ($2.40) seniors/students; free for everyone first Thurs of the month; extra fee for special exhibits. Open: Tues–Sat 10 a.m.–7 p.m., Sun and holidays 10 a.m.–2:30 p.m.*

Museu Picasso
Ciutat Vella

Although born in Andalusia, Picasso moved to Barcelona at age 14, and it was here, in the academy where his father taught, that he learned his craft. Barcelona was lucky enough when opening this museum to secure from the master himself many of his earliest works, which his sister had preserved. The very first room disproves the tongue-in-cheek myth that Picasso invented cubism merely because he couldn't draw properly, for here you see remarkable drawings and paintings executed with a high degree of realism — all when Picasso was barely a teenager. Of the other 3,000 works in this collection, seek out his *Las Meninas* paintings and drawings, a series of cubist studies made of Velázquez's masterpiece in Madrid's Prado museum (see that entry in Chapter 22). The curious can run through the museum in half an hour; Picasso fans will want to spend one to two hours.

See map p. 512. Montcada 15–19. ☎ *93-319-6310.* www.museupicasso.bcn.es. *Metro: Jaume I, Liceu. Bus: 14, 17, 19, 22, 24, 40, 45, 51, or 59. Admission: 5€ ($5.75) adults, 2€ ($2.30) seniors/students/ages 12–16, free ages 12 and under; free for everyone first Sun of every month. Open: Tues–Sat and holidays 10 a.m.–8 p.m., Sun 10 a.m.–3 p.m.*

Park Güell/Casa-Museu Gaudí
Grácia

In the northern reaches of the Grácia district, north of the Eixample, rises one of architect Antoni Gaudí's most colorful creations. This idiosyncratic park was intended as an unusual little residential community, but only two houses were built. The city bought the property in 1926 and turned it into a public park filled with Gaudí's colonnades of crooked columns (they look like tree trunks), narrow gardens, small fountains, and whimsical animals. A large, spectacular curving bench brightened by a patterned mosaic of tile and mirror dominates one sitting area; from this spot, you get great views of the city. Two mosaicked pavilions designed by Gaudí flank the entrance, but the Casa-Museu Gaudí (☎ **93-284-6446**), where the master lived from 1906 to 1926, was built by Ramón Berenguer. Gaudí's models, furnishings, and drawings fill the interior.

See map p. 512. Carrer d'Olot. ☎ *93-219-3811. Metro: Vallcarca. Bus: 24. Admission: The park is free; the museum costs 4€ ($4.60). Open: Park daily 10 a.m. to sunset, museum daily Oct–Mar 10 a.m.–6 p.m., Apr–Sept 10 a.m.–8 p.m.*

Sagrada Familia
Eixample

The Sagrada Familia is reminiscent of a giant, drippy sand castle — kids get a kick out of the bizarre style. Certainly the weirdest-looking church in Europe, this ongoing project represents the architect Antoni Gaudí's creativity at its whimsical, feverish best. Only 8 of what will be 13 spires and the two lesser facades are finished. The Civil War interrupted construction, but it has been picked up again as a slow trickle of donated funds allows work to continue on the nave, remaining towers, and main facade. You may only need an hour to tour this work-in-progress, but you can easily spend three just climbing up and down, and across the lithe bridges joining its multitude of spires.

The architectural details are almost Gothic in their intricacy, but with a modern, fluid twist — rosy brown and gray stone is flecked with the colors of Gaudí's signature tile-chip mosaics. You can climb conch-shell spiral staircases (or take elevators) up several of the spires to look through the rose windows with no panes. Admire the rounded-off grid of the Eixample around you, and examine up close the funky gargoyles — over here is the Virgin Mary, there a snail creeps up the building's side, and around the corner a stone cypress tree seems to flutter with white stone doves.

Gaudí or gaudy?

Around the turn of this century, Art Nouveau arrived in Barcelona in the form of *modernismo*, a particularly fluid and idiosyncratic Catalán version of a larger architectural revolution. The high priest of modernismo, Antoni Gaudí, apprenticed as a blacksmith before taking up architecture. Creative wrought-iron patterns became just one of the many signature details Gaudí incorporated into his flowing, organic structures; he was especially fond of creating colorful mosaics out of chips of ceramic and mirror.

If you see only a handful of modernismo buildings, make them Gaudí's most famous trio: the **Sagrada Familia** (see listing earlier in this chapter); the colorful **Casa Battlò** (Passeig de Gràcia 43; ☎ 93-216-0306; Admission: 10€/$12, including audioguide; Open: Daily 9 a.m.–8 p.m.) with a roof shaped like a dragon's back and theater-mask balconies; and **Casa Milà** (Passeig de Gràcia 92; ☎ 93-484-5979 or 93-484-5995), often called La Pedrera ("the quarry") for its undulating rocky shape. Here, especially, Gaudí seemed to avoid straight lines at all costs — the place looks like it's melting. Casa Milà contains an exhibition on Gaudí and modernismo; and for the 6€ ($6.90) admission you can also tour the architectural fun park and swirly, ice-cream chimneys. Hours are daily from 10 a.m. to 8 p.m.

Two other modernismo architects of note were Domènech i Montaner and Puig i Cadafalch. To compare them to each other, and to master Gaudí, take a walk down the Illa de la Discòrdia ("the block of discord") on Passeig de Gràcia between Carrer del Consell de Cent and Carrer d'Arago. Here, their interpretations of modernismo compete in the form of apartment buildings. At no. 35 is Montaner's **Casa Lleo Morera,** at no. 41 is Cadafalch's **Casa Amatller,** and at no. 43 is Gaudí's **Casa Battlò.** (For these and Casa Milà, take the Metro to Passeig de Gracia or Diagonal, which is closer to Casa Milà.)

Montaner also designed the gorgeous venue **Palau de la Música Catalana,** Carrer de Sant Francesc de Paula 2 (☎ 93-295-7200; www.palaumusica.org), now a UNESCO World Heritage Site. Go inside to see the sky-lit stained glass of the inverse dome in the auditorium; 50-minute guided tours depart Wednesday and weekends every half hour from 10:00 a.m. to 3:30 p.m. for 5€ ($5.75). One of Cadafalch's other major works is **Els Quatre Gats,** a restaurant (see "Barcelona's top restaurants," earlier in this chapter).

In the crypt is a museum that details the ongoing construction and shows, through models and drawings, what Gaudí's original plans were and how the finished building will appear. Gaudí got the Sagrada Familia commission in 1883, and it consumed him. He poured every peseta he had into the project and went begging door to door when funds ran out. He even lived on the site for 16 years. Gaudí died in 1926, after being run over by a trolley, but left behind no master plan for the church. Although his final design was unclear, workers inch toward finishing his masterpiece. Many (often vocal) critics believe the church should remain unfinished. You can be sure Gaudí is keeping a sharp (albeit posthumous) eye on the proceedings — he is buried in the church crypt.

See map p. 512. Carrer de Majorca 401. ☎ *93-207-3031.* www.sagradafamilia. org. *Metro: Sagrada Familia. Bus: 15, 18, 19, 33, 43, 44, 50, or 51. Admission: 8€ ($9.20) adults, 5€ ($5.75) seniors/students, 3€ ($3.45) children ages 7–10, free for ages 7 and under; 1.50€ ($1.75) for the elevator to the top. Open: Daily Apr–Aug 9 a.m.–8 p.m.; Mar, Sept, and Oct 9 a.m.–7 p.m., Nov–Feb 9 a.m.–6 p.m.*

More cool things to see and do

✔ **Touring Spain in a nutshell at the Poble Espanyol:** For the 1929 World's Fair, Barcelona created a simulated Spanish village high on top of Montjuïc, where 115 houses and structures reproduce Spanish monuments and buildings from over the last 1,000 years. Many of the replicas are crafts and souvenir shops, but over a dozen have been converted into restaurants that serve cuisines from Spain's various regions. With others housing discos, bars, and a flamenco club, the Poble Espanyol (☎ **93-508-6300;** www.poble-espanyol.com) is an entertaining spot for an evening out. Take the Metro to Espanya then Bus 61. Admission is 7€ ($8.05), 3.90€ ($4.50) for children under 12, and it's open Monday from 9 a.m. to 8 p.m., Tuesday through Thursday from 9 a.m. to 2 a.m., Friday and Saturday from 9 a.m. to 4 a.m., and Sunday from 9 a.m. to midnight.

✔ **Enjoying a *tapeo*:** When in Spain, do like the Spanish — indulge in an early-evening *tapeo* (tapas-bar crawl). For more details on this most Spanish of activities (tapas rank somewhere between a snack and a passion), see Madrid's dining section in Chapter 22. One of Barcelona's best *tascas* (tapas bars) is **Sagardi** at Argenteria 62 in the bustling Born section of La Ribera. Basque-style finger foods and traditional cider make a great pre-dinner social event, or a full meal. Just off the Ramblas, look for the building with all the umbrellas and double-back behind it to find the **Taverna Basca Irati** at Cardenal Casanyes 17, known for homemade *pintxos* (tapas) and some carefully selected wines.

✔ **Breaking out the castanets:** Inspired by the medieval tribulations of Spain's Jews and Moors, and influenced by gypsy rhythms and styles, the exotically fluid dance known as the flamenco heats up the night in two of Barcelona's bars. Admittedly, these shows are put on for the tourists — you have to head to Madrid or even Andalusia, the birthplace of flamenco, for more-authentic versions.

But if Barcelona is your only chance to experience the hand-clapping, guitar-strumming lifebeat of this folk art, try the **Tablao Flamenco Cordobés,** Las Ramblas 35 (☎ **93-317-5711**), or **El Tablao de Carmen** (☎ **93-325-6895**) in the Poble Espanyol. Call to confirm show times and prices, but a dinner performance usually happens around 8:30 or 9:30 p.m. for 55€ ($63), with a late show with just drinks around 11 p.m. for 29€ ($33).

✔ **Discoing 'til dawn with Barcelona's pulsing nightlife:** Like most of Spain, Barcelona loves late-night action, be it bar-hopping, dancing, or just general partying until the wee hours. The most traditional evening can be had in the modernismo architectural triumph of the **Palau de la Musica Catalán,** San Francest de Paula 2 (☎ 93-295-7200; www.palaumusica.org), which features year-round classical, jazz, and pop concerts as well as recitals. You can stay passive in your after-dark pleasures at a flamenco bar such as those listed previously or dance your own socks off at clubs: **Jamboree** (☎ 93-301-7564), a soul-oriented basement venue at Plaça Reial 17; historic **Sala Apolo,** Nou de la Rambla 113, (☎ 93-441-4001); perpetually "in" **City Hall** (☎ 93-317-2177), at Rambla Catalunya 2–4; sleek-chic **Baja Beach,** Passeig Marítim 34 (☎ 93-225-9100); or the fashionable waterside dance-club **Mojito Bar,** Maremagnum, Port Vell 3 (☎ 93-352-8746). Or hang out at the Born's classically atmospheric **Miramelindo** bar, Passeig del Born 15, (☎ 93-310-3727), just one of many wonderful spots in this ultracool neighborhood.

Guided tours

The public **Bus Turistic** (www.tmb.net) is a hop-on/hop-off service with two different routes: a northerly red route and a southerly blue one. With more than 30 stops and buses every 10 to 30 minutes (9 a.m.–8 p.m. daily; closed Dec 25 and Jan 1), the service effectively covers all the major points of interest in Barcelona. The cost is 16€ ($18) for one day and 20€ ($23) for two days. You receive an info booklet, and an attendant on board lets you know what's available at each stop. You also get around 10 to 20 percent off at many sights. The easiest place to start is at Plaça Catalunya, in front of **El Corte Inglés** department store.

Pullmantur, Gran Via de les Corts Catalanes 635 (☎ 93-318-0241; www.pullmantur.com), offers, daily, a morning guided bus tour of the old city and Montjuïc, and an afternoon tour of Eixample architectural sights, including Sagrada Familia, the Park Güell, and the Picasso Museum. Either tour costs 34€ ($39), or the two together (including lunch) cost 89€ ($102).

Suggested itineraries

If you're the type who'd rather organize your own tours, this section offers some tips for building your own Barcelona itineraries. Two full days gives you a good taste of what the city has to offer.

If you have one day

Begin early in the morning at the only grand cathedral of Europe still in the midst of being built, Gaudí's **Sagrada Familia.** Take 90 minutes or so to clamber around its spires and admire the whimsical sculpture adorning its odd hidden corners. Then take the Metro to Diagonal for more modernismo masterpieces in Gaudí's **Casa Milà** and the famed **Illa de la Discòrdia** along Passeig de Gràcia.

Hop back on the Metro at the Passeig de Gràcia stop to tunnel to the Jaume stop so that, after grabbing some lunch on the go, you can pop into the **Museu Picasso,** a museum honoring Barcelona's other artistic giant of the 20th century. Backtrack along Carrer de la Princesa/Carrer de Jaume I to turn right on Carrer de la Dagueria, which becomes Carrer Freneria as it passes some Roman columns and, eventually, spills into the square in front of Barcelona's massive Gothic **Catedral.**

As evening draws near, make your way over to the grand promenade of **Las Ramblas** to watch the street performers, the locals out for their *paseo* (evening walk), and to simply stroll one of the greatest pedestrian boulevards in Europe. Cut out by 6 p.m. or so to *tapeo* before heading back to your hotel to rest up from your full day, before a 10 p.m. dinner at **Los Caracoles.**

If you have two days

Begin Day 1 seeing perhaps Barcelona's greatest sight: **Las Ramblas,** that long, wide, pedestrian boulevard that glides right through the heart of the old city, from Plaça de Catalunya to the port. Start at the port end, at the Drassanes Metro stop. Stop into **La Boqueria** market to see the string beans stacked perfectly and the dried salt cod piled high. Pause at the twittering, tweeting cages of the tiny portable bird market; toss coins to the performers who pose as statues and only move when the clinks of change hit their hats. Follow Las Ramblas all the way to Carrer de Portaferrisa and turn right until you get to the **Catedral.**

For lunch, work your way south through the back streets of the medieval Barri Gòtic to **Los Caracoles.** Then head over to the **Museu Picasso.** Be out of there by 3:30 or 4:00 p.m. so you have plenty of time to get up to Montjuïc and the **Museu Nacional d'Art de Catalunya** (it doesn't close until 7 p.m.). Afterward, you can take in a flamenco show and dine in the nearby **Poble Espanyol.**

Day 2 is the day for modernismo. Start it off by proceeding to **Sagrada Familia** and the Art Nouveau wonderland of **Passeig de Gràcia.** You're in luck that **L'Hostal de Rita** is just a block away from the Illa de la Discòrdia for lunch.

Now, because the last day-and-a-half have been pretty packed (and you've done lots of walking), take the afternoon to relax while still sightseeing. Head up to the Gaudí-designed **Park Güell,** a wonderful place to wander, full of whimsical architectural accents, plus the **Casa-Museu Gaudí,** where the master once lived.

Fast Facts: Barcelona

Area Code

The country code in Spain is **34**. What was Barcelona's separate city code of **93** is now incorporated as part of the full number, which means you must always dial it (no matter where you're calling from). To call Barcelona from the United States, dial ☎ **011-34** followed by the number.

American Express

The American Express office, Passeig de Gràcia 101 (☎ 93-217-0070), is open Monday through Friday from 9:30 a.m. to 6:00 p.m. and Saturday from 10 a.m. to noon.

Currency

In 2002, the euro, the new European currency, became the legal tender in Spain, replacing the peseta. The exchange rate used to calculate the dollar values given in this chapter is 1€ = $1.15. Amounts greater than $10 are rounded to the nearest dollar.

Doctors and Dentists

Dial ☎ 061 to find a doctor. The U.S. Consulate has a list of English-speaking physicians. For a dentist, call ☎ 93-415-9922.

Embassies and Consulates

The U.S. Consulate is at Passeig Reina Elisenda 23 (☎ 93-280-2227).

Emergency

Dial ☎ **092** for the police. For a medical emergency, call ☎ **061** or 93-329-9701 for an ambulance. To report a fire, call ☎ **080**.

Hospitals

Three hospitals have emergency departments *(urgencias):* Hospital Clínic, Villarroel 170 (☎ 93-227-5400; Metro: Hospital Clínic); Hospital Creu Roja de Barcelona, Dos de Maig 301 (☎ 93-507-2700; Metro: Hospital de Sant Pau); and Hospital de la Santa Creu I Sant Pau, Sant Antoni Maria Claret 167 (☎ 93-291-9000; Metro: Hospital de Sant Pau).

Information

The most central and helpful of the several information offices is the subterranean Centre d'Informació, at the southeast corner of Plaça Catalunya (☎ 93-368-9730; www.barcelonaturisme.com; Metro: Catalunya). For details on it and other tourist offices in Barcelona, see "Finding information after you arrive," near the beginning of this chapter.

For transit info call ☎ 010 or check online at www.tmb.net for city public transport. Call ☎ 93-478-5000 for flight info.

Internet Access and Cybercafes

Not far from the University and La Rambla, the CyberMundo Internet Centre has two adjacent locations — Bergara 3 (☎ 93-317-7142; E-mail: info@cybermundo.es; Metro: Plaça de Catalunya), and around the corner at Balmes 8 — both open daily from 9 a.m. to midnight or 1 a.m. They serve coffee and other drinks and have some 200 computers in all. Another excellent center is EasyEverything, La Rambla dels Caputxins 29 (☎ 93-318-2435, Metro: Liceu or Drassenes), open daily 7 a.m. to 2 a.m., featuring drinks, sandwiches, ice cream, and 260 computers.

Maps

All tourist centers have helpful free maps, of course, but you can also get them from any major hotel reception desk and many bars and shops, including the El Corte Inglés department store right on Plaça Catalunya. The city's layout is a very quick study; orienting yourself is always easy, because the streets slope down, toward the sea, and up, toward the mountains.

Newspapers/Magazines

The most useful weekly guide is the *Guíaocio,* available at any newsstand for 1€ ($1.15), which includes an English-language section at the back; but there are also a host of English-language freebies to be found lying around in every shop, restaurant, and bar. One of the best is the monthly *Guide Out,* specializing in dining and entertainment options. The monthly *Metropolitan,* available at the Cinema Verdi in Gracia and other expat spots, is also excellent, providing a local's-eye-view of Barcelona.

Pharmacies

Pharmacies *(farmàcias)* rotate the duty of staying open late. The *farmàcias de guardia* (night pharmacies) are listed in daily newspapers and on the doors of all drugstores, or call ☎ 010. A very central pharmacy is open 24/7, Farmàcia Alvarez, at Passeig de Gràcia 26 (☎ 93-302-1124).

Police

Dial ☎ 092 for the police.

Post Office

Barcelona's main post office (☎ 93-318-3507) is on Plaça d'Antoni López, where Via Laietana meets Passeig de Colom. Hours are Monday through Friday from 8 a.m. to 9 p.m. and Saturday from 8 a.m. to 2 p.m.

Safety

The street crime for which Barcelona once drew unwanted attention has diminished, due in part to an increased police presence and new lighting on dark streets in the Old Town. Some wariness is still required, however, especially in the Raval after dark and whenever you're in transit — when your mind is focused on the sights and sounds, and simply finding your way. A favorite maneuver of criminals is to spit or spill a messy substance on you — while one member of the team offers to "help," another relieves you of valuables. Men are more likely to suffer this; women are often the victims of purse snatchings. Be especially alert in the older parts of town and around major sights. Take the usual urban precautions, including using hotel safes for jewelry, traveler's checks, extra credit cards, and any cash not required for each excursion.

Turisme Atenció (Tourist Attention), La Rambla 43 (☎ 93-344-1300; Metro: Liceu), has English-speaking attendants who can aid crime victims in reporting losses and obtaining new documents. The office is open 24/7.

Taxes

The government sales tax, known as IVA (value-added tax), is levied nationwide on all goods and services, and ranges from 7 to 33 percent.

Telephone

A local call is .25€ (30¢). Most public phone *cabinas* provide clear instructions in English. If you're calling long-distance from a hotel, expect a hefty surcharge.

To make an international call, dial ☎ 00, wait for the tone, and dial the country code, the area code, and the number.

Phone cards worth 12€ ($14) are good for 150 minutes. Use them to make international calls from properly equipped booths, which are clearly identified. Phone cards are available at tobacco shops *(estancos)* and post offices. Or you can make calls and pay for them after completion at the currency-exchange booth at La Rambla 88, open Monday through Saturday from 10 a.m. to 11 p.m. and Sunday from 10:00 a.m. to 1:30 p.m. Contact MCI at ☎ 800-099-357, AT&T at ☎ 900-99-0011, or Sprint at ☎ 900-99-0013, dialing directly from any phone.

Transit Info

See "Getting Around Barcelona," earlier in this chapter.

Chapter 24

Athens and the Greek Islands

. . . .

In This Chapter

▶ Getting to Athens and the Greek islands
▶ Learning the lay of the land
▶ Locating the best hotel, restaurants, and historical sights
▶ Side-tripping to the best beaches outside the big city

. . . .

*B*y the fifth century B.C., when the rest of Western civilization was still in its infancy, Athens was already a thriving metropolis, the site of one of the world's first successful democracies. The city gave birth to influential schools of art, architecture, literature, drama, and philosophy that continue to be the touchstones of modern culture.

Three magnificent sights from ancient times are preserved in Athens: the Acropolis Hill, whose Parthenon to Athena is the world's most famous ancient temple; a huge archaeological museum; and the Ancient Agora, the civic laboratory in which contemporary democracy was first developed and tested.

Even though Athens has one of the most sacred cultural heritages in Europe, I recommend that visitors see these icons quickly and then venture out into the rest of Greece. Honestly, the rest of the fabled city now leaves much to be desired; it's a tangled, polluted mess of over-development and traffic.

As I write this, Athens has just come out of the limelight after hosting the 2004 Olympic Games, but changes made for the Games will shape the city for years to come. In preparation for the games a new airport was built, an extended Metro system and a new ring road were constructed, sidewalks near Sýntagma Square were widened, roads were repaved, and traffic patterns were rerouted. One project completed just before press time was designed to "unify" Athens's archaeological sites — focusing on the four major squares, Sýntagma, Omónia, Monastiráki, and Koumoundourou — by refurbishing facades throughout these areas and permanently closing the sites' access roads to vehicular traffic.

All this work was done with the visitor's experience in mind, but because so many transformations to Athens are ongoing, you may find that hours and prices listed in this chapter have changed by the time you visit. In addition, price hikes that typically accompany the Olympics may be in place for some time to come — whether they'll return to pre-Olympic levels remains to be seen.

Because Athens is much farther from the heart of Europe than most people realize, first-time visitors to the Continent and those on a whirl-wind trip should seriously consider whether to invest the time it takes to visit Greece. They can either fly here from a more-central European city (luckily, new no-frills airlines — see Chapter 6 — now make this affordable for many travelers) or be prepared to spend a full six days on a train and ferry just to get from Rome to Athens and back. Don't let me talk you out of seeing Greece if you have your heart set on it. Just remember this: If you try to squeeze it in, you may be sorely disap-pointed. But if you're able to devote the time it takes to get out of Athens and explore this beautiful, complex, and history-laden country and its ancient culture, by all means make the trip.

Getting There

In addition to the usual options for getting to a major European city — plane, train, bus, and (for adventuresome travelers) automobile — Athens offers another mode of entry: ferry. But the marine route is not for everyone; schedules are erratic, and the crossing can be quite long. Flying is still the best alternative.

After you get to Athens, your feet and taxis are likely to be your best transportation bets.

Arriving by air

The new **Athens International Airport Eleftherios Venizelos** (☎ 210-353-0000; www.aia.gr), 17 miles east of the city at Spata, opened in March 2001 — a major milestone in Athens's preparation for the 2004 Olympics (and ahead of schedule, no less).

In the arrivals hall are two airport information desks (one at each end), three ATMs (near the exits), and two free Internet kiosks. The Greek National Tourist Organization (GNTO — sometimes abbreviated to the Greek acronym EOT) occupies a desk between exits two and three in the arrivals hall, adjacent to the travel agencies. There you can ask about hotels and transportation into Athens.

A **taxi** into central Athens will cost 20€ to 30€ ($23–$35); expect the fare to include a 2€ ($2.30) surcharge for trips to or from the airport and a 0.29€ (35¢) charge for each suitcase.

Greece

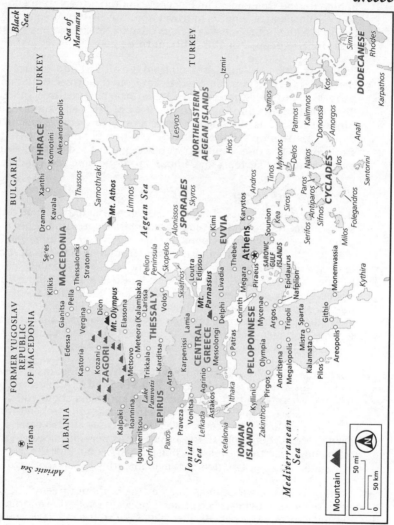

 If you decide to take a taxi, ask an airline official or a policeman what the fare should be, and let the taxi driver know you've been told the official rate before you begin your journey. If you're taking a taxi to the airport, try to have the desk clerk at your hotel order it for you well in advance of your departure. Many taxis refuse to go to the airport, fearing that they'll have a long wait before they get a return fare.

The airport-Athens **rail link,** part of the Suburban Rail, was finished just in time for the Olympics. The link connects the airport to line two of the Metro, allowing passengers to travel from the airport to central Athens in about a half-hour. One-way tickets cost 8€ ($9.20) for one person, 12€ ($14) for two people, or 16€ ($18) for three people.

Buses (☎ 195; www.oasa.gr/uk) from the airport into central Athens cost 2.90€ ($3.35); you can buy a ticket from the driver. Both bus E94 and E95 run to the Ethniki Amyna Metro stop on line three, but E95 continues on to Sýntagma Square in the heart of Athens, about a 70-minute trip. Bus E96 stops at the Faliro Metro stop before continuing on to the Piraeus Metro stop at Athens's port, southwest of the city; both those stops are on line one. Your airport bus ticket is good on any of Athens's public-transport systems for 24 hours from the time you validate it.

Arriving by ferry

Hordes of travelers take the ferry to Greece from Italy, so you'd think ferry operators would have standardized their fares and schedules, but you'd be wrong. The most popular crossing is from Brindisi (on the heel of Italy's "boot," a seven-hour train ride from Rome) to the port of Patras in Greece. This boat trip takes 10 to 17 hours; ferries usually leave Brindisi between 7 and 11 p.m. (be on board at least two hours early). Prices, ranging anywhere from $44 for a deck chair and a restless night outside (*not* recommended in poor weather) to $385 for the best cabins, are highest from late June through August. Eurail-pass holders can ride for free on Hellenic Mediterranean Lines (HML; www.hml.gr), although there may be a 20€ ($23) surcharge, plus port charges.

To get to Athens from Patras, you can catch a bus that leaves every 30 to 45 minutes; the trip on **Achaia** (☎ 210-514-7310 in Athens or 210-623-887 in Patras) takes two and a half hours and costs about 13€ ($15). You can also take one of eight daily trains that makes the trek in three and a half to four hours and costs 5.30€ ($6.10). You can also catch a bus to Delphi. Make your connections as quickly as possible, because the last train and bus of the day usually pull out very soon after the ferry arrives, stranding unsuspecting travelers in uninspiring Patras overnight.

Getting from Rome to Athens this way takes about three full days. Many people find that flying is the easiest and least expensive alternative for getting to Athens (especially after you tally all the rail, ferry, meal, and accommodation costs).

Arriving by rail

Trains (☎ 210-524-0646 or 210-512-4913; www.ose.gr) from Patras and southern Greece arrive in Athens at **Stathmós Peloponníssou** (Peloponnese Station), about a mile northwest of Omónia Square. Across the tracks is **Larissa Station,** Athens's main train station. This is the arrival spot for trains from the north and, therefore, also from other countries. From this station, you can take Trolley 1 to Sýntagma Square or you can get on the Metro (you're at the Larissa stop).

Arriving by bus

Regional buses pull into Athens at one of two unimaginatively named bus terminals. **Terminal A** (for buses from Patras; northern, southern, and western Greece; and the Peloponnese) is at 100 Kifíssiou Street (☎ 210-512-4910); from there, city bus 51 runs to a station just west of Omónia Square. **Terminal B** (for buses from central Greece, including Delphi, Thebes, and Meteóra) is at 260 Liossíon St. (☎ 210-512-4910; www.ktel.org); from this terminal, a dozen city buses go to Attiki Metro stop, from which you can catch lines one or two.

Orienting Yourself in Athens

Athens is a sprawling metropolis with an insatiable appetite for the surrounding countryside, which it continues to devour at a rapid pace. Still, the center of the city preserves the **Acropolis** and many other ancient ruins scattered among Byzantine churches, Turkish buildings, 19th-century boulevards, and modern metropolitan gridlock. And the work done to prepare for the 2004 Olympic Games should clean up and make more user-friendly many parts of the historic center of town. The one Athens landmark you have to locate and remember is **S; ntagma Square,** the political, geographical, and traffic center of the city.

Introducing the neighborhoods

From **S; ntagma Square,** the **Pláka** stretches to the southwest; this largely pedestrian- and tourist-friendly quarter is one of the most color-ful old sections of town. I recommend that you spend the bulk of your visit here.

The southwest corner of the Pláka is bounded by the **Acropolis Hill,** which draws visitors with its majestic **Parthenon** temple and other famous ancient ruins from the time when Athens was the center of Western civilization. The **Monastiráki** neighborhood, which features a flea market and shop-lined street, lies north of the Acropolis and west of the Pláka, next to the **Ancient Agora.**

North of the Pláka and Sýntagma Square, all roads lead to **Omónia Square,** the hub of a district that was once the commercial heart of the city. The square was redone for the Olympics, so returning visitors may notice fewer car lanes choking the area with traffic.

Northeast of Sýntagma Square you find the shopping and residential zone called **Kolonáki.** Although no longer the city's trendy hotspot (newer suburbs have stolen that title), the district is still a chic, happen-ing spot. Due south of Sýntagma Square is **Mets,** a trendy residential and intellectual quarter.

The relatively undiscovered neighborhood of **Makriyánni,** south of the Acropolis, is a moderately upscale area, full of good hotels, restaurants, and shopping. Southwest of this neighborhood is an even bigger secret — the **Koukáki** residential zone, with inexpensive hotels and a modest, thoroughly Athenian restaurant scene.

Finding information after you arrive

The **Greek National Tourist Organization** (often shortened to the Greek acronym EOT), at 7 Tsochas St., is open Monday through Friday from 8 a.m. to 3 p.m. (☎ **210-870-0000;** www.gnto.gr). It offers maps and information about Athens.

Getting Around Athens

I find that the best way to get around town is usually to use my feet and hail the occasional taxi. Except for a few longer excursions to visit museums, you may spend most of your time in or near the pedestrian-friendly Pláka.

The traffic in Athens is worse than in any other European city. The horn-honking, erratic driving, pollution, and daily congestion are worse in Athens than even in Rome and Naples. Drivers routinely turn left from the far right lane of a multilane boulevard, or use a string of empty parking spots as their own personal passing lane. I definitely urge you not to drive here.

By Metro (Subway)

The Metro (☎ **210-679-2399;** www.ametro.gr) system in Athens is clean and efficient but not quite finished. Line one begins at Piraeus, Athens's seaport, and runs through central Athens before terminating north of the city at Kifissia, an upscale suburb. Lines two and three make a large X across the city, meeting at Sýntagma Square, and each is currently being extended on either end. For tourists, the most useful stops are Sýntagma Square, Akropoli, and Monastiráki, each of which is centrally located and offers access to two of the Metro lines.

A **single ticket** costs 0.70€ (80¢); a **day pass** is 2.90€ ($3.35). Children under 6 ride free. Buy tickets at machines and booths inside the stations. Keep your ticket (good for one trip, including transfers, and valid for 90 minutes from the time you stamp it) with you until you exit the Metro.

By bus and trolley

Athens has several overlapping bus and bus-trolley networks. Blue minibuses stop at red signs every two blocks. Both minibus 100 and 200 stop on the north side of Sýntagma Square before continuing to the commercial district just north. The 200 minibus cuts a wider perimeter around the district, though, and also stops at the National Archaeological Museum, making it especially useful for visitors.

Bus and trolley tickets, which are sold in the Metro stations and at ticket kiosks, cost .45€ (50¢) and are good for one trip only, no transfers.

Athens has expanded and reconfigured its public-transportation system to accommodate the increased traffic that typically accompanies the Olympics. Now that the Games are over, there may be even more changes, as the city exhales its collective breath and returns to "normal." Upon your arrival in the city, pick up transportation maps to help you sort out the bus and bus-trolley routes.

By taxi

Taxis are cheaper in Athens than in any major European city — if you pay close attention to avoid getting charged improperly high rates. Taxis are the simplest way to get from doorstep to doorstep, and they occasionally provide the added bonus of a white-knuckle thrill ride. The charge for taxis is .75€ (85¢), plus .26€ (30¢) per kilometer. If you leave the city limits, the per-kilometer charge rises to .50€ (60¢). The fee for luggage is .30€ (35¢) per piece. The night rate (between midnight and 5 a.m.) is .50€ (60¢) per kilometer. The surcharge for stopping at the airport is 2€ ($2.30).

The number of unlicensed cab drivers around Athens is increasing. Usually, these pirate cabbies (many from Eastern Europe) don't drive the standard gray Athens taxi, but a similar gray car. Making sure your cab driver has a meter and a photo ID is a good idea. Make sure the meter rate reads "1" — it should only read "2" if you're going well outside the central city. And don't be shocked if your driver picks up other passengers during your ride. A taxi can carry other customers to destinations that are on the way, but everyone pays separately. Just check the amount on the meter when you climb in, and pay the difference when you get out.

You can hail a taxi on the street or call ☎ **210-363-6508,** 645-7000, or 222-1623. You pay a small surcharge of 1.30€ ($1.50) when you call a taxi.

By foot

Many of Athens's tourist attractions are concentrated in the city center, and some areas, such as the Pláka, are pedestrianized, so expect to see much of the city on foot. A new 2½-mile cobblestone promenade (part of that "unification" of Athens) wends its way around the base of the Acropolis and past many ancient ruins. A word of warning: Drivers here are aggressive, so as a pedestrian, be especially cautious.

Staying in Athens

Almost all the hotels in Athens are simple and basic. Although you can find some pretty shabby places if you stick to the low end of the price ladder, you'll find plenty of clean options if you look around. If you want to stay near the sightseeing and nightlife, the Pláka or Monastiráki are your best bets. The Koukáki and Makriyánni residential zones have plenty of good, clean hotels, which are cheaper than those in the city center. The **Hellenic Chamber of Hotels,** 24 Stadiou St., 4 blocks north of Sýntagma Square (☎ 210-323-7193 or 210-322-9912; www.grhotels.gr/english.html), can help you book a hotel anywhere in Greece.

You should steer clear of only one area: the downtrodden **Omónia Square** zone. Once a haven for budget inns, most people now find it too seedy.

Hoteliers increased their prices for the Olympic Games. Although those prices should have been in place only for the games, there's no knowing how long it will take for rates to return to pre-Olympic (read: more reasonable) levels.

Note: Hotels can ask you for a deposit of 25 percent of one night's stay. In the tourism off-season, by all means bargain.

Athens's top hotels

Acropolis View Hotel
$$$ **Makriyánni**

This nice hotel, snuggled into a quiet side street on Philopáppou Hill, has small and unspectacular, but modern rooms with televisions and air-conditioning. A few rooms even live up to the hotel's name. But if your room lacks a view, head up to the roof terrace, where you can get outstanding Acropolis vistas, especially at sunset.

See map p. 539. 10 Webster St. (off Rovértou Gálli, 2 blocks down from its intersection with Dionysíou Aeropayítou). ☎ *210-921-7303. Fax: 210-923-0705. Metro: Akropoli. Bus/trolley: A2, A2e, A3, 1, 5, 9, 15, 40, 57, 110, 126, or 230. Rates: 100€–160€ ($115–$184) double. Rates include breakfast. AE, MC, V.*

Andromeda Hotel
$$$$$ **Embassy District**

The city's only boutique hotel is easily the most charming in Athens, with a staff that makes you feel like this is your home away from home. Rooms are large and elegantly decorated. The only drawbacks: It's a serious hike (20 to 30 minutes) or a ten-minute taxi ride to Sýntagma, and few restaurants are in this residential neighborhood.

See map p. 539. 15 Timoleontos Vassou St. ☎ *210-641-5000. Fax: 210-646-6361. www.andromedaathens.gr or www.slh.com/andromeda. Metro: Megaron. Bus: 1, 3, 7, 8, 13. Rates: 435€–465€ ($500–$535) double. Rates include breakfast. AE, DC, MC, V.*

Athens Cypria
$$ Pláka

After extensive renovations, the former Diomia Hotel was reborn in 2000 as the Athens Cypria, an excellent addition to Athens's moderately priced hotels — and in a neighborhood where most hotels are seriously expensive. The street suffers little traffic, so most of the pleasantly modernized rooms are quiet, but book early so you can snag one (rooms 604–607) with a stunning view of the Acropolis. Sadly, the renovations don't seem to have extended to doing something about the quality of the lackluster and inattentive staff (but in fairness, this is a drawback the Cypria shares with many Athens hotels — not to be snooty, but they can leave you dangling for weeks after a reservation request).

See map p. 539. Odos Diomias 5 (2 blocks from Sýntagma Square). ☎ *210-323-8034 or 210-323-0470. Fax: 210-324-8792.* www.athenscypria.com. *Metro: Sýntagma Square. Bus/trolley: A2, A3, B2, E2, A2e, A95, 1, 2, 4, 5, 9, 11, 12, 15, 40 or 230. Rates: 110€–120€ ($127–$138) double. Rates include breakfast. AE, MC, V.*

Attalos Hotel
$ Monastiráki

Plain-but-nice rooms, cheerful service, and air-conditioning keep the Attalos popular among budget-conscious travelers. The roof terrace has a bar for snacks and ice cream and a lovely view to the Acropolis across the city (best when seen at night). This view is also available in 37 of the upper-floor rooms, many of which have balconies. Streetside rooms have soundproofed windows (which are pretty effective), and a recent renovation upgraded the very clean rooms to include televisions, hair dryers, and in-room safes. Tha Attalos is just a few minutes from the Pláka.

See map p. 539. 29 Athinás St. (1½ blocks from Monastiráki Square). ☎ *210-321-2801. Fax: 210-324-3124.* www.attalos.gr. *Metro: Monastiráki. Bus/trolley: 25, 26, 27, 35, 200, or 731. Rates: 83€–96€ ($95–$110) double. Rates include breakfast. AE, V.*

Divani-Palace Acropolis
$$$$ Near the Acropolis

Just 3 blocks south of the Acropolis, in a quiet residential neighborhood, the Divani Palace Acropolis does a brisk tour business, but welcomes independent travelers. The blandly decorated rooms are large and comfortable with generous bathrooms and private balconies; all were recently redone. A section of Athens's fifth-century B.C. defense wall is preserved behind glass in the basement. Nearby amenities include a Veropoulos SPAR supermarket a block away at 4 Parthenonos St. and a shop at 7 Parthenonos St. that sells American and English newspapers.

See map p. 539. 19–25 Parthenonos St., Makriyanni (from Sýntagma Square take Amalias Avenue to pedestrianized Dionysiou Areopagitou; turn left into Parthenonos; the hotel is on your left after about 3 blocks). ☎ *210-928-0100. Fax: 210-921-4993.*

Accommodations, Dining, and Attractions in Athens

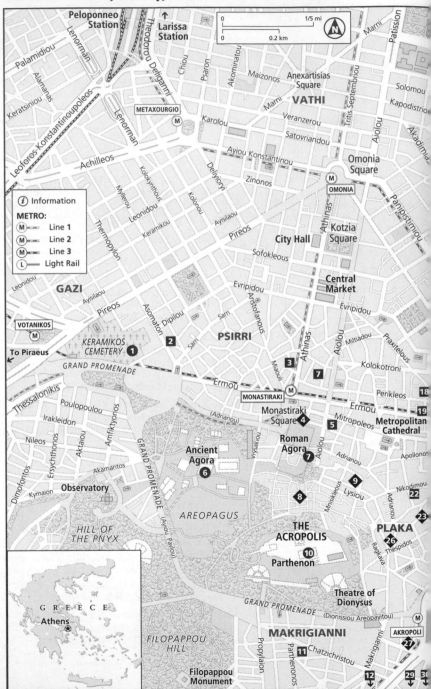

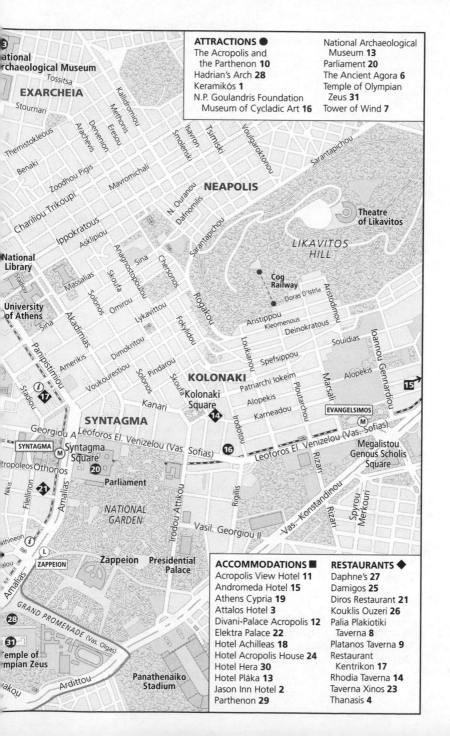

ATTRACTIONS ●
The Acropolis and
   the Parthenon **10**
Hadrian's Arch **28**
Keramikós **1**
N.P. Goulandris Foundation
   Museum of Cycladic Art **16**

National Archaeological
   Museum **13**
Parliament **20**
The Ancient Agora **6**
Temple of Olympian
   Zeus **31**
Tower of Wind **7**

ACCOMMODATIONS ■
Acropolis View Hotel **11**
Andromeda Hotel **15**
Athens Cypria **19**
Attalos Hotel **3**
Divani-Palace Acropolis **12**
Elektra Palace **22**
Hotel Achilleas **18**
Hotel Acropolis House **24**
Hotel Hera **30**
Hotel Pláka **13**
Jason Inn Hotel **2**
Parthenon **29**

RESTAURANTS ◆
Daphne's **27**
Damigos **25**
Diros Restaurant **21**
Kouklis Ouzeri **26**
Palia Plakiotiki
   Taverna **8**
Platanos Taverna **9**
Restaurant
   Kentrikon **17**
Rhodia Taverna **14**
Taverna Xinos **23**
Thanasis **4**

EXARCHEIA
NEAPOLIS
LIKAVITOS HILL
Theatre of Likavitos
Cog Railway
KOLONAKI
Kolonaki Square
SYNTAGMA
Syntagma Square
Parliament
NATIONAL GARDEN
Zappeion
Presidential Palace
GRAND PROMENADE
Temple of Olympian Zeus
Panathenaiko Stadium
National Archaeological Museum
National Library
University of Athens
Megalistou Genous Scholis Square
EVANGELSIMOS

www.divaniacropolis.gr. *Metro: Akropoli. Bus/trolley: 1, 5, 15, or 230. Rates: 230€–300€ ($265–$345) double. Rates include breakfast. AE, DC, MC, V.*

Elektra Palace
$$$$ Pláka

For the price, you can't beat this hotel's location — just southwest of Sýntagma Square in the colorful Pláka. The higher the floor, the smaller these clean, contemporarily furnished rooms get (although none is tiny by any stretch). The good news is that the balconies get proportionately larger. The nicest feature is the rooftop pool, with its sweeping Acropolis view and bar and barbecue service in summer. About 20 rooms, many of them suites, get the Acropolis view, too, but the hotel won't guarantee these when booking.

See map p. 539. 18 Nikodímou St. (near Adrianoú Street). ☎ *210-324-1401 or 210-337-0000. Fax: 210-324-1875. Metro: Akropoli or Sýntagma Square. Bus/trolley: A2, A3, B2, E2, A2e, A95, 1, 2, 4, 5, 9, 11, 12, 15, 40 or 230. Rates: 200€–250€ ($230–$288) double. Rates include breakfast. AE, DC, MC, V.*

Hotel Acropolis House
$ Pláka

Many original moldings and other classic architectural details adorn this 150-year-old villa in the pedestrian heart of the Pláka. The newer wing of this restored structure is not as charming as the rest, although its bathrooms are more modern. You can store your picnic supplies in fridges in the hall.

See map p. 539. 6–8 Odós Kodroú St. (the southern extension of Voulís Street, after it crosses Nikodímou). ☎ *210-322-2344. Fax: 210-324-4143. Bus/trolley: 1, 2, 4, 5, 9, 11, 12, 15, 25, 26, 27, 40, 57, or 110. Rates: 60€ ($69) double without bathroom, 75€ ($86) double with bathroom. 10€ ($12) per-day surcharge for A/C. Rates include breakfast. V.*

Athens's runner-up accommodations

Hotel Achilleas
$$$ Pláka This sister to the Hotel Pláka was renovated in 2001 and is a nice 3-star property with modern minimalist lines, but what makes it really stand out is the general friendliness and helpfulness of the staff. *See map p. 539. 21 Lekka St.* ☎ *210-323-3197. Fax: 210-322-2412.* www.achilleashotel.gr.

Hotel Hera
$$$ Makriyánni This hotel really has some of the best Acropolis views in town from the lush rooftop garden. Rooms are boring but have balconies. The location is in a quiet part of town. *See map p. 539. Odos Falirou 9 (between Odos Petmeza and Odos Donta).* ☎ *210-923-6682. Fax: 210-924-7334.*

Hotel Pláka

$$ Pláka This place offers breezy, modern accommodations with comfy amenities and balconies in the heart of the Pláka. Get a room on the fifth or sixth floor on the back side for a great view of the Acropolis. *See map p. 539. 7 Odos Kapnikareas (at Mitropoleos).* ☎ *210-322-2096. Fax: 210-322-2412.* www.plakahotel.gr.

Jason Inn Hotel

$ Near Monastiráki On the north side of the Agora, this hotel is simple, clean, comfortable, relatively quiet, and cheap. What more could you ask for? Rates include breakfast, served on the rooftop garden terrace. *See map p. 539. 12 Odos Asomaton (a block off Ermou).* ☎ *210-325-1106. Fax: 210-523-4786.*

Parthenon

$$$ Pláka Literally steps from the Acropolis, this modern hotel on the southern edge of the Pláka offers cut-rate prices. *See map p. 539. Odos Makri 6 (just south of Odos Dionissiou Aeropagitou and Hadrian's Arch).* ☎ *210-923-4594. Fax: 210-644-1084.*

Dining in Athens

Greeks are more concerned about the quality and freshness of the food than the appearance of the restaurant. The old travel adage, "Seek out the place crowded with local families having a good time," definitely holds true in Athens. Lots of eateries look like dives but serve food fit for the gods on Mount Olympus. The dinner hour is rather late, starting anywhere from 9 to 11 p.m., so be sure to drop by a *taverna* (a Greek cafe) in the early evening to tide you over.

A key part of the Greek diet are *mezédes,* appetizers served before the meal or on their own (similar to Spain's tapas). Greeks eat *mezédes* with wine at a laid-back *taverna* or with *ouzo* (a popular anise-flavored hard drink) at an *ouzerie* (a cafe where you find *ouzo,* wine, and *mezédes*). The tastiest are *tzatzíki* (a yogurt, cucumber, garlic, and mint dip), *melitzanosaláta* (eggplant salad), grilled *kalamarákia* (squid), *oktapódi* (octopus), and *loukánika* (sausage).

Other outstanding dishes served either as *mezédes* or as entrees are *dolmádes* (grape leaves stuffed with rice, pine nuts, and currants), *souvlaki* (shish kebabs of pork or lamb), *keftédes* (coriander- and cumin-spiced fried meatballs), *spanokópita* (spinach and feta pie), *moussaká* (an eggplant, potato, and minced meat casserole with a melted cheese crust), and other dishes of *arní* (lamb), *kotópoulo* (chicken), or *choirinó* (pork).

Greek *giaoúrti* (yogurt) is the creamiest and most delicious I've ever tasted. My favorite Greek meal is apple slices dipped in thick, plain yogurt. The ancient Greeks liked *méli* (honey) mixed with nectar so much they called it *ambrosia,* "food of the gods." You may feel the same way after drizzling some over your yogurt for dessert. *Baklavá* is flaky, thin pastry dough called *phyllo* layered with nuts and soaked in honey. *S; ka Mavrodáfni* is figs baked in red wine and served in a spice, orange-water, and honey sauce.

The quality of the seafood isn't always what you would expect it to be in Athens; overfishing and the resulting restrictions have led to high prices and freshness concerns. The port city of Piraeus boasts the best seafood restaurants in the area.

Wine may have been invented by the Greeks, but you wouldn't know it from the turpentine-flavored *retsina,* which is flavored with pine resin and has mysteriously become Greece's most famous wine. Un-resined *krasí* may be more palatable to your tastes. Although most Greeks prefer whiskey these days, the national alcoholic beverage is *ouzo,* a clear, anise-flavored liqueur that turns milky white when you add water.

For lunch on the run, gobble a *gyro* — a pocket of pita bread filled with strips of roasted spiced meat — there are countless gyro joints every-where around town. Otherwise, you can stop by any *taverna* for a nour-ishing round of *mezédes.*

Athens's top restaurants

Daphne's
$$$$ Pláka   ELEGANT GREEK/NOUVELLE

This neoclassical 1830s former home features frescoes on the walls, a shady garden with bits of ancient marble found on site when the restau-rant was built, and sophisticated Athenians at many tables. The cuisine here gives you all the old favorites (try the zesty eggplant salad) with new distinction, and combines familiar ingredients in innovative ways (deli-cious hot pepper and feta cheese dip). Most nights a pair of strolling musi-cians performs their repertoire that ranges from Greek favorites to "My Darling Clementine."

See map p. 539. 4 Lysikratous St. (across from Hadrian's Gate). ☎ *and Fax: 210-322-7971. Reservations recommended. Metro: Akropoli. Bus/trolley: A2, A2e, A3, 1, 5, 9, 15, 40, 57, 110, 126, or 230. Main courses: 16€–25€ ($18–$29). Open: Dinner daily. AE, DC, MC, V. Closed Dec 20–Jan 15.*

Diros Restaurant
$$$$ Near Sýntagma Square   GREEK

What more could you want? It's not expensive, it's right off Sýntagma Square, it has both an air-conditioned interior and sidewalk tables, it's been around forever (technically, the original Diros closed some years back, but the staff stuck together and reopened a new "Diros" just like the old one in this location) and the food couldn't be more satisfying. If you need a break from Greek food, this family-friendly joint also serves more familiar dishes such as spaghetti and roast chicken with french fries.

See map p. 539. 10 Odos Xenofóndos (one block south of Sýntagma Square). ☎ 210-323-2392. Reservations suggested. Metro: Sýntagma Square. Bus/trolley: A2, A3, B2, B3, E2, E6, 1, 2, 4, 5, 9, 11, 12, 15, 25, 26, 27, 40, 57, or 110. Main courses: 10€–18€ ($12–$21). Fixed-price menus: 13€–19€ ($15–$22). AE, DC, MC, V. Open: Lunch and dinner daily.

Platanos Taverna
$$ Pláka   GREEK

This classic Greek *taverna* is located on a tree-lined bend in a residential street. The interior features a simple mix of paintings, photos, and old-fashioned Greek ambience. Platanos serves hearty mainstays of Greek cuisine cooked simply but with a keen eye for freshness and quality.

See map p. 539. 4 Odos Dioyénous (near the intersection of Adrianoú and Eólou). ☎ 210-322-0666. Metro: Monastiráki. Bus: 25, 26, or 27. Main courses: 7€–15€ ($8.05–$17). No credit cards. Open: Lunch and dinner Mon–Sat; also lunch Sun Mar–May and Sept–Oct.

Restaurant Kentrikon
$$$ Near Sýntagma Square   INTERNATIONAL

Locals find that the excellent food at this huge restaurant is worth the comparatively high prices. The best bets on the menu include the lamb ragout with spinach, chicken with okra, and the special macaroni. Although everything at this air-conditioned, 1960s joint is quite informal, the service is top-notch.

See map p. 539. 3 Odos Kolokotróni (one block up from Stadíou). ☎ 210-323-2482. Metro: Sýntagma Square. Bus: 1, 2, 4, 5, 9, 11, 12, 15, 25, 26, 27, 40, 100, or 200. Main courses: 7€–17€ ($8.05–$20). AE, DC, MC, V. Open: Lunch Mon–Fri.

Rhodia Taverna
$$$ Kolonáki   GREEK

The atmosphere at this relatively cheap restaurant is among the best in Athens. The décor includes lacy curtains, dark wood paneling, wine kegs, and a vine-sheltered garden in back. Yet the ambience can't steal the show from the superb food; try the octopus in mustard sauce, light *bourékis* (vegetable-filled pastries), or lemon-tinged beef.

See map p. 539. 44 Odos Aristípou (off Kolonáki Square). ☎ 210-722-9883. Reservations suggested. Bus: 22, 60, or 200. Main courses: 7.50€–16€ ($8.65–$18). No credit cards. Open: Dinner Mon–Sat.

Taverna Xinos
$$$ Pláka GREEK

Live music and folksy murals give this place an informal feel, but this is one of the city's best restaurants. For a real cultural treat, arrive after 9 p.m. — that's when the locals and connoisseurs arrive — and sit back, relax, and enjoy a liesurely dinner. The *dolmádes, moussaká,* and lamb fricassee are all delicious.

See map p. 539. 4 Angélou Yéronda (sometimes spelled "Geronta;" either way, it's in the heart of the Pláka, between Kidathinéon and Iperídou). ☎ *210-322-1065. Metro: Akropoli. Bus/trolley: A2, A2e, A3, 1, 5, 9, 15, 40, 57, 110, 126, or 230. Main courses: 7€–16€ ($8.05–$18). No credit cards. Open: Dinner daily (sometimes closes Sun). Closed part of July and Aug.*

Athens's runner-up restaurants

Damigos
$ **Pláka** This cellar taverna has specialized in deep-fried codfish and eggplant for almost 150 years. Add in the cheap meats and stews, and you've got one of the best values on the Pláka's main drag. *See map p. 539. Odos Kidathineon 41.* ☎ *210-322-5084.*

Kouklis Ouzeri
$ **Pláka** Kouklis is the best Pláka joint for mezédes of all shapes and sizes. Pick and choose from the dozen presented on the platter or go all out and splurge on the whole shebang. *See map p. 539. Odos Tripodon 14 (between Flessa and Thespidos).* ☎ *210-324-7605.*

Palia Plakiotiki Taverna
$$$ **Pláka** This series of beautiful flowering terraces, complete with a band playing traditional Greek tunes, may look contrived, but this place is the genuine article. Locals come to this ancient taverna for good food and a rousing good time singing along with the music. Prices are a bit high, but think of it as cheap admission for the floor show. Try to book ahead. *See map p. 539. Odos Lissou 26.* ☎ *010-322-8722.*

Thanasis
$ **Pláka** Thanasis sells great souvlaki with a pita for just 1.45€ ($1.65). Get the food to go or eat at an outdoor table amid the throngs at this bustling corner of the Pláka. Good fries, too. *See map p. 539. 69 Odos Metropóleon (just off Monastiráki Square).* ☎ *210-324-4705.*

Exploring Athens

The congested, sprawling, and polluted appearance of Athens today can't hide the fact that it was once the center of Western culture. The world-class sights located here are a testament to the city's history as the seat of European civilization, and they mustn't be missed.

Athens's top sights

The Acropolis and the Parthenon

Located right in the heart of Athens, the Acropolis Hill is where, mythology tells us, the gods Athena and Poseidon squared off to see who could take better care of the local citizens and thus become the city's guardian and namesake. (Poseidon produced a saltwater spring from the ground; Athena topped him by inventing the versatile olive tree.)

The Acropolis is part of Greece's identity, a landmark that symbolizes the country itself. At the top rests the mighty **Parthenon,** a temple that rises nobly above Athens, reminding the modern city of its ancient heritage. Allow a good two to three hours to tour the Acropolis and its museum.

You enter by climbing stairs to the Beulé Gate, built by the Roman Emperor Valerian in A.D. 267. The cute little Ionic temple of Athena Nike (built 424 B.C., rebuilt A.D. 1940) is perched on your right as you climb.

The world has bigger and better-preserved ancient shrines, but the Parthenon still remains the poster child of Greek temples. Between 447 and 438 B.C., the Athenians spent lavishly to build this shrine to their patron. A 40-foot statue of Athena (a small Roman copy of it is in the National Archaeological Museum) once graced this all-marble temple. The structure is perfectly proportioned, and a few architectural tricks make it appear flawless to the naked eye. To compensate for the eye's natural tendency to create illusions, the horizontal surfaces are bowed slightly upward in the middle to appear perfectly level, the columns lean slightly inward to appear parallel, and each is thicker in the middle so it looks like a textbook cylinder to you and me.

The Parthenon remained virtually intact through the Middle Ages. It became an Orthodox church in the sixth century, a Catholic church during the Crusades, and an Islamic mosque when the Turks occupied the region. But its luck ran out when the Venetians attacked the Turkish city in 1687. The Turks stored ammunition in the old temple, and when a Venetian cannonball hit the stockpile, the armaments exploded and blew the Parthenon to pieces.

Although the temple was once covered almost entirely with sculptures and ornamental carvings, only a few sculptured spots remain on the Parthenon today. British Lord Elgin collected almost all the other sculpted friezes and pediment pieces from the rubble — destroying many in the process — and shipped them to England from 1801 to 1811. These bits of the original Parthenon remain in the British Museum, even though the Greek government has asked for their return many times. British officials have repeatedly refused, citing Athens's lack of a suitable museum in which to display the marbles. In response, Athens has begun to construct such a museum at the foot of the Acropolis. Although the hope was that it would be completed in time for the Olympics (and the Greeks could use the international attention to once again pressure the Brits), the structure is, as of this writing, still just a construction site.

If you look down the Acropolis's south side, you see the half-moon shapes of two theaters. The huge one to the east that is mostly in ruins is the **Theater of Dionysus,** built in 330 B.C. (entrance on Dionyssíou Aeropayítou; ☎ 010-322-4625). Near the entrance to the Acropolis lies the **Odeum of Heródes Átticus,** which was built in A.D. 174 and restored in recent centuries to stage concerts during the Athens Festival from June to October (for information, call the festival office at ☎ **010-322-1459** or the Odeum at ☎ **010-323-2771**).

The 12€ ($14) admission ticket is valid for seven days and includes admission to the Acropolis, the Acropolis Museum, the Ancient Agora, the Theater of Dionysus, the Temple of Olympian Zeus, and the Karameikos Cemetery as well as the Roman Forum and the Tower of the Winds. It is still possible for visitors to buy individual tickets at sights other than the Acropolis.

See map p. 539. The Acropolis entrance is on the west side of the hill and can be reached from a path off Dioskoúon and Theorías streets. ☎ 210-321-0219; 010-323-6665 for the museum. Metro: Acropolis. Bus/trolley: A2, A2e, A3, 1, 5, 9, 15, 40, 57, 110, 126, or 230. Admission: 12€ ($14) ; free first Sun of the months Oct–June and every Sun Nov–Mar. Acropolis open: Summer, Tues–Sun 8 a.m.–7 p.m., Mon noon to 7 p.m.; winter, daily 8:30 a.m.–2:30 p.m.; closed occasionally in the early afternoon. Acropolis Museum open: Mon 11 a.m.–7 p.m., Tues– Sun 8 a.m.– 7 p.m. Call the Greek National Tourism Organization (☎ 210-331-0437) for details and precise hours for this year.

The Ancient Agora (Market)

The everyday life of ancient Athenians revolved around the Agora, or marketplace. But like the Forum in Rome, not much is left of the historic market today; it appears as little more than a dusty bowl filled with mangy trees, broken-down pediments among the grass, and rows of broken column stubs marking the borders of temples and buildings from a bygone era. Still, the Agora takes a good two hours to sift through the rubble and study the reconstructed bits — longer for real students of history.

The **Hephaisteion,** built between 449 and 444 B.C. (and one of the world's best-preserved Greek temples), and the reconstructed **Stoa of Attalos** are the two most remarkable remains. A *stoa* was a series of columns spaced evenly apart supporting a long roof under which shopkeepers set up business, people met, and philosophers held court in the shade. One famous thinker named Zeno held classes under a *stoa* so often that his disciples were known as the Stoics.

The Agora's interesting museum is in the huge Stoa of Attalos, which was built in the second century B.C. and rebuilt in the 1950s. In many ways, the Agora is a museum of modern democracy; the most fascinating artifacts document systems the ancients used to carry out their famous democratic processes. For example, you can see bronze jury ballots — jurors voted with a bronze wheel with a solid axle if they felt the man on trial was innocent, with an empty axle if they found the defendant's story as hollow as the rod.

The museum also has a marble *kleroterion* (allotment machine) that looks very much like a modern lotto machine. Bronze tickets bearing the names of government officials were inserted into slots, and colored balls would fall from a tube and randomly determine who among those names would fulfill various civic duties, such as serving on a committee.

The museum also has a collection of pottery shards called *óstraka,* on which, once a year, Athenians could write the name of any man they thought had gained too much power and, thus, threatened the democracy. If any person's name appeared on the majority of *óstraka,* he would be *ostracized,* or banished, from Athens for ten years. (And now you know where the term came from.)

See map p. 539. The entrance to the Ancient Agora is on Andrianou Street at Ayiou Philippou Square, just east of Monastiráki Square and below the Acropolis. Metro: Thiseio or Monastiráki. Bus/trolley: 35 or 731. ☎ 210-321-0185. Admission: 4€ ($4.60) adults. Open: Daily 8:30 a.m.–7:30 p.m.

National Archaeological Museum
Neapolis

This museum is one of the greatest archaeological museums in the world — a testament to all of Greece's eminence and beauty hundreds of years before the rise of Rome and thousands of years before Columbus set sail for the New World.

You need three hours for even a perfunctory run-through. Aspiring archaeologists may want to stay most of a day and maybe even part of a second. The collections are hard to understand fully or enjoy without plenty of background info, so I recommend you invest in a catalog guide.

Life-sized and oversized bronze statues from Athens's Golden Age (400s B.C.) are the most striking artifacts in the museum. These include Poseidon about to throw his (now missing) trident, a tiny child jockey atop a galloping horse, and the "Marathon Boy" striking a disco pose. Most of these bronzes were found at the bottom of the ocean in shipwrecks by divers in the late 19th and 20th centuries.

Representing the sixth and seventh centuries B.C., the museum presents statues of *kouroi* — attractive young men with cornrow hair, taking one step forward with their arms rigidly at their sides. These figures, adapted from Egyptian models, set the standard in Greek art until the Classical period ushered in more anatomically correct and naturalistic sculpture.

See map p. 539. 44 Patissíon (October 28 Ave.; several long blocks north of Omónia Square). ☎ 210-821-7717 or 210-821-7724. www.culture.gr. Bus/trolley: A5, A8, 2, 3, 4, 5, 6, 7, 8, 9, 11, 13, 15, 22, 60, or 200. Admission: 6€ ($6.90) adults, free under 18 and for all the first Sun of each month. Open: In summer, Tues–Thurs 8:30 a.m.–3 p.m. and Fri–Sun 8 a.m.–7 p.m.; in winter Mon 10:30 a.m.–7 p.m., Tues–Sun 8:30 a.m.–3 p.m.

N. P. Goulandris Foundation Museum of Cycladic Art
Kolonáki

If you have an hour to spare, this museum is the best of all the others in town after the National Archaeological Museum. The Goulandris has wonderfully informative plaques describing each piece in a collection that celebrates the art and simple sculpture of the Cycladic tradition, which began in about 3000 B.C. Famed 20th-century artists such as Brancusi, Henry Moore, Modigliani, and Picasso were all inspired by these sculptures. The museum's second floor houses ancient Greek pieces, many from the fifth century B.C.

See map p. 539. 4 Neophýtou Douká Kolonáki. ☎ 210-722-8321 or 210-722-8323. www.cycladic-m.gr. *Metro: Evangelismos. Bus/trolley: A5, A6, A95, E7, 3, 7, 8, 13, 200, 214, 220, 221, 222, or 235. Admission: 3.50€ ($4.05) adults, 1.80€ ($2.05) students. Open: Mon and Wed–Fri 10 a.m.–4 p.m., Sat 10 a.m.–3 p.m.*

More cool things to see and do

✔ **Wandering the city in search of less touristy ruins:** It seems that everyone who visits Athens makes a beeline to the Acropolis, and most also find their way to the Agora and the National Archaeological Museum, but then many travelers set sail for the islands, leaving the rest of the city's vast archaeological heritage to the few who stay an extra day and explore a bit.

The best of the remaining ancient sites includes **Hadrian's Arch** (on Amalías Avenue, between Vasilissis Olgas and Dionissiou streets), through which the Roman emperor marched in A.D. 132 to dedicate the gigantic **Temple of the Olympian Zeus** (☎ 210-922-6330). Built a little bit at a time between 515 B.C. and A.D. 132, the temple measures 360 by 143 feet. Fifteen of the original 104 columns are still standing, each an impressive 56 feet high. The sight is open daily from 8 a.m. to 7 p.m.; admission is 2€ ($2.30).

The octagonal **Tower of the Wind** (where Eolou Avenue ends at Pelopída Street) was built in the first century B.C. and once held a water clock, which measured time by the fall or flow of water. In the 18th century, whirling dervishes did their religious spinning dance at the tower.

An ancient cemetery called the **Keramikós** (☎ 210-346-3553), 500 yards from the Agora at 148 Ermoú St., was outside the walls of the ancient city. You can still see some of the old walls here, as well as the ancient city gates. The cemetery site has roads lined with tombs and includes a section of the Sacred Way. Hours are Tuesday through Sunday from 8:30 a.m. to 3:00 p.m.; admission is 2€ ($2.30).

✔ **Seeing the changing of the guard:** Athens's version of this tradition is much more entertaining than its London counterpart. The guards wear shoes with pom-poms on the toes and march in a comical, stiff-legged style. They stand at attention in front of the

Parliament building and march back and forth in front of the Tomb of the Unknown Soldier (both are on Sýntagma Square). The duty-rotation ceremony occurs every Sunday at 10:30 a.m.

✔ **Enjoying some Greek music and dancing:** All over Athens, *bouzoúki* clubs — named after a mandolin-type instrument often played in them — can give you a tase of traditional folk music and dancing. The musical styles include the *rebétika* tunes of the urban lower class or *dimotiká,* upbeat country folk music. Greeks traditionally show their appreciation for the music by smashing plates, but you should check with the staff before you do this because many clubs don't allow this anymore. (Places that still do charge you or let you buy them before the show.)

As you get farther from the Pláka neighborhood, the clubs get more authentically Greek. Still, most clubs are used to seeing a lot of tourists, and the waiters can teach you some simple dances. Things really get busy around 11 p.m., but if you want a good seat you'd better arrive early.

For good *rebétika* music, try **Rebétiki Istorís,** 181 Odos Ippókratous (☎ 210-642-4937); **Taximi,** 29 Odos Isávron (☎ 210-363-9919); or **Stoa Athanaton,** 19 Sofokleous in the Centrsal Meat Market (☎ 010-321-4362). **Taverna Mostroú,** 22 Odos Mnissikléos (☎ 010-324-2441), is a top-notch *dimotiká* club. More club info is available in *Athenscope* magazine, which you can get at news kiosks.

You can see the most authentic, artistic folk dancing in the open-air shows put on by performers from the **Dora Stratou Folk Dance Theater** (☎ 210-924-4395 or 210-922-6210), May through September nightly at 9 p.m. (plus 8:15 p.m. Wed and Sun) on Philopáppou Hill.

Guided tours

Hop-in sightseeing tours (☎ 210-428-5500; www.hopin.com) make the rounds of 25 Athenian stops in a two-hour circuit between 9 a.m. and 4 p.m., and you can get on and off at will (and make use of a free tour guide at the Acropolis, where admission is extra). The bus stops at all the major sights in this chapter and on Sýntagma Square.

Tickets cost a steep 42€ ($48) and are good for two days; you can get them at travel agents or on the bus. Hop-in also offers variants on the bus tour for 46€ to 64€ ($53–$74); the higher price is for a tour that includes either lunch at a Pláka tavern or a two-hour guided tour at the Acropolis and a stop at the National Archaeological Museum (the cost of the tour covers admission fees).

Key Tours (☎ 210-923-3166; www.keytours.com) offers half-day tours of Athens that include the Acropolis, the University, Tomb of the Unknown Soldier, the Academy, Temple of Olympian Zeus. Tours cost $50. A night tour that includes dinner in the Pláka runs $58.

Following an itinerary

If you're the type who'd rather organize your own tours, this section offers some tips for building your own Athens itineraries.

If you have one day

If you see only one sight in Athens, it has to be the **Acropolis,** with its mighty **Parthenon,** the most famous Greek temple in the world and the symbol of the city itself. Spend the whole morning here admiring the work of the ancients, their temples and theaters, and the sculpture and other artifacts in the on-site museum.

After lunch (grab a *souvlaki* to go and some pita), trolley up to the incredible **National Archaeological Museum,** housing one of the richest collections of antiquities in the world.

In the late afternoon, head to the **Pláka** to explore its alleyways and nightlife. Have dinner under the sycamores of **Platanos Taverna,** and, if you're there between May and September, head to Philopáppou Hill before 10:15 p.m. to take in a performance of the **Dora Stratou Folk Dance Theater.** In winter, just find a traditional *bouzoúki* club after dinner and clap along.

If you have two days

Spend **Day 1** as described in the previous section. On **Day 2,** start off at the **Ancient Agora,** exploring its ruins and visiting the museum inside the famed Stoa of Attalos to see, literally, the machinery of the world's first democracy.

Afterward, delve briefly into the **Pláka** for an early lunch at one of its sidewalk *tavernas* (**Thanasis** is excellent). Make sure you get to the **N. P. Goulandris Foundation Museum of Cycladic Art** by 2:30 p.m. so you can admire its beautiful and highly stylized ancient statues.

Return to the Pláka in the late afternoon to seek out some of the less famous ancient architectural ruins hidden in its back alleys, such as **Hadrian's Arch.** Then rustle up some dinner at **Palia Plakiotiki Taverna** or **Taverna Xinos,** and find a *bouzoúki* club to plant yourself in for an evening of *retsina, ouzo,* and song.

If you have three days

If you can manage it, I would definitely give Athens only the two days described previously and spend the third day in **Delphi** (see the next section, "Traveling Beyond Athens").

The best way to do this, if you're arriving in Greece by ferry, is to take the bus from Patras to Delphi the night you arrive. (I'm not counting this as one of your three days because the boats arrive in the late afternoon.) Stay the night in Delphi, and then spend **Day 1** clambering around the evocative ruins, consulting the oracle (at least in your imagination), and touring the museum before hopping a late afternoon (or evening) bus to Athens. Then you can spend **Day 2** and **Day 3** of your Greek odyssey in Athens.

If you arrive in Greece by plane, spend **Day 1** and **Day 2** as described in the preceding section, but leave Athens on the evening of the second day for Delphi. Spend the night there before exploring the mountainside the next day, returning to Athens in the evening again for a late dinner.

Traveling Beyond Athens

Most visitors come to Greece to study the remains of an ancient culture or relax on a sun-drenched island. Archaeology buffs have a relatively easy choice — it's hard to beat Delphi's interesting artifacts and beautiful mountain setting. But if you're into island-hopping, you've got a dizzying number of choices. Greece has more than 6,000 islands, although fewer than 200 are inhabited. So here's my advice: Visit Santoríni (its Greek name is Thira, but everyone recognizes it by its Venetian moniker). Even though it's the farthest island from Athens, its tourist infrastructure makes the island easy for first-time visitors to negotiate. Santoríni has quite a few interesting ancient sites, as well as quaint seaside villages and a hopping nightlife — and let's not forget the beautiful beaches.

Delphi: The center of the ancient world

If I only had time to visit one archaeological site in Greece, I would choose Delphi. It's a no-brainer. The ancients couldn't have picked a prettier spot for the place they considered the center of the world. Delphi lies halfway up a mountainside, with the impressive Mount Parnassos surrounding the site and a lush, narrow valley of olive trees stretching down to the Gulf of Corinth.

You can do Delphi in one long daytrip from Athens, but you really should stay the night to make the trip less hectic and much more fun. After some time in the manic city, you may welcome Delphi's small-town beauty and pace.

Getting there

Buses make the three-hour trip from Athens six times a day. If you're taking the ferry to Greece, I suggest that you bus here right from the ferry terminal in Patras. After spending the next day and night in Delphi, continue on to Athens the following morning.

The **tourism office** (☎ 22650-82-900) is at 44 Odós Frideríkis and is usually open from 8 a.m. to 3 p.m. The office of the **Tourist Police** is nearby at 46 Odós Apollonos (☎ 22650-82-220).

Seeing the sights

Delphi is a two-road town with little side streets connecting the two. The bus drops you off at the west end of town, and the archaeological site is a five- to ten-minute walk from town. (Parking spaces are sparse at the sight, so if you *must* drive, head out early.) Many visitors start at the museum, which is along the way to the ruins, but if you want to beat the heat and the crowds, you should rush straight to the outdoor archaeological area first thing in the morning. The ruins will put you in the right frame of mind for the more intellectual experience of examining the museum's treasures.

The main ruins area is the **Sanctuary of Apollo** (☎ 22650-82-313), which extends up the lower slopes of Mount Parnassos. You follow the **Sacred Way,** a marble path lined with the ruined treasuries of Greek city-states that tried to outdo each other in their efforts to offer the greatest riches to the sanctuary. The Athenian Treasury, located just past the first bend in the Sacred Way, is a remarkably well-preserved example.

The Sacred Way hits a plateau at what was once the inner sanctum of the **Temple of Apollo.** Pilgrims from all over the Western world came here to seek advice or have their fortunes told by a seer called the Oracle of Delphi, who spoke the wisdom of Apollo in tongues. Earthquakes, looting, and landslides have pretty much destroyed the temple's partially underground chambers.

The fourth-century-B.C. **theater** at the top of the sanctuary is the best-preserved of its kind in Greece. (Of course, the Romans helped the preservation process by rebuilding it about 2,000 years ago.) Musicians and performers competed here in the Pythian Games, which emphasized culture more than the Olympic Games because they were held in honor of Apollo, god of poets and inventor of the lyre. The view of the whole archaeological site is fantastic from the theater, but you can climb even farther up to the long, tree-lined stadium, which dates to the sixth century B.C. and was the site of the Pythian Games's athletic contests.

After you leave the Sanctuary of Apollo, if you keep walking down the main road, you see Delphi's most beautiful ruins below you. These ruins are in the **Marmaria** — so named because later Greeks used the area as a marble quarry. The most striking sight is the remains of the small, round temple called **Tholos,** built in 380 B.C. In the 1930s, three of the original 20 columns in the temple's outer shell were re-erected and a section of the *lintel* (the horizontal connecting span) was replaced on top. The temple is at its most beautiful when the sun sets behind it.

Admission to the ruins is 6€ ($6.90). The ruins are open in summer Monday through Friday from 7:30 a.m. to 6:30 p.m.; in winter and Saturday, Sunday, and holidays, hours are usually from 8:30 a.m. to 3:00 p.m.

Delphi's **Archaeological Museum** (☎ 22650-82-312) is nearly as good as the one in Athens. *Kouri* (stylized statues of youths) from the seventh century B.C. and gifts that once were part of the Sacred Way's treasuries are among its artifacts. Don't miss the winged sphinx of the Naxians or the pride of the museum, a bronze statue of a charioteer from 474 B.C. that still has a few of the reins that once controlled a group of horse statues. The museum also houses the **Omphalós,** or "Navel Stone," a piece of rock that once marked the spot under the Temple to Apollo that the Greeks believed was the center of the world. Naturally, the Greeks relied on myths to settle on this location for the world's belly button. Zeus was said to have released two eagles at opposite ends of the earth (which was flat then). Because the birds flew toward each other at identical speeds, the point where they crashed into each other and fell to the ground marked the world's central point.

Admission is 6€ ($6.90), and the museum is open in summer Monday from noon to 5:30 p.m.; Tuesday to Friday 7:30 a.m. to 6:30 p.m.; Saturday and Sunday 8:30 a.m. to 3:00 pm. In winter, the museum is usually open daily from 8:30 a.m. to 3:00 p.m.

Where to stay and dine

The **Taverna Vackchos** (☎ **22650-82-448**), near the bus stop at 31 Odós Apóllonos, is a simple but delicious and inexpensive restaurant with great views. Spend the night at the **Hotel Varonos,** 27 Pavlou and Frederikis, Delphi's main street (☎ and fax: **22650-82-345**), where the rooms have spectacular views and doubles run 75€–90€ ($86–$104).

Santoríni: Sun, sun, and more sun

Santoríni (*Thíra* in Greek) is the last island in the Cyclades, a long string of isles in the Aegean Sea littered with ruins and populated by fishermen and sun-worshippers. The island consists of a steep black cliff with streaks of red stone that curves around a *caldera* (volcanic crater) of green water where newer volcano cones still sometimes hiss and smoke. Black-sand beaches, vineyards, whitewashed villages, and the excavations of ancient cities dot this spit of land.

Santoríni's charms — sunny beaches and the excesses of the "good life" — are not a secret; it's one of the most heavily visited Greek islands. It can get maddeningly crowded and seem like one big disco in July and August, a modern symbol of mythical hedonism. But in the spring and fall, when the visiting hordes diminish, Santoríni shines with the quaint feeling of a small fishing village.

Some people actually make Santoríni a daytrip by plane from Athens. These day-trippers, and the hordes that stop for an afternoon cruise break, make noon the most crowded time on Santoríni. If you stay overnight, you can get a friendlier, slightly less-crowded perspective on this crescent-shaped volcanic island. Santoríni is worth a two- to four-day stay if you can swing it, but remember that it virtually shuts down from late October to Easter.

Santoríni

Getting there and getting around

Several flights make the easy 50-minute trip from Athens each day. Call **Olympic Airways** (☎ **210-966-6666** or 210-936-9111; www.olympic-airways.com) or **Aegean Air** (☎ **0801-112-0000**; www.aegeanair.com). Fares start around 94€ ($108) round-trip, and — unless you plan on doing other island-hopping along the way — are generally worth the time you save over taking the ferry.

Between the various ferry companies, two to six boats depart daily to Santoríni from Athens's Piraeus port for 25€ ($29) in the summer. For information on the ferry companies and their schedules, visit a travel agent (the Pláka overflows with them) or call the **Port Authority** in Piraeus at ☎ **210-451-1310** or 210-451-1311. The trip takes 9 to 12 hours, depending on how many stops the ferry makes at other Cycladic islands along the way. An interminably long staircase connects the ferry port up to Fira, Santoríni's main town; you can also take a cable car that runs every 20 to 30 minutes for about 5€ ($5.75).

Buses (☎ **22860-25-404**) on the island connect the main town of Fira with the airport, the ruins of Akrotiri, and most villages and popular beaches. Tickets cost from .90€ to 1.50€ ($1.05–$1.75), paid on the bus, and most buses leave every 30 to 60 minutes (schedules are posted at the depot in Fira). Taxis (☎ **22860-22-555** or 22860-23-951) from the airport to Fira should cost around 7€ to 10€ ($8.05–$12).

Santoríni has no official tourism office, but dozens of private travel agents distribute free info; one of the best is **Kamari Tours** (☎ **22860-31-390**), located 2 blocks south of Fira's main square. It can help you get a hotel or schedule guided tours of the island. For additional information about the island, visit www.santorini.com.

Seeing the sights

If you don't want to take care of making the sightseeing connections yourself, stop by one of Fira's multitude of travel agencies, who make their living selling half- and full-day bus tours to all the island's villages and sights.

The island's best waterfront is **Kamári Beach,** a 4½-mile-long stretch of black pebbles and sand on the southeast shore of the island (it gets horribly crowded in July and August).

Other popular activities include shopping at the island's overabundance of boutiques and sampling the tasty wine produced with the help of the rich volcanic soil. **Boutari winery** (☎ **22860-81-011** or 22-860-81-607; www.boutari.gr) offers tours that include sampling of several wines. The tours cost about 6€ ($6.90) and run from April through September, Monday through Saturday from 10 a.m. to sunset. Ask the driver of the bus from Fira to Akrotiri to let you off at the winery.

But try also to fit in an excursion to Santoríni's two most impressive archaeological sites. The ruins of the wealthy Minoan city of **Ancient Akrotíri** (☎ **22860-81-366**) lie on the southern tip of the island. Since the 1930s, archaeologists have conducted covered excavations of the streets and buildings in this almost-6,000-year-old city (although the parts we can see today are from a settlement from 1500 B.C.). You can wander this emerging ghost town on a plank walkway. Buses run here regularly, and admission is 6€ ($6.90). The site is open Tuesday through Sunday from 8:30 a.m. to 3:00 p.m.; visit early in the morning to beat the crowds and the heat. The nearby Red Beach is a good place to swim and have lunch afterward.

After most of the island was destroyed in a volcanic explosion in the 1600s B.C., a second civilization started around 900 B.C. The capital was **Ancient Thíra** (☎ **02860-22-217** or 02860-22-366), which lies 1,200 feet above Kamári Beach. The ruins here are not covered, so considerably less is left standing than at Akrotíri. But after searching through the buildings (300 to 145 B.C.), you can have a picnic overlooking the sea and shaded by trees or an ancient portico still supported by Doric columns.

Ancient Thíra is open Tuesday through Friday from 8:00 a.m. to 2:30 p.m. and Sunday from 8:00 a.m. to 2:30 p.m.; it's also sometimes open on Saturday from 8:00 a.m. to 2:30 p.m.

Ancient Thíra charges 2€ ($2.30) adults, 1€ ($1.15) students, free under 18. It's free for everyone the first Sunday of the month from April through June and October, the second Sunday in September, and every Sunday between November and March. There are a few ways to get there, but it's well off the beaten path. You can take the bus to Kamári, which lets you off at the bottom of a difficult and steep 2½-mile hike up to the site. Or you can pay a mule driver at the bus stop around 16€ ($18) to take you up and around on a half-day tour. Other alternatives are taking a tour offered by one of the island's many travel agents, or paying for a taxi to take you to the site, which should cost about 45€ ($52) round-trip from Fira. Hours are Tuesday through Sunday from 8:30 a.m. to 3:00 p.m.

The main town of Fira also has a small but outstanding **archaeological museum** (☎ 22860-22-217), with artifacts from digs on the island as well as early Cycladic figurines. Admission is 3€ ($3.45); hours are Tuesday through Sunday from 8:30 a.m. to 3:00 p.m.

Where to stay

You find the most hotels in Fira — but you also hear the most noise and run into the most tourists. (Stay in a smaller village if you want to see the true colors of Santoríni.) Try to get a room with a view of the caldera, which is what you get in the 150€ to 175€ ($173–$201) doubles at **Loucas Hotel** (☎ **22860-22-480** or 22860-22-680; Fax: 22860-24-882; E-mail: loucas@ath.forthnet.gr).

If you want to stay on the beach at Kamári, try the **Kamári Beach Hotel** (☎ **22860-31-216** or 22860-31-243; Fax: 2286-32-120). Many of the 83€ to 129€ ($95–$148) doubles have balconies for enjoying the beach and the sea vistas.

As on most Greek islands, people who want to rent you a room in their house greet most boats. This can often work in your favor in Greece, as long as you ask questions before you head off with the person and don't commit to anything until you've seen the place. These private rooms can be your only option if you arrive without reservations in July or August. Most rooms cost from 25€ ($29) in the off-season to 50€ or 60€ ($58 or $69) in summer.

Many hotels on Santoríni are open only April 15 to October 15. In the off-season, the demand for hotel rooms is less than the supply, plus you can negotiate a good deal on a private room.

Where to dine

For light dining in Fira, try **Kástro** (☎ **22860-22-503**), which attracts scads of day-trippers because of its location across from the cable-car terminal, but the snacks, sandwiches, and beautiful views of the volcanic

The island that blew its top

Santoríni was a circular volcano until an eruption in the 1600s B.C. blew half the island into the air. This created massive tidal waves, spewed ash all over the region, and sparked earthquakes that swept the Aegean — an event that may have helped destroy the Minoan civilization, which was centered on Crete. A wealthy Minoan city called Akrotíri was on Santoríni, and some historians think that this city's volcanic destruction, just at the dawn of recorded history, fueled the mythology about a "lost continent." In other words, it could be the basis of the myth of Atlantis.

crater are worth the hassle. For one of the best meals in Greece, hit **Selene** (☎ 22860-22-249) in Fira (in the passageway between the Atlantis and Aressana hotels), which is known for dishes such as a delicious eggplant salad with octopus and tomato and sea bass grilled with pink peppers.

If you're at Kamári Beach and want a snack, check out **Alexis Grille** (no phone), located in a pine grove at the beach's north end. For more-elegant international fare, try **Camille Stephani** (☎ 02860-31-716), just 500 yards from the bus stop.

Fast Facts: Athens

Area Code

The country code for Greece is **30**. As of November 2002, all phone numbers in Greece require dialing ten digits. All (except for mobile phones, that is — see later in this section) also require you to precede the city/area code with a 2 and follow it with a 0, then dial the local phone number.

For example, to dial a number in Athens from outside Greece, dial **30** (the country code) + **2** + **1** (Athens) + **0** + the 7-digit Athens number. To dial Athens from within Greece, dial **0210** + the 7-digit Athens number. To dial a number outside of Athens from outside Greece, dial 30 (Greece) + local area code + 0 + local number. To dial a number outside of Athens from within Greece, dial the local area code + 0 + the local number.

Calling a mobile phone in Greece requires substituting a 6 for the 2 that precedes the area code.

The Greek phone system is notoriously unreliable. You may call a number in this book and hear a "Your call cannot be completed as dialed" message four or five times, as if you had the wrong number, before suddenly it just goes through on the sixth try. Be patient and persistent.

American Express

The American Express office, 2 Ermoú St. (☎ 010-324-4975), above the McDonald's in Sýntagma Square, is open Monday through Friday from 8:30 a.m. to 4:00 p.m. On Saturday only the travel and mail desks are open from 8:30 a.m. to 1:30 p.m.

Currency

In 2002, the monetary unit in Greece became the euro (€). The rate of exchange used to calculate the dollar values given in this chapter is 1€ = $1.15. Amounts over $10 are rounded to the nearest dollar.

Doctors and Dentists

If you need an English-speaking doctor or dentist, call your embassy for advice or try SOS Doctor (☎ 210-331-0310 or 010-331-0311). The English-language *Athens News,* available at news kiosks, lists some American- and British-trained doctors and hospitals offering emergency services. Most of the larger hotels have doctors whom they can call for you in an emergency.

Embassies and Consulates

The U.S. Embassy (☎ 210-721-2951; www.usembassy.gr) is at 91 Vassilíssis Sophías Ave. If you need emergency help after the embassy is closed, call ☎ 210-729-4301.

Emergency

In an emergency, dial ☎ 100 for fast police assistance and ☎ 171 for the Tourism Police (see "Police," later in "Fast Facts" for a description of the Tourism Police). Dial ☎ 199 to report a fire and ☎ 166 for an ambulance or a hospital. For hospitals, dial 106.

Hospitals

For emergency care in Athens, head to the Euroclinic (☎ 210-641-6600; www.euroclinic.gr) at 9 Athanasiadou St.

Information

The Greek National Tourist Organization, is at 7 Tsochas St. (☎ 210-870-0000; www.gnto.gr). For details on it, see "Finding information after you arrive," near the beginning of this chapter. Two good online resources are the Hellenic Ministry of Culture's www.culture.gr, and the privately maintained www.greecetravel.com.

Yet another very handy resource is the Tourist Police, 43 Veikou St. (☎ 171 or 210-920-0724), south of the Acropolis. This service offers round-the-clock visitor support in English and is the place to turn if you encounter any problems.

Internet Access and Cybercafes

The very efficient Sofokleous.com Internet C@fe, Stadiou 5, a block off Sýntagma Square (☎ and fax: 210-324-8105; www.sofokleous.com), is open daily from 10 a.m. to 10 p.m. The Astor Internet Café, Odos Patission 27, a block off Omónia Square (☎ 210-523-8546), is open Monday through Saturday from 10 a.m. to 10 p.m. and Sunday from 10 a.m. to 4 p.m. Across from the National Archaeological Museum is the Museum Internet Cafe, Odos Octobriou 28, also called Odos Patission (☎ 010-883-3418; www.museumcafe.gr), open daily from 9 a.m. to 11 p.m.

Maps

The Greek Archaeological Service's Historical Map of Athens includes the Pláka and the city center and shows the major archaeological sites. You'll find the map, which costs about 4€ ($4.60), in bookstores, at museums and ancient sites, and at newspaper kiosks.

The GNTO provides maps to tourists (see "Finding information after you arrive," near the beginning of this chapter.

Newspapers/Magazines

The *Athens News* (www.athensnews.gr) is Greece's English-language newspaper. *Kathimerini* (www.ekathimerini.com) is a compendium of English translations from the Greek press; the print edition is found inside the *International Herald Tribune*. The weekly *Athenscope* magazine lists cultural events in English. You can buy it at news kiosks.

Pharmacies

Pharmakia are marked by green crosses. They're usually open from 8 a.m. to 2 p.m., but if you need one after-hours, the location of the nearest 24-hour pharmacy is posted on all pharmacies' doors. You can also find a round-the-clock pharmacy by dialing ☎ 107 or by picking up a copy of the *Athens News*.

Police

In an emergency, dial ☎ 100. For help dealing with a troublesome taxi driver or hotel, restaurant, or shop owner, call the Tourist Police at ☎ 171; they're on call 24 hours and usually speak English, as well as other foreign languages.

Post Office

Athens's main post office is on Sýntagma Square at Odos Mitropoleos. Hours are Monday through Friday from 7:30 a.m. to 8:00 p.m., Saturday from 7:30 a.m. to 2:00 p.m., and Sunday from 9 a.m. to 1 p.m. The parcel post office, 4 Stadiou, inside the arcade (☎ 210-322-8940), is open Monday through Friday from 7:30 a.m. to 8:00 p.m. Parcels must be open for inspection before you seal them (bring your own tape and string) at the post office.

Safety

Visitors who are able to dodge the maniacal Athenian drivers really have only a few minor concerns. Women, single women in particular, often get hassled and rudely propositioned by leering shopkeepers (especially in the Pláka). And single men should be aware that unscrupulous bar owners sometimes try to distract them with beautiful women while the bartender keeps pouring ridiculously expensive drinks. The huge bill comes without any warning of the prices, and the unsuspecting visitor is forced to pay up. Although Greece has a low crime rate and Athens is considered a safe city, visitors should be aware that pickpocketing has become a real problem. Stash your valuables in your money belt and secure it under your clothes.

Taxes

A value-added tax (VAT) is included in the price of all goods and services in Athens, ranging from 4 percent on books to 36 percent on certain luxury items. Although in theory you should be able to get a refund on VAT at the airport, the red tape involved makes it virtually impossible in practice. If you want to try for a refund, keep all your receipts and look for the VAT booth (usually closed) at the airport. For more on the VAT, see Chapter 4.

Taxis

See "Getting Around Athens," earlier in this chapter.

Telephone

Many of the city's public phones now accept only phone cards, available at newsstands and tourist offices in several denominations starting at 5€ ($5.75). The card works for 100 short local calls (fewer long-distance or international calls). Some kiosks still have metered phones; you pay what the meter records. Local phone calls cost 0.09€ (10¢) for the first three minutes,

0.06€ (7@¢) for each minute after that. You can phone home directly by contacting AT&T (☎ 00-800-1311), MCI (☎ 00-800-1211), or Sprint (☎ 00-800-1411).

For recorded telephone assistance in English, dial ☎ 169.

Transit Info

For local bus schedules, dial ☎ 185; for bus schedules in the rest of Greece, call ☎ 142, 01-512-4910, or 01-831- 7158. For train info, call ☎ 145 (domestic), 147 (international), or 01-362-4402. For flight info, dial ☎ 01-936-9111 (domestic) or 01-969-4466 (international). For domestic ship info, call ☎ 143. For more information, see "Getting Around Athens," earlier in this chapter.

Part VI
The Part of Tens

The 5th Wave   By Rich Tennant

"Get your room key ready, Margaret!"

In this part . . .

*T*he final four chapters are *For Dummies* top-ten lists of Europe's bests, worsts, and little-known wonders. I want you to be better prepared than the next guy, who bought one of those densely written guides that lists dozens of hotels (usually without saying anything useful about them) and explains the history of every painting in the museum.

Chapter 25

The Ten Most Overrated Sights and Attractions in Europe

. . . .

In This Chapter

▶ London's changing of the guard and Madame Tussaud's

▶ Madrid's flamenco shows

▶ The city of Athens

▶ Famed boulevards and beaches

▶ Big-ticket shopping

. . . .

The sights listed in this chapter don't always live up to their hype. Nevertheless, I still include some of them in this book, because they're too popular to ignore. Plus, this list is subjective. I think these places are overrated — but you may enjoy the heck out of them, and that's okay, too.

Some of the sights listed in this chapter are so unjustly famous that I simply didn't include them in the book at all. So if you're wondering why the French Riviera is missing, read on and find out.

London's Changing of the Guard at Buckingham Palace

On the yawn scale, I give it about an eight out of ten. The changing of the guard features diffident pomp, halfhearted ceremony, and a clearly bored marching band. And it's crowded, too.

If you absolutely must take part in this tourist tradition, see Chapter 10 for the details.

London's Madame Tussaud's Wax Museum

Pay $37 to ogle wax portraits (albeit expertly executed) of famous dead people? Kitschy, maybe. A must-see? Never. This place is only famous because it has been franchised around the world — sort of a fast-food approach to culture for a museum that's only of marginal historical interest in the first place.

If you want to judge for yourself, see Chapter 10 for the details.

Paris's Champs-Elysées and Rome's Via Veneto

These boulevards — world-class public living rooms where the rich and famous went to sip coffee at a sidewalk cafe and to see and be seen — were the talk of the town into the 1960s.

Now the Champs-Elysées that once welcomed the carriage of Catherine de' Medici has become Paris's main drag for fast-food chains and movie multiplexes. The Via Veneto of Fellini's *La Dolce Vita* (the film that coined the term *paparazzi*) has gone from glitterati ground zero to a string of overpriced, internationally affiliated hotels booked only by tour-bus companies.

The French Riviera

From a beachgoing point of view, the French Riviera is a disappointment. Americans are used to vast expanses of glittering sand. In Europe, sand is a precious commodity, and the beaches — sand, shingle, pebbles, or outright rocks — are mostly private, crowded, narrow strips of shoreline with tightly packed regiments of umbrellas and changing cabins. Come to the Riviera for the casinos or nightlife, if that's your sort of thing. But don't come for the beaches.

Madrid's Flamenco Shows

The shows given for tourists are often of poor quality and overpriced. In Chapter 23, you find my recommendations for some of the more authentic flamenco shows, but remember that the real thing (a spontaneous nighttime ritual) is in Andalusia.

Athens, Greece

Yes, you definitely want to see the Acropolis and the Parthenon, the Ancient Agora, and the National Archaeological Museum if you visit

Athens (Chapter 24), but be forewarned that the city itself is dirty, crowded, and boring. And getting there is no easy task — you must spend three days of your trip traveling by train or ferry if you choose not to fly. Exploring Greece's fascinating interior is a much better use of your time. Or you can island-hop for loads of fun.

Four Shopping Disappointments: the "Big Names" in London, Paris, Rome, and Florence

Harrods was an incredible, almost unbelievable institution when it first opened — a block-long, multilevel building packed to the gills with every imaginable item that you may want to buy (and many that you never thought of), all in one place. We have a term for that today: *department store.* Sure, Harrods is still extraordinarily classy when compared to even top-end chains like Macy's, and it has a nifty food section, but you can actually find more variety (if not quality) these days at the Mall of America in Minnesota.

Paris's **Rue du Faubourg St-Honoré** is, indeed, lined with remarkable shops and high-end boutiques. But one of the cardinal rules of elite shopping in Europe is that high fashion costs no less in its country of origin (France or Italy) than it does in a New York boutique or upscale factory outlet in the United States. This applies to the other streets mentioned in this section, as well as any other street and city in Europe. Yes, buying that little black dress in Paris or leather shoes in Florence has cachet, but don't make the mistake of thinking that you're coming here for a bargain (those are found in stock shops and Europe's outdoor markets).

Via Condotti, the main shopping drag that shoots like an arrow from the base of Rome's Spanish Steps, is now home to a Foot Locker and a Disney Store. The big names of Italian fashion (not to mention the small "Made in Italy" boutiques) have slipped around the corners onto the side streets and parallels of Via Condotti.

Via de' Tornabuoni in Florence has similar problems (though Florence's new Foot Locker and Disney Store are actually located 2 blocks over on Via de' Calzaiuoli). Aside from Ferragamo's massive medieval palace/ flagship anchoring one end, and the original Gucci store in the middle of it, most of the best shops — big-name or not — are not on Via de' Tornabuoni. Instead, they reside on tributaries and side streets like Via della Vigna Vecchia.

Fair warning.

Chapter 26

Ten Overlooked Gems

In This Chapter

▶ Making discoveries in England and Ireland

▶ Going to off-the-beaten-path museums in Paris

▶ Heading to the woods in the Netherlands and Austria

▶ Finding solitude in Ostia Antica and the Venetian Lagoon

▶ Discovering a whole country — Spain! — or just a little hamlet

This chapter lists ten unforgettable places where you can avoid the tourists and see some cool sights to boot. Some of these recommendations don't appear elsewhere in this book, but all are within easy striking distance from the major cities, and I let you know where to begin your journey in each case.

Avebury, England

Okay, so it's not entirely unknown, but compared to Stonehenge, just 20 miles to the north, Avebury (☎ 01672-539-250; www.nationaltrust.org.uk) receives perhaps one-twentieth the number of visitors. Believe me, a prehistoric circle of stones feels much more mystical without throngs of camera-toting tourists posing around it.

But the relative lack of crowds is not the only thing that makes Avebury so special. The Avebury circle is absolutely huge; you even find a small village built halfway into it, with a pub, restaurant, and fine little archaeology museum. And unlike at Stonehenge you can actually wander around amid the stones.

Buses leave regularly from Salisbury station for Avebury. For details on getting to Salisbury (and Stonehenge), see Chapter 10.

Dingle Peninsula, Ireland

Almost everyone flocking to southeastern Ireland heads out of the main town of Killarney to ride around the famed Ring of Kerry. Far fewer know that, just one inlet to the north, the road looping around the Dingle

Peninsula has the same sort of fishing hamlets, village pubs, ancient ruins, and stunning vistas as the Ring of Kerry, but with almost none of the crowds.

Getting to Killarney from Ireland's big cities is easy. For details on visiting Dingle Peninsula, see Chapter 12.

Paris's Lesser-Known Museums

Everyone piles into Paris's Louvre and Musée d'Orsay — and with good reason. But Paris has more than 145 other museums, many of them unknown to the average tourist. At the beautiful little **Rodin Museum**, 77 rue de Varenne (☎ 01-44-18-61-10; www.musee-rodin.fr), castings of Rodin's greatest works fill the rooms, while his *Thinker* ponders in the lush garden. Or you can search out the **Musée du Moyen Age** (Museum of the Middle Ages), 6 place Paul Painlevé (☎ 01-53-73-78-00; www.musee-moyenage.fr), installed in the remains of a bathhouse built almost 2,000 years ago during the city's Roman era.

The Marais's **Musée Carnavalet**, 23 rue de Sévigné (☎ 01-44-59-58-58; www.paris.fr/musees/musee_carnavalet), is dedicated to the history of Paris. The **Musée Marmottan**, 2 rue Louis-Boilly (☎ 01-44-96-50-33; www.marmottan.com), on the edge of the Bois de Boulogne woods, houses Monet's *Impression, Sol Levant,* the painting whose title was taken to coin the term *Impressionism.* And don't leave out the **Musée Picasso,** 5 rue de Thorigny (☎ 01-42-71-25-21; www.musee-picasso.fr) or the **Orangerie,** just off place de la Concorde (☎ 01-42-61-30-82), with its 360° painting of *Waterlilies* by Monet (closed until 2005). For more on the Rodin Museum and Musée Picasso, see Chapter 13.

Hoge Veluwe Park, Netherlands

At this large national park outside Arnhem, you can borrow a bike for free and ride around the park's many roads and trails, exploring a microcosm of the many environments of the Netherlands, from sand dunes to forests to meadows to formal gardens. Make sure that you stop into the Kröller-Müller Museum, a fantastic and underrated gallery of modern art in the middle of the park. It features more than 270 works by van Gogh and hundreds of other works by 20th-century and contemporary artists, plus one of the most beautiful outdoor sculpture gardens in the world. For more on the park, see Chapter 14.

The Heuriger of Grinzig, Austria

If you ride Vienna's no. 38 trolley out to the end of the line, you arrive at the edge of the fabled Vienna Woods in the wine hamlet of Grinzig. Here, almost every block is home to a different *heurige,* a small vineyard that produces limited quantities of white wine and will serve some to you along with platters of roast sausages, dumplings, goulash, pastries, and other hearty Austrian dishes. You can enjoy your feast under aged, wood-beamed ceilings or, in warm weather, in wine gardens crowded by locals. For more on Austria, see Chapter 16.

Ostia Antica, Italy

At the crack of dawn each morning in Rome, lines of tour buses set out for a long daytrip to Pompeii. Take my advice and sleep late, and then take the B metro line for a less than 1-hour trip to another excavated ancient city called Ostia Antica, near the Italian shore.

In Ostia Antica, the cracked mosaic pavements and crumbling brick walls of 1,800-year-old houses, shops, and public buildings flutter with wildflowers; weeds grow in the flagstone roads; and the headless statues lean nonchalantly amidst tall grasses as if simply forgotten. And that's what the town was — forgotten — as the empire fell, the coast receded, and malaria infested the area. Explore it all here: abandoned temples, an empty theatre and amphitheater, windswept streets, and the broken remains of wealthy villas, simple flour mills, and public bathhouses. For more on Ancient Ostia, see Chapter 19.

Venetian Islands, Italy

Glorious St. Mark's Basilica, the pink and white Doge's Palace, the Carnival mask makers — the touristy side of Venice is all fine and well, but for a more authentic experience — and a slower pace — head to a series of smaller islands strung throughout the vast Venetian lagoon.

Hop a *vaporetto* (one of the ferries that serve as Venice's public buses) and in half an hour you can chug out to bustling **Murano,** where the art of Venetian glass-blowing was born and its main factories still reside. After wandering its canals and poking into its marvelous Byzantine/ Renaissance churches, continue on to the islet of **Burano,** a fishing village of brightly colored houses and tiny boats bobbing in the little canals where lace making is the local specialty.

Another vaporetto leaves from here to carry you to isolated **Torcello,** where the earliest lagoon settlement was established (older than Venice itself). Now all that's left are a few houses, a scraggly vineyard, and a Byzantine cathedral with a tipsy bell tower and gorgeous, glittering mosaics carpeting the apse and the entrance wall. The island is also the improbable home to Locanda Cipriani, a refined restaurant (same owners as Venice's Harry's Bar) that Hemingway used to frequent. Headed back to Venice proper on the last vaporetto, the sun setting over the lagoon, you now know how Venice lives outside the tourist trade.

For more on visiting the islands of Venice, see Chapter 21.

Arena Chapel, Padova, Italy

At the start of the 14th century, Giotto, a shepherd turned Gothic painter, kick-started the artistic revolution that would eventually flower into the Renaissance. His famous frescoes in Assisi attract plenty of visitors, but few people visit this beautiful chapel, covered almost from floor to ceiling with the master's vibrant painting, in Padova, just a 20-minute train ride from Venice. For details on visiting Padova, see Chapter 21.

Spain — All of It

Spain spent much of the last century under a dictatorship, so it didn't end up on most tourist itineraries. Although the backpackers are slowly rediscovering it, and in summer the Brits flock to the coastal resorts, Spain is still woefully overlooked by most travelers — their loss.

This country's rich history and heritage of Celtic, Roman, Moorish, Basque, and other influences make it one of the most diverse and culturally dense nations in Europe. **Madrid** is stuffed with museums, and **Barcelona** is an eminently livable city where life centers on a park-like pedestrian boulevard that runs through the very heart of town.

But if you have to pick one region to explore, choose the southlands of **Andalusia** (www.andalucia.org), full of genteel Moorish castles, Christian cathedrals, medieval quarters, Renaissance and baroque palaces and churches, and whitewashed villages. Bullfights, flamenco dancing, and fine sherries all hail originally from Andalusia, and there's nowhere better to experience life *a l'Española* than in the cities of Seville, Granada, and Córdoba; the hill towns northeast of Jerez (home of sherry); and the beaches of the Costa del Sol around Málaga.

For details on Madrid or Barcelona, see Chapters 22 and 23, respectively.

Medieval Hamlets and Hill Towns

If you want to turn back the clock and see villages and small towns where the leisurely pace of life has helped keep the winding stone streets in a veritable time capsule, Europe is the place to go. And many of these, dare I call them "quaint," old villages are just a short bus or train ride outside major cities.

San Gimignano, in Tuscany, bristles with 14 medieval stone towers just a hop, skip, and a jump from Florence (see Chapter 20). **Chartres,** with its glorious Gothic cathedral, is just an hour from Paris on the train (see Chapter 13). **Salisbury** and its massive Gothic cathedral is a similar easy daytrip from London (see Chapter 10). **Toledo** once the capital of Castille, is today a bright, oversized village full of El Greco paintings that's an easy day's jaunt out from Madrid (see Chapter 22).

The hamlets high in the **Lauterbrunnen Valley** of the Swiss Alps are centuries away in attitude from the grand business-capital cities of Switzerland, and even from the busy and modernized resort town of **Interlaken** at the valley's mouth (see Chapter 17). And the tidy Tyrolean town of **Innsbruck** nestles its medieval alleyways and baroque facades amid the Austrian Alps halfway between Vienna and Munich, making for a perfect stop between the two cities (see Chapter 16).

Chapter 27

The Top Ten Gifts for $20 or Less

In This Chapter

▶ Wheels of French cheese and European wines
▶ Scottish tartans and Italian leather wallets
▶ Dutch tulip bulbs, Venetian glass, Swiss army knives, and more

T hese gifts may be for a friend, a loved one, or (hey, why not?) yourself! Whatever the occasion, you *can* bring home something memorable from Europe without busting your budget.

A Bottle of Wine

You wouldn't know it from the criminal markups in most U.S. restaurants, but the vast majority of even the finer wines in France, Italy, Germany, and elsewhere cost less than $10 a bottle. Sadly, the United States has ridiculously strict puritanical laws about how much liquor you can bring back without being taxed on it (see Chapter 9), but one bottle is A-OK.

Marbleized Paper from Florence

For more than 500 years, Florentines have used sure hands and basins of ink floating on water to marbleize paper (creating colorful, peacock-feather designs or asymmetrical patterns), and they paste their creations onto just about anything, from notebooks to pencils to gift boxes. Or you can just buy the paper itself, as gift wrap, and let your friends back home stick it on the objects of their choice.

Tulip Bulbs from Holland

Gone are the heady 17th-century days when some bulbs sold for their weight in gold. However, for your gardening friends back home, what better gift can you find than tulips direct from Holland? Be sure to check with U.S. Customs first (see Chapter 9) about which kinds you're allowed to bring into the United States.

Soviet-Era Kitschy Trinkets

Sidewalk vendors in the Czech Republic and around the Brandenburg Gate in Berlin hawk watches, lighters, and the like emblazoned with the hammer and sickle. Prove your party loyalty by coming back to this seething den of capitalism you call America wearing a bona-fide communist souvenir.

A Small Wheel of Cheese from France or Italy

Edible souvenirs! U.S. Customs lets you bring home any cheese so long as it's not liquidy, like a mascarpone or particularly runny brie.

You *cannot* bring home any type of meat — cured, vacuum-packed, or otherwise — no matter what the shopkeep in Europe tells you. For food safety and health reasons, U.S. Customs officials will confiscate your salami if they discover it. (They keep little pâté-loving beagles at Customs checkpoints and baggage-claim areas of airports just to sniff this stuff out — I kid you not.) Packaged salmon is okay, though.

A Leather Wallet from Florence's San Lorenzo Street Market

You may have to bargain hard to get one for around $20, but it can be done. And what better gift? It's leather, it's from Florence, and it's genuinely useful.

A Glass Trinket from a Venetian Shop

Venice is famous for its Murano blown glass. Although you can lay out thousands of dollars for a chandelier or hand-crafted set of champagne flutes, many of the souvenir-sized objects crowding the display windows of shops all over Venice can be had for under $20, whether the object of your desire is a delicate perfume bottle or a teensy, tiny glass gondola.

Religious Objects from Shops around the Vatican

Many items sold in the stores and stands that crowd around the Vatican walls may be considered movingly religious or supremely silly, depending on your religious leanings and sense of humor. Whatever your tastes, a spin through one or two of these shops can prove a worthwhile diversion from a day spent at St. Peter's.

You can find stuff here to make good gifts for faithful and agnostic friends alike. Take a tasteful little gold-plated cross or crucifix on a chain to the Wednesday audience with the Pope so it, too, gets blessed when he does his benediction over the crowd, and then give it to a Catholic friend back home.

A Tartan Scarf from Scotland

If your friend has Scottish blood, you can find a scarf in his clan pattern. (Shops always have books, posters, or charts on hand to help you figure out which clan matches a particular surname.) You usually have four patterns to choose from: ancient hunting, ancient dress, modern hunting, and modern dress. If you have no clan, you're even luckier; you can just pick the tartan that you like the best.

If your budget can handle more than $20, go wild and get the whole kilt-and-caboodle (a nice kilt set will run you well over $600).

A Swiss Army Knife from — You Guessed It — Switzerland

The smallest, simplest knives do, indeed, cost less than $20. It's hard to believe that Switzerland has been able to stay neutral this long with a military unit armed solely with 2-inch blades, corkscrews, and removable tweezers.

Chapter 28

Ten Ways to Break Out of the Tourist Mold

● ●

In This Chapter

▶ Doing as the locals do
▶ Going to a soccer match
▶ Tuning into local TV
▶ Leaving this book behind (I mean it!)

● ●

Sometimes it pays to be less touristy when you travel to foreign countries. I take my inspiration from Michael Palin in his BBC series *Around the World in 80 Days;* when he arrived in Venice, after a nap, he decided to cruise the canals . . . in a Venetian garbage scow.

To enjoy the "real" Europe, do something other than what all the other travel books recommend. You'll be rewarded with a unique experience that travelers who stick solely to the major sights never have. Here are my suggestions for finding the road less traveled.

Do as the Locals Do

Find out how the locals live by exploring their neighborhoods. Be the first on your block to discover the upscale but thoroughly untouristy **17th Arrondisement in Paris.** Regale your friends back home with tales from **London's Clerkenwell,** where you can still have beer with breakfast and see the spot where Braveheart was executed outside Smithfield meat market; or **London's East End,** where amidst the immigrant families working to achieve the good life you can still find pockets of proud working-class Londoners speaking genuine Cockney. As you wander **Rome's Parioli district,** admire the funky architecture and join the well-heeled matrons strolling down to the cafe in their de rigueur fur coats.

Drink coffee (or something stronger) with the regulars in the corner bar. Sit on the edge of one of those clearly endless daily games of cards, backgammon, or bocce ball, watching carefully to get an idea of how the game is played. One of the grizzled old men may eventually gesture you over, and everyone will get a kick out of trying to pantomime to the foreigner the rules of the game as you proceed to lose spectacularly.

Find that local version of Wal-Mart or Target and just wander the aisles, checking out the daily essentials of the French or the Austrians, for example; as a souvenir, pick up a brand of toothpaste you've never heard of. If you're a music fan, wander into a European music store, most of which have listening stations. Pick up a CD by what seems to be the hottest native pop group.

Take a Dip in Bern's Aare River

Few capital cities in the world have river water that's actually clean enough for swimming. Bern (see Chapter 17) is proud to be one of them. On warm summer days, the locals troop partway upstream, jump in, and let the surprisingly swift current float them down river into the heart of town, where a public bathing complex awaits. Upon arrival, they clamber out and relax poolside or hike 20 minutes back up the tree-shaded path to jump back in the river.

Rent an Apartment or Villa

Instead of staying at several hotels in different cities or towns, pick a city or region to explore more fully and rent an apartment or villa. If you choose a small town or a place in the country, rent a car and settle down to life, European-style. Not only can you save money, but you'll also become a temporary native of sorts. Become a "regular" at the cafe on the corner and the little grocery store down the street. Get to know your neighbors; maybe they'll teach you the family recipe for spaghetti sauce. You may enjoy the lifestyle so much that you find yourself pausing at the windows of local realtors to peruse the offerings and check on property values.

Visit a Small Private Museum

You wouldn't believe the places you can find where wealthy collectors left behind dusty old mansions jumbled with valuable bric-a-brac ranging from Ming vases and Roman reliefs to medieval suits of armor and occasional paintings by Renaissance masters. Although few of the individual pieces, or the collections as a whole, tend to be first-rate, they offer fascinating insights into one man or family's tastes and styles — and often as not these places are preserved exactly as the collector left them in 1754 or 1892 or whatever, and as such offer a glimpse into the lives and times of a different era.

And before you pooh-pooh the idea of a private collection, remember the names of a few larger ones installed in the personal residences of Europe's richest past collectors: the Louvre (the French monarchs' collection in their city palace), the Uffizi (the Medicis' artwork installed in their old office building), and the Vatican (the Pope's best heirlooms in his private digs). . . .

Jog with the Locals

Europeans may not be as health-nutty or exercise-driven as your modern American, but the concept of a good cardio workout seems to be catching on. Find out where the locals jog, and join them for a morning (or evening) run. You can clear your head, explore a city park or two, and perhaps make some new friends.

Hike in the Countryside

Leave the crowds of the big city behind, and explore the country on foot. Buy the best, most detailed small-scale map you can find that shows all the unpaved roads and trails (if any). The tourist office of most smaller towns can help you out with maps, and sometimes even itineraries, or can point you toward the local trekking group. A few cities are so small (Florence comes to mind) that you can start many country walks right outside your doorstep — or from the end of a local bus line.

Catch a Soccer Match

In Europe, soccer is like packing all the cheers, joys, agonies, and devoted fandom of American baseball, football, basketball, and hockey into one sport and one season. Except for a few oddball games — cricket in England, or hurling in Ireland — this is the only sport that most Europeans follow, making it a close second to Christianity as the national religion in each country.

Find out when the big game takes place (often Sunday) and where the die-hard fans of the home team sit in the stadium. Then get a seat near them and root, root, root for the home team (unless you seem to be seated amidst fans of the opposing team, in which case scream your bloody lungs out for the visitors). Just avoid any obvious hooligans and any sign that a brawl's about to break out.

Pick Grapes or Olives

During harvest seasons, you're bound to see people out working their fields or small plots. Often, they're more than happy to accept any help you offer, and you can spend a day picking grapes or olives — both of which are a lot harder on your fingers and, in the case of grapes, your back, than you may imagine. But the experience can be fun, and you may even get to pass around the wine bottle with the farmers during breaks.

Watch Some Local Television Programs

Watching TV in Europe doesn't make you a couch potato. Tell your friends that you're having a cultural experience! You may be amazed by what they put on TV in other countries — a whole lot more nudity, for one thing. Plus, you get awful slapstick comedies (which are pretty easy to follow in any language), oddball game shows, and commercials for chewing gum or spring water. You can discover that the Germans love *Star Trek,* the Italians have an unhealthy fixation on the (poorly dubbed) *Fresh Prince of Bel Air,* and Bart Simpson is a beloved bad boy in every country.

Liberate Yourself from Your Guidebook

Yes! I really said it! Once in a while, stow away this and any other guidebooks you may have. Check out sights and restaurants without following my advice. If the bistro is cheap and full of Frenchmen, chances are it's good. Wander into a church without even checking to see if it's listed in your book and admire the baroque altarpiece and paintings for their aesthetic value alone, not because you know someone famous made them.

Try a dish that your menu translator doesn't cover. (Okay, that can be risky, but if the locals are willing to eat it, it probably isn't poison — just don't hold me responsible if it involves more tentacles than you're comfortable with.) Enjoy the thrill of discovery. Turn tourism into travel and your vacation into an adventure. The memories will be more than worth it.

Appendix

Quick Concierge

Average Travel Times by Rail

Amsterdam to
Munich   8½ hours
Paris   4¼ hours
Zurich   10 hours

Athens to
Munich   42½ hours
Vienna   43 hours

Barcelona to
Madrid   7 hours
Paris   11½ hours

Bath to
London   1¼ hours

Bern to
Interlaken   1 hour
Paris   4½ hours
Zurich   1½ hours

Edinburgh to
London   4 hours

Florence to
Paris   12½ hours
Rome   1½ hours
Venice   3 hours
Zurich   8 hours

Glasgow to
London   5 hours

Innsbruck to
Munich   3 hours
Vienna   8 hours
Zurich   5 hours

Interlaken to
Bern   1 hour

London to
Bath   1¼ hours
Edinburgh   4 hours
Glasgow   5 hours
Paris   3 hours

Madrid to
Barcelona   7 hours

Munich to
Amsterdam   8½ hours
Athens   42½ hours
Innsbruck   3 hours
Paris   8½ hours
Prague   7½ hours
Rome   11 hours
Venice   9 hours
Vienna   4¾ hours
Zurich   5 hours

Paris to
Amsterdam   4¼ hours
Bern   4½ hours
Barcelona   11½ hours
Florence   12½ hours
London   3 hours

Munich 8½ hours
Rome 15 hours
Venice 12¼ hours
Vienna 13½ hours
Zurich 6 hours

Pisa to

Rome 4 hours

Prague to

Munich 7½ hours
Vienna 5 hours

Rome to

Florence 1½ hours
Munich 11 hours
Paris 15 hours
Pisa 4 hours
Siena 3 hours
Venice 4½ hours
Zurich 8½ hours

Siena to

Rome 3 hours

Venice to

Florence 3 hours
Munich 9 hours
Paris 12¼ hours
Rome 4½ hours
Vienna 8 hours

Vienna to

Athens 43 hours
Innsbruck 8 hours
Munich 4¾ hours
Paris 13½ hours
Prague 5 hours
Zurich 12 hours

Zurich to

Amsterdam 10 hours
Bern 1½ hours
Florence 8 hours
Innsbruck 5 hours
Munich 5 hours
Paris 6 hours
Rome 8½ hours
Vienna 12 hours

Metric Conversions

Liquid Volume	
To convert	*Multiply by*
U.S. gallons to liters	3.8
Liters to U.S. gallons	.26
U.S. gallons to imperial gallons	.83
Imperial gallons to U.S. gallons	1.20
Imperial gallons to liters	4.55

Distance

To convert	Multiply by
Inches to centimeters	2.54
Centimeters to inches	.39
Feet to meters	.30
Meters to feet	3.28
Yards to meters	.91
Meters to yards	1.09
Miles to kilometers	1.61
Kilometers to miles	.62

Weight

To convert	Multiply by
Ounces to grams	28.35
Grams to ounces	.035
Pounds to kilograms	.45
Kilograms to pounds	2.20

Temperature

To **convert °F to °C,** subtract 32 and multiply by $\frac{5}{9}$ (.555).

To **convert °C to °F,** multiply by 1.8 and add 32.

32°F = 0°C

Clothing Size Conversions

Women's Clothing

American	Continental	British
6	36	8
8	38	10
10	40	12

American	Continental	British
12	42	14
14	44	16
16	46	18

Women's Shoes

American	Continental	British
5	36	4
6	37	5
7	38	6
8	39	7
9	40	8
10	41	9

Children's Clothing

American	Continental	British
3	98	18
4	104	20
5	110	22
6	116	24
6X	122	26

Children's Shoes

American	Continental	British
8	24	7
9	25	8
10	27	9
11	28	10

(continued)

Children's Shoes *(continued)*

American	Continental	British
12	29	11
13	30	12
1	32	13
2	33	1
3	34	2

Men's Suits

American	Continental	British
34	44	34
36	46	36
38	48	38
40	50	40
42	52	42
44	54	44
46	56	46
48	58	48

Men's Shirts

American	Continental	British
14½	37	14½
15	38	15
15½	39	15½
16	41	16
16½	42	16½
17	43	17
17½	44	17½
18	45	18

Men's Shoes

American	Continental	British
7	39½	6
8	41	7
9	42	8
10	43	9
11	44½	10
12	46	11
13	47	12

Toll-Free Numbers and Web Sites

Major North American carriers

Air Canada
☎ 888-247-2262
www.aircanada.com

American Airlines
☎ 800-433-7300
www.aa.com

Continental Airlines
☎ 800-231-0856
www.continental.com

Delta Air Lines
☎ 800-241-4141
www.delta.com

Northwest/KLM Airlines
☎ 800-447-4747
www.nwa.com

United Air Lines
☎ 800-538-2929
www.united.com

US Airways
☎ 800-622-1015
www.usairways.com

Major European carriers

Aer Lingus (Ireland)
☎ 800-474-7424 (U.S., Canada)
☎ 0845-084-4444 (U.K.)
☎ 01-886-8888 (Ireland)
www.aerlingus.com

Air France
☎ 800-237-2747 (U.S.)
☎ 800-667-2747 (Canada)
☎ 0845-359-1000 (U.K.)
☎ 1300-361-400 (Australia)
☎ 649-308-3352 (N.Z.)
☎ 0820-820-820 (France)
www.airfrance.com

Alitalia (Italy)
☎ 800-223-5730 (U.S.)
☎ 800-268-9277 (Canada)
☎ 0870-544-8259 (U.K.)
☎ 8488-65641 (Italy)
www.alitalia.com

Austrian Airlines
☎ 888-817-4444 (U.S., Canada)
☎ 0870-124-2625 (U.K.)
☎ 800-642-438 (Australia)
☎ 43-(0)5-1789 (Austria)
www.aua.com

British Airways (U.K.)
☎ 800-247-9297 (U.S., Canada)
☎ 034-522-2111 or 111 or
0845-77-333-77 (U.K.)
☎ 1300-767-177 (Australia)
www.ba.com

CSA Czech Airlines
☎ 800-223-2365 (U.S.)
☎ 416-363-3174 or 514-844-6376
(Canada)
☎ 870-444-3747 (U.K.)
☎ 420-224-81-04-26 (Czech Republic)
www.czechairlines.com

EasyJet (U.K)
☎ 0870-6000-000 (overseas)
0871-750-0100 (U.K.)
www.easyjet.com

Iberia (Spain)
☎ 800-772-4642 (U.S.)
☎ 800-363-4534 (Canada)
☎ 0845-850-9000 (U.K.)
☎ 902-400-500 (Spain)
www.iberia.com

**KLM Royal Dutch Airlines/
Northwest (The Netherlands)**
☎ 800-447-4747 (U.S. and Canada)
☎ 0870-507-4074 (U.K.)
☎ 1-300-787-747 (Australia)
☎ 09-309-1782 (N.Z.)
☎ 020-4-747-747 (Netherlands)
www.klm.com or www.nwa.com

Lufthansa (Germany)
☎ 800-399-5838 (U.S.)
☎ 800-563-5954 (Canada)
☎ 0870-837-7747 (U.K.)
☎ 1-300-655-727 (Australia)
☎ 0-800-945-200 (N.Z.)
☎ 49-(0)-180-5-8384267 (Germany)
www.lufthansa.com

Olympic Airways (Greece)
☎ 800-223-1226 (U.S.)
☎ 416-964-7137 (Canada)

☎ 0970-606-0460 (U.K.)
☎ 02-9251-2044 (Australia)
☎ 80-111-44444 (Greece)
www.olympic-airways.com

Ryanair (U.K. and Ireland)
☎ 0818-303-030 or 353-1-249-7851
(U.S., Canada, Australia)
☎ 0871-246-0000 (U.K.) 10p/min.
☎ 0818-303-030 (Ireland)
www.ryanair.com

Swiss (Switzerland)
☎ 877-359-7947 (U.S., Canada)
☎ 0845-601-0956 (U.K.)
☎ 1-800-883-199 (Australia)
☎ 0848-85-2000 (Switzerland)
www.swiss.com

Virgin Atlantic (U.K.)
☎ 800-862-8621 (U.S., Canada)
☎ 0870-380-2007 (U.K.)
☎ 0293-747-747 in Britain
☎ 02-9244-2747 (Australia)
www.virgin-atlantic.com

Major Pacific Rim carriers
Air New Zealand
☎ 800-262-1234 (U.S.)
☎ 800-663-5494 (Canada)
☎ 0800-028-4149 (U.K.)
☎ 132-476 (Australia)
☎ 0800-737-000 (N.Z.)
www.airnewzealand.com

Qantas (Australia)
☎ 800-227-4500 (U.S., Canada)
☎ 0845-774-7767
☎ 131-131 (Australia)
www.qantas.com

Car-rental agencies
Advantage
☎ 800-777-5500
www.advantagerentacar.com

Alamo
☎ 800-462-5266
www.alamo.com

Auto Europe
☎ 888-223-5555
www.autoeurope.com

Avis
☎ 800-230-4898 (U.S.)
☎ 800-272-5871 (Canada)
www.avis.com

Budget
☎ 800-527-0700 (U.S.)
☎ 800-268-8900 (Canada)
www.budget.com

Enterprise
☎ 800-261-7331 (U.S., Canada)
☎ 0870-350-3000 (U.K.)
www.enterprise.com

Europe by Car
☎ 800-223-1516
www.europebycar.com

Hertz
☎ 800-654-3001
www.hertz.com

Kemwel Holiday Auto (KHA)
☎ 800-678-0678
www.kemwel.com

National
☎ 800-CAR-RENT
www.nationalcar.com

Sixt
☎ 1-888-SIXTCAR
www.sixt-europe.com

Thrifty
☎ 800-847-4389
www.thrifty.com

Where to Get More Information

National tourist boards exist to help you plan a trip to their country. If you e-mail or call, they'll gladly send you a big envelope stuffed with brochures and information packets. Many of them are helpful enough to address specific questions and concerns you may have. Even more useful are their Web sites, which are loaded with country-specific information and links to other sites.

That said, take any mailing from a tourist office with a grain of salt. Most of the material is promotional literature and always puts the best spin possible on every aspect of the country. Read between the lines and rely on a quality, impartial third-party guidebook (like this one!) for the real, opinionated scoop on the local scene.

For local tourist boards, see the Fast Facts sections of Chapters 10 through 24. These offices can also send you tons of useful information — but again, view these materials with a critical eye.

International tourist office

European Travel Commission

www.visiteurope.com

National tourism offices

Austrian National Tourist Office

In the U.S.: P.O. Box 1142, New York, NY 10108-1142 (☎ 212-944-6880); 11601 Wilshire Blvd., Suite 2480, Los Angeles, CA 90025 (☎ 818-999-4030).

In Canada: 2 Bloor St. E., Suite 3330, Toronto, ON M4W 1A8 (☎ 416-967-3381); 1010 Sherbrooke St. W., Suite 1410, Montréal, PQ H3A 2R7 (☎ 514-849-3708); Suite 1380, Granville Square, 200 Granville St., Vancouver, BC V6C 1S4 (☎ 604-683-5808).

In the U.K.: Mail to: P.O. Box 2363, London W1A 2QB. Office at: 14 Cork St., London W1X 1PF (☎ 020-7629-0461).

In Australia: 36 Carrington St., 1st Floor, Sydney NSW 2000 (☎ 02-9299-3621).

www.austriatourism.com

Visit Britain (formerly the British Tourist Authority)

In the U.S.: ☎ 800-462-2748. 551 Fifth Ave., Suite 701, New York, NY 10176 (☎ 212-986-2200); 625 N. Michigan Ave., Suite 1510, Chicago, IL 60611 (☎ 312-787-0464).

In Canada: ☎ 888-VISIT-UK. 5915 Airport Rd., Suite 120, Mississauga, ON L4V 1T1 (☎ 905-405-1720).

In the U.K.: 1 Lower Regent St., Piccadilly Circus, London SW1Y 4XT (☎ 020-7808-3864).

In Australia: Level 2, 15 Blue St., North Sydney, NSW 2060 (☎ 02-9021-4400 or 1-300-858-589).

In New Zealand: 151 Queen St., 17th Floor, Auckland 1 (☎ 0800-700-741).

www.visitbritain.com

Czech Tourist Authority

In the U.S.: 1109 Madison Ave., New York, NY 10028 (☎ 212-288-0830).

In Canada: 401 Bay St., Suite 1510, Toronto, ON M5H 2Y4 (☎ 416-363-9928).

In the U.K.: 95 Great Portland St., London W1M 5RA (☎ 020-7291-9920).

www.czechtourism.com or www.czechcenter.com

French Government Tourist Office

In the U.S.: 444 Madison Ave., 16th Floor, New York, NY 10022 (☎ 212-838-7800); 205 N. Michigan Ave., Suite 3770, Chicago, IL 60601 (☎ 312-751-7800); 9454 Wilshire Blvd., Suite 715, Beverly Hills, CA 90212 (☎ 310-271-6665). To request information at any of these offices, call ☎ 410-286-8310.

In Canada: Maison de la France/French Government Tourist Office, 1981 av. McGill College, Suite 490, Montréal, PQ H3A 2W9 (☎ 514-876-9881).

In the U.K.: Maison de la France/French Tourist Office, 178 Piccadilly, London, W1J 9AL (☎ 09068-244-123, 60p/min).

In Australia: French Tourist Bureau, Level 20, 25 Bligh St., Sydney, NSW 2000 (☎ 02-9231-5244).

www.franceguide.com or www.francetourism.com

German National Tourist Office

In the U.S.: 122 E. 42nd St., 52nd Floor, New York, NY 10168 (☎ 212-661-7200).

In Canada: 480 University Ave., Suite 1410, Toronto, ON M5G 1V2 (☎ 416-968-1685).

In the U.K.: Nightingale House, 65 Curzon St., London, W1Y 8NE (☎ 020-7371-0908).

In Australia: Lufthansa House, 143 Macquarie St., 12th Floor, Sydney, NSW 2000 (☎ 02-8296-0488).

www.germany-tourism.de or www.cometogermany.com

Greek National Tourist Organization

In the U.S.: Olympic Tower, 645 Fifth Ave., Suite 903, New York, NY 10022 (☎ 212-421-5777).

In Canada: 91 Scollard St., 2nd Floor, Toronto, ON M5R 1G4 (☎ 416-968-2220).

In the U.K.: 4 Conduit St., London W1R OD (☎ 171-499-4976 or 171-734-5997).

In Australia: 51–57 Pitt St., Sydney, NWS 2000 (☎ 02-9241-1663 or 02-9252-1441).

www.greektourism.com

Irish Tourist Board

In the U.S.: 345 Park Ave., New York, NY 10154 (☎ 800-223-6470 or 212-418-0800).

In Canada: 2 Bloor St. W., Suite 1501, Toronto, ON M4W 3E2 (☎ 0800-223-6470).

In the U.K.: Nations House, 103 Wigmore St., London W1U 1QS (☎ 0800-039-7000).

In Australia: 5th Level, 36 Carrington St., Sydney, NSW 2000 (☎ 02-9299-6177).

In New Zealand: 6th Floor, 18 Shortland St., Private Bag 92136, Auckland 1 (☎ 09-379-8720).

www.tourismireland.com or www.ireland.travel.ie

Italian Government Tourist Board

In the U.S.: 630 Fifth Ave., Suite 1565, New York, NY 10111 (☎ 212-245-5618 or 212-245-4822); 500 N. Michigan Ave., Suite 2240, Chicago, IL 60611 (☎ 312-644-0996 or 312-644-0990); 12400 Wilshire Blvd., Suite 550, Beverly Hills, CA 90025 (☎ 310-820-1898 or 310-820-6357).

In Canada: 175 Bloor St. E., Suite 907, South Tower, Toronto, ON M4W 3R8 (☎ 416-925-4882).

In the U.K.: 1 Princes St., London W1B 2AY (☎ 020-7399-3562).

In Australia: Level 26, 44 Market Street, Sydney, NSW 2000 (☎ 02-9262-1666).

www.italiantourism.com or www.enit.it

Netherlands Board of Tourism

In the U.S.: ☎ 212-557-3500; 355 Lexington Ave., 21st Floor, New York, NY 10017 (☎ 212-370-7360).

In Canada: 25 Adelaide St. E., Suite 710, Toronto, ON M5C 1Y2 (☎ 416-363-1577).

In the U.K.: 18 Buckingham Gate, P.O. Box 523, London, SW1E 6NT (☎ 020-7539-7950 or 0906-871-7777, 60p/min).

www.holland.com

Scottish Tourist Board

Outside the U.K., the Scottish Tourist Board falls under Visit Britain (formerly the British Tourist Authority; see listing earlier in this section).

www.visitscotland.com

Tourist Office of Spain

In the U.S.: 666 Fifth Ave., 35th Floor, New York, NY 10103 (☎ 212-265-8822); 845 N. Michigan Ave., Suite 915E, Chicago, IL 60611 (☎ 312-642-1992); 8383 Wilshire Blvd., Suite 956, Beverly Hills, CA 90211 (☎ 323-658-7188); 1395 Brickell Ave., Suite 1130, Miami, FL 33131 (☎ 305-358-1992).

In Canada: 2 Bloor St. W., 34th Floor, Toronto, ON M4W 3E2 (☎ 416-961-3131).

In the U.K.: 22–23 Manchester Square, London W1U 3PX (☎ 020-7486-8077).

www.okspain.org

Switzerland Tourism

In the U.S. and Canada: ☎ 877-794-8037. Swiss Center, 608 Fifth Ave., New York, NY 10020 (☎ 212-757-5944); 222 N. Sepulveda Blvd., Suite 1570, El Segundo, CA 90245 (☎ 310-335-5980).

In the U.K.: Swiss Centre, 10 Wardour St., London W1D 6QF (☎ 0800-1002-0030020-7792-1550).

www.switzerlandtourism.com or www.myswitzerland.com

Index

• *W* •

USINESS, CAREERS & PERSONAL FINANCE

Grant Writing

Home Buying

0-7645-5307-0   0-7645-5331-3 *†

Also available:
- Accounting For Dummies †
  0-7645-5314-3
- Business Plans Kit For Dummies †
  0-7645-5365-8
- Cover Letters For Dummies
  0-7645-5224-4
- Frugal Living For Dummies
  0-7645-5403-4
- Leadership For Dummies
  0-7645-5176-0
- Managing For Dummies
  0-7645-1771-6

- Marketing For Dummies
  0-7645-5600-2
- Personal Finance For Dummies *
  0-7645-2590-5
- Project Management
  For Dummies
  0-7645-5283-X
- Resumes For Dummies †
  0-7645-5471-9
- Selling For Dummies
  0-7645-5363-1
- Small Business Kit For Dummies *†
  0-7645-5093-4

OME & BUSINESS COMPUTER BASICS

Windows XP

Excel 2003

-7645-4074-2   0-7645-3758-X

Also available:
- ACT! 6 For Dummies
  0-7645-2645-6
- iLife '04 All-in-One Desk Reference
  For Dummies
  0-7645-7347-0
- iPAQ For Dummies
  0-7645-6769-1
- Mac OS X Panther Timesaving
  Techniques For Dummies
  0-7645-5812-9
- Macs For Dummies
  0-7645-5656-8
- Microsoft Money 2004 For Dummies
  0-7645-4195-1

- Office 2003 All-in-One Desk
  Reference For Dummies
  0-7645-3883-7
- Outlook 2003 For Dummies
  0-7645-3759-8
- PCs For Dummies
  0-7645-4074-2
- TiVo For Dummies
  0-7645-6923-6
- Upgrading and Fixing PCs
  For Dummies
  0-7645-1665-5
- Windows XP Timesaving
  Techniques For Dummies
  0-7645-3748-2

OD, HOME, GARDEN, HOBBIES, MUSIC & PETS

Feng Shui

Poker

-7645-5295-3   0-7645-5232-5

Also available:
- Bass Guitar For Dummies
  0-7645-2487-9
- Diabetes Cookbook For Dummies
  0-7645-5230-9
- Gardening For Dummies *
  0-7645-5130-2
- Guitar For Dummies
  0-7645-5106-X
- Holiday Decorating For Dummies
  0-7645-2570-0
- Home Improvement All-in-One
  For Dummies
  0-7645-5680-0

- Knitting For Dummies
  0-7645-5395-X
- Piano For Dummies
  0-7645-5105-1
- Puppies For Dummies
  0-7645-5255-4
- Scrapbooking For Dummies
  0-7645-7208-3
- Senior Dogs For Dummies
  0-7645-5818-8
- Singing For Dummies
  0-7645-2475-5
- 30-Minute Meals For Dummies
  0-7645-2589-1

TERNET & DIGITAL MEDIA

Digital Photography

Starting an eBay Business

7645-1664-7   0-7645-6924-4

Also available:
- 2005 Online Shopping Directory
  For Dummies
  0-7645-7495-7
- CD & DVD Recording For Dummies
  0-7645-5956-7
- eBay For Dummies
  0-7645-5654-1
- Fighting Spam For Dummies
  0-7645-5965-6
- Genealogy Online For Dummies
  0-7645-5964-8
- Google For Dummies
  0-7645-4420-9

- Home Recording For Musicians
  For Dummies
  0-7645-1634-5
- The Internet For Dummies
  0-7645-4173-0
- iPod & iTunes For Dummies
  0-7645-7772-7
- Preventing Identity Theft
  For Dummies
  0-7645-7336-5
- Pro Tools All-in-One Desk
  Reference For Dummies
  0-7645-5714-9
- Roxio Easy Media Creator
  For Dummies
  0-7645-7131-1

WILEY

SPORTS, FITNESS, PARENTING, RELIGION & SPIRITUALITY

0-7645-5146-9

0-7645-5418-2

Also available:
- Adoption For Dummies
  0-7645-5488-3
- Basketball For Dummies
  0-7645-5248-1
- The Bible For Dummies
  0-7645-5296-1
- Buddhism For Dummies
  0-7645-5359-3
- Catholicism For Dummies
  0-7645-5391-7
- Hockey For Dummies
  0-7645-5228-7

- Judaism For Dummies
  0-7645-5299-6
- Martial Arts For Dummies
  0-7645-5358-5
- Pilates For Dummies
  0-7645-5397-6
- Religion For Dummies
  0-7645-5264-3
- Teaching Kids to Read
  For Dummies
  0-7645-4043-2
- Weight Training For Dummies
  0-7645-5168-X
- Yoga For Dummies
  0-7645-5117-5

TRAVEL

0-7645-5438-7

0-7645-5453-0

Also available:
- Alaska For Dummies
  0-7645-1761-9
- Arizona For Dummies
  0-7645-6938-4
- Cancún and the Yucatán
  For Dummies
  0-7645-2437-2
- Cruise Vacations For Dummies
  0-7645-6941-4
- Europe For Dummies
  0-7645-5456-5
- Ireland For Dummies
  0-7645-5455-7

- Las Vegas For Dummies
  0-7645-5448-4
- London For Dummies
  0-7645-4277-X
- New York City For Dummies
  0-7645-6945-7
- Paris For Dummies
  0-7645-5494-8
- RV Vacations For Dummies
  0-7645-5443-3
- Walt Disney World & Orlando
  For Dummies
  0-7645-6943-0

GRAPHICS, DESIGN & WEB DEVELOPMENT

0-7645-4345-8

0-7645-5589-8

Also available:
- Adobe Acrobat 6 PDF
  For Dummies
  0-7645-3760-1
- Building a Web Site For Dummies
  0-7645-7144-3
- Dreamweaver MX 2004
  For Dummies
  0-7645-4342-3
- FrontPage 2003 For Dummies
  0-7645-3882-9
- HTML 4 For Dummies
  0-7645-1995-6
- Illustrator CS For Dummies
  0-7645-4084-X

- Macromedia Flash MX 2004
  For Dummies
  0-7645-4358-X
- Photoshop 7 All-in-One Desk
  Reference For Dummies
  0-7645-1667-1
- Photoshop CS Timesaving
  Techniques For Dummies
  0-7645-6782-9
- PHP 5 For Dummies
  0-7645-4166-8
- PowerPoint 2003 For Dummies
  0-7645-3908-6
- QuarkXPress 6 For Dummies
  0-7645-2593-X

NETWORKING, SECURITY, PROGRAMMING & DATABASES

0-7645-6852-3

0-7645-5784-X

Also available:
- A+ Certification For Dummies
  0-7645-4187-0
- Access 2003 All-in-One Desk
  Reference For Dummies
  0-7645-3988-4
- Beginning Programming
  For Dummies
  0-7645-4997-9
- C For Dummies
  0-7645-7068-4
- Firewalls For Dummies
  0-7645-4048-4
- Home Networking For Dummies
  0-7645-42796

- Network Security For Dummies
  0-7645-1679-5
- Networking For Dummies
  0-7645-1677-9
- TCP/IP For Dummies
  0-7645-1760-0
- VBA For Dummies
  0-7645-3989-2
- Wireless All In-One Desk Reference
  For Dummies
  0-7645-7496-5
- Wireless Home Networking
  For Dummies
  0-7645-3910-8

HEALTH & SELF-HELP

-7645-6820-5 *†   0-7645-2566-2

Also available:

- ✔ Alzheimer's For Dummies
  0-7645-3899-3
- ✔ Asthma For Dummies
  0-7645-4233-8
- ✔ Controlling Cholesterol For Dummies
  0-7645-5440-9
- ✔ Depression For Dummies
  0-7645-3900-0
- ✔ Dieting For Dummies
  0-7645-4149-8
- ✔ Fertility For Dummies
  0-7645-2549-2

- ✔ Fibromyalgia For Dummies
  0-7645-5441-7
- ✔ Improving Your Memory For Dummies
  0-7645-5435-2
- ✔ Pregnancy For Dummies †
  0-7645-4483-7
- ✔ Quitting Smoking For Dummies
  0-7645-2629-4
- ✔ Relationships For Dummies
  0-7645-5384-4
- ✔ Thyroid For Dummies
  0-7645-5385-2

EDUCATION, HISTORY, REFERENCE & TEST PREPARATION

0-7645-5194-9   0-7645-4186-2

Also available:

- ✔ Algebra For Dummies
  0-7645-5325-9
- ✔ British History For Dummies
  0-7645-7021-8
- ✔ Calculus For Dummies
  0-7645-2498-4
- ✔ English Grammar For Dummies
  0-7645-5322-4
- ✔ Forensics For Dummies
  0-7645-5580-4
- ✔ The GMAT For Dummies
  0-7645-5251-1
- ✔ Inglés Para Dummies
  0-7645-5427-1

- ✔ Italian For Dummies
  0-7645-5196-5
- ✔ Latin For Dummies
  0-7645-5431-X
- ✔ Lewis & Clark For Dummies
  0-7645-2545-X
- ✔ Research Papers For Dummies
  0-7645-5426-3
- ✔ The SAT I For Dummies
  0-7645-7193-1
- ✔ Science Fair Projects For Dummies
  0-7645-5460-3
- ✔ U.S. History For Dummies
  0-7645-5249-X

Get smart @ dummies.com®

- **Find a full list of Dummies titles**
- **Look into loads of FREE on-site articles**
- **Sign up for FREE eTips e-mailed to you weekly**
- **See what other products carry the Dummies name**
- **Shop directly from the Dummies bookstore**
- **Enter to win new prizes every month!**

* Separate Canadian edition also available
† Separate U.K. edition also available

Available wherever books are sold. For more information or to order direct: U.S. customers visit www.dummies.com or call 1-877-762-2974.
U.K. customers visit www.wileyeurope.com or call 0800 243407. Canadian customers visit www.wiley.ca or call 1-800-567-4797.